"*Luke–Acts in Modern Interpretation* is an important collection of studies in the Milestones in New Testament Scholarship series. The two-volume work known as Luke–Acts warrants scholarly scrutiny not only because this work represents almost one quarter of the entire New Testament, but because it preserves a vital link between Jesus, his life and ministry, and the first generation of the church that emerged in the aftermath of his death and resurrection. Editors Stanley Porter and Ron Fay have assembled an impressive roster of contributors who have reviewed the history of scholarship concerned with Luke–Acts and have done so with critical judgment and keen insight."

—Craig A. Evans,
John Bisagno Distinguished Professor of Christian Origins,
Houston Baptist University

"*Luke–Acts in Modern Interpretation* is a well-conceived and readable high-level introduction to the history of the study of Luke–Acts. The pattern of introduction, survey of scholarship, and evaluation for each scholar serves well, and is supplemented by an introduction that reaches earlier and wider than the scholars chosen for inclusion."

—John Nolland, former Vice-Principal and Academic Dean at Trinity College
Bristol and Visiting Professor at the University of Bristol

"Luke–Acts represents the largest portion of the New Testament. It was long neglected but has been at the center of much New Testament discussion in recent times. This survey of major contributors provides a wonderful orientation to the issues that swirl around these two important parts of the New Testament. It prepares one well for engagement with the issues tied to these books."

—Darrell L. Bock, Executive Director for Cultural Engagement,
Howard G. Hendricks Center for Christian Leadership and Cultural Engagement;
Senior Research Professor of New Testament Studies, Dallas Theological Seminary

"This book is a handy guide to many of the most prominent and influential figures in critical Luke–Acts scholarship. For those wanting to get their feet wet in the world of Lukan studies, this is a great place to start."

—Craig S. Keener,
F. M. and Ada Thompson Professor of Biblical Studies,
Asbury Theological Seminary

LUKE-ACTS
IN MODERN
INTERPRETATION

Stanley E. Porter and Ron C. Fay

EDITORS

KREGEL
ACADEMIC

Luke–Acts in Modern Interpretation
© 2021 by Stanley E. Porter and Ron C. Fay

Published by Kregel Academic, an imprint of Kregel Publications, 2450 Oak Industrial Dr. NE, Grand Rapids, MI 49505–6020.

The Hebrew font, NewJerusalemU, and the Greek font, GraecaU, are available from www.linguistsoftware.com/lgku.htm, +1-425-775-1130.

ISBN 978-0-8254-4569-9

Printed in the United States of America

21 22 23 24 25 / 5 4 3 2 1

To all those Luke–Acts scholars
who have gone before us

CONTENTS

SERIES INTRODUCTION

The *Milestones in New Testament Scholarship* (MNTS) series fills a necessary place between a proper biography and a dictionary entry. Each person chosen as a subject of a chapter has had a major influence upon how scholarship, and usually along with it lay readers, have thought about a specific book, group of books, or topic in the New Testament. The history of scholarship leaves certain fingerprints that stand out more than others; yet many times some important makers of fingerprints are overlooked due to the time period in which they lived, the circumstances in which they wrote, or the influence of one of their contemporaries. MNTS will often shine a light on significant scholars who have been overlooked, while also giving space to those whose names are nearly synonymous with the books they studied.

The vision for this series is to cover numerous books and topics in the New Testament, with each volume providing a small snapshot of milestones in New Testament scholarship. We seek to balance canonical studies with textual and theological studies. This series will produce brief biographies of scholars who have had an impact on the study of a given book, corpus, or major issue in New Testament studies, and thereby established a milestone in the area. By looking at the lives of these scholars, the impact of their work can be felt. We have intentionally utilized an extended chronology for the chosen scholars, in order to show how their impact is felt by subsequent generations. Each article tells the story of a single person. It communicates the life circumstances, the influences on the person, and how that person impacted the specific area in New Testament studies. In turn, each volume of this series then tells multiple stories forming a timeline, and thus a narrative of the subject of each volume can be seen through the intellectual progression within the topic.

These volumes will then create a history of New Testament studies. In order to see how work in the Johannine literature has progressed, one would read the volume on John. To see how New Testament studies in general have progressed and to diagnose general trends, the entire series would be necessary. This allows both a deeper understanding of each individual subject and a more comprehensive view of how change in each subfield of New Testament studies has occurred. This makes MNTS perfect for those studying for comprehensive exams; those examining why certain trends in specific fields have occurred, wanting to understand the history of New Testament studies; or those wishing to see ideas embodied in the stories of the participants rather than simply in didactic material.

Our goal for MNTS, to fit in scope between a single biography of a certain scholar and an encyclopedia or dictionary of various New Testament interpreters, means that these volumes allow for a quicker read than a biography[1] but greater depth than a dictionary.[2] Each volume also allows the reader to approach each chapter individually, as each is a story with a beginning and an end. Since the chosen scholars are treated separately, researchers have a place to start when working on bibliographies. Since each chapter is written by someone working in the field, the nonspecialist gains a glimpse at how an expert understands and assesses an important scholar.

The purpose of MNTS is to open historical vistas normally closed to nonexperts, without having to dig into sources not readily available. This approach gives the student shoulders on which to stand, the expert a quick reference tool, and the biographer a short sample. Our hope is that MNTS brings joy and information to all who use the series.

—Stanley E. Porter and Ron C. Fay

1. For example, Konrad Hammann, *Rudolf Bultmann: A Biography* (Farmington, MN: Polebridge Press, 2012).
2. For example, William Baird, *History of New Testament Research*, 3 vols. (Minneapolis: Fortress Press, 1993–2013).

PREFACE

We are pleased to present this second set of essays in the Milestones in New Testament Scholarship series, this volume focused upon Luke–Acts. The chapters are freshly written essays commissioned for this book by authors who are closely connected with scholarship on Luke–Acts. Some, in fact, have more than passing acquaintance with the authors on whom they have written in terms of research and writing interests. We are pleased that the individual authors were willing to contribute their essays to this volume. Enthusiasm for Luke–Acts as an area of scholarly interest has risen and fallen over the course of the last two centuries of modern scholarship. However, as this volume attempts to make clear, there has always been scholarship done on one or both of these important New Testament books. Sometimes there has been more scholarship on Luke's Gospel and sometimes more on the Acts of the Apostles, and sometimes more on both of them together. Nevertheless, Luke–Acts as the significant corpus of writing that it is within the New Testament continues to demand that scholars return to it. We hope that this volume will play a role in this continuing discussion as we revisit the contributions of a number of scholars who are milestone figures within Luke–Acts scholarship. The varied figures included within this volume reflect both continuity and discontinuity within Lukan scholarship. On the one hand, there are a number of recurring questions that continue to be raised within critical scholarship, including such issues as authorship, historicity, theology, genre, and the like. On the other hand, there are always new questions being raised—or at least new perspectives being suggested—in light of continuing discussion. We see the latter in some of the literary approaches that have come to the fore in more recent studies of Luke–Acts. We wish for this volume to help to inspire further questions and new perspectives in the study of these two major New Testament books.

This volume, however, is not geared toward the future of Luke–Acts scholarship, but to its past. We believe that a volume such as this helps to further inform scholarship as we critically assess the contributions of major figures in the history of discussion. We have included ten scholars who rightly belong in a volume that attempts to represent milestones in previous interpretation of Luke–Acts. Not all have focused equally on both books; some have concentrated upon Luke's Gospel and some on Acts. It appears, as a matter of fact, that more of them have concentrated on Acts than Luke's Gospel, but that is not the result of an attempt to skew the orientation of the volume. Nevertheless, each has made a contribution to study of the Lukan corpus. The scope of their work extends well over a century and a half, from the mid-nineteenth century to the twenty-first. We do not believe that any of these scholars requires justification—even if some of them are more widely known than others, some of their positions are more positively viewed than others, and some fit more widely known or endorsed theological paradigms.

The introduction to this volume attempts to set the ten authors treated in this volume into their larger context. We begin the introduction by discussing F. C. Baur, whose theories regarding Acts, as well as Luke, have had an enduring effect upon study of Luke–Acts. In many respects, his interests shaped the agenda for study of Luke–Acts, in Germany and elsewhere. In the course of situating the authors discussed within this volume, we also include brief descriptions of the contributions of a number of other Luke–Acts scholars. This discussion provides a context in which to consider those treated here. Adolf Harnack will always be remembered as one of the greatest scholars of his or of any generation. The breadth of his knowledge and writing is astounding, and he towered above most of his peers in an age of many accomplished scholars. Harnack would merit mention in any number of different volumes on milestones in scholarship. He made a significant contribution to Luke–Acts as well. Although a theological liberal, he argued for some surprisingly early dates for composition of both Luke and Acts, which put him at odds with the mainstream of German scholarship of his time. Martin Dibelius was at the forefront of a surprisingly prolific period in German scholarship, with the rise to significance of form criticism. Dibelius was instrumental in shaping the agenda for future work in Luke–Acts with his form-critical study of both the Gospel and Acts. Dibelius's approach is still reflected in much subsequent scholarship, German or otherwise. Henry J. Cadbury, an American scholar with

Quaker perspectives, represents an independent and innovative voice in Luke–Acts scholarship. Cadbury is probably less well-known than some of the other authors studied in this volume, but his contribution was highly significant. Cadbury was on the forefront of appreciating the stylistic and other innovations of the Lukan author, while attempting to fit the corpus of Luke–Acts within its contemporary context. Ernst Haenchen remains best known in scholarship for his commentary on the book of Acts, a commentary that has continued to play a significant role in reflecting the views of much German scholarship and providing a foil for others. Although a theologian by profession before being a New Testament scholar, Haenchen became a leading New Testament scholar as a proponent of redaction criticism, which he used in his study of Acts. F. F. Bruce exemplifies a British perspective on scholarship on Luke–Acts that runs contrary to the major stream of German scholarship. Whereas German scholarship was skeptical of Lukan historicity, Bruce was highly influenced by his classical education and saw Luke as a reliable historian. Bruce was instrumental in establishing a conservative (even evangelical) approach to Luke–Acts as a respectable perspective from which to do biblical scholarship. Bruce represents a trend in British scholarship that has continued to be developed to the present. Hans Conzelmann and Haenchen were in many ways closely aligned in their scholarship on Luke–Acts. Conzelmann formulated a clear outline of salvation-history that encompasses both Luke and Acts, and this formulation has had an enduring effect upon New Testament scholarship, not least in the influence that it had on Haenchen in his commentary. C. K. Barrett, one of the most significant British New Testament scholars of the twentieth century, approached Luke–Acts with recognition of the issues raised in German scholarship but without some of its extremes. His concern for the effects of critical scholarship on Christian belief is readily seen in his scholarship on Acts. Jacob Jervell, a Norwegian scholar, represents a major break from the main trends in German scholarship. Whereas much German scholarship had emphasized the conciliatory role of Acts in the tension between Jew and Gentile, with the author approaching this tension from a position of Gentile universalism, Jervell reinterpreted the Lukan corpus, with Acts focusing upon the Jewish mission of the church that only later spread to the Gentiles. Jervell's major commentary on Acts was written to succeed Haenchen's, thus pitting two different perspectives on Acts against each other in the same commentary series. Richard I. Pervo challenged many of the standard theories regarding Acts and revived a number of ideas that have not been at the forefront of Acts studies—until recently. He reopened questions regarding genre, unity, authorship, and especially date of composition. It appears that many of these questions will grow in importance in the years to come. Finally, Loveday C. A. Alexander is the scholar with whom we close this volume and bring it up to the present. In some ways, Alexander returns to the emphasis upon classical study of Acts, while she also has a methodological awareness that pushes her into new arenas of scholarship. We wait to see if and how these ideas are further developed within Acts studies.

We have included essays on the above ten authors in this volume, as well as referred to a number of others in the introduction and elsewhere. We realize that there are many other worthy and able scholars who could have been included in this discussion. We cannot attempt to list such names here. We realize that any similar volumes, and those who edit them, will have various opinions on what constitutes true milestones in Luke–Acts scholarship, but the list of worthy scholars to consider would exceed the confines of a single volume such as this one. We, however, are satisfied with our list. These scholars represent a variety of methods, some of them being innovators and others solidifiers. They represent various current issues in Lukan scholarship of their times, some of them being on the avant-garde and others in defensive response to the onslaught. They represent some new departures and some well-established paths of endeavor. They also represent some new findings and able defenses of traditional viewpoints. One of the common threads that emerges in this series of essays is that each of these scholars endeavored to interpret the Lukan literature for their day and age, and as a result brought insights to the discussion. Our contributors are to be commended for their efforts to capture the sense of each of these scholars.

The editors wish to thank the individual contributors for their chapters in this volume and their willingness to share their expertise. By doing so, they help to advance discussion of Luke–Acts and bring to mind those who have established this discipline as the vibrant area of scholarly endeavor that it is. We also wish to thank our friends at Kregel for their continuing support of this series of volumes. In particular, we thank Laura Bartlett for her suggestions on various dimensions of the series and how it can continually be refined and improved, and Robert Hand for his fine editorial work on this volume. We also want to thank Shawn Vander Lugt for typesetting this volume and for his work on the index.

LIST OF CONTRIBUTORS

Karl L. Armstrong, McMaster Divinity College, Hamilton, Ontario

David K. Bryan, Trinity Evangelical Divinity School, Deerfield, Illinois

John Byron, Ashland Theological Seminary, Ashland, Ohio

Zachary K. Dawson, Regent University, Virginia Beach, Virginia

James D. Dvorak, Oklahoma Christian University, Edmond, Oklahoma

Ron C. Fay, Liberty School of Divinity, Lynchburg, Virginia

Laura J. Hunt, Spring Arbor University, Spring Arbor, Michigan

Osvaldo Padilla, Beeson Divinity School, Samford University, Birmingham, Alabama

Stanley E. Porter, McMaster Divinity College, Hamilton, Ontario

Alan J. Thompson, Sydney Missionary and Bible College, Croydon, New South Wales

INTRODUCTION TO *LUKE-ACTS* IN MODERN INTERPRETATION

Stanley E. Porter and Ron C. Fay

The Gospel of Luke and the Acts of the Apostles, two books that have historically been linked whether by authorship, chronology, or canon, comprise nearly one third of the content of the Greek New Testament. These two books, the longest and second longest in the New Testament, have occupied a provocative place within the history of New Testament scholarship. As this introduction will indicate, and as a number of the essays in this volume will further illustrate, many significant scholarly controversies involving some of the most significant New Testament scholars in the history of critical scholarship have focused serious efforts on discussing these books, whether individually or together. As a result of their study, we are able to observe some of the major trends in the history and development of New Testament scholarship, because of the implications of their research on Luke and Acts. The significance of these two books in the history of the development of early Christianity, and the critical scholarship that has accompanied them, has meant that many fine scholars in the history of New Testament scholarship have devoted their not inconsiderable talents and abilities to their critical analysis. Sometimes these scholars agree and sometimes, in fact, many times, they do not. Nevertheless, they continue to visit and revisit important historical, theological, literary, and textual issues that attend to these two books. In this introduction, we attempt to lay out, even if only briefly and incompletely, the history of scholarship on Luke–Acts. Because a volume such as this cannot include every important scholar, to say nothing of treat them in detail, we will attempt to mention—and sometimes that is all that we can do—the major scholars who, in the history of scholarship, have made a noteworthy and enduring contribution to study of Luke–Acts.[1] This higher level picture of Luke–Acts scholarship will then provide the basis for a contextual understanding of the individual scholars discussed in far greater detail in the chapters that follow.

The history of New Testament scholarship on Luke–Acts can be conveniently divided into four major periods, each one representing a period of time in which there were currents and countercurrents in the various opinions advocated and refuted. It is perhaps appropriate in a discussion of Luke–Acts that this dialectic of proposals and counterproposals is used as a framework for further discussion, as such a Hegelian idealistic analysis stands at the advent of major critical study of Luke–Acts, in particular the book of Acts. Much of the history of discussion of these two books continues to be performed in light of this original dialectic. This introduction focuses upon scholars who have established their reputations in Luke–Acts studies over the course of time and hence only considers for sustained consideration those who have either died or concluded the vast bulk of their careers, since attempting to assess our contemporaries is often difficult. Because of the nature of our audience, we also tend to concentrate upon scholars who write in English, especially when considering contemporary scholars.

---

1. There are several volumes that survey scholarship on Luke and/or Acts. Those most valuable to us in this study, in chronological order, are: W. Ward Gasque, *A History of the Criticism of the Acts of the Apostles* (repr., Grand Rapids: Eerdmans, 1975); François Bovon, *Luke the Theologian*, 2nd rev. ed. (Waco, TX: Baylor University Press, 2006 [1978]); Mikeal C. Parsons and Joseph B. Tyson, eds., *Cadbury, Knox, and Talbert: American Contributions to the Study of Acts*, SBLBSNA (Atlanta: Scholars Press, 1992), although we do not include John Knox in our survey; and Joseph B. Tyson, *Luke, Judaism, and the Scholars: Critical Approaches to Luke–Acts* (Columbia: University of South Carolina Press, 1999), but we do not include Adolf Schlatter, because his contribution was more to the debate over Judaism rather than to study of Luke–Acts.

SETTING THE FOUNDATIONS IN THE NINETEENTH CENTURY

The foundations of subsequent Luke–Acts scholarship were clearly laid in the mid-nineteenth century, and in particular in German scholarship. We do not wish to minimize the significance of other scholars who studied Luke–Acts before that time. Such scholars include: some of the Reformers, who wrote commentaries on Luke and Acts, with Jean Calvin's (1509–1564) commentaries on Luke and especially on Acts being noteworthy; Johann Albrecht Bengel (1687–1752) and his *Gnomon*, a commentary on the Greek text of the entire New Testament;[2] Friedrich Schleiermacher (1768–1834) and his famous 1817 essay on Luke's Gospel as a work of collection and reporting of the accounts of others, including the incorporation of another's travel narrative (Luke 9:51–19:49);[3] and Wilhelm Martin Leberecht de Wette (1780–1849), one of the great scholars of the nineteenth century, who wrote on a wide range of topics, including a significant introduction to the New Testament and a short commentary on the book of Acts, both of which reflect his view that the book was far less programmatic and planned than was thought by other scholars.[4]

The most important figure in the history of Luke–Acts scholarship is Ferdinand Christian Baur (1792–1860).[5] Baur, a church historian, wrote on the New Testament as part of his set of wider theological interests that focused upon the thoroughly historical nature of Christianity. One can see the influence of German idealism, probably including

---

2. John Albert Bengel, *Gnomon of the New Testament*, 5 vols., trans. Andrew R. Fausset (Edinburgh: T&T Clark, 1857–1858), esp. vol. 2, with both Luke and Acts (as well as John's Gospel).

3. William Baird, *History of New Testament Research*, 3 vols. (Minneapolis: Fortress, 1992–2013), 1:215–16, citing Schleiermacher, *A Critical Essay on the Gospel of St. Luke*, trans. Connop Thirlwall (London: J. Taylor, 1825).

4. Gasque, *History of the Criticism*, 24–26, citing W. M. L. de Wette, *Lehrbuch der historisch kritischen Einleitung in die Bibel Alten und Neuen Testaments. Zweyter Theil: Die Einleitung in das Neue Testament enthaltend* (Berlin: Reimer, 1826); and de Wette, *Kurze Erklärung der Apostelgeschichte* (Leipzig: Weidmann, 1838).

5. See Baird, *History of New Testament Research*, 1:258–69; Horton Harris, *The Tübingen School: A Historical and Theological Investigation of the School of F. C. Baur* (repr., Leicester: Apollos, 1990 [1975]), 11–54, 137–80; J. C. O'Neill, *The Bible's Authority: A Portrait Gallery of Thinkers from Lessing to Bultmann* (Edinburgh: T&T Clark, 1991), 117–25 (with 95–107 on Hegel); Tyson, *Luke*, 12–29; Roy A. Harrisville and Walter Sundberg, *The Bible in Modern Culture: Baruch Spinoza to Brevard Childs*, 2nd ed. (Grand Rapids: Eerdmans, 2002), 104–22; Hughson T. Ong, "Ferdinand Christian Baur's Historical Criticism and *Tendenzkritik*," in *Pillars in the History of Biblical Interpretation, Volume 1: Prevailing Methods before 1980*, eds. Stanley E. Porter and Sean A. Adams, MBSS 2 (Eugene, OR: Pickwick, 2016), 118–38.

that of the philosopher Hegel, whose dialectic approach seems to have influenced Baur's conception of the development of thought as the development of Absolute Spirit, a dialectic that had an influence upon much of Baur's criticism. His critical approach is called *Tendenzkritik*, or tendency criticism, which emphasizes the intention of the author, a literary-critical position very much at home in the nineteenth century.[6] Although Baur wrote only a relatively small number of books dedicated to New Testament studies, the entire corpus of his work was concerned with historically accounting for the development of Christian thought. Within this body of work, he wrote on major areas of the New Testament, including the Synoptic Gospels, John's Gospel, Acts, and Paul. Baur's theories are well-known in New Testament studies but bear brief repetition here.

Baur posited that there were two major factions within early Christianity: the Pauline and the Petrine Christians, or the Hellenistic and the Judaistic Christians, with the Pauline view found in the Pauline letters and the Petrine Christians centered upon Jerusalem.[7] The first group focused upon justification and the second on circumcision, which tension resulted in conflict depicted within the Corinthian church. The height of the conflict between the parties is represented in Luke's Gospel, which is, next to Paul's letters, the best source of the Pauline perspective. Written after AD 70 (Baur thought AD 130–140), Luke's Gospel depicts the destruction of Jerusalem and represents Jesus as the redeemer of humanity. This tendency toward universalism (against Matthew's particularism) is seen in Jewish rejection and Gentile acceptance of Jesus, the mission of the seventy, and Jesus's trips to Galilee. Luke's Gospel declares the Mosaic law ended and excludes Peter's declaration regarding Jesus.[8] In that sense, Luke's Gospel is further from Matthew's Gospel and closer to John's Gospel, which Baur posits was written possibly as late as AD 160–170. Marcion, apart from Luke's Gospel, is the greatest

---

6. See Ong, "Ferdinand Christian Baur's Historical Criticism," 131.
7. F. C. Baur, "Die Christuspartei in der korinthischen Gemeinde, der Gegensatz des petrinischen und paulinischen Christentums in der ältesten Kirche, der Apostel Petrus in Rom," *Tübinger Zeitschrift für Theologie* 4 (1831): 61–206. The entire sweep of the history of the development of the first three centuries of the church, from the foundational events to its theology, is found in Baur, *The Church History of the First Three Centuries*, 3rd ed., 2 vols., trans. Allan Menzies (London: Williams and Norgate, 1878–1879); ET of Baur, *Das Christenthum und die christliche Kirche der drei ersten Jahrhunderte* (Tübingen: Fues, 1853; *Kirchengeschichte der drei ersten Jahrhunderte*, 3rd ed., 1863), and followed in the recounting here.
8. See Baur, *Church History*, 1:77–81.

advocate of Paulinism, taken to its extremes in his Gnosticism and his rejection of the Old Testament.[9]

These two parties, Pauline and Petrine, remained at odds with each other until into the second century, when there were efforts to reconcile them brought about by both sides, with intermediate positions attempting to mediate the extremes. One of the major developments was baptism replacing circumcision. A number of New Testament books reflect attempts to reconcile these two parties (e.g. Hebrews, Ephesians, Colossians, Philippians, the Pastoral Epistles, James, and 1 Peter), but the major reconciliatory book was Acts. The foundational tension between the early apostles threatened the church, so it became incumbent, once there was more unity between the parties, to show that this unity had existed from the start. Acts, written by a member of the Pauline party in the second century (c. AD 130–140), was a literary work that also influenced the history of these movements by depicting Paul in relation to the earliest apostles. Acts retains the Paulinist perspective by defending Christian universalism, in which Gentiles, without needing to follow the law, are depicted as equal with Jews. Even if Jews are to follow the law, Gentile Christians were free from following the law apart from cases of greatest offense (see Acts 15:28–29).[10]

Even though Baur does not treat Luke and Acts as a two-part work for the purposes of his reconstruction, he clearly identifies them with important moments and movements within the development of early Christianity. Baur's hypothesis about factions within early Christianity has had continuing significance throughout New Testament scholarship to the present. Several of the major ways it has influenced New Testament criticism include identifying rival factions within the earliest events of Christianity, defining them around major figures in the New Testament, equating the divisions with important cultural and theological beliefs, and seeing the books of the New Testament, in this instance Luke and Acts, in relationship to this fundamental tension. Luke's Gospel represents an encapsulation of Pauline Christianity that stands opposed to the Petrine party, while Acts attempts to rewrite the history of their tension, although from the Pauline perspective.

The effects of Baur's reconstruction of the history of Christianity was seen in two immediate ways, by those who supported his

---

9. Baur, *Church History*, 1:82–84.
10. Baur, *Church History*, 1:131–33.

conclusions and those who opposed them. As one can imagine, Baur's conclusions regarding early Christianity—and in particular the role that Luke and Acts played within it—aroused significant response within scholarship, much of it negative. Baur's position was often rejected outside of Tübingen and led to many of Baur's direct followers having difficulties in securing academic positions. Nevertheless, there were a number of scholars in the mid-nineteenth century connected with Tübingen who accepted and developed his theories regarding the divisions within the early church, to the point that there became what has been called the Tübingen School (1831–1860).[11] Despite its actual demise, many of its suppositions regarding diversity and reconciliation came to characterize New Testament study long after Baur's particular reconstruction was no longer commonly accepted. The follower who was arguably the most radical of all was Bruno Bauer (1809–1888), whom Ward Gasque labels "one of the tragic figures in the history of New Testament interpretation."[12] Baur was so radical in his perspectives that he even alienated David Friedrich Strauss (1808–1874), who was closely aligned with Baur, and thought that Baur had not taken his conclusions far enough. Bauer argued that both Paul and the book of Acts were not historical accounts of early Christianity (and he disputed the authorship of *all* of the Pauline letters). The purpose of Acts is to show how a Jewish group became a universal religion, a view in line with Baur. Written after any contention was long past (but not as a mediating position), Acts depicts a conservative Judaism with Gentile Christianity.[13] Gustav Volkmar (1809–1893) was also a radical among a group that was known in its day for being radical. He assumed most of Baur's presuppositions, such as the Pauline and Petrine parties, and then took them to extremes that even others of the Tübingen school commented upon. As Horton Harris states, "when Volkmar discovers everywhere in the New Testament Pauline and Jewish Christians, Gnostics and anti-gnostics; when Paul entreats Euodia and Syntyche to agree in the Lord (Phil. 4:1) and Volkmar argues that the names refer not to two individuals but to the Pauline and Jewish parties; when he expresses the view that the stories about Jesus in the Gospels are actually descriptions of Paul, then he is only

---

11.   See Harris, *Tübingen School*, 238–39; cf. 181–237.
12.   Gasque, *History of the Criticism*, 73. Cf. O'Neill, *Bible's Authority*, 150–66.
13.   Gasque, *History of the Criticism*, 74–77, citing Bruno Bauer, *Die Apostelgeschichte: Eine Ausgleichung des Paulinismus und des Judenthums innerhalb der christlichen Kirche* (Berlin: Gustav Hempel, 1850).

carrying Baur's principles to their logical conclusion."[14] One of the most significant of the Tübingen scholars who wrote on Luke and/or Acts was Eduard Zeller (1814–1908), Baur's son-in-law. Zeller is probably best known for his work on Acts in which he (perhaps not too surprisingly) "confirms Baur's reconstruction of early Christianity and his assessment of Acts as a tendency document."[15] Before Baur himself wrote his own history of the early church, one of the Tübingen school, Albert Schwegler (1819–1857), published a history of the post-apostolic period in which he attempted to fill out Baur's reconstruction. The work was not well received and so he abandoned writing in the area of theology, even though Baur and Schwegler probably had the closest viewpoint and Schwegler represented the fullness of the position in the mid-nineteenth century. Schwegler was apparently a troubled and generally unpopular person who never held a full-time academic position.[16] Karl Reinhold Köstlin (1819–1893) was more successful in securing academic positions even if he made only a modest contribution to scholarship, including a large two-part article in which he argued for a mediating position regarding the development of the early church. He posited that there was a growing and significant middle party rather than the tension between Paulinism and Petrinism or the triumph of Paulinism (argued by Ritschl; see below).[17] Finally, although he was not associated with the study of Luke or Acts in particular, Adolf Hilgenfeld (1823–1907) was probably the most prolific scholar of Baur's followers. Even though he had some difficulties with all of Baur's presuppositions (e.g., he argued for the authenticity of 1 Thessalonians, which would upset Baur's historical scheme), he generally supported the Tübingen position.[18]

Reaction to and rejection of the Tübingen school was not long in coming, with one of its most important figures being a person who began his academic life as a member. Albrecht Ritschl (1822–1889) made a special effort to move from the north of Germany to Tübingen in the south so that he could study with Baur. Although at first he accepted the Tübingen approach, he soon began publishing works that

---

14. Harris, *Tübingen School*, 133; cf. 127–33.
15. Baird, *History of New Testament Research*, 1:271.
16. Harris, *Tübingen School*, 78–88, esp. 84, referring to Albert Schwegler, *Das Nachapostolische Zeitalter in den Hauptmomenten seiner Entwicklung* (Tübingen: Fues, 1846).
17. Harris, *Tübingen School*, 96–100, esp. 98, referring to Karl Reinhold Köstlin, "Zur Geschichte des Urchristenthums," *Theologische Jahrbücher* (1850): 1–62, 235–302.
18. Harris, *Tübingen School*, 113–26, esp. 119–20.

rejected its major suppositions regarding the major factions within the early church. This criticism began in Ritschl's well-known book on Marcion that included some criticism of Schwegler's book on the post-apostolic church and then continued in a variety of writings, including a critical review of Baur's major work on the apostle Paul.[19] Ritschl questioned such elements of the position as Baur's rejection of authenticity of the Thessalonian letters and 2 Timothy and Titus until the point where Ritschl recognized that, although he had respect for Baur and his approach, he could not accept his views regarding authorship and hence his reconstruction of early Christianity. Ritschl's work was followed by that of others who directly attacked the Tübingen position and developed their own opinions in other directions.[20] Ritschl is known today as the leading figure in the development of theological liberalism. One could argue that Philip Schaff (1819–1893) and Joseph Barber Lightfoot (1828–1889) reflect a more conservative reaction to Baur and the Tübingen approach, although their work on Luke and Acts is contained within their history of the early church. Educated at Tübingen and appreciative of Baur's historical approach, Schaff however was much more conservative in his approach to the history of early Christianity.[21] Lightfoot reacted directly to Baur's hypotheses in his multivolume treatment of the Apostolic Fathers, in which he directly challenged the historical reconstruction of the second century and the development of early Christianity by the Tübingen school.[22] In the few things that he directly wrote on Acts, Lightfoot endorses traditional views of Lukan authorship, historicity, and early date.[23]

---

19. Albrecht Ritschl, *Das Evangelium Marcions und das kanonische Evangelium des Lucas* (Tübingen: Osiander, 1846) and Ritschl, review of Baur in *Allgemeine Literatur-Zeitung* (Halle and Leipzig, 1847), 124–27, reviewing Ferdinand Christian Baur, *Paulus, der Apostel Jesu Christi: Sein Leben und Wirken, seine Briefe und seine Lehre* (Stuttgart: Becker & Müller, 1845; 2nd ed., 1866–1867); ET Baur, *Paul, the Apostle of Jesus Christ: His Life and Works, His Epistles and Teachings*, 2 vols. in one (repr., Peabody, MA: Hendrickson, 2003 [1873–1875]).

20. See Harris, *Tübingen School*, 238–48.

21. Baird, *History of New Testament Research*, 2:43–52.

22. Baird, *History of New Testament Research*, 2:66–73, esp. 71–73, with reference to J. B. Lightfoot, *The Apostolic Fathers*, 2 parts in 5 vols. (London: Macmillan, 1890, 1885); and Gasque, *History of the Criticism*, 116–23.

23. Several of Lightfoot's publications on Acts, including his article on it in Smith's *Dictionary of the Bible* and his incomplete commentary based on lecture notes, have recently been published in J. B. Lightfoot, *The Acts of the Apostles: A Newly Discovered Commentary*, Lightfoot Legacy Set 1, ed. Ben Witherington III and Todd D. Still (Downers Grove, IL: InterVarsity, 2014). The dictionary article is on pp. 279–326 (without full publication information).

There are several different ways in which the history of scholarship on Luke–Acts, and those who have had the greatest impact on such scholarship, may be told from this point to the present. One way would be to treat the discussion of Luke and Acts separately, as there are numerous issues that focus more upon one book than another. These include issues related to the Synoptics and Luke and the Gentile mission of the church in Acts. A second way is simply to identify a number of different topics within Luke–Acts scholarship and treat them synchronically. A third way is to treat them together according to major topics within Luke–Acts scholarship as it has diachronically progressed. Rather than treating the two books separately, we will treat them together and we will diachronically trace the history of research. Out of the history of Luke–Acts scholarship, however, two major topics have emerged. These are the importance of theology and history. The two have been intertwined in Luke–Acts scholarship since at least the time of Baur and continue to be important in contemporary discussion. We will focus upon these two topics, while also noting others of importance.

THE LATE-NINETEENTH AND EARLY TWENTIETH CENTURIES

As we move into the post-Baur and Tübingen period, there was an increasing diversity in New Testament scholarship as centers of study developed not just in Germany and Britain but in North America and elsewhere. There began to emerge some clear, diverse lines of thought regarding Luke–Acts. The late nineteenth and early twentieth century was a period in which some of the major lines of thought became significant.

A strong line of continuity with the dominant Tübingen trend in earlier nineteenth-century scholarship is found in the work of Franz Overbeck (1837–1905).[24] Although a professor of theology in Basel, Overbeck was an agnostic who had little regard for Christianity and was a good friend of Friedrich Nietzsche (1844–1900). Overbeck identified with the Tübingen approach to history with its developmentalism and anti-supernaturalism, although without the same Hegelian assumptions. Overbeck argued for a rigorous historiography that, in many respects, arguably takes the Tübingen approach to its logical conclusions. His

---

24. Baird, *History of New Testament Research*, 2:138–44, esp. 140–41; O'Neill, *Bible's Authority*, 179–90 (on Nietzsche, see 191–97).

major work on the book of Acts was to expand de Wette's commentary on Acts, including adding a new introduction.[25] Gasque observes that Overbeck's expanded version of de Wette's commentary amounts to a new work, especially when Overbeck places his contradictory ideas next to those of de Wette. This would have been the only commentary on Acts written by the Tübingen school. Overbeck follows Zeller in many ways, Gasque contends, except for the fact that he does not follow Baur in the purpose of Acts but instead follows a line closer to that of Bauer.[26] In other words, Overbeck sees Acts as an attempt to depict the Gentile Christianity of anywhere from AD 120–140 not as reflecting Paulinism but as reflecting Jewish thought. Another of the Tübingen followers was Otto Pfleiderer (1839–1908), although he is not so closely identified with Luke–Acts in particular.[27] Pfleiderer was the last of Baur's important students at Tübingen. His major accomplishment was a major work on the history of early Christianity, one of whose four volumes is dedicated to the Synoptic Gospels and Acts.[28] He argues that Acts was written as a conciliatory document, although he does not endorse Baur's two-parties hypothesis.

In contrast to Overbeck and Pfleiderer, Friedrich Blass (1843–1907) made a significant contribution to scholarship on Luke–Acts, one that is now often overlooked. Blass, although he is associated with the grammar written under his name,[29] was better known in his own day and age as a major textual scholar. Blass was a classical philologist, with a specialization in Greek oratory, who edited editions of a variety of ancient authors including Andocides, Antiphon, Hyperides, Demosthenes in multiple editions, Isocrates, Dinarchus, Aeschines, and Lycurgus.[30] His contribution to Luke–Acts studies (besides any contribution to study of its Greek grammar) is his Greek editions of

25. See Baird, *History of New Testament Research*, 2:140–41, referring to W. M. L. de Wette, *Kurze Erklärung der Apostelgeschichte*, 4th ed., rev. and expanded Frans Overbeck (Leipzig: Hirzel, 1870). Cf. Gasque, *History of the Criticism*, 80–86.

26. Gasque, *History of the Criticism*, 82, 83.

27. Baird, *History of New Testament Research*, 2:213–20.

28. Baird, *History of New Testament Research*, 2:217–18, citing Otto Pfleiderer, *Primitive Christianity: Its Writings and Teachings in Their Historical Connections*, trans. W. Montgomery, ed. W. D. Morrison, 4 vols., TTL (London: Williams & Norgate, 1906–1911 [1887]).

29. He is treated as a grammarian in Baird, *History of New Testament Research*, 2:184–85 and even Gasque, *History of the Criticism*, 97.

30. See Ryder A. Wishart, "Friedrich Blass and A. T. Robertson: Comprehensive and Comparative Greek Grammars from the Modern Vantage Point," in *Pillars in the History of Biblical Interpretation, Volume 3: Further Essays on Prevailing Methods*, eds. Stanley E. Porter and Zachary K. Dawson, MBSS 6 (Eugene, OR: Pickwick, 2021), 89–109, esp. 90.

Luke and of Acts—but more than that, his theory of two authoritative early editions of both Luke and Acts, with the so-called Western text of both Luke and Acts reflecting one of those traditions, and the Alexandrian the other.[31] Blass argues that Luke was responsible for both traditions, possibly accounting for the Gospel being in one form when written and sent to Theophilus and then in a different form when presented to the church in Rome, with a similar pattern for Acts of one presented to Rome and then one sent to Theophilus (and hence early dates for both).[32] Whereas Blass's view on Acts is well-known (he was not the only one to hold it), and has been revived and enhanced in more recent scholarship,[33] the fact that he took the same view on Luke's Gospel has virtually disappeared from scholarship[34]—a striking contrast to the persistence of Baur's views.

One of the most important scholars of this time, or any time, was the Berlin scholar Adolf Harnack (1851–1930).[35] On the one hand, Harnack in many ways represents the culmination of the liberal thought of Ritschl. On the other hand, Harnack functioned on the outskirts of the religious establishment of his times. Harnack reflects many of the principles of the Tübingen school, especially in his developmental views regarding history and how Christianity should be treated as a historical problem. As a result, Harnack emphasizes the importance of history as reflection of the human spirit, was skeptical of miracles, and, in true liberal fashion, was "anthropocentric and

---

31.   This view is reflected in his editions of the Gospel and of Acts: Friedrich Blass, *Euangelium secundum Lucam sive Lucae ad Theophilum liber prior secundam formam quae videtur romanam* (Leipzig: Teubner, 1897) and Blass, *Acta apostolorum sive Lucae ad Theophilum liber alter* (Göttingen: Vandenhoeck & Ruprecht, 1895; 2nd ed., 1896).

32.   Friedrich Blass, *Philology of the Gospels* (London: Macmillan, 1898), esp. 100–101. Blass defends his view for both Luke's Gospel and Acts at various points throughout this volume.

33.   Blass is followed on Acts but not Luke's Gospel by Theodor Zahn, *Introduction to the New Testament*, trans. Melancthon Williams Jacobus, et al., 3 vols. (Edinburgh: T&T Clark, 1909), 3:8–41. The most rigorous defense of such a two-version view of Acts is probably M. E. Boismard and A. Lamouille, *Texte occidental: Des Actes des Apôtres*, 2 vols. (Paris: Recherche sur le civilisations, 1984) and extended further in Boismard and Lamouille, *Les Actes des Deux Apôtres*, 3 vols., EB 12–14 (Paris: Gabalda, 1990).

34.   A survey of more than twenty-five commentaries on Luke's Gospel written since Blass published his work reveals only one who discusses his theory for the Gospel: M.-J. Lagrange, *Évangile selon Saint Luc*, EB (Paris: Gabalda, 1948), clii–cliii, but who rejects it as arbitrary.

35.   Baird, *History of New Testament Research*, 2:122–35; Gasque, *History of the Criticism*, 146–55; O'Neill, *Bible's Authority*, 214–29; Tyson, *Luke*, 30–42. Another scholar who wrote on Luke–Acts was Theodor Zahn (1838–1933). However, Zahn wrote on most of the New Testament, and his areas of recognized expertise were in the realms of canon and introduction. See Baird, *History of New Testament Research*, 2:367–73.

Christocentric."[36] Harnack's historiographic method includes a mix of attention to data and the influence of German theories of history. Harnack was one of the most productive scholars of his or any era. Most important for this volume is that he wrote significant works on the history of the development of Christianity and most importantly on both Luke and Acts, where he finally arrived at surprisingly early dates for the composition of both Luke's Gospel and Acts.[37] Harnack is the earliest scholar represented in this volume on milestone figures in Luke–Acts and more details about his life and work are found in the essay in this volume.

In both comparison and contrast, one might point to a line of scholars in Luke–Acts scholarship who in some respects follow Harnack with their conservative conclusions, but who are quite distinct from his theological liberalism and to be identified with the developments of evangelical Christianity. This line of scholarship begins with William Ramsay (1851–1939), the Scottish archaeologist and early Christian historian.[38] In the early years of his career, Ramsay, who studied in Germany, came under the influence of the Tübingen school, as he admits in his own writings. He began his study of Asia Minor with the view that the book of Acts was not a reliable historical source for his study. However, as he investigated Asia Minor more carefully in light of the book of Acts, he came to believe that Acts reflected an accurate picture of the time of Paul. He apparently began with Acts 14 and extended his work and view of its reliability from there, enlarging his study to Paul and his letters.[39] One of the major topics Ramsay took up was defense of the so-called Southern Galatian hypothesis. Ramsay did not contribute nearly so much to the study of Luke's Gospel,

36. Baird, *History of New Testament Research*, 2:124.
37. Adolf Harnack, *Luke the Physician: The Author of the Third Gospel and the Acts of the Apostles*, trans. J. R. Wilkinson (London: Williams & Norgate, 1908); Harnack, *The Sayings of Jesus: The Second Source of St. Matthew and St. Luke*, trans. J. R. Wilkinson (London: Williams & Norgate, 1908); Harnack, *The Acts of the Apostles*, trans. J. R. Wilkinson (London: Williams & Norgate, 1909); and Harnack, *The Date of the Acts and of the Synoptic Gospels*, trans. J. R. Wilkinson (London: Williams & Norgate, 1911).
38. See Gasque, *History of the Criticism*, 136–42; W. Ward Gasque, *Sir William M. Ramsay, Archaeologist and New Testament Scholar* (Grand Rapids: Baker, 1966). For a comparison of Ramsay with Ernst Haenchen, see Daniel So, "William Ramsay and Ernst Haenchen," in *Pillars in the History of Biblical Interpretation, Volume 1*, 302–20.
39. W. M. Ramsay, *The Bearing of Recent Discovery on the Trustworthiness of the New Testament* (London: Hodder & Stoughton, 1905), 39–52. He concludes: "Acts rightly understood is the best commentary on the letters of Paul, and the letters on the Acts" (52). See also Ramsay, *St. Paul the Traveller and the Roman Citizen* (London: Hodder & Stoughton, 1897) and numerous articles in Hastings's *Dictionary of the Bible* (see Gasque, *Ramsay*, 88–91, for references).

although he did write on some issues related to Luke as author, such as the identity of Luke and the Lukan census.[40]

At the end of the nineteenth century and the beginning of the twentieth century, we see that there were two major perspectives reflected in study of Luke–Acts. The mainstream of critical scholarship had clearly been influenced by the perspective of Baur and the Tübingen school, with its historical skepticism and emphasis upon the theological agenda of the author of Luke–Acts. There was, however, some resurgence during this time of an effort to defend the historical reliability of Luke and Acts, especially Acts, as an important record of the development of the early church.

THE FLOURISHING OF THE
EARLY TO MID-TWENTIETH CENTURY

The early to middle years of the twentieth century marked a period of flourishing within Luke–Acts studies. There were a number of scholars and projects on Luke–Acts that generated major research that is worth noting. As a result, it is understandable that the majority of the scholars discussed in this volume belong to this period.

We begin this period by noting the major five-volume work on Acts edited by F. J. Foakes Jackson (1855–1941) and Kirsopp Lake (1872–1946).[41] This five-volume set is not written by a single person, but it certainly stands as a milestone in the history of Luke–Acts scholarship. Published over the course of thirteen years (1920–1933), these five volumes were an anticipated but never realized inception of a greater series of volumes on the beginnings of Christianity.[42] Foakes Jackson, who taught at Cambridge for much of his career and then at Union Theological Seminary in New York, was a church historian who wrote a number of works on the history and development of Christianity well into the post-apostolic period, as well as writing a popular level commentary on Acts.[43] Lake, who taught at Harvard Divinity

---

40. See W. M. Ramsay, *Luke the Physician and Other Studies in the History of Religion* (London: Hodder & Stoughton, 1908), esp. 1–68, 71–101; and Ramsay, *Was Christ Born at Bethlehem? A Study on the Credibility of St. Luke* (London: Hodder & Stoughton, 1898).
41. This collection is examined in Gasque, *History of the Criticism*, 171–85 along with his treatment of Cadbury.
42. F. J. Foakes Jackson and Kirsopp Lake, eds., *The Beginnings of Christianity. Part 1: The Acts of the Apostles*, 5 vols. (London: Macmillan, 1920–1933).
43. F. J. Foakes-Jackson, *The Acts of the Apostles*, MNTC (London: Hodder & Stoughton, 1931).

School, was a New Testament scholar who is probably best remembered today for his work in textual criticism, including publishing the photographs of the Sinaiticus codex, and his translation of the Apostolic Fathers for the Loeb Classical Library.[44] Nevertheless, their efforts at promoting scholarship in the book of Acts endure. Volumes one and two include prolegomena and criticism. Volume one contains essays on Jewish, Gentile, and primitive Christian backgrounds. It includes ten essays and five appendixes. Six of the ten essays are written by the editors, as are three of the appendixes. These essays lay out the foundations of this set of volumes, which are designed to be full historical-critical examinations of major topics and issues in the beginnings of Christianity. Hence the essays in this volume discuss such topics as Jewish historical background (the editors); the spirit of Judaism (C. G. Montefiore); the variety of thought within Judaism (the editors); the dispersion of the Jews (the editors); the Roman system of provinces (H. T. F. Duckworth); life in the Roman era (Clifford H. Moore); the teaching of Jesus (the editors); the disciples and rise of Gentile Christianity (the editors); Christian thought on the Spirit, church, and baptism (the editors); and Christology (the editors). Volume two continues questions of prolegomena and criticism with essays on the composition and purpose of Acts and the identity of the editor of Luke and Acts. In the first section, there are essays on the Greek and Jewish traditions, the Greek used in Acts, the Septuagint, use of Mark in Luke's Gospel, and internal evidence of Acts. Two of these essays are by the editors, but other authors include Henry J. Cadbury (see below), J. de Zwaan, W. K. L. Clarke, and F. C. Burkitt. The second section includes four essays on tradition, by the editors, Cadbury, C. W. Emmet, and H. Windisch. The criticism section includes an essay on historical criticism on Acts in Germany by A. C. McGiffert and British criticism by J. W. Hunkin. There are also three appendixes, the last a commentary on Luke's preface by Cadbury. Volume three stands out for its being an edition by J. H. Ropes (1866–1933) of the book of Acts from both codex Vaticanus and codex Bezae (on facing pages), preceded by an introduction of 320 pages on textual criticism—one of the fullest introductions to manuscripts and issues, at least at the time, that is available—and followed by nearly two hundred pages of

---

44. Baird, *History of New Testament Research*, 2:406–10.

further notes.[45] Ropes, who taught at Harvard Divinity School, is now lesser known in New Testament scholarship apart from his commentary on James (ICC), although his work on Acts represents enduring scholarship. Volume four, in some ways an independent volume like volume three, is a translation and commentary on Acts by Lake and Cadbury.[46] Cadbury is noted elsewhere in this introduction, and he has an entire essay devoted to him in this volume. The fifth and final volume is a collection of thirty-seven (one is coauthored) essays on a range of topics. Eighteen of the essays are written by Lake, and eleven by Cadbury. The rest are written by Robert P. Casey (two), Silva New (two), Lily Ross Taylor (two), Arthur Darby Nock, Vincent Scramuzza, and T. R. S. Broughton. They cover a wide variety of specialized topics within Acts, such as the preface, the ascension, the apostles, God-fearers, the Holy Spirit, Simon Magus, the apostolic council, the unknown god, Artemis, Asiarchs, Roman law and Paul's trial, titles of Jesus, speeches in Acts, chronology, and other topics. This five-volume set remains one of the greatest accomplishments in Acts scholarship because of the both breadth and depth that it brings to discussion of Acts. It remains unreplaced as a single location for this kind of suitable information, written by scholars of recognized expertise and competence.

One of the major movements within twentieth-century biblical scholarship was the rise of form and redaction criticism in relation to the Gospels and Acts.[47] These forms of criticism definitely had their roots in the nineteenth century, and some would even say that they developed during that time. Therefore, one sees early versions of form criticism in scholars such as Julius Wellhausen (1844–1918), William Wrede (1859–1906), Benjamin Wisner Bacon (1860–1932), Hermann Gunkel (1862–1932), and Eduard Norden (1868–1941),[48]

---

45. James Hardy Ropes, *The Text of Acts*, vol. 3 of *The Beginnings of Christianity*, eds. F. J. Foakes Jackson and Kirsopp Lake (London: Macmillan, 1926).

46. Kirsopp Lake and Henry J. Cadbury, *English Translation and Commentary*, vol. 4 of *The Beginnings of Christianity*, eds. F. J. Foakes Jackson and Kirsopp Lake (London: Macmillan, 1933).

47. Gospel source criticism has a much longer history in scholarly discussion, with the rise of critical Gospel source criticism gaining most of its impetus in the nineteenth century and then carrying into the twentieth century. Most of the scholars important in the rise and development of Gospel source criticism do not appear to have made a significant impact on Luke–Acts studies, apart from their treatment of Luke within discussion of the Synoptic problem. Some of the most important in this discussion are Heinrich Holtzmann (1832–1910) and B. H. Streeter (1874–1937).

48. See Baird, *History of New Testament Research*, 2:238–39, 151–56, 144–51, 300–305, respectively. Baird does not treat Norden in any detail.

and redaction criticism in Wrede, R. H. Lightfoot (1883–1953), Ned B. Stonehouse (1902–1962), and A. M. Farrer (1904–1968), among others.[49] However, self-conscious advocacy of their approach emerged more clearly in the early twentieth century. Some of the most important names in this regard—although by no means the only ones who might be mentioned—are the major form critics, the Germans Martin Dibelius (see below for discussion), Rudolf Bultmann (1884–1976),[50] Karl Ludwig Schmidt (1891–1956),[51] and, so far as English scholarship is concerned, Vincent Taylor (1887–1968),[52] followed by the German redaction critics Günther Bornkamm (1905–1990),[53] Hans Conzelmann (see discussion below), Willi Marxsen (1919–1993),[54] and Ernst Haenchen (see discussion below). These types of criticism are all related, as is seen in their works. Form criticism is concerned to examine the literary forms used to transmit the oral tradition of the early church while redaction criticism is concerned with how these traditions are theologically interpreted by the Gospel writers. The interaction between the two becomes obvious in how form critics differentiate theological tendencies within Gospel writers and how redaction critics base their theological interpretations upon form-critical assumptions within the Gospel accounts.

Of these scholars, several of them were not only major advocates of various forms of criticism but were major contributors to discussion of Luke–Acts. Of these, Martin Dibelius (1883–1947) must be mentioned first.[55] A professor at the University of Heidelberg, Dibelius wrote in the period from the First World War through the Second

---

49. Besides Wrede (see note above), Baird does not treat any of the other of these authors in any detail, not even mentioning Stonehouse.

50. Baird, *History of New Testament Research*, 2:280–86 and 3:85–117. See Rudolf Bultmann, *History of the Synoptic Tradition*, trans. John Marsh (Oxford: Blackwell, 1963 [1921]), where the final section, entitled "Die Redaktion des Erzählungsstoffes und die Komposition der Evangelien" (German ed., 362–92; ET 337–67), shows how redaction criticism grows out of form criticism.

51. Baird, *History of New Testament Research*, 2:270–73. See Karl Ludwig Schmidt, *Der Rahmen der Geschichte Jesu: Literarkritische Untersuchungen zur ältesten Jesusüberlieferung* (Berlin: Trowitzsch, 1919).

52. Darlene Seal, "Vincent Taylor and Form Criticism," in *Pillars in the History of Biblical Interpretation, Volume 3*, 201–26. Baird does not treat Taylor in detail.

53. Baird, *History of New Testament Research*, 3:147–68. See Günther Bornkamm, "The Stilling of the Storm in Matthew" (1948) and "End-Expectation and Church in Matthew" (1954), in Bornkamm, Gerhard Barth, and Heinz Joachim Held, *Tradition and Interpretation in Matthew*, NTL, trans. Percy Scott (Philadelphia: Westminster, 1963), 52–57 and 15–51, respectively.

54. Baird, *History of New Testament Research*, 3:360–65. See Willi Marxsen, *Mark the Evangelist: Studies on the Redaction History of the Gospel*, trans. John Boyce, et al. (Nashville: Abingdon, 1969 [1956]).

55. Baird, *History of New Testament Research*, 2:273–79; Gasque, *History of the Criticism*, 201–35.

World War and its many privations. He wrote on a variety of topics, including well-known commentaries on the Pastoral Epistles (HNT/ Hermeneia), James (KEK/Hermeneia), and Colossians, Ephesians, Philemon, Thessalonians, and Philippians (these last in the HNT series). However, he is probably best known for his form-critical work on both the Gospels and Acts, although his work on Acts for which he is best known was not published until four years after his death (1951).[56] Dibelius laid out basic criteria of form criticism, or what is called in the first chapter (in English) "the Criticism of Literary Form," that were further developed and responded to by other scholars, German and elsewhere. These forms include sermons, paradigms, tales (Novelle), legends, and analogies including *chriae*. Dibelius also defined the passion story as a separate identifiable unit. His book on Acts was a later composite of mostly but not entirely previously published essays (written and published from 1923 up to the time of his death), reflecting an overall form-critical orientation that Dibelius lays out in the initial essay in the volume on "style criticism" in Acts. A consistent thread in Dibelius's treatment of episodes in Acts, such as the Areopagus speech, Athens, apostolic council, Cornelius, and other speeches, is that the historical element is strongly tempered in each situation by the theological interpretation within the book of Acts. Dibelius occupies a major place in Luke–Acts studies within the last century and a chapter in this volume is dedicated to his work.

A further, important figure to mention at this point is Henry Cadbury (1883–1974).[57] In some ways like the better-known German form and redaction critics, Cadbury arguably utilized a form of redaction criticism while critically appropriating form criticism.[58] Cadbury was a devout Quaker and devoted to Quaker causes throughout his

---

56. Martin Dibelius, *Die Formgeschichte des Evangeliums* (Tübingen: Mohr Siebeck, 1919; 6th ed., ed. Günther Bornkamm, 1971); ET of 2nd ed. as Dibelius, *From Tradition to Gospel*, trans. Bertram Lee Woolf (London: Ivor Nicholson and Watson, 1934); and Dibelius, *Aufsätze zur Apostelgeschichte*, ed. Heinrich Greeven, FRLANT 42 (Göttingen: Vandenhoeck & Ruprecht, 1951); ET Dibelius, *Studies in the Acts of the Apostles*, ed. Heinrich Greeven, trans. Mary Ling and Paul Schubert (London: SCM, 1951).
57. Baird, *History of New Testament Research*, 3:16–26; Gasque, *History of the Criticism*, 168–94 (along with treatment of the five volumes of *Beginnings*); Zachary K. Dawson, "Henry J. Cadbury and the Composition of Luke–Acts," in *Pillars in the History of Interpretation, Volume 3*, 173–200; cf. the essays in Parsons and Tyson, eds., *Cadbury, Knox, and Talbert*, 7–51.
58. See Henry J. Cadbury, "Between Jesus and the Gospels," *HTR* 16 (1923): 81–92. Baird, *History of New Testament Research*, 3:19 notes that this essay appeared a decade before Vincent Taylor wrote on form criticism for the English-speaking world.

life, including receiving the Nobel Peace Prize on behalf of the American Friends Service Committee. Having received his doctorate at Harvard, Cadbury eventually became professor at Harvard Divinity School, succeeding Ropes. It is reportedly to Cadbury that we owe the hyphenated reference to Luke–Acts, and Luke–Acts was clearly Cadbury's area of scholarly interest. As already noted above, Cadbury was a major contributor to the five-volume collection of essays on Acts edited by Foakes Jackson and Lake, including not only a number of essays but a commentary on Acts. However, Cadbury is known for having written three important monographs on Luke–Acts. The first is his *The Style and Literary Method of Luke*,[59] which was originally his doctoral dissertation at Harvard. The volume is divided into two parts. The first deals with the lexis of Luke–Acts. Cadbury shows that the author used a vocabulary with Attic influence and reflective of the kind of language found in other accomplished Hellenistic authors of the time. This vocabulary is not, however, more medical than that of other writers who were not doctors, thus disputing the claims that Luke was a physician. The second part deals with Luke's sources. In an early form of redaction criticism, insofar as Cadbury considers theological reasons, he shows the various ways in which the author treats Mark. Cadbury expanded his treatment of Luke–Acts in his second major work, *The Making of Luke–Acts*,[60] where he indicates that he was responsible for the titular hyphenation. One of the major purposes of the volume is to illustrate and establish the unity of the two volumes by exploring their materials, common methods, author, and purpose. Cadbury's final contribution to the discussion was his *The Book of Acts in History*,[61] which in a number of ways is a continuation of the work he did in the Foakes Jackson and Lake series. He treats Acts as a reliable source for its environment. He deals with the various environments in which Acts functioned, including Greek, Roman, Jewish, and Christian. Cadbury clearly remains one of the underestimated significant figures in scholarship on Luke–Acts. However, he is studied in more detail in a chapter in this volume.

---

59. Henry J. Cadbury, *The Style and Literary Method of Luke*, HTS 6 (Cambridge, MA: Harvard University Press, 1920).
60. Henry J. Cadbury, *The Making of Luke–Acts* (New York: Macmillan, 1927; 2nd ed., London: SPCK, 1958). See the "Preface to the Second Edition" (ix–x, esp. x) for reference to the hyphenated phrase.
61. Henry J. Cadbury, *The Book of Acts in History* (London: A&C Black, 1955).

By contrast, in German scholarship, many scholars tended to follow the course of thought promoted by Dibelius. The earliest major redaction critic who was also a noteworthy Luke–Acts scholar was Hans Conzelmann (1915–1989).[62] A student of Bultmann, and then of Bultmann's student Bornkamm, Conzelmann fought in World War II in both Russia and France and was wounded and lost a leg. Conzelmann was a prolific scholar, writing commentaries on a number of books (he revised Dibelius's commentary on the Pastoral Epistles in HNT/Hermeneia, wrote his own on 1 Corinthians in KEK/Hermeneia, and wrote commentaries on Ephesians and Colossians in NTD), as well as publishing an "outline" of New Testament theology. Conzelmann is best known, however, for his redaction-critical analysis of Luke's theology. In his volume *Die Mitte der Zeit* (nondescriptively translated as *The Theology of St Luke*),[63] Conzelmann argues against the prevailing motif of promise and fulfillment and sees Luke–Acts as portraying salvation history. Luke writes in response to the delayed parousia and depicts three stages in the history of salvation: Israel, Jesus Christ, and the church. The period of Jesus Christ is thus in the middle of time. Luke thereby reflects his own theological orientation to the Jesus tradition and interprets it theologically. Conzelmann's commentary on Acts, published in the Handbuch zum Neuen Testament (HNT) and then translated for the Hermeneia series,[64] shows the influence of Haenchen with whom he carried on a longstanding correspondence (see below). Conzelmann concentrates on commenting on the text from a philological and historical standpoint. Despite this, Conzelmann sees Acts as following the same salvation-historical schema as in the Gospel. The biblical author conveys his own theological and historical positions throughout the work, as is reflected in the speeches as literary products. Conzelmann is discussed in more detail in a chapter within this volume.

A major figure closely associated with Conzelmann is Ernst Haenchen (1894–1975), whose commentary on Acts has been one of the most enduring critical commentaries in both German and English

62. Baird, *History of New Testament Research*, 3:353–59; Gasque, *History of the Criticism*, 247–50, 291–96; Tyson, *Luke*, 76–90.
63. Hans Conzelmann, *Die Mitte der Zeit: Studien zur Theologie des Lukas*, BHT 17 (Tübingen: Mohr Siebeck, 1953; 6th ed., 1964); ET Conzelmann, *The Theology of St Luke*, trans. Geoffrey Buswell (London: Faber and Faber, 1960).
64. Hans Conzelmann, *Die Apostelgeschichte*, HNT 7 (Tübingen: Mohr Siebeck, 1963); ET Conzelmann, *Acts of the Apostles*, trans. James Limburg, et al., Hermeneia (Philadelphia: Fortress, 1987).

scholarship.[65] Like Dibelius, of whom he was a student, Haenchen was dramatically affected by both world wars, as well as by numerous recurring health problems. In the First World War, Haenchen was seriously injured, requiring numerous surgeries and losing one of his legs, and in the second he chose to align himself with the National Socialists, even though he was medically unable to participate in the war. Haenchen also suffered from tuberculosis over the course of many years. Haenchen was a professor of systematic theology in the mid-war period, and his theological and philosophical interests had an abiding influence upon his scholarship. He only turned to New Testament teaching during the Second World War when there was a lack of New Testament professors in Germany, an interest that he continued after the war when he no longer held a full-time academic position. Haenchen is aligned with the redaction critics on the basis of his work on Mark's Gospel, *Der Weg Jesu*, that displays a type of redaction criticism.[66] He also was working on a major commentary on the Gospel of John at the time of his death, which commentary was later published in both German and English editions (Hermeneia). However, the major work for which Haenchen is known is his commentary on Acts, first published in the Meyer commentary series and then translated into English.[67] This commentary went through seven editions in the Meyer series from 1956 to 1977, until it was replaced in 1998 by a new commentary by Jacob Jervell (on whom see below). In many ways, Haenchen's commentary was an extension of the kind of historical skepticism found in Dibelius's earlier work and represented the mainstream of German thought maintained in the second half of the twentieth century. Haenchen's contribution to Luke–Acts scholarship is considered more fully in a chapter in this volume.

The strength and endurance of the views of Dibelius, Conzelmann, and Haenchen, as a moderated endorsement of the Baur school, cannot be underestimated. This position has come to dominate critical scholarship on Luke and Acts, including its universalism,

65. See James Robinson, "Foreword," in Ernst Haenchen, *John*, 2 vols., trans. Robert W. Funk, eds. Robert W. Funk with Ulrich Busse, Hermeneia (Philadelphia: Fortress, 1984), 1:ix–xiii; Gasque, *History of the Criticism*, 235–47; Tyson, *Luke*, 66–76. Haenchen is not discussed in detail in Baird.
66. Ernst Haenchen, *Der Weg Jesu: Eine Erklärung des Markus-Evangeliums und der kanonischen Parallelen* (Berlin: Alfred Töpelmann, 1966; 2nd ed., Berlin: de Gruyter, 1968).
67. Ernst Haenchen, *Die Apostelgeschichte*, KEK 3 (Göttingen: Vandenhoeck & Ruprecht, 1956); ET of the 14th ed. of 1965 as Haenchen, *The Acts of the Apostles: A Commentary*, trans. Bernard Noble and Gerald Shinn, rev. R. McL. Wilson (Oxford: Blackwell; Philadelphia: Westminster, 1971).

its eschatology, and its questioning of historicity. There was a conservative scholarly reaction to this position, in large part following the kind of archaeologically based but common-sensical view of history that Ramsay endorsed. This position came to characterize a major stream in British and American scholarship on Luke–Acts that, at least in some ways, has also continued to the present. This stream is seen, perhaps most significantly, in three major Luke–Acts scholars: F. F. Bruce, Colin Hemer, and I. Howard Marshall. Bruce (1910–1990) served a very important role in the development of evangelical scholarship especially in Britain but also in the rest of the English-speaking world.[68] Like Ramsay, Bruce, also a Scot, was educated as a classicist and taught in this area until he accepted a position as the founding head of department in biblical studies at the University of Sheffield. He went on to become the Rylands Professor in Biblical Criticism and Exegesis at the University of Manchester. Although Bruce is not very well known for scholarship on Luke's Gospel (and in fact only wrote on the Gospel occasionally), he is still highly regarded for his work on various dimensions of Acts scholarship. He wrote two major commentaries on Acts, as well as addressing some of the major issues regarding Acts, such as the speeches and historical reliability (where he opposed the views of Dibelius, Conzelmann, and Haenchen).[69] Bruce was surprisingly open in his interpretations, not taking a standard line in a number of areas (such as dating of Daniel), but on the major questions in Luke–Acts scholarship he was a proponent of Luke as a reliable historian who used his sources well and faithfully represented the speeches of the figures in Acts. There is a chapter on Bruce included within this volume, so we need not say more about him here.

Although the major lines of Luke–Acts scholarship were already laid in the nineteenth century, a number of major Luke–Acts scholars continued to develop some of the lines of the Baur hypothesis, although with a number of new dimensions especially concerning Lukan theology. The skepticism that often accompanied such views

---

68. Tim Grass, *F. F. Bruce: A Life* (Grand Rapids: Eerdmans, 2011); Gasque, *History of the Criticism*, 257–64.
69. See, e.g., F. F. Bruce, *The Speeches in the Acts of the Apostles* (London: Tyndale, 1943), the first of several works on the speeches; Bruce, *The Acts of the Apostles: The Greek Text with Introduction and Commentary* (London: Tyndale; Grand Rapids: Eerdmans, 1951; 2nd ed., 1952; Grand Rapids: Eerdmans; Leicester: Apollos, 3rd ed., 1990); and Bruce, *Commentary on the Book of the Acts*, NICNT (Grand Rapids: Eerdmans, 1954; *The Book of the Acts*, 2nd ed., 1988).

was also opposed in some more conservative circles by scholars who approached the text from classical historical perspectives.

THE SOLIDIFICATION AND INNOVATION OF THE MID- TO LATE TWENTIETH CENTURY

The mid-to-end of the twentieth century witnessed a mix of approaches to the study of Luke–Acts. On the one hand, it was a time of consolidation of the major perspectives that had been outlined in the previous periods. On the other hand, there were several innovations that marked serious progress in the study of these two books. In this section, we will briefly trace the course of the developments in these areas.

Much of the mainstream discussion of Luke–Acts during the mid-to-late twentieth century continued the major emphases of the previous periods. This means that there was a significant amount of research and writing on Luke–Acts that developed the view that saw the books as less historical and more theological expositions of developments within the early church. Even if many scholars had already pulled away from the timeframe outlined by Baur, they continued to argue for Luke–Acts as works that promoted the author's theological interests, with less attention to historical reliability. There were a number of scholars, however, who rejected this perspective and continued to argue for the fundamental historical reliability of Luke–Acts, even if Luke was also to be appreciated as a significant theological writer within the early church; he was a theologian who wrote in light of faithfully recounting the events of early Christianity.

In the previous section, we discussed the contribution of Bruce, who followed in the path of Ramsay as a staunch defender of the historical reliability of the New Testament, in particular Acts. Bruce himself left such a legacy. Bruce had many doctoral students during his time in Sheffield and especially Manchester. One of those who directly continued his work was the classicist Colin J. Hemer (1930–1987). At first a secondary school teacher, Hemer never held a permanent postsecondary academic position but apart from occasional lecturing spent much of his career as a researcher. His lasting contribution to the study of Luke–Acts was a major volume that appears very much to be in the mode of both Ramsay and Bruce. Although the volume touches on Luke's Gospel, it is a thorough study of Acts from the standpoint of justifying its historical reliability. Hemer discusses topics such as historicity, historiography, and a variety of historical evidence in Acts, including details, names, the Pauline letters, the Galatian question, authorship, sources, and date.[70] This volume remains a compendium of important and helpful information for not just the exegete but the scholar pursuing matters of historicity.

Although I. Howard Marshall (1934–2015) is often rightly linked with Bruce and others within the evangelical tradition, his work on Luke–Acts was more encompassing, even if he tended to emphasize the Gospel.[71] Marshall and Bruce had much in common—they were both Scots, educated at the Universities of Aberdeen and Cambridge, and important leaders within the emerging and then strong period of evangelical scholarship within the British scholarly scene. Marshall represents the next generation, who picked up the torch from Bruce.[72] Marshall spent virtually all of his academic career at Aberdeen, where he began teaching in 1964, became professor in 1979, and retired in 1999. Just as Bruce supervised numerous students who had an impact upon emerging evangelical scholarship, so did Marshall during his time at Aberdeen, where he was known to supervise students in a wide range of topics. Although Marshall wrote commentaries on a number of books (in a range of respected series), including the Johannine epistles (NICNT), 1 and 2 Thessalonians (NCB), 1 Peter (IVP), Philippians (Epworth), and the Pastoral Epistles (ICC), he also made a significant contribution to scholarship on Luke–Acts with his commentaries on Luke's Gospel (NIGNT) and the Acts of the Apostles (TNTC), a guide to Acts, and his classic work on *Luke: Historian and Theologian*, among other lesser works.[73] One of the subjects on which Marshall wrote that appears to have influenced his views on the biblical text

70. Colin J. Hemer, *The Book of Acts in the Setting of Hellenistic History*, ed. Conrad H. Gempf, WUNT 47 (Tübingen: Mohr Siebeck, 1989; repr., Winona Lake, IN: Eisenbrauns, 1990). Hemer also wrote a number of articles on historical matters, especially related to Acts (see the bibliography in his *Book of Acts*).

71. See Stanley E. Porter, "Hermeneutics, Biblical Interpretation, and Theology: Hunch, Holy Spirit, or Hard Work?" in I. Howard Marshall, *Beyond the Bible: Moving from Scripture to Theology* (Grand Rapids: Baker, 2004), 97–127, esp. 98–101. For bibliography, see Jon C. Laansma, Grant Osborne, and Ray Van Neste, eds., *New Testament Theology in Light of the Church's Mission: Essays in Honor of I. Howard Marshall* (Eugene, OR: Cascade, 2011), 11–24.

72. Some of the other evangelical scholars of that generation would include Richard T. France, John Drane, and Anthony C. Thiselton, none of them known for their Luke–Acts scholarship as was Marshall.

73. I. Howard Marshall, *The Gospel of Luke: A Commentary on the Greek Text*, NIGTC (Grand Rapids: Eerdmans, 1978); Marshall, *The Acts of the Apostles*, TNTC (Grand Rapids: Eerdmans, 1980); Marshall, *The Acts of the Apostles*, New Testament Guides (Sheffield: JSOT Press, 1992); and Marshall, *Luke: Historian and Theologian* (Grand Rapids: Zondervan, 1971; 2nd ed. 1979; 3rd ed., 1988).

is his work on some of the larger topics of biblical interpretation.[74] The title of his last work mentioned above probably best summarizes Marshall's approach to Luke–Acts, in distinction to the kind of position represented by mainstream German scholarship such as that found in Dibelius, Haenchen, and especially Conzelmann. Without taking a narrow and dogmatic approach, Marshall affirms the historicity of both Luke and Acts, while recognizing the limitations of ancient historiography, and he endorses Luke as a significant theologian in the early church, while questioning Conzelmann's salvation-historical schema. The result is that Marshall, while clearly well-respected as a major scholar within the field of Luke–Acts (and other areas of New Testament study), has posed something of an enigma both to more liberal scholars and to some evangelicals (especially in North America), where both sides are much more doctrinaire in their approaches. As a consequence, Marshall clearly moved against the mainstream when he opposed Ernst Käsemann's (1906–1998) views of early Catholicism and apocalyptic being the mother of Christianity,[75] but he also infuriated many evangelicals in his not finding inerrancy as a necessary doctrine in relation to inspiration. Nevertheless, Marshall demonstrated a reasoned and serious scholarly approach to the issues that he treated. There are very few so clearly evangelical scholars who have had the kind of widespread scholarly recognition and acceptance as did Marshall. His scholarship appeared in major places within the mainstream of criticism, while he also continued to publish in distinctively evangelical venues, especially those that reflected British evangelicalism. Marshall also attracted a large number of doctoral students from North American evangelical circles. Several of these students undertook Luke and Acts as their major areas of study. We can perhaps envision future volumes on milestones in scholarship featuring some of these students, as well as others within the evangelical sphere.

In many ways, Marshall's work culminated in the six-volume set of volumes on Acts produced by Tyndale House in Cambridge, England,

---

74. For example, I. Howard Marshall, *Biblical Inspiration* (Grand Rapids: Eerdmans, 1982); and Marshall, *Beyond the Bible*, 11–79. Cf. also Marshall, ed., *New Testament Interpretation: Essays on Principles and Methods* (Grand Rapids: Eerdmans, 1977), a still fine collection of essays on the topic.
75. I. Howard Marshall, "'Early Catholicism' in the New Testament," in *New Dimensions in New Testament Study*, eds. Richard N. Longenecker and Merrill C. Tenney (Grand Rapids: Zondervan, 1974), 217–31; Marshall, "Is Apocalyptic the Mother of Christian Theology?" in *Tradition and Interpretation in the New Testament: Essays in Honor of E. Earle Ellis for His 60th Birthday*, eds. Gerald F. Hawthorne with Otto Betz (Grand Rapids: Eerdmans, 1987), 33–42.

from 1993 to 1998 (for which he was an advisor and a coeditor of one of the volumes). A group of scholars was convened to study the kinds of questions that had been raised by the scholarship of Dibelius and Haenchen, and a series of volumes was planned in response more along the lines of the scholarship in German circles as exemplified by Martin Hengel.[76] Whereas it took the earlier group of Acts scholars thirteen years to produce their five volumes, this project resulted in a similar mix of volumes but in a shorter amount of time. Whereas the earlier collection had a relatively limited number of contributors, the later project drew on a greater number of scholars. The first volume of this new series was concerned with Acts in its ancient literary setting and so dealt with such topics as Acts in relationship to ancient history, biography, biblical history, subsequent writings, Luke, the Pauline letters, speeches and rhetoric, and modern literary criticism.[77] The range of contributors extends beyond the usual boundaries of evangelicalism, even though the conclusions are generally favorable to Acts in relationship to the topic concerned. The second volume is also a collection of essays, this one on Acts in its Greco-Roman setting. It deals with Acts and cultural and social issues such as travel, food, religion, and urban life; Acts and the provinces of Syria, Cyprus, and Asia, along with the Asiarchs, Galatia, Macedonia, along with the Politarchs, Achaia, Rome and Italy, and Luke's geography, as well as the "we" passages.[78] As in the first volume, the conclusions are generally favorable to the presentation of events in the book of Acts. The third volume is a monograph on Paul's Roman imprisonments by Brian Rapske. The volume concentrates on Paul's trials and his imprisonments in Acts, from the standpoint that Acts provides a reliable account of

76. See David W. J. Gill, I. Howard Marshall, and Bruce W. Winter, "Preface," in *The Book of Acts in Its Ancient Literary Setting*, eds. Bruce W. Winter and Andrew D. Clarke, BAFCS 1 (Grand Rapids: Eerdmans; Carlisle: Paternoster, 1993), ix–xii, esp. x–xi. They cite Martin Hengel, *Acts and the History of Earliest Christianity*, trans. John Bowden (London: SCM, 1979). However, they also cite Gerd Lüdemann, *Early Christianity according to the Traditions in Acts: A Commentary* (London: SCM, 1989), who takes a much less historical view than does Hengel.
77. Winter and Clarke, eds., *Book of Acts in Its Ancient Literary Setting*. The contributors include: Loveday Alexander (see below for discussion), Richard Bauckham, Conrad Gempf, Peter Head, T. W. Hillard, I. Howard Marshall, Alanna Nobbs, Darryl Palmer, David Peterson, Brian S. Rosner, Philip E. Satterthwaite, F. Scott Spencer, David Wenham, and Bruce W. Winter.
78. David W. J. Gill and Conrad Gempf, eds., *The Book of Acts in Its Graeco-Roman Setting*, BAFCS 2 (Grand Rapids: Eerdmans; Carlisle: Paternoster, 1994). The contributors include: Brad Blue, Andrew Clarke, David French, David Gill, Walter Hansen, G. H. R. Horsley, R. A. Kearsley, Alanna Nobbs, Stanley E. Porter, Brian Rapske, James M. Scott, Robyn Tracey, Paul Trebilco, and Bruce W. Winter.

such events.[79] The fourth volume is another collection of essays, this one on Acts and its Palestinian context. The topics here include treatment with reference to Palestine of the various cultures in the Second Temple period, Roman policy, geography, personal names, religious leaders, synagogues, the Jerusalem church, demographics, Jewish prayer, topography, Christian community of goods, Jewish antagonism, Paul's pre-Christian life, Peter in Lydda, and James.[80] Framed as an attempt to update Cadbury's volume on Acts and history,[81] this volume deals with a good number of topics about the context of Acts rather than about Acts itself. The fifth volume is a monograph on Acts and its diaspora setting by Irina Levinskaya.[82] This volume deals at length with proselytes and the God-fearers and then with the nature of Jewish diaspora communities throughout the Mediterranean world. The sixth and final volume is on the theology of Acts.[83] After an essay on how one writes on the theology of Acts by Marshall, the volume is divided into three parts. Part one is on salvation, part two on God's call, and part three on God's renewing work, with a total of twenty-three essays in these three parts. There is a conclusion on Luke's theology by David Peterson, another of the editors. Whereas the fourth volume includes a wide range of contributors on what surrounds Acts, this sixth volume deals directly with theological topics and is written by a generally clearly identifiable group of evangelical scholars. It is difficult to comment on the long-term impact of this series (especially

79. Brian Rapske, *The Book of Acts and Paul in Roman Custody*, BAFCS 3 (Grand Rapids: Eerdmans; Carlisle: Paternoster, 1994).

80. Richard Bauckham, ed., *The Book of Acts in Its Palestinian Setting*, BAFCS 4 (Grand Rapids: Eerdmans; Carlisle: Paternoster, 1995). The contributors include: Ernst Bammel, Richard Bauckham, Brian J. Capper, Daniel K. Falk, David A. Fiensy, David W. J. Gill, Martin Hengel, Simon Légasse, Steve Mason, Jerome Murphy-O'Connor, Tessa Rajak, Wolfgang Reinhardt, Rainer Riesner, Joshua Schwartz, and Margaret H. Williams.

81. See Bauckham, "Preface," in *Book of Acts in Its Palestinian Setting*, xiii–xiv, esp. xiii.

82. Irina Levinskaya, *The Book of Acts in Its Diaspora Setting*, BAFCS 5 (Grand Rapids: Eerdmans; Carlisle: Paternoster, 1996).

83. I. Howard Marshall and David Peterson, eds., *Witness to the Gospel: The Theology of Acts* (Grand Rapids: Eerdmans, 1998). This volume is not overtly advertised as part of the series on The Book of Acts in Its First Century Setting, although the format of the book is similar. There is reference to the series in the editors' preface, where the status of this sixth volume appears to be ambiguous. However, the previous volumes all advertised a sixth volume on the theology of Acts. The contributors include: Stephen C. Barton, Hans F. Bayer, Craig L. Blomberg, Brad Blue, Darrell Bock, Peter Bold, Douglas Buckwalter, Brian Capper, Andrew C. Clark, Joel Green, G. Walter Hansen, I. Howard Marshall, Heinz-Werner Neudorfer, John Nolland, David Peterson, Brian M. Rapske, Brian S. Rosner, David Seccombe, John Squires, Christoph Stenschke, Philip H. Towner, Max Turner, Robert Wall, and Ben Witherington III.

with one of the authors of this introduction a contributor to one of the volumes). The volumes are occasionally uneven, and there is clearly some attempt to direct the theological outcomes. Nevertheless, the clear focus throughout the volumes is on defending the historical and theological reliability and significance of the book of Acts.

We now turn to several distinguished Luke–Acts scholars from a number of different countries who flourished during the mid-to-late twentieth century. The mainstream of critical scholarship on Luke–Acts has not followed the line of more conservative scholars represented in the collection of volumes discussed above but has tended to take a more skeptical view of the historicity of the two books, even if they are not nearly as skeptical as Baur and his immediate followers and are more comfortable arguing for a view in line with Dibelius, Conzelmann, and Haenchen. One of the most important British scholars of the mid-to-late twentieth century was C. K. Barrett (1917–2011).[84] A devout Methodist, Barrett was educated at Cambridge University and is thought by some to be the most significant New Testament scholar of this period in Britain. Barrett is distinguished by having written several important and enduring commentaries on central books in the New Testament, including Romans, 1 and 2 Corinthians (all in BNTC), and his very thorough freestanding commentary on John's Gospel, still one of the most important commentaries on the book, known for its attention to Greek language matters as few since have been. As a result, Barrett was probably best known throughout much of his career as a Pauline and a Johannine scholar, in support of which he also wrote numerous other articles and chapters, although he wrote on other topics as well. However, relatively early in his career Barrett published an important but often overlooked book on *Luke the Historian in Recent Study*.[85] This volume is concerned with both Luke and Acts, which Barrett describes as being a history influenced by the writer's religious convictions. In many respects, he follows German thought on Luke and Acts by endorsing the salvation-historical view of Conzelmann and Haenchen who see the author as standing between

84. Baird, *History of New Testament Research*, 3:538–48.
85. C. K. Barrett, *Luke the Historian in Recent Study* (London: Epworth, 1961). Cf. his later Barrett, "Quomodo Historia Conscribenda Sit," *NTS* 28 (1982): 303–20, repr. as "How History Should Be Written," in *History, Literature and Society in the Book of Acts*, ed. Ben Witherington, III (Cambridge: Cambridge University Press, 1996), 33–57.

eras.[86] At the end of his life, Barrett published what is thought by some to be his culminating work, his two-volume commentary on Acts in the ICC series.[87] The commentary continues the same perspective as in Barrett's earlier work, demonstrating how a common sense form of British scholarship is able to incorporate—minus the extremes and rough edges—the major propositions of German scholarship, especially regarding reconciling Jewish and Gentile elements. He places Acts earlier than did Baur but finds Luke as an interpretive historian of the major tensions within early Christianity. Barrett is discussed in greater detail in an essay devoted to him in this volume.

A second British scholar to note is Michael Goulder (1927–2010).[88] Goulder was an Eton and Oxford educated businessman who worked in Hong Kong, became a priest in the Anglican church, then pursued scholarship, resigned his clerical orders when he became an atheist, and eventually became a professor of Bible in the school of continuing studies at the University of Birmingham in the UK. What is noteworthy is that he never held a professorship in a department of Bible or theology in the UK, which some attribute to the fact that he had parted ways with establishment religion, especially British establishment religion, which never forgave him. Despite some physical handicaps, Goulder was an innovative thinker and robust defender of a series of provocative ideas. Even if they were not unique to him, he gave them renewed life in his exposition of them. Besides his earlier involvement in theological debate over Christology and the existence of God,[89] Goulder is known for several major, unconventional hypotheses. Goulder wrote several volumes in Old Testament studies, in particular on the Psalms. Better known perhaps are his lectionary hypothesis regarding the origins of the Gospels, evidenced in his *Midrash and Lection in Matthew* and *The Evangelists' Calendar*, and his defense of the Baur hypothesis by seeing two major factions in the church in his *Tale of Two Missions* and

---

86. Barrett, *Luke the Historian*, 26–50, acknowledges his indebtedness to six major Luke–Acts scholars, Dibelius, Bertil Gärtner, Arnold Ehrhardt, Robert Morgenthaler, Conzelmann, and Haenchen.

87. C. K. Barrett, *A Critical and Exegetical Commentary on the Acts of the Apostles*, 2 vols., ICC (London: T&T Clark, 1994–1998). This work was followed by a more popular summary in a single volume: Barrett, *Acts: A Shorter Commentary* (London: T&T Clark, 2002).

88. See Dennis Nineham, "Foreword," in *Crossing the Boundaries: Essays in Biblical Interpretation in Honour of Michael D. Goulder*, eds. Stanley E. Porter, Paul Joyce, and David E. Orton, BINS 8 (Leiden: Brill, 1994), x–xv; and Baird, *History of New Testament Research*, 3:373–76.

89. Goulder was involved in the myth of God incarnate debate. See Michael D. Goulder, ed., *Incarnation and Myth: The Debate Continued* (London: SCM; Grand Rapids: Eerdmans, 1979).

Paul and the Competing Mission in Corinth.[90] Goulder's first published volume was on the book of Acts, although he is probably least well-known for this work. In his *Type and History in Acts*, Goulder examines Acts by means of typological criticism.[91] He recognizes that this approach is not widely known or used (then or now). His examination of Acts is an effort to identify the types that stand behind the New Testament account. This displays itself in Acts being organized into four sections, each one depicting the life of Jesus. Acts is, thereby, a typological construction by the author. Goulder's best-known hypothesis, however, is to dispense with Q, following in the line of his Oxford teacher Farrer.[92] In his two-volume commentary on Luke's Gospel, Goulder argues that Luke, the last Gospel written, was the product of the author using Mark and Matthew, not any other sayings source or other posited sources.[93] Goulder believes that it can be shown that Luke uses Matthew (e.g., Luke 22:63–64), and so there is no need for Q. Luke's Gospel is thus the redactional product of the author interpreting these sources. This is an extension of Goulder's lectionary hypothesis in the sense that Matthew expands Mark, and Luke joins Mark and Matthew together, along with making his own additions. The strength of Goulder's work is recognized in the view of Markan priority without use of Q as the Farrer–Goulder hypothesis. However, as important as source criticism was to Goulder's work, to limit it to this singular hypothesis is overly narrow. His work on Luke–Acts, although admittedly less so in Acts, demonstrates a consistent implementation of developmental hypotheses that are related to the Baur hypothesis of Christian origins in a way that few contemporary scholars have developed such a hypothesis until lately.

In the United States in the mid to late twentieth century, the major scholar in Luke–Acts was arguably the Jesuit priest Joseph A. Fitzmyer (1920–2016).[94] Fitzmyer had a wide educational background in both New Testament and Semitic studies, including a PhD from Johns

---

90. Michael D. Goulder, *Midrash and Lection in Matthew* (London: SPCK, 1974); Goulder, *The Evangelists' Calendar: A Lectionary Explanation of the Development of Scripture* (London: SPCK, 1978); Goulder, *A Tale of Two Missions* (London: SCM, 1994); and Goulder, *Paul and the Competing Mission in Corinth* (Peabody, MA: Hendrickson, 2001).

91. M. D. Goulder, *Type and History in Acts* (London: SPCK, 1964).

92. Goulder was strongly influenced by Farrer. A. M. Farrer wrote "Dispensing with Q," in *Studies in the Gospels: Essays in Memory of R. H. Lightfoot*, ed. D. E. Nineham (Oxford: Blackwell, 1955), 55–88.

93. Michael D. Goulder, *Luke: A New Paradigm*, 2 vols., JSNTSup 20 (Sheffield: JSOT, 1989).

94. John R. Donahue, "Joseph A. Fitzmyer, S.J. (1920–2016)," *BAR* May/June 2017 (online).

Hopkins University, and was an accomplished scholar in both areas (he also prided himself on being an expert on crayfish). He taught at several institutions, before retiring from the Catholic University of America. Fitzmyer was in the first wave of Roman Catholic scholars who openly engaged in historical criticism of the Bible when restrictions were lifted after the Second Vatican Council. Fitzmyer established a strong reputation in Dead Sea Scrolls studies (he was in Jerusalem in the 1950s when the Scrolls were first being examined) and Pauline studies. In the area of Pauline studies, he wrote major commentaries on Romans (AB), 1 Corinthians (AB), and Philemon (AB). He also wrote a number of significant articles, later collected into several volumes of essays on the Semitic background of the New Testament. However, among all these writings, Fitzmyer also established himself as a major figure in Luke–Acts studies through his commentaries both on Luke and on Acts (both AB). In that sense, Fitzmyer represents several scholars who have made their contribution to study of Luke–Acts through writing commentaries (along with other works), although few have achieved the same level of significance. We hesitate to mention others, for fear that any list will run the risk of excluding worthy candidates. Fitzmyer's two-volume commentary on Luke's Gospel was part of the wave of contributions to the Anchor Bible that transformed the commentary from a set of notes on a translation to a full-blooded critical commentary.[95] Fitzmyer told one of the authors of this introduction that his commentary on Acts could have been in two volumes as well but he was prohibited from such length by the publisher.[96] One of the distinguishing features of Fitzmyer's commentaries, not only those on Luke–Acts but others in the Anchor Bible, is his lengthy and detailed introductions to critical issues. Over one-third of the first volume on Luke comprises the introduction, which includes sections on Lukan studies, the identity of Luke and his readers, composition of the Gospel, Lukan language and style (a section still rarely surpassed), the text, an outline, and then a one-hundred page "sketch" of Lukan theology, before a select bibliography

95. Joseph A. Fitzmyer, *The Gospel According to Luke*, 2 vols., AB 28, 28A (Garden City, NY: Doubleday, 1981–1983). The first to mark this transformation in size was Raymond Brown's two-volume commentary on John's Gospel (1966–1970) followed by Markus Barth's two volumes on Ephesians (1974).

96. One notes that a subsequent New Testament book, Mark, was treated in two volumes.

that includes reference to earlier commentaries among other works.[97] Fitzmyer's perspective on Luke is a moderate historical-critical one. He appreciates Luke as a theologian and attempts to synthesize his theology. He also attempts to avoid the extremes of both the traditional German position as indicated by Dibelius and Haenchen and the kind of view promoted by Bruce and his followers. While attributing both Luke and Acts to the traditional Luke, Fitzmyer also distances him from Paul so as to give him a position of independence. In his commentary on Acts, Fitzmyer has a relatively shorter introduction but treats many of the same issues.[98] Appropriate for Acts, he includes sections on the "Historical Character of Acts" and "The Lucan Story of Paul."[99] Repeating his previous perspective, Fitzmyer takes a middle course between what we might call the German and British extremes. He sees Luke as providing a generally reliable account in the book of Acts, although he also makes errors along the way. Fitzmyer provides a model of a moderate view of commentary writing that established him as a milestone figure within study of Luke–Acts.

In the period from around 1980 on, there was an expansion in the analytic frameworks utilized in New Testament studies. Whereas within mainstream scholarship forms of the historical-critical method had generally reigned supreme, the last twenty or so years of the twentieth century marked a reassessment of what was meant by biblical criticism. As a result, a number of new methods were developed. One of these came to be called literary interpretation or literary readings, and later narrative criticism. Several well-known scholars engaged in this kind of literary interpretation, including Jack Dean Kingsbury, David Rhoads, and Alan Culpepper, with all of them writing around the same time (their work began in the early 1980s and extended into the 1990s). Two of them were especially significant in the study of Luke–Acts. In 1982, Charles H. Talbert,[100] who taught mostly at Wake Forest University and later at Baylor University, published a

---

97. Fitzmyer, *Luke*, 1:3–283, with the theological sketch on 143–270. Cf. Fitzmyer, *Luke the Theologian: Aspects of His Teaching* (New York: Paulist, 1989).
98. Joseph A. Fitzmyer, *The Acts of the Apostles*, AB 31 (New York: Doubleday, 1998). Fitzmyer's volume replaces the one by Johannes Munck, *The Acts of the Apostles*, AB 31 (Garden City, NY: Doubleday, 1967), who made a contribution to Acts studies, but whose legacy has not endured as it has in Pauline studies.
99. Fitzmyer, *Acts*, 124–47.
100. See the essays in Parsons and Tyson, eds., *Cadbury, Knox, and Talbert*, 133–51, with a response by Talbert.

literary and theological commentary on Luke's Gospel.[101] This was the first of several literary and theological commentaries that he published (he also published them on the Corinthian letters and John's Gospel, as well as writing several other commentaries). Talbert published a similar commentary on Acts in 1997.[102] Talbert's body of research on Luke–Acts, although earlier in his career more from a historical-critical than literary perspective, went back to his dissertation in the mid 1960s and continued throughout his career.[103] However, Talbert's literary approach to interpretation, in particular of Luke and Acts, went back to the 1970s, and is what he describes as "reading as a participant in the authorial audience."[104] This approach reflects a form of literary interpretation derived from what had developed more widely in literary criticism in North America, with emphasis upon close reading of the text and appreciation of the role of the reader. Talbert himself has attributed this approach to "American pragmatism" and his indebtedness to the New Criticism in literary theory.[105] A second Luke–Acts scholar to pioneer the use of literary interpretation was Robert Tannehill.[106] Like Talbert's, Tannehill's interests in literary interpretation began before he published his major work of Luke–Acts scholarship. In *The Sword of His Mouth*, Tannehill attributes his interest in the literary and theological dimensions of the parables to earlier literary interpretations of the parables by Robert Funk (1926–2005), Dan Otto Via, and John Dominic Crossan.[107] Tannehill, who spent virtually all of his career at Methodist Theological School in Ohio, published his major two-volume work on the

---

101. Charles H. Talbert, *Reading Luke: A Literary and Theological Commentary on the Third Gospel* (New York: Crossroad, 1982; rev. 2002).

102. Charles H. Talbert, *Reading Acts: A Literary and Theological Commentary on the Acts of the Apostles* (New York: Crossroad, 1997). Talbert had earlier published *Acts*, Knox Preaching Guides (Atlanta: John Knox, 1984). See also Talbert, "The Acts of the Apostles: Monograph or *Bios*?" in *History, Literature and Society*, 58–72.

103. Charles H. Talbert, *Luke and the Gnostics: An Examination of the Lukan Purpose* (Nashville: Abingdon, 1966); Talbert, *Literary Patterns, Theological Themes and the Genre of Luke–Acts*, SBLMS 20 (Missoula, MT: SBL and Scholars Press, 1974), as well as several edited volumes.

104. Charles H. Talbert, "Preface," in *Reading Luke–Acts in its Mediterranean Milieu*, NovTSup 107 (Leiden: Brill, 2003), ix. This is a collection of Talbert's essays from the 1970s to the time of publication.

105. Charles H. Talbert, "Reading Chance, Moessner, and Parsons," in *Cadbury, Knox, and Talbert*, 229–40, esp. 237.

106. Tyson, *Luke*, 127–33.

107. Robert C. Tannehill, *The Sword of His Mouth*, SBL Semeia Supplements 1 (Philadelphia: Fortress; Missoula, MT: Scholars Press, 1975), 1–10, esp. 2, but also 7–10, where he distinguishes his approach from the form criticism of Dibelius and Bultmann.

narrative unity of Luke–Acts in 1986 and 1990.[108] He uses a form of "narrative criticism" in which he attends to matters of plot and character to show the narrative unity of the two works.[109] One of the major features of Tannehill's work on Luke–Acts is that he treats the two books as a single entity and applies the same approach to both. As with Talbert, the approach that he uses is methodologically fairly basic but has had a lasting influence upon New Testament interpretation. While literary interpretation has become a part of New Testament studies, the earlier enthusiasm for literary readings has clearly diminished over time.

We close the discussion of the twentieth century by treating two continental European scholars, neither German, who have made significant contributions to the study of Luke–Acts. The first is the Norwegian scholar Jacob Jervell (1925–2014), who spent the vast bulk of his career at the University of Oslo as professor of New Testament.[110] Jervell is probably not as well known in New Testament scholarship as are some of the other scholars mentioned in this introduction, because much of his scholarship has not been published in English. He wrote on a range of subjects, including Paul and John's Gospel, but his major area of focus was Luke–Acts. Two of Jervell's significant books in English on Luke–Acts are collections of mostly previously published essays. These two volumes, *Luke and the People of God* and *The Unknown Paul*, draw together essays in which he argues a position that is significantly different from many of his predecessors in study of Luke–Acts.[111] Rather than seeing the emphasis on Luke's universalism in Luke and Acts, Jervell argues for a Jewish perspective, in which the early church that Luke represents is a thoroughly Jewish institution. The mission to the Jews constitutes the basis of the mission to the Gentiles, with the Jews responding positively to the

---

108. Robert C. Tannehill, *The Narrative Unity of Luke–Acts: A Literary Interpretation*, 2 vols. (Philadelphia: Fortress, 1986–1990). Tannehill also later published a collection of essays on a range of topics, some with overlap to his work in Luke–Acts, in Tannehill, *The Shape of the Gospel: New Testament Essays* (Eugene, OR: Cascade, 2007). Another scholar who made a contribution to Luke–Acts during this time, and from a literary approach, is Joseph B. Tyson, *The Death of Jesus in Luke–Acts* (Columbia: University of South Carolina Press, 1986); and Tyson, *Images of Judaism in Luke–Acts* (Columbia: University of South Carolina Press, 1992).

109. Tannehill, *Narrative Unity*, 1:1.

110. Tyson, *Luke*, 91–109.

111. Jacob Jervell, *Luke and the People of God: A New Look at Luke–Acts* (Minneapolis: Augsburg, 1972); Jervell, *The Unknown Paul: Essays on Luke–Acts and Early Christian History* (Minneapolis: Augsburg, 1984).

gospel and the church remaining faithful to Jewish belief. In his small book on the theology of the book of Acts, Jervell further defends the Jewish perspective in Acts, in which the church's mission begins with the Jews before being extended to the Gentiles.[112] Jervell's largest work in Luke–Acts studies is his commentary on the book of Acts.[113] This volume, in the Meyer commentary series, is the replacement volume for Haenchen's commentary. However, Jervell clearly does not simply assume the interpretive tradition from Baur to Dibelius to Conzelmann to Haenchen. As he says in the introduction to the commentary, the theological understanding of Acts has a distinctly Jewish stamp on it. Luke does not begin from a non-Jewish standpoint but from deeply within Jewish tradition, with a distinct Jewish Christianity after AD 70 when the author wrote. Jervell sees this displayed in Luke's Christology, ecclesiology, and soteriology, the view of the law, the use of Jewish words and concepts, a biblically influenced language, and, perhaps most interestingly, a depiction of the story of Paul as apostle of the Jews and of the Diaspora.[114] As interesting as some of Jervell's views are—and there is some merit in some of his positions regarding not juxtaposing Judaism and Gentile Christianity—the surprising response to his scholarship has, for the most part, been neglect, especially among German scholarship, where he has obviously had the audacity to try to counter the prevailing norm.[115] Jervell is treated in more detail in an essay dedicated to him in this volume.

The final scholar to mention in this section is the French Swiss scholar François Bovon (1938–2013).[116] Bovon was educated in Switzerland and taught at the University of Geneva for more than twenty-five years before moving to Harvard Divinity School, where he finished his career. Bovon did a significant amount of work in apocryphal texts, including apocryphal Acts (he discovered an important manuscript of the *Acts of Philip*),[117] but especially on Luke–Acts. He

---

112. Jacob Jervell, *The Theology of the Acts of the Apostles*, NTT (Cambridge: Cambridge University Press, 1996).

113. Jacob Jervell, *Die Apostelgeschichte*, KEK 3 (Göttingen: Vandenhoeck & Ruprecht, 1998). This is the seventeenth edition of Acts within the series but the first edition by Jervell.

114. Jervell, *Apostelgeschichte*, 50–51.

115. Tyson, *Luke*, 102; cf. 102–109, where he evaluates Jervell's perspective. One who has critiqued it is Bovon, *Luke*, 377–81.

116. David W. Pao and David H. Warren, "Always a Student: Remembering François Bovon," *Marginalia* November 14, 2013 (online).

117. See François Bovon, Ann Graham Brock, and Christopher R. Matthews, eds., *The Apocryphal Acts of the Apostles: Harvard Divinity School Studies* (Cambridge, MA: Harvard University Press, 1999), for a representative work in this area.

was also interested in questions of exegetical method. Bovon's first major work on Luke–Acts was his summative evaluation of scholarship on Luke. First published in French in 1978, this volume treated scholarship on Luke and Acts from 1950–1975. This initial volume was followed by an English translation in 1987 that brought scholarship up to 1983. A second English edition was then published in 2006 that added material to cover 1980–2005. The work is topical, and hence treats the theological emphases of Luke including the plan of God, Israel's Scriptures, Christology, the Holy Spirit, salvation and its reception, the church, and then additional entries that bring the work up to the date of publication. More important, however, is Bovon's major commentary on Acts. This commentary has an interesting history of having been written in German (EKK), and then translated into a variety of other languages, including French (the author's first language), English (Hermeneia), Spanish, and Italian, each of them a four-volume edition except for the three volumes in English.[118] The commentary itself, despite its size, is not as detailed as some other commentaries on the books of Luke or Acts. The introduction in English is only eleven pages, where Bovon lays out his basic assumptions. He endorses Markan priority with Q, describes the author as a historian of sorts, but sees authorship ascribed to Luke probably to create an apostolic connection, linking the commentary with the apocryphal Acts by means of posited . authorship. The commentary itself is written within the German tradition, even if more moderate in its conclusions than many, with attention to form-critical identification of pericopes and comments on sources, in which Bovon sees Luke as not hesitating to take his sources and supplement them with his own redactional comments.

There are many other authors who wrote on Luke and Acts in this period, with a number of commentaries being produced in the closing years of the century. However, many of the authors are still actively engaged in scholarship, so it is premature to identify those whose legacy will remain significant. Despite the work of several other scholars, the close of the century left the major categories of critical scholarship in place. A distinctive minority voice continued to argue for the historicity

---

118. François Bovon, *Das Evangelium nach Lukas*, 4 vols., EKK (Zürich: Benziger; Neukirchen: Neukirchener, 1989–2008); ET Bovon, *Luke*, 3 vols., Hermeneia, trans. Christine M. Thomas, Donald S. Deer, and James Crouch (Minneapolis: Fortress, 2002–2012).

of Luke–Acts while recognizing its theological significance, while much of mainstream scholarship continued to endorse a broad German tradition, even if without the extremes of the earlier Tübingen school. There were also other approaches that attempted to make themselves heard among the jostling for position within Luke–Acts studies.

INTO THE TWENTY-FIRST CENTURY

We are only twenty or so years into the twenty-first century, so it is premature to identify milestone figures in Luke–Acts studies in the same way as we have identified them above. Nevertheless, there have been several figures who have emerged on the scene that at least merit attention. There are two that we mention here, although we are aware that this section might well need to be rewritten and expanded in the years to come as other scholars establish themselves through their work on Luke–Acts.

The person who has arguably caused much more debate in Luke–Acts study than any other over the last thirty-five years or so is Richard Pervo (1942–2017). Beginning with his first book *Profit with Delight*, a revision of his Harvard Divinity School doctoral dissertation, Pervo constantly engaged in a career of reassessing critical views on Acts, as well as of later Christian writings. In this first volume, Pervo examines the literary genre of Acts as a popular form of novelistic literature, very much related to the apocryphal Acts that followed.[119] On the basis of his view of Acts, Pervo then published a more popular level retelling of the story of Acts, especially its account of Paul, on the basis of Acts alone, without reference to the Pauline letters, in order to appreciate the literary qualities and characteristics of the author we call Luke.[120] This volume was followed by a coauthored book, with Mikeal Parsons, that developed further Pervo's view of the independence of Acts, by addressing one of the consistent ideas in study of Luke–Acts, their unity.[121] The authors call into question Cadbury's hyphen, indicating unity, by examining the supposed generic, narrative, and theological

119. Richard I. Pervo, *Profit with Delight: The Literary Genre of the Acts of the Apostles* (Philadelphia: Fortress, 1987).
120. Richard I. Pervo, *Luke's Story of Paul* (Minneapolis: Fortress, 1990).
121. Mikeal C. Parsons and Richard I. Pervo, *Rethinking the Unity of Luke and Acts* (Minneapolis: Fortress, 1993). Cf. also Richard I. Pervo, *The Gospel of Luke*, The Scholars Bible (Salem, OR: Polebridge, 2014).

unity of Luke and Acts. Having tackled the major topic of the kind of literature that Acts is, Pervo then turned in earnest to *Dating Acts*.[122] In this attempt at a comprehensive treatment of the topic, Pervo discusses a wide range of issues regarding Acts in relationship to its sources, other literature, Paul's letters, early church writers, and especially Josephus, to arrive at the conclusion that Acts was written in the early second century, sometime around AD 110–120. The dating of Acts to the second century in some ways has brought some of the issues raised by Baur back to the fore in Acts studies.[123] The culmination of Pervo's work on Acts is found in his Hermeneia commentary.[124] Pervo works from similar assumptions as he does in his earlier works, including seeing Acts as a work of popular history even if a romanticized one (although he seems to give Luke more credit than earlier as a historian, even if as a creator rather than recorder of history),[125] examining his use of Mark, the Septuagint, Paul's letters, and Josephus as sources, positing a date in the second century, and noting its differences from the Gospel.[126] Despite some of his more extreme conclusions not gaining widespread acceptance, Pervo's commentary has established itself as probably the major critical commentary on Acts in English (or at least North American) scholarship. Although there appears to be a growing number of scholars who are entertaining many of Pervo's conclusions, the number still remains in the minority. Pervo is treated in more detail in a dedicated essay in this volume.

We conclude this introduction with the last scholar we mention, Loveday C. A. Alexander. Alexander first studied classics at Oxford and then turned to theology for her doctorate. She spent virtually all of her active teaching career at the University of Sheffield.[127] Soon after

122. Richard I Pervo, *Dating Acts: Between the Evangelists and the Apologists* (Salem, OR: Polebridge, 2006). Pervo revisited some of these issues in his "Acts in the Suburbs of the Apologists," in *Contemporary Studies in Acts*, ed. Thomas E. Phillips (Macon, GA: Mercer University Press, 2009), 29–46. Cf. Pervo's more popular *The Mystery of Acts: Unraveling Its Story* (San Rosa, CA: Polebridge, 2008).
123. See, e.g., Joseph B. Tyson, *Marcion and Luke–Acts: A Defining Struggle* (Columbia: University of South Carolina Press, 2006), who admits to taking Pervo further and to connections with Baur.
124. Richard I. Pervo, *Acts*, Hermeneia (Minneapolis: Fortress, 2009).
125. Pervo, *Acts*, 15, 18. Cf. the critique of Pervo's original position in Stanley E. Porter, *The Paul of Acts: Essays in Literary Criticism, Rhetoric, and Theology*, WUNT 115 (Tübingen: Mohr Siebeck, 1999), 14–21.
126. See Pervo, *Acts*, 1–26, for his introduction.
127. See Lloyd K. Pietersen, "Introduction: The Honouree—Loveday Alexander," in *Reading Acts Today: Essays in Honour of Loveday C. A. Alexander*, eds. Steve Walton, Thomas E. Phillips, Lloyd Keith Pietersen, and F. Scott Spencer, LNTS 427 (London: T&T Clark, 2011), xv–xxiii; Sean A. Adams, "Loveday Alexander, David Rhoads, and Literary Criticism of the New Testament," in *Pillars in the*

earning her doctorate and in the year she arrived at Sheffield, Alexander published an important article on Luke's preface,[128] a topic to which she would return. Nevertheless, this article forecast the general course of her career, which has been primarily devoted to the study of Acts within its ancient context, especially its ancient Greco-Roman context. In 1993, Alexander published a revised version of her dissertation as *The Preface to Luke's Gospel* that also included discussion of the preface to Acts.[129] Alexander examines the prefaces to Luke and Acts—the only books in the New Testament with such formal prefaces—and compares them to various other suggested parallels, such as Jewish prefaces or classical prefaces. She concludes that the Lukan prefaces resemble the kind of scientific writing that would have been recognizable at the time. In 2005, Alexander published a collection of her (all but one) previously published essays on *Acts in Its Ancient Literary Context*, with the subtitle *A Classicist Looks at the Acts of the Apostles*.[130] In this volume, she includes essays on ancient literary context, the preface to Acts, Acts and ancient intellectual biography, the voyage motif in Acts, the toponomy of Acts, several essays on genre, the unity of Luke–Acts, and its language. In some ways, Alexander falls within a stream of Acts scholarship that emphasizes its position within the ancient Greco-Roman world, in line with scholars with classical backgrounds such as Bruce, Hemer, and others. However, in other ways, Alexander moves outside the traditional classical constraints and posits new solutions to old questions by appealing to new bodies of literature (such as scientific prose, rather than traditional classical texts) and new constructs for understanding (e.g. Gérard Genette's notion of paratext).[131] Alexander is treated in more detail in an essay dedicated to her work in this volume.

History of Biblical Interpretation, Volume 2: Prevailing Methods after 1980, eds. Stanley E. Porter and Sean A. Adams, MBSS 2 (Eugene, OR: Pickwick, 2016), 441–57, esp. 447–51.

128. Loveday C. A. Alexander, "Luke's Preface in the Pattern of Greek Preface-Writing," *NovT* 28 (1986): 48–74.

129. Loveday C. A. Alexander, *The Preface to Luke's Gospel: Literary Convention and Social Context in Luke 1.1–4 and Acts 1.1*, SNTSMS 78 (Cambridge: Cambridge University Press, 1993).

130. Loveday C. A. Alexander, *Acts in Its Ancient Literary Context: A Classicist Looks at the Acts of the Apostles*, LNTS 289 (London: T&T Clark, 2005). Alexander also published popular commentaries on Acts in "Acts," in *The Oxford Bible Commentary*, eds. John Barton and John Muddiman (Oxford: Oxford University Press, 2001), 1028–61 and *Acts*, The People's Bible Commentary (Oxford: Bible Reading Fellowship, 2006).

131. Loveday C. A. Alexander, "Reading Luke–Acts from Back to Front," in *Acts in Its Ancient Literary Context*, 207–29.

We are currently still at the relative beginning of this century within Luke–Acts research. There will be other scholars who will establish their reputations and become milestone figures in the discussion. However, at this point, the line of scholarship—despite its various shifts and adjustments—from Baur to Pervo by means of Dibelius, Conzelmann, and Haenchen, remains robust and productive, while there are also those who are attempting to examine Luke and Acts by other means, including placing them within their ancient historical and theological contexts.

CONCLUSION

We conclude this introduction by noting how important Baur and the Tübingen hypothesis has been, not only in Pauline studies, where it is certainly well-known and remains influential, but also in study of Luke–Acts. Baur and his followers transformed study of Luke–Acts in a variety of ways, especially in relation to date and purpose, but also in terms of historical reliability and theology. As a result, much of subsequent study of Luke–Acts has been driven by the issues identified and promoted by Baur. In some sense, one can speak of a wave effect of Baur's work. The surge of early interest subsided in the next generation of scholars, such as Ritschl and theological liberalism, although even here there was a residual effect of Baur's hypotheses. As Baur's influence ebbed, there were reassertions of the historical reliability of especially Acts, with important concomitant influence upon Luke's Gospel. Nevertheless, the flow of the Baur hypothesis, although modified in various ways by its proponents, again surged in the early-to-mid twentieth century, even if it was again countered by renewed interest in Luke as both a historian and theologian. As we close this account, we see another surge in Baur-influenced hypotheses, countered by a re-assertion of the significance of understanding Luke–Acts within its historical context. The essays in this volume provide more detailed pictures of a number of the significant scholars who have been a part of this scholarly historical and theological dialogue about Luke and Acts.

ADOLF HARNACK AND LUKAN SCHOLARSHIP AT THE HEIGHT OF CLASSICAL LIBERALISM

Zachary K. Dawson

INTRODUCTION

Only a select few scholars in the history of New Testament research have achieved the level of stature that Adolf Harnack enjoyed in the eyes of the academic guild of his day. Harnack's importance is often measured with regard to his historical-theological works on church history, the history of doctrine, and the essence of Christianity as defined within the paradigm of classical liberalism. The impact of his scholarship, however, was not limited to these areas of focus. He also made substantial contributions to New Testament research, not least to Lukan studies. In the first half of this essay, I will describe the various areas of Harnack's scholarly endeavors within the context of his life, major influences, and academic career. This will set the stage for the second half of this essay where, having situated Harnack's contributions to Lukan scholarship within the context of his life and intellectual environment, I will present the content and arguments in his major works on the Third Gospel and book of Acts to critically assess their strengths and weaknesses and gauge their enduring value.

HARNACK'S LIFE AND WORKS

The Dorpat and Erlangen Years

Karl Gustav Adolf Harnack (1851–1930) was born May 7, 1851, to Theodosius Andreas Harnack (1817–1889) and Anna Caroline Maria Ewers (called Maria) (1828–1857) in the Baltic city of Dorpat in Livonia, then a province of Imperial Russia, now Tartu, Estonia.[1] Adolf grew up in a full household. He and his twin brother Karl Gustav Axel Harnack (called Axel) (1851–1888), who became a professor of mathematics at Dresden, were two of Theodosius and Maria's five children; the eldest was a daughter, Anna Harnack (1849–1868), who died of pneumonia at the age of nineteen, and the two youngest were sons, Friedrich Moritz Erich Harnack (1852–1915), who became a professor of pharmacology at Halle, and Rudolf Gottfried Otto Harnack (1857–1914), who became a professor of history, literature, and aesthetics at Stuttgart. The Harnacks were orthodox Lutherans and, with respect to education and social position, belonged to "the ruling minority of Prussians who maintained the language and customs of Germany in [the] far outpost of German ecclesial and commercial missionary work" in which they lived.[2] Theodosius, who preceded his four sons as a university professor, began his teaching career at the University of Dorpat in 1843 and in 1848 became a professor of practical theology and, later, of systematic theology. He held this post until moving the family to the orthodox Lutheran university town of Erlangen in Bavaria (now Germany) in 1853 to assume a new position as a professor at Friedrich-Alexander University. This is where Adolf spent the early years of his childhood.

---

1. For biographical information, I have found the following sources to be the most helpful: Agnes Zahn-Harnack, *Adolf von Harnack* (Berlin: Hans Bott, 1936), who, being Harnack's daughter, compiled what is still the most comprehensive biography of her father; G. Wayne Glick, *The Reality of Christianity: A Study of Adolf von Harnack as Historian and Theologian* (New York: Harper & Row, 1967), whose critical evaluation of Harnack's formative influences and description of his theological program, though dated, is still perhaps the best treatment; Martin Rumscheidt, ed., *Adolf von Harnack, Liberal Theology at Its Height*, The Making of Modern Theology (London: Collins, 1988); Wilhelm Pauck, *Harnack and Troeltsch: Two Historical Theologians* (New York: Oxford University Press, 1968); William A. Mueller, "Adolf von Harnack, Church Historian and Theologian," in *The Teacher's Yoke: Studies in Memory of Henry Trantham*, eds. E. Jerry Vardaman and James Leo Garrett, Jr. (Waco, TX: Baylor University Press, 1964), 287–97; William Baird, *History of New Testament Research*, 3 vols. (Minneapolis: Fortress, 1992–2013), 2:122–35.
2. Rumscheidt, *Adolf von Harnack*, 10.

Four years later, on November 23, 1857, Maria, Adolf's mother, died after giving birth to her youngest at the age of forty-nine; Adolf was only six years old at the time. She is remembered as a woman of superior intelligence, a trait that lived on in her children.[3] For nearly seven years the full responsibility of rearing five children fell entirely to Theodosius, who impressed his staunch Lutheran confessionalism and steadfast patterns of devotion upon his children, shaping them to become God-fearing, well-behaved, upstanding citizens. These patterns of discipline and devotion remained ingrained in them into adulthood, as is evident in each of their academic achievements.[4]

When Adolf was thirteen years old, Theodosius married Helene Klementine Amalie Maydell (1834–1923). In 1866, the family moved back to Dorpat when Theodosius accepted a position again at the university, which is where he would finish his career.[5] Back in Dorpat, Adolf finished his secondary education. In addition to already having received a rich heritage of Lutheran confessionalism, Adolf was also well educated in historical, philosophical, and literary subjects upon the insistence of his father.[6] When it came time in Adolf's final year at the Gymnasium, he chose theology as his major area of study and matriculated at the University of Dorpat, a choice that in itself attests to the great personal influence of his father. Not until he developed his own conception of history and broke with his Lutheran heritage while

---

3. Mueller, "Adolf von Harnack," 287.
4. Christoffer H. Grundmann, "Theodosius Andreas Harnack (1817–1889)," in *Nineteenth-Century Lutheran Theologians*, REFO500 Academic Studies 31, ed. Matthew L. Becker (Göttingen: Vandenhoeck & Ruprecht, 2015), 255–74 (259–60).
5. Theodosius Harnack had a remarkably successful career as a preacher, professor, and prolific writer. In addition to his professorships, he served as the university preacher at Dorpat. He also treated a number of theological topics in print, with most of his emphases centering on the church and its ministry. For his major works, see Theodosius Harnack, *Alles und in allem Christus: Zwei Predigten* (Elberfeld: Hassel, 1841); Harnack, *Grundbekenntnisse der evangelisch-lutherischen Kirche: Die drei ökumenischen Symbole und die Augsburgische Konfession: Für die Glieder dieser Kirche, mit einer ausführlichen Einleitung und mit Anmerkungen herausgegeben* (Dorpat: W. Gläser, 1845); Harnack, *Der christliche Gemeindegottesdienst im apostolischen und altkatholischen Zeitalter* (Erlangen: Theodor Bläsing, 1854); Harnack, *Tabellarische Übersicht über die Geschichte der Liturgie des christlichen Hauptgottesdienstes* (Erlangen: Theodor Bläsing, 1858); Harnack, *Die lutherische Kirche Livlands und die herrnhutische Brüdergemeinde* (Erlangen: Theodor Bläsing, 1860); Harnack, *Die Kirche, ihr Amt, ihr Regiment* (Nürnberg: U. E. Sebald, 1862); Harnack, *Luthers Theologie: Mit besonderer Beziehung auf seine Versöhnungs- und Erlösungslehre*, 2 vols. (Erlangen: Theodor Bläsing, 1862–1886); Harnack, *Praktische Theologie*, 4 vols. (Erlangen: Theodor Bläsing, 1877–1878); Harnack, *Über den Kanon und die Inspiration der Heiligen Schrift: Ein Wort zum Frieden* (Erlangen: Theodor Bläsing, 1885).
6. Zahn-Harnack, *Adolf von Harnack*, 37.

in Leipzig was there any indications of the conflict that would come to define his relationship with his father later in life.

While at the University of Dorpat, Adolf (hereafter Harnack) sat under the tutelage of Moritz Engelhardt, who, apart from Theodosius, was Harnack's most important personal influence during his formative years. Engelhardt was professor of church history at the University of Dorpat from 1858 until 1881 when he died. It was from this professor that Harnack learned and became fascinated with the methods of textual and source criticism that he used throughout much of his academic life, not least in his studies on the Gospels and Acts. Moreover, Harnack's intellectual attraction to Engelhardt's teaching and scholarship was also reinforced by his sincere and pastoral disposition toward his students. Commenting on his character, Harnack once wrote, "Anyone who had come into contact with this professor would never forget him, and to this day this Baltic country owes a great part of its ethical strength to the influence of a single man."[7] To sum up the qualities of this teacher, Harnack succinctly described him as *"magister, patronus, und amicus"*—master, patron, and friend.[8] Harnack's two major influential figures, Theodosius and Engelhardt, would remain significant to him as he emerged as a scholar of history and theology over the next several years, but in quite different ways as will be explained below.

The Leipzig Years

Harnack left home in October 1872 to complete his formal education at the University of Leipzig. Over the course of the year 1873, he wrote his doctoral dissertation on "Source Criticism of the History of Gnosticism."[9] The next year, within the span of only five months, he wrote his *Habilitationsschrift*, which, according to the regulations of the university, had to be written in Latin. This work was in church history and was titled *De Appelis Gnosi monarchica*.[10] After passing a final set of oral examinations, he now qualified to teach at a

---

7.   Glick, *Reality of Christianity*, 30, translated from Adolf von Harnack, *Reden und Aufsätze*, vol. 5 (Giessen: Töpelmann, 1930), 152.

8.   Zahn-Harnack, *Adolf von Harnack*, 54, and for a fuller description of the role Engelhardt played in Harnack's early development as a scholar, see esp. 53–55; Glick, *Reality of Christianity*, 29–34.

9.   Later published as Adolf Harnack, *Zur Quellenkritik der Geschichte des Gnostizismus* (Leipzig: Bidder, 1873; Tübingen: Mohr, 1899).

10.   Rumscheidt, *Adolf von Harnack*, 11.

university. As an early church historian, Harnack began his career in 1874 as a *Privatdozent* in Leipzig, and then was raised to a *Professor extraordinarius* in 1876.

Despite his own success, Harnack's first impressions of Leipzig were less than favorable. In a letter to Engelhardt, he laments of a dire situation where threads of the Christian and the worldly life were so bound up together in a mess of church politics and other matters that, to his mind, the church was wholly debilitated in carrying out true Christian service, and this extended into the theological education sector.[11] The theological situation began to change, however, as Harnack entered his teaching career. It would seem, in fact, that he contributed to bringing about the change he so desired, not only by attracting numerous exceptional students to the area (most of whom were from orthodox-pietistic backgrounds) and dedicating himself to their instruction,[12] but also by taking on the various historical, theological, and ethical problems he identified through a rigorous publishing agenda. Friedrich Smend's bibliography accounts for more than one hundred pieces of writing Harnack published by the time he left Leipzig in 1879.[13] In 1875, he also became a coeditor with Oscar Leopold Gebhardt and Theodor Zahn of the *Patrum apostolicorum opera* and established a "church history society" that regularly met at his apartment. Moreover, in 1876, with the help of Emil Schürer, he cofounded the *Theologische Literaturzeitung*, which became the most important review journal for theological literature in Germany.[14] His

---

11.   Zahn-Harnack, *Adolf von Harnack*, 59–60.

12.   Harnack's attractiveness followed him wherever he moved, drawing students along with him in his placements in Giessen, Marburg, and Berlin. Glick notes that "to list the students of Harnack who later became renowned would be, practically, to compile a 'Who's Who' of late nineteenth- and twentieth-century theologians" (*Reality of Christianity*, 36). The *Festschrift* for Harnack's seventieth birthday was presented to him on behalf of 215 theologians, 155 of whom he had taught as students (see *Harnack-Ehrung: Beiträge zur Kirchengeschichte ihrem Lehrer Adolf von Harnack zu seinem siebzigsten Geburtstage (7. Mai 1921)* (Leipzig: J. C. Hinrichs, 1921). Several of the contributing scholars who studied under Harnack include Martin Dibelius (1903–1906), Otto Dibelius (1900–1904), Edgar Johnson Goodspeed (1898–1899), Otto Ritschl (1882–1884), James Hardy Ropes (1894–1895), Karl Ludwig Schmidt (1910–1913), Hans Freiherr von Soden (1900–1905), and Hans Windisch (1906–1907), among numerous others; the years in parentheses denote the time period when each sat under Harnack's tutelage.

13.   Friedrich Smend, *Adolf von Harnack: Verzeichnis seiner Schriften* (Leipzig: J. C. Hinrichs, 1931).

14.   Horton Harris, "Harnack, Adolf von," in *Dictionary of Biblical Criticism and Inte.pretation*, ed. Stanley E. Porter (London: Routledge, 2007), 143–45. In 1881, Harnack, now in Giessen, accepted a one-year appointment as the review's editor, but would go on to keep the position for twenty-eight more years. See Glick, *Reality of Christianity*, 16.

other efforts included providing critical editions of texts and revising others that he deemed as not meeting a sufficient standard.[15]

Chief among the problems that Harnack saw with the church of his day was the role of dogma, particularly how it was used to legitimate a particular view of history and perpetuate an ecclesiastical hierarchy and theological paradigm that failed to produce the practical and ethical outcomes envisioned by the gospel as preached by Jesus. This problem fueled Harnack's interest in church history, which he endeavored to map out in relation to the entire intellectual history of humanity. He believed that the same method used in studying human history should also be used for church history, even though God's revelation is specific to the latter. A major question that arises, then, is: "How are creeds and dogmas to be studied as being both of individual faith and public history?"[16] For Harnack, this question was best answered in accordance with the intellectual climate of classical liberalism that had swept across Germany over the course of the nineteenth century as a result of the influence of Schleiermacher and Hegel, which entailed a rejection of the authority of tradition to control theology. It was while at Leipzig that Harnack made his full conversion to liberal theology, having by this time come under the influence of Albrecht Ritschl the "architect of modern liberalism."[17] It was in 1877 that Harnack first met Ritschl, who was teaching at Göttingen at the time. Regarding this figure, Rumscheidt remarks, "It was this theologian in whom Harnack saw genuine potential for Christianity as an ecclesial institution in the modern intellectual climate. . . . To his life's end Harnack pointed to him as an example and point of orientation which would rescue theology from romantic diversions and irrationalism."[18] Ritschl's major three-volume work, *The Christian Doctrine of Justification and Reconciliation*, was published over the course of five years, 1870–1874, which overlaps when Harnack was receiving his education in Leipzig. The impact of Ritschl's work was immediate within the German theological guild, and his influence on Harnack's thought

---

15. Rumscheidt, *Adolf von Harnack*, 12.
16. Rumscheidt, *Adolf von Harnack*, 12.
17. Baird, *History of New Testament Research*, 2:86.
18. Rumscheidt, *Adolf von Harnack*, 12. However, Glick notes that Harnack must have been introduced to Ritschl's work first while still in Dorpat, as Engelhardt was "one of the first to understand the significance of Ritschl's work and to give it extensive study" (*Reality of Christianity*, 38). Cf. Reinhold Seeberg, *Die Kirche Deutschlands im neunzehnten Jahrhundert* (Leipzig: Deichert, 1903), 344–45.

contributed significantly to his break with his orthodox Lutheran heritage and move to liberalism.

To gain an understanding of why Harnack embraced liberalism, it is helpful to digress momentarily to explain what characterized this movement in Germany. In general usage today, liberalism is something of a protean notion; it can mean what we want it to mean, and it often resists a firm definition. For a view to be "liberal," it only has to be "left" of one's conception of what is conservative. However, liberalism, as a movement in nineteenth- and twentieth-century German theological thought, can be described according to a few features that create cohesion within what was still a convoluted intellectual paradigm. First, following Schleiermacher, liberal theologians "were committed to the task of reconstructing Christian belief in the light of modern knowledge."[19] In other words, given the progress in the areas of philosophy and science since the Enlightenment, Christian theology could not persist independently from cultural developments; faith had to be reconfigured to make sense in light of modern thought. Second, liberalism emphasized freedom of thought, and "this freedom holds fast to its higher vantage-point where comparing, assessing, discussing and judging remain forever open possibilities."[20] This included the freedom to critically question age-old doctrines.[21] Thus, with respect to the question of dogma and creeds raised above, liberalism did not reject the value of teaching and creed-like affirmations of faith, but simply reserved the rights to reject traditional beliefs when it seemed appropriate and to replace them with new ones. Third, liberalism tended to focus on the ethical and practical dimensions of Christian theology.[22] Fourth, liberal theologians grounded their theology on something other than the authority of the Bible, such as, with the case of Harnack, historical investigation.[23] Lastly, according to Stanley Grenz and Roger Olson, "liberal theology continued to drift toward divine immanence at the expense of transcendence begun by the Enlightenment and continued by the great German thinkers of the early nineteenth century."[24]

---

19. Stanley J. Grenz and Roger E. Olson, *20th Century Theology: God and the World in a Transitional Age* (Downers Grove, IL: IVP, 1992), 52.
20. Rumscheidt, *Adolf von Harnack*, 35.
21. Grenz and Olson, *20th Century Theology*, 52.
22. Grenz and Olson, *20th Century Theology*, 52.
23. Grenz and Olson, *20th Century Theology*, 52.
24. Grenz and Olson, *20th Century Theology*, 52.

Exemplifying these features of liberalism, Harnack evidenced several distinct ways in which he broke with his Lutheran heritage while at Leipzig, and some of these are worth mentioning here as they point towards the kind of scholar he was becoming. The first major way involves the doctrine of the person of Christ in which he could no longer affirm his preexistence. In a letter to Engelhardt in 1873 he wrote:

> I cannot . . . comprehend how one can hold the doctrine of preexistence. If I should hold it, I should have to assume that revelations of God which are to be esteemed very highly have taken place among heathen peoples; for from all which I can perceive, this doctrine comes out of heathen philosophy, which at about the turn of the ancient period mixed noticeably with Semitic ideas of angels and of preexistence.[25]

In other words, Harnack believed the earliest Christians would have known nothing of the notion of the eternal Christ; it was rather a result of a development in the history of Christian dogma. A corollary of this stance was Harnack's denial of the dual nature of Christ; he rejected the divinity of Christ and only affirmed his humanity.[26] The second way he broke with his heritage pertained to the way he valued tradition, and dogma by extension. Harnack held to the conviction that every historical movement's means of establishing a tradition worked through a process of "rationalizing, leveling, and deteriorating"[27] to the point that tradition is only ever loosely based on what first instigated its establishment. He also could not convince himself that God had so protected the Lutheran tradition to inoculate it from the natural tendencies of tradition, and so his view of history became determinative for his stance towards the doctrine of his own Lutheran background.[28] The third way involved the sacraments, which he concluded were only symbolic tokens that offered comfort to believing Christians concerning the forgiveness of their sins. In addition, Harnack remained uncommitted to any view regarding the saving efficacy of

---

25. Zahn-Harnack, *Adolf von Harnack*, 93, translated in Glick, *Reality of Christianity*, 38.
26. See Ernst Bammel, "The Jesus of History in the Theology of Adolf v. Harnack," *Modern Churchman* 19 (1976): 90–112.
27. In German: *rationalisierend, nivellierend und verschlechternd* (Zahn-Harnack, *Adolf von Harnack*, 96).
28. Zahn-Harnack, *Adolf von Harnack*, 96; Glick, *Reality of Christianity*, 39.

child baptism, his main reservation being that it did not include a person's capacity to think or believe.[29]

These ideas began occupying his thoughts as early as 1873 (Harnack was only twenty-one years old), and he would continue developing them after he left Leipzig. Harnack evidently corresponded with his father regarding his theological leanings throughout this time, and Theodosius was unreserved in expressing his great concern for his son. In one letter he wrote:

> Had I been more faithful, you would take a more positive position than you do. I beg of you, my dearest Adolf, for the sake of everything which is of worth and dear to you, neither to allow yourself to be imposed upon, nor to suffer your vanity to be charmed by the negative criticism of the modern theology, in which a leaf can be torn from the Bible, or the whole Bible can be thrown away. Do not follow the consciousness of the time, but rather that of the church, for our only choice is between these two.[30]

Harnack was not dissuaded from his historical convictions, which created a great point of tension in his relationship with his father.

The Giessen Years

In 1879 Harnack accepted a professorship at the University of Giessen where he would remain until 1886. Approaching the end of his tenure at Giessen, the first installment of his monumental three-volume *Lehrbuch der Dogmengeschichte* (*History of Dogma*) was published in December 1885 (copyright 1886), the work which constituted his *magnum opus*.[31] The influence of Ritschl on Harnack's thought is plainly evident in this work, which officially solidified his break with his orthodox Lutheran

---

29. Zahn-Harnack, *Adolf von Harnack*, 97; Glick, *Reality of Christianity*, 39–40.

30. Zahn-Harnack, *Adolf von Harnack*, 106–107, translated in Glick, *Reality of Christianity*, 26.

31. Adolf Harnack, *Lehrbuch der Dogmengeschichte*, 3 vols. (Leipzig: Mohr, 1886–1890); ET Harnack, *History of Dogma*, 7 vols., trans. Neil Buchanan (London: Williams and Norgate, 1895–1899). A shorter version of this work was published several years later in Harnack, *Grundriss der Dogmengeschichte: Die Entstehung des Dogmas und seine Entwickelung im Rahmen der morgenländischen Kirche* (Freiberg: J. C. B. Mohr, 1889). For the English translation of this work, see Harnack, *Outlines of the History of Dogma*, trans. Edwin Knox Mitchell, with an Introduction by Philip Rieff (Boston: Beacon, 1957). Much of the same material was condensed and presented in the form of a lecture series. See Harnack, *Die Entstehung der christlichen Theologie und des kirchlichen Dogmas: Sechs Vorlesungen*, Bücherei der christlichen Welt (Gotha: Leopold Plotz, 1927).

heritage. The work itself set out to accomplish three objectives: (1) to investigate where the church's theology began and where the onset of ecclesiastical dogma originated; (2) to trace the development of dogma until the time of Augustine in the West and until the year 787 in the East; and (3) to trace the development of dogma in Tridentine-Vatican Roman Catholicism, followed by its critique by Socinians and humanistic Enlightenment thinkers and, lastly, the Reformers' response to traditional Roman Catholic dogma. "With respect to the latter," Mueller explains, "Harnack believed himself to be able to establish the thesis that the Reformation should have effected a break with traditional dogmatic Catholic positions far more radical than was actually achieved."[32] The objectives of the work, however, were not the matters that concerned others nearly as much as the presuppositions operative in it and the way Harnack presents the trajectory of Christian history.

In the first volume of *History of Dogma*, Harnack discusses his presuppositions regarding the preaching of Jesus, the teaching of Paul, and the theology of John—the three traditions that express "the richest contents of the earliest history of the Gospel."[33] Regarding the preaching of Jesus, Harnack held that Jesus professed to be the Messiah, but this did not carry with it anything of the high Christology that developed later in the church. Instead, the primary meaning of "Messiah" consisted of the relationship between Jesus's person and the message he carried, the message being that God himself comes to his people, who are given the opportunity to be embraced by him. This is the good news that Jesus embodied, which Harnack summarizes as follows:

> Jesus Christ brought no new doctrine, but he set forth in his own person a holy life with God and before God, and gave himself in virtue of this life to the service of his brethren in order to win them for the Kingdom of God, that is, to lead them out of selfishness and the world to God, out of the natural connections and contrasts to a union in love, and prepare them for an eternal kingdom and an eternal life.[34]

That which Jesus embodied he also preached, the message of which Harnack summarizes elsewhere:

32. Mueller, "Harnack," 290.
33. Harnack, *History of Dogma*, 1:97.
34. Harnack, *History of Dogma*, 1:42.

The individual is called upon to listen to the glad message of mercy and the Fatherhood of God, and to make up his mind whether he will be on God's side and the Eternal's or on the side of the world and of time. The Gospel, as Jesus proclaimed it, has to do with the Father only and not with the Son. This is no paradox, nor, on the other hand, is it "rationalism," but the simple expression of the actual fact as the evangelists give it.[35]

Jesus's preaching, then, expresses the apocalyptic eschatological message that the kingdom of God will be consummated in the future, but those who accept Jesus's message can experience it at present.[36] According to Harnack, this message was largely rejected by the Jews and was proclaimed to the Gentiles. Paul, as the Apostle to the Gentiles, played an integral role in shaping Christianity in its Hellenistic environment where it transitioned from religion to theology—that is, from a set of beliefs and practices by which a group defines its collective identity and relationship to a deity, to a set of systematic statements about the nature and character of God.[37] More specifically, Paul taught that the death of Christ was the end of the law and that faith in Christ was the means of obtaining the righteousness the Gospel promised.[38] Christianity developed, then, according to the influence of Paulinism (synonymous with "Gentile Christianity" in Harnack's writings), which centered around this Christocentric doctrine.[39] John's contribution to the New Testament, according to Harnack, also reveals Christianity's shift toward Hellenistic thought. However, "the peculiar and lofty conception of Christ and of the Gospel, which stands out in the writings of John, has directly exercised no demonstrable influence on the succeeding development—with the exception of one peculiar movement, the Montanistic, which, however, does not rest on a true understanding of these writings."[40]

In the early development of ecclesiastical dogma, Harnack, still in the first volume of *History of Dogma*, identifies Gnosticism and

---

35. Adolf Harnack, *What Is Christianity?*, trans. Thomas Bailey Saunders with an introduction by Rudolf Bultmann (Gloucester, MA: Peter Smith, 1978), 143–44.
36. See Baird, *History of New Testament Research*, 2:126.
37. Baird, *History of New Testament Research*, 2:126.
38. Harnack, *History of Dogma*, 1:86–87.
39. Harnack, *History of Dogma*, 1:92.
40. Harnack, *History of Dogma*, 1:97.

Marcionism as profound agencies of influence.[41] With respect to Gnosticism's influence, he finds, "the decisive thing [to be] the conversion of the Gospel into a doctrine, into an absolute philosophy of religion, the transforming of the *disciplina Evangelii* into an asceticism based on a dualistic conception, and into a practice of mysteries."[42] Marcion, on the other hand, whom Harnack took great personal interest in and even admired,[43] "deserves the credit for having first grasped and actualized the idea of a canonical collection of Christian writings."[44] Marcion's canon was made up of a collection of Paul's letters and the Gospel of Luke. He also rejected the Old Testament as a source that spoke of a different God other than the God of love revealed through Jesus, and he attempted to sever Christianity from it. The church in the second century reacted strongly against Gnosticism and Marcionism, and this instigated the process of the canonization of the New Testament. Despite this being a part of the unfortunate development of Christian dogma, Harnack believes "the witness of the literature of the NT to the original, dynamic gospel remained a positive force in the continuing history of Christianity."[45] The church also reacted against the Montanist heresy, which Harnack understands as the point where the church crystallized "the apostolic gospel into the rigid Christianity of creed, canon, and episcopacy. The fatal step . . . was taken by the apologists who secularized the gospel and degraded

---

41. On the influence of Gnosticism, see Harnack, *History of Dogma*, 222–65. On Marcion's influence, see pp. 266–86.

42. Harnack, *History of Dogma*, 1:252.

43. As a nineteen-year-old student at the University of Dorpat, Harnack won a gold medal for a paper he wrote on Marcion and Tertullian's response to his teachings. From then on Harnack wished to write a longer work on Marcion, which he finally accomplished fifty years later in 1920 (copyright 1921) (Rumscheidt, *Adolf von Harnack*, 28; see Adolf von Harnack, *Marcion: Das Evangelium vom fremden Gott: Eine Monographie zur Geschichte der Grundlegung der katholischen Kirche* [Leipzig: J. C. Hinrichs, 1921]). In his monograph on Marcion, Harnack approves of Marcion's attempt to decanonize the Old Testament because the New Testament speaks of an alien God who redeems and is altogether different from the God of the Old Testament who has little to do with his miserable and corrupt creation apart from imposing a hopelessly unattainable legalism. Harnack states his thesis as follows: "the rejection of the Old Testament in the second century was a mistake which the great church rightly avoided; to maintain it in the sixteenth century was a fate from which the Reformation was not yet able to escape; but still to preserve it in Protestantism as a canonical document since the nineteenth century is the consequence of a religious and ecclesiastical crippling" (Adolf von Harnack, *Marcion: The Gospel of the Alien God*, trans. John E. Steely and Lyle D. Bierma [Durham, NC: Labyrinth, 1990], 134).

44. Harnack, *Marcion* [English translation], 132.

45. Baird, *History of New Testament Research*, 2:128. Cf. Harnack, *Entstehung der christlichen Theologie*, 73.

Christianity into dogma."[46] As the first volume of *History of Dogma* is described here, and all throughout the two subsequent volumes, with the rare exceptions of Augustine and Luther, Harnack depicts "the whole saga of early Christian history as a story of tragic decline."[47]

Harnack's *History of Dogma* made him famous, and after its publication there resulted a great divide between Harnack and his father that would never again be bridged. Some time thereafter he received a letter from Theodosius, which read:

> Our difference is not simply a theological one, but one so profoundly and directly Christian that if I should pass over it lightly, I would be denying Christ; that no one can desire or expect of me, even if he stands as close to me, my son, as you do. To mention only the most decisive issue, whoever takes the position which you take on the Resurrection is in my eyes no longer a Christian theologian. I simply do not understand how anyone can appeal to history when he indulges in such historical machination, or I understand it only if one thereby degrades Christianity.[48]

Even though Harnack's relationship with his father caused him great sorrow, his time in Giessen was also marked by the personal joy of marrying Amalie Thiersch in December 1879. Together they had three daughters and one son, all of which were born in Giessen between 1881 and 1886. It is quite remarkable that Harnack remained as productive as he was during these years. By the time Harnack left Giessen in 1886 he had published 367 items. He was only thirty-five years old.

The Marburg and Berlin Years

Upon leaving Giessen, Harnack accepted a call to a position in Marburg in 1886. Then, two years later in 1888, by unanimous recommendation of the faculty, he was called to Berlin to assume the chair of history. This appointment, unlike any of those previous, became a matter of significant controversy as it was contested by the Evangelical *Oberkirchenrat*, which, as the highest office of the state church of Prussia, possessed this right over the theological chairs in universities. The

---

46.   Baird, *History of New Testament Research*, 2:128.

47.   Baird, *History of New Testament Research*, 2:128.

48.   Zahn-Harnack, *Adolf von Harnack*, 143, translated in Glick, *Reality of Christianity*, 27.

concern of the church officials was largely based on the views Harnack articulated in the two volumes of *History of Dogma* that had been published thus far (the final volume was yet to appear in 1889). There were three counts in particular on which the council voted against Harnack. First, Harnack was charged with dismantling the New Testament canon because he argued that certain books were not written by their traditional authors. In particular, these included the Gospel of John, the Letter to the Ephesians, and First Peter. Second, he denied the existence of miracles and proposed unconventional interpretations of Christ's virgin birth, resurrection, and ascension. Third, he denied that Jesus instituted the Trinitarian formula for baptism. Pauck notes that "no attempt was made to refute these views on the basis of historical scholarship from which they were derived, only the irreconcilability of Harnack's views with doctrinal authority of the church was stated."[49] The controversy went on for nine bitter months, but the veto was overruled, in the end, by Emperor William II, who signed the document of Harnack's appointment on September 17, 1888.[50]

This episode, Pauck also explains, "cast a shadow upon Harnack's academic position. Indeed, it darkened his entire career."[51] The most disappointing aspect of Harnack's controversy with the ecclesial hierarchy was that he remained labeled a *persona non grata* by the Protestant church with which he still considered himself faithfully committed. He was even disallowed participation in the process of evaluating his own students in their preparedness for service in the church,[52] including students who spoke highly of their teacher as one who "combined a fine understanding of the nature and needs of youth, a friendly approach and unselfish encouragement, a strict scholarly passion for truth and religious ardor, [and] earnest work and a free unruffled easiness of manner."[53] Since he was not able to work for the church from within its ranks, he resolved still to labor alongside it through his support of foreign missions in his writing, through eight years of service as the

49.   Pauck, *Harnack and Troeltsch*, 5.
50.   Pauck, *Harnack and Troeltsch*, 4–5.
51.   Pauck, *Harnack and Troeltsch*, 5.
52.   Rumscheidt, *Adolf von Harnack*, 21.
53.   Zahn-Harnack, *Adolf von Harnack*, 74–75, translated in Glick, *Reality of Christianity*, 36. The comment was made by Wilhelm Bornemann, who later became a professor in Frankfurt. See also Kurt Aland, Walter Elliger, and Otto Dibelius, *Adolf Harnack: in memoriam: Reden zum 100. Geburtstag am 7. Mai 1951 gehalten bei der Gedenkfeier der Theologischen Fakultät der Humboldt-Universität Berlin* (Berlin: Evangelische Verlagsanstalt, n.d.).

president of the *Evangelisch-Soziale Kongress*, through active involvement in the Inner Mission, and through being a cofounder and president of the Evangelical Union.[54] Harnack also dedicated much of his time to administrative responsibilities in the government of Kaiser Wilhelm II, with whom he became a close confidant.[55] Among these responsibilities included his appointment as Director-General of the Royal Library in Berlin in March 1905. His successful management of the library resulted in the staff increasing from 150 to more than 300 individuals and enlarging the budget exponentially over the course of nine years, at which time on March 22, 1914, the Emperor granted him a knighthood.[56] From the point of this ennoblement on, Harnack and his family became known as "von Harnack." In 1910 he also became president of the *Kaiser Wilhelm Gesellschaft zur Förderung der Wissenschaften* and continued in this post for several years.

Harnack's appointment was not the only theological controversy in which he became involved while in Berlin. Several more were to follow, the first occurring in 1892 when a dispute over the Apostles' Creed broke out. Harnack had previously spoken of his wish for a new expression of the Christian faith that would supersede the Apostles' Creed as a more credible statement of belief in the nineteenth century, though he had remained out of public discussion on the issue until he was approached by a group of students who sought his advice in their plans to promote a new creed.[57] He published his response to them, prefaced with a separate study on the Creed, in the liberal journal *Christliche Welt*, which, as Rumscheidt describes, "landed like a fox in a henhouse."[58] As a testament to this short study's public interest, Zahn-Harnack points out that it enjoyed twenty-seven editions but was simultaneously met with unbridled backlash from the Catholic press in particular.[59]

Another controversy ensued over the sixteen public lectures Harnack delivered in the winter semester of 1899/1900 that were subsequently published in his book *Das Wesen des Christentums* (in English *What Is Christianity?*).[60] This work, as his contemporaries

---

54.   Glick, *Reality of Christianity*, 59.
55.   Rumscheidt, *Adolf von Harnack*, 22.
56.   Rumscheidt, *Adolf von Harnack*, 21.
57.   Rumscheidt, *Adolf von Harnack*, 17. See also Harris, "Harnack, Adolf von," 144.
58.   Rumscheidt, *Adolf von Harnack*, 17.
59.   Zahn-Harnack, *Adolf von Harnack*, 151.
60.   Adolf von Harnack, *Das Wesen des Christentums* (Leipzig: J. C. Hinrichs, 1900); ET Harnack, *What Is Christianity?*

described it, was a distillate of Harnack's theological convictions.[61] It is organized in a similar way to his *History of Dogma*, beginning with an introductory section but then followed by two major parts: "The Gospel" and "The Gospel in History." The first part on the Gospel is further divided into two parts: "The Main Features of Jesus' Message," and "The Gospel in Relation to Certain Problems," the problems being asceticism, the social question, questions of public order, civilization, Christology, and creed. The second major part of the book discusses Christianity and its development throughout history, with attention given to the Apostolic Age, Catholicism (both its Eastern and Western forms), and Protestantism. The whole work is oriented to answer the question: Can one be a Christian today? To answer this question, Harnack believes that Christianity must be understood historically in order to uncover its essence: "It is solely in its historical sense that we shall try to answer this question here; that is to say, we shall employ the methods of historical science and the experience of life which is earned by witnessing history. We must thus exclude the view of the question taken by the apologist and the religious philosopher."[62] From Christianity's essence—that is, what is of permanent value—the spirit of the gospel can be appropriately applied to each new age and culture. Throughout the work Jesus remains the central focus, but Harnack makes an important distinction between the gospel *of* Jesus and the gospel *about* Jesus. Clarifying this point, Mueller writes,

> Harnack held that the Gospel *of* Jesus may be summed up under these three heads: first, the Kingdom of God and its coming; secondly, faith in God the Father and the infinite value of the human soul; thirdly, the higher righteousness and the commandment of love. Jesus has brought about a transvaluation of all values. What Jesus revealed about the Father and the preciousness of the human soul, ennobled through its union with God, "shows that the Gospel is in no wise a positive religion like the rest; that it contains no statutory or particularistic elements; *that it is, therefore, religion itself.*" Harnack even went so far as to avow that Jesus is indeed "the way to the Father, and as he is the appointed of the Father, so he is the judge as well. . . . It is not as a mere factor that

---

61.   Glick, *Reality of Christianity,* 263.
62.   Harnack, *What Is Christianity?*, 5–6.

he is connected with the Gospel; he was its personal realization and its strength, and this he is felt to be still." [63]

Thus, according to Harnack, the person of Jesus is not an integral part of the gospel itself as much as he is the quintessential testimony to the gospel. From this view stemmed much controversy, not only because Harnack's historical conclusions railed against orthodox doctrines such as the Trinity and atonement, [64] but because these views were articulated so clearly and sincerely at a level that the laity could easily apprehend the implications of Harnack's views. The lectures themselves sparked such excitement that "immediately on their publication, the railway station at Leipzig was crowded with immense consignments of the books about to be dispatched to every corner of the world." [65] The success of the book added both to the feud with the ecclesiastical authorities on the one hand, and Harnack's fame throughout Germany and beyond on the other.

Other controversies would follow in the years to come, including the so-called "Jatho-affair" in 1911, [66] the publication of *Marcion* in 1921, and Harnack's response to the emergence of dialectical theology in 1923. [67] Despite these struggles, the years at Berlin were the most productive yet for Harnack's scholarship. His major works during this time include his two-volume *The Expansion of Christianity in the First Three Centuries*, [68] his three-volume *History of Ancient Christian*

---

63. Mueller, "Harnack," 293, quoting Harnack, *What Is Christianity?*, 154.

64. Harnack's challenge to orthodox views regarding Christology are incapsulated in his summative statement "the Father alone, and not the Son, belongs in the Gospel as Jesus preached it" (*What Is Christianity?*, 125).

65. Stephen Neill and Tom Wright, *The Interpretation of the New Testament, 1861–1986*, 2nd ed. (Oxford: Oxford University Press, 1988). Rudolph Bultmann, in his "Introduction" to the Stuttgart 1950 reprint (English translation 1957) of the book comments that "by 1927 the volume had already been through fourteen printings, and had been translated into as many languages."

66. This affair involved the Lutheran clergyman Karl Jatho, who had become outspoken in his denial of the fundamental doctrines of the Lutheran Church. While in the process of being dismissed by the Lutheran governing body, Harnack disseminated a brochure expressing that while Jatho's theology was irreconcilable with the beliefs of the Lutheran Church, he should not be removed from his position. Despite Harnack's advocacy for Jatho, controversy arose between the two since Harnack, in the same brochure, described Jatho's deviant theology as unbearable. Jatho took issue with Harnack because he believed their theologies to be essentially the same, and so he received Harnack's brochure as more of an insult than advocacy (Harris, "Harnack, Adolf von," 144). For a full account of the Jatho affair, see Zahn-Harnack, *Adolf von Harnack*, 395–401.

67. See Glick, *Reality of Christianity*, 19; Harris, "Harnack, Adolf von," 144.

68. Adolf von Harnack, *Die Mission und Ausbreitung des Christentums in den ersten drei Jahrhunderten*, 2 vols. (Leipzig: J. C. Hinrichs, 1902); ET Harnack, *The Expansion of Christianity in the First Three Centuries*, 2 vols., trans. James Moffatt (New York: G. P. Putnam's Sons, 1904).

Literature,[69] and his six-volume *New Testament Studies*, which contains his major historical-critical contribution to Lukan scholarship.[70] He also wrote a massive history on the Prussian Empire, which appeared first in 1900 (copyright 1901) in four large volumes.[71] In all, from 1900 to 1914, his published pieces number 455.

During World War I, Harnack's publication rate slowed. On many occasions he wrote and presented public addresses on the War at the request of the Emperor, and he believed that the War assured "a peace which would be more noble than the peace which had led to the War in the first place."[72] Germany's eventual defeat did not come as a surprise, but Harnack was not prepared for the reality that came after the War. He had grown deeply troubled with the way the Emperor and his ministers had conducted the war effort and believed it did not align with the values of German scholarship. Harnack supported the move to a democratic order but was not naïve to the fact that such a move would not be enough to heal the broken nation.[73]

In 1921, Harnack, now seventy years old, retired from the directorship of the Royal Library and from the university, though he

69. Adolf von Harnack, *Geschichte der altchristlichen Literatur bis Eusebius*, 3 vols. (Leipzig: J. C. Hinrichs, 1893–1904). Pauck notes that this work "laid the foundation for all further critical studies in patristics" (Pauck, *Harnack and Troeltsch*, 8.)
70. This series of books includes the following: Adolf von Harnack, *Beiträge zur Einleitung in das Neue Testament I: Lukas der Arzt: Der Verfasser des dritten Evangeliums und der Apostelgeschichte* (Leipzig: J. C. Hinrichs, 1906); ET Harnack, *New Testament Studies I: Luke the Physician: The Author of the Third Gospel and the Acts of the Apostles*, trans. J. R. Wilkinson (London: Williams & Norgate, 1908); Harnack, *Beiträge zur Einleitung in das Neue Testament II: Sprüche und Reden Jesu: Die zweite Quelle des Matthäus und Lukas* (Leipzig: J. C. Hinrichs, 1907); ET Harnack, *New Testament Studies II: The Sayings of Jesus: The Second Source of St. Matthew and St. Luke*, trans. J. R. Wilkinson (London: Williams & Norgate, 1908); Harnack, *Beiträge zur Einleitung in das Neue Testament III: Die Apostelgeschichte* (Leipzig: J. C. Hinrichs, 1908); ET Harnack, *New Testament Studies III: The Acts of the Apostles*, trans. J. R. Wilkinson (London: Williams & Norgate, 1909); Harnack, *Beiträge zur Einleitung in das Neue Testament IV: Neue Untersuchungen zur Apostelgeschichte und zur Abfassungszeit der synoptischen Evangelien* (Leipzig: J. C. Hinrichs, 1911); ET Harnack, *New Testament Studies IV: The Date of the Acts and of the Synoptic Gospels*, trans. J. R. Wilkinson (London: Williams & Norgate, 1911); Harnack, *Beiträge zur Einleitung in das Neue Testament V: Über den privaten Gebrauch der Heiligen Schriften in der alten Kirche* (Leipzig: J. C. Hinrichs, 1912); ET Harnack, *New Testament Studies V: Bible Reading in the Early Church*, trans. J. R. Wilkinson (London: Williams & Norgate, 1912); Harnack, *Beiträge zur Einleitung in das Neue Testament VI: Die Entstehung des Neuen Testaments und die wichtigsten Folgen der neuen Schöpfung* (Leipzig: J. C. Hinrichs, 1914); ET Harnack, *New Testament Studies VI: The Origin of the New Testament and the Most Important Consequences of the New Creation*, trans. J. R. Wilkinson (London: Williams & Norgate, 1925).
71. Adolf von Harnack, *Geschichte der Königlich Preussischen Akademie der Wissenschaften zu Berlin*, 4 vols. (Berlin: Georg Stilke, 1901).
72. Rumscheidt, *Adolf von Harnack*, 26.
73. Rumscheidt, *Adolf von Harnack*, 26–27.

continued filling the same teaching post for the next two years until the appointment of his replacement, Hans Lietzmann, was ratified.[74] He continued to accept invitations to lecture, and these were often used to express his concern for the growing trends in theology, which did not afford sufficient respect or attention to history. For Harnack, such a view was exemplified in the work of his former student Karl Barth.[75] Harnack continued to write and present lectures up until the last few weeks of his life. Then, on June 10, 1930, his life came to its end.

Attempting to keep the totality of Harnack's life and works in view, how might his vision as a historian and theologian be succinctly expressed? The aim of his scholarship as Harnack conceived it can be summed up as follows: the object of the historian is to find the "kernel" of true Christianity amidst the "husk" of Greek influence and all the unessential baggage that has been added to Christian doctrine down through the centuries. The object of the theologian is then to abstract what is essential to Christianity and then interpret how the spirit of Christ is to be applied anew in each culture.[76] This is best accomplished through applying rationalistic thought that is free from the strictures of dogma. Harnack did just this, not only with his *History of Dogma*, but with all three areas of his work—the study of the New Testament, early Christian literature, and the development of church doctrine[77]—to an extent hitherto unparalleled in German scholarship. Such an accomplishment earned Harnack the credit of bringing liberalism to its height.

Now I will turn attention to Harnack's work on Lukan studies to survey and evaluate his contribution to two of the earliest documents of Christian history—Luke and Acts.

HARNACK'S CONTRIBUTIONS TO LUKAN STUDIES

Harnack made significant contributions to several areas of Lukan scholarship, especially those related to the standard critical issues of authorship, language features/style, sources, and date of composition.

---

74.   Rumscheidt, *Adolf von Harnack*, 30.
75.   See Zahn-Harnack, *Adolf von Harnack*, 415.
76.   For a brief summary of this view, see Adolf Harnack, *Christianity and History*, trans. Thomas Bailey Saunders (London: A&C Black, 1907).
77.   According to George S. Duncan, all of Harnack's biblical and the theological writings can be organized into one of these three groups ("The Contribution of Adolf von Harnack to Theological and Biblical Learning," *Christian Education* 14, no. 6 [1931]: 694–98).

In a seemingly ironic contrast with his reputation as a liberal theologian, he helped to support many of the positions that have come to be, for the most part, the majority conservative views on these issues. The importance of this is that Harnack, as one who thought independently in the spirit of liberalism, cannot be accused of any sort of bias that favors orthodox views, which makes him one of the most significant figures in the history of criticism as one who advocated for Luke's reputation as a (mostly) reliable historian.[78] I will survey a selection of topics from Harnack's major works on the Gospel of Luke and Acts to show how he contributed to this area of study and has had lasting influence in the field.

LUKE THE PHYSICIAN, AUTHOR, AND COMPANION OF PAUL

Harnack's major works on the Third Gospel and the Acts of the Apostles consist of the first four volumes in his historical-critical *New Testament Studies* series. In the first of these volumes, *Luke the Physician*, Harnack investigates the possibility of whether "Luke the Greek physician of Antioch, the companion and fellow-worker of St. Paul, composed the third gospel and the Acts of the Apostles."[79] Most German scholars at the time denied the traditional view of authorship, and there was a reason for this; despite the fact that F. C. Baur's theories had been overturned, the influence of the Tübingen school still exercised great sway in New Testament criticism, one way being the view that the Acts of the Apostles was written in the middle of the second century and not by a fellow worker of Paul.[80] Harnack even comments that "the indefensibility of the tradition is regarded as being so clearly established that nowadays it is thought scarcely worthwhile to reprove this indefensibility, or even to notice the arguments

78. W. Ward Gasque, *A History of the Criticism of the Acts of the Apostles* (repr., Grand Rapids: Eerdmans, 1975), 146.

79. Harnack, *Luke the Physician*, 8.

80. See F. C. Baur, *Paul the Apostle of Jesus Christ: His Life and Works, His Epistles and His Doctrine; A Contribution to a Critical History of Primitive Christianity*, trans. Allan Menzies, 2 vols. (London: Williams & Norgate, 1875; repr., Peabody, MA: Hendrickson, 2003). For an explanation of the decline of Baur's theories regarding *Tendenzkritik* and the issues with his Hegelian philosophical framework of thesis, antithesis, and synthesis, see Neill and Wright, *New Testament Interpretation*, 35–60. See also Hughson T. Ong, "Ferdinand Christian Baur's Historical Criticism and *Tendenzkritik*," in *Pillars in the History of Biblical Interpretation, Volume 1: Prevailing Methods before 1980*, eds. Stanley E. Porter and Sean A. Adams, MBSS 2 (Eugene, OR: Pickwick, 2016), 118–38.

of conservative opponents."[81] Against the critical consensus of his day, Harnack affirmed each aspect of the traditional view: Luke was a native of Antioch, a physician, a fellow-worker of Paul, and authored both works ascribed to him. Each of these conclusions requires some consideration to grasp what lengths Harnack took to argue the traditional view. Further, since Harnack's *Luke the Physician* in some way relates to most of the major issues on Lukan scholarship, or at least those that occupied Harnack's time, this work and my evaluation of it will be the main focus of this section, while his other works on the Third Gospel and Acts will be discussed where they factor into the topics discussed below.

Luke, a Native of Antioch

Harnack defends the traditional view that Luke was a native of Syrian Antioch (i.e., Antioch on the Orontes), citing the external evidence found in Eusebius and the ancient *Anti-Marcionite Prologue to the Gospel of Luke*.[82] He also seeks support in the internal details of Acts. Even though Luke never describes himself as an Antiochean in the sections in Acts where he presumably portrays himself as an eyewitness (i.e., the "we" passages),[83] Harnack believes the knowledge Luke shows for this city, as well as the special interest he takes in its community, lends support to the external evidence. He interprets a number of details as indicative of Luke's special knowledge of Antioch: Luke knows that those who first preached to the Gentiles in Antioch were from Cyprus and Cyrene (11:20); this city was where the name "Christian" was first used to refer to believers in Jesus (11:26); he enumerates a list of prophets and teachers in Antioch in Acts 13:1 with some other distinguishing details; and Paul and Barnabas's missionary journey is portrayed as an Antiochean undertaking (13:2).[84] "All these instances," Harnack states, "surely permit the conclusion that the testimony of the Acts is not only not opposed to the tradition that its author was a

---

81. Harnack, *Luke the Physician*, 6.
82. Harnack, *Luke the Physician*, 4. Cf. Eusebius, *Hist. Ecc.* 3.4, 6. It may be an oversight that Harnack, who understood the "we" passages as indicative of Luke's presence in the narrative, fails to mention that in the Western recension (e.g. Codex Bezae [D05]) the first instance of the pronoun "we" is in Antioch (Acts 11:28). See also August Strobel, "Lukas der Antiochener (Bemerkungen zu Act 11, 28 D)," *ZNW* 49 (1958): 131–34 (132).
83. I discuss Harnack's view of the "we" passages below.
84. Harnack, *Luke the Physician*, 22–23.

native of Antioch, but even admirably accommodates itself thereto."[85]
This view from tradition bears no apologetic or theological concern,[86]
and its plausibility has continued to be argued by scholars who draw
on Harnack's argument.[87]

However, there is, perhaps, one weakness in Harnack's evaluation
of the internal evidence. Harnack explains that the book of Acts in a
number of places increases in the level of detail and assumes a greater
assuredness in its tone, and "every time that this happens (chap. xii.
excepted) he finds himself in Antioch or concerned with a narrative
which points his attention to that city."[88] One challenge to Harnack's
impression of Luke's assuredness regarding Antioch is implicitly made
in Colin J. Hemer's more than fifty-page catalogue of the instances of
specialized local knowledge in Acts 13–28. Of the numerous precise
details found throughout the latter half of Acts, Hemer's meticulous
analysis yields zero references to Antioch, and this is perhaps made
significant in that of the six main episodes in Acts that involve Antioch,
five of them occur in Acts 13–28 (cf. 11:19–20; 13:1–4; 14:26–28;
15:1–3, 13–40; 18:22–23).[89] It may be that Luke's concern with
Antioch derives directly from the importance of events that took place
in and around that city. The general caution should be kept in mind
here that in using internal evidence to support a claim, it is often easy
to find supportive details when one hopes to find them. But if Hemer's
work has revealed anything, it is that Luke displays much specialized
local knowledge throughout the whole of his narrative, not just about
Antioch. Nevertheless, there stands no good reason to doubt the external evidence that Luke was a native of Antioch.

Luke as Physician and Author

Harnack's arguments that Luke was a physician and the author of both
the Third Gospel and Acts are bound up together as the consistent linguistic features and style of both volumes point to the author's specialized
medical knowledge, which, in turn, lends credence to the view that the
author is indeed Luke, Paul's companion, who is identified as a physician

85. Harnack, *Luke the Physician*, 23.
86. Joseph A. Fitzmyer, *Luke the Theologian: Aspects of His Teaching* (New York: Paulist, 1989), 3.
87. See Strobel, "Lukas der Antiochener"; Richard Glover, "'Luke the Antiochene' and Acts," *NTS* 11
     (1964): 97–106.
88. Harnack, *Luke the Physician*, 21.
89. Colin J. Hemer, *The Book of Acts in the Setting of Hellenistic History*, ed. Conrad H. Gempf (repr.,
     Winona Lake, IN: Eisenbrauns, 1990), 108–58.

in Colossians 4:14. Harnack accepts the thesis of William Kirk Hobart that the specialized medical vocabulary pervasive throughout the Third Gospel and Acts supports two facts: that both books were written by the same man and the author was a Greek physician.[90] Hobart's thesis was accepted by some of Harnack's contemporaries, such as Theodor Zahn and John C. Hawkins, and was considered the definitive work of the time. The first serious challenge to Hobart did not come until some years later with the published doctoral dissertation of Henry J. Cadbury entitled *The Style and Literary Method of Luke*, where he refutes Hobart's argument, showing that the various "medical" words that Luke employs are not used exclusively by physicians but, to the contrary, are found among many writers who had no medical background.[91] While there are still many who see Luke's vocabulary as indicative of his vocation and education, this stance can no longer be taken for granted; one must address the compelling work of Cadbury.

Also relevant to the question of authorship is the prologue to the Third Gospel (Luke 1:1–4). Regarding the prologue, Harnack believes that of necessity it "must have contained in its title the name of its author."[92] If Luke was not the author, then the real author must have been purposely suppressed. However, Harnack deems this possibility unlikely because it would be strange for a work published either anonymously or pseudonymously to contain a dedication to a specific person. Moreover, if the author's name was for some reason suppressed, then it would have been likely that the name of a more prominent person than Luke would have been used.[93]

---

90. Harnack, *Luke the Physician*, 14. Cf. William Kirk Hobart, *Medical Language of St. Luke: A Proof from Internal Evidence That "The Gospel according to St. Luke" and "The Acts of the Apostles" Were Written by the Same Person and That Person Was a Medical Man*, Dublin University Press Series (Dublin: Hodges, Figgis, 1882).

91. See Henry J. Cadbury, *The Style and Literary Method of Luke*, HTS 6 (Cambridge, MA: Harvard University Press, 1920), 39–50. Cf. Zachary K. Dawson, "Henry J. Cadbury and the Composition of Luke–Acts," in *Pillars in the History of Biblical Interpretation, Volume 3: Further Essays on Prevailing Methods*, eds. Stanley E. Porter and Zachary K. Dawson, MBSS 6 (Eugene, OR: Pickwick, 2021), 173–200.

92. Harnack, *Luke the Physician*, 2.

93. Supporting this view is the opinion of B. H. Streeter, who states, "In the second century the bias was very strongly in the direction of attributing Apostolic authorship to documents accepted into the Canon. The burden, then, of proof lies with those who would assert the traditional authorship of Matthew and John, but on those who would deny it in the case of Mark and Luke" (*The Four Gospels: A Study in Origins—Treating of the Manuscript Tradition, Sources, Authorship and Dates* [London: Macmillan 1924], 530). Cf. Gasque, *History*, 147.

That the autograph would have contained Luke's name in its title is a view that has not always been well accepted, but it perhaps carries more weight than some have been willing to concede. While the titles of the earliest extant manuscripts of the Third Gospel and Acts may be secondary in form, this does not necessarily mean that the original documents were formally anonymous. As Simon Gathercole has recently shown, the alleged anonymity of the Gospels cannot be inferred from the lack of self-reference in the body of the texts, nor does the absence of the authors' names in the extant manuscripts exclude the possibility that authorship was attributed in a different way. In fact, the numerous references throughout second-century Christian literature that attest to the Gospel writers being Matthew, Mark, Luke, and John should be considered significant evidence that the Gospels (and Acts by extension) were not originally formally anonymous documents, but from the beginning were attributed to their authors.[94] Moreover, of all the Gospels, Gathercole states, "Luke is perhaps the least likely to be anonymous, given the first-person references (ἐν ἡμῖν, καθὼς παρέδοσαν ἡμῖν, ἔδοξεν κἀμοὶ παρηκολουθηκότι) and dedication (κράτιστε Θεόφιλε) in the preface to the Gospel (Luke 1:1–4) as well as in Acts 1:1 (ἐποιησάμην . . . ὦ Θεόφιλε) and the 'we-passages.'"[95] Thus, it seems that Harnack's view is receiving fresh support in recent scholarship on issues of authorship and the Gospels.

Luke as Author and Companion of Paul: Evaluating the "We" Passages

One of the main pillars of Harnack's argument for Lukan authorship of the Third Gospel and Acts is the character of the so-called "we" passages in Acts. Nearly one hundred pages of Harnack's *Luke the Physician* are devoted to the "we" passages[96] in which he argues that Luke was a companion of and fellow missionary with Paul. He supports this view by showing that the theological perspective and content of the "we" source, as well as its homogeneity in vocabulary, syntax, and style with the rest of Acts, point to the likelihood that the "we" source was written by the same person and "in close connection with the composition and writing of the whole work."[97] There are a

---

94. Simon Gathercole, "The Alleged Anonymity of the Canonical Gospels," *JTS* 69.2 (2018): 447–76.

95. Gathercole, "Alleged Anonymity," 475–76.

96. Harnack, *Luke the Physician*, 26–120.

97. Harnack, *Luke the Physician*, 53.

number of moving parts in this argument, and so it will be helpful to explain and assess multiple aspects of this argument one at a time.

First, it is helpful to clarify a number of matters, including what the "we" passages are, where they are located, and why they factor so significantly into Lukan critical issues. The "we" passages refer to the sections in Acts where the narrative shifts in grammatical person from third person to first-person plural. Aside from the traditional view (also Harnack's view) that understands Luke as now present in his own narrative, the text gives no explicit indication as to who is included in these first-person plural references—though Paul is often clearly excluded—nor is there any contextual means of recovering to whom the "we" refers. In each case the first-person plural appears suddenly and then disappears without a clear contextual reason as to why. Scholars have also long debated how many "we" passages Acts contains, ranging from three to five. There is general agreement, however, that the first of these passages begins in Acts 16:10 with the verb ἐζητήσαμεν ("we sought") and extends to 16:17. There is dispute over which span of text constitutes the second "we" passage. Some take the whole of Acts 20:5—21:28 as one passage,[98] while others see 20:5–15 and 21:1–18 as two separate passages. Harnack argues for the latter, which many others have followed. The next section, usually identified as the final "we" passage, begins in 27:1 and extends to 28:16. Harnack held to this view and so counted four "we" passages in total. However, Stanley E. Porter, for example, argues for splitting this section into two and omitting 27:30–44 from the "we" source.[99] The significance of identifying the number of "we" passages is that it affects the way the sections are interpreted when viewed in isolation, such as what characteristics they have when compared to the rest of Acts, and to what extent they exhibit the same or different perspective and linguistic features. The

---

98. For example, see F. S. Spenser, *The Portrait of Philip in Acts: A Study of Roles and Relations*, JSNTSup 67 (Sheffield: JSOT, 1992), 247.

99. The only problem with this solution, as I see it, is that there is a use of the first-person plural in 27:37, which Porter dismisses as incidental and trivial, much like the use of "we" in sea voyage narratives (Stanley E. Porter, *Paul in Acts* [repr., Peabody, MA: Hendrickson, 1999], 32). However, earlier in the same essay, Porter heavily critiques those who explain the "we" passages in relation to the way sea voyages were narrated in Hellenistic literature. Therefore, some may not be convinced by the line of argumentation that Acts 27:37 should not be viewed as part of the "we" section in 27:1–28:16 (see pp. 20–24). Apart from this, Porter makes a compelling case that the "we" passages were a previously written source used by the author of Acts, but probably not originating with him, and so "the 'we' passages can also be used as a reliable guide to establishing sources in Acts without necessarily speaking to their historical reliability or authorship" (11).

conclusions scholars reach on these questions inform larger questions about sources, authorship, and the work's historical reliability.[100] As for Harnack, he argues that the "we" passages possess the same theological perspective and characterization of Paul as the rest of Acts, and they do not differ in linguistic vocabulary, syntax, or style. Both of these points need further consideration.

In the first part of the second chapter in *Luke the Physician*, Harnack sketches the details of the four (by his count) "we" passages to show how they conform in theological perspective and content with the whole book. He makes the following conclusions:

> The "we" sections thus contain narratives of an exorcism, of the healing by laying on of hands of a man stricken with fever, of a miraculous deliverance from the effects of snake-bite. They include also a summary account of many cases of healing, they tell of one who was raised from the dead, of prophecies delivered by brethren in Tyre, of a prophecy of the prophet Agabus, of the prophesying daughters of Philip, of several prophecies of St. Paul himself, of the appearance of an angel to St. Paul in the ship, and of a vision of Troas. Could one wish for more miracles within the compass of so few verses? *The author shows himself just as fond of the miraculous—and in particular just as deeply interested in miracles of healing, in manifestations of the "Spirit," and in appearances of angels—as the author of the third gospel and the Acts.* So far as regards the subject matter of the narrative, the relationship could scarcely be closer than it is.[101]

Harnack indeed demonstrates a number of ways in which the "we" passages share in content and perspective with the rest of Acts. However, despite his claim that "no difference worthy of mention can be discovered,"[102] several important distinguishing features of the "we" passages have since been brought to light. Porter identifies several that I will now discuss.[103] First, in the "we" passages, the perspective of the author shifts in how he portrays divine guidance—that is, in both the way divine guidance is given and received it is more understated. For

---

100. See Jacques Dupont, *The Sources of Acts: The Present Position*, trans. Kathleen Pond (London: Darton, Longman & Todd, 1964), 76–165; Hemer, *Book of Acts*, 311–34.

101. Harnack, *Luke the Physician*, 33, italics original.

102. Harnack, *Luke the Physician*, 33.

103. For the full discussion, see Porter, *Paul in Acts*, 51–62.

example, regarding the vision at Troas (16:9), which Harnack cites as evidence of the author's fondness for miracles, the presentation should not be lost on the reader that the narrative does not depict the vision but rather focuses on the response to the vision.[104] Moreover, Porter notes that "in none of the purported visions or divine communications in the 'we' passages is God (or Christ) quoted directly; either an angel is said to have spoken or God's words are quoted secondhand," and this contrasts with, "for example, 18:9–10, where God is directly quoted when he speaks to Paul."[105]

Second, the author of the "we" passages reflects a strikingly Hellenistic perspective, tending to minimize any distinctive importance of the Jews or Judaism.[106] One example, among others, is that the "we" source virtually only includes non-Jewish cities, and this even includes when Paul is in Palestine. For example, in the third "we" passage (21:1–18), the narrative depicts Paul and his companions spending the majority of their time in Caesarea, "a center of Hellenistic and Roman culture in Palestine."[107] And even though traveling to Jerusalem is the goal of the journey, events in Jerusalem do not factor into the "we" source; after arriving in the city and immediately going up to see James and the elders (21:17–18), the first-person plural ceases and Jewish concerns are at once reintroduced into the text (cf. 21:20).[108] While Harnack supports the view that Luke was a Greek and reveals elements of his Hellenistic background through his language and knowledge of events and places, he does not recognize any such shift in perspective in the "we" passages where a concern for Jews and Judaism is almost entirely absent.

Third, the "we" perspective presents Paul's competence in an understated manner and does not emphasize his missionary efforts as an orator.[109] In fact, Paul's speaking in the "we" passages is limited to a meager nine verses (20:10; 21:13; 27:10, 21–26).[110] Moreover, none of

---

104. Porter, *Paul in Acts*, 51.
105. Porter, *Paul in Acts*, 51.
106. Porter, *Paul in Acts*, 55–58.
107. Porter, *Paul in Acts*, 57.
108. Porter, *Paul in Acts*, 57.
109. Porter, *Paul in Acts*, 58–60.
110. This count is contingent upon where one believes the "we" passages begin and end. Harnack in his *Acts of the Apostles*, published only two years after *Luke the Physician*, suggests at one place that "the two passages [Acts] xx. 23 and 28 belong to a speech of St. Paul which in all probability must be assigned to the we-sections—seeing that it stands in their midst and that St. Luke was present on the occasion" (141). Thus, Paul would retain his more vocal characterization as a speechmaker, but

Paul's missionary speeches nor his apologetic speeches fall within the confines of a "we" passage, and the fact that a couple of the speeches are located in close proximity to the "we" passages[111] only serves to draw a starker contrast with the muted Paul of the "we" source and the great orator of other parts of the book.[112] No such observations are entertained in Harnack's work.

Fourth, Paul is not portrayed as a miracle worker in the "we" passages, or at least not in the same way as he is elsewhere in the book.[113] This point is perhaps the strongest rebuttal to Harnack's conclusions because he uses Paul's involvement in supernatural events as evidence that the "we" passages reflect the same perspective as the rest of Acts. Harnack accounts for four miraculous events in the "we" passages: (1) the exorcism of a female ventriloquist, (2) the resurrection of Eutychus, (3) the snake bite that left no mark, and (4) the healing of Publius's father.[114] Somewhat puzzling is that Harnack includes the exorcism in his list of events of the first "we" passage, the end of which he marks as 16:17. This is puzzling because Paul's exorcism does not occur until 16:18. Thus, according to the textual boundaries Harnack draws, the exorcism itself does not belong to the "we" source, and so it should not be used to support the "we" source's affinity for miracles. The miracles in the "we" passages thus shrink to three. The second miracle Harnack identifies is the resurrection of Eutychus after he had fallen asleep and fallen out of the window to the ground (20:9). Following this the Greek then reads: καὶ ἤρθη νεκρός ("and he was taken up dead"). Harnack takes this statement at face value and thus interprets Paul's words, "Do not be troubled, for his life is in him"[115] (20:10) as indicative of Paul's act of raising him from the dead.[116] However, as Porter rightly points out, verses 10–12, when taken together, make it difficult to conclude that Paul thought that Eutychus was dead; that he says his life is in him could be interpreted

---

Harnack's argument rests on nothing else than logical inference. There is no textual backing to his claim as the first-person plural clearly discontinues after 20:15 and does not resume again until 22:1.

111. Paul's address to the Ephesian elders (20:18–36) follows on the heals but is clearly separated from the second "we" passage (20:5–15). Also, Paul's address to the Jews in Rome (28:17–20) begins soon after the final "we" passage.
112. Porter, *Paul in Acts*, 58–59.
113. Porter, *Paul in Acts*, 60.
114. Harnack, *Luke the Physician*, 28–29, 32.
115. In Greek: μὴ θορυβεῖσθε, ἡ γὰρ ψυχὴ αὐτοῦ ἐν αὐτῷ ἐστιν (NA28).
116. In Harnack's own words, Eutychus "is called back to life by St. Paul" (*Luke the Physician*, 29).

as Paul's realization that, upon embracing him, Eutychus was still alive.[117] Even if Paul raised Eutychus from the dead, the ambiguity in the episode only further substantiates the view that miraculous events are understated in the "we" passages. In the third miracle, when Paul encounters the viper, he is entirely a passive agent, and "the rhetorical possibilities of the miracle are not exploited to their fullest extent, but kept understated and matter-of-factly opposed to superstition."[118] The fourth miracle, the healing of Publius's father from fever and dysentery is the most detailed miracle in the "we" passages. Paul lays his hands on Publius's father and prays and he is healed. However, not much can be made of one enthusiastic healing on the part of Paul, especially when "the results are hardly impressive, being conveyed in summary fashion."[119] This critique, however, should be considered in light of Harnack's own observations that when the "we" sections are omitted there are only ten instances of miraculous events in the second half of Acts, "and even these suffer serious reduction when we consider that the earthquake in Philippi was a natural occurrence treated as a special instance of Providential interference and used in the narrative."[120] Thus, if Porter's critique is to stand, it must be considered in light of the fact that the second half of Acts does not relate miracles to the extent that the first half does.

Each of the points mentioned above supports the view that Harnack underanalyzes the perspective expressed in the "we" passages. However, this is only one part of his study in which he attempts to argue that the "we" source originated with Luke; it is necessary also to consider his linguistic argument. Aside from the use of first-person plural, Harnack believes the "we" passages conform to the same style as the rest of Acts. To conclude his lengthy linguistic analysis of the first "we" passage, Harnack writes,

> After this demonstration those who declare that this passage (xvi. 10–17) was derived from a source, and so was not composed by the author of the whole work, take up a most difficult position. What may we suppose the author to have left unaltered in the source? Only the "we"? For, in fact, nothing else remains! In regard to vocabulary,

---

117. Porter, *Paul in Acts*, 61.
118. Porter, *Paul in Acts*, 61–62.
119. Porter, *Paul in Acts*, 62.
120. Harnack, *Acts of the Apostles*, 141.

syntax, and style he must have transformed everything else into his own language! As such a procedure is absolutely unimaginable, we are simply left to infer that the author is here himself speaking.[121]

Here we see the confident judgment of Harnack as a seasoned source critic. Still today, most scholars would concur that Harnack is correct that the linguistic features of the "we" source resemble much of the rest of Acts, though not all agree that the "we" source can be definitely proven to have originated with Luke. To assess Harnack's argument here, a brief sketch of his source-critical work on the rest of Acts and the Gospels will be helpful.

Based on the quantified analyses of Gospel source criticism, it is well accepted that the author of the Third Gospel redacted his sources, which he openly admits to using in the preface to the Third Gospel. There is no reason to doubt that Acts, too, is informed by a number of sources, though Harnack believes that Luke relied more heavily on oral tradition to write the first half of Acts and primarily on written sources for the second half.[122] Because continuity in style is integral to Harnack's view of the "we" passages, a source-critical question arises here as to how Luke would have handled different kinds of sources. Was Luke more likely to impose his own vernacular when using oral tradition than he was when working with a written source? If so, then this would seem to require the two halves of Acts to be treated differently in matters of source criticism. Moreover, this question becomes complexified due to the way Harnack characterizes Luke's handling of written sources. In the second volume of his *New Testament Studies* series, *The Sayings of Jesus*, Harnack conducts an analysis of Matthew and Luke's common usages of non-Markan material and concludes Luke "has thoroughly revised the text of the ["Q"] source."[123] Thus, according to Harnack's findings, wherever Luke makes use of a source, he transforms it into his own style.[124] Elsewhere, he makes the similar statement that "St. Luke is an artist in style, and always modifies his style in accordance with the content of his narrative and the geographical scene of action; from this established fact it follows that differences

121. Harnack, *Luke the Physician*, 52–53.
122. Harnack, *Acts of the Apostles*, 162–202.
123. Harnack, *Sayings of Jesus*, 115.
124. Harnack, *Luke the Physician*, 84.

of style do not necessarily imply different sources."[125] How then can continuity in style act as a criterion for identifying where Luke used a source? Whereas the Gospel of Matthew exists to demonstrate that Luke is not the originator of the "Q" source, there is no other comparable document for Acts by which to eliminate the possibility that Luke is the original author of the "we" passages. So then, by what criterion can Harnack determine that the "we" source contains the original words of Luke?

Despite the complexities, Harnack believes the problem can still be solved on linguistic grounds. In his judgment, the book of Acts, as well as parts of Luke's Gospel (e.g., Luke 1–2), are so thoroughly Lukan in style that no written source could have been used. As a result, Harnack argues that Luke is dependent on oral tradition for these sections.[126] In other words, Luke reproduces oral tradition in his own literary style to a greater extent than he achieves with his written sources. Taking Luke's use of the "Q" source for example, Harnack states, "Although the stylistic corrections of St. Luke are so numerous, we cannot say that he has completely obliterated the characteristics of his exemplar. Indeed, in spite of all, we cannot but recognise that his work of revision is ever carried out in a conservative spirit, and that his readers receive from him a just impression of our Lord's style of discourse." [127] The "we" passages, then, being a written source, must be from the author's own hand because the same "style and vocabulary of the writer is everywhere so unmistakably recognizable, even in the minutest details, this excludes the possibility that Luke has used a Greek source for the 'we' sections."[128]

According to Harnack's own description, when Luke uses a written source, he does not completely overwrite its style. Thus, it follows that if the linguistic features in the "we" source can be shown to contrast with Luke's style, then this can be used as evidence against Harnack.

---

125. Harnack, *Acts of the Apostles*, 163.
126. Harnack (*Acts of the Apostles*, 188) attributes Acts 2 and 5:17–42 to an oral source he calls "Jerusalem B." He finds it worthless because it combines things that have no real connection to each other, and where it is trustworthy, it often confuses the order of events (194). Another partly oral source, "Jerusalem A" or the Jerusalem-Caesarean or Petro-Philippine source, is used in 3:1—5:16; 8:5–40; 9:31—11:18; and 12:1–23. Harnack believes this source to be trustworthy and to have originated with Philip, or from him and his daughters (192). The "Jerusalem-Antiochean" source is used in 6:1—8:4; 11:19–30; 12:25—15:35, and, according to Harnack, is a written source of high historical value (195). For a summary of these sources, see Harnack, *Acts of the Apostles*, 188–89.
127. Harnack, *Sayings of Jesus*, 115.
128. Harnack, *Luke the Physician*, 103.

Here the issue of the *hapax legomena* in the "we" passages becomes most salient. In his analysis, Harnack notes that there are "111 words that are not found elsewhere in the Acts, and St. Luke's gospel. This proportion is much greater than in the remaining parts of the work."[129] There are, in fact, "two and a half times as many as we should expect."[130] Harnack tries to explain away the disproportionate instances of *hapax legomena* by pointing to the peculiar contexts and subject matter the "we" passages relate, such as sea voyages and the shipwreck in Acts 27, which itself makes up about half of the content of the "we" passages.[131] Thus, in Harnack's estimation, once these factors are taken into account, the *hapax legomena* do not exceed their usual expected frequency. This conclusion has come under criticism by several scholars, and not least by Gerd Lüdemann who questions whether the use of vocabulary statistics is a sufficient criterion for determining whether the "we" passages were composed by the author of Acts.[132] In any case, Harnack's method of calculating lexical and syntactical features to determine source and author is woefully underdeveloped; linguistic conclusions such as these need to be based on corpus data far larger than the New Testament offers, let alone the Third Gospel and Acts.[133] We know that Luke edited his sources, and Harnack appears to be inconsistent with himself when he admits that apart from initial καί, Luke, in the writing of his Gospel, is able to completely recast the Gospel of Mark in his own style: "Otherwise the narrative is in detail (in style) so much altered and polished that the special character of the source is not immediately discernible."[134] If Luke did this with his use of Mark, then why could he have not also have thoroughly revised the "we" source? Since Harnack's method of determining authorship based on lexis and syntax has been shown to be lacking in enough data, one should be cautious in appealing to his work to support Luke's presence in the "we" passages as an eyewitness and companion of Paul.

---

129. Harnack, *Luke the Physician*, 85.

130. Harnack, *Luke the Physician*, 85.

131. Harnack, *Luke the Physician*, 85.

132. Gerd Lüdemann, *Early Christianity according to the Traditions in Acts: A Commentary*, trans. John Bowden (Minneapolis: Fortress, 1987), 9. Cf. Porter, *Paul in Acts*, 34–36.

133. See Porter, *Paul in Acts*, 35; Matthew Brook O'Donnell, "Linguistic Fingerprints or Style by Numbers? An Evaluation of the Use of Statistics for New Testament Authorship," in *Linguistics and the New Testament: Critical Junctures*, eds. Stanley E. Porter and D. A. Carson, JSNTSup 168, SNTG 5 (Sheffield: Sheffield Academic, 1999), 206–63.

134. Harnack, *Luke the Physician*, 93.

THE DATE OF ACTS

Another significant critical issue Harnack advanced was the dating of Acts, as well as the Synoptic Gospels. His final argument on dates for these documents is made in the fourth volume of his *New Testament Studies* series, *The Date of the Acts and the Synoptic Gospels*.[135] However, his views on the dates of these books changed even during the couple of years between the publications of *Luke the Physician* and *Acts of the Apostles*, and the reasons for this change of mind are worth recounting. When Harnack published *Luke the Physician*, he was committed to the view that the composition of the book of Acts was limited to 78–93 CE: "The book must have been written before the persecution of Domitian, before the epistles of St. Paul had been widely circulated, before the name 'Christians' had firmly established itself in Christian phraseology, before the canonising of the idea of ἐκκλησία, before the use of the word μαρτύς in the special sense of 'martyr,' but some time after the destruction of Jerusalem."[136] In his *Chronologie der altchristlichen Literatur bis Eusebius*, published a few years prior in 1897, Harnack gave three additional reasons for a late first-century date for Luke's writings: (1) the prologue of Luke's Gospel seems to require that at least half a century had passed since Jesus's death; (2) the detailed prophecies about the destruction of Jerusalem in Luke's Gospel seem to indicate a post-70 CE date; and (3) the legends regarding the Resurrection and Ascension are difficult to explain, unless they postdate the destruction of Jerusalem.[137]

Upon further reflection, however, Harnack became convinced that the book of Acts was composed much earlier, around the year 62 CE. He provides six reasons for this date. First, the problem with the conclusion of Acts (or lack thereof) is mitigated in the simplest way if Luke wrote shortly after Paul's Roman imprisonment and while he was still living. Second, an earlier date clears up the discrepancy in Acts 20:25, where Paul prophesies, "I know that all of you will see my face no more, among whom I have preached the kingdom," with the information in 2 Timothy; Luke permits Paul to say something about the future that is

---

135. The whole first section of this work recapitulates Harnack's defense of Lukan authorship for Acts; see Harnack, *Date of Acts*, 1–89.

136. Harnack, *Luke the Physician*, 24.

137. Adolf Harnack, *Die Chronologie der altchristlichen Literatur bis Eusebius*, 2 vols. (Leipzig: J. C. Hinrichs, 1897–1904), 1:246–50, 718.

later proved wrong. Third, the Jews are never the group who are persecuted in the book of Acts, but rather are always the ones who persecute. To Harnack, it now seems most probable that Acts was written prior to 70 CE, and even 66 CE, since Luke makes no indication of the disaster that befell the Jews in both Jerusalem and the Diaspora. Fourth, in the same way as Mark and Matthew, Luke combines the final catastrophe (21:25ff.) with the coming of the Son of Man (21:27–28) and concludes these events with Jesus saying, "Truly, I say to you, this generation will not pass away until all things take place" (21:32). Harnack cannot allow for the explanation that these events were so arranged if the destruction of Jerusalem had already occurred. It would seem that a corollary of this argument is that Matthew, too, should be dated before the destruction of Jerusalem, though Harnack is unsure on this and believes the book was composed in close proximity to the destruction of Jerusalem.[138] Fifth, moving the date to the early 60s better explains why Luke was unfamiliar with Paul's epistles.[139] Sixth, Luke's use of the word "Christ" is even more primitive than the Pauline usage; it has not assumed the status of a title, but always means, "the Messiah."[140] Harnack finds these six arguments the most important in locating the date of Acts, and his observations, especially that Acts nowhere presupposes the Jewish revolt, have continued to be cited by scholars who support an early date for Acts.[141]

Harnack's dating of Acts also bears implications for when the Synoptic Gospels must have taken shape, and these he explains at the end of his book *The Date of Acts*. He assigns a date to an early version of Mark's Gospel to the early 50s, and this was the version Luke used when composing his own Gospel.[142] Mark later revised his Gospel, which was

138. Harnack, *Date of Acts*, 134.
139. Though not in direct support, this observation is consistent with Harnack's hypothesis that Paul's letters were not immediately copied and circulated together but were gradually gathered together as their enduring value was realized. See Adolf Harnack, *Die Briefsammlung des Apostels Paulus und die anderen vorkonstantinischen christlichen Briefsammlungen* (Leipzig: J. C. Hinrichs, 1926), 6–27. See also Theodor Zahn, *Geschichte des Neutestamentlichen Kanons*, 2 vols. (Erlangen: Deichert, 1888–1892), 1:811–39; Zahn, *Grundriss der Geschichte des Neutestamentlichen Kanons: Eine Ergänzung zu der Einleitung in das Neue Testament* (Leipzig: Deichert, 1904), 35–37. Cf. Stanley E. Porter, *The Apostle Paul: His Life, Thought, and Letters* (Grand Rapids: Eerdmans, 2016), 170–71, for a summary of the "gradual collection" theory.
140. Harnack, *Acts of the Apostles*, 293–96; Harnack, *Date of Acts*, 90–113.
141. For a full list of those who build on Harnack's deductions on the dating of Acts, see Karl L. Armstrong, "A New Plea for an Early Date of Acts," *JGRChJ* 13 (2017): 79–110 (98–101).
142. Harnack, *Date of Acts*, 126–33.

then used by Matthew, who composed his Gospel around 70 CE.[143] The book concludes on a confident note: "Our conclusion [is] that we have found nothing to upset the verdict, to which we have been led by critical investigation of the Acts of the Apostles, that the second and third gospels, as well as the Acts, were composed while St Paul was still alive, and that the first gospel came into being only a few years later."[144]

CONCLUSION

So much more could be written on Harnack's life and scholarship. Neill and Wright state venerably, "For nearly forty years he bestrode [the world of theological scholarship] like a colossus."[145] And Baird likewise wittily comments that "to accomplish all he did, he must have been an academic Briareus—the mythological giant with a hundred arms and fifty heads."[146] He wrote prolifically, taught numerous students who would go on to be the next generation's leaders in biblical and theological studies, and was involved in many political affairs and church organizations, despite being labelled a heretic by the orthodox Lutheran church in Germany. I have attempted to give a broad survey of his works in the various areas to which he contributed, including his theological, historical, and biblical publications, with a focused treatment of his major works in Lukan scholarship. Harnack addressed many of the critical issues still debated among Lukan scholars. It is significant that his liberal mindset led him to many of the conclusions of today's conservative scholars. His positions, however, are not above criticism, and I have demonstrated a number of the strengths and weaknesses that characterize his work. In any case, Harnack will continue to be relevant for Lukan scholarship, not simply as one of the foremost scholars in the history of New Testament research, but as a figure whose arguments still hold weight for a number of issues.

---

143. Harnack, *Date of Acts*, 133–35.
144. Harnack, *Date of Acts*, 162.
145. Neill and Wright, *Interpretation of the New Testament*, 140.
146. Baird, *History of New Testament Research*, 2:123.

MARTIN DIBELIUS ON THE GOSPEL OF LUKE AND THE ACTS OF THE APOSTLES

The Most Literary Writings in the New Testament

James D. Dvorak

Although perhaps not as prolific as a number of his contemporaries (e.g., Rudolf Bultmann), Martin Dibelius (1883–1947) was certainly not overshadowed by any one of them in terms of the significance of his contributions to the discipline of biblical studies. Actually, over the course of his relatively short academic career, Dibelius published a number of important works.[1] Between 1911 and 1913, he contributed three commentaries to the series founded and edited by Hans Lietzmann, Handbuch zum Neuen Testament (HNT). These included commentaries on 1–2 Thessalonians and Philippians (*An die Thessalonicher I, II, An die Philipper*, 1911);[2] Colossians, Ephesians, and Philemon (*An die Kolosser, Epheser, An Philemon*, 1912);[3] and

---

1. See D. B. Peabody, "Dibelius, Martin Franz," in *Dictionary of Major Biblical Interpreters*, ed. Donald K. McKim (Downers Grove, IL: InterVarsity, 2007), 368.
2. Martin Dibelius, *An die Thessalonicher I, II, An die Philipper*, 2nd ed., HNT 11 (Tübingen: Mohr Siebeck, 1925).
3. Martin Dibelius, *An Kolosser, Epheser, An Philemon*, HNT 12 (Tübingen: Mohr Siebeck, 1912).

1–2 Timothy and Titus (*Die Pastoralbriefe*, 1913).[4] In 1921, the well-respected series Meyer's Kritisch-Exegetischer Kommentar (KEK) published Dibelius's commentary on the Epistle of James (*Der Brief des Jakobus*, 1921).[5] This commentary, which many consider to be Dibelius's best, continues to demand the engagement of Jacobean scholars even though nearly a century has passed since it was first published in German.[6] In addition to these critical and scholarly commentaries, Dibelius also published a number of monographs that were aimed at a broader yet still educated audience; a sampling of these works includes *Jesus* (1939),[7] *The Sermon on the Mount* (1940),[8] and *Paul* (completed and edited by W. G. Kümmel and published posthumously in 1951).[9]

These important contributions notwithstanding, Dibelius continues to be most well-known for developing the interpretive methodology that he called *Formgeschichte* (known in English as "Form Criticism")[10] and for its use in the analysis of the Synoptic Gospels. *Formgeschichte* methodology was intended to provide an analytical model by which the original (or at least the oldest) form, style, and meaning of the Christian tradition could be recovered, but without the accretions that had become attached to it over time (more on this below).[11] An early form of the methodology was laid out by Dibelius in 1919 in a volume bearing

---

4.   Martin Dibelius, *Die Pastoralbriefe*, 2nd ed., HNT 13 (Tübingen: Mohr Siebeck, 1931); ET Dibelius and Hans Conzelmann, *The Pastoral Epistles*, Hermeneia (Philadelphia: Fortress, 1972).

5.   Martin Dibelius, *Der Brief des Jakobus*, KEK 15 (Göttingen: Vandenhoeck & Ruprecht, 1921). The eleventh edition was revised by Heinrich Greeven and published in English in the Hermeneia series: *James: A Commentary on the Epistle of James*, Hermeneia (Philadelphia: Fortress, 1976).

6.   See, e.g., Stanley E. Porter, "Cohesion in James: A Response to Martin Dibelius," in *The Epistle of James: Linguistic Exegesis of an Early Christian Letter*, eds. James D. Dvorak and Zachary K. Dawson, Linguistic Exegesis of the New Testament 1 (Eugene, OR: Pickwick, 2019), 45–68.

7.   Martin Dibelius, *Jesus*, trans. Charles B. Hedrick and Frederick C. Grant (Philadelphia: Westminster, 1949).

8.   Martin Dibelius, *The Sermon on the Mount* (New York: Scribners, 1940).

9.   Martin Dibelius, *Paulus*, ed. Werner Georg Kümmel, Sammlung Göschen 1160 (Berlin: Walter de Gruyter, 1951); ET Dibelius, *Paul*, ed. Werner Georg Kümmel, trans. Frank Clarke (London: Longmans, Green, 1953).

10. A better English rendering would be "history of literary forms." G. T. Sheppard ("Biblical Interpretation in Europe in the 20th Century," in *Historical Handbook of Major Biblical Interpreters*, ed. Donald M. McKim [Downers Grove, IL: InterVarsity, 1998], 415) says that the term *Formgeschichte* was used by Dibelius to identify Gunkel's methodology; however, Dibelius himself intimates that his choosing of this word was based at least in part on Eduard Norden's use of it in the subtitle of his book *Agnostos Theos*, viz., *Untersuchungen zur Formengeschichte religiöser Rede* (see Martin Dibelius, *From Tradition to Gospel*, trans. Benjamin Lee Woolf [New York: Scribners, 1935], 4).

11. Dibelius, *From Tradition to Gospel*, 1–36; Dibelius, *The Message of Jesus Christ*, trans. Frederick C. Grant, The International Library of Christian Knowledge (New York: Scribners, 1939), xvii.

the title *Die Formgeschichte des Evangeliums*.[12] A more fully developed version of the method was described in a second, enlarged edition of this work, which was published in 1933.[13] Two years later an English translation of the second German edition was released bearing the title *From Tradition to Gospel*.[14] Shortly thereafter in 1935, Dibelius published *Die Botschaft von Jesus Christus*, which was translated into English and published in 1939 as *The Message of Jesus Christ*.[15] This volume contains the first complete record of the results of *Formgeschichte* analysis of the Synoptic Gospels. In Part I of this book, Dibelius provides the texts of the earliest tradition after having utilized meticulously his methodology to remove any of the Evangelists' scaffolding; each of these is categorized according to its form, from oldest to youngest (i.e., old stories [= paradigms], parables and sayings of Jesus [= exhortations], tales, and legends).[16] Part II of the book offers up an explanation as to why the texts were categorized in the way that they were. At heart, part II is a concise restatement of the *Formgeschichte* methodology.

The purpose of the present essay is to investigate Dibelius's analyses of both the Gospel of Luke and the Acts of the Apostles. Interestingly, Dibelius never wrote a commentary or any sort of full-scale monograph on either Luke's Gospel or the book of Acts. Despite this fact, Dibelius had much to say about both. Most of what he offered in regard to the Gospel of Luke is wrapped into the development and application of *Formgeschichte* and a few other sources; thus, these comments must be excavated from those quarries. In regards to Acts, between 1923 and 1947, Dibelius did write a number of seminal essays that, as Gasque puts it, "have served as the basic catalyst of scholarly debate concerning the book of Acts from 1950 to the present."[17] These essays were

---

12.   Martin Dibelius, *Die Formgeschichte des Evangeliums* (Tübingen: Mohr Siebeck, 1919).

13.   Martin Dibelius, *Die Formgeschichte des Evangeliums,* 2nd ed. (Tübingen: Mohr Siebeck, 1933) (cited below in this essay).

14.   Dibelius, *From Tradition to Gospel*. W. G. Kümmel says the English title is a paraphrase of "the form history of the Gospel," a more wooden gloss of the German title (*The New Testament: The History of the Investigation of Its Problems*, trans. S. McLean Gilmour and H. C. Kee [Nashville: Abingdon, 1972], 330).

15.   Martin Dibelius, *Die Botschaft von Jesus Christus: Die alte Überlieferung der Gemeinde in Geschichten, Sprüchen, und Reden* (Tübingen: Mohr Siebeck, 1935); Dibelius, *Message of Jesus Christ*.

16.   For descriptions of each of these, see Dibelius, *From Tradition to Gospel*, 37–132; James D. Dvorak, "Martin Dibelius and Rudolf Bultmann," in *Pillars in the History of Biblical Interpretation, Volume 1: Prevailing Methods before 1980*, eds. Stanley E. Porter and Sean A. Adams, MBSS 2 (Eugene, OR: Pickwick, 2016), 263–67.

17.   W. Ward Gasque, *A History of the Interpretation of the Acts of the Apostles* (repr., Eugene, OR: Wipf & Stock, 2000 [1975]), 202.

first collected and published in 1951 in German as *Aufsätze zur Apostelgeschichte*, and they were subsequently published in English in 1956 with the title *Studies in the Acts of the Apostles*.[18] These will serve as the primary sources containing Dibelius's thoughts on Acts.[19]

Principled interpretation, whether of biblical texts or the writings of a biblical scholar, requires the interpreter to understand the context in which the work(s) under investigation were produced. Thus, this essay will proceed with a brief sketch of Dibelius's biography, with emphasis on his academic advancement. This is followed by a capsulized description of the development of scholarly thought leading up to Dibelius. This is intended not only to aid the reader in placing Dibelius in the history of interpretation, but also to gain a sense of the analytical and interpretive paradigm within which he operated. On the heels of this is a basic description of Dibelius's model and methodology, which will provide the scaffolding necessary for getting a handle on his analytical efforts in relation to the Gospel of Luke and the Acts of the Apostles.

BIOGRAPHY

Martin Franz Dibelius was born in Dresden, Germany, on September 14, 1883 to parents Franz Wilhelm and Martha (Hoffman) Dibelius.[20] His father Franz, a conservative Lutheran pastor who had himself studied at Berlin and had successfully published a number of works,[21] appears to have been a positive influence on his son in regards to the value of education.[22] Upon reaching university age, Martin spent a semester studying theology at Neuchâtel, Switzerland, after which he returned to

---

18.   Martin Dibelius, *Aufsätze zur Apostelgeschichte*, ed. Heinrich Greeven, FRLANT 42 (Göttingen: Vandenhoeck & Ruprecht, 1951); ET Dibelius, *Studies in the Acts of the Apostles*, ed. Heinrich Greeven, trans. Mary Ling and Paul Schubert (London: SCM, 1956).

19.   In 2004, these essays were published a second time in English in a book edited by K. C. Hanson: *The Book of Acts: Form, Style, and Theology*, Fortress Classics in Biblical Studies (Minneapolis: Fortress, 2004). One difference between this edition and Greeven's edition is that instead of ordering the essays chronologically, Hanson arranged them thematically in three parts. Part one contains essays that are concerned with style and content; part two contains essays that are concerned with literary turning points in Acts, particularly as they relate to Peter and Paul; and part three contains the single essay that deals with the difference between the text of Acts, the synoptics, and the Paulines.

20.   Matthias Wolfes, "Schuld und Verantwortung: Die Auseinandersetzung des Heidelberger Theologen Martin Dibelius mit dem Dritten Reich. Mit einer aus dem Nachlass heraugegebenen 'Lebensbeschreibung' aus dem Jahre 1946," *ZKG* 111 (2000): 186. According to Peabody ("Dibelius," 366), Martha died when Martin was around four years old; his father remarried Elsbeth Köhler.

21.   See Peabody, "Dibelius," 366.

22.   Peabody, "Dibelius," 366.

Germany to continue his studies first at Leipzig, then at Tübingen, and finally at Berlin.[23] He earned his *Dr phil promoviert* (= PhD) in 1905 at Tübingen; his dissertation, an investigation stimulated by Hermann Gunkel's methodology, was published in 1906 with the title *Die Lade Jahves: Eine religionsgeschichtliche Untersuchung* (*The Ark of Yahweh: A History of Religion Investigation*).[24] In 1908, under the guidance of Otto Pfleiderer, Dibelius completed his Lic. theol., producing a thesis that was published in 1909 as *Die Geisterwelt im Glauben des Paulus* (*The Spirit World in the Faith of Paul*).[25] For his habilitation, Dibelius wrote a thesis in which he investigated the early Christian tradition regarding John the Baptist, but according to Wolfes the evaluating faculty were not pleased with it, which resulted in Dibelius withdrawing it.[26] However, Adolf Deissmann came to Dibelius's aid, arguing that he be granted habilitation on the basis of the licentiate work that he had completed in 1908.[27] Apparently the faculty agreed, for Dibelius was granted the habilitation degree (required for teaching) in 1910 and joined the theological faculty at Friedrich Wilhelms University in Berlin.[28] In the summer of 1915, Dibelius accepted a position as Professor of New Testament Exegesis and Criticism at the University of Heidelberg as the successor to Johannes Weiss, a position that he held until 1947.[29] Dibelius died of tuberculosis on November 11, 1947.[30] He was married to Dorothea (Wittich); they had four children.[31]

PARADIGM AND PERSPECTIVE

Early twentieth-century interpretation displayed a number of traits that had been passed down through its epistemological ancestry, and many of these characteristics are manifest in Dibelius's methodology.

---

23. Wolfes, "Schuld und Verantwortung," 187.
24. Martin Dibelius, *Die Lade Jahves: Eine religionsgeschichtliche Untersuchung* (Göttingen: E. A. Huth, 1906). See Wolfes, "Schuld und Verantwortung," 187.
25. Martin Dibelius, *Die Geisterwelt im Glauben des Paulus* (Göttingen: Vandenhoeck & Ruprecht, 1909). Wolfes, "Schuld und Verantwortung," 187.
26. Wolfes, "Schuld und Verantwortung," 187. Dibelius later published the rejected thesis as *Die urchristliche Überlieferung von Johannes dem Täufer*, FRLANT 15 (Göttingen: Vandenhoeck & Ruprecht, 1911).
27. Wolfes, "Schuld und Verantwortung," 187.
28. Wolfes, "Schuld und Verantwortung," 187.
29. Wolfes, "Schuld und Verantwortung," 187.
30. Wolfes, "Schuld und Verantwortung," 188; Peabody, "Dibelius," 367.
31. Wolfes, "Schuld und Verantwortung," 206 (under the heading "*Lebensbeschreibung von Prof. Dr. Martin Dibelius*").

Thus, before diving into the specifics of Dibelius's work on Luke and Acts, it will be beneficial first to consider the critical-hermeneutical paradigm into which Dibelius was enculturated and how that paradigm informed his style of theorizing and shaped his analytical model and methodology.

The points of view and practices that eventually matured into modern critical biblical interpretation are often traced to late seventeenth-century Western Europe. Due in large part to divisions in the church in that time frame, the religious culture that had theretofore centered upon an unquestioned acceptance of a Judeo-Christian understanding of God and attendant beliefs about the Bible and the church were fracturing under the weight of rationalism.[32] As rationalism became more firmly entrenched and human reason was elevated to the standard by which everything was to be tested and measured[33]— the hallmark notion of the so-called Enlightenment era[34]—the paradigm of biblical analysis and interpretation increasingly shifted away from an acceptance of the established traditions of the church to only those things that could be established by critical, historical investigations of the Bible and its world.[35] It became characteristic that "intellectuals were no longer willing to accept statements in the Bible as true merely because they were in the Bible."[36]

Two key figures played significant roles in this shift, namely J. S. Semler (1725–1791) and W. M. L. de Wette (1780–1849): Semler,

---

32. Robert Morgan and John Barton, *Biblical Interpretation*, The Oxford Bible Series (Oxford: Oxford University Press, 1988), 17.

33. This sentiment is often illustrated with a quotation of John Locke, who penned the following words toward the end of the seventeenth century: "Religious enthusiasm takes away both reason and revelation and substitutes in place of them the ungrounded fancies of a man's own brain, and assumes them for a foundation both of opinion and conduct. . . . Reason must be our last judge and guide in everything" (*An Essay Concerning Human Understanding* [Raleigh, NC: Generic NL Freebook Publisher, http://proxy.oc.edu:2184/login.aspx?direct=true&db=nlebk&AN=1085946 &site=ehost-live], IV.19.3, 14). Anthony Thiselton ("New Testament Interpretation in Historical Perspective," in *Hearing the New Testament: Strategies for Interpretation*, ed. Joel B. Green [Grand Rapids: Eerdmans, 1995], 12) adds a very important point regarding this quotation: "[Locke's] motivation was not a 'secular world view' as such; he was a religious man. . . . He appealed to reason not against genuine faith as such, but against *manipulative* religion, whether from the political and religious left or from the political and religious right" (italics original).

34. *Aufklärung* in German (*Siècle des Lumières* in French), generally dated in the period between 1650 and 1789.

35. See Morgan and Barton, *Biblical Interpretation*, 17–18. See also Colin Brown, "Enlightenment Period," in *Dictionary of Biblical Criticism and Interpretation*, ed. Stanley E. Porter (New York: Routledge, 2007), 91–101; John Rogerson, "Post-Enlightenment Criticism," in *Dictionary of Biblical Criticism and Interpretation*, 280.

36. Rogerson, "Post-Enlightenment Criticism," 280.

who is often considered the father of biblical criticism,[37] promoted an "objective" approach to biblical studies,[38] arguing that the biblical text and canon were the result of *historical* factors and conditions.[39] Thus, for him the primary task of biblical criticism and interpretation is to reconstruct the historical circumstances that precipitated the production of the biblical texts, and to do so without theological (i.e., dogmatic) input.[40] A little more than fifty years after the publication of Semler's *Abhandlung*, de Wette published a thesis in which he argued that Deuteronomy had been produced at a much later time than the other writings of the Pentateuch.[41] Along the way to making this point, he suggested that the actual history of Israelite religion and sacrificial system had been different from that presented in the Old Testament and that it was more likely the end product of a long process of development rather than being completely in place from the beginning.[42] Critical biblical scholars of the time latched on to this notion and applied it more broadly to all of the religious traditions that are described in the Bible. Consequently, it quickly became a matter of course to seek the "preliterary history" of the biblical texts, which came to include the search for any "outside" influences and primitive traditions that may have influenced ancient Israel, later Judaism, and

---

37. Anthony C. Thiselton, *Hermeneutics: An Introduction* (Grand Rapids: Eerdmans, 2009), 138–39. He also says of Semler, "If the beginnings of modern biblical criticism can be traced to any individual thinker or book, the strongest candidate would be Johann Salomo Semler . . ." ("New Testament Interpretation in Historical Perspective," 10–11).

38. See esp. J. S. Semler, *Abhandlung von frier Untersuchung des Canon*, 4 vols. (Halle: Hemmerde, 1771–1775). In Semler's words, "An interpreter ought not to interject anything of his own ideas into the writing he wishes to interpret, but to make all he gets from it part of his current thinking and make himself sufficiently certain concerning it solely on the basis of its content and meaning. Nevertheless, it is obvious that the very attitude and intention is assumed that makes the application of that fundamental rule actually and really no longer possible" (ET Kümmel, *New Testament*, 66). See also Thiselton, "New Testament in Historical Perspective," 12–13; Thiselton, *Hermeneutics*, 140.

39. Thiselton rightly says that this point of view clearly expresses the ethos of the Enlightenment (*Hermeneutics*, 139). See also Kümmel, *New Testament*, 63, 68; Brown, "Enlightenment Period," 97–99.

40. See Thiselton, *Hermeneutics*, 139. See also William Baird, *History of New Testament Research, Volume 1: From Deism to Tübingen* (Minneapolis: Fortress, 2003), 120–21. This historical penchant eventually became the central tenet of "historical criticism proper," which is not to be confused with "historical-critical methodology" as it is known today. See James A. Loader and Oda Wischmeyer, "Twentieth Century Interpretation," in *Dictionary of Biblical Criticism and Interpretation*, 372.

41. Published (in Latin) in W. M. L. de Wette, *Opuscula Theologica* (Berlin: G. Reimer, 1830), 149–68.

42. Rogerson, "Post-Enlightenment Criticism," 282. See de Wette, *Opuscula Theologica*, 164–65n5, where he argues that Deuteronomy's prohibition of worship at local shrines was a later development than what is expressed in Exodus 20:24. See also Eugene H. Merrill, "Deuteronomy and de Wette: A Fresh Look at a Fallacious Premise," *JESOT* 1 (2012): 26n3; Thiselton, *Hermeneutics*, 143.

early Christianity, and how those influences are manifest in the final forms of the biblical texts.[43]

In view of de Wette, Semler's presumption that primitive Christianity had developed in almost complete isolation within its cultural and historical environment was largely left behind.[44] Scholars broadened their field of vision and began to consider the ways in which Judaism[45] in its various forms and the complex manifestations of Hellenism[46] may have influenced the development of the Christian religion.[47] There developed a fundamental presupposition that "in order to understand the Bible aright, one must try to describe the *religion* . . . of ancient Israel and early Christianity, and that an accurate description required a comparative and strictly historical method."[48] It was in this hermeneutical soil that the *religionsgeschichtliche Schule* (History of Religion School)[49] germinated and grew a substantial taproot. This development

43. See W. Randolph Tate, *Interpreting the Bible: A Handbook of Terms and Methods* (Peabody, MA: Hendrickson, 2006), 374–75 (under "Tradition Criticism"). Perhaps the most well-known example of this is Julius Wellhausen's *Die Composition des Hexateuchs und der historischen bücher des Alten Testaments* (Berlin: Reimer, 1899), in which he argued that four sources stood behind the Pentateuch (an idea that was not actually new with Wellhausen but with Simon in 1678 and Astruc in 1753 [see Bradford A. Anderson, *An Introduction to the Study of the Pentateuch*, 2nd ed., T&T Clark Approaches to Biblical Studies (London: Bloomsbury T&T Clark, 2017), 39; also Merrill, "Deuteronomy and de Wette," 25–26]), namely the Yahwist (J), Elohist (E), Deuteronomic (D), and Priestly (P) sources, and that these strands of tradition developed chronologically with J being the oldest and most primitive, followed closely by E, then D, and finally P (Anderson, *Introduction to the Study of the Pentateuch*, 40).

44. Kümmel, *New Testament*, 206.

45. For example, Emil Schürer asserted that "since it was from Judaism that Christianity had emerged . . . nothing in the Gospel account is understandable apart from its setting in Jewish history, no word of Jesus [is] meaningful unless inserted into its natural context of contemporary Jewish thought," so that "the task of the New Testament scholar . . . is to relate Jesus and the Gospel, not only to the Old Testament, but also, and above all, to the Jewish world of his time" (Schürer, *Geschichte des jüdischen Volkes im Zeitalter Jesu Christi* [Leipzig: Hinrichs, 1901], 1 [my translation]).

46. C. F. G. Heinrici exemplifies this perspective. According to Kümmel (*New Testament*, 210), Heinrici was "the first to make extensive use of parallels from Hellenism to help in the understanding of Paul's language and the social forms of the Pauline congregations," especially the Corinthian congregation. He "compared the symptoms of community life at Corinth with information from Greek and Roman social groups" (Heinrici, *Das zweite Sendschreiben des Apostels Paulus an die Korinthier* [Berlin: Hertz, 1887], 556–57), and followed this same principle when investigating Paul's ideas and vocabulary.

47. See Kümmel, *New Testament*, 206–10.

48. Wayne A. Meeks, "The History of Religions School," in *The New Cambridge History of the Bible, Vol. 4, From 1750 to the Present*, ed. John Riches (New York: Cambridge University Press, 2015), 127 (italics his).

49. Ernst Troeltsch claims that even though the German term *religionsgeschichtlich* has no exact English equivalent, "the method of investigation is . . . well known to English-speaking scholars," with "the nearest approach" being "comparative religions" (Troeltsch, "The Dogmatics of the 'Religionsgeschichtliche Schule,'" *AJT* 17 [1913]: 1n1).

is significant in relation to Dibelius's methodological paradigm and perspective, because his enculturation into the world of biblical criticism occurred during the time in which the history of religion approach gained prominence in the academy, and he sat at the feet of two of the approach's leading proponents, Otto Pfleiderer (1839–1908)[50] and Hermann Gunkel (1862–1932),[51] the latter of whom appears to have had the greatest impact on Dibelius.

With a view to Dibelius, it is quite significant that Gunkel distinguished between history proper (*strenge Geschichtsschreibung*) and popular tradition (*volkstümliche Tradition*), and that such a distinction was made on the basis of a text's literary form and style as well as its content.[52] Gunkel argues further that the recording of history proper

---

50. Pfleiderer, often called the father of the history of religion approach (see Kümmel, *New Testament*, 207; Stephen Neill and Tom Wright, *Interpretation of the New Testament 1861–1986*, 2nd ed. [Oxford: Oxford University Press, 1988], 169), embraced philosophical idealism and believed that truth (or the divine spirit) is revealed in history, that history is the evolutionary process of the realization of the divine purpose, and that Christianity is the historical expression of universal truth. See also William Baird, *History of New Testament Research, Vol. 2: From Jonathan Edwards to Rudolf Bultmann* (Minneapolis: Fortress, 2003), 213–20, esp. 214. See also Otto Pfleiderer, *Christian Origins*, trans. Daniel A. Huebsch (New York: B. W. Huebsch, 1906), 20–25. He believed that in order to understand primitive Christianity one must determine whence it developed and what traditional influences were involved in its development. This requires the comparison of the biblical text "with extra-biblical Jewish, and heathen, religious history" as an "indispensable" step "for the elucidation of some of the most important questions" about early Christianity. Otto Pfleiderer, *Primitive Christianity: Its Writings and Teachings in their Historical Connections*, trans. W. Montgomery, 4 vols., Library of Religious and Philosophic Thought (Clifton, NJ: Reference Book Publishers, 1965), 1:vi. See also Baird, *New Testament Research*, 2:214.

51. Gunkel maintained the core tenet that all traditions grow out of and reflect the symbolic world of the communities that produce them (Tate, *Interpreting the Bible*, 375). He presumed that the "religion of the earliest Christian Church" was "syncretistic. . . . Christianity, born of syncretistic Judaism, has strong syncretistic traits. Early Christianity is like a river that has come together from two large tributaries: one is specifically Israelite, which originates in the Old Testament, while the other flows through Judaism from foreign, oriental religions. Then to this, in the West, is added the Greek element" (Hermann Gunkel, *Zum religionsgeschichtlichen Verständnis des Neuen Testaments* [Göttingen: Vandenhoeck & Ruprecht, 1903], 35–36 [my translation]; see also Kümmel, *New Testament*, 258–59). Most of Gunkel's academic efforts are geared toward discovering the origins of these "tributaries" of tradition and explaining how they developed and found their way into Israelite tradition, into the Hebrew Bible, and eventually into the New Testament. A survey of his major works confirms this perspective; see at least the following: Hermann Gunkel, *Schöpfung und Chaos in Urzeit und Endzeit: Eine religionsgeschichtliche Untersuchung über Gen 1 und Ap Joh 12* (Göttingen: Vandenhoeck & Ruprecht, 1895); ET Gunkel, *Creation and Chaos in the Primeval Era and the Eschaton: A Religio-Historical Study of Genesis 1 and Revelation 12*, trans. K. William Whitney, Jr. (Grand Rapids: Eerdmans, 2006); Gunkel, *Genesis*, 2nd ed., HKAT 1/1 (Göttingen: Vandenhoeck & Ruprecht, 1902); Gunkel, *Die Sagen der Genesis* (Göttingen: Vandenhoeck & Ruprecht, 1901); ET Gunkel, *The Legends of Genesis*, trans. W. H. Carruth (Chicago: Open Court Publishing, 1907); Gunkel, *Zum religionsgeschichtlichen Verständnis*, 36.

52. For example, in his work on Genesis, Gunkel argues that history proper consists principally of "national" records of "great public events," especially as they relate to "the deeds of popular kings,

most likely developed as a written form of communication while, on the other hand, popular tradition derives from the older oral presentations of kin and fictive kin groups as they handed down to subsequent generations the values, norms, and chief identity markers of their groups through various stories about their ancestors and their activities.[53] Over time, these smaller social groups began to see the benefit of inscribing their families' traditional stories for subsequent generations, but because these stories had to that point been primarily oral, they remained fairly malleable as they began to be recorded in writing. People's experiences and imaginations, according to Gunkel, become enmeshed and to some extent indistinguishable, with the result that what gets inscribed, being essentially "poetic" in nature, ends up being written either in the literary form of song (*Lieder*) or of legend (*Saga*).[54] Thus, as Gunkel's argument goes, legends are not the free constructions of an author(s); rather, they are the compilation of "popular oral tradition written down"[55] that have been stitched together and redacted by compilers and editors—and this in accordance with the needs of their own time.[56] The "preliterary history" of

---

and especially to wars" (Gunkel, *Legends of Genesis*, 2; Gunkel, *Sagen der Genesis*, 1). By contrast, popular tradition has a more focused sphere of interest, namely the goings on in the lives of specific social groups such as families or tribes or even fictive kin groups (see Gunkel, *Legends of Genesis*, 4–5). Gunkel, *Sagen der Genesis*, 3: "Another distinguishing feature is the sphere of interest of legend and of history. History deals with the great public events; but the legend speaks of things that the people are interested in, the personal and the private, and it likes to conceive of political things and personalities in such a way that a popular interest can be connected with them" (my translation).

53. Gunkel, *Legends of Genesis*, 3; Gunkel, *Sagen der Genesis*, 2: "A distinctive feature is that legend is originally oral tradition; history tends to exist in written form" (my translation). See also Gunkel, *Legends of Genesis*, 5; Gunkel, *Sagen der Genesis*, 3.

54. "Was sie erleben, verfärbt sich ihnen unter der Hand, Erfahrung und Phantasie mischt sich; und nur in poetischer Form, in Liedern und Sagen vermögen sie es, geschichtliche Begebenheiten darzustellen" (Gunkel, *Genesis*, 1). Special thanks to Dr. Curt Niccum (e-mail message to author, September 27, 2019), who rightly suggested that in context Gunkel's phrase "verfärbt sich ihnen unter der Hand" ("subtly changes its color") is a metaphor by which Gunkel likely intends "subtly changes its *form*." On the notion that legend is poetry, see Gunkel, *Legends of Genesis*, 10–12, 88–122 (*Sagen der Genesis*, 5–6, 40–55). See also Gunkel, *Reden und Aufsätze* (Göttingen: Vandenhoeck & Ruprecht, 1913), 33–35. Genesis, as Gunkel's argument goes, "contains the final sublimation into writing a body of oral traditions," and these appear in the form of legends (Gunkel, *Sagen der Genesis*, 2). See Gunkel, *Legends of Genesis*, 4. See also the discussion in Gunkel, *Introduction to Psalms: The Genres of the Religious Lyric of Israel*, trans. James D. Nogalski, Mercer Library of Biblical Studies (Macon, GA: Mercer University Press, 1998), 1–21. It is worth noting that Gunkel did say that Gen. 14 was an exception; it is, in his view, the only account in Genesis that contains a political event and may, thus, qualify as history proper (*Legends of Genesis*, 5; *Sagen der Genesis*, 3).

55. Gunkel, *Legends of Genesis*, 39.

56. See the discussion in Gunkel, *Legends of Genesis*, 123–60; Gunkel, *Sagen der Genesis*, 55–71. Gunkel, *Schöpfung und Chaos*, 6: "Auch hat PC in der Genesis im allgemeinen nicht seine willkürlichen Erfindungen niedergelegt, sondern er hat den überkommenen Stoff in dem Sinne seiner Zeit neu bearbeitet."

the legends of Genesis is this oral popular tradition, and it is the task of the practitioner of *Religionsgeschichte* to "get behind" each legend to determine its *Sitz im Leben*, which, in turn, will open the possibility for discovering whence the tradition that the legend transmits originated as well as its relative age and trajectory of development.

The influence of Gunkel and the basic tenets of the *Religionsgeschichte* paradigm become apparent in two fundamental presuppositions that factor greatly in Dibelius's *Formgeschichte* method (more on this below), both of which mirror Gunkel's distinction between history proper and popular tradition. The first presupposition is that the Gospels were not "authored" by the evangelists "upon their own responsibility."[57] Rather, their efforts were confined to "the choice, the limitation, and the final shaping of the material, but not with the original moulding," for they "took over material which already possessed a form of its own" and "had possessed a certain independent completeness."[58] This presupposition is still in play in his approach to Acts (and other New Testament writings) where he foregrounds the analysis of style, which he calls *Stilkritik* (style criticism), over the identification of forms or sources of tradition (more on this below). Even though the *Stilkritik Methode* demonstrates that "in Acts there is a greater depth of original composition," it still demonstrates that Luke "fitted together, joined, and framed fragments of tradition, as in a mosaic."[59] Thus Dibelius views the construction of both the Synoptic Gospels and Acts in a way that is very similar to the way Gunkel understood the construction of Genesis. Also similar to Gunkel, Dibelius believes that literary analysis is the most appropriate means for identifying these fragments of tradition and opening the way to getting to the *Sitz im Leben* that prompted their telling and their relative age.

The second presupposition "consists in the view that the origin of early tradition is most closely connected with the faith of those early Christians, but not so closely with their knowledge—or their desire for knowledge."[60] Dibelius asserts that the evangelists and those who had begun collecting the tradition that had formed before their time were not interested in producing a *bios* of the historical Jesus because they believed that their generation would experience immanently the

---

57. Dibelius, *Message of Jesus Christ*, 123.
58. Dibelius, *Tradition to Gospel*, 3, 4; Dibelius, *Formgeschichte des Evangeliums*, 3.
59. Dibelius, *Studies in Acts*, 2.
60. Dibelius, *Message of Jesus Christ*, 124.

apocalypse of God and the end of all things; thus, they saw no need to provide written accounts of the past since "there was to be no posterity for whose benefit such narratives ought to be provided."[61] Moreover, Dibelius argues, the disciples were "for the most part Galilean fishermen, tax gatherers, perhaps also farm-labourers, unfamiliar with the literary practices of the world and probably not even accustomed to writing."[62] Instead, being motivated by their faith, they shared orally their reminiscences of Jesus and his teachings and eventually began collecting the fragments of tradition as a means of sustaining and promoting faith in Jesus as the Messiah, as the one in and through whom God had revealed himself.[63] This is redolent of what Gunkel said about the spheres of interest of legends, that they deal with things that interest common people, namely personal and private matters, particularly the matters of family such as values, norms, and identity markers. These are also the main items connected with faith. Additionally, Gunkel says that too often interpreters treat such material "too much like 'books,'" and do not take into account the contexts of situation in which the legends (traditions) were recited.[64] Dibelius seems to extend this idea to the study of how the Synoptics came together and, given that they are based on popular tradition, the manner in which they present Jesus.

Despite these and other notable influences that Gunkel had upon his mentee, Dibelius certainly developed and exercised his own theoretical perspective while remaining within the bounds of the *Religionsgeschichte* paradigm. His perspective—that is, his style of theorizing—differed from that of Gunkel in significant ways. Perhaps the most significant difference has to do with what each thought should be the scope of *religionsgeschichtlich* investigations. As pointed out above, Gunkel was most interested in showing the development of tradition over a long span of time, creating a genealogy, of sorts, of the tradition. Thus, for him, the *Religionsgeschichte* methodology served first and foremost as a means of diachronic investigation. Of course, Dibelius, too, engaged in diachronic studies given that he, like his mentor, was interested in tracing the development of tradition. However,

61. Dibelius, *Message of Jesus Christ*, 124–25.
62. Dibelius, *Message of Jesus Christ*, 125.
63. See now Dibelius, *Jesus*, 9–15. Note here the classic history of religion distinction of the Jesus of history and the Christ of faith, with which Martin Kähler famously struggled (see his *Der Sogenannte Historische Jesus und der Geschichtliche, Biblische Christus*, Vortrag auf der Wuppertaler Pastoralkonferenz [Leipzig: A. Deichert, 1892]).
64. See Gunkel, *Legends of Genesis*, 40.

in his perspective the scope of the history of religion methodology was certainly not only, if even primarily, diachronic. As he described his methodology in *Die Geisterwelt im Glauben des Paulus*, Dibelius argues that history of religion investigations must not merely assume that ideas or teachings had migrated from earlier times; some, he says, may have arisen as "autochthonous."[65] Thus, those who utilize *Religionsgeschichte* methodology must not ask solely about the "genealogy" of an idea or practice, but also about "analogy."[66]

This brings up a second related difference, namely the way in which the data obtained by the methodology is treated. Kümmel rightly points out that in *Die Geisterwelt*, Dibelius set out "to show the connection between certain features of Pauline Christology with gnostic concepts, and endeavored to demonstrate in particular the *connection* between these concepts and the activity of the spirit world and Pauline theology."[67] In prosecuting a history of religion approach to this end, Dibelius was not satisfied to make connections between Paul's thought and gnostic concepts merely for "genealogical" purposes or even to point out analogues from other thought systems. Instead, as he pointed out,

> The ultimate goal of [such a study] is to demonstrate the *importance* of the ideas of spirits *in the faith* of Paul. It was necessary to establish the connection between Paul's belief in spirits and his other religious and theological ideas. . . . But the place of belief in spirits is of special importance in Paul's religion for his eschatology and Christology. We must not exclude these things as peripheral, for individual ideas are found at the very heart of piety: We lose a segment of Pauline faith if we scorn them.[68]

Thus, Dibelius interrogated the data he had obtained with the methodology "with respect to its material significance"—in this case, how the connections actually impacted Paul and his teachings—and "as

---

65. Dibelius, *Geisterwelt im Glauben des Paulus*, 4.
66. Dibelius, *Geisterwelt im Glauben des Paulus*, 4: "Es gilt das große Problem aller vergleichenden Religionsgeschichte: Analogie oder Genealogie? an einzelnen Punkten zu entscheiden. Hat Ideenwanderung stattgefunden? Sind die Vorstellungen autochthon entstanden?"
67. Kümmel, *New Testament*, 263.
68. Dibelius, *Die Geisterwelt im Glauben des Paulus*, 4 (translation from Kümmel, *New Testament*, 264).

a consequence the *theological* goal of religio-historical research" was once again foregrounded.[69]

A third major difference in perspective pertains to procedure. Even a cursory reading of Gunkel's work reveals that he preferred a bottom-up analytical procedure. In fact, Dibelius even reports that "the researches of Gunkel and his school made the analysis of 'the smallest details' an axiom of research."[70] However, Dibelius did not necessarily think that an analytical approach was the only or even most appropriate way to proceed in determining what motivated the early believers to spread their reminiscences about Jesus and his teachings, or what standards governed both their spread and ultimately their preservation in writing. He says that

> an analytical method which starts from the texts and goes back to the sources and isolated elements of tradition is not satisfactory. Rather one requires a constructive method which attempts to include the conditions and activities of life of the first Christian Churches. If we leave this work on one side, the sources and the small details which are brought forward by the analytical method hang in the air, and their sociological relationships, or "Sitz im Leben," is not clear.[71]

In other words, a major problem of analytical approaches like Gunkel's and those of his contemporaries, Wrede and Bultmann—as valuable as they may be in what they may discover—is that their results remain largely disconnected from the "historical and social stratum" (or socio-historical [*geschichtlich-soziale*] context) in which the analyzed texts were produced.[72] Without this connection, Dibelius believes that it becomes impossible to determine what motivated the early believers to spread stories about Jesus or what social process governed the formal structuring of the stories. Of course, this does not mean that Dibelius neglects the analysis of "the smallest details" or that he judged the conclusions of all analytical researches to be without value; his corpus of work clearly demonstrates both his own careful and tedious analysis as well as an assumed reliability of and dependence upon the

---

69. Kümmel, *New Testament*, 263.
70. Dibelius, *Tradition to Gospel*, 5; Dibelius, *Formgeschichte des Evangeliums*, 5.
71. Dibelius, *Tradition to Gospel*, 10; Dibelius, *Formgeschichte des Evangeliums*, 9.
72. Dibelius, *Tradition to Gospel*, 7; Dibelius, *Formgeschichte des Evangeliums*, 7.

results of others' analytical investigations,[73] not to mention the fact that he characterizes his *Formgeschichte* method as both a constructive and analytical methodology being brought together for a single purpose.[74] Rather, Dibelius wishes to express why he prefers a top-down "constructive" (in some ways "abductive" or "retroductive" may be a more appropriate descriptor)[75] approach. In such an approach, he first imagines a context of situation—a *Sitz im Leben*—in which the desire to tell others about Jesus (first among the group of believers but also, over time, beyond that group) and eventually to fix them into distinct forms and even to record them in writing would make sense. This reconstruction would then be tested through an analysis of the details to see if it would be supported or if it would require modification or reformulation.[76]

MODEL AND METHOD:
DIBELIUS'S READING OF LUKE AND ACTS

Because of his preference for a constructive approach, it is typical of Dibelius to begin any of his investigations and discussions about methodology with a description of the "conditions and activities of life [*Lebensbedingungen und Lebensfunktionen*] of the first Christian churches"[77] that best explain both the existence and the form of the biblical data he sets out to interpret.[78] In fact, *Formgeschichte* and its trimmed-down version, *Stilkritik*, are formulated in accordance with the abductively reconstructed *Sitz im Leben* of each text or corpus. In

---

73.   For example, Dibelius adopts the "Theory of Two Sources" as "a relatively sure result" of the "analytic method" behind the source criticism of the Synoptic Gospels (see Dibelius, *Tradition to Gospel*, 9; Dibelius, *Formgeschichte des Evangeliums*, 8; Martin Dibelius, *A Fresh Approach to the New Testament and Early Christian Literature*, International Library of Christian Knowledge [London: Ivor Nicholson and Watson, 1936; repr., Westport, CT: Greenwood, 1979], 53–56). Another example, which is significant in regard to how he views Acts, is Dibelius's acceptance of Henry Cadbury's stance that an ancient historian "readily interpolated his record with speeches which he himself introduced, speeches which were composed by him" (Dibelius, *Tradition to Gospel*, 16; Dibelius, *Formgeschichte des Evangeliums*, 15).

74.   Dibelius, *Tradition to Gospel*, 41; Dibelius, *Formgeschichte des Evangeliums*, 38.

75.   On abductive or retroductive reasoning, see John H. Elliott, *What Is Social-Scientific Criticism?*, GBS (Minneapolis: Fortress, 1993), 48–49; James D. Dvorak, "John H. Elliott's Social-Scientific Criticism," *TJ* 28 (2007): 251–78.

76.   See Dibelius, *Tradition to Gospel*, 41; Dibelius, *Formgeschichte des Evangeliums*, 38.

77.   Dibelius, *Tradition to Gospel*, 10; Dibelius, *Formgeschichte des Evangeliums*, 9.

78.   This is true not only in his more technical works, but also in his more accessible works such as *Jesus* and *Sermon on the Mount*.

this section I briefly set out Dibelius's reconstructions of the situations behind the productions of Luke and Acts, followed by the specific methodology he puts to use for analysis in light of the reconstructed *Sitz im Leben* of each.

The *Sitz im Leben* of the Gospel of Luke

As Dibelius sees it, the situation behind the production of the Gospel of Luke is the same in essence as that of the Gospels of Mark and Matthew, so he treats them all together.[79] An important leaping off point in the discussion has to do with the nature of these accounts. On the one hand, Dibelius is unwilling to classify them as "literature proper" (*großen Literatur*), for they lack the characteristic features of literary and polished writing, and they do not appear to be written for publication and dissemination to the masses.[80] On the other hand, the Evangelists do exhibit some amount of creativity in regards to the "choice, the limitation, and the final shaping of the material, but not with the original moulding."[81] Moreover, their accounts were clearly something other than private communications such as letters or notes.[82] Thus, in the end, Dibelius calls them *Kleinliteratur*, which is variously glossed in English as "humbler forms of literature" or "unpretentious literature."[83] By this he means literature belonging to "that lower stratum which accords no place to the artistic devices and tendencies of literary and polished writing" because it is written for

79. Dibelius believed that the "John" who authored the Fourth Gospel "was an author in the true meaning of the term," exercising much more freedom in regard to arrangement of materials and elaboration upon the tradition in order to fulfill his stated purpose, "that you may believe that Jesus is the Messiah, the Son of God" (John 20:31) (Dibelius, *Fresh Approach*, 95–96). See Dvorak, "Martin Dibelius and Rudolf Bultmann," 261–63.

80. Dibelius, *Tradition to Gospel*, 1; Dibelius, *Formgeschichte des Evangeliums*, 1.

81. Dibelius, *Tradition to Gospel*, 3; Dibelius, *Formgeschichte des Evangeliums*, 3. Note, however, that Dibelius viewed the Gospel of Luke as "essentially of a more literary character than the other two synoptic Gospels"; with the addition of a prologue and the transformation of his sources "by using more refined and educated modes of expression," Luke "makes an attempt at a genuine style, firstly in the framework into which he places the tradition" and secondly by endeavoring "to employ the material offered him by his sources in the manner of a biography" (Dibelius, *Fresh Approach*, 62–63). Yet see also Dibelius, *Studies in the Acts*, 146, where he comments on Luke's Gospel account: "Luke has revised the texts of his sources from a linguistic point of view; in interests of probability and clarity he has also re-arranged their presentation; he has added observations and supplementary passages which provide connecting-links and continuity, but all this has not essentially changed the character of the Gospel. It remains a book which contains collected material, stories and sayings, in addition to the story of the Passion and traditions of the community, revised certainly, but not newly formed."

82. Dibelius, *Tradition to Gospel*, 1; Dibelius, *Formgeschichte des Evangeliums*, 1.

83. Dibelius, *Tradition to Gospel*, 1–2. See Dvorak, "Martin Dibelius and Rudolf Bultmann," 263n52.

people "in circles not touched by literature proper."[84] Moreover, the Gospel accounts were assembled "for a definite publicity" and not merely for "the circle of the author's acquaintance"—but, still, not for the masses.[85] If it is, indeed, the case that the Evangelists did not engage in the creative authorship of their Gospel accounts but instead intended to gather and to assemble the traditional materials that had taken shape between the lifetime of Jesus (AD 30) and the writing of the oldest Gospel account (AD 70, in Dibelius's view),[86] then two questions emerge: (1) What was the motive (*Anlaß*) that compelled the circle of earliest disciples to spread the teachings of Jesus and stories about his life that became the traditional materials (*Stoffes*)[87] with which the Evangelists worked?[88] and (2) What was the "law" or principle (*Gesetz*) that governed the fixing of the early disciples' reminiscences about Jesus into their various forms—"if not of word yet of outer and inner structure"?[89] These two questions reveal the *religionsgeschichtlich* nature of Dibelius's investigation.

In answering these questions, Dibelius takes for granted a number of significant points. First, he presumes that if the circle of the earliest disciples passed around the words of Jesus and stories about him merely as a means of reminding each other of the things they had experienced together, "there would have been no order in the propagation, no formulation of the material, in short, no tradition,"[90] for the "fixation [of tradition] is only to be accepted where the handing down takes place either in the regulated activity of teaching and of learning, or under the control of immanent laws."[91] But fixation did, indeed, occur, and as evidence Dibelius claims:

---

84. Dibelius, *Tradition to Gospel*, 1; Dibelius, *Formgeschichte des Evangeliums*, 1.
85. Dibelius, *Tradition to Gospel*, 1; Dibelius, *Formgeschichte des Evangeliums*, 1.
86. Dibelius, *Tradition to Gospel*, 9–10; Dibelius, *Formgeschichte des Evangeliums*, 9.
87. Dibelius, *Formgeschichte des Evangeliums*, 3–4: "Die Formgeschichte des Evangeliums, d. h., dieses Stoffes, beginnt also nicht etwa mit der Arbeit der Evangelisten, sondern sie erreicht in der Formwerdung der Evangelien-Bücher bereits einen gewissen Abschluß. Was auf die Abfassung der ersten Evangelien-Bücher folgt, ist die Entwicklung dieser Gattung bis hin zu den Sammlungen verwilderter und absichtsvoll zurechtgemachter Tradition. . . ."
88. Especially if the earliest disciples were certain that the end of the age was imminent and that what was to come was to be so much more glorious than anything they had experienced to that point (see Dibelius, *Tradition to Gospel*, 10; Dibelius, *Formgeschichte des Evangeliums*, 10).
89. Dibelius, *Tradition to Gospel*, 10; Dibelius, *Formgeschichte des Evangeliums*, 9.
90. Dibelius, *Tradition to Gospel*, 13; Dibelius, *Formgeschichte des Evangeliums*, 12.
91. Dibelius, *Tradition to Gospel*, 11; Dibelius, *Formgeschichte des Evangeliums*, 10: "Fixierung ist immer nur dort anzunehmen, wo entweder in geordnetem Lehr- und Lernbetrieb oder aber unter der Kontrolle immanenter Gesetze überliefert wird."

synoptic Gospels themselves fill out and prove these observations. Numerous cases of parallel tradition indicate that the narrative material had not been subject merely to accident, that it had neither fluttered about nor split up, but that it had crystallized out in different places under similar conditions.[92]

He also cites for support both Luke's and Paul's uses of the terms παραδίδωμι (Luke 1:2; 1 Cor. 15:3) and παραλαμβάνω (1 Cor. 15:1, 3), which Dibelius says "are the equivalent for the official Jewish terms for the taking over and passing on of tradition."[93]

Second, Dibelius presumes that those within the earliest circle of believers actively engaged in preaching (*Predigt*). Here, Dibelius turns specifically to the prologue of Luke's Gospel for support. Luke refers to the accounts that were "passed along to us" (παρέδοσαν ἡμῖν) by "those being eyewitnesses and servants of the word from the beginning" (οἱ ἀπ' ἀρχῆς αὐτόπται καὶ ὑπηρέται γενόμενοι τοῦ λόγου [Luke 1:2]). On the one hand, argues Dibelius, Luke likely did not intend "eyewitnesses and servants" (*Augenzeugen und Diener*) to describe two distinct groups, "for he unites them by means of the common definite article."[94] Yet, on the other hand, he says that it cannot be that the groups are identical, for over time not all of the preachers were able to claim eyewitness status.[95] Nevertheless, Dibelius thinks that this reference demonstrates that Luke was certain that the early eyewitnesses "also preached as ministers of the word."[96]

Third, by "preaching," Dibelius does not have in mind a specific type of sermon "with which the whole tradition would find its place"; rather,

the dependence of the formation of tradition upon the preaching is to be conceived somewhat in this fashion: the material of tradition gave objectivity to the preaching of salvation; it explained, expanded, and, in accordance therewith, was either introduced into the preaching, or related at its close.[97]

---

92. Dibelius, *Tradition to Gospel*, 13; Dibelius, *Formgeschichte des Evangeliums*, 12.
93. Dibelius, *Tradition to Gospel*, 21; Dibelius, *Formgeschichte des Evangeliums*, 20.
94. Dibelius, *Tradition to Gospel*, 12; Dibelius, *Formgeschichte des Evangeliums*, 11. It should be noted, however, that the article more likely substantivizes the participle γενόμενοι rather than acting as a specifier of αὐτόπται ("eyewitnesses") and ὑπηρέται ("servants").
95. Dibelius, *Tradition to Gospel*, 12; Dibelius, *Formgeschichte des Evangeliums*, 11.
96. Dibelius, *Tradition to Gospel*, 12; Dibelius, *Formgeschichte des Evangeliums*, 11.
97. Dibelius, *Tradition to Gospel*, 15; Dibelius, *Formgeschichte des Evangeliums*, 14. See also Dibelius, *Message of Jesus Christ*, 129–34.

Additionally, he says, "if I speak of preaching in this connection, all possible forms of Christian propaganda [*Verkündigung*] are included: mission preaching, preaching during worship, and catechumen instruction."[98] It is in these various types of preaching that Dibelius finds both the motive and the organizing principle by which the early believers' recollections of the sayings of Jesus and their reminiscences of his deeds eventuated into the traditional materials that Mark, Matthew, and Luke then drew upon to construct their Gospel accounts:[99]

> And so, naturally, in connection with such preaching, certain fixed forms emerged, types of stories which were told—by one missionary just as by another—regarding the Lord. . . . Hence if neither consideration for a later age nor the urge toward literary creation led the Christians to form and preserve their tradition, nevertheless the requirements of mission preaching, of public worship, and the instruction of new converts compelled them to set forth the old reminiscences in definite form and finally to write them down.[100]

Formgeschichte and Dibelius's Take on the Gospel of Luke

The *Formgeschichte*[101] method is a variety of "literary criticism"[102] to which Dibelius has added "style criticism" (*Stilkritik*).[103] Its purpose is to identify the units which comprise the teachings about Jesus and

---

98. Dibelius, *Tradition to Gospel*, 15; Dibelius, *Formgeschichte des Evangeliums*, 14.

99. Dibelius, *Tradition to Gospel*, 37: "The paradox has become probable to us that unliterary men created a definite style. In so doing they followed, of course, not some need of making an artistic form but a compulsion of their life. It arose out of the only practical activity which these men, who belonged to a new realm in the old world, were really acquainted with, viz. propaganda on behalf of their faith. The words, 'We cannot but speak the things which we saw and heard' (Acts 4:20) express the tendency which influenced this unliterary process of development."

100. Dibelius, *Message of Jesus Christ*, 126.

101. It is interesting to note that Gunkel, apparently, was not overly fond of this term, and neither does he seem too pleased with the way that Dibelius (or Bultmann and Schmidt for that matter) had adapted his methodology for the analysis of the New Testament. In a letter to Adolf Jülicher, Gunkel said that he found the word "*form*geschichtlich" and even "*stilkritisch*" to be "particularly unpleasant" to him ("Besonders unangenehm ist mir das Wort '*form*geschichtlich' oder gar '*stilkritisch*'"). Moreover, he criticized his New Testament students for having "blurred" the "tediously established, clear lines" of his methodology ("meine neutestamentlichen Schüler meine so mühsam erworbenen, klaren Linien verwischt haben"). See Hans Rollmann, "Zwei Briefe Hermann Gunkels an Adolf Jülicher zur religionsgeschichtlichen und formgeschichtlichen Methode," *ZTK* 78.3 (1981): 276–88, here 283, 285.

102. See Dibelius, *Tradition to Gospel*, 7.

103. Dibelius, *Tradition to Gospel*, 6–7, 41; Dibelius, *Formgeschichte des Evangeliums*, 6–7, 38. The two become disconnected when Dibelius reads Acts (and other texts outside the Synoptic Gospels). See below.

the teachings of Jesus and "to detach them from their framework and to study their original meaning."[104] Care must be taken to define these terms. For Dibelius, "literary criticism" (*Literarkritik*) refers to a methodology that has more recently been lumped together with source criticism. Patterned after Gunkel's approach for Old Testament analysis, it is an analysis that attempts to identify the sources and/or traditional elements used in the composition of the Synoptic Gospels, as well as the extent to which the writers (compilers) may have adapted those sources for their own purposes. One must not confuse it with what is now called literary criticism, which *assumes* that the biblical writers were "the imaginative, creative crafters of art employing structural elements and literary devices usually associated with the poetics of literature (i.e., the creation of literature) and [literary] genre."[105] Similarly, one must not think of "style criticism" as some sort of "flirtation with aesthetic standards" or as an analysis that "deals only with vocabulary and construction"; rather, it is to be understood in terms of identifying the writer's "whole way of speaking."[106] To accomplish this certainly requires taking into account vocabulary and construction, but it adds to this a consideration of wordiness or brevity, of the nature of the description, of how stories and/or sayings are introduced into the text, and of how the textual unit concludes as the means of determining the purpose of the writer: to arouse interest, to make converts, or to instruct those who are already believers.[107] Thus, the method identifies forms on the basis of two features: from the literary critical point of view, the method looks for "seams" in the text that signal the beginning and ending of a story or saying; from the style critical perspective, the method considers both *how much* of a story is told and the *manner* in which it is told.

In Dibelius's hands, the model identifies four main forms used throughout the Synoptics: paradigms (*Paradigma*); paraenesis (*Paränese*);

---

104. Dibelius, *Sermon on the Mount*, 42.
105. Tate, *Interpreting the Bible*, 199.
106. Dibelius, *Tradition to Gospel*, 7; Dibelius, *Formgeschichte des Evangeliums*, 7.
107. Dibelius, *Formgeschichte des Evangeliums*, 7: "Der Begriff 'Stil' ist dabei selbstverständlich nicht nur in jenem engen Sinn gefaßt, der sich auf Wortwahl und Satzkonstruktion bezieht. Vielmehr ist unter Stil die gesamte Vortragsart zu verstehen, die—mindestens bei dieser volkstümlichen Kleinliteratur—konstitutiv für die Gattung ist. Denn die Unbekannten, die diesen Stil hervorbringen, schaffen nach überindividuellen Gesetzen. Darum kennzeichnet der Stil die Gattung. Ob die Verfasser Interesse oder Anhängerschaft wecken wollen, ist unter Umständen auch an Wortwahl und Satzbau, ebenso aber auch an Breite oder Spärlichkeit der Schilderung, an der Art der Charakteristik, an Einleitung und Ausleitung zu erkennen."

tales (*Novelle*); and legends (*Legende*).[108] Briefly,[109] paradigms are essentially anecdotes; they are the relatively brief stories about Jesus that traveled about relatively disconnected from their original historical context,[110] so that they could more easily be "plugged in" to sermons for the purpose of illustrating particular points about Jesus.[111] When the Evangelists made use of these bits of tradition, they provided the scaffolding (i.e., introductions and conclusions) necessary for stitching them into their accounts.[112] Based on the evolutionary principle, Dibelius takes the paradigm—being the least complex and least accreted of the forms—as the oldest type of form and closest to the origin of the Christian tradition and, thus, the standard against which the other forms are compared.

Paraenesis, or "exhortations," are similar to the paradigms in terms of structure and function, but they had defining characteristics of their own. First, these appear principally in Matthew and Luke and more rarely in Mark.[113] Second, these sayings were handed down through the various mechanisms of tradition in accordance with a different governing principle than were paradigms and other forms.[114] Rather

---

108. Note that the 1919 edition of *Formgeschichte des Evangeliums* did not contain a section describing legends.

109. I will not provide here full descriptions of each form. For an overview, see Dvorak, "Martin Dibelius and Rudolf Bultmann." For Dibelius's discussions of each, see the following: on paradigms, see Dibelius, *Tradition to Gospel*, 37–69; Dibelius, *Formgeschichte des Evangeliums*, 34–66; Dibelius, *Message of Jesus Christ*, 135–47; on paraenesis, see Dibelius, *Tradition to Gospel*, 233–65; Dibelius, *Formgeschichte des Evangeliums*, 234–65; Dibelius, *Message of Jesus Christ*, 148–65 (under "parables" and "sayings"); on tales, see Dibelius, *Tradition to Gospel*, 70–103; Dibelius, *Formgeschichte des Evangeliums*, 66–100; Dibelius, *Message of Jesus Christ*, 166–73; on legends, see Dibelius, *Tradition to Gospel*, 104–32; Dibelius, *Formgeschichte des Evangeliums*, 101–29; Dibelius, *Message of Jesus Christ*, 174–87. Dibelius also discusses the "myth" form (*Mythus*) (*Tradition to Gospel*, 266–86; Dibelius, *Formgeschichte des Evangeliums*, 265–87; see Dvorak, "Martin Dibelius and Rudolf Bultmann," 266). However, "only to the smallest extent is the tradition assembled in the Gospel [of Mark] of a mythological character and this is confined to the epiphany narratives and a few Tales" (*Tradition to Gospel*, 279). However, Dibelius thinks that the Gospel of John is much more mythological than the Synoptic Gospels (*Tradition to Gospel*, 285–86).

110. See Dibelius, *Message of Jesus Christ*, 136.

111. Dibelius, *Tradition to Gospel*, 42; Dibelius, *Formgeschichte des Evangeliums*, 39; Dibelius, *Message of Jesus Christ*, 136.

112. In this regard, Dibelius sees an analogy between rabbinic theodicy-legends and paradigms. See the discussion in Dibelius, *Tradition to Gospel*, 133–48; Dibelius, *Formgeschichte des Evangeliums*, 131–46.

113. In *Fresh Approach* (58–59), Dibelius says that it was the aim of Matthew's Gospel to interweave with Mark's account "a large part of the tradition of Jesus' words which was current in the church—most of which was in the form found in the 'Sayings Source' Q." See Dibelius, *Tradition to Gospel*, 233; Dibelius, *Formgeschichte des Evangeliums*, 234; Dibelius, *Fresh Approach*, 53–56; and Dibelius, *Sermon on the Mount*, 26–28 for brief discussions of the two-source theory and the Q hypothesis. Dibelius comments that no matter how helpful the Q hypothesis may be, in other ways it still "remains an unsolved problem."

114. Dibelius, *Tradition to Gospel*, 237; Dibelius, *Formgeschichte des Evangeliums*, 239.

than serving as illustrations or examples for sermons, the exhortations were passed down as a sort of Christian Halakha as a means of guiding or directing one's life,[115] with the so-called Sermon on the Mount as the paramount example:[116]

> It is perfectly certain that the sayings were not brought together at first for the sake of their Christological interest. Indeed, the passages which are to be claimed for Q show themselves on the whole to have a completely different interest. It is the same interest as we have . . . observed in Paul, viz. *the sayings of Jesus were originally gathered together for a hortatory end*, to give the Churches advice, help, and commandment by means of the Master's words. This typical interest was dominant both in the origin of this special source and also in the gathering together of the words of Jesus everywhere. The nature of the formulation and of the collection prove this interest.[117]

Tales, according to Dibelius, are like paradigms in that they are independent stories that are complete in themselves; however, tales have a completely different stylistic character. "There is found here [in Tales] that descriptiveness which we missed in the Paradigms; that breadth, which a paradigmatic application makes impossible; that technique, which reveals a certain pleasure in the narrative itself; and that topical character, which brings these narratives nearer to the corresponding categories as they were to be found in the world outside Christianity."[118] The telltale characteristic of tales is that they are marked by the Evangelist's addition of richer content and other narrative elements (e.g., dialogue) such that the stories take on what Dibelius calls a "secular motive" or coloring.[119] The stories in the Synoptic Gospels that Dibelius places into this category are, in the main, the miracle stories. This is because the miracle stories are not necessarily told for didactic purposes; that is, "it is not Jesus as the herald of the Kingdom of

---

115. See Dibelius, *Sermon on the Mount*, 28.
116. See now Dibelius, *Sermon on the Mount*, 13–30.
117. Dibelius, *Tradition to Gospel*, 246 (italics original); Dibelius, *Formgeschichte des Evangeliums*, 247 (with emphasis on "man hat die Jesussprüche ursprünglich zu paränetischem Zweck gesammelt").
118. Dibelius, *Tradition to Gospel*, 70; Dibelius, *Formgeschichte des Evangeliums*, 66–67. "Above all else [tales] rest upon the *breadth* of the description . . . and makes one think of writers who understand their art and who love to exercise it" (Dibelius, *Tradition to Gospel*, 76 [italics original]; Dibelius, *Formgeschichte des Evangeliums*, 73).
119. Dibelius, *Tradition to Gospel*, 78, 99; Dibelius, *Formgeschichte des Evangeliums*, 74, 96.

God with His signs, demands, threats and promises, who stands at the center of these stories, but Jesus the miracle-worker."[120] Whereas "the 'old' stories [i.e., paradigms] aim to preach the gospel; these [i.e., tales] try to picture Jesus as the greatest wonder-worker of the time," and this became important over time as the followers of Jesus began to venture out into the world asserting their claims about Jesus and, as they went, encountered others who claimed to work miracles.[121]

Legends[122] in Dibelius's scheme are stories that describe the deeds of holy men or women, with particular attention given to the human elements (e.g., circumstances, other human participants) associated with their piety (even if their lives are said to have been guided and protected by God), as if the storyteller was following a "law of biographical analogy."[123] In this way, they are distinct from paradigms and tales:

> The essential interest is not directed toward the greatness of a more or less miraculous fact, as in the case of the Tales, but to the edifying character of the whole. But it is not the message by word or by deed which is intended to be edifying, as in the Paradigms, so much as the religious-ness and sanctity of the hero together with the protection granted him by God. . . . above all, his life is decorated with characters and scenes which correspond to the very nature of legendary biography.[124]

It should be noted that, according to Dibelius, it is rare in the Synoptic Gospels to find legends that are strictly about Jesus. One exception to this may be the story of Jesus when he was twelve years old (Luke 2:41–50).[125] Instead, legends tend to focus on others besides Jesus. Dibelius explains:

---

120. Dibelius, *Tradition to Gospel*, 79–80; Dibelius, *Formgeschichte des Evangeliums*, 76.

121. Dibelius, *Message of Jesus Christ*, 168. Dibelius investigates whether rabbinic personal legends (stories about miracles effected by Rabbis) are appropriate analogues for what he describes as tales. He admits that the connection is tenuous, but that despite the tension, there are still a few similarities between them. See Dibelius, *Tradition to Gospel*, 148–51; Dibelius, *Formgeschichte des Evangeliums*, 146–49.

122. On the question of historicity in relation to legends, see Dibelius, *Message of Jesus Christ*, 174–77; Dibelius, *Tradition to Gospel*, 108–9; Dibelius, *Formgeschichte des Evangeliums*, 105–7.

123. Dibelius, *Tradition to Gospel*, 108; Dibelius, *Formgeschichte des Evangeliums*, 105–6. See also Dibelius, *Message of Jesus Christ*, 174–77.

124. Dibelius, *Tradition to Gospel*, 108; Dibelius, *Formgeschichte des Evangeliums*, 105.

125. Dibelius, *Tradition to Gospel*, 106–7; Dibelius, *Formgeschichte des Evangeliums*, 103–4.

The gospel does not present Jesus as a "pious" man, but as a man with divine authority, who by virtue of this authority is in a position to disregard the traditional standards of piety. Certain features of the Passion Narrative, especially in its Lucan revision, would of course be understood as showing how Jesus manifested heroic human virtue in the midst of suffering. But elsewhere the narratives from the period of his life-work are silent regarding his virtue or piety; they have nothing to say of his participation in the temple worship; they make no mention of his prayers—what we read about them is from the editorial connections supplied by the evangelists. And it is significant of the attitude of the old narrators that we have only one legend in the New Testament that tries to describe Jesus' piety; and this relates to his childhood, i.e., to the period concerning which the preaching the gospel knew nothing and had naught to say. It is the story of the twelve-year-old Jesus in the temple. Yet even here the main interest is not the participation of the child in the discussions of the learned, but the motive that led him to remain in the sanctuary; and this is not designed to suggest the love of a pious soul for the temple, but rather Jesus' peculiar right to be in the house of his Father.[126]

So what does *Formgeschichte* reveal to Dibelius that shapes how he reads the Gospel of Luke? Before specifically addressing this question, it must be noted that *Formgeschichte* points out that each of the types of forms appears in each of the Synoptic Gospels.[127] One might expect Dibelius to take to counting or to statistical analysis of these findings as a means of establishing claims of lesser to greater accretion of the tradition contained in the Synoptic accounts, where a greater number of paradigms and fewer tales and legends might perhaps suggest less accretion and greater "purity," and vice versa. However, Dibelius seems little concerned with raw or normed tallies; instead, he remains centrally interested in the extent to which the Evangelists adapt the stories and/or fashion contextual frameworks into which they fit the story. So then, rather than pointing out that Mark has three times as many paradigms as Luke and that Luke as twice as many legends as Mark and subsequently judging Mark to be a better steward of the forms of tradition at his disposal (or some such judgment), Dibelius,

126. Dibelius, *Message of Jesus Christ*, 178.
127. See now Dibelius, *Message of Jesus Christ*, 9–120.

instead, looks at the manner in which each Evangelist uses and/or modifies the traditional forms and fits them together—sometimes fabricating contexts or connections between them—into a more or less unitary story as a means of showing how each developed the tradition and what may have motivated that development.[128]

Dibelius notes a number of idiosyncrasies in Luke especially compared to Mark but also with Matthew. He begins with a look at Luke's handling of paradigms and paraenesis (including the parables) and argues that Luke has styled many of the sayings into "chria-like formulations."[129] Chriae are short, pointed, or pithy sayings with seemingly universal meaning and significance, which are attributed to a particular person and derived from a particular situation;[130] they are fairly common stock in the biographies of philosophers,[131] and often they were used to create connections—albeit sometimes very loose connections—between independent short stories or sayings.[132] Dibelius lists six parables to which, he says, Luke supplied "data of a situation in the way that the Chriae would have given them in sentences";[133] I summarize four here:

- At Luke 10:29 a νομικός (i.e., an interpreter of the Law) who had attempted to test Jesus but ended up looking foolish, in an attempt to justify himself, asks a pithy, universalizing question—"And who is my neighbor?"—that Luke uses to connect this story to the so-called Parable of the Good Samaritan.

- At Luke 12:13 someone (τις) in the crowd calls upon Jesus to tell his brother to divide the inheritance with him, to which Jesus responds with the pointed question, "Who made me

---

128. This is one instance where Dibelius's emphasis on finding rabbinic and Greek analogies becomes important. In one sense, the validity of his method disintegrates if he cannot show that tradition outside Christianity did not develop in similar ways.

129. Dibelius, *Tradition to Gospel*, 161; Dibelius, *Formgeschichte des Evangeliums*, 161.

130. Dibelius, *Formgeschichte des Evangeliums*, 150: "Es ist die Wiedergabe eines kurzen pointierten Ausspruchs von allgemeiner Bedeutung, der auf eine bestimmte Person zurückgeführt und aus einer bestimmten Situation abgeleitet wird." See also Dibelius, *Tradition to Gospel*, 152.

131. Dibelius discusses biographies of philosophers written by Diogenes and Philostratus as well as the biography of Demonax by Lucian. He also included those occurring in the anecdotes of Socrates that are preserved in Xenophon's *Memorabilia* (Dibelius, *Tradition to Gospel*, 153–56; Dibelius, *Formgeschichte des Evangeliums*, 151–56).

132. Dibelius makes this observation in commenting on a portion of Philostratus's biography of Herod Atticus (Dibelius, *Tradition to Gospel*, 154–55; Dibelius, *Formgeschichte des Evangeliums*, 153–54).

133. Dibelius, *Tradition to Gospel*, 161; Dibelius, *Formgeschichte des Evangeliums*, 161.

judge or arbitrator over you [two]?" which Luke connects to a general, sweeping saying of Jesus about the dangers of covetousness: "Watch out and protect yourselves from every form of covetousness, for a person's life is not in the abundance of anything from among his possessions."

- At Luke 14:15, following a parable to the fellows who had been invited to eat in the home of the rulers of the Pharisees and a parable to the one who had invited him, Luke has one who was reclining with the group make the laconic remark, "Whoever will eat a meal in the kingdom of God is honorable" (μακάριος), which connects the previous sayings to the parable in verses 16–24.

- At Luke 15:1–2, seeing that many tax collectors and deviants were coming to hear Jesus, Luke says that both the Pharisees and the scribes were gossiping (διεγόγγυζον)[134] about it stating, "He receives deviants and he eats with them."

Dibelius also claims that there are a "large number of cases" (he counts eight, but does not explain why he considers this a "large number," again demonstrating that he is not overly interested in statistical analysis) of these chria-like formulations in which Luke makes the words of Jesus serve as answers or responses to others' short questions or assertions, such as at Luke 11:27–28, about which Dibelius comments:

> A woman in the crowd cries, "Blessed is the womb that bare thee and the breasts which thou didst suck"; Jesus answers, "Blessed are they that hear the word of God and keep it." Whereas we receive the impression here and in xiii, I, xix, 39 that the situation may have been handed down to the evangelist and that only the pregnant style is due to him. . . . We see that Luke artificially created constructions of that character.[135]

Perhaps more significant in the shaping of Dibelius's view of Luke's Gospel account is Luke's use of legends. *Formgeschichte* identifies the

---

134. See Richard L. Rohrbaugh, "Gossip in the New Testament," in *Social Scientific Models for Interpreting the Bible: Essays by the Context Group in Honor of Bruce J. Malina*, ed. John J. Pilch, BibInt 53 (Atlanta: SBL, 2001), 239–59.
135. Dibelius, *Tradition to Gospel*, 162; Dibelius, *Formgeschichte des Evangeliums*, 162.

following stories as legends, according to Dibelius:[136] the Virgin Mary (Luke 1:26–35, 38); the shepherds (Luke 2:4–19); Simeon (Luke 2:25–32); Jesus in the temple at the age of twelve (Luke 2:41–49); the baptism of Jesus (Mark 1:9–11); the contest with Satan (Matt. 4:1–10; Luke 4:1–12); the transfiguration (Mark 9:2–9); the great catch of fish (Luke 5:3–6, 8–10); Zacchaeus (Luke 19:1–9); the entry into Jerusalem (Mark 11:1–10); the empty tomb (Mark 16:1–6, 8); and the walk to Emmaus (Luke 24:13–21, 25–32). Notably, the majority of these are from Luke's account, which suggests that Luke is doing something different with the traditional materials that he was handling than what Mark and Matthew were doing. The stories in this list are, it appears, the "purer" legendary forms; there are additional stories that, in Dibelius's view, have been transformed into legends by Luke.[137] An example of this is the pericope about Jesus returning to his hometown (Mark 6:1–6 and Luke 4:16–30). Mark's version of this story is categorized by Dibelius as a paradigm with some amount of transformation of its ending by Mark; however, the core portion of the story is brief, and it ends with a saying of Jesus that, in Dibelius's view, is intended to edify.[138] Yet Dibelius thinks that Luke heavily modifies this story in his account. Although the whole narrative is "by no means new as a legend," since it follows the basic skeleton of the story as laid out by Mark (i.e., the amazement, the offense, and the saying about the despised prophet),[139] Luke transforms it into the form of a legend in several ways. First, he has the annoyance that Jesus causes result in an angry mob that drags him to the "brow of the hill" (ὀφρύος τοῦ ὄρους) in order to throw him off, yet, in the style of a genuine legend, Jesus miraculously escapes. The bit about the despised prophet is located more centrally in Luke's story, "as it would not correspond with the violent conclusion of the action."[140] Additionally, Luke leaves connected with the saying about the despised prophet the maxim "Physician, heal yourself," which is extraordinarily similar to what is found in the late second or early third century P.Oxy. I 1.30–35.[141] In

---

136. This list is based on Dibelius, *Message of Jesus Christ*, 107–20.
137. For these other legendary stories, see the discussion of legends in Dibelius, *Tradition to Gospel*, 104–32; Dibelius, *Formgeschichte des Evangeliums*, 101–29.
138. Dibelius, *Tradition to Gospel*, 109; Dibelius, *Formgeschichte des Evangeliums*, 106–7.
139. Dibelius, *Tradition to Gospel*, 110; Dibelius, *Formgeschichte des Evangeliums*, 106–7.
140. Dibelius, *Tradition to Gospel*, 110; Dibelius, *Formgeschichte des Evangeliums*, 106–7.
141. P.Oxy. I 1.30–35: "Jesus says, 'A prophet is not received in his homeland, and neither does a doctor do cures among those who know him'" (my translation; see Dibelius, *Tradition to Gospel*, 110;

the end, as Dibelius sees it, the point of this story is to provide at least partial insight into the human grounds for the rejection of Jesus.[142]

Setting aside for now a critique of Dibelius's model, method, and results, it is important to point out how these findings shaped his thinking about the Gospel of Luke. If one reads through *Tradition to Gospel* (*Formgeschichte des Evangeliums*) too quickly, she or he may miss the connections that Dibelius makes between chriae (and chria-like formulations) and legends on the one hand and biography on the other.[143] When Luke develops the tradition that he is working with to present the sayings of Jesus as chria-like and other stories in the form of legends, he follows what Dibelius calls a "law of biographical analogy,"[144] which results in a work that is "essentially of a more literary character than the other two Synoptic Gospels."[145] In sum,

> [Luke's gospel] is introduced by a genuine prologue in the form of a dedication to a certain Theophilus. Both the existence of this prologue and its wording correspond with the literary usage of the time, and this correspondence extends to the choice of expressions. By his use of Mark we perceive, and for his use of Q we may conclude, that in spite of all connections of content, Luke transformed his sources by using more refined and educated modes of expression. . . . He makes an attempt at genuine style, firstly in the framework into which he places the tradition. He ventures to bind together matters which are distinct from each other, e.g. he points out at the end of the Temptation that the devil leaves Jesus until an opportune moment, and that he takes possession of Judas at the beginning of the Passion. He prepares for the appearance of the women beneath the cross by introducing them as fellow-travelers of Jesus even in Galilee (Luke viii, 1–3). By interpolations he can set up historical connections, e.g. he concludes the story of the Baptist with a notice of his arrest (iii, 19, 20), introduces the public ministry of Jesus with detailed chronological data (iii, 1–2), and begins his account

---

Dibelius, *Formgeschichte des Evangeliums*, 107). Dibelius did not know at the time that this papyrus is a fragment of the Greek version of the *Gospel of Thomas*.

142. Dibelius, *Tradition to Gospel*, 110; Dibelius, *Formgeschichte des Evangeliums*, 106–7.

143. See Dibelius, *Tradition to Gospel*, 108–9, 155–56; Dibelius, *Formgeschichte des Evangeliums*, 105–6, 151–56.

144. Dibelius, *Tradition to Gospel*, 108–9; Dibelius, *Formgeschichte des Evangeliums*, 106 ("Gesetz der biographischen Analogie").

145. Dibelius, *Fresh Approach*, 62.

of Pilate by giving the points of accusation which had been brought against Jesus (xx, 2).[146]

All of these things weighed together lead Dibelius to conclude that Luke, in his Gospel account, "endeavors to employ the material offered him by his sources in the manner of biography."[147] This is the kind of "sociological result" that *Formgeschichte* was intended to reveal.

The *Sitz im Leben* of the Acts of the Apostles

Although Luke connects the Acts of the Apostles with his Gospel account (see Acts 1:1–2), Dibelius argues that the two texts are substantially different enough that "both these works by the same author do not belong in one class."[148] "Acts is dedicated by the same author to the same Theophilus, and is *even more literary than the Gospel.*"[149] In the Gospel account "it was a case of framing and piecing together fragments of tradition" that had taken shape through the preaching of the earliest disciples so that Luke "could . . . restrict himself to little interpolations, chiefly of an editorial nature."[150] However, such is not the case with Acts. Here, Luke "has employed a much higher standard of writing than in the Gospel,"[151] and the primary reason Dibelius gives for this is that Luke had very little traditional material with which to work in regard to the progress of the Christian message and the concomitant growth of the church from Jerusalem to Rome.[152] He writes,

> In writing the Gospel [Luke] had predecessors, whose work he used and whose technique of piecing together the tradition provided a model also for his more reflective and pragmatic style; indeed, one of them, Mark, had even, to a fair extent, authoritatively determined the sequence of the Lukan narrative. Of predecessors of the Acts of the Apostles we know nothing. Moreover, its special plan is not evident in

---

146. Dibelius, *Fresh Approach*, 62–63.
147. Dibelius, *Fresh Approach*, 63.
148. Dibelius, "Style Criticism in the Book of Acts," in *Studies in the Acts of the Apostles*, 2; Dibelius, "Stilkritisches zur Apostelgeschichte," in *Aufsätze zur Apostelgeschichte*, 10.
149. Dibelius, *Fresh Approach*, 261 (italics added).
150. Dibelius, "Style Criticism," 2.
151. Dibelius, "Style Criticism," 2; Dibelius, "Stilkritisches," 10: "Vor allem hat sich Lukas in der Apostelgeschichte in viel höherem Grade schriftstellerisch betätigt als im Evangelium." See also Gasque, *History of Interpretation of Acts*, 203.
152. Dibelius, *Fresh Approach*, 261–62. See also Gasque, *History of Interpretation of Acts*, 203.

itself, and its main theme—somewhat in the sense of 1:8—one could imagine treated quite differently. From all of this we may conclude that Luke was the first to set himself to the task of describing the progress of the gospel from Jerusalem to Rome, and that we thus have before us in Acts a work of more individual stamp than the Gospel of Luke.[153]

Without the traditional material acting as both guide and restraint, it was up to Luke to provide many of the details about the spread of the gospel and growth of the church. How he proceeded to do so, at least insofar as Dibelius describes it, explains more fully why Dibelius sees Acts as possessing the literary character that propels it to the brink of "'great' literature" (*"großen" Literatur*).[154] Dibelius's assertion in the preceding quotation about what Luke was trying to accomplish with Acts must not be missed: "Luke . . . set himself to the task of describing the progress of the gospel from Jerusalem to Rome." This raises an important question for Dibelius: Was Luke attempting to write a piece of contemporary history such that it should be taken as proper literature? The answer to this question has important methodological implications much in the same way that the reconstructed *Sitz im Leben* of the early believers' preaching (*Predigt*) had on Dibelius's method for reading Luke's Gospel account.

Initially, Dibelius points out that Acts appears to "present pragmatically and evidently according to a plan a portion of contemporary history."[155] He lists as evidence for this such things as its "literary prologue" (Acts 1:1–2) and the speeches (*Reden*) that Luke "puts . . . into the mouths of its heroes."[156] He notes contrapuntally, however, that Acts is "not really uniform in style" and that, although Luke works hard to give the events he writes about a sense of universal importance on par with other significant events of world history, these events, nevertheless, remain legendary given that they were relatively minor and their import was limited to a movement that was, at the time, relatively obscure.[157] Thus, on the one hand, Dibelius appraises Acts as something less than a proper literary production, yet on the

153. Dibelius, "Style Criticism," 3; Dibelius, "Stilkritisches," 11.
154. See Dibelius, "The First Christian Historian," in *Studies in the Acts of the Apostles*, 124; Dibelius, "Der Erste Christliche Historiker," in *Aufsätze zur Apostelgeschichte*, 109.
155. Dibelius, "Style Criticism," 1; Dibelius, "Stilkritisches," 9.
156. Dibelius, "Style Criticism," 1; Dibelius, "Stilkritisches," 9.
157. Dibelius, "Style Criticism," 2; Dibelius, "Stilkritisches," 9. Note Gunkel's influence here; recall how he distinguished between history proper and legend.

other hand—primarily because he views the speeches in Acts as literary compositions of Luke and secondarily because of Luke's use of the legend form (and a few tales)—he considers Acts to be "*the most literary book in the New Testament.*"[158]

Stilkritik and Dibelius's Take on the Acts of the Apostles

To garner support for this view, Dibelius turns again to his methodology, but in dealing with Acts he cannot apply *Formgeschichte* in the same way that he had with the Gospel of Luke. There, he aimed to demonstrate that preaching was the primary mechanism in the formation of the oldest tradition about Jesus, and that the Evangelists used that material to assemble their Gospel accounts—and in so doing, further developed the tradition to a greater or lesser extent. The least accreted form of the tradition with which the Evangelists worked was the paradigm (stories of Jesus's deeds); second to this was paraenesis (the teachings of Jesus). Both of these appear in Luke's Gospel, but, according to Dibelius, they are conspicuously rare in Acts.[159] In the latter, the function of these forms—evangelism and instruction—was taken up and almost completely subsumed by the speeches and legends.[160] This requires that *Formgeschichte* be recalibrated somewhat so that it focuses more on *style* than on *form*. In order to highlight this recalibration, Dibelius tweaks the name of his method and calls it *Stilkritik* (style criticism).[161]

In regards to the speeches in Acts, Dibelius takes the view that they must have been invented by Luke rather than being word-for-word reproductions or even condensed accounts[162] of speech material that he had in his possession. Because he cannot imagine how Luke would have gained access to any portion of the speech material, let alone the actual word-for-word accounts, he adopts what some have called the "Thucydidean view."[163] In this view, Luke

---

158. Dibelius, *Fresh Approach*, 262 (italics original).
159. Dibelius, "Style Criticism," 4; Dibelius, "Stilkritisches," 11.
160. Dibelius, "Style Criticism," 4; Dibelius, "Stilkritisches," 11.
161. *Stilkritik* is not a completely new methodology; in fact, Dibelius has really only adjusted the aperture of the *Formgeschichte* lens so that literary style is given more focus than form. Of course, form is still significant, as the discussion of the speech and legend forms demonstrates.
162. See F. F. Bruce, *The Speeches in the Acts of the Apostles* (London: Tyndale, 1942).
163. See now Martin Dibelius, "The Speeches in Acts and Ancient Historiography," in *Studies in the Acts of the Apostles*, 138–85; Dibelius, "Die Reden der Apostelgeschichte und die antike Geschichtsschreibung," in *Aufsätze zur Apostelgeschichte*, 120–62. Others define the so-called Thucydidean view differently.

plays a role closer to that of an ancient historian or, more specifically, historiographer,[164] who, according to Dibelius, "was not aware
of any obligation to reproduce only, or even preferably, the text of
a speech which was actually made; perhaps [because] he did not
know whether a speech was in fact made at the time; sometimes
he did know, but he did not know the text of it; perhaps [because]
he could not have known if the speech was made, for example, in
the enemy's camp to a limited audience."[165] Speeches were written
for reasons other than tedious historical record keeping including,
but not limited to, providing greater context to enable a necessary insight into a specific situation; marking the significance of an
historical moment, without trepidation in regards to going beyond
the facts of that moment; providing insight into a particular character; to introduce explanations of a situation from the mouth of a
significant character.[166] These serve the larger purpose of the historical narrative, and, in the case of Acts, this purpose appears to be not
only to tell of the events but to convince Theophilus and his group
that the spread of the gospel and the growth of the church is really
the work of God through the followers of Jesus, especially the likes
of Peter and Paul.[167]

Dibelius grounds this perspective about speeches in a statement
made by Thucydides in 1.22.1. In his reading of Thucydides,[168] Dibelius understands him to say that it was difficult for him to remember exactly what was said (χαλεπὸν τὴν ἀκρίβειαν αὐτὴν τῶν
λεχθέντων διαμνημονεῦσαι), so "he had therefore allowed the
speakers to express themselves in a way he thought individuals would
have found it necessary to speak on the subject to be discussed."[169] He
goes on to say that Thucydides's phrase ξύμπασα γνώμη (roughly "the

164. Historiography is the writing of history in narrative form/arrangement, usually guided by some agenda or ideology (see Tate, *Interpreting the Bible*, 168–69).
165. Dibelius, "Speeches in Acts," 139; Dibelius, "Die Reden der Apostelgeschichte," 121.
166. Dibelius, "Speeches in Acts," 139–40; Dibelius, "Die Reden der Apostelgeschichte," 121.
167. Or, as Dibelius puts it, Acts "is above all a *religious* book," in which Luke "is trying to show the powers of the Christian spirit with which the persons in his narrative are charged, and which he wished to make live in his readers"; additionally, "the book was intended . . . to serve Christendom as an apologetic writing" (*Fresh Approach*, 265).
168. For an excellent coverage of the difficulties surrounding the interpretation of Thucydides's statement, see Stanley E. Porter, "Thucydides 1.22.1 and Speeches in Acts: Is There a Thucydidean View?" in *Studies in the Greek New Testament: Theory and Practice*, SBG 6 (New York: Peter Lang, 1996), 173–93 and sources cited there.
169. Dibelius, "Speeches in Acts," 141; Dibelius, "Die Reden der Apostelgeschichte," 122.

general scope [of a speech]"),[170] the meaning of which is debated,[171] refers not to the general content of the authentic speeches but the literary or historiographical intention of the reconstructed speeches.[172] In short, taking Thucydides as a comparative analogue—just like he used Greek chriae and rabbinic legends to substantiate a "law of biographical analogy"—Dibelius concludes that Luke, like ancient historians, did not operate by the modern concern of recording the precise details of speeches as they are given; rather, he invented the speeches, using them to achieve his desired literary and/or historiographical purpose.[173]

In regard to legends, recall that these are "pious tales of pious persons"[174] that are told for edifying purposes and that zero in on the "religiousness and sanctity of the hero together with the protection granted him by God."[175] Dibelius highlights a number of legends from Acts. The raising of Tabitha (Acts 9:36–42) first appears to be a tale, since it focuses on the miracle and gives some particular details regarding how it was enacted (Peter prayed and spoke to Tabitha's body, v. 40). However, the story takes personal interest in Peter (primarily) and Tabitha and is rounded out with the statement that the miracle "became known throughout Joppa, and many believed in the Lord" (v. 42); these two features indicate that the story "is entirely calculated to edify," which *Stilkritik* categorizes as a legend.

Dibelius's take on the conversion of Cornelius (Acts 10:1–11:18) is noteworthy. The story begins with Cornelius seeing a vision in which the angel praises the Gentile centurion for offering prayers and alms, which have "ascended as a memorial before God" (v. 4). This befits the form of legend, focusing as it does on the piety of Cornelius, as does the content of verses 9–26. Peter's speech in 10:34–43, a "literary elaboration" according to Dibelius, ends up functioning here not as a proof that the mission to the Gentiles was justified (although it appears that the story is alluded to later in Acts for this purpose [15:7–11]) but as a testimony of God's effective power and, it may be added, a testimony in regard to the piety of Cornelius.[176]

---

170. See LSJ, s.v. "ξύμπασα."
171. See Porter, "Thucydides," 189–91.
172. Dibelius, "Speeches in Acts," 141; Dibelius, "Die Reden der Apostelgeschichte," 122. See also Porter, "Thucydides," 175–76.
173. See Dibelius, "Speeches in Acts," 144; Dibelius, "Die Reden der Apostelgeschichte," 124–25.
174. Dibelius, *Message of Jesus Christ*, 174.
175. Dibelius, *Tradition to Gospel*, 108; Dibelius, *Formgeschichte des Evangeliums*, 105.
176. See Dibelius, "Style Criticism," 13–14; Dibelius, "Stilkritisches," 19.

Stilkritik would categorize several other stories in the central portion of Acts as legends, among which are: the story of Ananias and Sapphira (Acts 5:1–11); the conversion of the eunuch (Acts 8:26–39); the death of Herod (Acts 12:20–23); Peter's release (Acts 12:5–17); and the release of Paul and Silas from prison in Philippi (Acts 16:25–34).[177] But the question remains: Why would Luke choose to write in this manner? Here is where Dibelius, again taking a constructive approach, offers a possible *Sitz im Leben: both* Luke's Gospel *and* Acts were written not just for the humble Christian community who were likely generally uninterested in literary stylings but also for a circle of people of higher social standing who would be more likely to take interest in literary flourish:

> We must reckon that Luke's gospel had from the beginning (speaking in a modern idiom) two market outlets: it was intended as a book to be read by the Christian community, in the same way as Mark, Matthew, and other books now lost to us (the πολλοί of the prologue to Luke), but also, at the same time, intended for the private reading of people of literary education.[178]

In the end, Dibelius's style criticism of Acts demonstrates, at least as Dibelius sees it, that it occupies a unique place in the diachrony of Christian tradition. Not being tethered to traditional materials as he was when writing his Gospel, Luke acts more as an independent author. He utilizes literary forms such as legends (as well as a few tales) and, in Dibelius's view, follows a method of speech writing that befits ancient historiography. As a result, he writes a document that is on the very edge of literature proper. This is done with his audience in view, which includes both the honorable Theophilus (and persons of higher status) and the humble Christian community. The purpose of Acts was to demonstrate God's activity in the world through the narrative of the spread of the gospel and the growth of the church by the power of the Holy Spirit. Acts, thus, "Signifies a long stride in the evolution of primitive Christian literature."[179]

---

177. See Dibelius, "Style Criticism," 14–23; Dibelius, "Stilkritisches," 21–28.
178. Dibelius, "Speeches in Acts," 147; Dibelius, "Die Reden der Apostelgeschichte," 127.
179. Dibelius, *Fresh Approach*, 266.

CONCLUSION

The goal of this chapter has been to discuss how Martin Dibelius viewed both the Gospel of Luke and the Acts of the Apostles and to show how his theoretical upbringing in the *religionsgeschichtliche Schule* shaped the way he approached these texts and considered their meaning. At the same time, Dibelius certainly cleared a path for himself, and this is most clearly seen in his constructive perspective and the particulars of his *Formgeschichte* methodology. While still fitting into the broader History of Religion approach, Dibelius focused his attention on the question of how the Christian tradition took shape prior to the Synoptists' work, as well as how these Evangelists developed that traditional material in their Gospel accounts. Dibelius believed Luke to be the most literary of the Evangelists, utilizing a style that pushed the Gospel nearer to a biography and the Acts nearer to historiography.

Over the years, scholarly opinion regarding Dibelius's treatments of Luke and Acts has oscillated from positive to cautious to negative and back. Not surprisingly, when his work first appeared on the scholarly scene, especially at a time when the *Religionsgeschichte* paradigm was in vogue, it was heralded as particularly insightful, providing both a sharper image of the earliest teachings of Jesus and the earliest believers and a fuller picture of how Christian tradition developed over time. As time has passed and a number of the key tenets of the *religionsgeschichtliche Schule* have been scrutinized and challenged, claims that Dibelius's insights are perhaps interesting but outmoded have increased.

Perhaps, however, the weight of Dibelius's contributions to studies in Luke–Acts is better measured on the basis of how their impact has continued to live on in studies of Luke and Acts. As Hanson has pointed out,

> His form-critical work was foundational for Gospel studies, which moved on after the war to redaction criticism. His focus on literary aspects of the book of Acts was a precursor to much of the work in New Testament literary criticism today. And questions of setting in life (*Sitz im Leben*) were important for laying the foundation of current emphases in social history and social-scientific criticism. . . . And while the exegesis of the book of Acts continues, it does so on the shoulders of Dibelius and the work presented in [his essays on Acts].[180]

---

180. Hanson, "Editor's Foreward," in Dibelius, *The Book of Acts*, ix.

With specific regard to both Luke and Acts, it is rare that a scholarly study or commentary comes along that does not engage Dibelius's work. In fact, many would argue that it is impossible for a work to ignore Dibelius and still be considered "scholarly."

HENRY JOEL CADBURY AND THE STUDY OF LUKE–ACTS

Osvaldo Padilla

Henry J. Cadbury's contribution to New Testament scholarship is discussed within a period called "The Zenith of Enlightenment Criticism" by William Baird in his standard work on the history of New Testament research.[1] This is a strong claim in light of the fact that in the same period Baird places luminaries such as C. H. Dodd and T. W. Manson, whose works were characterized not just by rare depth of development but also by breadth of contributions to different aspects of New Testament studies. A close look at Cadbury's productive career, however, does suggest that he belongs in this group. Consider the following accomplishments:

- President of the Society of Biblical Literature (1936)
- President of the *Studiorum Novi Testamenti Societas* (1957–1958)
- Revised Standard Version committee
- Numerous books and essays on Luke–Acts, the life of Jesus, and New Testament research
- Hollis Chair of Divinity at Harvard for twenty years[2]

---

1. William Baird, *History of New Testament Research, Volume Three: From C. H. Dodd to Hans Dieter Betz* (Minneapolis: Fortress, 2013), 7–62.
2. On these accomplishments see further Baird, *History of New Testament Research*, 17.

Bullet point four represents original, careful work published in prestigious venues, and could thus be significantly enlarged. For example, I could list the numerous, seminal contributions Cadbury made to the volumes of the momentous *Beginnings of Christianity*, contributions which—although requiring some updating now—continue to play a significant role in contemporary research, particularly Luke–Acts. I will come back to Cadbury's contribution to this series.[3]

The chapter at hand explores Cadbury's influence on New Testament scholarship primarily by discussing his contribution to the study of Luke–Acts. I will proceed in the following manner: (1) a biographical sketch of Cadbury's life, (2) contributions to Luke–Acts, and (3) his conception of scientific scholarship.

BIOGRAPHICAL SKETCH[4]

Henry Joel Cadbury was born in Philadelphia on December 1, 1883, to parents who were devoted to the Religious Society of Friends, that is, Quakers.[5] They could trace their roots to Quaker thought back to mid-seventeenth-century England. Prior to Cadbury's birth, Quakers in Philadelphia had been split into two factions. On the one hand, there were the so-called Orthodox Quakers, who had been influenced by Protestantism in general and the English evangelical movement specifically. On the other hand, there were the more old-fashioned Quakers, who believed that some of the ideas of the Orthodox were not in keeping with traditional Quakerism.[6] Cadbury's family belonged to the Orthodox wing of Philadelphia Quakers.

Under the preaching of Joseph John Gurney, a more evangelically inclined teacher from England, the Orthodox Quakers received

---

3. For now I list the major contributions by Henry Cadbury in F. J. Foakes Jackson and Kirsopp Lake, eds., *The Beginnings of Christianity, Part One: The Acts of the Apostles*, 5 vols. (London: Macmillan, 1920–1933), vol. 2: "The Greek and Jewish Traditions of Writing History," 7–29; "The Tradition," 209–64; "Commentary on the Preface to Luke," 489–510; vol. 4: "English Translation and Commentary" (cowritten with Kirsopp Lake); vol. 5: "The Hellenists," 59–73; "Roman Law and the Trial of Paul," 297–337; "The Speeches in Acts," 402–27.

4. For this section, I draw on the following: Margaret Hope Bacon, *Let This Life Speak: The Legacy of Henry Joel Cadbury* (Philadelphia: University of Pennsylvania Press, 1987); Paul Anderson, "Henry Joel Cadbury," in *The Routledge Encyclopedia of the Historical Jesus*, ed. Craig A. Evans (New York: Routledge, 2008), 85–86; Haverford College Library, Haverford, PA, Special Collections, Quaker Collection, Henry J. Cadbury papers, Coll. No. 1121.

5. I will return in Section 3 to Quaker history and provide more information on the type of Quakerism that was manifest in Henry Cadbury.

6. See Bacon, *Let This Life Speak*, 2–3.

teaching that was more in keeping with Protestantism.[7] For example, Gurney was more inclined than many Quakers to view revelation as coming from Scripture. Furthermore, his view of the death of Jesus as redemptive was nearer Protestantism than other Quakers. We are not sure of Cadbury's judgment of the Orthodox Quakers when he was a child. Presumably, he followed his parents' view on the matter. However, as Cadbury developed intellectually, he began to follow the more traditional Quaker path, where as a matter of principle praxis came before doctrine. By the time Cadbury reached adolescence he no longer believed in the divinity of Christ nor in salvation as stemming from faith in Christ. In the words of Bacon, Cadbury began "to feel that obedience to the teaching and example of Jesus was for him the prime emphasis of the life of the spirit."[8] We will come back to this under the third major section.

Cadbury's early education took place at Quaker institutions. At age seven he entered Penn Charter School, where he was educated in Latin, Greek, and French. He graduated at age fifteen.[9] One year later he entered Haverford College, founded in 1833 in part to function as the Quaker alternative to Yale, Harvard, and Princeton.[10] While at Haverford he was heavily influenced by the liberal Quaker Rufus Jones, who taught philosophy, psychology, and Bible.[11] In particular, Cadbury became convinced by Jones that higher criticism was the proper, objective manner of studying the Bible.[12] Jones would later become Cadbury's brother-in-law. Cadbury's further education differed from family members and other close friends in that he attended a non-Quaker institution when he entered Harvard for the MA with a concentration in classics. After graduating from Harvard, Cadbury dedicated the next four years to teaching classics at the Latin School of Chicago and Westtown School in Chester County (PA). In 1908 he returned to Harvard to begin a PhD in biblical studies. While

---

7. On Gurney and the manner in which he was influenced by orthodox Protestants, including Charles Simeon, see David E. Swift, *Joseph John Gurney: Banker, Reformer, and Quaker* (Middletown, CT: Wesleyan University Press, 1962), 125–28.
8. Bacon, *Let This Life Speak*, 7.
9. Bacon, *Let This Life Speak*, 8.
10. Bacon, *Let This Life Speak*, 8.
11. On Rufus Jones's intellectual leadership in Quakerism in North America, particularly the liberal wing of Quakerism, see Thomas D. Hamm and Isaac Barns May, "Conflict and Transformation, 1808–1920," in *The Cambridge Companion to Quakerism*, eds. Stephen W. Angell and Pink Dandelion (Cambridge: Cambridge University Press, 2018), 31–48, at 40–42.
12. Bacon, *Let This Life Speak*, 9–10.

at Harvard, Cadbury learned New Testament under William Ryder, Religion of Israel under William Arnold,[13] and New Testament introduction with the famous text-critic James Hardy Ropes.[14] Cadbury completed the PhD in 1914 with a brilliant dissertation, which would later be published and have a strong effect on Lukan studies: *The Style and Literary Method of Luke*.[15] After teaching for some time at Andover Theological Seminary and Bryn Mawr, Cadbury succeeded James Hardy Ropes as Hollis Chair of Divinity in 1934. He taught at Harvard until his retirement in 1954.[16]

A sketch of Cadbury's life would be woefully incomplete if it did not also highlight his ardent commitment to the Religious Society of Friends. Indeed, it could be argued that his contributions to the Quakers were as many, if not more, than his contributions to biblical studies. While reading Cadbury's writings as well as what others have written of him, it is not difficult to form the impression that the ideals of the Society of Friends formed the core of Henry Joel Cadbury. His devotion to activism, civil liberties, and pacifism were propelled by his commitment to the Quaker ideal.[17] I will argue under the third section below that his approach to the Bible was equally constituted by the religious views of what can broadly be called liberal Quakerism.

CONTRIBUTION TO THE STUDY OF LUKE–ACTS

With respect to the historical and literary dimensions of the Lukan corpus, there are few areas where Cadbury has not left his fingerprints. The hyphenated expression "Luke–Acts" itself probably goes back to Cadbury.[18] In light of the goal of this chapter I will concentrate on his most original and enduring contributions.

---

13. The title of the course already clearly indicates Harvard's commitment to higher criticism.
14. Bacon, *Let This Life Speak*, 15–18.
15. Bacon, *Let This Life Speak*, 27–28.
16. Baird, *History of New Testament Research*, 16–17. Baird notes that prior to 1934 Cadbury had received invitations from both Yale and Harvard but had declined both.
17. In 1947, Cadbury received the Nobel Peace Prize on behalf of the American Friends Service Committee (see Bacon, *Let This Life Speak*, 2).
18. See Cadbury, *The Making of Luke–Acts*, 2nd ed. (London: SPCK, 1968), 11, where he states that, although necessary to communicate the essential unity of the two works, he preferred to avoid hyphenated expressions due to their lack of elegance.

The Author and Language of Luke–Acts

Cadbury was interested in the literary standard of Luke's vocabulary, as the question of the nature of New Testament Greek was an important topic at the beginning of the twentieth century. Related to this was the question of the identity of the author of Luke–Acts.[19] The tradition, going back to Irenaeus in the second century, was that the author was a constant companion of Paul and the apostles and, furthermore, that Paul referred to him as "Luke, the beloved physician," in Col 4:14.[20] This tradition was not questioned until the rise of higher criticism in the eighteenth-nineteenth centuries.[21] In 1882, an apologetic and popular work to defend the traditional view of the author of Luke–Acts was written by William Hobart.[22] This erudite work compared Luke's language to that of Greek medical writers of the classical and Hellenistic periods (e.g., Hippocrates, Aretaeus, Galen), concluding that the similarities were such that Luke should also be viewed as a physician. The work convinced many, including Adolf Harnack, who stated that Hobart's work had "proved" (*beweisen*) that the author of Luke's work was familiar with the language of Greek medicine.[23] This would mean that the author of Luke–Acts was a doctor (the "beloved physician"), possessed significant education, and thus was identical with the author posited by the early church. This was a conclusion that Cadbury wanted to question in his Harvard PhD dissertation.[24]

---

19. Note that Cadbury was persuaded that the two works were written by the same author, communicating this by the use of the hyphen (see above). This conclusion remains the standard, even if the repercussions for exegesis are questioned by a thoughtful minority: Mikeal C. Parsons and Richard I. Pervo, *Rethinking the Unity of Luke and Acts* (Minneapolis: Fortress, 1993); Andrew Gregory, *The Reception of Luke and Acts in the Period Before Irenaeus* (Tübingen: Mohr Siebeck, 2003); Patricia Walters, *The Assumed Authorial Unity of Luke and Acts: A Reassessment of the Evidence*, SNTSMS 145 (Cambridge: Cambridge University Press, 2009). See also issue 4 of *JSNT* 2007, which is dedicated to the question of the unity of Luke–Acts.

20. For a detailed discussion, see Osvaldo Padilla, *The Acts of the Apostles: Interpretation, History and Theology* (Downers Grove, IL: InterVarsity, 2016), 21–37. Note that P. Bodmer 75 (P⁷⁵), which dates between 175–225, has the words εὐαγγέλιον κατὰ Λουκᾶν at the end of the Gospel of Luke. Of course, we are not sure if this is the same "Luke" that Paul and Irenaeus refer to.

21. On the critical study of the Acts of the Apostles, see W. W. Gasque, *A History of the Criticism of the Acts of the Apostles* (Tübingen: Mohr Siebeck, 1975).

22. William Hobart, *The Medical Language of St. Luke* (London: Longmans, Green, 1882). See xxix for the explicit goal of the book.

23. Reference stems from Annette Weissenrieder, *Images of Illness in the Gospel of Luke: Insights of Ancient Medical Texts* (Tübingen: Mohr Siebeck, 2003), 332–33.

24. Henry Joel Cadbury, *The Style and Literary Method of Luke*, vol. 1: *The Diction of Luke and Acts*; vol. 2: *The Treatment of Sources in the Gospel* (Cambridge, MA: Harvard University Press, 1920). By making this statement I am not thereby suggesting that Cadbury was motivated *solely* by the apologetic question regarding the authorship of Luke–Acts. It seems to me that Cadbury was

And so Cadbury had to enter the heated discussion on the nature of New Testament Greek.[25] Discoveries of papyri from Egypt at the turn of the century led Adolf Deissmann to important conclusions regarding the language of the New Testament. He believed he could give a more specific explanation of the linguistic context of the Greek, namely that its language belonged to the common (*koiné*) Greek of the Hellenistic period.[26] As far as the level of sophistication of this Greek, it fell far short of the Attic Greek of the classical period. And this would seem to contradict the repercussions of Hobart's work above in that the Greek of the New Testament (including Luke's double-work) was not written by men with a high level of education. It is in this context that we must understand Cadbury's contribution to the language of the New Testament and Luke–Acts.

Cadbury began by sharpening his method of examination. In his opinion one could not speak of the Greek of the New Testament if one first did not make careful differentiations between the different levels of Greek represented in the New Testament.[27] Cadbury made Luke–Acts the focus of his research. His reading of the data led him to conclude that Luke–Acts was an example of post-classical Greek, as was the Septuagint, which he considered to be Luke's favorite book. In this respect Cadbury made a helpful contribution to the language of the New Testament and Luke–Acts. Their Greek was not a "Holy Ghost" language or a Jewish Greek dialect from Alexandria. Rather, it was more or less the Greek of the Septuagint, itself at times overlapping with post-classical Greek.[28] In this way Cadbury anticipated—but with less nuancing—the contributions of authors like Albert Wifstrand.[29]

---

also genuinely curious about the language of the New Testament as a whole and Luke–Acts in particular.

25. A very good introduction to this subject remains Stanley E. Porter, ed., *The Language of the New Testament: Classic Essays*, JSNTSup 60 (Sheffield: Sheffield Academic, 1991).

26. Adolf Deissmann, "Hellenistic Greek with Special Consideration of the Greek Bible," in *Language of the New Testament*, 39–59.

27. Cadbury, *Style and Literary Method*, 4–5.

28. Cadbury, *Style and Literary Method*, 38–39.

29. Wifstrand viewed the Greek of Luke as imitation of the Septuagint. The Greek of the epistles of James, Peter, and Hebrews he believed stemmed from "the edifying language of the Hellenized synagogue" ("Stylistic Problems in the Epistles of James and Peter," in *Epochs and Styles: Selected Writings on the New Testament, Greek Language and Greek Culture in the Post-Classical Era*, eds. Lars Rydbeck and Stanley E. Porter, WUNT 179 [Tübingen: Mohr Siebeck, 2005], 57). As to where the Greek of the Hellenized synagogue *itself* came from: ". . . in phonology, accidence, syntax, word formation and many significations of words their language was ordinary koine" (ibid.)

What, then, does the language of the New Testament and Luke–Acts in particular say about the author "Luke"? Does it demonstrate that he was a doctor? Cadbury's answer was in the negative. He states: "If we are to accept the definition of Hobart as to what constitutes a medical term, we have already seen that many such words are found in the LXX, Josephus, Plutarch, and Lucian."[30] The best explanation of the data according to Cadbury is to recognize that many so-called medical words had spread to the common vocabulary of the period. Otherwise one would have to argue that Josephus, Plutarch, and Lucian also were physicians, a proposition for which there is no evidence. For Cadbury, it was more likely that Hobart's method was incorrect and therefore his conclusions were misleading.

Cadbury's sound method, painstaking research, and clarity of argument led to a general rejection of Hobart's conclusion. The joke circulated that "Cadbury earned his doctorate by depriving St. Luke of his!"[31] On a more serious note, it is worth clarifying that Cadbury did not prove that Luke was not a doctor; he only proved that his *vocabulary* was not privy to doctors alone. If one does not believe it is possible to prove that Luke was a doctor by language *alone*, one should also believe that it is not possible to *disprove* that Luke was a doctor by language alone. In fact, some have pointed out that the linguistic register of the preface to Luke points to a context of crafts and professions—which included the study of medicine. And this takes us to Cadbury's second contribution.

The Preface to Luke and the Genre of Acts

How a book begins remains an important aspect in the reader's determination of what that book is about. The opening lines of a work can give us a hint about what the genre of a work is: poetry, science fiction, political history, and so on. In a way, the importance of opening lines for the guessing of a genre is more attenuated today. For we can generally discover the genre of a book by looking at the copyright page or the dustjacket or the section of the bookstore or library where the book is shelved. In the ancient world, although there were factors that would have aided in the learning of a book's genre (not least the setting and community in which it was read), the external amount of

---

30. Cadbury, *Style and Literary Method*, 49.
31. Baird, *History of New Testament Research*, 19.

material to help in a quick generic classification was not as plentiful as is the case today due to the publishing industry and the different media of the printed word. Without these external aids, the beginnings of works in the ancient world served as the primary *internal* signal in aiding a reader to grasp the genre of the work.[32]

Apart from John 19:35, 20:30–31, and 21:24–25, the preface to the Gospel of Luke is unique in the canonical Gospels in that the implied author speaks directly to his audience. In Luke 1:1–4 we hear the author addressing Theophilus in the second person, where the former gives those tantalizing words about his method and purpose in composing his Gospel.[33] In principle, therefore, it would appear that a careful study of the preface may yield useful information about the genre of the book and its author. This is one of the reasons why it is important to study carefully Cadbury's contribution in the second volume of *Beginnings of Christianity*, to which he contributed perhaps the most erudite piece in English on the preface of Luke's Gospel.[34] His work was held as authoritative in the field of Luke–Acts for many years; and it was not until the monograph of Loveday Alexander on the topic, published in 1993, that a new work appeared with comparable mastery of the material.[35] It is worth summarizing Cadbury's most important conclusions from his study of the preface to Luke.

Cadbury's commentary on the preface does not put forth a general thesis that covers the entirety of the preface. Rather, the essay consists of *ad hoc* observations and explanations of particular terms and phrases. Nevertheless, a number of themes do emerge, which help us better understand Cadbury's contribution to this important section of Luke's work.

First, Cadbury continues to reinforce his *linguistic* assessment of Luke–Acts: and that is that Luke's Greek is representative of Hellenistic,

32. For the importance of the first sentences of a book in the identification of its genre in the Greco-Roman period, see Sean A. Adams, *The Genre of Acts and Collected Biography*, SNTSMS 156 (Cambridge: Cambridge University Press, 2013), 48–49, 120–24.
33. It is probable that these words are also applicable to the composition of the Acts of the Apostles. Of the voluminous literature on the subject, I have found I. Howard Marshall's essay, "Acts and the 'Former Treatise,' " in *The Book of Acts in Its Ancient Literary Setting*, eds. Andrew D. Clarke and Bruce Winter, BAFCS 1 (Grand Rapids: Eerdmans, 1993), 163–82, particularly thoughtful.
34. Cadbury, "Commentary on the Preface to Luke," in *Beginnings of Christianity*, 2:489–510.
35. Loveday C. A. Alexander, *The Preface to Luke's Gospel: Literary Convention and Social Context in Luke 1.1–4 and Acts 1.1*, SNTSMS 78 (Cambridge: Cambridge University Press, 1993). Again, this comment refers only to work published in English.

post-classical Greek. To be sure, in the preface Luke uses words and constructions that are common in Attic Greek.[36] However, these words are also found in works fairly contemporary with Luke which had no Atticistic ambitions. In addition, there are other words and grammatical features in the preface that belong primarily to Hellenistic Greek usage.[37] Thus, the preface strengthens Cadbury's previous conclusions on Luke's Greek—it is a postclassical form, common in the Hellenistic period.

Second, Cadbury notes that many features of the preface line-up with those of historical works.[38] Thus, Cadbury continues the tradition of using the language of the preface as evidence that the genre of Luke–Acts is history. It should be noted that this conclusion with respect to genre, based on the preface, has been questioned by more recent works, particularly those of Alexander[39] and Richard Pervo.[40] The former, in particular, seems to have downplayed some of the evidence marshalled by Cadbury. More recent commentators have returned to the traditional view of the genre of Luke–Acts on the basis of the preface's language.[41] In this respect, Cadbury's conclusion has been vindicated—at least for the moment.

Third, and without question Cadbury's major stress point on the preface, is his observation that the use of a preface and the language used demonstrate the author's following of convention.[42] That is, Luke is employing many of the "buzzwords" and concepts that *historians* used in their prefaces. This is partly what led Cadbury (see above) to conclude that the genre of Luke–Acts is history. At just this very juncture we

---

36. See, e.g., ἐπειδήπερ, ἐπεχείρησαν ("This is a good classical word . . ." 493), and the construction περὶ ὧν κατήχηθης λόγων, etc.

37. See, e.g., καθώς (condemned by Atticists) as well as the use of adverbs with prepositions.

38. See esp. "Commentary on the Preface to Luke," 2:498–99, where Cadbury notes the concept of *autopsia* present in Luke's preface. Cadbury also notes the use of ἀκριβῶς as a marker of historical prefaces.

39. In her 1993 monograph, *Preface to Luke's Gospel*, Alexander made the argument that the language of Luke's preface is actually more attuned to the language of scientific treatises, not history. In subsequent work Alexander is more open to the preface as equally pointing to a historical genre: see Alexander, *Acts in Its Ancient Literary Context: A Classicist Looks at the Acts of the Apostles*, LNTS 289 (London: T&T Clark, 2006), 21–42.

40. Richard I. Pervo, *Acts*, Hermeneia (Minneapolis: Fortress, 2008).

41. See, e.g., Michael Wolter, *Das Lukasevangelium* (Tübingen: Mohr Siebeck, 2008), 59–60, with criticism of Alexander's earlier insistence that the preface's language aligns closer with scientific prose. While Wolter acknowledges the technical language of the preface, he reminds us that technical language is also part of historical prefaces, and that Luke's expression about composing a narrative (διήγησιν) must be taken into consideration. Thus, "the alternative constructed by Alexander appears to be dualistic."

42. Cadbury, "Commentary on the Preface to Luke," 2:490–92, 499, 509–10.

should observe, however, that Cadbury's conception of ancient history explicitly enters the discussion, leading him to conclude that the rhetorical fullness of the preface may actually call into question the very things claimed in the preface. Consider the following statements: "Even the specific purpose expressed in the preface—apparently that of defending Christianity—must not be applied too seriously to the work as a whole." Later he states: "Thus again we are reminded not to lay too great stress on the selection of ideas contained in it."[43] On the one hand, this leads Cadbury to a "soft" reading of the "many" who were Luke's predecessors in writing about Jesus. That is, the conventional use of "many" and other terms at the beginning of historical works more than likely means that Luke is not disparaging his predecessors. With respect to the verb ἐπεχείρησαν ("to attempt"), for example, Cadbury states, "By itself [it] cannot prove that Luke is making odious comparisons."[44] On the other hand, Luke makes a number of truth-claims whose validity is of great importance for Christians who believe—on the basis of the text itself—that eyewitness testimony is essential for the truthfulness of the Gospel account.[45] Luke talks about the "events that have been fulfilled among us" (v. 1); those who were "eyewitnesses and servants of the word" (v. 2); and his goal that Theophilus "may know the truth" of the things he has been taught (v. 4). Are these statements also conventional *simpliciter*? This appears to be Cadbury's judgment. Thus, on the concept of *autopsia* invoked by Luke's language in verse 2, Cadbury is inclined to view it as no more than a "commonplace."[46] This ultimately carries him to the opinion—expressed with careful measure—that Luke was not an eyewitness to any of the events he narrates.[47]

By way of assessment, I do not wish to dispute that even the statements of truth-claims in Luke's preface are conventional. If successful communication largely hangs on the use of "commonplaces" that permit the receiver to follow the author, then conventions are always necessary. But consider the following example: it may be a convention to say "thank you" when a family member passes the food down the table—but that does not mean that every time I say it I do not mean it, simply because it is a convention! Cadbury's conclusion of ancient

43. Cadbury, "Commentary on the Preface to Luke," 2:490.
44. Cadbury, "Commentary on the Preface to Luke," 2:493.
45. On this, see further Padilla, *The Acts of the Apostles*, 32–36, 200–43.
46. Cadbury, "Commentary on the Preface to Luke," 2:499.
47. Cadbury, "Commentary on the Preface to Luke," 2:498–500.

history, then, leads him simultaneously to say too little and too much about Luke's preface. He says too little in that his understanding of the *conventions* of historiography so swallow the *content* of the preface that little of referential meaning is left. He says too much in that the conventions employed are themselves more or less all that can be interpreted with any measure of confidence.

The Speeches in Acts

One of the striking features of Acts is the amount of direct speech present. Each chapter of Acts in our modern Bible chapter divisions contains some form of direct speech. If we compare Acts in this respect to some of the classical Greek historians—Herodotus and Thucydides, for example—Luke has included many more speeches. Naturally, the sheer number of speeches (among other things) has led to a considerable amount of work on the subject.[48] Scholars have found that investigation of the speeches is important because the latter help us understand many of the central aspects of Acts: genre, poetics, theology, history, and so on. We are fortunate, therefore, that Cadbury dedicated a chapter in the *Beginnings of Christianity* to the speeches in Acts.[49]

Cadbury's relatively brief essay on the many speeches in Acts brims with erudition and thoughtfulness. As a result, the reader comes away stimulated. The main preoccupation of the essay is historical—or more specifically, historicity. Cadbury canvasses the method of speech-reporting in a group of authors from the Greco-Roman period (e.g., Dionysius of Halicarnassus, Josephus, Dio Cassius, Tacitus); explores the use of the Old Testament in the speeches; examines the relationship of one speech to another; and discusses Luke's method of handling his sources from a look back at the Gospel of Luke. All this is done to answer the following question: are the speeches the free composition of Luke; or are they ultimately based on solid historical tradition, which Luke conveys faithfully? Although Cadbury is measured in his response, he ultimately opts for the former option: the speeches, as a

---

48. The literature here is massive. A helpful, general entry remains Marion Soards, *The Speeches in Acts: Their Content, Context, and Concerns* (Louisville, KY: Westminster/John Knox, 1994). For more detailed work on the speeches, see the current author's work, *The Speeches of Outsiders in Acts: Poetics, Theology and Historiography*, SNTSMS 144 (Cambridge: Cambridge University Press, 2008); idem, *The Acts of the Apostles*, 123–49.

49. Cadbury, "The Speeches in Acts," in *Beginnings of Christianity*, 5:402–27.

whole, are free compositions of Luke, thus putting into question their historical reliability.

How should we respond to Cadbury's conclusion? On the one hand, judging that the speeches are in their final shape the work of Luke should not be controversial: the weight of classical studies would favor such a conclusion. Scholars of the Greco-Roman period have shown that the ancient concept of speech-reporting was the following: historians were free to compose a speech as long as it generally corresponded with the personality of the speaker and the situation being reported.[50] There was no expectation of reproducing speeches word for word; quotation marks did not exist. Therefore, responsible historians, while they would reproduce the essence of what a speaker might have said had the evidence been available, more than likely felt that their obligation was no more than to faithfully represent the character of the speaker and the situation which prompted the speech. It would actually appear from the castigating statements of Polybius (12.25a3–5; 12.25b1–4) and Lucian (*How to Write History* 2–9) that *few* historians were committed to operating to this standard: most simply *invented* speeches and put them in the mouths of historical characters in order to show off their rhetorical polish. In any case, Cadbury is correct when he says that the speeches in Acts are not *verbatim* reports (a rarity in antiquity): comparison of the speeches by Peter and Paul, for example, yields such lexical correspondence that it is clear that the final product is from Luke.

On the other hand, recognition of Luke's "touch" on the speeches need not yield to Cadbury's skepticism, as when he judges that the speeches in Acts are "devoid of historical basis in genuine tradition."[51] An example of someone who views the speeches as Lukan productions *and at the same time* as reliable statements of the speakers of the early church (based on genuine tradition) is Rudolf Pesch in his commentary on Acts.[52] And he is not alone. Many other scholars could be marshalled who, while recognizing Luke's redactional activity

---

50. For arguments from both primary and secondary sources in support of the statement above, see Padilla, *The Acts of the Apostles*, 123–49.

51. Cadbury, "The Speeches in Acts," 5:427.

52. Rudolf Pesch, *Die Apostelgeschichte*, 2nd ed., EKK (Neukirchen-Vluyn: Neukirchener, 1994), 42–45, with criticisms of Dibelius and his influential work on the speeches in Acts, which has led to skepticism of their historical reliability in much of German-speaking scholarship (e.g., G. Schneider and J. Roloff). I choose Pesch as an example because he is someone who would not adopt the more conservative view of the speeches (e.g., F. F. Bruce), and yet does not go to the extreme skepticism of Cadbury.

on the speeches,[53] conclude that Luke provides us with the gist of what the speakers said.[54] I have proposed elsewhere that a comparison of Luke's *performance* in speech-reporting with Greco-Roman historians (including Hellenistic-Jewish works like Second Maccabees) yields two significant differences, suggesting that it is probable that Luke not only meets the criterion of "fit" mentioned above but actually goes beyond that to report the gist of what the speakers actually said. While this is not the place to give detailed arguments for this conclusion, I will briefly mention two.[55]

First, there is the matter of *length*. When one reads side by side the speeches of Greco-Roman histories with Acts, the former are considerably longer. To use Acts' longest speech—that of Stephen—as an example, it takes approximately five to six minutes to read this speech. Reading a speech of "normal" length in, say, Thucydides or Josephus, usually takes longer than the longest (and really the exception, lengthwise) speech in Acts. The shortness of the speeches in Acts suggests (and no more than that) that here we have an author who is not overly preoccupied to demonstrate his rhetorical ability, which would normally necessitate a longer speech in order to insert the different necessary *topoi*. On the contrary, even the "long" speeches in Acts read like compressed accounts of what surely took longer to say in real life.

In the book of Acts, we find only one significant example of pairing of speeches, between Tertullus and Paul (24:1–27). Otherwise, we hear only one side of the argument, despite there being excellent opportunities for Luke to pair speeches. One situation where Luke could have provided counter-speeches is the apologetic one. Especially in the second half of Acts we hear of accusations from both Jews and Gentiles against the sect of the Nazarenes (cf. Acts 24:5). At Thessalonica the believers are accused of "turning the world upside down" (17:6), more than likely a charge of sedition. At Corinth Paul is accused of "persuading people to worship God in ways that are contrary to the law" (18:13; the Jewish law or Roman law?). At Ephesus, Demetrius the silversmith effectively tells his fellow craftsmen that Paul is inviting

---

53. This statement assumes that Luke did possess some sources for his speeches. I would add that as a traveling, missionary companion of Paul (see Irenaeus, *Haer.* 3.1.1; 3.14.1), Luke would have remembered what Paul said in his proclamation and criminal defense.
54. See, e.g., Craig S. Keener, *Acts: An Exegetical Commentary: Volume 1: Introduction and 1:1–2:47* (Grand Rapids: Baker, 2012), 258–319.
55. See Padilla, *The Acts of the Apostles*, 139–46.

hubris on the city by denying the gods, particularly Artemis (19:23–28). This is an accusation of "atheism" and of affronting religion (*pietas*), a very serious accusation in the Greco-Roman world (cf. Socrates at Athens). It is remarkable, in the context of rhetoric in the historical writing of the period, that Luke does not provide a counter speech to defend the innocence of Christians. This comes later, perhaps too late (Acts 24 and 26)! As one author puts it,

> Paul, certainly, is presented as innocent of the particular charge on which he was tried in Caesarea. . . . But he and his associates have incurred a number of charges along the way which have never in so many words— that is, in the explicit terms we would expect of apologetic speech—been refuted. Mud has a disturbing tendency to stick, and it is a dangerous strategy for an apologetic writer to bring accusations to the reader's attention without taking the trouble to refute them.[56]

I would suggest as likely that Luke does not provide us with counter speeches because there probably were none delivered at the moment, and he probably did not want to invent a speech. This may suggest that Luke was a conservative historian, committed to a high standard of speech-reporting, unlike those historians who are denounced by Polybius, Lucian, and others.

To conclude this subsection, it is worth stating that Cadbury does not seem at all bothered by the possibility (in his judgment, the *probability*) that Luke was not really reporting the words and sentiments of the apostles and early Christian leaders. His understanding of the manner in which historians operated in the New Testament period apparently freed him from that expectation. In my opinion, however, the matter goes beyond the protocols of history. We may now give in full the statement from Cadbury that we in part quoted above:

> Even though devoid of historical basis in genuine tradition the speeches in Acts have nevertheless considerable historical value. There is reason to suppose that the talented author of Acts expended upon them not only his artistic skill, but also a considerable amount of historic imagination. . . . Probably these addresses give us a better idea of the early church than if Luke had striven for realism. . . . They indicate at least

---

56. Alexander, *Acts in Its Ancient Literary Context*, 198.

what seemed to a well-informed Christian of the next generation the main outline of the Christian message as first presented by Jesus' followers in Palestine and in the cities of the Mediterranean world.[57]

From a theological perspective, this statement would likely be alarming to Christians who believe that in the speeches of Peter and Paul we have access at least to a summary of what these apostles proclaimed. The reason for this is that the New Testament and church tradition believe that the canonicity of the New Testament is tied to apostolic speech. The New Testament is ultimately the written word of God because it is based on the words of the apostles and prophets, whom God in his freedom chose to speak through (cf. Eph. 2:20; 2 Peter 1:16–20). For Cadbury, by contrast, revelation is not exclusively tied to God speaking through canonical scriptures. As we will explain more fully below, Cadbury understood revelation as in principle the domain of humanity. Hence, if all we have in Acts' speeches is an "idea" of the early church, our knowledge of God is none the worse. It should be noted that I am not criticizing Cadbury here (although of course I have a profound disagreement with him theologically!); he set out in his essay on the speeches in Acts to provide a "purely historical" explanation—and that was certainly his prerogative as a student of the Bible. I am simply suggesting, in light of a global reading of Cadbury's work, that it is possible that his theological views play a part in the way he expresses his conclusions.[58]

In summing up this section on Cadbury's contributions to Luke–Acts, we should note that there were many other areas of study where Cadbury produced work that has remained authoritative to the present.[59] When researching subjects such as the identity of the Hellenists of Acts 6, the summaries of Acts, Roman law, etc., consultation of Cadbury is often one of the first steps to ensure that the researcher is

---

57.   Cadbury, "The Speeches in Acts," 5:426–27.

58.   In describing the *religionsgeschichtliche Schule* of the eighteenth to nineteenth centuries, Ulrich Wilckens finds as its basis the "purely historical" (*rein historischer*), non-theological explanation of the Bible and early Christianity (Wilckens, *Theologie des Neuen Testaments. Band 1: Geschichte der Urchristlichen Theologie* [Neukirchen-Vluyn: Neukirchener, 2002], 15–18 and *passim*). Cadbury would have fit well in this movement (e.g., William Wrede) to the extent that he did not want to limit the study of Christianity to the canon but also wanted to include the early Christianity of the second and third centuries. A recent example is Klaus Berger's *Theologie-geschichte des Urchristentums*, 2nd ed. (Tübingen: Francke, 1995).

59.   Consult n3 above.

performing thorough work. Even if his contributions were limited to the subjects examined in this subsection, they are of such importance in interpreting Acts that if Cadbury had not written much else on the matter, he would still have a place as one of the giants of Luke–Acts. One of the remarkable things about Cadbury's work is its duration. In a time (the present) when there is such an explosion of data, Cadbury's ideas remain—and usually they are directly attributed to him. This is the more remarkable considering that Cadbury wrote most of his work in the early to mid-twentieth century. How can we explain such constancy? The answer to this takes us to the third and final section.

CADBURY THE SCIENTIFIC SCHOLAR

Both the methodical manner in which Cadbury executed his work and his language have led to a reception-history (*Wirkungsgeschichte*) of objectivity.[60] That is, Cadbury's work has been received in posterity as an example of impeccable credibility. As a result, many of the scholars who presently build on his work often give Cadbury the credit for working without impartiality, namely, theological bias. This *persona* of unbiased, precise, and scientific scholarship, free from ecclesiastical pressures, is something Cadbury himself cultivated. On the other hand, Cadbury recognized that in our motives for conducting biblical scholarship there does not exist an either/or: a purely religious drive (read: apologetic) or a pure pursuit for the truth (read: unapologetic scholarship to be followed wherever the results lead). There is usually a mixture of both. Cadbury concluded his presidential address to the SBL in 1936 with the following words: "Fidelity to the best in our professional tradition, both of piety and of open-minded, honest quest for the truth, may prove in the end one of the most satisfying motives for us all."[61] It must have been this intellectual largesse in Cadbury that allowed for a happy time for evangelical scholars who completed their research under him.[62]

---

60. In what follows I draw from my essay, "The *Wirkungsgeschichte* of Henry Joel Cadbury as an Objective Historian: An Exploration of America's Premiere Luke–Acts Scholar," *BBR* 29 (2019): 499–510.

61. Henry Joel Cadbury, "Motives of Biblical Scholarship," *JBL* 56 (1937): 1–16, at 16.

62. A great example is George Ladd, who, according to John A. D'Elia, loved Cadbury "as a son would love a father" (John A. D'Elia, *A Place at the Table: George Eldon Ladd and the Rehabilitation of Evangelical Scholarship in America* [Oxford: Oxford University Press, 2008], 25).

I want to suggest that one of the main reasons why Cadbury has remained one of the primary scholars when studying any aspect of Acts was just this intellectual honesty mentioned above. Cadbury appeared to his contemporaries and posteriority as the pinnacle of scientific and objective scholarship. When I use the verb "appear" in the previous sentence I am not at all suggesting that Cadbury was attempting to deceive his audience; on the contrary, from his writings, lectures, letters, and testimony of others, Cadbury truly did aspire and often achieved a high level of objectivity and exactness in his work. And yet—and here begins the final theme of this chapter—Cadbury's greatest weakness was his conception that scientific and objective was coterminous with *nontheological*. He believed that a conscious theological aim or framework was the enemy of objective historical work. This mentality of Cadbury is overlooked by the majority of New Testament scholars today. I was relieved, therefore, to find that it was not overlooked by William Baird: "Cadbury acknowledges that he has not considered theology in his assessment of the authorship of Ephesians, an issue he believes to be clouded by subjectivity. Thus the address discloses *Cadbury's strength and also his weaknesses*: his passion for objectivity and his antipathy for theology."[63] In the final paragraphs of this chapter, I would like to explore this by looking at the roots of this attitude of Cadbury, its concretization in his book *The Making of Luke–Acts*, and the theological/philosophical counterparts of his antipathy to theology.

Cadbury the Quaker

As mentioned at the beginning of this chapter, Cadbury's intellectual and spiritual formation was indebted to Quakerism. To put this religious movement in the singular is misleading; for just as there are many "branches" or movements within Christianity, so there are in Quakerism.[64] As mentioned above, while at Haverford, Cadbury studied under Rufus Jones (who would later become his brother-in-law), well known as one of the leaders of the modernist wing of Quakerism.[65] Although

---

63. Baird, *History of New Testament Research*, 26. Emphasis added.
64. I found the following two works very helpful in beginning to understand Quaker thought: Pink Dandelion, *The Quakers: A Very Short Introduction* (Oxford: Oxford University Press, 2008); and Angell and Dandelion, eds., *The Cambridge Companion to Quakerism*.
65. See Dandelion, *The Quakers*, 34–36, 65 and n11 above. According to J. William Frost, the apogee of liberal Quakerism covers the years 1887–2010: "Modernist and Liberal Quakers: 1887–2010," in *The Oxford Handbook of Quaker Studies*, eds. Pink Dandelion and Stephen Angell (Oxford: Oxford University Press, 2015), 78–92.

liberal Quakerism prefers deeds over creeds, thereby showing hesitation to produce an authoritative list of necessary beliefs, nevertheless the following have emerged *ad hoc* as its basic tenets or theology: (1) the priority of experience over Scripture for religious knowledge; (2) the necessity for Quakerism to adapt according to the period in which it lives; (3) the openness to new ideas; and (4) progressivism, the concept that knowledge of God would increase as history moved forward.[66] If some of these statements are similar to the liberal theology of the nineteenth century, that is because this wing of Quakerism drew significantly from this movement. We will come back to this shortly.

In this respect it is important to note Cadbury's attitude towards the traditional Christian understanding of revelation. He puts the Quaker understanding of revelation in contrast to the orthodox Christian understanding in his lecture, "A Quaker Approach to the Bible."[67] Cadbury argues on the basis of Quaker primary sources that for many Quakers, revelation, while having one source, is experienced in a duality of equal proportion. The source of revelation is the Holy Spirit, and it is experienced in Scripture and religious activity. Unlike Protestants, Cadbury argues, Quakers view experience as a continuation of revelation:

> In using the Old Testament apocrypha they [Quakers] were not unlike other Protestants of their day, for the Protestant aversion to those books has increased more recently. Friends' curiosity about still other books, lost or professing early date, was a natural expression of their feeling that Divine revelation neither began with Moses nor ended with the Apostles.

Cadbury continues his explanation of the Quaker understanding of revelation by using an analogy from the dictionary:

> Or one might name this [Quaker] approach Operation Dictionary, though the dictionary, like the Bible, is often misunderstood. The dictionary is not the authority which dictates how words ought to be used. It is rather the record of how words are used and what they commonly mean. In like manner, the Bible is not the dictator of our conduct and faith. It is rather the record of persons who exemplified faith and virtue.

---

66. Dandelion, *The Quakers*, 65.
67. The essay was originally the Ward Lecture at Guilford College, delivered in 1953. Easy access is found in the following website, which this author consulted: https://universalistfriends.org/cadbury-1.html. There is no pagination provided in this electronic format.

He then makes a statement that is strikingly similar to the words of G. E. Lessing: "What is true in the Bible is there because it is true, not true because it is there. Its experiences answer to ours, that is, they correspond to ours." Lessing, the father of rationalism in Germany, had said the following in 1777 when speaking of the nature of revelation: "[R]eligion is not true because the evangelists and apostles taught it; on the contrary, they taught it because it is true. The written records must be explained by its inner truth, and none of the written records can give it any inner truth if it does not already have it."[68]

Did Cadbury consciously operate with this understanding of the Bible when he researched and wrote on Luke–Acts? Or did he "suspend" these beliefs, lest they contaminate the purity of scientific scholarship? It might be impossible to answer this question with certainty. In the following subsection, however, I would suggest that there is likely a connection between Cadbury's Quaker understanding of revelation and (what has been judged as) his most important book on Luke–Acts.

The Making of Luke–Acts and Cadbury's "Theology"

Unlike many monographs on Luke–Acts, which are preoccupied with the theological subject(s) matter of the double work, Cadbury is clear that this is not his concern in composing this book. He states that his aim is not theological—and therefore not apologetic.[69] It is clear from this statement and others that Cadbury understood theological work as essentially defensive: either to defend the traditional, conservative theology of the church or to defend the liberal philosophical translation of the New Testament in purely immanent categories (e.g., in the philosophy of Kant). Cadbury's aim is the following: "The present study does not aim to deal as such with the events narrated by this writer ['Luke'], but with an event of greater significance than many which he records—the making of this work itself."[70] In some ways this is not at all a controversial statement. It is similar to the aim of, say, form criticism, where the scholar's goal is to label the different stories of the Gospels in order then to inquire into the situation in the church

---

68. Gotthold Lessing, *Lessing: Philosophical and Theological Writings*, ed. H. B. Nisbet (Cambridge: Cambridge University Press, 2005), 63.
69. Cadbury, *Making of Luke–Acts*, 1–2.
70. Cadbury, *Making of Luke–Acts*, 3.

that gave rise to such stories. In fact, the hallmark of Enlightenment-based higher criticism of the Bible is just this concept that the meaning of the Bible is to be found, not in the final text, but in reconstructions behind the text.[71] Cadbury's aim in *The Making of Luke–Acts* could thus just be viewed as a modern historical interpretation of the text of Acts. To the extent that this was the sort of critical study of the Bible that was being practiced in universities across Europe and North America, Cadbury's work should not be viewed as unique.

On the other hand, we should note the value judgment that Cadbury attaches to his aim. His investigation is "an event of greater significance than many which he records—the making of this work itself." This is without question a *truth-claim* on the part of Cadbury. Why should the composition of Luke–Acts be of "greater significance" than the final work? Note Cadbury's clarification: "These works [of other scholars writing on Luke–Acts] and others like them all contribute to our understanding of the making of Luke–Acts. But their scope is not identical with the present inquiry. *Their ultimate interest is not the author and his times, but the subject matter of history.*"[72] Again we ask, why should the "subject matter" of Acts be of less significance than the author himself?

Cadbury's Nontheology as an Example of Modern Philosophy

In light of Cadbury's comments, I contend the following: Cadbury's aim in *The Making of Luke–Acts* is related to his understanding of revelation as expressed in "A Quaker Approach to the Bible"—and this approach is ultimately based on the philosophies that constitute the modern, "professional" study of the Bible.[73] While this approach was

71. Helpfully, Hans Frei, *The Eclipse of Biblical Narrative: A Study in Eighteenth and Nineteenth Century Hermeneutics* (New Haven: Yale University Press, 1974); John Rogerson, *Old Testament Criticism in the Nineteenth Century: England and Germany* (Philadelphia: Fortress, 1985); Mark Gignilliat, *A Brief History of Old Testament Criticism: From Benedict Spinoza to Brevard Childs* (Grand Rapids: Zondervan, 2012). In German, the work of Ulrich Wilckens, *Theologie des Neuen Testaments. Band III: Historische Kritik der historisch-kritischen Exegese. Von der Aufklärung bis zur Gegenwart* (Göttingen: Vandenhoeck & Ruprecht, 2017), is both a story of higher-criticism and a trenchant critique. More popular and openly critical is Berger, *Die Bibelfälscher: Wie wir um die Wahrheit betrogen werden* (Munich: Pattloch, 2013).

72. Cadbury, *Making of Luke–Acts*, 7.

73. I argue elsewhere that these philosophies are: rationalism, Kantian idealism, romanticism, and historicism. See Osvaldo Padilla, *The Vicarious Life of Jesus*, Studies in Christian Doctrine and Scripture (Downers Grove, IL: InterVarsity, forthcoming).

viewed (at least in the United States) during Cadbury's life as nontheological (and therefore objective and scientific), today it is recognized as very theological—just not the theology confessed in the great creeds of the church.

Cadbury's insistence that the composition of Luke–Acts is more significant than the actual contents of Acts can be understood as an example of historicism. Consider the following explanation of historicism: "The historicist holds . . . that the *essence, identity or nature* of everything in the human world is made by history, so that it is *entirely* the product of the particular historical processes that brought it into being."[74] In this philosophy, knowledge of reality can be obtained by observing the immanent chain of events that lie behind a historical work and that took place in the composition of the work. This is where "revelation" is to be found.

Another philosophy that is latent in Cadbury's work is romanticism. The most significant theological work composed in this key is of course *The Christian Faith* of Friedrich Schleiermacher (originally published in 1830), the basis of Protestant liberalism. The relationship[75] of Schleiermacher's thought and Cadbury's expressions above is found in the assertation that religious *experience* is an authoritative source of revelation. This would be a reason to be preoccupied primarily with Luke the person, for revelation is found—not in his Gospel and Acts, as the church has believed—but in the person's individual experience.

The great irony—or weakness, as Baird saw it—of Cadbury's *oeuvre* is this single-minded ambition to write scientifically of the Bible by putting aside theology. Yet precisely this attitude—the heritage of liberal Quakerism in the case of Cadbury—ultimately puts Cadbury in a position that is actually not scientifically superior to confessing scholarship. It is to the great credit of Cadbury that the philosophies that constituted his underlying approach to the Bible did not often emerge in scathing critiques of confessional scholarship.

---

74. Frederick Beiser, *The German Historicist Tradition* (Oxford: Oxford University Press, 2011), 2.

75. I am not arguing for a genetic relationship between Schleiermacher's work and Cadbury! I am not aware that the latter read and/or reflected on Schleiermacher. The relationship between the two, I would guess, is indirect.

CONCLUSION

In completing this chapter, the power of Cadbury's scholarship was brought back as I read the latest issue of the journal *New Testament Studies*. The opening article explores an aspect of the Acts of the Apostles—and Cadbury's articles are often cited in authoritative fashion! Even after nearly a century, Cadbury continues to shape the field of Luke–Acts.

I have argued in this chapter that Henry Cadbury is one of the giants of Luke–Acts scholarship, perhaps internationally the most influential scholar from the United States. Cadbury was erudite and intelligent, and he wrote in a clear and winsome manner. In the area of the language of the New Testament he was ahead of his times; in many areas of Luke–Acts his contributions must still be carefully read. Cadbury strived for the freedom of those who often were undermined in American society. His kindness and openness as a scholar allowed many who disagreed with him confessionally to work happily with him and under him.

My greatest criticism of Cadbury was what appears to have been a blind spot in his scholarship. This was his belief, probably stemming from his Quaker roots, that true scientific study of the Bible could only be possible when theology was put aside entirely. For Cadbury, theological study of the Bible was inherently apologetic—and this was incompatible with the type of detached, objective, historical study of the Bible that was his ambition. Yet a closer look at Cadbury's work appears to reveal that his nontheology was actually an example of philosophical historicism and romanticism, where revelation from God is purely in the form of immanent religious experience. As a result, even while consulting and admiring Cadbury's work, I suggest we do not give it instant credibility over the work of confessional scholars.

ERNST HAENCHEN AND HIS IMPACT ON LUKE–ACTS SCHOLARSHIP

Karl L. Armstrong

There can be no doubt that Ernst Haenchen made a profound impact on New Testament studies in general, and Luke–Acts scholarship in particular.[1] He was a prolific writer and his insights continue to shape the way that many scholars go about the business of interpreting the New Testament. In order for Luke–Acts scholarship to move forward, we must be willing to engage and understand some of the ways that Haenchen has, for better or worse, steered our thinking into the present day.

That being said, the goal of this essay is much more modest—it merely provides an introduction to and overview of Haenchen's life and scholarship with a special emphasis on the ways that he interpreted the book of Acts. In the first major section below, the reader is provided with a summary of Haenchen's biography and some of the significant teachers and events in his life that shaped his thinking and

---

1. Where Tyson credits Hans Conzelmann with his "ground-breaking study on the theology of Luke," he aptly recognizes the great impact Haenchen had on the study of Acts. See Joseph B. Tyson, *Luke, Judaism, and the Scholars: Critical Approaches to Luke–Acts* (Columbia: University of South Carolina Press, 1999), 66. See especially his chapter 5 (pp. 66–90): "Ernst Haenchen (1894–1975) and Hans Conzelmann (1915–1989)."

theology. The next section, "Haenchen's Contribution to Luke–Acts Study," examines his approach to some of the major issues in Luke–Acts scholarship that continue to be discussed and debated. In this section, I address three interlinking areas with the purpose of acquiring Haenchen's perspective and influence: (1) the sources of Acts; (2) Luke as theologian, historian, and writer; and (3) Luke and Paul. Last, I have included a section devoted to some of the critical responses to Haenchen's work along with a long-awaited reappraisal of his work.

AN INTRODUCTION TO THE LIFE AND SCHOLARSHIP OF ERNST HAENCHEN

Ernst Haenchen was born on December 10, 1894 in Czarnikau in the (then) western Prussian province of Posen. He was the third and youngest child of the Royal Prussian district secretary Karl Haenchen and his wife Ehefrau Elfriede.[2] When Ernst was only three years old, his father passed away and after this the family moved to Breslau.[3] There he attended community school for four years until the family moved to Berlin in 1904.[4]

From Easter of 1905 onward, he attended the local Joachimsthal Gymnasium beginning with grade nine through to graduation. For his first parish exam he wrote about his school years and admits that "[t]he learning was easy, and the old languages made me very happy, so that my relatives expected, I would study classical philology like my eleven year older brother."[5] Since the sixth grade, Haenchen was apparently plagued by doubts regarding the religious views of his parents and their church. Modern views of astronomy had also eroded some aspects of his faith in God—although his study of the Old Testament prophets revealed another world to him beyond the physical realm.

Haenchen by this time had a greater desire to study theology, but he continued to have doubts with regards to the relationship between the omniscience of God and human freedom. Subsequently, he attended Humboldt University in Berlin during the summer semester

---

2. With regards to the life and career of Haenchen, I rely extensively on Ulrich Busse, "Ernst Haenchen und sein Johanneskommentar," *ETL* 57 (1981): 125–43 (here 125).
3. Breslau (in German) is the modern-day capital of Poland's lower region of Silesia (Wrocław).
4. Busse, "Ernst Haenchen," 125.
5. Busse, "Ernst Haenchen," 125.

of 1914 after passing his secondary school graduation exams. His struggles with theology continued after hearing the lectures of Hugo Gressmann and Graf Baudissin (who both saw the Old Testament filled with myth and legends), as well as Adolf Harnack's lectures on the history of dogma. Under Martin Dibelius's supervision, Haenchen found solace in philology and biblical studies and the texts of the ecumenical councils.[6]

After the start of the First World War, Haenchen was rejected as a volunteer for the military due to his poor health and thus was able to continue his studies with Dibelius at Heidelberg in the spring of 1915.[7] However, he received his draft notice on May 21, 1915 and first served on the eastern front in Poland, then in Serbia. Later that same year on October 22, Haenchen was seriously wounded for the first time. He was able to recover at the garrison of Landsberg where he had the chance to work a little on Dibelius's lecture notes on the Gospel of John.[8] In August 1917, he returned to the battlefield and was stationed in Riga and Wolhynia where he was promoted to Lieu-tenant of the Reserve after a brief period of officer training.

A month later Haenchen fought in the battle of Somme (France) and lost his right leg during the German offensive on July 7, 1918.[9] He was not able to leave the hospital in Berlin until August 1919 after a series of operations (eleven in total). After his release he began to attend lectures again and resume his studies. During this time, Haenchen read the writings of Albert Schweitzer, which revealed to him that the *religionsgeschichtliche* (history of religion) method did not actually solve his questions from his earlier studies in Berlin but merely deferred them.[10] Haenchen's resolve is commendable as he was able to finish his studies and his first theological examination in spite

---

6. Among New Testament scholars, Haenchen seems to have been influenced greatly by Dibelius as can be seen in his later dedication to him (along with Karl Heim) in his commentary on Mark: "Gewidmet ist das Buch dem Andenken meiner alten Lehrer in Heidelberg und Tübingen." See Ernst Haenchen, *Der Weg Jesu: Eine Erklärung des Markus-Evangeliums und der kanonischen Parallelen* (Berlin: Töpelmann, 1966), viii. Gasque explains that the "dependence of Haenchen on the work of Dibelius is obvious from the start." See W. Ward Gasque, *A History of the Criticism of the Acts of the Apostles* (repr., Grand Rapids: Eerdmans, 1975), 235.
7. Busse, "Ernst Haenchen," 126. Tyson (*Luke*, 66) glosses over some of the details from Busse and in this instance Tyson wrongly implies that Haenchen's studies were interrupted at the start of the war.
8. Busse, "Ernst Haenchen," 126.
9. Busse ("Ernst Haenchen," 126) explains that this was the third time he was wounded although an earlier wound in 1917 was only minor.
10. Busse, "Ernst Haenchen," 126.

of his significant health issues that also caused him to suffer from various neurovegetative disorders throughout his life.

Haenchen then left Berlin for Tübingen so he could then focus on New Testament studies during the winter and spring sessions of 1922–1923 and summer of 1925.[11] Haenchen then worked for the Evangelical Church of the Old-Prussian Union as a pastor and then became Karl Heim's teaching assistant in Tübingen during the winter semester of 1926–1927. While Haenchen was teaching at Friedeberg (Neumark), Tübingen accepted his doctoral thesis and on January 15, 1926 he was awarded a doctorate in theology (*summa cum laude*).

Haenchen passed his second theological examination later that year in Berlin.[12] It was during the winter semester of 1926–1927 that Haenchen first met Ernst Käsemann, who, like Haenchen, was interested in Bultmann's work on the Gospel of John. Despite their differing views on some important points of interpretation, their friendship continued with their mutual interest in the study of John's Gospel.

Haenchen's early teaching career was unfortunately fraught with difficulties. In February of 1928, he developed tuberculosis as a result of an old war wound. He then moved to Davos, Switzerland for two years in order to heal from his illness. It was here that he became engaged to the daughter of a protestant minister; Marguerite Fahrenberger gave Ernst renewed courage to resume teaching (on a trial basis) at Tübingen for the summer semester of 1930.[13] They married the following year.

Part of Haenchen's success as a professor was due to his ability to simplify for his students the complex dialectical theologies of Friedrich Gogarten, Eduard Thurneysen, Karl Barth, Emil Brunner, and Rudolf Bultmann—and he apparently did so without using any unnecessary arcane words. His teaching style resulted in his being shortlisted for the Chair of Systematic Theology in Giessen, where he was competing against notable scholars such as Emil Brunner.[14] Haenchen was offered

---

11. I am assuming Busse ("Ernst Haenchen," 127) indicates these dates with his abbreviations: "WS 1922/23 — SS 1925." WS = Winter Session and SS = Summer Session.
12. Busse, "Ernst Haenchen," 127. The date is entirely unclear except that it was in 1926.
13. Busse, "Ernst Haenchen," 127. He did so initially "with a collapsed lung"!
14. Haenchen's work began in philosophy and systematic theology long before his well-known studies on the New Testament. See Daniel So, "William Ramsay and Ernst Haenchen," in *Pillars in the History of Biblical Interpretation, Volume 1: Prevailing Methods before 1980*, eds. Stanley E. Porter and Sean A. Adams, MBSS 2 (Eugene, OR: Pickwick, 2016), 302–20 (303).

and accepted the position in Giessen, and taught there starting in the summer semester of 1933.[15]

In fact, 1933 represents a major turn of events in German history. Busse remarks that "[t]he time of National Socialism brought a period of temptation and testing for Ernst Haenchen."[16] He faced temptation because he was a very gifted Prussian educated professor who sacrificed both his youth and his health for the 'fatherland.' Moreover, the rise of National Socialism would also have been enticing for Haenchen because of the promise of a greater Germany and the call to Christians to help achieve this end. His relationship with Emanuel Hirsch in Freudenstadt, with whom he shared common interests, would only have strengthened this desire.[17]

In the years leading up to World War II, Haenchen became active in church politics both as a dean of Giessen and as a member of the Theological Chamber of the German Protestant Church in 1936.[18] He taught at the University of Münster for only one semester before the German invasion of Poland on September 1, 1939. Many of the students and faculty were drafted. Haenchen, however, continued (almost singlehandedly) to teach while he focused on ethics as well as Paul's letters to the Romans and Galatians in the winter semester of 1933–1934. The content of his teaching reflected much of what the remaining (and wounded) students wished to learn.

Since Münster eventually came into the range of enemy aircraft, Haenchen was forced to teach in the basement of the Fürstenberghaus, which was one of the University of Münster's buildings.[19] The university finally closed after the summer semester of 1944, and Haenchen went back to Switzerland (at the instigation of his Swiss relatives) for a time to heal since he had become physically weak. Meanwhile he managed to smuggle in a copy of the Nestle Greek text of the New Testament, despite there being a prohibition on importing printed

---

15.   It was during this year that Haenchen published: "Volk und Staat in der Lehre der Kirche," in *Volk, Staat, Kirche: Ein Lehrgang der theologischen Fakultät Giessen*, eds. H. Bornkamm, et al. (Giessen: Töpelmann, 1933), 53–72. For a discussion of this essay and Haenchen's "struggle with Nazi ideology," see Tyson, *Luke*, 67–69. Although Tyson finds the "lack of a vigorous critique of Nazi doctrines of *Volk* and law" disappointing there is "little sign of anti-Judaism" in the article (pp. 67 and 68 respectively).

16.   Busse, "Ernst Haenchen," 128.

17.   Busse ("Ernst Haenchen," 129) highlights the fact that both had a common interest in Søren Kierkegaard.

18.   Busse ("Ernst Haenchen," 129) explains that Haenchen's political commitment did not go beyond his church appointment.

19.   Busse, "Ernst Haenchen," 129.

German products into Switzerland. This event in effect launched his "second career" as a "NT exegete."[20] In particular, his reading of the Greek text of Acts on the train ride seems to represent the definitive start of Haenchen's later and greater work on Acts, and also on Mark and John.[21]

Haenchen returned to Münster in 1948 after four very productive years and this time represented a transition into a new phase of his scholarship where he did not rely on any secondary literature.[22] Beyond his preparatory work in Switzerland, in 1949 (and at the faculty's request) he taught the third-level Greek course for the next ten years as an emeritus professor until his retirement in 1959. During this time, he became more focused on the Gospel of John and worked almost daily at the task of preparing his commentary. Unfortunately, he died on April 30, 1975 and was not able to finish this work himself. However, Haenchen's commentary on John was finished through the combined efforts of his wife, friends, and students—all in an attempt to reflect his original purpose.[23]

HAENCHEN'S CONTRIBUTION TO LUKE–ACTS STUDY

Haenchen's influence on Luke–Acts scholarship is unequivocally far reaching and the jewel of the crown is his commentary on Acts.[24]

---

20. Tyson, *Luke*, 67.
21. Richard I. Pervo, *Acts*, Hermeneia (Minneapolis: Fortress, 2009), xv; So, "Ramsay and Haenchen," 303. Tyson (*Luke*, 67) seems to imply that Haenchen published his commentary on Mark at this time but the first edition did not appear until 1966. See Haenchen, *Der Weg Jesu*. For a handy chronological list of Haenchen's publications (until 1964) see: Walther Eltester and Franz H. Kettler, eds., *Apophoreta: Festschrift für Ernst Haenchen zu seinem siebzigsten Geburtstag am 10. Dezember 1964* (Berlin: Töpelmann, 1964), 1–6. See also Ernst Haenchen, *Das Johannesevangelium: Ein Kommentar*, ed. Ulrich Busse (Tübingen: Mohr Siebeck, 1980) and Haenchaen, *Die Apostelgeschichte*, 10th ed., KEK 3 (Göttingen: Vandenhoeck & Ruprecht, 1956). The English version represents the 14th German edition from 1965. See Ernst Haenchen, *The Acts of the Apostles* (Oxford: Blackwell, 1971).
22. Busse ("Ernst Haenchen," 129) considers this to be a "unique stroke of luck" ("ein einmaliger Glücksfall").
23. Busse, "Ernst Haenchen," 131. See the rest of Busse's essay that discusses the history and evolution of the commentary editions, Haenchen's theological position, and the invitation to continue his work on John.
24. For further study on Haenchen's contribution to the study of Acts, see Gasque, *History*, 235–50; C. K. Barrett, *Luke the Historian in Recent Study* (London: Epworth, 1961), 46–50; Jacques Dupont, *The Sources of Acts: The Present Position* (London: Darton, Longman & Todd, 1964), 126–32, 140–47; Busse, "Ernst Haenchen," 125–43; Tyson, *Luke*, 66–90 (his chapter 5 but esp. 66–76 on Haenchen); and So, "Ramsay and Haenchen," 302–20 (esp. 308–18).

Fitzmyer claims that, aside from two key works by Hans Conzelmann, "no book has so influenced the study of Acts in recent decades as Haenchen's massive commentary *Die Apostelgeschichte.*"[25] Fitzmyer goes on to say that this work is to the English-speaking world "one of the great NT commentaries of the third quarter of this century; no one who would study Acts can do without it."[26] Bruce calls it a "magnificent commentary" where "[n]o charge of parochialism can be laid against him, such as is incurred from time to time by German theologians."[27] Edwards in his conclusion boasts that "it is the most satisfactory commentary on a biblical book that I have ever read."[28]

Accolades aside, it is worth revisiting this watershed work directly and without the added layers of secondary opinion which in time can become subjective and stifling. Let us endeavor to read and digest Haenchen in his own words. Writing in November of 1970, he opens his preface with some important history as to how his landmark work came about:

> Fifty-six years ago, in my first semester, I bought as my first books the Nestle *Novum Testamentum Graece* and Wendt's commentary on Acts, which had just appeared in its 9th edition in the Meyer commentary series. At that time I did not suspect that Acts one day would claim the major part of my time and effort for 20 years on end, and that as author of the 10th edition I was to be Wendt's successor.[29]

Immediately one is struck by the weight of academic investment that went into this commentary. It is commendable that Haenchen

---

25. Cf. Joseph A. Fitzmyer, Review of *The Acts of the Apostles: A Commentary*, by Ernst Haenchen, *TS* 33 (1972): 582–85 (582); Hans Conzelmann, *Die Mitte der Zeit: Studien zur Theologie des Lukas*, BHT 17 (Tübingen: Mohr Siebeck, 1954) ET Conzelmann, *The Theology of St. Luke*, trans. Geoffrey Buswell (London: Faber & Faber, 1960); Conzelmann, *Die Apostelgeschichte*, HNT 7 (Tübingen: Mohr Siebeck 1963).

26. Fitzmyer, Review of *The Acts of the Apostles*, 582.

27. F. F. Bruce, Review of *The Acts of the Apostles: A Commentary*, by Ernst Haenchen, *ExpTim* 83 (1972): 153–54 (153). See also E. Earle Ellis, Review of *The Acts of the Apostles*, by Ernst Haenchen, *RTR* 26 (1972): 197; S. G. Wilson, Review of *The Acts of the Apostles*, by Ernst Haenchen, *Theol* 75 (1972): 268–70.

28. O. C. Edwards, Jr., "The Exegesis of Acts 8:4–25 and Its Implications for Confirmation and Glossalalia: A Review Article on Haenchen's Acts Commentary," *ATR* (Supplement Series) 2 (1973): 100–112.

29. Haenchen, *Acts*, vii. He explains that "[p]robably neither of these things would have come about had I not had to travel to Switzerland for a cure in 1944." See also Hans Hinrich Wendt, *Die Apostelgeschichte*, 9th ed., KEK 3 (Göttingen: Vandenhoeck & Ruprecht, 1913).

invested fifty-six years of general study, with twenty years specifically dedicated to the book of Acts. That is commendable.

During his train ride to Switzerland after the summer semester of 1944, and armed with only a single, thin-paper edition copy of Nestle's *Novum Testamentum Graece*, Haenchen "sought to penetrate more deeply into Acts."[30] Accordingly, he says that this was "all I had when I began to occupy the time of my convalescence with some serious work. That was a great blessing."[31] In this way, he could study Acts without the influence of secondary works which were "primarily interested in Luke's sources."[32] This lack of external influence meant that Haenchen's mind was open to the crucial question of what Luke was trying to say to his readers through the book of Acts.[33] We will revisit the value of Haenchen's questioning process in the section below. See "Critical Responses and a Reappraisal of Haenchen's Work in Luke–Acts."

By 1946, and after his time in Switzerland, Haenchen produced an outline of his first commentary on Luke–Acts that later grew from a monograph to a comprehensive volume.[34] The questions raised at this point fuelled his search for answers that would later appear in the "twice substantially revised" work by the time of its fifteenth edition in 1968 while the English edition procured new insights as well.[35]

Haenchen's train ride represents the start of a pendulum swing in Luke–Acts scholarship. Rather than simply focusing on Luke the historian, the emerging focus would begin to see Luke as an edifying writer and theologian—thus plunging Luke–Acts into a "storm center in contemporary scholarship."[36] Although Haenchen is by no

---

30. Haenchen, *Acts*, vii. Here he says that it was then "strictly forbidden to take books across the frontier."
31. Haenchen, *Acts*, vii.
32. Haenchen, *Acts*, vii. See "The Sources of Acts" below.
33. Haenchen, *Acts*, vii.
34. Haenchen, *Acts*, vii.
35. Haenchen, *Acts*, vii–viii. Under the supervision of Hugh Anderson, Haenchen credits Bernard Noble and Gerald Shinn with the translation from the fourteenth German edition and R. McL. Wilson with the final revised English translation. Further, Haenchen says that Joachim Jeremias and Ernst Käsemann "read the entire manuscript of the first edition in its various stages with a critical eye" (vii). He gives credit to H. J. Cadbury and Jacques Dupont for scholarship outside of Germany. He dedicates his book to Cadbury while he refers to his work rather frequently.
36. W. C. van Unnik, "Luke–Acts, a Storm Center in Contemporary Scholarship," in *Studies in Luke–Acts: Essays in Honour of Paul Schubert*, eds. Leander E. Keck and J. Louis Martyn (Nashville: Abingdon, 1966), 15–32. Certainly others contributed to this shift such as Martin Dibelius, Ernst Käsemann, Philipp Vielhauer, and Paul Schubert (as noted by Fitzmyer, Review of *The Acts of the Apostles*, 583).

means the sole cause of this shift we need to understand his work in Acts in light of this momentous shift.[37] Since this is the case, we will explore the core of Haenchen's contribution through the major areas of Haenchen's research. Before the conclusion, I will engage some of the general criticisms of Haenchen's work while also providing a fresh defense of his approach.

The Sources of Acts

Among the several interpretive issues pertaining to Acts, the source debate is one area where Haenchen offers some valuable comments for discussion. He suggests that the primary reason as to why this subject remains such a thorny issue is due to the risky business of comparing Acts with the Third Gospel.

> For the situation in Acts is utterly different. We are in possession of one of the sources for Luke: the Gospel of Mark. Another—Q—can to a large extent be inferred. In the case of Acts we are not in the happy position of possessing one of its sources. This is the more regrettable since Luke, as we have learned from comparing him with Mark, subjects his sources to a stylistic revision which renders their reconstitution impossible from his text alone. We may assume that he did not treat the underlying sources of Acts any differently. No sources can therefore be discerned in Acts by stylistic criteria.[38]

Far from being silenced, the traditional questions raised concerning the author of Acts and his sources became livelier than ever in Haenchen's mind.[39] Although the source discussion has fallen strangely quiet since

---

37. Fitzmyer, Review of *The Acts of the Apostles*, 583.

38. Haenchen, *Acts*, 81.

39. Haenchen, *Acts*, 117. He states that scholars have "long been in suspense over the question of sources in Acts. Even today it has not been finally answered." Haenchen, *Acts*, 81 (see his full discussion in section 6 "The Source Question," 81–90). After referring to the earlier work by Wendt in the KEK series, Pervo discusses Haenchen's commentary who sent "reams of source theory up the chimney by showing a generation of scholars and clergy that Wendt had wasted his time." See Richard I. Pervo, *Dating Acts: Between the Evangelists and the Apologists* (Santa Rosa, CA: Polebridge, 2006), 1. Here Pervo claims that "about one half" of Wendt's introduction relates to the question of sources. See Hans H. Wendt, *Die Apostelgeschichte*, 8th ed., KEK 3 (Göttingen: Vandenhoeck & Ruprecht, 1899). Pervo seems to be overreaching in his comments here not only in light of Haenchen's expressed view (*Acts*, 117) but also because Wendt clearly had some valid source ideas. For example, Wendt (in relation to 'an' Antioch theory of sorts) hypothesized that the "rewriting" of the 'we' sections demonstrates how the author of these sections should *not* "be identified with the writer of Acts." See Dupont, *Sources*, 63; Wendt, *Die Apostelgeschichte* and also Hans H. Wendt,

his time, some have been willing to revisit the theories and enter into what should remain a necessary discussion.[40]

The source discussion led to a consideration of a greater source at Luke's disposal which would account for the "linking of the pericopes in a considerable part of the book."[41] Namely, this record of Paul's "missions" was thought to depend in part on an 'itinerary' that was "written in the first person plural" as previously discussed by Dibelius and subsequently borrowed by Haenchen as one of his students.[42] However, over the course of Haenchen's publications, he came to question (in greater intensity) the itinerary/travel-journal hypothesis originally proposed by Dibelius.[43] In the beginning Haenchen supported Dibelius's hypothesis but later rejected it.

Given Haenchen's skepticism in general—and against source theory in particular—his views on some aspects of the source discussion are somewhat surprising.[44] For example, he maintains that the author was clearly relying on some form of source(s) and did not invent all of the stories and speeches in the narrative for some imaginative purpose.[45] Although Haenchen is hesitant to name specific sources, he

---

"Die Hauptquelle der Apostelgeschichte," *ZAW* 24 (1925): 293–305. More recently, Stanley E. Porter (*Paul in Acts* [repr., Peabody, MA: Hendrickson, 1999], 39) argues along similar lines as Wendt. Earlier, Bultmann addressed Haenchen's views on the sources for Acts and claimed that it is in fact easier to understand certain passages (such as Acts 15:1–35) if there is in fact a written source behind it. See Rudolf Bultmann, "Zur Frage nach den Quellen der Apostelgeschichte," in *New Testament Essays: Studies in Memory of Thomas Walter Manson*, ed. Angus J. Brockhurst Higgins (Manchester: Manchester University Press, 1959), 68–80 (68).

40. Pervo, *Dating Acts*, 1. Unfortunately, some Luke–Acts scholars do not think it is worth exploring. For example, Pervo refers to Talbert who "efficiently dispenses with questions about the sources and date of Acts before he has completed the first page." See Charles H. Talbert, *Reading Acts: A Literary and Theological Commentary on the Acts of the Apostles*, RNTS (New York: Crossroads, 1997), 2. For further study see Craig S. Keener, *Acts: An Exegetical Commentary*, 4 vols. (Grand Rapids: Baker Academic, 2012–2015), 1:166–220 ("Approaching Acts as a Historical Source") and, more recently, Karl L. Armstrong, *Dating Acts in Its Jewish and Greco-Roman Contexts*, LNTS 637 (London: T&T Clark, 2021), 47–73.

41. See Dupont, *Sources*, 67.

42. Dupont, *Sources*, 67 and Martin Dibelius, *Studies in the Acts of the Apostles*, ed. Heinrich Greeven, trans. Mary Ling and Paul Schubert (London: SCM, 1956), 73–74.

43. Haenchen, *Acts*, 86. Gasque (*History*, 239) says that from 1959 onward Haenchen "completely parts company with Dibelius over the question of the itinerary" and so Haenchen came to "reject the *Itinerar*-hypothesis altogether" (italics original). However, if we consider Dibelius's original and broadly defined theory of an itinerary there are good reasons to revisit it once again. See Dibelius, *Studies*, 5–6 and Dupont, *Sources*, 114–15.

44. Gasque (*History*, 236) credits Haenchen's disdain of the older "source-critical" perspective between "tradition and composition in Acts" primarily to Dibelius. See also Tyson, *Luke*, 69–70.

45. See Haenchen, *Acts*, 81–90 and his section on "The Source-Question." See also Ernst Haenchen, "Tradition und Komposition in der Apostelgeschichte," *ZTK* 52 (1955): 205–25 and Haenchen, "The Book of Acts as Source Material for the History of Earliest Christianity," in *Studies in Luke–Acts*, 258–78.

does not dismiss the likelihood that such sources existed.[46] Even the longstanding Antioch source theory he does not reject outright but instead challenges its veracity—while also weighing the possibility of Paul's companions as legitimate sources.[47]

Haenchen thought there were both oral and written traditions that originated with certain Christians and their associated church communities:

> But have we in fact only the choice between a travel-journal and the chronicle of Antioch? Not at all. When, years after Paul had run his course, Luke set about the task of describing the era of primitive Christianity, various possibilities of collecting the required material lay open to him. He could himself, for example, look up the most important Pauline communities—say Philippi, Corinth, Ephesus, Antioch. He might even visit Jerusalem. But it was also possible for him to ask other Christians travelling to these places to glean for him whatever was still known of the old times (if he was preparing Acts about the year 75, twenty years would not yet have elapsed since Paul's death, and perhaps forty from the foundation of the community in Antioch). Lastly, he could have written to the congregations in question and asked them for information.[48]

This appears to be an entirely plausible scenario except that he assumes this date of Acts (c. AD 75), rather than arguing for it.[49] Given Haenchen's skepticism, it is significant that he sees Luke writing as early as AD 75 in relation to Paul's death.

Haenchen refers back to his explanation of source theories in his introduction (discussed immediately above) and he applies this specifically to the situation at Philippi in Acts 16:11–40. He thinks

---

46. Haenchen, *Acts*, 86.
47. Haenchen, *Acts*, 87, 369.
48. Haenchen, *Acts*, 86.
49. In fairness to Haenchen, he is not alone with respect to assumptions on the date of Acts. A core issue in this debate is the death of Paul that likely occurred as early as AD 63/64 but no later than the end of Nero's reign in AD 68. See Harry W. Tajra, *The Martyrdom of St. Paul*, WUNT 67 (Tübingen: Mohr Siebeck, 1994), 199. In a note of disappointment, Pervo (*Dating Acts*, 461) admits that Haenchen "does not argue for a 'late date' for Acts. . . . he does not depart from the 'consensus.'" Haenchen's comments imply a date of AD 75 but also a date of 80 and possibly AD 85. See Haenchen, *Acts*, 86, 164, 244–45, 257. Elsewhere Haenchen ("Source Material," 266) implies a date "toward the end of the first century in which Luke lived." For a recent treatment on this critical issue, see Karl L. Armstrong, "A New Plea for an Early Date of Acts," *JGRChJ* 13 (2017): 79–110; Armstrong, "The End of Acts and the Comparable Age of Its Variants," *FN* 31 (2018): 87–110; and Armstrong, *Dating Acts*.

that Luke "probably received the information concerning Philippi—directly or indirectly—from an eyewitness of the Pauline mission."[50] Additionally, he surmises that Luke "gives the reader to understand this valuable source of his material through the fact that he reports the history of the mission in Philippi whenever possible in the 'we' style."[51] In addition to information about the "founding of the community and the expulsion of the Apostle," Luke may also have received information about the "stories which circulated about Paul in Philippi."[52] It seems then that Haenchen wanted to be critical of source theories on the one hand, but on the other, he kept the door open to a very plausible scenario of how Luke gathered his sources. On this point Haenchen's perspective deserves greater attention and presents an opportunity for further research.

Luke as Theologian, Historian, and Writer

Beyond the thorny topic of Luke and his sources, Haenchen's greatest contribution to Luke–Acts scholarship is probably his work relating to the conjectural relationship between Luke as a theologian, historian, *and* writer. Haenchen explains that, since there is such an "uncommonly close tie" between these three aspects of Luke as an author,

> [o]ne cannot avoid treating the three separately, but that remains an expedient. Scholars of past generations regarded Luke as above all a historian. . . . More recently the worthy labours of Vielhauer and especially Conzelmann . . . have done much to bring his theology to light. It is the *art of the writer* which now stands most in need of evaluation.[53]

---

50. Haenchen, *Acts*, 503.
51. Haenchen, *Acts*, 503. On the problem with the 'we' passages, see Henry J. Cadbury, "'We' and 'I' Passages in Luke–Acts," *NTS* 3 (1957): 128–32; Dupont, *Sources*, 75–112 (esp. 75–93); Susan M. Praeder, "The Problem of First Person Narration in Acts," *NovT* 29 (1987) 193–218; Colin J. Hemer, *The Book of Acts in the Setting of Hellenistic History* (Tübingen: Mohr Siebeck, 1989), 308–34; Porter, *Paul in Acts*, 10–46; William S. Campbell, *The "We" Passages in the Acts of the Apostles: The Narrator as Narrative Character* (Atlanta: SBL, 2007); and William S. Campbell, "The Narrator as 'He,' 'Me,' and 'We': Grammatical Person in Ancient Histories and in the Acts of the Apostles," *JBL* 129 (2010): 385–407; and more recently Armstrong, "The 'We' Source Theories," in *Dating Acts*, 52–65.
52. Haenchen, *Acts*, 503.
53. Haenchen, *Acts*, 90–91 (my emphasis, see 12–24 with regards to those who view Luke primarily as a historian).

Haenchen's emphasis upon Luke's prowess as a writer requires further exploration and conversation. The backdrop to this discussion is especially significant as we can see the continuity (and variance) between his teacher Dibelius and the more recent developments presented by his contemporaries: Vielhauer and Conzelmann.

Prior to Vielhauer and Conzelmann, Dibelius demonstrated that Luke, as an author *and* historian, was able to reproduce "reality in an altered form in order to illuminate its meaning."[54] Here it is necessary to note just how much credit Haenchen gives Dibelius for giving due prominence to Luke as a New Testament writer.[55] No longer was Luke simply a "'compiler or transmitter'" of information—due prominence was given to him as a writer and theologian with "his own positive characteristics."[56] Scholars were now free to discard the well-ingrained belief that Acts was simply a "quarry to furnish material for the reconstruction of primitive Christianity."[57] Since Dibelius's watershed work scholars were free to ask what a biblical writer was "trying to tell his readers"—instead of myopically researching the "historical reliability" of the text.[58] Nearly fifty years later there does not seem to be any major shift in this trend that focuses upon Luke as a creative writer in Luke–Acts studies. At the same time, the measure of Luke as a historian should not be excluded from any consideration of Luke as a writer and theologian.

Furthermore, Haenchen expected that Dibelius and "his followers must expect to encounter strong resistance."[59] He explains that the kind of freedom that Dibelius ascribed to the "writer Luke is hard to stomach"—and not only for "Catholic scholars" but also for those in England where "scholarship is governed by the spirit of conservatism."[60] However, this is not only a matter of overcoming deeply held church traditions; it is a question of "disappointing the longing for historical information" that has been habitually and historically gleaned from every verse in Acts.[61] Consequently, Haenchen remarks that the "purely historical outlook, after a reign of two hundred years, could

---

54. Haenchen, *Acts*, 48.
55. See Haenchen, *Acts*, 34–42 and his unpacking of Dibelius in the context of the first and second phase of form-criticism that occurred after 1945.
56. Haenchen, *Acts*, 41.
57. Haenchen, *Acts*, 41.
58. Haenchen, *Acts*, 41.
59. Haenchen, *Acts*, 41.
60. Haenchen, *Acts*, 41.
61. Haenchen, *Acts*, 41.

scarcely be dethroned overnight."[62] With this in mind, Haenchen, in line with Dibelius, pushed to share this new perspective that saw Luke as an edifying writer and theologian—and not simply an unbiased purveyor of history.[63]

In many ways, Haenchen went far beyond Dibelius's thought whereby three substantial scholars provided additional building material for his argument that Luke was an edifying writer: Vielhauer, Conzelmann, and Käsemann. By the 1950s it was Luke the theologian (and not the historian) who became the focus of "Protestant" research on Acts in Germany.[64] Specifically, it was Vielhauer's key essay on the differences between the theology of Luke and Paul that garnered widespread attention.[65] Vielhauer argued that Luke, the "supposed companion of Paul, is everywhere at odds with the Apostle: he lends a positive tendency to the *theologia naturalis*, plays down the redemptive significance of the Cross and abandons expectation of the End."[66]

Meanwhile, Conzelmann's studies in Lukan theology further illustrated the shift from Luke the historian to seeing Luke (in greater measure) as a creative theological writer.[67] Conzelmann argued that Luke wrote a theology of "saving history" instead of the earlier Christian teaching that was myopically focused on the "imminent End."[68] Accordingly, Luke narrated three periods of history starting with (1) the "law and the prophets," (2) the "time of salvation" that focuses on Jesus, and (3) the "time of the Church" that culminates with the future parousia.[69] Alternately, Käsemann estimated that Luke's "real theme was to represent the hour of the Church as the middle of time."[70] Haenchen deduced that the "."

---

62. Haenchen, *Acts*, 41.
63. Haenchen, *Acts*, 103–10.
64. Haenchen, *Acts*, 48.
65. Cf. Philipp Vielhauer, "Zum 'Paulinismus' der Apostelgeschichte," *EvTh*10 (1950–1951): 1–15.
66. Haenchen, *Acts*, 48.
67. Hans Conzelmann, *Die Mitte der Zeit*; Conzelmann, *The Theology of St. Luke*. See his earlier essay: Conzelmann, "Zur Lukasanalyse," *ZTK* 49 (1952): 16–33.
68. Haenchen (*Acts*, 48) is drawing from Conzelmann, *Die Mitte der Zeit* (and the English translation: *St. Luke*); Conzelmann, "Zur Lukasanalyse"; and Conzelmann, "Die Rede des Paulus auf dem Areopag," *Gymnasium Helveticum* 12 (1958): 18–32.
69. Haenchen, *Acts*, 48.
70. Haenchen, *Acts*, 48–49. "Luke is . . . the first representative of evolving early Catholicism." See Ernst Käsemann, "Neutestamentliche Fragen von heute," *ZTK* 54 (1957): 1–21 (20, as cited by Haenchen, *Acts*, 49).

with Luke's theology was that he essentially "replaces the *theologia crucis* with the *theologia gloriae*."[71]

Over and above the work of Dibelius, it was the works by Vielhauer, Conzelmann, and Käsemann who had a profound impact on Haenchen's thought—although he admits that his views presented "some moderation."[72] Haenchen is being modest here since his own work seems to represent a critical expansion of thought that supersedes the ideas of Dibelius, Vielhauer, Conzelmann, and Käsemann. The first reason for Haenchen's moderation is that (in his commentary) he did not treat the "theology of Acts as the only theme of this book."[73] His concern was to "expound the composition of the writer Luke both as a whole and in detail, a composition which at times appears almost to create *ex nihilo*. It is only by virtue of this astounding freedom that Luke's historical narrative can become the trusty tool of Lucan theology."[74]

The second reason for Haenchen's moderation is that (in anticipation of his section on "Luke as Theologian, Historian and Writer") Luke does "not yet present, like the Ignatian letters, a theology of the episcopal office" but rather he "outlines no theory of all-embracing ecclesiastical organization."[75] Haenchen is adamant that the "real subject of Acts" is the word of God and its growth.[76] He goes on to explain that the word of God is "certainly proclaimed by men and authenticated by God through signs and miracles."[77] Even a casual reading of Acts seems to support this observation.

Haenchen explains how Luke's theology never reached the same heights as Paul and that his teaching is "one of the many variants of Gentile Christian theology which—more or less independent of the great Apostle to the gentiles—grew up alongside and after the theology of Paul."[78] The core of this "gentile theology" that came with a "tendency

---

71. Haenchen, *Acts*, 49. There appears to be a change in Luke's emphasis from Paul's focus on the cross at Corinth (1 Cor. 2:2).
72. Haenchen, *Acts*, 49. He points to his tenth edition as representing this new shift. Cf. also Ernst Haenchen, "Schriftzitate und Textüberlieferung in der Apostelgeschichte," *ZTK* 51 (1954): 153–67; Haenchen, "Tradition und Komposition," 205–25; Haenchen, "Zum Text der Apostelgeschichte," *ZTK* 54 (1957): 22–55; and Haenchen, "Source Material," 258–78.
73. Haenchen, *Acts*, 49.
74. Haenchen, *Acts*, 49 (original emphasis).
75. Haenchen, *Acts*, 49. Here he points to Acts 9:31 as indicative of the church simply meaning "individual community" without any development of sacramentalism.
76. Haenchen, *Acts*, 49.
77. Haenchen, *Acts*, 49.
78. Haenchen, *Acts*, 49.

to law and observances" gradually morphed into early Catholicism.[79]
For Haenchen then, the true voice of the gospel can only be found in
Paul's theology of the cross.

Luke as Theologian

Haenchen clarifies an important factor in his quest to understand Luke
as a theological writer. He claims that Luke is "no systematic theologian" and that he "does not seek to develop any unified doctrine, the
product of thorough reflection."[80] However, even though his theology may not be systematic, Haenchen does indicate that Luke clearly
presents a theology of his own. Luke begins with "definite theological
premises" that were a going concern in his day; and yet, he does not
present his theology in a systematic fashion but rather his concerns
are "suggested to the reader in his historical presentation by means of
vivid scenes."[81] Haenchen reinforces his position by offering a nuanced
presentation of the kinds of theological issues that seem to underline
Luke's theological program.[82]

In the first part of Haenchen's argument for "Luke as Theologian,"
he observes how Luke at times has been "praised for presenting so
faithful a picture of the primitive theology of early Christian times."[83]
Contrary to this long-held belief, Haenchen demonstrates that behind
Luke's presentation in Acts the careful reader discovers a shared "simple
theology" that undergirds the prayers, speeches, and other theological expressions and comments.[84] He then discusses the centrality of
God the father in Luke's perspective and the nuances found relating
to Jesus and the Holy Spirit. In regards to the Spirit, Luke does "not
yet show the balance attained by later theology in the doctrine of the
Trinity."[85] Furthermore, apparently Luke "elaborates no doctrine of
the *Church*"—and Haenchen explains that it is only at Acts 9:31 do
we find a "meaning beyond 'local congregation'" for ἐκκλησία—

79. Haenchen, *Acts*, 49.
80. Haenchen, *Acts*, 91.
81. Haenchen, *Acts*, 91, vii.
82. See Haenchen, *Acts*, 91–94 ("A. The Theological Premises").
83. This is contrary to Foakes-Jackson's earlier view where "Luke seems to have been able to give us
an extraordinarily accurate picture of the undeveloped theology of the earliest Christians." See
Frederick John Foakes-Jackson, *The Acts of the Apostles*, MNTC (New York: Harper, 1931), xvi (as
cited by Haenchen).
84. Haenchen, *Acts*, 91.
85. Haenchen, *Acts*, 92.

and even then it "simply covers the Church in Judaea, Galilee and Samaria."[86] He points out—and I think correctly—that with regards to Lukan ecclesiology we have to "fall back upon scattered clues in the historical narrative."[87] Then again this is no surprise as Haenchen reasoned above that Luke is no systematic theologian.

What we have in Acts is a record of primitive Christianity. Even with the appointing of elders we "cannot speak of an 'apostolic succession': the elders are regarded rather as holding their authority from the Holy Spirit, and as entrusted by the Spirit with the leadership of the congregation."[88] Haenchen further adduces that Luke does not offer any "systematic teaching on how one becomes a *Christian*" and so rightly cautions us with any claim to the label of "'early Catholicism.'"[89] Furthermore, even the "sacramental piety" found in the Lord's supper which was performed "with gladness" (Acts 2:46) demonstrates that there is "little mention in Acts as of a monarchical episcopate."[90]

Haenchen's second argument in support of his view of 'Luke as Theologian' originates from two "theological questions of the day" that draw considerable attention in Acts; first, the "expectation of the imminent end of the world," and second, the "mission to the Gentiles without the law."[91] Here Haenchen addresses the first "eschatological problem" that made Luke's "writing of history intrinsically possible" while the second issue is "so inextricable from the course of the historical narrative."[92]

A key aspect of his argument rests on how the first generation of Christians saw the world, as they were "convinced that they stood amid the decisive revolution of the ages; this world, the present era, was passing away; and the era to come was upon them."[93] Haenchen alleges that due to the "short interval" after the advent of Jesus, and prior to the parousia and coming judgment, the disciples must "spread the glad tidings as wide as possible."[94] However, this earlier view of history was about to change in Acts:

---

86.   Haenchen, *Acts*, 93.
87.   Haenchen, *Acts*, 93.
88.   Haenchen, *Acts*, 93–94.
89.   Haenchen, *Acts*, 94 (original emphasis).
90.   Haenchen, *Acts*, 94.
91.   Haenchen, *Acts*, 94 (see also 94–98 for his section: "B. Theological Questions of the Day").
92.   Haenchen, *Acts*, 94. Haenchen deals with Luke as a historian in his third section (see 98–103: "II. Luke the Historian in Acts").
93.   Haenchen, *Acts*, 95.
94.   Haenchen, *Acts*, 95. The approaching reign of God was already at work through the miracles and healings.

This expectation of the imminent end was not fulfilled. When Luke wrote Acts, Paul had been executed and James the brother of the Lord had died a martyr; Christians had burned as living torches in the gardens of Nero; the Holy City and its Temple lay in rubble. Yet the world went on. By this many Christians recognized that the imminent expectation of the end was false. If, however, the end was not to come soon, when would it come?

If Haenchen is correct, then this naturally follows an expectation that the Gospel writers (including Luke) would need to adapt their writings to these notable events and unfulfilled expectations.[95]

Haenchen considers two possible literary responses—first, that a Gospel writer "might see the last things happening here and now," or second, they "might expect their realization only in a remote, indefinite future."[96] Accordingly, the Fourth Evangelist endeavored to demonstrate how the reader did not have to wait since they could embrace the "resurrection and the life" here in the present.[97] Everything from the resurrection to damnation was wound up in the present time—there was no need to be watching the skies and waiting anxiously for the "Son of Man descending with clouds" since in John's mind the Father and Son were already "dwelling with him."[98]

The Third Evangelist also "denied the imminent expectation" as he left such dates and times up to God, for Christians should refrain from such eschatological speculations about the end of the world and should instead "reckon with the world's survival."[99] For Luke's Gospel, it was easier to deal with eschatology and expectation since it all happened in the past and so Luke (as a historian) did his best with his sources.[100] When it comes to the book of Acts, Luke focuses on the "'*Word of God*' which fills the time after Pentecost; this Word is furthermore the message concerning Jesus, belief in whom brings forgiveness of sins

---

95. If Luke was unaware of these events when he wrote Acts then this would present a serious difficulty to Haenchen's argument. The problem is that a study of the historical context shows that there are good reasons to suggest he was not aware of these events. See Armstrong, "A New Plea," 79–110; Armstrong, "The End of Acts," 87–110; Armstrong, *Dating Acts*.

96. Haenchen, *Acts*, 95.

97. Haenchen, *Acts*, 95.

98. Haenchen, *Acts*, 95–96.

99. Haenchen, *Acts*, 96; Acts 1:7. He also refers to Acts 1:11 "despite 2.20"!

100. Haenchen, *Acts*, 97.

and deliverance in the judgment."[101] This is the "clamp which fastens the two eras together," according to Haenchen, and this clamp is what "justifies, indeed demands, the continuation of the first book."[102]

Haenchen then asks, "[A]t what point should this portrayal stop?" and he goes on to explain how the proper ending for Luke would include the "return of Jesus" but this is "hidden from us in an unknown future."[103] Luke then stops short of his true historical conclusion since Paul was a "witness before the emperor" and consequently "suffered martyrdom."[104] Rather than including this event, Luke chose to end his story with the portrait of an unhindered Paul in Rome.[105]

Luke's story of the gospel marching forth from Jerusalem to Rome came full circle while also comforting the faithful since God was still active and in control right up to the last verse of Acts.[106] Much ink has been spilled over what Luke did or did not allude to with respect to the martyrdom of Paul and what he determined he should write at the end.[107] However, it seems clear that the end to Luke's grand history did relay a sense of comfort to the faithful while at the same time encouraging his readers to continue the work of the gospel.[108]

Luke as Historian

In this section, we will consider Haenchen's perspective on "Luke as Historian."[109] Haenchen claims that it was Luke's "familiarity with the theological situation, and his understanding of what it required, that led Luke to turn historian and write a historical work in two

---

101. Haenchen, *Acts*, 98 (original emphasis).
102. Haenchen, *Acts*, 98.
103. Haenchen, *Acts*, 98.
104. Haenchen, *Acts*, 98. He says that the "alert reader" is aware of this martyrdom because of Acts 20:25, 38 and 27:24.
105. Haenchen, *Acts*, 98.
106. Haenchen, *Acts*, 98; Pervo, *Acts*, 686.
107. Haenchen, *Acts*, 98, 732. See also Pervo, *Acts*, 688; Joseph A. Fitzmyer, *The Acts of the Apostles*, AB 31 (New York: Doubleday, 1998), 52–53 and 674–76. More recently see Rainer Riesner, "Paul's Trial and End according to Second Timothy, *1 Clement*, the Canon Muratori, and the Apocryphal Acts," in *The Last Years of Paul: Essays from the Tarragona Conference, June 2013*, eds. Armand Puig i Tàrrech, et al., WUNT 352 (Tübingen: Mohr Siebeck, 2015), 391–409 (395). See Armstrong, *Dating Acts*, 113–116, for arguments against Luke's use of foreshadowing.
108. For further reading on the end of Acts, see Charles B. Puskas, *The Conclusion of Luke–Acts: The Significance of Acts 28:16–31* (Eugene, OR: Pickwick, 2009); Troy M. Troftgruben, *A Conclusion Unhindered: A Study of the Ending of Acts within Its Literary Environment*, WUNT 2/280 (Tübingen: Mohr Siebeck, 2010). See more recently the instructive essays in Armand Puig i Tàrrech, et al., eds., *The Last Years of Paul*, and a reappraisal of the various perspectives in Armstrong, *Dating Acts*, 97–123.
109. See Haenchen, *Acts*, 98–103.

volumes."[110] He argues that the picture of the "history of primitive Christianity" that Luke paints is characterized by "astonishing uniformity and simplicity" and that any difficulties are either
smoothed over or simply omitted.[111]

Haenchen then examines Luke's proclivity for smoothing out
his writing by working through a selection of issues that surround
the account of mission and expansion of the gospel from Jerusalem
(Acts 1) to Rome (Acts 28).[112] He espouses that Luke is giving the
impression of a "problem-free, victorious progress on the part of the
Christian mission."[113] However, from the "first page to the last" we
can observe how Luke the historian is "wrestling" with the difficulty
of the "*mission to the Gentiles without the law*."[114] He considers this
to be such an issue that Luke's "entire presentation is influenced" by
this problem.[115] Consequently, Haenchen begins to suggest what is
really going on behind the narrative.[116]

Problem-free seems to be a bit of an exaggeration, but in defense
of Haenchen, every chapter of Acts does appear to present the
victorious progress of the gospel right to the very end. We see this
victorious march culminate with the final picture of Paul in Rome
under house arrest for two whole years, preaching "with all boldness
and without hindrance" (μετὰ πάσης παρρησίας ἀκωλύτως).[117]
Haenchen goes on to explain that the problem of the 'mission to
the Gentiles without the law' consists of a "theological" as well as a
"political" element:[118]

---

110. Haenchen, *Acts*, 98–99.
111. Haenchen, *Acts*, 99.
112. Haenchen, *Acts*, 99–100. Some have seen in the end of Acts some kind of fitting narrative
      conclusion with Paul in Rome. For further reading, see Darrell L. Bock, *Acts*, BECNT (Grand
      Rapids: Baker, 2007), 758; Pervo, *Acts*, 686; and Troftgruben's (*Conclusion Unhindered*, 24–26)
      assessment and caution.
113. Haenchen, *Acts*, 100.
114. Haenchen, *Acts*, 100 (original emphasis). In his note 11 he claims that "[t]his problem is heralded as
      early as 1.8 and remains a burning question right up to 28.28." This concept remains an outstanding
      problem for Haenchen that lends to the unhistorical nature of Acts via differences between the Paul
      in Acts and Paul in his letters (see "Luke and Paul" below).
115. Haenchen, *Acts*, 100.
116. Although this method of questioning is natural for historians—this can be seen as dangerous to
      some conservative scholars. See I. Howard Marshall, *The Acts of the Apostles*, TNTC (repr., Downers
      Grove, IL: InterVarsity, 2008), 36.
117. See Haenchen, *Acts*, 98, 732 and David L. Mealand, "The Close of Acts and Its Hellenistic Greek
      Vocabulary," *NTS* 36 (1990): 583–97.
118. Haenchen, *Acts*, 100.

> By forsaking observance of the Jewish law Christianity parts company
> with Judaism; does this not break the continuity of the history of Salva-
> tion? That is the theological aspect. But in cutting adrift from Judaism
> Christianity also loses the toleration which the Jewish religion enjoys.[119]
> Denounced by the Jews as hostile to the state, it becomes the object
> of suspicion to Rome. That is the political aspect. Acts takes both
> constantly into account.[120]

For Haenchen then, the interpretive solution rests in seeing Luke
struggling with what to do with the Gentile mission (without the law)
in Luke's "own time."[121] The real Paul is essentially replaced with a
Paul that reflects a later stage of the church and as such we should "not
expect the Lukan Paul to resemble the Paul of the epistles."[122]

According to Haenchen, the "problem's true solution" for Luke
lies in showing how the "instigators and leaders of the Christian
mission" retained their Jewish faith while "God unmistakably and
irresistibly steered them into the mission to the Gentiles."[123] In order
to support this view Haenchen focuses upon the "irresistible will of
God" motif in Acts and cites the example of the "Cornelius episode"
and the "conversion and apologies with regard to Paul."[124] He asks, "If
God has endowed Gentile audiences with the Spirit, who can deny
them baptism? In the same way Paul, the Jewish missionary who was
brought up in Jerusalem, must bow to the irresistible will of God: it is
no use his kicking against the pricks!"[125]

Haenchen then claims that the "Christian mission need not have
to become the purely Gentile mission" that it was in Luke's time.[126]
The reason it became this way was because the offer of salvation was
given to the Jews "again and again."[127] However, it was not until "they

---

119. Here Haenchen draws from Burton S. Easton, *Early Christianity: The Purpose of Acts and Other Papers* (London: SPCK, 1955), 41–57.
120. Haenchen, *Acts*, 100.
121. Tyson, *Luke*, 71.
122. Tyson, *Luke*, 71. Haenchen (*Acts*, 116) explains how the "real Paul . . . has been replaced by a Paul seen through the eyes of a later age" and that "primitive age of Christianity is not described here by one who lived through the greater part of it."
123. Haenchen, *Acts*, 100. He claims that Luke supports this with "a number of auxiliary ideas."
124. Haenchen, *Acts*, 101. He brings this up later (113) as discussed in the section "Luke and Paul" below.
125. Haenchen, *Acts*, 101.
126. Haenchen, *Acts*, 101; my note 49. A common assumption for Haenchen (and many others) is that Luke is writing at a much later time than the events he is narrating.
127. Haenchen, *Acts*, 101.

refused it [i.e. salvation] by their vilification of Jesus that the emissaries of Christianity turned to the Gentiles."[128] Therefore, according to Haenchen this rejection motif is what undergirds Luke's narration of the spread of the gospel.[129]

Along with other factors, "Luke as a historian solved as best he could the theological problem posed by the mission to the Gentiles without the law."[130] Next, Haenchen explains how Luke managed to solve the political problem.[131] Since both Christianity and Judaism beforehand are "religion[s] of resurrection" the Roman Empire would be unmoved by such "theological niceties alien to its concern"—especially since Christianity does not "imply any transgression of Roman laws."[132] As a result, the illuminated Romans consistently viewed the Christian mission as a positive enterprise.[133] Haenchen then considers Luke's account to be a "simplification of the course of history, for thus mastering the problem of the mission, Luke the historian was obliged to pay a heavy price—one heavier than he suspected."[134]

Haenchen also takes issue with the way that Christianity spreads in Acts, saying that a reader would mistakenly think it was a "simple uniform process."[135] Moreover, he finds the way that Acts ends to be

---

128. Haenchen, *Acts*, 101. Here he cites Acts 13:46; 18:6; and 28:28 as justification for his theory. Haenchen (*Acts*, 417) with respect to Acts 13:46 claims that "[t]his is the moment of divorce between the gospel and Judaism." Additionally, the "shaking of the clothes" in Acts 18:6 demonstrates how Paul "completely repudiates any fellowship with the Jews and so is exempted from any further responsibility concerning them. As in 13:46 and 28:28 this renunciation makes it clear to the reader that Israel by her own fault has forfeited salvation and made the proclamation to the Gentiles necessary, so that now Paul can go to them with a clear conscience" (535).

129. See my recent survey of this issue in Karl L. Armstrong, "The End of Acts and the Jewish Response: Condemnation, Tragedy, or Hope?" *CBR* 17 (2019): 209–30.

130. Haenchen, *Acts*, 102. Van Unnik may be referring to Haenchen (102) when he states that "Luke is often dismissed as a historian but treated as a theologian"—straight away van Unnik asks: "Is this valid?" See Clare K. Rothschild, *Luke–Acts and the Rhetoric of History: An Investigation of Early Christian Historiography*, WUNT 2/175 (Tübingen: Mohr Siebeck, 2004), 46 (n94) and van Unnik, "Storm Center," 27. Van Unnik (along with Haenchen) "claims that the author of Luke–Acts did not write history for history's sake but 'to serve the church of his own day amid the questions and perils that beset her.'" Rothschild (*Luke–Acts*, 46) is here quoting van Unnik, "Storm Center," 23–24.

131. Haenchen, *Acts*, 102.

132. Haenchen, *Acts*, 102.

133. Haenchen, *Acts*, 102. Here he lists several pieces of evidence such as: the conversion of Sergius, Gallio's dismissal of a Jewish complaint against Paul, the friendly Asiarchs, the town clerk of Ephesus, the tribune of Jerusalem (Claudius Lysias), and how both governors Felix and Festus "refuse to condemn Paul out of hand." In addition, he (102) cites Paul the prisoner and his unhindered missionary work in Rome.

134. Haenchen, *Acts*, 102.

135. Haenchen, *Acts*, 103. I am not sure if Luke gives the impression that the spread of the gospel is a simple process. Although Luke provides obvious summary statements that indicate a general growth

problematic since it requires Luke to "suppress the fact that long before Paul ever reached Rome the Christian mission had got a foothold and created a community there."[136] However, in fairness to Luke he does not suppress this fact (Acts 18:1–2 and esp. 28:14). As far as the question of the "unhistorical character of Luke's presentation of Paul" this is addressed in the section "Luke and Paul" below.[137]

Luke as Writer

Haenchen's third component of his overall argument focuses on how Luke is primarily an edifying writer.[138] He remarks how the "elegant exordium of the third gospel has left many scholars with the impression that Luke would have been capable of writing the history of the dawn of Christianity in the style of a Xenophon, if not a Thucydides."[139] Accordingly, Haenchen contends that there are two things missing that would permit Luke to write on this level—"an adequate historical foundation" and the "right readers":[140]

> Any book he might conceivably offer his readers—especially as a sequel to the third gospel had to be a work of *edification*. Of course Luke firmly believed that the history of Christian beginnings was edifying in itself, but to present it as such he had to employ a special technique and offer his readers history in the guise of stories. Everything he knew concerning apostolic times, or thought himself entitled to infer, he had to translate into the language of vivid and dramatic scenes.[141]

One of the examples Haenchen uses to demonstrate this is the report on Matthias's replacement of Judas in Acts 1:12–26.

Haenchen theorizes that this report could have consisted of a simple sentence, but this would not have "conveyed much significance to the readers. So *Luke the writer* sets about it another way: he causes

---

and spread of the church (e.g. Acts 6:7) he also offers details of persecution that indicate it was not so simple (i.e. Acts 8:1).

136. Haenchen, *Acts*, 103.

137. Haenchen, *Acts*, 112–16 (see "8. Luke and Paul").

138. Haenchen, *Acts*, 103 (see 103–12, "III. Luke the Writer and Edifier"). Although he sees Luke as a theologian and historian his essential contribution to scholarship is that Luke is primarily a great storyteller.

139. Haenchen, *Acts*, 103.

140. Haenchen, *Acts*, 103.

141. Haenchen, *Acts*, 103 (original emphasis).

a *living scene* to rise before their eyes."[142] Luke capitalizes on this information by creating a living scene where Peter offers a speech about the manner of Judas's death and the need to replace him—and all of the justification for this event can be readily found in the Scriptures.

According to Haenchen, this account provides a chance for Peter to describe what it means to be an apostle—that in order to be a witness to the resurrection of Jesus he must be a follower of Jesus from baptism to ascension.[143] After the lots are cast between the two officially qualifying disciples the Holy Spirit guides the process as they pray for the "man of his choice," which happens to be Matthias.[144] Therefore, in Haenchen's view, this example "serves to show Luke's ability to transform a simple report into action and to weave a speech into the course of such an action."[145]

In addition to Luke's creative ability as a writer, he is equally skilled in condensing events into "a single scene" that otherwise represents a much longer period of time.[146] For one of Haenchen's examples he uses the incident of the two disciples at Emmaus in Luke 24:13–35 to justify this point. Although he recognizes that Luke is here "using a tradition" he finds it rather peculiar that in the "course of conversation the strange fellow-traveller should expound to the two disciples the whole of the scriptures concerning himself" (i.e., Luke 24:25–27).[147] Haenchen's suspicions seem plausible since the early church was "not presented with its scriptural proofs complete in one single moment."[148] In truth, this was a gradual process of illumination as each new piece of the Gospel story was interpreted in light of the OT prophecies concerning Christ.[149] For Haenchen, the difference between Luke and the church's reporting is this "single scene" attribution of "scriptural proofs" to the disciples at Emmaus.[150]

Furthermore, Haenchen claims that this condensing process can be observed throughout the book of Acts. He looks to the apostles

---

142. Haenchen, *Acts*, 104 (my emphasis); see earlier Dibelius, *Studies*, 150.
143. Haenchen, *Acts*, 104.
144. Haenchen, *Acts*, 104.
145. Haenchen, *Acts*, 104. That Luke is the creator of the speech is supported by the fact that "only the Septuagint text of Psalms 69 and 109 gives the meanings required" (104).
146. Haenchen, *Acts*, 104–5 (105).
147. Haenchen, *Acts*, 105.
148. Haenchen, *Acts*, 105.
149. Haenchen, *Acts*, 105.
150. Haenchen, *Acts*, 105. His point is well made but, after all, Luke (as a theologian, historian, and writer) is reporting and interpreting this tradition as a part of the church.

in Palestine where there had been "much unrest and frequent insurrection."[151] He wonders at the turbulent accounts of Palestine and how we have so little description in Acts with all of the known activities of the *Sicarii*.[152] While referring to the Egyptian rebel in Acts 21:38 Haenchen sees Luke's account of this incident as an attempt to paint Christianity as having nothing to do with "any political revolution."[153] He argues that it would be wrong for us to interpret such a "'condensed sentence as historical information" or for us to identify the "unarmed pilgrims of the wilderness with the dagger-men of Jerusalem."[154]

Another key argument for Haenchen is that Luke was "most anxious to impress upon his readers that the Roman authorities treated the Christian missionaries with benevolence and acknowledged them to be politically harmless."[155] There seems to be plenty of merit in support of this point but Haenchen believes that in the "form of a general conten-tion" this would not carry much weight since the "fate finally suffered by both Peter and Paul spoke clearly against it."[156] Therefore, Luke needed to demonstrate in "concrete stories how friendly and correct had been the behaviour of Roman officials towards Paul."[157]

Therefore, in order to show Paul's "innocence" and the "justness of the Roman," Luke "like a dramatist . . . produces a rapid succession of *vivid* and *lively scenes*" from Acts 25:14 to 26:32.[158] Haenchen then works through three scenes in the palace of the Roman governor with governor Festus, King Agrippa, and his sister Berenice. With regards to Paul's second testimony, Haenchen highlights Paul's obedience to the "commands of Christ" before the "dramatic by-play between Paul and Festus" who are unable to "make neither head nor tail of the resurrection message."[159] At this point Haenchen highlights the

---

151. Haenchen, *Acts*, 105.
152. Haenchen, *Acts*, 105. Luke does mention this movement in Luke 6:13 and Acts 1:13; 21:28. See Morton Smith, "Zealots and Sicarii: Their Origins and Relation," *HTR* 64 (1971): 1–19 and Peter Schäfer, *The History of the Jews in the Greco-Roman World*, rev. ed. (London: Routledge, 2003), 117.
153. Haenchen, *Acts*, 105.
154. Haenchen, *Acts*, 106.
155. Haenchen, *Acts*, 106.
156. Haenchen, *Acts*, 106. This naturally assumes that Luke was writing *after* the death of Peter (AD 64–67) and Paul (AD 63–64). See Armstrong, *Dating Acts*; Mittelstaedt, *Lukas als Historiker*, 165–220; Tajra, *Martyrdom*, 199.
157. Haenchen, *Acts*, 106.
158. Haenchen, *Acts*, 106 (my emphasis).
159. Haenchen, *Acts*, 107 (cf. also 106).

friendly (but noncommittal) note of "appreciation ·to the Christian" when Paul converses with the king.[160] Haenchen further observes Agrippa's summary statement that "Paul could have gone free had he not appealed to the emperor" (Acts 26:32).[161]

Consequently, we are able to "clearly discern Luke's dramatic technique of *scene-writing* in an episode where, untrammelled by tradition, he enjoyed freedom of movement."[162] This is in contrast to scholars who overlook Luke's "technique" and find in this scene an "eyewitness-report by a companion of Paul."[163] For Haenchen the real issue is that once Festus appealed to the emperor it really didn't make any difference whether or not Festus found Paul culpable.[164] According to Haenchen this is evidence that Luke was not "slavishly bound" to a given tradition.[165]

Haenchen further argues that "[t]radition is not petrified but still molten lava, and the conjuncture of circumstances may permit its transformation, the realization of its many latent possibilities."[166] Afterwards, he points to the three different accounts of Paul's conversion as evidence to how Luke molds a given tradition for his own literary purpose. In contrast to an *external* explanation that Luke had "differing sources before him and reproduced now this one, now that" Haenchen says that we should rather "ascribe this diversity to *internal* causes, the changing necessities of the literary situation."[167] While acknowledging the recurring elements in each version of Paul's conversion account, Haenchen argues that each one needed to be "told differently according to the context . . . [b]ut every other feature of the story may be changed if necessary. And it is necessary."[168]

In the first conversion account (ch. 9), Haenchen remarks how Paul is referred to in the third person so as to bring a greater significance to the episode.[169] Haenchen then estimates that a "present-day narrator" would simply draw attention to Paul as a "persecutor becoming

---

160. Haenchen, *Acts*, 107.
161. Haenchen, *Acts*, 107.
162. Haenchen, *Acts*, 107 (my emphasis).
163. Haenchen, *Acts*, 107. He refers to Zahn specifically but without reference.
164. Haenchen, *Acts*, 107.
165. Haenchen, *Acts*, 107.
166. Haenchen, *Acts*, 107.
167. Haenchen, *Acts*, 108 (my emphasis).
168. Haenchen, *Acts*, 108.
169. Haenchen, *Acts*, 108.

the missionary of the persecuted."[170] Instead, Luke employs a different strategy since he "puts everything he wishes to say to the reader in the mouths of the protagonists themselves."[171] Haenchen explains how the words must come from "Ananias or of the Lord himself" to present an effective account for his readers.[172]

At this point he proposes that Luke is using a Hellenistic narrative technique known as the "double dream" whereby he is able to "show at one and the same time how Paul behaved during the three days in question, and how it came about that Ananias rescued him."[173] Accordingly, Luke uses a dialogue where Ananias paints Saul as the "dreaded persecutor who has come with full authority to launch a reign of terror."[174] This creates a grand contrast where Saul the persecutor becomes Christ's suffering apostle who represents him before Jew and Gentile.[175] It seems that Haenchen is arguing that Luke is a far more creative writer than many scholars up to this time realized.

Since the readers are already well aware of Paul's conversion by the twenty-second chapter of Acts, Haenchen interprets another literary purpose for this second account. This conversion account is really about "vindicating the gentile mission in the teeth of the fanatical Jews" that is "achieved by a Pauline autobiography: he who carried the mission to the Gentiles recounts his life and his vocation."[176] Haenchen argues that Luke is employing the *captatio benevolentiae* in the same manner as "every speech of antiquity" whereby Paul relates to his readers who are connected to Jerusalem and trained by Gamaliel who "instilled in him the strict observance of the law."[177]

This time, there are important differences in the conversion account such as the lack of attention to Jesus (since this audience was fanatical) and a nuanced mention of Ananias where he is presented as a "pious Jew whom the Damascus Jewish community

---

170. Haenchen, *Acts*, 108.
171. Haenchen, *Acts*, 108. Haenchen (108) insists that Luke does the same thing in Acts 1:18 where it is Peter who announces the "fate of Judas" and in Acts 2:8–11 it is the "actual witnesses of the events of Pentecost who enumerate the peoples" and in 21:21 it is the "elders in Jerusalem who inform Paul of the Jews' accusations against him." This does not, however, preclude the possibility that Luke is drawing from sources who were familiar with these events.
172. Haenchen, *Acts*, 108.
173. Haenchen, *Acts*, 108.
174. Haenchen, *Acts*, 108.
175. Haenchen, *Acts*, 108.
176. Haenchen, *Acts*, 109.
177. Haenchen, *Acts*, 109.

holds in high esteem."[178] This version is key in this context because it shows that if one becomes a Christian it does "not mean cutting oneself off from one's people as a renegade."[179] However a "second scene" is needed whereby Paul is then narrated as "praying on the holy ground of the Temple" where he fell into a trance and his sole goal was to witness to Christ as he went forth from Jerusalem.[180] For Haenchen, Luke's point has been made: "Christ made Paul a missionary to the Gentiles against Paul's own wish and on account of Jewish unbelief."[181]

Moving on to Paul's third conversion account in Acts 26 Haenchen remarks how this is "once again a question of justifying the Christian mission to the Gentiles" in front of the expert in Jewish affairs: King Agrippa.[182] Here there is no need to reconstruct the familiar events that have been described earlier by Luke since the purpose is to present Paul as a "man of Jerusalem and a strict Pharisee."[183] At this point, Luke intensifies the maltreatment that the Christians endured in Jerusalem in order to sharpen the "contrast with the vision before Damascus."[184] Via the well-known Greek proverb of the goads Luke emphasized that "fate was irresistible."[185]

Similarly, Luke's Jewish audience—who knew the Old Testament Scriptures—realized the fulfilment of Paul's "call to the Gentile mission" whereby he simply "cannot disobey this direct command of God."[186] It is indeed very curious that everyone else who has seen the light falls to the ground "but nobody is blinded" (Acts 26:13).[187] As a result, despite the blinding of Paul being known by the whole church, and being at the core of his conversion story, Luke, as the narrator, is free to shape the story as he sees fit.[188]

This may seem to be a reckless method of dealing with tradition, but for Haenchen he figures that this boils down to a difference

---

178. Haenchen, *Acts*, 109.
179. Haenchen, *Acts*, 109.
180. Haenchen, *Acts*, 109.
181. Haenchen, *Acts*, 109.
182. Haenchen, *Acts*, 109.
183. Haenchen, *Acts*, 109.
184. Haenchen, *Acts*, 109.
185. Haenchen, *Acts*, 109.
186. Haenchen, *Acts*, 109.
187. Haenchen, *Acts*, 110.
188. Haenchen, *Acts*, 110.

between how Luke would narrate an event and how we would.[189] In Luke's world, a "narration should not describe an event with the precision of a police-report, but must make the listener or reader aware of the inner significance of what happened, and impress upon him, unforgettably, the truth of the power of God made manifest in it."[190] He concludes by asserting that Luke's "obedience is indeed fulfilled in the very freedom of his rendering."[191] Despite some of the later criticisms, Haenchen's observations and questions are worth considering when we reexamine the Lukan writings.[192]

Luke and Paul

Next to Vielhauer, Haenchen is considered to be the most influential and pioneering proponent of the differences that exist between the Paul in Acts and Paul in his letters.[193] Haenchen's work in this regard has been greatly influential in German and English speaking circles to such a degree that "several of the assured results of scholarship" are now open to question—namely that the book of Acts is "anything but primarily a historical document" and that its "depiction of Paul is at odds with that of the Pauline letters."[194] Since this perceived dissonance remains such a divisive issue among New Testament scholars, it is worth unpacking some of Haenchen's arguments in order to facilitate further discussion on this important issue.

Where Vielhauer focuses on the alleged theological differences between Paul in Acts and Paul in his letters, Haenchen instead emphasizes the differences with respect to the "representation" of Paul.[195] Haenchen begins his discussion by calling attention to the ancient second-century tradition that "Luke, the beloved physician" (Col. 4:14) was a companion of the apostle Paul.[196] Haenchen does

---

189. Haenchen, *Acts*, 110. This position he explains in greater detail in an earlier essay: Haenchen, "Tradition und Komposition," 205–25.

190. Haenchen, *Acts*, 110.

191. Haenchen, *Acts*, 110.

192. See "Critical Responses and a Reappraisal of Haenchen's Work in Luke–Acts" below.

193. Haenchen, *Acts*, 112–16 and Philipp Vielhauer, "On the 'Paulinism' of Acts," in *Studies in Luke–Acts*, 33–50 (originally published as "Zum 'Paulinismus' der Apostelgeschichte").

194. Porter, *Paul in Acts*, 188. Gasque (*History*, 246) for example, highlights what he perceives to be Haenchen's bias in favor of Paul's theology instead of Luke's. See also Thomas E. Phillips, *Paul, His Letters, and Acts* (Peabody, MA: Hendrickson, 2009).

195. Haenchen, *Acts*, 116. Or the "person or depiction" of Paul as noted by Porter (*Paul in Acts*, 189—see 189–99 for a summary and critique of these arguments). See also Vielhauer, "'Paulinism,'" 33–50.

196. Haenchen, *Acts*, 112. Irenaeus, *Her.* 3.1.1; 3.13.3; 3.14.1; Col. 4:14; *Muratorian Fragment*, 2–8 (the gospel), 34–39 (of Acts); Philem. 23–24 and 2 Tim. 4:11. As noted by Dupont (*Sources*,

not dispute Luke's authorship but he does question the assertion that
Luke really was "that companion of Paul, or any companion of his at
all."[197] Haenchen explores three avenues that potentially weakens the
traditional view that sees Luke as a companion of Paul.

According to Haenchen the first "overriding problem" for both
Luke and Paul was that of the *"mission to the Gentiles without the
law"*—and since Luke is *"unaware of Paul's solution"* he was able to
"justify the mission without the law on internal evidence: the law leads
not to God, but into sin."[198] Furthermore, Haenchen highlights other
Pauline points that show the higher purposes of the law that Luke
appears to be unaware of.[199]

We can see what Haenchen refers to as the 'internal' evidence in
Paul's letters where the "sinner places his trust in Christ" but there is
no evidence of this interpretation of the law in Acts.[200] It's not that
Luke is unaware of the Gentile mission but the problem for Haenchen
is that Luke is "incapable of justifying it" internally as Paul did:[201]

> [Luke] must therefore seize on a justification 'from without'—God
> willed the mission, and that was sufficient. One can speak here of
> a majestic divine will that will brook no discussion; nevertheless,

---

118–19), Dibelius subscribed to the traditional view that the author was Luke the physician who
was a companion of Paul, and possibly from Antioch. See also Keener, *Acts*, 1:410–11.

197. Haenchen, *Acts*, 112.

198. Haenchen, *Acts*, 112 (emphasis original). He brings up the central issue of the 'mission to the
Gentiles without the law' earlier (see 94, 102–103). See also Gal. 3:19; Rom. 4:13–16; 10:3–4; 2
Cor. 3:6; 1 Cor. 15:56 and also Fitzmyer, Review of *The Acts of the Apostles*, 583.

199. Haenchen, *Acts*, 112; Rom. 10:3–4; Gal. 3:21–22.

200. Haenchen, *Acts*, 113. Haenchen could be right but then again Luke's narrative purpose is different
from Paul's. Where the latter is addressing theological matters of salvation and practical matters for
the church, Luke is endeavoring to write the history of the early church from its birth in Jerusalem,
its expansion into Asia Minor and Greece, until the last recorded phase in Rome. Where theology
is more of a concern for Paul, Luke is especially concerned with chronicling the acceptance and
progress of the gospel. Where Luke is trying to write history (i.e., Luke 1:1–4; Acts 1:1–3), Paul is
explaining what it means to believe in and follow Christ in his letters.

201. Haenchen, *Acts*, 113. For proponents of the 'new perspective,' all of the Jewish elements of Paul
in Acts simply show "continuity between the Paul of Acts and his letters." Cf. Porter, *Paul in Acts*,
191. However, if we hold to a traditional understanding of the law (and I agree with Porter), then
Haenchen's criticism remains in force. And yet, just because Luke does not clearly lay out all of Paul's
theological 'internal' justifications this does not necessarily mean he has a different Paul in mind or
a lack of awareness of Paul's view of law and grace in his letters. See Porter, *Paul in Acts*, 192. For
further study on the 'new perspective,' see E. P. Sanders, *Paul and Palestinian Judaism* (Minneapolis:
Fortress, 1977); James D. G. Dunn, *Jesus, Paul and the Law: Studies in Mark and Galatians* (Louisville:
Westminster John Knox, 1990), 183–214; and Stephen Westerholm, *Perspectives Old and New on
Paul: The "Lutheran" Paul and His Critiques* (Grand Rapids: Eerdmans, 2004).

> inasmuch as men cannot grasp it on its inward side, it smacks of that ineluctable destiny known to pagan belief. Be that as it may, Luke was not greatly helped by the bare reference to the will of God: how could he persuade his *readers* that God really willed *this* and no other thing?[202]

In Haenchen's thought, this is where the miracles and signs enter into the narrative. The miracles that "play so dominant a role in the work of Luke" give legitimacy to the broader community and the Gentile mission.[203] In essence, the miracles provide the Gentile mission with the "good conscience that 'it is God's will.'"[204]

A second contention for Haenchen is that there is a *"discrepancy between the 'Lucan' Paul and the Paul of the epistles."*[205] Haenchen offers three subpoints that support this conclusion. His subpoint (a) is that while Paul (in Acts) is the "great *miracle worker*," he is far less so in his letters.[206] Haenchen lists several examples in Acts that identify Paul—along with Peter in the earlier passages—as a miracle worker extraordinaire.[207] Haenchen reflects on the fact that, in his letters, Paul acknowledges the power of an apostle (2 Cor. 12:12), and yet they were of the ordinary sort to the extent that his "opponents flatly denied his ability to perform miracles."[208] The main thing for Haenchen was that miracles (and especially overcoming obstacles by miracles) were not central for the real Paul since the apostolic experience must relate to suffering and the necessity of being helped by Christ (2 Cor. 12:10).[209]

Haenchen's subpoint (b) is that while the Lukan Paul is an *"outstanding orator,"* his "enemies are obliged" to engage him as Paul

---

202. Haenchen, *Acts*, 113 (original emphasis).
203. Haenchen, *Acts*, 113. Here he notes how the miracles are there from Acts 2 onward as they accompany the development of the Gentile mission.
204. Haenchen, *Acts*, 113. However, Paul, in a similar fashion to Luke, relates everything to God's will and guidance as he frequently reasoned from the Scriptures (e.g. Rom. 15:30–32).
205. Haenchen, *Acts*, 113 (original emphasis).
206. Haenchen, *Acts*, 113 (original emphasis).
207. Haenchen, *Acts*, 113. Some of the examples he gives are: (1) the blinding of Elymas (Acts 13:6–12), (2) the cripple at Lystra (Acts 14:8–10), (3) Paul surviving being stoned to death (Acts 14:19–20), (4) Paul's healings and exorcisms along with the superfluous power of his direct and indirect touch (Acts 19:12), (5) Paul's miraculous deadly snake bite survival (Acts 28:3–6), and (6) Paul's apparent raising of Eutychus (Acts 20:7–12; cf. 1 Kings 17:21; 2 Kings 4:34).
208. Haenchen, *Acts*, 113.
209. Haenchen, *Acts*, 113. Although being helped by Christ can also be seen as a miracle. One has to admit there are supernatural elements at work with respect to Paul's life and mission in his letters—such as his own miraculous conversion story or his discussion of spiritual gifts (e.g. Gal. 1:16; 1 Cor. 12:4–11; 15:8–10). Cf. Porter, *Paul in Acts*, 193–94.

"defends himself with convincing eloquence" (Acts 24:10–21).[210] In
fact, Paul was barely "snatched from the rough handling of the raging
mob" as he "steps forward once again *with* the orator's raised hand, and
the turbulent throng is hushed" (Acts 21:40; 22:1–21).[211] Haenchen
argues that it doesn't seem to matter whether he speaks before "Jews or
Gentiles, governors, or philosophers"—Paul in Acts is "never at a loss
for the right word" and Luke presents him as a "born orator, imposing
himself with the eloquence of a Demosthenes."[212]

On the contrary, according to his letters, the "real" Paul was
"anything but a master of the improvised speech . . . as a speaker he
was feeble, unimpressive" (2 Cor. 10:10).[213] Haenchen further argues
that Luke "paints so different a portrait of him, it is not the alchemy
of remembrance which is at work, but the presumption, so tempting
for the later generation, that Paul the great missionary must also have
been Paul the great orator."[214] As a result, the portrait of Paul in Acts
paints a different picture from what we gather from Paul's letters—just
how different remains the question.[215]

Haenchen's subpoint (c) is that despite all the "splendour in which
Luke has bathed the figure of Paul" Luke did "*not affirm Paul's real
claim*" as an apostle.[216] Accordingly, it was during Paul's European
mission that he insisted that he should be considered an apostle to
the same degree as Peter was (Gal. 2:8).[217] Furthermore, Paul highlights the fact that next to Peter and James, Christ "appeared also to

210. Haenchen, *Acts*, 114.
211. Haenchen, *Acts*, 114 (original emphasis).
212. Haenchen, *Acts*, 114. He cites the following Scriptures in support of his point with respect to Jews:
    Acts 13:16–41; 22:1–21; 23:1–11; 26:2–23, 27; 28:17–20, 26–28, Gentiles: Acts 14:15–17; 17:22–
    31, governors: Acts 13:9–11; 24:10–21; 25:10–12; 26:2–26, and philosophers: Acts 17:22–31.
213. Haenchen, *Acts*, 114 (and also p. 116 on "the real Paul"). Second Corinthians 10:10 appears to be
    a rhetorical comment whereby Paul conceivably wishes to demonstrate his humility as an orator.
    See Murray J. Harris, *The Second Epistle to the Corinthians*, NIGTC (Grand Rapids: Eerdmans,
    2005), 698–700. In the greater context of 2 Corinthians 10:10 one could argue that this is what
    his detractors were saying about him and that he does not personally believe this about himself. If
    anything, a better reference for Haenchen's argument would be Paul's admission of a lack of training
    as a speaker (2 Cor. 11:6). Then again (in the context of this verse) he is defending himself against
    the accusations of the "super-apostles" in verse 5.
214. Haenchen, *Acts*, 114.
215. Haenchen's point rests on the principle that Luke is not writing from "remembrance" but from a
    much later time than the events in the narrative. As noted above (in my note 49), Haenchen does
    not commit to a date for Acts, although his comments imply a date somewhere between AD 75 and
    "toward the end of the century." Haenchen, "Source Material," 266.
216. Haenchen, *Acts*, 114. It seems that Haenchen's insistence that Paul (in Acts) is a miracle worker
    weakens his argument here (recall Haenchen's subpoint [a] above).
217. Haenchen, *Acts*, 114.

me" (1 Cor. 15:5–8).[218] Haenchen points out that Paul received "from no man, not even from any of the Twelve—a unique commission: to bring the gospel to the Gentiles" (Gal. 2:7).[219]

Haenchen then claims that "Acts takes another view" where it was only the twelve who were considered apostles.[220] Unlike Paul it was the twelve who "lived in community *with* him from his baptism to the Ascension" and had "eaten and drunk with the risen Christ."[221] As a result, Haenchen argues that in Acts it was only the twelve who could "fulfil the conditions of apostolic witness" while Paul and "any other Christian missionary, must appeal to their authority."[222] Haenchen finds further discrepancies where, according to Paul, "Jesus was no longer 'flesh and blood' . . . after his resurrection"—it would have been blasphemous for Paul to hear of the risen Christ eating and drinking with the disciples.[223] Since Luke is "oblivious" of such "difficulties" he takes up a later generation's explanation of the resurrection since all the "witnesses had died and the reality of Jesus' resurrection had to be defended against gnostic docetism and Jewish or pagan scepticism at one and the same time." [224]

Haenchen's third and final point that reveals a different portrait of Paul in Acts is that Acts "draws a *picture of relations between Jews and Christians which contradicts that of the Pauline epistles*."[225] He claims that the reason for the conflict between Christians and the Jews in Acts is due to the preaching of the resurrection, which is understood differently between Pharisees and Christians.[226] He then claims that what brought Paul into conflict with the Jews in his letters was his "teaching with regard to the law and his corresponding missionary practice."[227]

---

218. Haenchen, *Acts*, 114.
219. Haenchen, *Acts*, 114.
220. Haenchen, *Acts*, 114. Here Haenchen states in his footnote (5) that it "makes no difference that in 14.4 & 14 Paul and Barnabas, as envoys from Antioch, are called 'Apostles.'" This seems to undercut his point unless one argues that in Acts 14 the sense of meaning relates to Paul and Barnabas as envoys (vs. a title). Cf. Porter, *Paul in Acts*, 197.
221. Haenchen, *Acts*, 114; Acts 1:21; 10:41 (emphasis original).
222. Haenchen, *Acts*, 114; Acts 13:31.
223. Haenchen, *Acts*, 114–15.
224. Haenchen, *Acts*, 115. Some have argued for the similar usage of the "resurrection of the dead" in Acts and Paul's letters. See Porter, *Paul in Acts*, 198–99.
225. Haenchen, *Acts*, 115 (original emphasis).
226. Haenchen, *Acts*, 115.
227. Haenchen, *Acts*, 115; 1 Thess. 2:15; Porter (*Paul in Acts*, 198) claims that this presents a false dilemma or a case of the "excluded middle (resurrection vs. law)." In fairness to Haenchen, he was not yet aware of the arguments in favor of the thematic and linguistic consistencies that exist between Acts and Paul's letters.

In essence, Haenchen argues that the obvious stumbling block for the Jews was Paul's view of the law and not his view of the resurrection, since this belief was already shared by the Jews.[228]

Haenchen offers a solution to this inconsistent picture of Jews and Christians by recognizing Luke as the "voice of a man of the sub-apostolic age."[229] Since, according to Haenchen, Christianity and Judaism had already parted ways we can safely conclude that only a Christian of the "sub-apostolic period" could have welcomed Luke's perspective that both religions were one and the same with their "resurrection faith."[230] Haenchen admits that a Jew would not be convinced by this line of reasoning, but then again, Luke's goal as a writer was not to "win Jews to the fold; it was designed to win over the Roman authorities."[231] For these reasons Haenchen concludes that the Paul in Acts leaves us with the impression that Luke was not a companion of Paul as believed by many:

> The time has come to strike the balance: *representation* of Paul in Acts— not to mention the overall picture of missionary beginnings—shows that here we have no collaborator of Paul telling his story, but someone of a *later generation* trying in his own way to give an account of things that can no longer be viewed in their true perspective. That this writer venerated Paul and sought in every way to bring his achievements to light, to make them "tell," that much is evident from every line he devotes to the Apostle—and quite half of Acts is concerned with Paul.[232]

We find then that the "real" Paul that is familiar to his "followers and opponents alike, has been replaced by a Paul seen through the eyes of a *later age*," and written by someone who has *not* lived through the "greater part" of the primitive age of Christianity.[233]

---

228. Haenchen, *Acts*, 115–16.
229. Haenchen, *Acts*, 116.
230. Haenchen, *Acts*, 116. And that it was simply an "unfortunate misunderstanding on the part of the Jews which caused the conflict to break out" (116). Although Haenchen's argument is entirely plausible his relegation of Luke to the sub-apostolic period requires further justification.
231. Haenchen, *Acts*, 116.
232. Haenchen, *Acts*, 116 (my emphasis) and my note 49. For Haenchen, the view that Luke was a companion of Paul is "wholly untenable." Gasque, *History*, 240. Porter (*Paul in Acts*, 199) contends that the "[d]ifferences between the two accounts seem easily to fall within the realm of the kinds of differences one would expect from two different authors writing in two different literary genres (narrative and epistle), even when writing about the same subject." Cf. also Keener, *Acts*, 1:257.
233. Haenchen, *Acts*, 116.

On the one hand Haenchen values Luke's contribution but on the other he asserts that this "ensures that the gospel according to Paul will not be robbed of its due."[234] Taken together, Haenchen's three points on the representation of Paul in Acts remain a milestone in Luke–Acts research.

CRITICAL RESPONSES AND A REAPPRAISAL OF HAENCHEN'S WORK IN LUKE–ACTS

Although Haenchen's work has been well received by many, there has been a substantial pushback especially with regard to his commentary on Acts.[235] Despite that, the purpose of this section is not to merely present a rehash of previously registered criticisms but to highlight a few concerns that scholars have already noted. At the same time, a second purpose is to suggest some reasons why we should revisit Haenchen's approach to Luke's writing and give him a fresh hearing. First, let us examine some of the pushback that has come from more traditional and conservative scholars in particular.[236]

With regards to Haenchen's commentary on Acts, Gasque claims it is in "every way a magnificently impressive piece of scholarship—a treasury of bibliographical, philological, and exegetical detail. . . . Even when one does not agree with the conclusions of the author (which will be, for most scholars, fairly often!) he must confess that Haenchen has made him look at the text and the problem raised by it from every possible angle."[237] Accolades aside, Gasque estimates that in the future Haenchen's commentary will be regarded "more as a historical phenomenon belonging to one era of the history of exegesis than as a lasting contribution to New Testament research."[238] Gasque then quips that after "two or three decades of research" scholars will be "able to see that the commentary of Haenchen is as tendentious and ultimately as unhistorical as he thinks the author of the book of Acts was."[239]

---

234. Haenchen, *Acts*, 116.
235. Cf. Fitzmyer, Review of *The Acts of the Apostles*, 582–85; Bruce, Review of *The Acts of the Apostles*, 153–54; Ellis, Review of *The Acts of the Apostles*, 197.
236. Haenchen fully expected conservative pushback. See Haenchen, *Acts*, 41.
237. Gasque, *History*, 243. Here Gasque calls Haenchen's work the "most elaborately conceived and carefully executed German commentary on the Book of Acts up to the present day."
238. Gasque, *History*, 243–44.
239. Gasque, *History*, 244. Here Gasque explains that if the Tübingen critics were essentially "wrong in their understanding of the nature of early Christianity and the problems of the Book of Acts"

Lukan scholars are naturally free to decide for themselves whether Gasque's harsh prediction came true; however, the existence of the latest Hermeneia commentary on Acts shows Henchen's influence and thought process is alive and well.[240] In fact, one could say that Haenchen's legacy is characterized by a renewed sense of historical skepticism. As Marshall exclaims, "[a]nyone who thought that R. Bultmann represented the ultimate in historical scepticism as regards the New Testament was in for a rude shock."[241] More recently, Daniel So remarks how Haenchen's skepticism was "even greater than in many New Testament scholars of his period."[242] Haenchen found that many of his contemporaries were "too preoccupied with history—whether it was the source critics who devoted their attention to hypothesizing about possible sources or the traditional scholars who refused to give up their dogmatic position on the accuracy of Acts as history."[243] In essence then, he was "only trying to counter this negative trend"—but the problem with his approach for some was that he was going too far in the "other direction."[244]

In essence, according to some scholars Haenchen found Luke to be nothing more than a "historical novelist" who had no desire to incorporate factual information into his narrative.[245] As we have seen above, Haenchen points to the varying accounts of Paul's conversion (Acts 9, 22, 26) as further evidence that Luke was a "deliberately creative writer" who shaped his narrative as he saw fit.[246] One of the perceived weaknesses of Haenchen's approach is due in part to Luke's

then "Haenchen is wrong . . . [on] the other hand, if Haenchen's basic understanding of the nature of the book of Acts is correct in its major details, then all these other scholars stand condemned." The other scholars he mentions are J. B. Lightfoot, William Ramsay, Harnack, Eduard Meyer, and Alfred Wikenhauser. Additionally, he thinks that "even if" the less radical critics (i.e. Foakes-Jackson, Cadbury, and Kirsopp Lake) who "refused to side wholeheartedly with the defenders" of the historical reliability of Acts were correct then Haenchen's theories would still contain "very little truth" (244).

240. Pervo, *Acts*, et passim.
241. Marshall, *Acts*, 36.
242. So, "Ramsay and Haenchen," 317. Some argue that Conzelmann was far more skeptical than Haenchen. See Gasque, *History*, 248.
243. So, "Ramsay and Haenchen," 317. In later years Hemer (*Acts*, 2) laments how the question of the historicity of Acts "has been strangely neglected."
244. So, "Ramsay and Haenchen," 317.
245. Marshall, *Acts*, 36.
246. Gasque, *History*, 237. According to Gasque it is typical for Haenchen to take a passage and emphasize "all the problems which he sees standing in the way of accepting the narrative as historically trustworthy" (246). Then once he finds the passage to be in serious error Haenchen delivers the "coup de grace" by explaining how Luke "would not have been interested in such questions anyway" (246)!

expressed purpose to carefully investigate "everything."[247] However, in defense of Haenchen, it is entirely possible that Luke was merely giving the impression of a careful historian. Either way, as we reexamine Haenchen's insights with respect to Luke as a theologian, historian, *and* writer we need to find a defensible balance—especially since some continue to argue that there is in fact a "strong case for regarding Acts as an essentially reliable account of what it reports."[248]

Our quest to find a proper balance and scholarly agreement between Luke as a theologian, historian, and writer may prove elusive, but it remains an important one. In fact, a way forward may be found at the very point where Marshall criticizes Haenchen for his questioning of Luke:

> Haenchen's method was to ask at every point in Acts "What was Luke trying to do?" and he found that he could explain most of Acts in terms of Luke producing an edifying account of the early church that owed nothing to written sources and was based on the scantiest of oral traditions.[249] The result was that Luke's historical accuracy was apparently torn in shreds; the narrative was claimed to have little basis in tradition, to be full of historical inconsistencies and improbabilities, and to be basically the product of the fertile mind of a historical novelist with little or no concern for such tiresome things as facts.[250]

The question raised by Haenchen: "What was Luke trying to do?" (as noted by Marshall), should not be considered something anathema to New Testament scholars.[251] In fact, it may prove to be exactly what we need to ask.

---

247. So, "Ramsay and Haenchen," 317. Luke 1:3: "it seemed good to me also, having investigated everything carefully from the beginning, to write to you in an orderly manner, most excellent Theophilus." See also Dupont, *Sources*, 102, 108. Haenchen (*Acts*, 136 [n3]) tries to navigate past this by stating that the "prologue to Luke applies only to the third gospel."

248. See Marshall, *Acts*, 43; Hemer, *Acts*, 102 and more recently Keener, *Acts*, 1:166–220.

249. I think that not only is Marshall (*Acts*, 36) embellishing his point, but Haenchen's view of Luke's sources has been misunderstood by critics and allies alike. See my section "The Sources of Acts" above.

250. Marshall, *Acts*, 36. Prior to Haenchen's commentary on Acts, Conzelmann tried to establish (and many followed suit) that Luke's concern was simply theology and he was not a very good historian. Cf. Marshall, *Acts*, 36. Marshall adduces that Conzelmann's commentary on Acts (*Die Apostelgeschichte*) tries to establish the same kind of skepticism but due to its brevity it "appears much more arbitrary and ill-founded than that of Haenchen" (36). Evidently Conzelmann as a redaction critic had a "great influence on Haenchen." Cf. So, "Ramsay and Haenchen," 303.

251. Marshall, *Acts* 36.

At a first glance, however, this kind of critical questioning could be viewed as a proverbial death knell for Luke as a historian (as Marshall seems to suggest). However, in light of the greater conversations that have occurred within the broader discipline of history over the past century, we should continue to ask these and other questions in conjunction with the historical context of Luke–Acts.[252] It is entirely defensible for us to join Haenchen and consider "what the author of Acts had wanted to say to his readers through the varied scenes of his book."[253] Neither should we relegate the "facts" (as Marshall seems to indicate) to such a clear and obvious place that they require no filtering or interpretation. As Haenchen also wrote, "It is not easy to deduce facts and lines of historical development from an ancient author. For in his decisions about selection, combination, and presentation of facts, he will have been influenced by his own view of the history about which he writes."[254]

As a contemporary of Haenchen, E. H. Carr wrote in the early 1960s that historical writing is "ultimately the product of the historian."[255] For Carr the "facts are available to the historian in documents, inscriptions and so on, like fish on the fishmonger's slab. The historian collects them, takes them home, and cooks and serves them in whatever style appeals to him."[256] Along with Haenchen and other New Testament scholars in the 1930s and 1940s, historians were asking very similar questions of both ancient and modern writers.[257] After all, Luke was not simply a *historian* and *theologian*, but as Haenchen has so well demonstrated, he was also a *writer*. Today, Haenchen's style of

---

252. See Munslow, *Deconstructing History,* 2nd ed. (London: Routledge, 2006), 45; John Tosh, *The Pursuit of History: Aims, Methods and New Directions in the Study of Modern History,* 6th ed. (London: Routledge, 2015), 10, 53, on the meaning of historical context. Although it is critical that we understand the historical context of our written sources, we can only achieve this by "reading other texts." Cf. Benjamin Ziemann and Miriam Dobson, "Introduction," in *Reading Primary Sources: The Interpretation of Texts from Nineteenth- and Twentieth-Century History,* eds. Miriam Dobson and Benjamin Ziemann, 2nd ed., RGHS (London: Routledge, 2020), 1–20 (14).

253. Haenchen, *Acts,* vii.

254. See Haenchen, "Source Material," 258–78 (258).

255. See Anna Green and Kathleen Troup, eds., *The Houses of History: A Critical Reader in Twentieth-Century History and Theory* (New York: New York University Press, 1999), 7; and E. H. Carr, *What Is History?,* 2nd ed. (repr., London: Penguin, 1990), et passim. Carr (*History?,* 22) says that the "facts of history never come to us 'pure' . . . they are always refracted through the mind of the recorder." Hence our "first concern" should not be with "the facts which it contains but with the historian who wrote it" (22).

256. Carr, *History?,* 9. See his further fishing analogy (23) where he explains what the historian catches depends on what "kind of fish he wants to catch" and "what part of the ocean he chooses to fish in and what tackle he chooses to use." In this way the historian will "get the kind of facts he wants" (23).

257. Cf. Charles A. Beard, "That Noble Dream," *AHR* 41 (1935): 74–87.

questioning and interpretation of the Lukan accounts in many ways is something that historians do on a regular basis—even if we disagree with those interpretations and conclusions.

It seems that much of our approach to Luke–Acts comes down to how we interpret and process our sources. However, like Haenchen, we should never read *any* ancient (or modern) account blindly and without respect to an author's tendency, motives, selection, and appropriation of the available sources.[258] The reality is that there is an incredible amount of subjectivity involved in the selection and interpretation of information by the ancient writer before it reaches the reader—and it seems that Haenchen as a New Testament scholar was a pioneer in recognizing this.

This does not mean we cannot know anything about ancient sources such as Luke–Acts, it just means that we need to interpret them carefully and realize that what we are reading is a compilation of interpreted sources (i.e., some combination of the author's firsthand experience, secondhand oral or written sources). Therefore, as we approach the fiftieth anniversary of the English version of Haenchen's commentary on Acts we should endeavor to shed some of our presuppositions for a moment and with Haenchen "become [Luke's] reader" once again in new and fresh ways.[259]

In summary, perhaps Bruce's assessment of Haenchen's commentary is not only a fair statement but worthy of repetition and reflection:

> As a fellow-commentator on Acts, the reviewer finds himself filling the margins of this commentary with question marks, while at the same

---

258. I have covered this extensively in Armstrong, *Dating Acts,* 23–46. There are very few examples of historiography applied to the New Testament. See, for example, Beth M. Sheppard, *The Craft of History and the Study of the New Testament,* SBLRBS 60 (Atlanta: SBL, 2012); Michael R. Licona, *The Resurrection of Jesus: A New Historiographical Approach* (Downers Grove, IL: InterVarsity, 2010). See also Stanley E. Porter, "The Witness of Extra-Gospel Literary Sources to the Infancy Narratives of the Synoptic Gospels," in *The Gospels: History and Christology. The Search of Joseph Ratzinger-Benedict XVI/ I Vangeli: Storia e Cristologia. La Ricerca di Joseph Ratzinger-Benedetto XVI,* eds. Bernardo Estrada, et al., 2 vols. (Rome: Libreria Editrice Vaticana, 2013), 1:419–65 who addresses a distinct lack of attention among New Testament scholars with regards to the important scholarship that has been occurring in historiography. For further study in historiographical theory and method, see the essays in Dobson and Ziemann, eds., *Reading Primary Sources*; Tosh, *Pursuit of History*; Alun A. Munslow, *History of History* (London: Routledge, 2012); Munslow, *Deconstructing History*; Munslow, *The New History* (Harlow, UK: Pearson-Longman, 2003); Munslow, ed., *The Routledge Companion to Historical Studies,* 2nd ed. (London: Routledge, 2006); and Jeannette Kamp, et al., eds., *Writing History! A Companion for Historians* (Amsterdam: Amsterdam University Press, 2018).

259. Haenchen, *Acts,* vii.

time the conviction grows on him that, in order to be anything like adequate nowadays, his work must receive thoroughgoing revision in the light of Haenchen's commentary.[260]

I could not agree with Bruce's assessment more and perhaps it is high time to revisit Haenchen's work with new methods and approaches. Although some of Haenchen's conclusions continue to be debated, his work on Acts in particular has remained on the forefront of historical criticism for close to a half-century in Germany and more than three decades in British and North American circles. Haenchen's approach continues to play a significant role in more recent studies in Luke–Acts and therefore we must treat it seriously and give it the respect that it deserves.[261]

CONCLUDING OBSERVATIONS ON THE LIFE AND SCHOLARSHIP OF ERNST HAENCHEN

Haenchen's impact has been felt across the entire breadth of New Testament scholarship, while his greatest influence has been upon the interpretation of the Acts of the Apostles. His greatest contribution to Acts scholarship began with his train ride to Switzerland in 1944 where he found a renewed sense of freedom to interpret the Acts and its sources based on the text itself without a reliance on secondary literature. There is great value in trying to understand the book of Acts (or any ancient text) first on its own terms and ask penetrating questions that can lead to new insights.

As a result of Haenchen's work, Lukan scholars are made to think a little deeper with regard to some of the more established positions on the interpretation of Luke's Gospel and his second volume on the Acts of the Apostles. In the future, perhaps the greatest opportunity for scholars will be to revisit and rediscover with greater clarity Luke's purpose in writing the history of the early church. If we can learn anything from Haenchen's contribution, we must be willing to consider his thoughts on Luke as theologian, historian, and (especially) writer. Where Haenchen's predecessors and contemporaries focused primarily on Luke's theology

---

260. Bruce, Review of *The Acts of the Apostles*, 154.
261. For example, Pervo's commentary on Acts draws from Haenchen frequently. Moreover, Pervo (*Acts*, xv) credits Haenchen's approach as a formative influence during the start of his career.

or his view of history, Haenchen expanded upon these two aspects in significant ways. And yet, his greatest contribution relates to his perspective on Luke's skill as a writer and storyteller. Since this requires a careful and balanced interpretation, we must not become too preoccupied with one aspect to the neglect of the other two.

Furthermore, Haenchen gave us much food for thought when it came to the differences with respect to the representation of Paul in Acts versus the Paul we know in his letters. These differences that Haenchen observed in many ways reset the clock on the arguments that saw Luke as a companion of Paul. That Luke was devoted to Paul was beyond question, but his account of Paul's mission and ministry was, for Haenchen, far removed from what we know of Paul to see a clear eyewitness connection. Although his methods and conclusions continue to be debated, Haenchen's scholarship on Luke is without a doubt a masterful attempt to explore the history and meaning of early Christianity and will no doubt be remembered as a milestone in interpretation for decades to come.

F. F. BRUCE, LUKE–ACTS, AND EARLY CHRISTIAN HISTORY

Stanley E. Porter

Frederick Fyvie Bruce (1910–1990) remains one of the most important evangelical New Testament scholars of last century, even if, it seems, his reputation has retreated in the twenty-first century. The following study, which does not attempt to address the full range of Bruce's scholarship, focuses upon Luke–Acts, for which he was and is, so far as he is remembered, still best known, even though he wrote on most if not all New Testament books and a wide range of topics in biblical studies. In some ways, Bruce was very much a person of the early to mid-twentieth century, especially in Britain. He was educated in the classics and then made a transition to biblical and particularly New Testament studies on the basis of his Christian convictions, but he brought his classics background to bear on his scholarship throughout his career, even as he expanded his interests to encompass Hebrew and Old Testament studies, to the point of occupying a chair in biblical studies that was, at that time, known for its holders being capable in both testaments. Bruce was instrumental in the revival of evangelical biblical scholarship within Great Britain in the twentieth century, even though he himself was not an Anglican. Perhaps because he was not an Anglican, but was instead a member of the Open Brethren, he was able to move in untraditional ways throughout his career.

Nevertheless, the area in which Bruce remains best known, and in which his scholarly publications probably best endure, is his research and writing on Luke–Acts. As I will discuss, his interest in Luke is less in the Gospel than it is in the man, especially as author of Acts, and his work on Acts has a legitimate claim to remain as some of the finest scholarship in English on this important book chronicling the development of early Christianity.

Bruce has been well served by several publications that offer insights into his life and scholarship. These include shorter works, such as biographical dictionaries, obituaries, or articles, but also a full biography that documents his life from start to finish and an autobiography.[1] His full biography offers a clear but charitable view of Bruce. It places Bruce into his cultural context much better than one can gain by reading one of his works. One is exposed to the influences of his youth, his theological contemplations, his education, his strength of character that enabled him to take unpopular and potentially disadvantageous positions, whether these were scholarly or personal, and his thorough and enduring commitment to the principles that he believed were important for life, scholarship, and the church. I only had one occasion to meet Bruce, when he visited Sheffield—a place important to his career and scholarship (note below)—when I was doing my PhD there. Bruce offered a public lecture and then a seminar. The personal portrait of Bruce that I saw, in the final stage of his life as an emeritus professor, was entirely consonant with the picture that is drawn by his various biographers. His public lecture was not scintillating, but during the question and answer time, his renowned abilities came to the fore. When one auditor—apparently attempting to trap Bruce—asked about

1.   See, e.g., I. Howard Marshall, "F. F. Bruce as a Biblical Scholar," *Christian Brethren Research Fellowship Journal* 22 (November 1971): 5–12; Marshall, "Frederick Fyvie Bruce 1910–1990," *Proceedings of the British Academy* 80 (1991): 246–60; A. R. Millard, "Frederick Fyvie Bruce 1910–1990," *JSS* 36 (1991): 1–6; J. J. Scott, Jr., "Bruce, Frederick Fyvie," in *Evangelical Dictionary of Theology*, ed. Walter A. Elwell (Grand Rapids: Eerdmans, 1984; rev. ed., 2001), 188–89; W. W. Gasque, "Bruce, F(rederick) F(yvie) (1910–1990)," in *Historical Handbook of Major Biblical Interpreters*, ed. Donald K. McKim (Downers Grove, IL: InterVarsity, 1998), 444–49; Peter Oakes, "F. F. Bruce and the Development of Evangelical Scholarship," *BJRL* 86.3 (2004): 99–124; Tim Grass, *F. F. Bruce: A Life* (Grand Rapids: Eerdmans, 2011); and F. F. Bruce, *In Retrospect: Remembrance of Things Past* (London: Marshall Pickering, 1980; rev. ed., 1993). I directly draw on these sources in the biographical summary below, especially Glass's excellent biography. Many of the studies of Bruce focus upon his relationship with evangelicalism and especially the Open Brethren or his ability to write for popular audiences. I only mention these as necessary to the primary topic of Luke–Acts scholarship. For a full bibliography of Bruce's work, see Grass, *Bruce*, 230–65, which I depend upon below. I also use various websites for factual information.

an obscure document that he apparently hoped would reveal Bruce's ignorance in order to drive home a contrary apologetic point, Bruce not only knew the work but responded by dating it (the tenth century and so not germane to the discussion of the biblical text), discussing its content and context, and then even citing some of it from memory. Bruce's response terminated that disingenuous point of discussion. In the departmental seminar later, Bruce was no more scintillating than before, but he was certainly on home territory as he discussed a matter in Acts related to the speeches. He repeated a view with which he is identified, confidently invoking what he called a Thucydidean view of the speeches in Acts, revealing the kind of historical view for which he is well known in both evangelical and nonevangelical circles. I will always remember that day and am thankful that I had the opportunity to witness Bruce in scholarly action.

In this chapter, I will focus upon Bruce's scholarship on Luke and Acts. In the first part, I will discuss Bruce's life and legacy, tracing the five major periods in his life as a context for his scholarship on Luke–Acts. Then, in the bulk of the chapter, I will discuss his major published works on Luke–Acts. There are, of course, many other references to passages in Luke and Acts scattered throughout Bruce's works, as would be expected for a person who wrote as widely as he did for both scholarly and popular publications. However, there are a number of major scholarly works that appropriately demand attention, and I will focus upon them. I will not examine his scholarship in other areas, as worthy as that might be. I will then offer an evaluation of Bruce's scholarly legacy.

THE LIFE AND WORK OF BRUCE

The life of Bruce may usefully be divided into five periods. While his major biographer divides Bruce's life into seven periods, these five will encompass the main important elements that inform his scholarship. These five periods are: his upbringing and education, his initial career as a classicist, his time at Sheffield, his time at Manchester, and then his retirement years.

Upbringing and Education
Frederick Fyvie Bruce was born on October 10, 1910, and reared in Elgin, Scotland, a market town about seventy miles from Aberdeen. His father, Peter, although not an educated man, was a well-known and

highly regarded figure in Open Brethren circles who placed emphasis upon biblical interpretation as the basis of his theological belief. The Brethren were a surprisingly well-informed theological group that had moderate Calvinistic tendencies but were far from doctrinaire. This appears to have formed a template for Bruce's own theological orientation, which was grounded in reformation thought but biblically based. Bruce himself studied first at a local school and then at the Elgin Academy, where he learned both Latin and Greek, subjects in which he excelled. On the basis of his academic achievement, Bruce received financial assistance that enabled him to attend the University of Aberdeen, where he concentrated on the study of Latin and Greek, but also a number of other subjects, including Hebrew. The Latin professor Alexander Souter (1873–1949) had a major influence upon Bruce,[2] as did the scholarship of a former Aberdonian William Ramsay (1852–1916), whose work on Asia Minor heavily influenced him, and Adolf Deissmann (1866–1937), the German scholar who drew strong links between koine Greek and the Greek of the New Testament.[3] Bruce won a number of prizes during his time at Aberdeen, most of them focusing upon the ancient languages, and graduated with first-class honours in 1932 with a MA. As was the custom then, Bruce was encouraged to study further in England, and so he undertook to study for an undergraduate degree in classics at Cambridge. In 1933, he received a first in part one of the Classical Tripos (the first portion of the Cambridge undergraduate curriculum), and then, in 1934, a first in part two, finishing the degree in two years. The comparative philologian and fellow Aberdonian Peter Giles (1860–1935) apparently had a significant influence upon Bruce while at Cambridge.[4] On the strength of his academic performance, Bruce was further encouraged to undertake an academic career, and

---

2. See Alexander Souter, *Novum Testamentum Graece*, 2nd ed. (Oxford: Oxford University Press, 1947), vii, where in the preface to the second edition, as his former teacher, he thanks Bruce, who then was lecturer at Leeds, for his reading of the text.
3. Bruce refers to the works of these scholars, especially Ramsay, at various places in his own works. See below.
4. Giles was also the teacher of James Hope Moulton, arguably the most significant Hellenistic Greek scholar of the comparative-historical period that Britain produced. Giles, whose career had a number of parallels with Bruce's (moving from the University of Aberdeen to Gonville and Caius College at Cambridge), was reader in comparative philology, and introduced the German New Grammarians to Britain. See his *A Short Manual of Comparative Philology for Classical Students* (London: Macmillan, 1895).

he was able, by winning scholarships,[5] to embark on postgraduate study for a possible doctorate at the University of Vienna under the well-known scholar of Indo-European and comparative philology, Paul Kretschmer (1865–1956),[6] during which time Bruce learned Hittite. Bruce only remained in Vienna for a year, 1934–1935, however, because of growing tensions over the rise of anti-Semitism and Nazism that would eventually result in the takeover of Austria. Some of these sentiments even reached into Brethren circles (Hitler's cousin was a member of the Brethren in Austria), in which Bruce continued to remain actively involved. Bruce was strongly opposed to this political shift. While back in Britain after his first year in Vienna, he heard of a position in classics, so he left Vienna without completing a degree and returned to Great Britain and thus undertook to begin his academic career.

Classical Career
Upon his return to Britain in 1935 in the midst of his studies in Vienna, Bruce was encouraged to apply for a position at the University of Edinburgh as assistant in Greek. He was hired for the position and hence never completed a doctorate, something not necessary in the academic climate of Britain at the time.[7] The position in Edinburgh was for a fixed term of three years, from 1935–1938, but the financial security allowed him in 1936 to marry Annie Davidson, with whom he had two children and to whom he was married until his death. Although Bruce had published a number of student items and in some denominational publications, it was at Edinburgh that he began a very modest academic publishing career in the classics, mostly as a Latinist. This included two articles from his Viennese doctoral work and an article

---

5. One of these was the Croom Robertson Fellowship from the University of Aberdeen, for which Bruce wrote a dissertation entitled "The Latinity of Gaius Marius Victorinus Afer," never published. See Marshall, "Frederick Fyvie Bruce," 247; cf. Glass, *Bruce*, 49, who may confuse Gaius Marius Victorinus with Victorinus of Pettau. Bruce wrote on both of them.

6. Paul Kretschmer was known for his belief in the influence of non-Indo-European languages upon Indo-European. Significant works include Kretschmer, *Einleitung in die Geschichte der Griechischen Sprache* (Göttingen: Vandenhoeck & Ruprecht, 1896); Kretschmer, *Sprache*, in *Einleitung in die Altertumswissenschaft*, eds. Alfred Gercke and Eduard Norden (Leipzig: Teubner, 1923); and Kretschmer, *Die indogermanische Sprachwissenschaft: Eine Einführung für die Schule* (Göttingen: Vandenhoeck & Ruprecht, 1925).

7. Academic doctorates were to a large extent an invention of the German universities and then imported into the USA. They came late to the UK. Bruce apparently shared the skepticism of others regarding their value.

on the earliest Latin commentary on the book of Revelation.[8] In anticipation of his position at Edinburgh coming to an end, Bruce needed
to find a new position, and secured one at the University of Leeds as
lecturer in Greek. Bruce stayed at Leeds from 1938–1947. Whereas
this was a position in teaching Greek and Latin, due to a variety of
circumstances Bruce began to do more work in the Bible. He also
became actively involved in the Biblical Research Committee (and later
chair from 1942–1951) of the Inter Varsity Fellowship, which brought
into being the Tyndale Fellowship as a means of supporting evangelical scholarship that would reach the wider academic community. This
involvement began to pay off in more opportunities for Bruce than in
his field of classics. In 1939, Bruce was awarded a scholarship to study
the Bible in its original languages, the Crombie Scholarship (he was the
only applicant!). During World War II, he taught on the Greek New
Testament for Methodist ordinands, since their local college was closed
during the war, and he was an internal examiner for biblical studies at
Leeds. The coming of the war put added burdens upon many people,
and Bruce, although rejected for military service, served as an air-raid
warden. It was apparently during his time in air-raid shelters, with only
his Greek New Testament, that Bruce began to write his first, and arguably best known, commentary on the Greek text of the book of Acts.
He also earned a diploma in Hebrew from Leeds in 1943.

While Bruce continued to write regularly for a variety of Brethren
and other popular-level publications, including Inter Varsity Fellowship in which he was increasingly active, his academic scholarship
significantly increased as well, but virtually entirely in biblical studies, not in classics. Bruce wrote a number of articles for such journals
as *The Expository Times* and the *Evangelical Quarterly*. In fact, during
the years 1938–1947, Bruce published nine articles in the *Evangelical Quarterly* (becoming associate editor in 1942, assistant in 1943,
and then editor from 1949–1980). More importantly, however, Bruce
began to publish what would become a total over his lifetime of about
fifty books, both popular and scholarly. His first published volume,
published in 1943, was a book that has become a classic within evangelical scholarship, *Are the New Testament Documents Reliable?*, which

---

8. F. F. Bruce, "Latin Participles as Slave Names," *Glotta* 25 (1936): 42–50; Bruce, "Some Roman
    Slave-Names," *Proceedings of the Leeds Philosophical Society: Literary and Historical Section* 5.1 (1938):
    44–60; Bruce, "The Earliest Latin Commentary on the Apocalypse," *EvQ* 10 (1938): 352–66; repr.
    in Bruce, *A Mind for What Matters: Collected Essays* (Grand Rapids: Eerdmans, 1990), 198–212.

went through six editions during Bruce's lifetime.[9] This volume reflects Bruce's interest in examining the New Testament from the standpoint of a classicist. He compares the evidence regarding the reliability of the New Testament documents with what is known about equivalent classical authors, and concludes that the basis for the reliability of the New Testament exceeds that of other ancient comparable documents. In the same year that he published this first book, Bruce also published his 1942 Tyndale New Testament Lecture, the first such lecture given under the auspices of the Tyndale Fellowship and his first major publication on the book of Acts, entitled *The Speeches in the Acts of the Apostles*.[10] I will examine this work more thoroughly below.

Even though Bruce emerged during this period as a leading British evangelical biblical scholar, heavily involved in the Tyndale Fellowship and a number of fledgling publishing projects to promote serious evangelical scholarship within the larger scholarly world, Bruce's own career as a classicist had essentially come to a halt. He unsuccessfully applied for the chair in Greek at Cardiff—not surprisingly since, after publication of his two articles based upon his incomplete doctoral research, he published nothing in classical studies.

Bruce at Sheffield

In 1947, the University of Sheffield inaugurated what was then called a Department of Biblical History and Literature within its Faculty of Arts, consciously deciding against forming a sectarian faculty of theology that would presumably be geared toward educating ordinands especially for the Anglican church. Bruce applied for the position and was interviewed, along with two Presbyterians, and was offered the position, which he eagerly accepted. The initial years as head of the department and initially as senior lecturer were modest, beginning with only a single student. However, the department rapidly grew from its one faculty member, Bruce, and then a second in the following year, to become a much more robust department educating undergraduates and then postgraduates, one that continued to thrive and grow to even greater heights after Bruce

---

9. F. F. Bruce, *Are the New Testament Documents Reliable?* (London: IVF, 1943; Grand Rapids: Eerdmans, 1945), retitled in the fifth edition as *The New Testament Documents: Are They Reliable?* (London: IVF; Grand Rapids: Eerdmans; Downers Grove, IL: IVP, 1960).

10. F. F. Bruce, *The Speeches in the Acts of the Apostles* (London: Tyndale, 1943).

left.[11] Bruce was promoted to professor in 1955 and remained in Sheffield as the head of department and professor until 1959. He considered his classical background and education a definite advantage in getting the position (as was the fact that he was not an Anglican or even ordained, but a Noncomformist), even though it meant that he was suddenly expected to lecture on a range of subjects, such as the book of Judges and Acts in his first year. He taught both testaments throughout his time in Sheffield. Bruce also threw himself into the wider field of biblical studies, joining the major professional societies (Society of Old Testament Studies and Society of New Testament Studies, both of which he eventually became president, one of only two people to hold both positions in their lifetimes). Bruce also began to be called upon to lecture at a wide range of institutions on diverse topics, such as the Dead Sea Scrolls and the history and development of the New Testament. Many of his lecture series became published books.

The Sheffield period was very significant in Bruce's academic and scholarly development in at least three areas: his scholarly publications, his editorial work, and his publishing of reviews and popular writings. Bruce's range of scholarly publications during this time reflects the diversity of his teaching. This period also reflects the beginning of his association with Paternoster Press, his primary publisher throughout his academic career, with his first volume appearing with them in 1950 and the last in 1992, two years after his death. It is difficult to judge but arguably many if not most of the works that Bruce is either still remembered for or that made their greatest contribution were either started or appeared during the Sheffield period of his life. Bruce began work on his commentary on the Greek text of Acts in 1939 and finished it in around 1944, but due to a change of publisher and a variety of delays it did not appear until 1951, with subsequent editions in 1952 and 1990.[12] I will say more about this work below, but this volume both

---

11. For Bruce's account of the department, see F. F. Bruce, "The Department of Biblical Studies: The Early Days," in *The Bible in Three Dimensions: Essays in Celebration of the Fortieth Anniversary of the Department of Biblical Studies in the University of Sheffield*, eds. David J. A. Clines, Stephen E. Fowl, and Stanley E. Porter, JSOTSup 87 (Sheffield: JSOT, 1990), 24–27. For a fuller history, see David J. A. Clines, "The Sheffield Department of Biblical Studies: An Intellectual Biography," in *Auguries: The Jubilee Volume of the Sheffield Department of Biblical Studies*, eds. David J. A. Clines and Stephen D. Moore, JSOTSup 269 (Sheffield: Sheffield Academic, 1998), 14–89.
12. F. F. Bruce, *The Acts of the Apostles: The Greek Text with Introduction and Commentary* (London: Tyndale; Grand Rapids: Eerdmans, 1951; 2nd ed., 1952; Grand Rapids: Eerdmans; Leicester: Apollos, 3rd ed., 1990).

reflects Bruce's classical education and established his reputation as a serious and important New Testament scholar, evangelical or otherwise. He followed this technical commentary on the Greek text with a volume on the English text of Acts (the American Standard Version of 1901) in the New International Commentary series in 1954, subsequently revised in 1988 (with his own translation).[13] During this period he also published, along with the Oxford scholar E. K. Simpson, a commentary on Ephesians and Colossians (Bruce on the latter), revised in 1984 with Bruce writing the entire commentary on Ephesians, Colossians, and the additional Philemon.[14] Bruce also became one of the first evangelical scholars, as well as a leading scholar, in the study of the Dead Sea Scrolls. Although his first (popular) publications in the area of the Dead Sea Scrolls appeared in 1950, just a few years after their initial discovery, he also published three significant works in this area, the first his *Second Thoughts on the Dead Sea Scrolls* in 1956, the second his *The Teacher of Righteousness in the Qumran Texts* in 1957, and the third his *Biblical Exegesis in the Qumran Texts* in 1959.[15] One of the first set of lectures that Bruce published, delivered at Calvin College and Seminary, was a book on Christian apologetic in the New Testament.[16] Bruce also published several works on the history and development of the New Testament and Christianity. His *The Books and the Parchments* began as some articles for a Brethren publication but was expanded into an account of the transmission of the Bible.[17] He also published three

13.   F. F. Bruce, *Commentary on the Book of the Acts*, NICNT (Grand Rapids: Eerdmans, 1954); *The Book of the Acts* (2nd ed., 1988).
14.   E. K. Simpson and F. F. Bruce, *Commentary on the Epistles to the Ephesians and the Colossians*, NICNT (Grand Rapids: Eerdmans, 1957); Bruce, *The Epistles to the Colossians, to Philemon and to the Ephesians*, NICNT (Grand Rapids: Eerdmans, 1984).
15.   F. F. Bruce, *Second Thoughts on the Dead Sea Scrolls* (London: Paternoster; Grand Rapids: Eerdmans, 1956; 2nd ed., 1961; 3rd ed., 1966/1968); Bruce, *The Teacher of Righteousness in the Qumran Texts* (London: Tyndale, 1957); and Bruce, *Biblical Exegesis in the Qumran Texts*, Exegetica 3/1 (The Hague: Van Keulen, 1959; 2nd ed., Grand Rapids: Eerdmans; London: Tyndale, 1959/1960). Note that with publication of the Tyndale Lecture in Biblical Archaeology, *Teacher of Righteousness*, Bruce had delivered and published the Tyndale New Testament, Old Testament, and Biblical Archaeology lectures. Bruce published on the Dead Sea Scrolls throughout his career, with his last publication in the field appearing in 1983. Bruce's status in the field was recognized by the fact that he edited the area for the *Encyclopedia Judaica*, which appeared in 1971. See Grass, *Bruce*, 80–81n46.
16.   F. F. Bruce, *The Defense of the Gospel in the New Testament* (Grand Rapids: Eerdmans, 1959; rev. ed., 1978); also as *The Apostolic Defense of the Gospel: Christian Apologetic in the New Testament* (London: Inter-Varsity Fellowship, 1959; 2nd ed., 1967; rev. ed., 1977 under new title).
17.   F. F. Bruce, *The Books and the Parchments: Some Chapters on the Transmission of the Bible* (London: Pickering & Inglis, 1950; 2nd ed., 1953/1955; 3rd ed., 1963; 4th ed., with title change, 1984; 5th ed., 1991), with different publishers in the subsequent editions.

books on the history of the development of Christianity in 1950, 1951, and 1952, gathered together into a single volume as *The Spreading Flame* published in 1953 (discussed below).[18] In 1957, Bruce was awarded an honorary DD degree by his alma mater, Aberdeen, and was commended as one of the most accomplished graduates of the university of his time. It is noteworthy that the Doctor of Divinity was given to a person who had never studied divinity in Aberdeen or elsewhere.

Bruce's time at Sheffield also involved his editing a variety of publications, mostly journals. His editorship of journals included *Yorkshire Celtic Studies* from 1945–1958, but which produced only three volumes during this time; the *Journal of the Transactions of the Victoria Institute* from 1950–1957, a journal founded in the nineteenth century to promote traditional Christian belief in light of contemporary philosophical and scientific thought; the *Palestine Exploration Quarterly* from 1957–1971, even though he did not make his first trip to Israel until 1970; and, most importantly perhaps, the *Evangelical Quarterly* from 1942–1980, assuming the senior editorial role in 1949, a journal that became important within the world of evangelical scholarship, and to which Bruce also contributed many articles and reviews. This was the time during which Bruce began to review a huge number of books, especially for the *Evangelical Quarterly*. He reviewed a wide variety of books, and in total probably published somewhere over two thousand reviews, not only in the *Evangelical Quarterly* but in other journals such as the *Journal of Semitic Studies*, the *Palestine Exploration Quarterly*, or other especially evangelical journals. He apparently had competence in German, French, Dutch, Italian, and Spanish, so as to review books in all of those languages, besides English. Bruce also expanded his popular appeal by writing regular columns for popular publications, especially a monthly journal of the Brethren church, *The Harvester*, from which he later collected such essays into a number of books.

During the Sheffield period, Bruce established his national and even international reputation as a scholar, although his scholarly renown was at least as much for his work outside the New Testament

18.   F. F. Bruce, *The Dawn of Christianity* (London: Paternoster, 1950); Bruce, *The Growing Day: The Progress of Christianity from the Fall of Jerusalem to the Accession of Constantine, A.D. 70–313* (London: Paternoster, 1951); Bruce, *Light in the West: The Progress of Christianity from the Accession of Constantine to the Conversion of the English* (London: Paternoster, 1952), brought together in *The Spreading Flame: The Rise and Progress of Christianity from Its First Beginnings to the Conversion of the English* (Grand Rapids: Eerdmans, 1953; 2nd ed., 1958; 3rd ed., 1981).

as in it, and at least as much for his work in the Dead Sea Scrolls as in any other area. However, it was also during this period that he brought to fruition some of the most important works that he wrote in the area of Luke–Acts studies, upon which I will comment more below.

Bruce and Manchester

When T. W. Manson (1893–1958) unexpectedly died as the Rylands Professor of Biblical Criticism and Exegesis, the University of Manchester had trouble filling this prestigious chair that had been held by two other well-known scholars, A. S. Peake (1865–1929) and C. H. Dodd (1884–1973), all Nonconformists. The chair was, at least at that time, designated for a person who had established competence in both testaments, and was the first chair in biblical studies or theology in a British university that did not have a religious requirement. As a result, it is not surprising that Bruce was on a list to be considered for it, even though his name was clearly not at the top, probably because he had a reputation for possibly being a fundamentalist due to his writing for Brethren publications.[19] By May of 1959, his name had emerged for direct consideration and he traveled to Manchester only for a conversation about the position not for a formal interview. He ended up being offered the position, with the apparent influence of the Baptist scholar H. H. Rowley (1890–1969), the recently retired professor of Old Testament at Manchester. Although he liked being in Sheffield, Bruce accepted the new position, one he held until his retirement in 1978, when he became professor emeritus. The Manchester department of biblical studies, which eventually united with the faculty of theology, was growing in size during this time and Bruce clearly helped it on its way. As part of his duties, Bruce as Rylands professor was expected to give public lectures, which he did from 1960–1986, many of which were published in the *Bulletin of the John Rylands Library*. Bruce was not known as a vibrant lecturer but was instead known to read to his students the manuscripts on which he was working, and later in life to read his books to his students. Despite Bruce's initial wariness of the value of the research doctorate—grounded in its association with German critical scholarship in his mind—Bruce attracted an enormous number of

---

19.   It is noteworthy that Bruce was not considered a fundamentalist by James Barr in either of his books on the topic: *Fundamentalism* (London: SCM, 1977) or *Escaping from Fundamentalism* (London: SCM, 1984), even though he is mentioned in each volume for his positions on topics.

doctoral students, eventually supervising as many as fifty during his time at Manchester, with most of them being foreign students and among those mostly North Americans. His supervisory style was known to be aloof, although he seemed to take the task seriously. Despite his short-comings, Bruce appears to have been popular with his students and they took his opinions and assessments of his work seriously. Bruce himself earned a MA in Hebrew language and literature at Manchester in 1963, followed by serving as president of SOTS in 1965 and then SNTS in 1975. On the basis of his growing recognition, seen by his colleagues, in 1970 Bruce was honored by the first of two *Festschriften*, the first one contributed to by fellow scholars.[20] He was also voted into membership in the British Academy as a Fellow in 1973, and then in 1979 awarded the Burkitt Medal in biblical studies by the academy for his contribu-tion to the field. With colleagues and former students located in diverse places, it is not surprising that Bruce was increasingly called upon to offer lectures on a variety of topics at many different institutions, with many of these lecture series becoming published volumes.

In terms of his scholarship, if one can characterize this period, there is a mix of work that Bruce published, but there are several note-worthy strands. These include his continued interest in history, his work that spans both testaments, and especially his publications on Paul and his epistles.[21] Bruce's first book after moving to Manchester was a history of the English Bible, published in 1961, written at the instigation of Dodd.[22] This book was designed to be published at the same time as the Revised English Bible, which Dodd edited. Bruce also published two books during this time that emphasized the history of the biblical peoples. The first was on the history of Israel, published in 1963, and the second was on New Testament history, published in 1969.[23] The latter is probably better known today than the former, as it provides a clear historical exposition written by a classicist, rather

20. W. Ward Gasque and Ralph P. Martin, eds., *Apostolic History and the Gospel: Biblical and Historical Essays Presented to F. F. Bruce on His 60th Birthday* (Exeter: Paternoster, 1970).
21. Bruce makes this point himself in F. F. Bruce, "Preface," to *Paul: Apostle of the Free Spirit* (Exeter: Paternoster 1977), published in the USA as *Paul: Apostle of the Heart Set Free* (Grand Rapids: Eerdmans, 1977; 2nd ed., 1980), 11.
22. F. F. Bruce, *The English Bible: A History of Translations* (London: Lutterworth; New York: Oxford University Press, 1961; 2nd ed., 1970; 3rd ed., 1978/1979, with an excerpt edition 1963).
23. F. F. Bruce, *Israel and the Nations from the Exodus to the Fall of the Second Temple* (Exeter: Paternoster; Grand Rapids: Eerdmans, 1963; ill. ed., 1969; 2nd ed., 1983; rev. David F. Payne, 1998); Bruce, *New Testament History* (London: Nelson, 1969; rev. ed., 1971; 2nd rev. ed., 1977; 3rd rev. ed., 1980; 4th ed., 1982), with various publishers.

than a theologian, despite some of its possible limitations in terms of contemporary scholarship.[24] A book that also falls within the historical stream is Bruce's work on Jesus and Christian origins, in which he treats Jesus in relationship to evidence outside of the New Testament, one of the first such treatments in this era of scholarship.[25] This is a volume that was published in 1974, long before the current wave of comparison of Jesus in the New Testament and extrabiblical traditions became fashionable. Bruce also published in 1968 a volume on how the New Testament develops Old Testament ideas, which originated with lectures delivered at Fuller Theological Seminary; then in 1970 he published a similar book on tradition in the Old and New Testaments, which originated with lectures delivered at The Southern Baptist Seminary in Louisville; and finally in 1978 he published a book on fulfillment of the Old Testament in the New based on lectures delivered at Moore College in Australia.[26] Several of these books have been criticized for following the lecture format and not drawing out the implications of the topics, but they nevertheless provide helpful summaries of their individual issues.

The final and by far most important stream of publications within this period is Bruce's writing on Paul and his epistles. Before I mention the commentaries and monographs, I should mention Bruce's expanded paraphrase of the Pauline letters side by side with the Revised Version.[27] This paraphrase, published in 1965, originated with articles first published in the *Evangelical Quarterly* from 1957–1964, and provides interesting reading for those who wish to see Bruce's take on the letters, as he arranges them chronologically, along with providing short introductions.[28] The major research works to note here are,

---

24. Note however the critical comments of it by Marshall, "Frederick Fyvie Bruce," 254.

25. F. F. Bruce, *Jesus and Christian Origins outside the New Testament* (London: Hodder & Stoughton; Grand Rapids: Eerdmans, 1974; 2nd ed., 1984).

26. F. F. Bruce, *This Is That: The New Testament Development of Some Old Testament Themes* (Exeter: Paternoster, 1968); also as *The New Testament Development of Old Testament Themes* (Grand Rapids: Eerdmans, 1969); Bruce, *Tradition Old and New* (Exeter: Paternoster; Grand Rapids: Zondervan, 1970); and Bruce, *The Time Is Fulfilled: Five Aspects of the Fulfilment of the Old Testament in the New* (Exeter: Paternoster, 1978; Grand Rapids: Eerdmans, 1979).

27. F. F. Bruce, *An Expanded Paraphrase of the Epistles of Paul* (Exeter: Paternoster, 1965); also as *The Epistles of Paul: An Expanded Paraphrase* (Grand Rapids: Eerdmans, 1965).

28. As an example for comparison, Bruce renders Romans 3:21–22 as: "But now a way to get right with God has been revealed, apart from the righteousness prescribed in the law. This way, which is attested by the law and the prophets, is provided by God, through faith in Jesus Christ, for all who believe in Him" (*Expanded Paraphrase*, 191). This reflects Bruce's orientation to Paul's theology, contrary to some other attempts at translating Paul.

first, his short commentary on the book of Ephesians published in 1961 (not to be confused with the one he published in 1984 for the New International Commentary),[29] followed by a more important commentary on the book of Romans that appeared in the Tyndale New Testament Commentary series in 1963, subsequently revised in 1985 (although to the disappointment of some not going far enough in recent developments in Pauline discussion).[30] This has proved to be a surprisingly resilient and useful volume for the study of this inexhaustible letter. Then, there is his commentary in the New Century Bible on 1 and 2 Corinthians, a volume consistent with the surprisingly brief commentaries found within the series in which it appeared in 1971.[31] Bruce's two monographs of this time on Paul are his short volume on Paul and Jesus,[32] which originated with lectures delivered at Ontario Bible College (now Tyndale University and Seminary) and, arguably, his magnum opus, *Paul: Apostle of the Free Spirit* (or in North America: *Paul: Apostle of the Heart Set Free*), published in 1977.[33] The British title of the work makes clear that Bruce saw Paul as an advocate of Christian freedom, perhaps not surprisingly in some harmony with Bruce's own position in relation to conformist church pressures. As a result, Bruce emphasizes Paul's proclamation of Christian freedom and emancipation from the law or other such constraints, a position in light of the soon to emerge New Perspective that has probably struck some as theologically naïve, although one can probably not accuse Bruce of being too heavily influenced by Lutheranism. The two other publications worth mentioning at this point are Bruce's commentary on Hebrews in the New International Commentary series, which appeared in 1964, soon after he took over as editor of the commentary series (based upon the American Standard Version, then his own translation in the revised edition), although he had begun it sometime around 1954, and an expositional commentary on the Johannine

---

29. F. F. Bruce, *The Epistle to the Ephesians* (London: Pickering & Inglis; Westwood, NJ: Revell, 1961). This entry is missing from Glass's bibliography.

30. F. F. Bruce, *The Epistle to the Romans*, TNTC (London: Tyndale; Grand Rapids: Eerdmans, 1963); 2nd ed., *The Letter of Paul to the Romans*, TNTC (Leicester: IVP; Grand Rapids: Eerdmans, 1985). Glass, *Bruce*, 203 rightly criticizes Bruce for not referring to E. P. Sanders's work on the New Perspective except in passing. However, not referring to an unpublished dissertation can hardly be criticized for a commentary of this level and type.

31. F. F. Bruce, *1 and 2 Corinthians*, NCB (London: Oliphants, 1971).

32. F. F. Bruce, *Paul and Jesus* (Grand Rapids: Baker, 1974).

33. See also Robert A. Mounce, "The Contribution of F. F. Bruce to Pauline Studies: A Review Article," *JETS* 23 (1980): 67–73.

epistles published in 1970.[34] Bruce's volume on Hebrews is still highly regarded as one of his finest commentaries.

Bruce was also very busy as an editor during his Manchester years. Not only did he continue as the editor of the *Evangelical Quarterly*, but he proofread the entirety of the English translation of the *Theological Dictionary of the New Testament*[35] and assumed editorship of the New International Commentary series from Ned Stonehouse in 1962, which he retained until shortly before his death in 1990. Bruce edited a small series of church history books for Paternoster from 1961–1964, in which his *The Spreading Flame* was the first of a number of volumes. Bruce along with the Glasgow scholar William Barclay (1907–1978), Bruce's contemporary,[36] also edited from 1961–1965 a series of Bible Study Guides. Bruce contributed a volume on the Thessalonian and Corinthian letters in 1962, later expanded to include Philippians as well.[37] His editing of these guides with Barclay, who despite his evangelical upbringing was far less conservative than Bruce, caused some consternation in Bruce's more conservative ecclesial circles. During this time Bruce continued a good portion of his popular writing, although near the end of this period he cut back on some of it, after being heavily engaged for decades.

During his Manchester years, Bruce further established and expanded his reputation as a mainstream New Testament scholar— even if his interests seemed to shift away from Acts, his major earlier focus, to Paul and his letters. This gave him even greater breadth to his interests. Nevertheless, despite this shift, he continued to write on a range of subjects and at a variety of levels, from monographs down to commentaries of varying levels to much more popular writing.

---

34. F. F. Bruce, *The Epistle to the Hebrews*, NICNT (Grand Rapids: Eerdmans, 1964; London: Marshall, Morgan & Scott, 1965; 2nd ed., Grand Rapids: Eerdmans, 1990); and Bruce, *The Epistles of John* (London: Pickering & Inglis, 1970). The volume on the Johannine epistles is not mentioned in Glass's bibliography.

35. Gerhard Kittel and Gerhard Friedrich, eds., *Theological Dictionary of the New Testament*, trans. and ed. Geoffrey W. Bromiley, 10 vols. (Grand Rapids: Eerdmans, 1964–1976). Bruce apparently did this while commuting by train from his home in Buxton to Manchester every day.

36. Barclay's career in some ways parallels that of Bruce. Barclay studied classics as an undergraduate before turning to divinity, and he studied for a year in Germany in the 1930s before returning to Great Britain to pursue his first church and then academic career. They both had evangelical upbringings, even if on opposite ends of the evangelical spectrum.

37. F. F. Bruce, *Paul and His Converts: 1 and 2 Thessalonians, 1 and 2 Corinthians*, Bible Guides 17 (London: Lutterworth; Nashville: Abingdon, 1962); rev. ed. with Philippians, *Paul and His Converts: How Paul Nurtured the Churches He Planted* (Downers Grove, IL: IVP; Crowborough: Highland, 1985).

Retirement

Bruce's retirement as emeritus professor from the University of Manchester in 1978, mandated by age, was met with high hopes and expectations by him as he had a number of scholarly projects that he wished to complete. He was able to continue to use the university's Rylands library and regularly gave lectures there, even though attendance at such lectures declined over the years. Bruce remained active during these years, especially in his publication of research, the delivery of lectures at various institutions and events, and the writing of popular level publications. In 1980, Bruce was honored by his second *Festschrift*, this one by his former students, focused upon Pauline studies, indicating the general direction of his scholarship over the last decade or more.[38] As incredible as it may seem, it was in 1983 that Bruce took his first trip to modern-day Turkey to see the sites of ancient Asia Minor that he had written so much about in his various volumes, especially on Paul and Acts. He was also awarded an honorary DLitt degree by the University of Sheffield in 1988, in recognition of his scholarship and the role he had played in the establishment of the department of biblical studies there. The first five or so years of his retirement were incredibly productive, mostly following along the lines of his previous period at Manchester.

In 1980, Bruce published an autobiographical volume that had originated in popular level articles written over the course of several years for a Brethren publication.[39] This volume contains a recounting of the people, places, and events in the author's life, even if it does not go into the personal side of Bruce's life as much as one would like (after all, he was a Scotsman of the early twentieth century, not given to such expression). Bruce was invited to give the first Didsbury Lectures at British Isles Nazarene College (Bruce had supervised a number of students in this theological tradition while at Manchester), lectures that combined some lectures from previous venues and that discussed people (men) of importance in the New Testament other than Paul and his circle, such as Peter, Stephen, James, and John.[40] Bruce also

---

38. D. A. Hagner and M. J. Harris, eds., *Pauline Studies: Essays Presented to F. F. Bruce on His 70th Birthday* (Exeter: Paternoster; Grand Rapids: Eerdmans, 1980).
39. Bruce, *In Retrospect.*
40. F. F. Bruce, *Men and Movements in the Primitive Church: Studies in Early Non-Pauline Christianity* (Exeter: Paternoster, 1979); also as *Peter, Stephen, James and John: Studies in Non-Pauline Christianity* (Grand Rapids: Eerdmans, 1980).

followed up on his large introduction to Paul by delivering lectures that resulted in a book that argues for continuity between the thinking of Jesus and Paul.[41] Several more popular books emerged during this time especially dependent upon his popular periodical writing for Brethren and other evangelical causes. These volumes include one on the work of Jesus that appeared in 1979, another on the hard sayings of Jesus that appeared in 1983 that was later combined with other volumes on hard sayings of Paul and the Old Testament by other authors, and an apologetic book affirming the historicity of the life and events in Jesus's life that appeared in 1985.[42] Bruce also wrote a companion book to the one mentioned above on those within the Pauline circle that appeared in 1985, this one including a number of women and illustrating the inclusive and egalitarian view of Bruce on women in ministry that had been characteristic of his stance from much earlier (and had sometimes caused controversy in his Brethren, as well as probably some other evangelical, circles).[43] Besides revising several of his commentaries (including both Acts commentaries, Romans, Hebrews, and the joint commentary on Ephesians and Colossians, also adding Philemon), Bruce wrote several more commentaries, several of them of distinction. These included the Galatians commentary in the New International Greek Testament Commentary Series, and the Thessalonians commentary in the Word Biblical Commentary series, both published in 1982.[44] The commentary on Galatians was begun by Bruce in 1967 and was not originally designed for the NIGTC, but Bruce's technical focus upon the Greek text was suitable for the series, although it has been noted that he was not as cognizant of more recent developments in Pauline scholarship (e.g., the New Perspective) as would have been warranted in a commentary on such a

---

41.   F. F. Bruce, *Paul and the Mind of Christ* (Leicester: Religious & Theological Studies Fellowship, 1985).

42.   F. F. Bruce, *I Want to Know What the Bible Says about the Work of Jesus* (Eastbourne: Kingsway, 1979); also as *What the Bible Teaches about What Jesus Did* (Wheaton, IL: Tyndale House, 1979), reissued under other titles; Bruce, *The Hard Sayings of Jesus* (London: Hodder & Stoughton; Downers Grove, IL: IVP, 1983), combined in Walter C. Kaiser, Jr., Peter H. Davids, F. F. Bruce, and Manfred T. Brauch, *Hard Sayings of the Bible* (Downers Grove, IL: IVP, 1996); and Bruce, *The Real Jesus: Who Is He?* (London: Hodder & Stoughton, 1985); also as *Jesus: Lord and Savior* (Downers Grove, IL: IVP, 1986).

43.   F. F. Bruce, *The Pauline Circle* (Grand Rapids: Eerdmans; Exeter: Paternoster, 1985), not listed in Grass's bibliography and dated to 1986 when he refers to it in his text.

44.   F. F. Bruce, *The Epistle of Paul to the Galatians: A Commentary on the Greek Text*, NIGTC (Exeter: Paternoster; Grand Rapids: Eerdmans, 1982); Bruce, *1 & 2 Thessalonians*, WBC 45 (Waco, TX: Word, 1982).

book.[45] The same year Bruce's commentary on the Thessalonian letters also appeared, but there has been some criticism of how he handled the divided format of the WBC. Whether that is a fault of Bruce or of the commentary series itself is probably a debatable issue, as others in the series have also used this format in varying ways. Bruce also published in 1983 a popular level commentary on the Gospel of John and also in 1983/1984 one that used the Good News Bible translation of Paul's letter to the Philippians, later revised to comment on the New International Version in 1989/1990.[46] Bruce's last major written project was the publication of his book on the canon of Scripture, a project that he had conceived as far back as 1944 and that he had lectured on at Manchester, including both testaments in his volume.[47] This book, which appeared in 1988, has many independent judgments in it by Bruce, who approaches the task as a historian.

Bruce had a heart attack in 1987 that slowed him down on all fronts, including his scholarly publishing, his popular writing, and his traveling. Apart from a few pleasurable trips in his last couple of years, he mostly concentrated upon his last major book project on the canon, wrote a couple of articles of importance, one on the canon for a dictionary on Jesus and the Gospels and another on Paul in Acts and his letters for a dictionary on Paul and his letters.[48] His final project was to gather together eighteen of his previously published essays in a collection, the preface for which he signed in June 1990.[49] Bruce had several major health incidents in 1990, including the removal of a kidney in May and then the discovery of stomach cancer in August, to which he eventually succumbed on September 11, 1990.

Bruce's academic career spanned more than fifty years in the heart of the twentieth century, an important time in the history of New

45. One might also criticize it for still using the same comparative-historical understanding of ancient Greek as was used in his 1951 commentary on Acts, even though the field of Greek language and linguistics had changed significantly during the intervening thirty years.

46. F. F. Bruce, *The Gospel of John* (Basingstoke: Pickering; Grand Rapids: Eerdmans, 1983); Bruce, *Philippians*, Good News Commentary (San Francisco: Harper & Row, 1983; Basingstoke: Pickering & Inglis, 1984); rev. ed., *Philippians*, New International Biblical Commentary 11 (Carlisle: Paternoster, 1989; Peabody, MA: Hendrickson, 1990).

47. F. F. Bruce, *The Canon of Scripture* (Downers Grove, IL: IVP; Glasgow: Chapter House, 1988).

48. F. F. Bruce, "Canon," in *Dictionary of Jesus and the Gospels*, eds. Joel B. Green, Scot McKnight, and I. Howard Marshall (Downers Grove, IL and Leicester: IVP, 1992), 93–100; and Bruce, "Paul in Acts and Letters," in *Dictionary of Paul and His Letters*, eds. Gerald F. Hawthorne and Ralph P. Martin (Downers Grove, IL and Leicester: IVP, 1993), 679–92. I note that in the second edition of the dictionary on Jesus in the replacement article on canon Bruce's book on canon is not even mentioned.

49. Bruce, *A Mind for What Matters*.

Testament scholarship. During that time, he established himself as a major scholar by means of his professorial position, his major scholarship, and his involvement in professional societies and other events. Within his body of work, however, Bruce perhaps remains best known for his work on Luke–Acts.

BRUCE AND LUKE–ACTS

The summary of Bruce's publishing career highlights the major periods within his life and scholarship, including his scholarship on Luke–Acts. In this section, I wish to examine in more detail his major scholarly works on Luke–Acts. I do not attempt to describe and assess all his work, but the major works that are pertinent to the topic. What emerges is that, although Bruce occasionally and then popularly writes on Luke's Gospel, the vast majority of his scholarly work, and of the work of enduring significance, is written on Acts in support of the notions of historical reliability and continuity with the Pauline letters. I divide this discussion into five sections: speeches in Acts, early Christian history, Greek and English commentaries on Acts, and supporting studies.

Speeches in Acts

Bruce's initial foray into Luke–Acts scholarship concerned the speeches in Acts. Bruce wrote four articles on the speeches in Acts that I wish to consider here, one during his early classical career, one in his Manchester period, and two during his retirement period. The first, mentioned above, was the initial 1942 Tyndale New Testament lecture, published in 1943 while Bruce was already engaged in writing his commentary on the Greek text of Acts.[50] There are several features of this published lecture that come to typify Bruce's position: (1) his explicitly approaching the issue as a classicist, (2) his distinction between those who believe the speeches of Acts are accurate reflections of what was said (here F. J. Foakes Jackson [1855–1941]) and those who do not (here Martin Dibelius [1883–1947]),[51] (3) his acceptance of the Thucydidean view of speeches (1.22.1), followed by Polybius (2.56.10–12), (4) his inclusion of the Gospel of Luke

---

50. Bruce, *Speeches in Acts*.
51. F. J. Foakes-Jackson, *The Acts of the Apostles*, MNTC (London: Hodder & Stoughton, 1931), xvi; and Martin Dibelius, *A Fresh Approach to the New Testament and Early Christian Literature* (New York: Scribners, 1936), 262.

within his discussion, even if only briefly, when he says that the same
pattern of reliable speeches is found there, and (5) his division of the
speeches into four rhetorical types: (a) evangelistic, including to Jews
and God-fearers (Peter's speeches in Acts 2, 3, 4, 5 and 10; Paul's at
Pisidian Antioch in Acts 13) and to pagans (Paul's speeches in Lystra
in Acts 14 and Athens in Acts 17), (b) deliberative (Peter's speech in
Acts 1:16–22 and the speeches in Acts 15), (c) apologetic (Stephen in
Acts 7; Peter's defense of eating with Cornelius in Acts 11:4–18; and
Paul's defenses before those in Jerusalem in Acts 22, the Sanhedrin in
Acts 23, Felix in Acts 24, Festus in Acts 25, Herod Agrippa II in Acts
26, and the Jews at Rome in Acts 28:17–21), and (d) hortatory (the
Miletus speech in Acts 20:18–35). Bruce concludes that the speeches
are not necessarily verbatim accounts but "faithful epitomes" of what
was said.[52] This view came to be identified with Bruce and his view of
not just the speeches but all of Acts.

When he wrote his second major essay on the speeches in Acts
thirty years later,[53] Bruce (1) refers to his earlier publication and reas-
serts the fact that he then was a classics teacher and received endorsement of his perspective from his classical colleagues, while his biblical colleagues were not as receptive (e.g., Jacque Dupont)[54] because,
so he claims, he (2) needed to further justify the speeches of Acts
as Thucydidean, which he does. Bruce (3) acknowledges that what
he calls the Dibelius–Haenchen–Conzelmann line of thought had
continued since he first wrote, in the writings of Dibelius and others,
such as Ulrich Wilckens.[55] Bruce (4) defends his previous position by

52. Bruce, *Speeches in Acts*, 27.
53. F. F. Bruce, "The Speeches in Acts—Thirty Years After," in *Reconciliation and Hope: New Testament Essays on Atonement and Eschatology Presented to L. L. Morris on His 60th Birthday*, ed. Robert Banks (Exeter: Paternoster, 1974), 53–68.
54. Jacques Dupont, *Les Problèmes du Livre des Actes d'après les Travaux Récents* (Louvain: Universitaires de Louvain, 1950), 47; repr. in Dupont, *Études sur les Actes des Apôtres*, LD 45 (Paris: Cerf, 1967), 42.
55. Bruce refers to these scholars elsewhere, including Dibelius, Ernst Haenchen (1894–1975), and Hans Conzelmann (1915–1989). Martin Dibelius, *Aufsätze zur Apostelgeschichte*, ed. Heinrich Greeven (Göttingen: Vandenhoeck & Ruprecht, 1951); ET Dibelius, *Studies in the Acts of the Apostles*, ed. Heinrich Greeven, trans. Mary Ling and Paul Schubert (London: SCM, 1956); Ernst Haenchen, *Die Apostelgeschichte*, KEK 3 (Göttingen: Vandenhoeck & Ruprecht, 1965); ET Haenchen, *The Acts of the Apostles: A Commentary*, trans. Bernard Noble and Gerald Shinn, rev. R. McL. Wilson (Oxford: Blackwell; Philadelphia: Westminster, 1971); Hans Conzelmann, *Die Apostelgeschichte*, HNT 7 (Tübingen: Mohr Siebeck, 1963); ET Conzelmann, *Acts of the Apostles*, trans. James Limburg, et al., Hermeneia (Philadelphia: Fortress, 1987); Conzelmann, *Die Mitte der Zeit* (Tübingen: Mohr Siebeck, 1954); ET Conzelmann, *The Theology of St Luke*, trans. Geoffrey Buswell (London: Faber and Faber, 1960); Ulrich Wilckens, *Die Missionsreden der Apostelgeschichte: Form- und traditionsgeschichtliche Untersuchungen* (Neukirchen: Neukirchener, 1961).

responding to the criticisms of the German alliance by noting a variety of factors such as unique wordings that point to authorship other than by Luke, and hence possibly by Paul.

In his third essay on the speeches in Acts, written more than ten years later,[56] Bruce (1) invokes a Thucydidean view that says that the Lukan compositions "reproduce the general purport of what was actually said,"[57] (2) summarizes Paul's intention to see Rome, which Bruce sees as the goal of Acts to exemplify, (3) analyzes six speeches in which Paul defends himself against his opponents (to the crowd in Jerusalem, Sanhedrin, Felix, Festus, Agrippa, and Jews in Rome), (4) assumes that Luke is providing a historical rather than an apologetic account, even if he ends up offering an apology for early Christianity as fulfillment of Judaism, and (5) counters many of the competing theories regarding Acts, such as offering a defense for Paul before Caesar or Christianity in the Roman Empire, or commending the empire to Christians.

In his final essay on the topic, published the year he died,[58] Bruce follows the format of his first essay by (1) endorsing a Thucydidean view of speeches, (2) seeing continuity in Luke's Gospel, and then (3) explicating speeches under the categories of (a) missionary speeches (by Peter at Pentecost in Acts 2:14–40 and in the temple court in Acts 3:12–26), (b) speeches to Gentiles (by Peter to Cornelius in Acts 10:34–43), (c) speeches to pagans (by Paul at Lystra in Acts 14 and at the Areopagus in Acts 17:22–31), (d) speeches in Jerusalem (at the council in Acts 15:6–29), (e) an exhortation at Miletus (by Paul in Acts 20:13–31), (f) Stephen's defense (Acts 7:2–53), and (g) Paul's apologetic speeches (Acts 22:1–21; 23:1–6; 24:10–21; 25:8–11; 26:2–23; 28:17–28).

We see a surprisingly high amount of consistency in Bruce's presentation, so much so that, apart from some reshuffling of the categories of speeches, the first and fourth essays are consistent throughout, reflecting no significant difference in approach. The second essay reflects some acknowledgment that, at least among New Testament scholars, Bruce's classical approach is not entirely convincing, but he ends up arguing the same conclusion nonetheless. He does so in direct opposition to major German scholars, whose work

---

56. F. F. Bruce, "Paul's Apologetic and the Purpose of Acts," *BJRL* 69 (1986–1987): 379–93; repr. in Bruce, *A Mind for What Matters*, 166–78 with notes (used here).
57. Bruce, "Paul's Apologetic," 166.
58. F. F. Bruce, "The Significance of the Speeches for Interpreting Acts," *SJT* 33 (1990): 20–28.

he appears to know in German. However much one might wish to commend such consistency, there are problems with Bruce's position. The first is that there are numerous assumptions in his appeal to being a classicist, which he implicitly acknowledges in his second essay, even if he turns the argument to a classicist's advantage. His classical approach makes assumptions regarding language, history, and method that Bruce only tacitly acknowledges in his second essay but retreats from quickly. The second problem, at least as significant as the first, is that Bruce continues to invoke a Thucydidean view of speeches throughout his career. He often does so by simply citing in translation Thucydides's statement (although not even that in the third essay), perhaps followed by a summary of what he believes this statement says (and only in the third essay citing a number of scholars in defense of his view).[59] However, this statement by Thucydides is highly problematic at almost every interpretive point, with scholarly opinion notoriously mixed on what exactly Thucydides meant.[60] The third problem is that Bruce does not face the significance of his belief that Luke provides a faithful summary of what was said, even though the speeches in Acts, as well as in Luke's Gospel, are much shorter than even summaries of speeches in classical sources such as Thucydides and arguably follow a regular pattern of presentation, such as Bruce discusses. Bruce's stature as a classical scholar probably helped to ensure that his view was taken seriously, but there are many points at which his approach and his conclusions could and should have been questioned and bolstered. Repetition of a view does not necessarily make it stronger.[61]

---

59. Bruce cites A. W. Gomme, "The Speeches in Thucydides," in *Essays in Greek History and Literature* (Oxford: Oxford University Press, 1957), 156–89; T. F. Glasson, "The Speeches in Acts and Thucydides," *ExpTim* 76 (1964–1965): 165; P. A. Stadter, ed., *The Speeches in Thucydides* (Chapel Hill, NC: University of North Carolina Press, 1973); M. I. Finley, *Ancient History: Evidence and Models* (London: Chatto & Windus, 1985), 13–15; and G. H. R. Horsley, "Speeches and Dialogue in Acts," *NTS* 32 (1986): 609–14. This is in fact a surprisingly limited and even shallow accounting of this passage.

60. See Stanley E. Porter, "Thucydides 1.22.1 and Speeches in Acts: Is there a Thucydidean View?" *NovT* 32 (1990): 121–42; repr. and revised in Porter, *Studies in the Greek New Testament: Theory and Practice*, SBG 6 (New York: Peter Lang, 1996), 173–93, where the wide range of possible interpretations of Thucydides's language is demonstrated (and seen in a variety of authors). A much broader range of evidence regarding Thucydides's statement is surveyed in this article.

61. Some have noted that classical studies does not undergo the same major conceptual changes every twenty to thirty years as New Testament studies does, and so there is less revisionism, something that perhaps influenced Bruce's approach to scholarship throughout his career.

Early Christian History

In several works, Bruce treated Luke–Acts as part of the development of early Christian history. These works were not works distinguished by their being focused treatments of either Luke or Acts, but the use he makes of them is instructive for his approach to them. The three volumes here are his *The Spreading Flame*, which brings into one volume three separate historical volumes, his *New Testament History*, and his *Paul: Apostle of the Free Spirit/Heart Set Free*. What all three of these works, Bruce's major historical writings, have in common is that they utilize the narrative framework found in Luke (as well as the other Gospels) and Acts. His first major historical work, *The Spreading Flame*, follows, apart from in chapter one, the general outline of the Gospels (including Luke's) and Acts for its first part on the advent of Christianity. The chapters are concerned with: "When the Time Was Ripe," the birth of Jesus; "A Light for the Nations," Jesus's ministry; "The Light Shines in the Darkness," Jesus's crucifixion; "The Darkness Did Not Put It Out," the resurrection; "The New Community," a transitional chapter between the Gospels and Acts; "The Rabbi of Tarsus," introducing Paul; "Antioch on the Orontes," following the Acts account of the missionary endeavor from Antioch; "Advance in Palestine," concerning Peter and the early Jewish missionary venture; "The Council of Jerusalem," emphasizing Acts 15; "Into Europe," the spread of Christianity into Europe; "Paul and His Converts," Paul in Corinth and Ephesus; "Diana of the Ephesians," with focus upon Ephesus; "Christianity at Rome," concerning Paul's trip to Rome; and "Palestine: The End of the Beginning," the years approaching the Jewish revolt. One might argue that as Bruce is presenting a history of early Christianity, he should use the Gospels and Acts for that history; however, implicit in that assumption is that these provide historically reliable documents upon which to base such a history.

The next historical work is Bruce's New Testament history. Because this work attempts to situate the rise of Christianity within a broader historical context, Bruce has chapters that set the stage for Christianity by treating Jewish history since the return from exile, Herodian and Roman rule, and the various major philosophical and religious groups of the times (including the Hasidim, Pharisees, Sadducees, Essenes, Zealots, and Qumraners). At this point, beginning with chapter 11 of thirty, Bruce begins to trace the narrative outline of the Gospels and Acts. The Gospels are followed for John the Baptist, the ministry

of Jesus, and his trial and execution (chs. 12–15). Then Bruce generally follows the outline of the book of Acts for the rest of his New
Testament history, apart from the last chapter and a half. He moves
from the primitive Jerusalem church to early figures such as Stephen
and Philip and then turns to Paul, with only an occasional interlude
(e.g. ch. 19 on Gaius, but even then it concludes with the eschatological passages of the Gospels). The story resumes with the spread
of the Pauline mission, the Jerusalem council, spread of Christianity
to Europe, and further developments in Judea and Rome, including
Paul's imprisonment in Jerusalem and then journey to Rome, before he
closes out the historical account with further historical developments
that go beyond the New Testament (in chs. 21 and 22). Bruce continues to reflect his classical background, in that he treats the documents
of the New Testament in a way that is very similar to the way that he
treats the other ancient sources available to him, whether those are the
Dead Sea Scrolls or Pliny or Tacitus. Even more so, even though he
cites Josephus frequently throughout his account, he does not base his
New Testament history upon Josephus's account, but draws selectively
upon him. The basic account that he gives of the development of New
Testament history is one that is found in the Gospels and Acts.

The third historical work is Bruce's account of the life and ministry of
Paul. One of the features that has commended Bruce's major treatment of
Paul is that he does not conform to the usual format of first introducing
a set of topics and then introducing the individual letters and debating
their issues. Instead, Bruce creates a narrative framework for his account
of Paul, to which he adds supporting and extra discussions. Bruce makes
clear in his introduction the approach he is going to take:

> From the first century we have one account of Paul composed (it
> appears) in complete independence of his letters; that is the account
> given in the Acts of the Apostles (a work which was designed as the
> second part of a history of Christian origins whose first part we know
> as the Gospel of Luke). This is our principal secondary source for the
> life and work of Paul, and the present work is based on the conviction
> (for which arguments have been set out elsewhere) that it is a source of
> high historical value.[62]

---

62. Bruce, *Paul*, 16. The reference in the second parentheses is to Bruce, *Acts* (Greek), 1st/2nd ed., 15ff.
    et passim.

Bruce then presents thirty-eight chapters, with especially chapters 7–37 following the Acts chronology with some interludes. Thus, he treats the beginning of "the way," Paul as persecutor and then convert, Paul in relationship to Jerusalem, the historical Jesus, the exalted Christ, and the Hellenistic mission. He then proceeds to the Jerusalem council, the mission to Asia Minor, then Antioch to Philippi to Thessalonica to Athens (he refers to Thucydides in his discussion of Paul's speech at the Areopagus)[63] and to Corinth and Ephesus, leaving Macedonia and Achaia and visiting Jerusalem before imprisonment in Caesarea and traveling to Rome and the last days of Paul. Bruce could not be any more explicit than he is in this volume that he relies upon Acts as the basis of his historical outline of Paul's life and ministry. In this, of course, he is not alone, as those far more skeptical than Bruce have also used the account of Acts as the basis of their outlines. Nevertheless, there is much predicated upon all of the other beliefs that Bruce has regarding Acts (and Luke's Gospel) that figure into this account, such as its literary genre, its reliability, its dating, and the ability to reconcile the presentation in Acts with what is found in the Pauline letters. This poses a problem even for Bruce, who gently dismisses authenticity of Ephesians and the Pastoral Epistles, but finds it difficult to place the Pastorals within his chronology.[64] One might well observe that it is interesting to note Bruce's willingness to accept so readily the historical reliability of Acts (and Luke) to the point of establishing a reliable Pauline chronology, when he is not willing to accept the Pauline authorship of at least some of the letters that are ostensibly claimed by Paul.

Greek Acts

At this point, we turn to Bruce's single most important work in Luke–Acts scholarship, his commentary on the Greek text of Acts. As noted earlier, this work was begun in around 1939, was finished in around 1944, but was not published until 1951, with a second edition the next year, and a third edition much later in 1990. In most ways, these several editions are clearly minor revisions of the same work, although there are also some interesting changes to note as well. The Preface to the first edition says that the commentary was written to be "neither too

---

63. Bruce, *Paul*, 245.
64. Bruce, *Paul*, 424–25 on authorship of Ephesians and 442–44 and other places, where the Pastorals are apparently distributed into the last two chapters on Paul's last days in history and tradition.

technical nor too popular for the requirements of ordinary students," in
which the "elementary character of many of the grammatical notes arises
out of experience in the lecture-room."[65] One then observes comments
on the words and phrases within Acts, provided in Greek often without
translation, in the tradition of J. B. Lightfoot's commentaries, with the
practice continued in the second and third editions (there is also plenty
of untranslated Latin that no doubt vexes modern students as well). It is
hard to imagine a commentary being written like this today for English
scholarship, in which supposedly major and significant commentaries
are frequently written with virtually no serious attention to language
(ones that would have qualified as popular style commentaries according to Bruce's criteria). I fear that there may be some students (and even
some of their professors) who are singularly unprepared to use and even
evaluate a commentary such as this.

Nevertheless, here are some of the conclusions that Bruce arrives at
in his first/second edition, with comparison to the third edition, of his
commentary on Greek Acts. (1) Since the commentary focuses upon
the Greek text, one might well expect comments upon the Greek. An
abundance of comments is found, most of them in the classical and
comparative-philological mode, with statements about Attic alternative forms, the possible influence of Semiticisms, and categories of
Aktionsart.[66] In a short section on language and style of Acts in the
introduction, Bruce cites some of Luke's language features, including the observation that Luke "makes an accurate distinction between
tenses . . . especially in the imperative,"[67] by which he means seeing
such categories as the continuous present, etc. There are surprisingly few references to Greek grammatical works, although the ones
cited, mostly Moulton and Howard (and later Turner) and Blass and
Debrunner (and later Funk), provide the vast majority of references.[68]

65. Bruce, *Acts* (Greek), Preface (to first ed.), vii, the first part of the quotation cited in the Preface to
the Revised Edition, xvi.
66. For those unfamiliar with such a category, see Stanley E. Porter, *Verbal Aspect in the Greek of the New
Testament, with Reference to Tense and Mood*, SBG 1 (New York: Peter Lang, 1989), 26–35.
67. Bruce, *Acts* (Greek), 1st/2nd ed., 27/3rd ed., 67.
68. See J. H. Moulton, *Prolegomena*, vol. 1 of *A Grammar of New Testament Greek* (Edinburgh: T&T
Clark, 1906; 3rd ed., 1908); Moulton and W. F. Howard, *Accidence and Word-Formation*, vol. 2 of
A Grammar of New Testament Greek (Edinburgh: T&T Clark, 1929); Nigel Turner, *Syntax*, vol. 3
of *A Grammar of New Testament Greek* (Edinburgh: T&T Clark, 1963); and Turner, *Style*, vol. 4
of *A Grammar of New Testament Greek* (Edinburgh: T&T Clark, 1976); Friedrich Blass and Albert
Debrunner, *A Greek Grammar of the New Testament and Other Early Christian Literature*, ed. and
trans. Robert W. Funk (Chicago: University of Chicago Press, 1961).

(2) The commentary takes an avowedly non-theological approach (as Bruce states in the preface to the second edition),[69] which is not to say that there are not theological comments, only that theology does not drive exegesis (as it so often does in some contemporary commentaries, where theological systems are all-too-readily imposed on the text) but theology, such as it is discussed, emerges from the exegesis. Some examples of pertinent and meaningful theological statements that arise from the text are those on the kingdom of God in Acts 1:3 or on glossolalia in 2:4, among some others.[70] Bruce does provide a section in his introduction on the theology of Acts that provides a conspectus of the major theological teachings of the book.

(3) On general introductory questions regarding Acts, Bruce affirms traditional Lukan authorship by a man who wrote two volumes of acts (one of Jesus and the other of the apostles, a view made clearer in the third edition), sees Luke as a historian in the Thucydidean mode (although he softens the view somewhat in the third edition), takes his previous Thucydidean view of the speeches in Acts (and in Luke's Gospel), does not see the influence of the Pauline letters or Josephus upon composition of Acts but recognizes other sources such as the "we" source, sees Acts and the Pauline letters as compatible, not contradictory or indicating late composition as the Tübingen school posited, presents a favorable view of Paul (Paul is Luke's hero according to Bruce), sees Luke as a theologian in his own right even if he does not emphasize theology at every turn in the commentary, and believes that the Alexandrian tradition represents more closely the earliest version of Acts (although he moves from Westcott and Hort's edition to the NA in the third edition). It is in the area of date of composition of Acts that the biggest change occurs in Bruce's work. In the first and second editions he endorses a date of composition soon after the writing of Luke's Gospel in AD 61, but in the third edition he endorses a date of late AD 70s to early AD 80s, in part because he has adjusted his date for composition of Luke's Gospel to later on the basis of the fall of Jerusalem. The change of date required a rewriting of the end of the third edition of the commentary, with the deletion of the last two paragraphs of the first and second editions.

69.   Bruce, *Acts* (Greek), Preface (to second ed.), viii.
70.   Bruce, *Acts* (Greek), 1st/2nd ed., 67–68/3rd ed., 100; 1st/2nd ed., 82/3rd ed., 114–15.

(4) Perhaps the most important feature of Bruce's commentary is its tendency to give the text of Acts the benefit of the doubt as a reliable text. This is seen in the introduction, but also in comments throughout the commentary. As a result, there are more references to Martin Hengel and as many to Colin Hemer as there are to Dibelius or Haenchen and many more than Conzelmann in the third edition.[71]

(5) The commentary is organized virtually the same in both earlier and later editions. The only major organizational difference to note is that in the earlier form, the fourth major section, titled "Paul's First Missionary Journey and the Apostolic Decree" in the first/second edition and "Church Extension from Antioch and Apostolic Decree at Jerusalem" in the third, includes Acts 12:25–16:5 in the earlier and 12:25–15:35 in the later, with later sections following on, with only a slight shift in title. This makes sense, as the second missionary journey begins at Acts 15:36, when Paul leaves Antioch. However, despite Bruce's earlier statement about Acts as Acts of the Apostles, he only uses this terminology for one section in his commentary, the third, "Acts of Peter" (9:32–12:24), and only uses the Pauline missionary journeys as a heading once in the earlier commentary and not in the later (he refers to the second missionary journey as a subheading for Acts 15:36–41 in the earlier commentary but not in the later).

We see that Bruce's perspective on Acts (and Luke's Gospel) is consistent with what we have seen in his other writings on Luke–Acts. We also see that, to the extent that Bruce's classical approach and assumption of a Thucydidean view of history and speeches can be questioned, to that same extent his approach to Acts as a whole can also be questioned. More importantly perhaps, Bruce's commentary, at least the first and second editions, was clearly written in the fashion of a single volume commentary on the Greek text to aid students of the text to understand the Greek. The standards for Greek knowledge were clearly significant at the time. As would be expected when the commentary was written, Bruce follows comparative and classical philological principles as seen in the standard New Testament Greek reference grammars and as would have been expected on the basis of his own education. Even though Ferdinand de Saussure published his

---

71. E.g. Martin Hengel, *Acts and the History of Earliest Christianity* (London: SCM, 1979) and Colin J. Hemer, *The Book of Acts in the Setting of Hellenistic History*, ed. Conrad Gempf, WUNT 49 (Tübingen: Mohr Siebeck, 1989; repr., Winona Lake, IN: Eisenbrauns, 1990).

Course in General Linguistics in 1916, and the Prague Linguistics Circle flourished in the between the war period, their influence upon language study as a whole and then other fields did not occur until much later, at least after World War II, as Saussure's work was not translated into English until 1959.[72] Nevertheless, even in the third edition, Bruce continues with the same understanding. As a result, there are possible misconstruals of the meanings of the tense-forms not by Luke but by Bruce, who endorses an *Aktionsart* and temporal model in which present tense-forms indicate continuous or iterative or similar action, etc. A good example of how his misconception affects understanding is in his interpretation of Acts 16:6.[73] The Greek text states: διῆλθον δὲ τὴν Φρυγίαν καὶ Γαλατικὴν χώραν, κωλυθέντες ὑπὸ τοῦ ἁγίου πνεύματος λαλῆσαι τὸν λόγον ἐν τῇ Ἀσίᾳ. Bruce makes several possible mistakes regarding the Greek of this passage. The first is that he interprets the aorist participle, κωλυθέντες, because it is an aorist, as indicating past time. That nonindicative verbs, including participles, are nontemporal has been recognized by some scholars since the early twentieth century. As a result of this first misinterpretation, the second mistake is to reconstruct an implausible scenario in which Paul and his companions received the prohibition by the Holy Spirit before they entered the region of Phrygia and Galatia. If Bruce had recognized that participles are nontemporal (even if he did not go as far as to recognize all tense-forms in Greek as nontemporal) and are temporally construed on the basis of syntax and context, then he could have interpreted this clause complex as indicating that Paul and his companions passed through Phrygia and Galatia, and at that time (either at the same time or subsequently) were hindered by the Holy Spirit from speaking the word in Asia, as Asia would have been the next area in which they would have entered. In other words, the syntax of the participle clause following its main verb supports the geographical configuration.[74]

The issue of Bruce's change of date of composition of Acts from an earlier to a later date (the middle date in most Acts scholarship) raises

---

72. For a review of how study of New Testament Greek fits within the history of linguistic thought, see Stanley E. Porter, *Linguistic Descriptions of the Greek New Testament: New Explorations in Systemic Functional Linguistics* (forthcoming).
73. Bruce, *Acts* (Greek), 1st/2nd ed. 310/3rd ed., 354.
74. Porter, *Verbal Aspect*, 377–88, esp. 386. See Richard Belward Rackham, *The Acts of the Apostles: An Exposition*, 8th ed. (London: Methuen, 1919 [1909]), 276; cf. 184n1.

its own set of questions. There are several factors to consider. The first is that it is not merely a matter of time between editions that results in the later date being endorsed, as the evidence that Bruce cites is essentially the same in both discussions. I believe that the difference is perhaps attributable to the different orientations of his writing as a classicist in the first and second editions and as a New Testament scholar in the third. When he first approached Acts, perhaps without as much consideration of the larger Synoptic Problem but on the basis of Acts and especially its extratextual references, Bruce imagined a work written in the early AD 60s. However, after becoming fully acculturated in New Testament scholarship, with seeing more of the interconnections of various areas of exploration, he was inclined to the later date. However, I think that it is important to note that the evidence itself has not changed, but the perspective on it has, in which Bruce is inclined to take Luke as writing after the fall of Jerusalem rather than before it, even though he is ambivalent in his arguments. Not only is there a problem with the fact that Bruce draws different conclusions from essentially the same evidence, but there is not a major argument created for why a date around AD 80 should be endorsed, other than his endorsing a date later than the fall of Jerusalem and not within the period in which the Pauline letters would have been known.[75] The third edition provides a less satisfactory explanation of the date of Acts than does the earlier version. Despite these criticisms, and if one takes some more recent developments into account especially in reference to Greek language study on which the commentary focuses, then Bruce's commentary remains one of the finest for its concentration upon understanding the Greek text of Acts.

English Acts

Bruce also published two editions of his English-language commentary on Acts. He indicates that he took seriously the task of communicating the meaning of a first-century text to a contemporary audience. In the preface to the commentary, he notes Karl Barth's (1886–1968) complaint in the preface to the second edition of his Romans commentary that many commentators perform critical biblical interpretation

75. On Bruce's later date as a typical compromise date in such discussions, see Stanley E. Porter, "Dating the Composition of New Testament Books and Their Influence upon Reconstructing the Origins of Christianity," in *In Mari Via Tua: Philological Studies in Honour of Antonio Piñero*, eds. Israel M. Gallarte and Jesús Peláez (Córdoba: Ediciones El Almendro, 2016), 553–74, esp. 557.

that is, according to Barth, "no commentary at all, but merely the first step towards a commentary."[76] Bruce admits that his commentary on the Greek text probably fell afoul of Barth's criticism, but also observes that one cannot take the second step without the first, even though he says that he has probably not achieved the second step in his English-language commentary either. I find it interesting that Bruce cites Barth in this way, and then admits that neither of his commentaries probably fulfills Barth's purpose, since Bruce's stated purpose is to hear not only "the voice of Luke" but "the word of God."[77] Whatever one thinks of Barth's comment and the purpose of commentaries, it would appear that hearing the word of God through the words of Luke would fulfill the purpose of providing meaningful commentary for the reader.[78]

The commentary is very simply arranged, with a brief introduction and then the section by section exposition, divided into groups of verses. The introduction deals with relatively few of the issues of interpretation: (1) canonical relationship and placement, (2) origin and purpose, including date, and (3) Paul in Acts. Regarding Paul in Acts, Bruce repeats his view that Paul is Luke's hero and sees Luke as a faithful historical recorder of the phenomenal mission of Paul in spreading the gospel. In discussion of date of composition, we see one of the most significant changes between the two editions of the commentary, similar to the one observed above in the Greek commentary. In the first edition, Bruce sees Acts as being written before the fall of Jerusalem and any indication of Roman persecution of Christians in the mid AD 60s. As a result, he dates Acts to before AD 64. In the second edition, Bruce recognizes the same evidence, but does not conclude that the fall of Jerusalem is compelling. He instead sees a date ranging within the Flavian period of AD 69–96. More specifically, he states

76. Bruce, *Acts* (English), 1st ed., 9/2nd ed., xvii, citing Karl Barth, *The Epistle to the Romans*, trans. Edwyn C. Hoskyns (London: Oxford University Press, 1933), 6. In the first edition, Bruce includes a trenchant footnote that has been deleted in the second edition: "May one dare to suggest that Barth's *Römerbrief* itself would have been a work of more abiding value if it had been preceded by such a 'first step'?" One can only wonder why such an apt statement was deleted in the second edition, as truer words have rarely been said of Barth's commentary.

77. Bruce, *Acts* (English), 10, xvii.

78. Barth used the example of Calvin's commentary on Romans as an ideal. Barth (*Romans*, 6–10, in a single paragraph) was rejecting the kind of higher criticism that grew out of the Enlightenment agenda that was concerned not with commentary but with reconstructing the text and making some philological notes and never really coming to terms with the text as text. One cannot accuse Bruce of failing in this regard, although one might well find many other contemporary commentators who focus on a variety of extraneous matters in commenting, such as rhetoric, intertextuality, and the imposition of entire theological systems.

that Ramsay's arguments for composition "about A. D. 80 are precarious, but nothing that has been discovered since then has pointed to a more probable dating."[79] Bruce apparently did not remember his own arguments in either the first/second edition of his Greek commentary or the first edition of his English commentary on Acts. One cannot help but think that he was at this point simply uncritically reflecting an easier consensus rather than maintaining the more independent position he had carved out earlier.

As for the commentary itself, in many ways Bruce's English-language commentary stands out as a model commentary. It is clearly based upon his understanding of the Greek text, even though reference to Greek is confined to footnotes (references to Moulton, Howard, and Turner still exceed those to Blass and Debrunner), and rather than discussing individual words or phrases, he engages in a discursive expositional style that summarizes a verse or set of verses and provides added explanation or detail regarding the context. The exposition itself is based upon the American Standard Version of 1901 in the first edition and Bruce's own translation in the second. The organization of the commentaries, including the shifts noted above, reflects the same changes as in the Greek commentaries, with one additional change. In the first edition of the English Acts, the third section, "The Acts of Peter and Beginnings of Gentile Christianity," extends from Acts 9:32–12:25, but in the second edition only to 12:24, with verse 25 placed in the next section.

In most regards Bruce follows a consistent perspective not just within this commentary from first to second edition (apart from the issue of date of composition), but also between both his Greek and English commentaries on Acts. For the most part, these are standard and repeated conclusions, even if they are subject to criticism. However, an example treated in both sets of commentaries provides a suitable test of his approach. In discussion of Acts 15:8–9, the Greek text reads: καὶ ὁ καρδιογνώστης θεὸς ἐμαρτύρησεν αὐτοῖς δοὺς τὸ πνεῦμα τὸ ἅγιον καθὼς καὶ ἡμῖν, καὶ οὐθὲν διέκρινεν μεταξὺ ἡμῶν τε καὶ αὐτῶν, τῇ πίστει καθαρίσας τὰς καρδίας αὐτῶν. In his Greek commentary, Bruce cryptically labels the use of the two aorist participles, δοὺς and καθαρίσας, as simultaneous or coincident aorist

79. Bruce, *Acts* (English), 2nd ed., 12, citing William M. Ramsay, *St. Paul the Traveller and the Roman Citizen* (London: Hodder & Stoughton, 1895), 386–87.

participles.[80] He does not explain his reasoning for this, especially in light of a comment such as he makes regarding Acts 16:6 (see above). He has an expanded similar comment in his English commentary: "Both these participles . . . are examples of the 'simultaneous' [or 'coincident,' added in 2nd ed.] aorist participle . . . : God testified to the genuineness of these people's faith by giving them the Spirit and cleansing their hearts in one regenerative moment."[81] Bruce apparently retains the idea of the aorist indicating a singular moment (akin to the notion of the punctiliar aorist, terminology from the comparative philology of the nineteenth century),[82] but he does not insist upon the past reference of the aorist participle. He does not give his rationale for not construing the aorists as past, but instead interprets them as simultaneous or coincidental, probably on the basis of context in which it makes less sense to have the events as antecedent. What he does not notice is that not only the context but also the syntax suggest this interpretation, as the aorist participle clauses appear after their main verb in both instances. This example, along with the one cited above on Acts 16:6, well illustrates that Bruce assumed the comparative-philological framework for understanding Greek, at least up to a point, where his interpretation demanded something else, but in which case he did not have a grammatical reason to suggest it, or at least that he included.

It is unclear to me what influence a different Greek interpretive model would have had on Bruce, that is, if he had availed himself of modern linguistic insights into Greek, but as seen in the two examples cited above, at the least they may have had an influence upon how he formulated his arguments and arrived at his interpretations. This is consistent with other observations above, in which Bruce seems to have had a fixed and consistent approach to many issues in Luke–Acts studies.

Supporting Studies

In this section, I turn to a number of further studies by Bruce that involved Luke–Acts. These consist of twelve journal articles or chapters that he published in a thirty-year span over the course of his career. I will not discuss each one in detail, but provide a summary assessment

---

80.   Bruce, *Acts* (Greek), 1st/2nd ed., 293/3rd ed., 336.
81.   Bruce, *Acts* (English), 1st ed., 306n25/2nd ed., 289–90n37.
82.   This notion was already disputed in mainstream New Testament scholarship by at least 1972 and Frank Stagg's article, "The Abused Aorist," *JBL* 91 (1972): 222–31. Bruce does not cite this article here, or anywhere else that I can find among the works I examined in detail for this chapter.

of each one, from earliest to latest, as a means of further establishing Bruce's approach to Luke–Acts.[83] Whereas Bruce published his major discussion of the speeches of Acts and his two major Acts commentaries relatively early in his career, that is, during his classical and then early Sheffield periods, his supporting studies fall into the end of his Sheffield period and later.

The first is Bruce's 1959 study of apostolic succession in the book of Acts, a summary of recent scholarship.[84] This article is followed by two intermediate reports Bruce published in 1982 and 1985 as assessments of current scholarship and is bookended by the final article in this traversal, a survey of commentaries on Acts, published in 1989. The article from 1959 is designed to help preachers be better informed in the pulpit, with Acts being their most important book since it describes how the church came into being at Pentecost. If we examine some of the books that Bruce discusses, we see what we noticed above—that he had high aspirations for preachers and students of the New Testament. His presentation reinforces a number of themes we have already encountered, including his emphasis upon Luke as author, and as both historian and theologian, although he emphasizes the historical discussion and other works that find Acts as historically reliable. He treats the speeches in Acts as contextually adapted comments that were delivered by the speaker, hence disputing the view of Dibelius, whose stylistic criticism he rejects. He says he is "in hearty agreement with [C. S. C. Williams] when he dates Acts before A.D. 70," showing that his shift to a later compositional date occurred

---

83. Bruce actually wrote a further article that I will do nothing more with than cite it and its conclusions. Bruce examines the literary and epigraphic evidence for the name of the Roman governor of Judea and concludes that his full name was probably Tiberius Claudius Felix (as Josephus indicates), not Tiberius Antonius Felix (as Tacitus indicates). See F. F. Bruce, "The Full Name of the Procurator Felix," *JSNT* 1 (1978): 33–36.

84. F. F. Bruce, "The True Apostolic Succession: Recent Study of the Book of Acts," *Int* 13 (1959): 129–43. The major works he refers to are: F. J. Foakes Jackson and Kirsopp Lake, eds., *The Beginnings of Christianity. Part 1: The Acts of the Apostles*, 5 vols. (London: Macmillan, 1920–1933), including a commentary on Acts by Lake and Henry J. Cadbury in volume 4 (1933); A. C. Clark, *The Acts of the Apostles* (Oxford: Clarendon, 1933); C. H. Dodd, "The Framework of the Gospel Narrative," *ExpTim* 43 (1932): 396–400; Dodd, *The Apostolic Preaching and Its Developments* (London: Hodder & Stoughton, 1936); Dibelius, *Studies*; Dibelius, *Paul*, ed. W. G. Kümmel (London: Longmans, Green, 1953); Roland Allen, *Missionary Methods: St. Paul's or Ours?* (London: R. Scott, 1912); G. W. H. Lampe, *The Seal of the Spirit* (London: Longmans, Green, 1951); John Knox, *Chapters in a Life of Paul* (Nashville: Abingdon, 1950); Wilfred L. Knox, *The Acts of the Apostles* (Cambridge: Cambridge University Press, 1948); William Ramsay, *The Bearing of Recent Discovery on the Trustworthiness of the New Testament* (London: Hodder & Stoughton, 1915); Henry J. Cadbury, *The Book of Acts in History* (London: A&C Black, 1955).

later.[85] Bruce also cites several works that emphasize the Greek text, in particular textual criticism. He concludes the article by assessing ten English commentaries on Acts from the late nineteenth century to his time of writing. The most highly commended is the one by Kirsopp Lake (1872–1946) and Henry J. Cadbury (1883–1974) in *The Beginnings of Christianity* collection of 1933, but also noteworthy is T. E. Page's commentary on the Greek text, very similar to Bruce's (and designed for students!).[86]

The second article appeared in 1973 on the Holy Spirit in Acts.[87] The article in fact is more than that. It presents Bruce's view of the Holy Spirit in Luke–Acts. Bruce distinguishes the view of Luke from the other Gospels and sees that only Jesus received the Holy Spirit before Pentecost. Luke's Gospel is the "time of Christ," and Acts is the "age of the Spirit," contrary to Conzelmann's view of Acts as the "time of the church."[88] Bruce sees similarities and differences in the view of the Spirit in Luke–Acts and at Qumran, with the Spirit in both marking a new age, but in Luke–Acts being personal (unlike at Qumran). Bruce notes examples of the work of the Spirit in a series of passages throughout Acts. He also sees a different emphasis in Paul than in Acts on the Spirit, with Acts emphasizing manifestations of the Spirit with which Paul is familiar but does not see as vital. Bruce also sees similarities between the view of the Spirit in John 14–16 and Acts 1–15. Bruce concludes that the progress of the gospel in Acts is directed by the Holy Spirit. As in previous work, Bruce defines his view against what he characterizes elsewhere as the German Dibelius–Haenchen–Conzelmann school of thought. Despite his treatment of a theological topic, his discussion is always closely tied to specific texts.

85. Bruce, "Apostolic Succession," 143, referring to C. S. C. Williams, *A Commentary on the Acts of the Apostles*, HNTC/BNTC (New York: Harper and Brothers, 1957).
86. Illustrating the ephemeral nature of commentaries, four of the ten are not mentioned in Craig S. Keener's exhausting bibliography of works on Acts (*Acts: An Exegetical Commentary*, vol. 4 [Grand Rapids: Baker, 2015]), including arguably one of the two best, the one by Page, *Acts of the Apostles* (London: Macmillan, 1886), the other being by Lake and Cadbury. The others are: R. J. Knowling, "The Acts of the Apostles," in *The Expositor's Greek Testament*, ed. W. Robertson Nicoll, vol. 2 (New York: Dodd, Mead, 1908); Rackham, *Acts*; A. W. F. Blunt, *The Acts of the Apostles*, Clarendon (Oxford: Clarendon, 1922); Foakes-Jackson, *Acts*; J. Alexander Findlay, *The Acts of the Apostles* (London: SCM, 1934); R. R. Williams, *The Acts of the Apostles*, Torch (London: SCM, 1953); G. H. C. Macgregor and Theodore P. Ferris, "The Acts of the Apostles," in *The Interpreter's Bible*, vol. 9, ed. George Arthur Buttrick (Nashville: Abingdon, 1954); Williams, *Acts*.
87. F. F. Bruce, "The Holy Spirit in the Acts of the Apostles," *Int* 27 (1973): 166–83. Bruce has a somewhat similar discussion at the end of his introduction to his *Acts* (Greek), 1st/2nd ed., 49–51.
88. Bruce, "Holy Spirit," 170, referring to Conzelmann, *Theology of St Luke*.

The next article, published in 1976, raises the question of whether the Paul of Acts is the real Paul.[89] Bruce frames this not as a disjunction but as the difference between a self-portrait and a portrait by someone else. The motivation for finding disjunction came from the Tübingen school of F. C. Baur (1792–1860), although it is still found in other manifestations, such as by those who see Acts as reflecting early Catholicism, such as Ernst Käsemann (1906–1998), Philipp Vielhauer (1914–1977), Conzelmann, and Haenchen.[90] Bruce turns to the two major sources for Paul: the letters and Acts. He first finds a large number of similar biographical details. As part of this mining of details, he examines Galatians 1:11–2:14, the only major autobiographical section in Paul's letters. Although he does not see reference to the decree of the Jerusalem council in Galatians, he states that he believes it is to be found in the background. Paul appears here to be unhappy with the decree, but is associated with it in Acts, which prompts Bruce to propose that the Acts account of the Jerusalem council is an "amalgamation" of two meetings, one attended by Paul and the other not.[91] The letters also help us to understand the Pauline collection for the Jerusalem church, in which Bruce rejects John Knox's (1901–1990) proposal for mitigating its significance.[92] Bruce then looks to Paul's resulting impression from his two sources, Acts and the letters. Paul is depicted as a truly emancipated person. Finally, Bruce discusses the theology of Paul as revealed in three speeches in Acts: at Pisidian Antioch (Acts 13:16–41), at the Areopagus (Acts 17), and to the Ephesian elders (Acts 20), where he sees consistency between Paul and Acts. This is the earliest of the essays that I have read that introduces the notion of Acts 15 being an amalgamated report, although Bruce does so without reference to any subsequent literature or teasing out any of its implications. This is an idea that Bruce develops more fully in a subsequent essay (see below). Bruce strongly argues for the Paul of Acts being the real Paul as depicted by an admirer and friend. Bruce's use of the speeches in support of his depiction and his reliance upon two sources, Acts and Paul's letters, provide the basis of Bruce's account.

---

89.   F. F. Bruce, "Is the Paul of Acts the Real Paul?" *BJRL* 58 (1975–1976): 282–305.

90.   Ernst Käsemann, *Essays on New Testament Themes* (London: SCM, 1964); Philipp Vielhauer, "On the 'Paulinism' of Acts," in *Studies in Luke-Acts*, eds. Leander E. Keck and J. Louis Martyn (Nashville: Abingdon, 1966), 33–50.

91.   Bruce, "Paul of Acts," 291.

92.   Knox, *Chapters*, 71.

The fourth article is on the Davidic Messiah in Luke–Acts, published in 1978.[93] Bruce admits that even though others may have wanted to make the connection of Jesus to the house of David, this is something that Luke did not make. As a result, the number of passages that emphasize a Davidic Messiah in Luke–Acts are relatively few. Luke only does so in Luke 1–2, especially the song of Zechariah, and the Lukan genealogy. The book of Acts, however, has three passages that emphasize the Davidic Messiah, all making use of testimonia. These are Peter's speech at Pentecost in Acts 2 that draws upon Joel 2, Paul's speech at Pisidian Antioch in Acts 13 that draws upon a variety of psalm passages and Isaiah servant passages, and the use of Amos 2 in Acts 15 at the Jerusalem council. The fact that Peter's and Paul's speeches resemble each other Bruce attributes to their relying upon primitive Christian tradition, as Dodd identified.[94] Bruce concludes by noting that, if the speeches in Acts are based upon earlier traditional material (and are not Lukan compositions), as he has argued earlier,[95] then this Davidic messianic interpretation of Jesus represents an early indication of this thought regarding Jesus.

Bruce returns to the topic of the state of Acts scholarship in an article published in 1982.[96] This essay is one in which he emphasizes contrasts, especially between those who endorse the historicity of Acts and those who do not. After noting that the beginning of the twentieth century was characterized by two works that contrasted with the previous work of Baur, those of Ramsay and Adolf Harnack (1851–1930),[97] Bruce begins his account in earnest with two major works that appeared after World War I. These are, first, an account of the rise of Christianity by the classical historian Eduard Meyer (1855–1930), who is commended because Meyer places Luke among the great historians

93. F. F. Bruce, "The Davidic Messiah in Luke–Acts," in *Biblical and Near Eastern Studies: Essays in Honor of William Sanford LaSor*, ed. Gary A. Tuttle (Grand Rapids: Eerdmans, 1978), 7–17.

94. C. H. Dodd, *The Apostolic Preaching and its Developments* (London: Hodder & Stoughton, 1944).

95. Bruce cites *Acts* (Greek), 1st/2nd ed., 18–21.

96. F. F. Bruce, "The Acts of the Apostles To-Day," *BJRL* 65.1 (1982): 36–56.

97. William M. Ramsay, *Historical Geography of Asia Minor* (London: John Murray, 1890); Ramsay, *The Cities and Bishoprics of Phrygia: Being an Essay of the Local History of Phrygia from the Earliest Time to the Turkish Conquest*, 2 vols. (Oxford: Clarendon, 1895–1897); Adolf Harnack, *Luke the Physician: The Author of the Third Gospel and the Acts of the Apostles*, trans. J. R. Wilkinson (London: Williams & Norgate, 1907); Harnack, *The Acts of the Apostles*, trans. J. R. Wilkinson (London: Williams & Norgate, 1909); and Harnack, *The Date of the Acts and of the Synoptic Gospels*, trans. J. R. Wilkinson (London: Williams & Norgate, 1911).

of antiquity.[98] The second is the five volumes edited by Foakes Jackson
and Lake on the beginnings of Christianity, which places study of Acts
at the forefront of investigation.[99] Those who have read the above will
not be surprised that Bruce sees these two major works as not the start
but the end of an era of Acts scholarship, at least one that he endorses.
Bruce then contrasts these works with German scholarship on Acts by
Dibelius, Haenchen, and Conzelmann, work that he recognizes but
clearly sees as taking a very different approach with Dibelius's style criticism, Haenchen's promotion of Acts as historical fiction, and Conzelmann's clear theological construction of time.[100] In contrast, Bruce cites
the most recent work on Acts by Cadbury, who provides an abundance
of historical evidence for interpreters, tending to favor a view compatible with eyewitnesses, and by A. N. Sherwin-White, who as an ancient
historian endorses the historical reliability of Acts.[101] Bruce continues
with Arnold Ehrhardt (1903–1965), a former colleague at Manchester
and a former German professor of Roman law who took a view similar
to that of Meyer and endorsed Luke as a historian who provided abun-
dant evidence for consideration by readers.[102] Bruce is skeptical of some
of the preliminary findings of C. K. Barrett (1917–2011) in the course
of writing his commentary on Acts for the ICC and more supportive
of I. H. Marshall's (1934–2015) commentary on Acts that follows
his book on Luke as historian and theologian and his commentary
on Luke's Gospel.[103] Bruce concludes by highly commending Martin
Hengel's (1916–2009) short work on Acts as a mainstream Greek
historical work.[104] Bruce concludes by welcoming what he sees as a trend

98. Eduard Meyer, *Ursprung und Anfänge des Christentums*, 3 vols. (Stuttgart: Cotta, 1921–1924).

99. Foakes Jackson and Lake, eds., *Beginnings of Christianity*.

100. Dibelius, *Studies*; Haenchen, *Acts*; Conzelmann, *Acts*; Conzelmann, *Theology of St Luke*, the last
of which Bruce notes has a "not entirely satisfactory title" in comparison to its more expressive
German title, *Die Mitte der Zeit*.

101. Cadbury, *Book of Acts in History*; A. N. Sherwin-White, *Roman Society and Roman Law in the New
Testament* (Oxford: Clarendon, 1963).

102. Arnold Ehrhardt, *The Framework of the New Testament Stories* (Manchester: Manchester University
Press, 1964); Ehrhardt, *The Acts of the Apostles: Ten Lectures* (Manchester: Manchester University
Press, 1969). Ehrhardt was Jewish and had to flee from Nazi Germany before the war. He refused
to return after the war, and Bruce had great respect for him.

103. C. K. Barrett, "Acts and the Pauline Corpus," *ExpTim* 88 (1976–1977): 2–5; I. H. Marshall,
The Acts of the Apostles: Introduction and Commentary, TNTC (Leicester: IVP, 1980); Marshall,
Luke: Historian and Theologian (Grand Rapids: Zondervan, 1970); Marshall, *The Gospel of Luke: A
Commentary on the Greek Text*, NIGTC (Grand Rapids: Eerdmans, 1978).

104. Martin Hengel, *Acts and the History of Earliest Christianity*, trans. John Bowden (London: SCM,
1979).

away from skepticism and toward appreciation of Acts as "a trustworthy source for our knowledge of the history as well as the theology of primitive Christianity."[105] The only surprise in this article (besides the fact that it must have been a rather uninteresting lecture, perhaps not unlike others by Bruce) is that Bruce does not invoke the Thucydidean view of Acts, although he does mention the speeches, but only in passing.

The next article, also a survey of scholarship on Acts, published in 1985,[106] has the character of an introduction to Acts that surveys most of Bruce's major areas of interest, along with many of the same supporting and contrasting works already noted above. In his introduction to Acts, Bruce now distinguishes Acts of the Apostles from the Gospel according to Luke (not Acts of Jesus), but he sees both Luke and Acts as "a history of the origins of Christianity,"[107] and then provides a summary of the contents of Acts. The article treats four topics: historicity, speeches, sources, and author, date, and purpose. Regarding historicity, Bruce endorses the views of classical historians regarding the historical reliability of Acts, citing numerous small details in support of this claim.[108] He further compares Acts to other early Christian sources, primarily the Pauline letters, and finds remarkable consonance between them at numerous points. This leads him to discuss speeches, where he immediately invokes a Thucydidean view: the speeches in Acts "are Thucydidean in the proper sense," which means that, even if not verbatim, they convey the gist of what was said.[109] Bruce takes exception to the views of Dibelius and Wilckens, and appeals to a previous interpretive tradition to which the author of Acts appeals.[110] At this point, part of Bruce's appeal is to G. Ernest Wright (1909–1974) of the Biblical Theology movement, who sees a supportive relationship between the Old Testament and the Christian kerygma.[111] Much of the discussion

---

105. Bruce, "Acts of the Apostles To-Day," 56.

106. F. F. Bruce, "The Acts of the Apostles: Historical Record or Theological Reconstruction?" in *Aufstieg und Niedergang der römischen Welt. II. Principat 25.3*, eds. Hildegard Temporini and Wolfgang Haase (Berlin: de Gruyter, 1985), 2569–2603.

107. Bruce, "Acts of the Apostles: Historical Record," 2570.

108. The scholars he cites include, from previous discussions, Sherwin-White and Ramsay, among some others, against the views, e.g., of Dibelius and Haenchen.

109. Bruce, "Acts of the Apostles: Historical Record," 2582.

110. Wilckens, *Die Missionsreden.*

111. G. Ernest Wright, *God Who Acts* (London: SCM, 1952). Bruce shared many ideas with this movement, even if he was not one of its apparent promoters. See Brevard Childs, *Biblical Theology in Crisis* (Philadelphia: Westminster, 1970); and its greatest critic, James Barr, *The Semantics of Biblical Language* (Oxford: Oxford University Press, 1961).

here is pitting skeptical comments against more positive ones by scholars like Meyer, Bertil Gärtner (1924–2009), and others.[112] Concerning sources in Acts, Bruce argues for sources, but not for an overspecification of them, such as is found in the theories of Harnack on two Jerusalem sources or Charles Cutler Torrey (1863–1956) on an Aramaic document for Acts 1–15 or Foakes Jackson and Lake for a Caesarean source,[113] and he definitely rejects Josephus as a source. Finally, under the category of authorship, date, and purpose, Bruce recognizes that both Luke and Acts are formally anonymous, but he believes the "we" sections of Acts point to the "I" of Acts 1:1, since the style of the "we" sections cannot be distinguished from the rest of the book, as indicated by Harnack and J. C. Hawkins.[114] However, tradition from the late second century points to Luke as the author. As for date, Bruce sees AD 62 as the earliest but, since there is no indication of Paul's death—which would have been mentioned—and due to the relationship of Luke to Acts, he indicates a date after AD 64/65, so in the late sixties. He is not more specific than this, although at this time he has apparently not shifted to a date in the AD 70s/80s as he does only a few years later in his commentary revisions. However, Bruce is very clear that dating Acts to the second century, as was done by Baur, is not plausible, as was argued by Harnack, Lake, Foakes Jackson, and even Dibelius. Many of Dibelius's followers, nevertheless, have argued for a later date, including Haenchen, Conzelmann, and others, such as John O'Neill (1930–2003), sometimes accompanied by the view that Acts reflects early Catholicism, found in Käsemann and others.[115] Bruce concludes that Acts has an apologetic purpose, while retaining its historical reliability. This essay is important in the sense that, not only does Bruce continue to take the same position on Acts, but he explicitly introduces Biblical Theology as a means of justifying his theological interpretation of Acts. The Biblical Theology movement saw unity between the testaments and emphasized the revelation of God in history, the latter a view compatible

---

112. Bertil Gärtner, *The Areopagus Speech and Natural Revelation*, trans. Carolyn Hannay King (Uppsala: Gleerup, 1955).

113. Harnack, *Acts of the Apostles*, 166–78; Charles Cutler Torrey, *The Composition and Date of Acts* (Cambridge, MA: Harvard University Press, 1916); Foakes Jackson and Lake, "The Internal Evidence of Acts," in *Beginnings of Christianity*, 2:121–204, esp. 152.

114. Harnack, *Luke the Physician*, 26–120; J. C. Hawkins, *Horae Synopticae*, 2nd ed. (Oxford: Clarendon, 1909), 182–89.

115. John Cochrane O'Neill, *The Theology of Acts in its Historical Setting*, 2nd ed. (London: SPCK, 1970); Ernst Käsemann, "Ephesians and Acts," in *Studies in Luke–Acts*, 288–97.

with Bruce's desire to affirm the historicity of Acts even as a theological document, and hence as a reliable revelation of God.

In 1985 also, Bruce published a study on the church of Jerusalem in Acts.[116] This article, unlike several of the previous ones, is not a review of scholarship on Acts but an exposition of Acts that reads much like his commentary on the English text of Acts. Since the topic is the church in Jerusalem, Bruce concentrates upon Jerusalem in Acts, recounting what the text says at several key junctures and supplementing it with further comments. He illustrates many of his same perspectives. The topics that he covers are the church in Jerusalem as the mother church first ruled by apostles and then elders; the founding of the church in Jerusalem at Pentecost and the matter of Hebrews and Hellenists, a primarily linguistic distinction with ramifications beyond Jerusalem; Paul's minimal contact with the Jerusalem church in Acts 9 that is recounted differently by Paul in Galatians 1:18–20; the attack upon the Jerusalem apostles caused by Peter's going to the Gentile Cornelius; the role of Jerusalem, and its council in Acts 15, in the Gentile mission; Paul's last trip to Jerusalem, when he is arrested; and the transition of Christianity from Jerusalem to Rome marked by Paul's arrest. Bruce's exposition often amounts to an informed retelling of the biblical account, as Bruce treats the Acts account as the primary reliable source for recounting the developments of early Christianity and he believes in its essential historical reliability. This article in some ways does not seem important enough to include in such a survey, but it was one of the articles he published in the *Bulletin of the John Rylands Library* and chose to reprint in his *A Mind for What Matters*, and it represents his expositional style as found in his English Acts commentary.

Bruce devoted further attention to the apostolic decree in Acts 15 in a chapter published in 1986 in a *Festschrift* for Heinrich Greeven, the scholar who edited Dibelius's *Studies in the Acts of the Apostles* for their original German publication.[117] In this chapter, Bruce primarily deals with the issue of how to understand Paul's relationship to the apostolic decree. The decree, according to Bruce, is a compromise position regarding Gentile believers in the church. Paul's position,

---

116. F. F. Bruce, "The Church of Jerusalem in the Acts of the Apostles," *BJRL* 67 (1984–1985): 641–61; repr. in Bruce, *A Mind for What Matters*, 150–65 plus notes (used here).

117. F. F. Bruce, "The Apostolic Decree of Acts 15," in *Studien zum Text und zur Ethik des Neuen Testaments: Festschrift zum 80. Geburtstag von Heinrich Greeven*, ed. Wolfgang Schrage, BZNW 47 (Berlin: de Gruyter, 1986), 115–24.

however, was not to give any authority to the law regarding salvation or even church status. Paul is said to be part of delivering the letter with the decree to Syria (Antioch) and elsewhere, but Paul's letters seem to indicate his not following its prescripts, so we have a conflict. Bruce examines both the Corinthian correspondence and Galatians. Paul appears to ignore the decree in Corinth and not know of it in writing to the Galatians, because the decree had not yet been issued. The Jerusalem council did not impose Jewish legal requirements, but later the Jerusalem church did, and this led to Paul's comments in Galatians regarding Peter's withdrawal. As a result, Bruce thinks it probable that Acts 15 "conflates two separate meetings at Jerusalem— an earlier one (at which Paul was present), which refused to require circumcision from Gentile converts, and a later one (at which Paul was not present), where the apostolic decree was drawn up," one that shows signs of Peter's involvement.[118] This is an interesting article that arrives at an unusual conclusion, especially unusual for Bruce. If one examines his Acts commentaries, the first and second editions of the Greek commentary do not, so far as I can determine, suggest the solution of conflation of two different episodes within Acts 15. Bruce takes the traditional view that the events in Galatians preceded the Jerusalem council that was called because of this situation and Paul would not have objected to the requirements of the decree, as they did not compromise the basis of faith. The third edition of the commentary on the Greek text takes a similar view but attaches a paragraph that states not that it is probable but that "It has been widely held that Ac. 15 combines records of two meetings at Jerusalem," using the same language as the article.[119] However, Bruce says that if Galatians 2:1–10 is not the meeting in Jerusalem (as he does not believe it is), then this view loses its pertinence. Thus, he rejects the conflation hypothesis in the commentary. In the first edition of his Acts commentary in English, Bruce takes essentially the same view as in the first/second editions of his Greek commentary, with the added comment that "To suppose that such an apostolic letter as Luke describes was drawn up, but that Paul had nothing to do with it, is to make Luke a writer of

---

118. Bruce, "Apostolic Decree," 121–22.
119. Bruce, *Acts* (Greek), 3rd ed., 331; see also 332. Many of the sources Bruce cites in the commentary at this point supporting this position are the same ones that he also cites in his article when he proposes the conflation.

historical fiction, in face of his own assurance about his methods."[120] In the second edition of the English Acts commentary, Bruce rewrites the introduction and does not include the statement above, but does include this statement: "Another suggestion is that in Acts 15 Luke combines into one narrative two originally separate meetings: one (recorded also in Gal. 2:1–10) at which Paul and Barnabas were present, and the other (which produced the decisions of Acts 15:28–30) at which Paul and Barnabas were not present. It is simpler to conclude that the occasion reported by Paul and that described by Luke were not the same."[121] It is hard to understand what has gone on here, apart from the fact that (in good Pauline fashion) Bruce is trying to be all things to all people. He unfortunately is satisfying none. Further strangeness is found in the relatively similar set of secondary sources that Bruce cites regardless of the position he takes on the conflation proposition. It appears that Bruce, at least temporarily, entertained the idea of Galatians 2:1–10 being reflected in Acts 15, but this is hard to countenance in light of his strong statements regarding the implications for his view of Luke as historian and his own conclusions in all of his commentaries.

In the ninth supporting study, Bruce also published in 1986 a paper regarding chronological questions in Acts.[122] Almost incidentally to the article itself, Bruce offers the view that Acts was written after the deaths of Peter, Paul, and James, a view he had rejected earlier (he thought Acts was not written at the time of Paul's death), and that it was written "a decade or two later than the last events which [Luke] records."[123] This is the earliest reference I have found in the material I have surveyed regarding Bruce's change of view on the date of composition of Acts. Bruce differentiates two types of chronological questions: date of composition of a work and internal chronological references, the latter of which this article focuses upon. He examines ten instances of "chronological data from apostolic history," of which eight occur in Acts.[124] These include: reign of Aretas, reign and death

---

120. Bruce, *Acts* (English), 1st ed., 299. He refers in a footnote earlier in the quotation to a number of the sources he cites in the article and in the *Acts* (Greek), 3rd ed. commentary.

121. Bruce, *Acts* (English), 2nd ed., 283–84. He refers in a footnote at the end of the penultimate sentence to many of the same works cited in his article at this point and in the *Acts* (Greek), 3rd ed. commentary.

122. F. F. Bruce, "Chronological Questions in the Acts of the Apostles," *BJRL* 68 (1985–1986): 273–95; repr. in *A Mind for What Matters*, 133–49 with notes (used here).

123. Bruce, "Chronological Questions," 133.

124. Bruce, "Chronological Questions," 135.

of Herod Agrippa I, famine during the reign of Claudius, Sergius Paullus as proconsul in Cyprus, Claudius's expulsion of the Jews from Rome, Gallio's proconsulship, the reign of Herod Agrippa II, Felix and Festus as procurators, reference to days of unleavened bread in Acts 19:6–7, and Nero's persecution of Christians. Bruce finds that very little is chronologically definitive in these episodes, so as to provide help in dating the Pauline chronology in the letters, where he disputes the compressed timing of Knox and the conflation of events into one location of Gerd Lüdemann on the basis of Gallio's proconsulship as a precise datum.[125] On the one hand, Bruce speaks with confidence regarding the reliability of the data in Acts for his purposes and treats it side by side with the Pauline letters. As a result, he takes a more flexible view of the dating of the Aretas incident, believing that Aretas's emissary may have been in charge of only a group of Nabateans. On the other hand, some of this confidence may be slightly overdrawn due to Bruce's appeal to the Greek language (he refers to Greek "past tense" and "future" as if they conveyed temporal values)[126] and belief that this supports what he concludes by calling it "the natural sense of Paul's language."[127]

The next year, 1987, Bruce published a chapter on Stephen's speech in Acts.[128] In this chapter, Bruce returns to comments that he made on Stephen's speech in his initial and final discussions of the speeches in Acts. In the first, he referred to Stephen's speech as apologetic and in the last as a defense. In this chapter, he examines the speech in more detail, concentrating upon how Stephen deals with the biblical material that he recounts. Bruce notes the two groups within the early Jerusalem church, the Hebrews and the Hellenists, both Jewish Christian groups, distinguished along linguistic lines that resulted in other cultural and related differences. Even if we do not know the origin of the Hellenistic group, Luke depicts them as having a view of the temple with which he is sympathetic. Stephen was apparently a

---

125. Knox, *Chapters*; and Gerd Lüdemann, *Paul, Apostle to the Gentiles: Studies in Chronology* (London: SCM, 1984).

126. Bruce, "Chronological Questions," 147. Greek does not have a past tense. It may have several different verbal forms that may be used to refer to the past, but that is not the same thing. The future form is also highly problematic and cannot be taken as a simple future (cf. English in this regard).

127. Bruce, "Chronological Questions," 149.

128. F. F. Bruce, "Stephen's Apologia," in *Scripture: Meaning and Method. Essays Presented to Anthony Tyrrell Hanson for his Seventieth Birthday*, ed. Barry P. Thompson (Hull: Hull University Press, 1987), 37–50.

leader of this Hellenistic group, who took a view that saw discontinuity rather than continuity between Jesus and Israel, with the temple being rendered obsolete. As a result, Stephen was charged with blasphemy and defended himself. Although the context is forensic, the speech is a form of *testimonia adversus Iudaeos*, here focusing on how to worship God. Bruce does not believe that Luke holds to the same view as Stephen but contends that Stephen presents a "manifesto" of a "segment of early Hellenistic Christianity."[129] The speech covers four topics: the patriarchs (Acts 7:2–16), the oppression in Egypt (7:17–34), the exodus (7:35–43), and the tabernacle and temple (7:44–50). Bruce then discusses how Stephen interprets the biblical tradition, including his editorial abridgments, departures from the Masoretic text and the Septuagint, and comments addressed to the contemporary audience. Stephen concludes with an invective directly addressed to the persecution of his hearers. Bruce concludes by noting that, whereas Luke did not hold to Stephen's view of the temple, he was sympathetic to it because God's messengers had been excluded from it. Although Bruce recognizes that there is interpretation on the part of Stephen, as well as Luke, he clearly assumes that the account of the speech in Acts reflects what Stephen said.

In 1988, Bruce published an essay on eschatology in the book of Acts[130] but makes clear from the outset that "eschatology" is not used in the narrower sense but in relation to three subjects in Acts concerned with the end of the old age and the beginning of the new. The first is the notion of the restored kingdom. Bruce here returns to his discussion of the Davidic Messiah, seeing it promoted in a variety of places in the New Testament, but especially in Luke 1 and Zechariah's canticle and fulfilled in Jesus as son of David, as is stated in Peter's speech at Pentecost in Acts 2 and the use of Amos 9:11–12 in James's summary of the Jerusalem council in Acts 15. The second subject is judgment and resurrection. Bruce here treats the Son of Man or one like a son of man found in Luke 12:8, John 5:27, and especially Mark 14:62, with Jesus sitting in judgment beside God (Ps. 110:1). The resurrection is seen in the later Pauline speeches of Acts, such as when Paul speaks before the council in Acts 23 or before the procurator Felix in Acts 24 or before

129. Bruce, "Stephen's Apologia," 40.
130. F. F. Bruce, "Eschatology in Acts," in *Eschatology and the New Testament: Essays in Honor of George Raymond Beasley-Murray*, ed. W. Hulitt Gloer (Peabody, MA Hendrickson, 1988), 51–63.

Herod Agrippa II in Acts 26. The third is the fulfillment of all that must occur before the return of Christ. Acts 3 speaks of the Messiah waiting in heaven until the words the prophets spoke regarding restoration of all things occurs, including the fulfillment of all prophecies. For Luke in Acts this eschatology does not seem to entail a restoration of Israel but fulfillment of a Gentile mission and preaching to all the nations, what Bruce calls "gospel expansion," without regard for what happens after this time.[131] Even though Bruce deals with a topic that is not usual for him, eschatology, he interprets it in relation to the book of Acts and some of the familiar topics or themes that he finds there, including the Davidic Messiah and the kind of schematization found in Conzelmann.

The last supporting study is a final assessment by Bruce of commentaries on Acts, published in 1989.[132] Thirty years after his first assessment, Bruce revisits the topic. He immediately begins with the commentary by Lake and Cadbury appearing in volume 4 of the *Beginnings of Christianity*, published in 1933, and followed by Cadbury in subsequent publications.[133] Bruce commends this latter work as it marks the end of an era that treated Acts as a historical source before turning to treating it as a theological source. Many subsequent commentaries were influenced by Dibelius's *Studies in the Acts of the Apostles*, including C. S. C. Williams's commentary that often disagreed with Dibelius. More favorable was Haenchen, whom Bruce labels as "unnecessarily skeptical" for attributing to Luke freedom to write "historical fiction."[134] Conzelmann then picked up where Haenchen left off, taking Paul's voyage to Rome as a Lukan construction. Bruce commends R. P. C. Hanson (1916–1988) for being as "independent a thinker" as Haenchen and Conzelmann but not as skeptical.[135] Bruce laments the unevenness of the commentary by Johannes Munck (1904–1965), which was written by an ill author who died two years before the commentary, which had to be finished by others, appeared.[136] Bruce commends the commentary by William Neil (1909–1979) for endorsing both historical reliability and theology.[137] Bruce then

131. Bruce, "Eschatology," 62; contra Conzelmann, *Theology of St Luke*.
132. F. F. Bruce, "Commentaries on Acts," *BT* 40.3 (1989): 315–21.
133. See Cadbury, *Book of Acts in History*.
134. Bruce, "Commentaries," 316.
135. Bruce, "Commentaries," 317, citing R. P. C. Hanson, *The Acts*, New Clarendon Bible (Oxford: Clarendon, 1967).
136. Johannes Munck, *The Acts of the Apostles*, AB 31 (Garden City, NY: Doubleday, 1967).
137. Bruce, "Commentaries," 318, citing William Neil, *The Acts of the Apostles*, NCB (London: Marshall, 1973).

notes a number of commentaries on Acts in one-volume commentaries, including by G. H. C. Macgregor (1892–1963), G. W. H. Lampe (1912–1980), Joseph A. Fitzmyer (1920–2016), and William Baird.[138] Bruce also interjects commendatory notes on several works that are not commentaries. The first is Ehrhardt's lectures on Acts followed by his work on the framework of the New Testament.[139] In both these books Ehrhardt endorses Luke as both historian and theologian. Bruce then turns to two German commentaries by Jürgen Roloff and by Gerhard Schneider.[140] He commends them for being less skeptical and more positive regarding Luke as a historian than Haenchen and Conzelmann. Bruce also notes Hengel's translated volume on Acts and the history of early Christianity, commending Hengel for treating Acts as a historical document, as well as explicitly arguing against Haenchen and Conzelmann. Even though Hengel argues that Luke may have smoothed out his sources, Bruce finds this acceptable within historical method. Bruce closes by commending two final commentaries. The first is the commentary on Acts by Marshall, who sees Luke as an evangelist rather than as a historian or theologian. Bruce evaluates Marshall and Hanson as the two best commentaries on the English text of Acts. He concludes by mentioning the anticipated commentary on Acts by Barrett for the International Critical Commentary, with the anticipation that it will be "the best available commentary on Acts."[141] There are several observations to make about this article. The first is how, even after thirty to nearly fifty years, Bruce still looks to and commends many of the same commentaries on Acts while also rejecting some of the same opponents. The second is that he evaluates them all primarily on the grounds of whether they argue for or against the historical reliability of the book of Acts, as that is the major presupposition with which Bruce approaches the study of

---

138. G. W. H. Lampe, "Acts of the Apostles," in *Peake's Commentary on the Bible*, 2nd ed., ed. Matthew Black (London: Thomas Nelson, 1963), 882–916 (Bruce wrote the articles on "The Epistles of Paul" and "Hebrews" for this commentary); Joseph A. Fitzmyer (and Richard J. Dillon), "Acts of the Apostles," in *Jerome's Bible Commentary*, eds. Raymond E. Brown, Joseph A. Fitzmyer, and Roland E. Murphy (Englewood Cliffs, NJ: Prentice-Hall, 1968), 165–214; and William Baird, "Acts of the Apostles," in *Interpreter's One-Volume Commentary on the Bible*, ed. Charles M. Laymon (Nashville: Abingdon, 1971), 729–67.
139. Ehrhardt, *Studies*; Ehrhardt, *Acts*.
140. Jürgen Roloff, *Die Apostelgeschichte*, NTD (Göttingen: Vandenhoeck & Ruprecht, 1981); Gerhard Schneider, *Die Apostelgeschichte*, 2 vols., HThKNT (Freiburg: Herder, 1980–1982).
141. Bruce, "Commentaries," 321 (emphasis original). The first volume appeared five years later, followed by the second four years after that. C. K. Barrett, *A Critical and Exegetical Commentary on the Acts of the Apostles*, 2 vols., ICC (Edinburgh: T&T Clark, 1994–1998).

Acts, even if he also entertains regard for theological value (but never at the expense of historical reliability). The third and final observation is that this article gives an indication of how the commentary industry has exploded since 1989. In this article, Bruce goes back to works published in the 1920s and 1930s, spanning sixty years. Since Bruce wrote this article, there have easily been more than twenty-five commentaries on Acts published, making the evaluative scene far more crowded, even if not more complex.

There is a surprisingly large amount of consistency within Bruce's essays on Acts, to the point of responding to the same group of scholars and categorizing his own position in relation to theirs. He assumes historical reliability and uses that to establish Acts as a source to be used alongside Paul's letters in recounting the development of the early church.

EVALUATION OF BRUCE'S SCHOLARSHIP ON LUKE–ACTS

Bruce was a major Luke–Acts scholar, probably because of a combination of his classical education, which made him confident in the use of original sources, during a time when there were several major transitions occurring within academic disciplines, the church, and New Testament scholarship, and his deep regard for the Scriptures based upon his Brethren background. As a result, Bruce was able to capitalize on his background and transition into New Testament scholarship that led to a highly productive career. Although Bruce never wrote a major monograph on Luke–Acts, his two major commentaries and his clearly articulated positions especially on the speeches in Acts, supported by a number of other volumes and some major articles, established his reputation in evangelicalism and then in wider New Testament scholarship. In light of this work, there are several observations to be made about Bruce's Luke–Acts scholarship.[142]

Common Ideas

Marshall rightly observes that Bruce did not have a major novel idea that distinguished his scholarship.[143] Instead, Bruce focused his Luke–Acts

---

142. I have benefited from the comments on Bruce's legacy in Grass, *Bruce*, 212–27. I note that in a handout for a lecture on Bruce, Grass refers to Bruce's method as inductive. See below.
143. Marshall, "Frederick Fyvie Bruce," 258; cf. also Grass, *Bruce*, 223.

scholarship around a relatively small number of fundamental beliefs, some of them assumptions and others of them direct results of other scholarly positions. These include the idea of Luke as a reliable historian, the speeches in Acts also being reliable as they reflected a Thucydidean view of historiography and of speech-giving, a textual focus especially on the Greek language seen through the eyes of nineteenth- and early twentieth-century comparative philology, and a clearly defined position that pitted itself against a number of well-known German scholars and their widely promulgated theories, perhaps among others. Although in some ways Bruce wanted to distinguish his view as progressive in relationship to trends in contemporary scholarship, his assumptions are conservative, and his preunderstandings are straightforward and relatively simple. However, he often repeated the major planks of his platform, to the point where he often simply invoked his conceptual framework and did not argue or sometimes even clearly state his assumptions.

Progressive Thought

Despite what I have just said, in some ways Bruce was a progressive in his thought, at least in the way in which he positioned his scholarship (whether he would have viewed himself this way is highly doubtful) and his own ecclesial beliefs. He believed that New Testament scholarship had been detrimentally influenced by the Baur Tübingen hypothesis, and its results were evidenced in the work of a number of contemporary scholars, such as Dibelius, Haenchen, and Conzelmann, who provided foils for his own thinking. In response to their domination, Bruce saw himself as arguing a minority position that corrected the direction that they had taken. His views on the speeches in Acts and especially his two commentaries provide a full-fledged response to the German status quo that had established itself within New Testament scholarship. This minority voice decrying mainstream (mostly German) scholarship is also found in Bruce's own ecclesial position. He was a convinced Nonconformist and was able to leverage this theological stance to secure the two major academic posts that he held in his career in biblical studies. He was considered either an outsider or a safe option as opposed to hiring an Anglican clergyman (Bruce was neither) to fill an academic post. Bruce therefore also positioned himself against the tide of contemporary theological scholarship. The same holds true within his own Brethren circles. Despite the complexities of Brethren relationships in Great Britain at the time, one might generalize by saying that the Brethren were theologically and socioculturally quite conservative. In many ways, so was Bruce, although in some theological matters Bruce was clearly outside the conservative norm, endorsing a late date of Daniel, multiple Isaiahs, and evolution as compatible with the Genesis account. In cultural issues, he was definitely a person of broader perspective than many of his generation and time within conservative Christianity. In matters of social justice, he fully exemplified what he believed was Paul's gospel of freedom. As a result, Bruce was in favor of gender equality within the church (remember, he was from a church that did not practice ordination) and racial equality within the church and society (his daughter married a man from Nigeria, which he fully supported and endorsed).

Methodology

Despite the perception of progressive thought, however, Bruce functioned within a relatively conservative Enlightenment-engendered methodological approach to New Testament studies, and this is especially evident in his studies of Luke–Acts. This is witnessed in several ways. Despite the appearance that he was using arguably the latest linguistic knowledge in his approach to Greek, Bruce in fact utilized the comparative philology of the mid-nineteenth to early twentieth centuries. Even though modern linguistics did not really emerge even in language studies until post World War II, Bruce was already firmly entrenched in the comparative-historical method in which he was educated, including his work with Kretschmer in Vienna, and he never seems to have deviated from it or shown signs of deviating from it. As evidence, Bruce wrote a very competent introduction to the character of the Greek language, in which he demonstrates a very enlightened comparative-historical view, but not a modern linguistic one.[144] However, there is more to consider than simply the linguistic method that Bruce demonstrates. There is the attitude that appears to be in place. Bruce's approach to language, as evidenced in his introduction to the language and especially in his commentaries, is unreflective, that is, he apparently does not critically reflect upon the categories of discussion in Greek, and hence appears to take a view that sees his description as the way to construe the language, without recognizing

---

144. Bruce, *Books and the Parchments*, 58–73. Note that subsequent editions provided opportunities to address some of these issues.

or acknowledging that there has been subsequent work in such areas as synchrony over diachrony, language as system, and differentiating between langue and parole, to name a few, that might have an influence upon his view of language.[145]

A similar attitude is seen in several other of the major areas in which Bruce treats Acts. I would not say that Bruce is a historical positivist, as on a few occasions he notes that Acts is a history from Luke's perspective and that there may be differences between Luke's account and others' accounts, such as Paul's. However, there is a distinct sense in which Bruce is very confident that he knows what history and historiography are and that Luke is writing not just history but reliable and dependable history, history that can be used as a primary source in not just discussing the development of early Christianity but also in presenting Paul. In his earlier work, Bruce invokes Thucydides as a historian as the ground for his belief in Luke as a historian, by claiming that, contrary to other scholars such as Dibelius, Haenchen, and Conzelmann, who emphasize Luke's creative abilities, Luke is a faithful and reliable historian in the Thucydidean mold. As he progresses in the course of his career, Bruce seems to argue less and less for the Thucydidean view and more and more simply asserts or merely assumes the position. This orientation is made clearest perhaps in Bruce's view of the speeches of Acts, a view that he subscribed to early in his career and persisted in until its end. As with Luke in general as a historian, Bruce argues that Luke took a Thucydidean view of speeches, in which the gist or essence of what was actually said on the occasion was reflected in the words in Acts. As indicated in the above discussion, the notion of a Thucydidean view of history and of speeches is highly problematic, as Thucydides's statement regarding speeches is subject to a wide variety of interpretations that vary from claiming that he captures the meaning of what was said to creating a meaning appropriate to the occasion, with views in between.

---

145. I find it interesting to note that one scholar who would have certainly made Bruce aware of such matters was his own doctoral student, Moisés Silva. Silva wrote his doctoral dissertation on "Semantic Change and Semitic Influence in the Greek Bible: With a Study of the Semantic Field of 'Mind'" (unpublished PhD thesis, University of Manchester, 1972), revised and expanded as *Biblical Words and Their Meaning: An Introduction to Lexical Semantics* (Grand Rapids: Zondervan, 1983), an introduction to structural linguistic lexical semantics, as well as publishing other articles related to this work. However, sometimes it is difficult for teachers to learn from their students, even in areas in which they are interested.

CONTEMPORARY ASSESSMENT

Bruce's reputation seems to have faded within the twenty-first century. This is perhaps the inevitable result of reconsideration of any scholar after one has passed from the scene, until subsequent generations revisit one's work and reestablish one's place within the critical landscape. I can imagine, however, that the reassessment of Bruce is influenced by several factors. One is that Bruce does not show much change or development in his major ideas regarding Luke–Acts—and as we have seen his major work is on Acts, not Luke—throughout his entire career. This is manifestly clear in his treatment of the speeches in Acts, but it is also seen in his overall perspective on Acts. Acts is a historically reliable presentation of the development of early Christianity by Luke, the early historian as well as theologian, who was a champion of Paul and who presented him in this light. The only two areas of significant shift that I have identified in his views concern the date of composition of Acts and the construction of Acts 15. Concerning the date of Acts, Bruce seemed to gravitate fairly late in his career toward a later date for Acts, along the way dismissing views that he had thought impregnable before, but not providing substantive new evidence for the later date. In this regard, I am not convinced that his later view is more convincing or more plausible than his former one. Concerning the composition of Acts 15, Bruce presents some ambiguous views on whether there were two meetings in Jerusalem, one with and one without Paul, but finally does not seem to endorse such a view in his revised commentaries, even if he entertains it earlier. There does not seem to be anything seriously gained by the revisionist view.

Another factor in his reassessment is that Bruce tended to identify and then position himself against a particular position within Luke–Acts scholarship, one identified with Baur originally but more recently with Dibelius, Haenchen, and Conzelmann. The major difference between Bruce and these scholars is not necessarily exegesis of particular points—although there are plenty of such differences if one mines Bruce's commentaries in comparison to their work—but their different assumptions regarding the historical reliability of Acts and Luke as a reliable historiographer. Dibelius, Haenchen, and Conzelmann were more concerned not with Luke as a preserver of what he inherited but with Luke as an innovator and developer of the tradition. Bruce and Dibelius, et al., were always going to find themselves on opposite sides of most questions, as Bruce points out in several of his articles on various topics in Luke–Acts studies. However, since Bruce wrote, even within more conservative circles, there has been growing acceptance of the creative initiative of the biblical authors, so that Bruce's opinion is probably not as widely held in its basic form as it once was, and the kind of creative viewpoint found in Dibelius, et al., such as regarding the "we" passages or ancient sea voyages, has come much more to the fore. The result can only be to reduce the profile of Bruce's work.

One of the recurring criticisms of Bruce has been that he is not as theologically robust as one might wish. Bruce himself seems to have been aware of this criticism, as noted above in his introduction to his English Acts commentary. This has perhaps helped to contribute to the lessening of his reputation in evangelicalism as the movement has become increasingly theological in most areas, to the point of theological interpretation being equated with interpretation in the Theological Interpretation of Scripture movement. However, there is serious question regarding the validity of this criticism of Bruce. First, it is true that Bruce was not formally theologically educated, which is perhaps one of the major reasons for the criticism of his work as not being theologically informed. Nevertheless, he was thoroughly entwined within the Brethren movement of the first half of the twentieth century. As a "nonconformist," and one might say embattled, theological movement within Anglican Britain, the Brethren of Bruce's time were often highly theologically informed, even if not formally theologically educated, as they had the constant battle of defending their movement and its beliefs in opposition to establishment Anglicanism. Second, the kind of theology that Bruce reflects is much more what might be called a textual or even (as Grass indicates) inductive approach, that is, one that emerges from the text rather than being imposed upon it systematically from the outside. As a result, Bruce is admittedly in many contexts less theological but what that really means, I believe, as opposed to so much contemporary theological commentary on Scripture, is that Bruce does not read a particular theological system into Acts or Paul, and so he does not answer the burning contemporary theological questions in the way that many desire. The kinds of theological statements that Bruce makes—and there are many of them as indicated in the discussion above—reflect what he sees as the theological interests of the biblical author. Bruce believed that Luke was a theologian, even if he was a historian first, and this is reflected in his comments on Acts, even if not to the degree that some might wish.

A final factor in the reassessment of Bruce is that the relative critical hegemony of the historical method, whether fully critical or not (Bruce would dispute that it was, and rightly so), has moved on to a much more complex methodological landscape, in which there is a greater variety of methods, most of which Bruce shows no awareness. Even within the areas that he functions, however, there is much greater recognized methodological complexity. Language studies have moved from the comparative to the modern linguistic paradigm, and with the move a shift from diachronic to synchronic concerns. The matter of historiography has been greatly complexified as historians have moved from a more positivist orientation to recognition of a variety of other approaches to history, including those influenced by society, culture, geography, and the linguistic turn. Bruce seems to assume the facts that he is going to discuss in his treatments of Acts, but historians are now debating the nature of facts in relation to data, to say nothing of scenarios that account for such facts. With greater methodological awareness, the relatively naïve, or at least naïve appearing, approach of Bruce, in which facts appear to be stable elements and history a fixed proposition, will inevitably be subject to revision.

CONCLUSION

Bruce was an important mid-century figure in the history of Luke–Acts—and especially Acts—studies, in particular for evangelical scholarship, where he had an important influence that is still felt in some circles. He emerged at a time when evangelical scholarship within Great Britain was looking for a scholar who could command the attention of others. Due to a variety of factors, including his education, his church affiliations, and his own interests and perspectives, Bruce emerged on the scene and flourished, not in classics his own original field of interest, but in New Testament and wider biblical studies, more in keeping with his theological upbringing and continuing religious commitments. As a result, Bruce was able to write in commanding ways over a period of time that convinced others of his position, and this led to him holding several important positions in British academia that allowed him to exercise influence over an entire generation of evangelical scholars. It is doubtful that contemporary evangelical scholarship could produce a scholar as convinced of or as consistent over time regarding one's positions as was Bruce, or who could exercise so much influence over a field of scholarship.

HANS CONZELMANN: LUKE AS THEOLOGIAN OF SALVATION HISTORY

Alan J. Thompson

M any consider Hans Conzelmann's (1915–1989) contribution to the study of Luke and Acts a landmark in Lukan studies and a major turning point that set the agenda for studies of Luke's writings. He is viewed as a pioneer in methodology and in the theology of Luke and Acts. In this chapter, I will summarize and briefly critique these contributions as well as suggest an overarching approach of Conzelmann's that is still profitable for Lukan studies today. Before I look more specifically at Conzelmann's contributions to Lukan studies and some areas of critique and appreciation, we must become briefly acquainted with Conzelmann the man and his broader work.

CONZELMANN'S LIFE AND WORK

Hans Conzelmann was born on October 27, 1915 in Tailfingen, Germany (just south of Tübingen). He excelled in his early studies at the universities of Tübingen and Marburg (1934–1938), moving from

Tübingen to Marburg to study under Rudolf Bultmann.[1] Bultmann would have a profound influence on Conzelmann's own work and approach to New Testament studies, and Conzelmann's theology of the New Testament was regarded by some "as the standard replacement for Bultmann's textbook in that area."[2] Conzelmann's university years took place during the rise of the Third Reich. After returning to Tübingen in these tumultuous years, Conzelmann joined the Church Theological Society, a group that was similar to the Confessing Church that opposed the Nazi party. Nevertheless, Conzelmann was drafted into the military and served as a foot soldier and then an officer in Russia. After getting married in 1944 he returned to fight in France (at the age of twenty-nine) where he was badly wounded and had to have a leg amputated. As I note below, his health suffered for years afterward.

After the war Conzelmann spent time in pastoral duties, taught religion and history in a high school, and then completed his doctorate at Tübingen and his postdoctoral *Habilitationsschrift* (required for university teaching) in Heidelberg under Günther Bornkamm. Ironically it is this postdoctoral work, published in 1954 before his call to begin his academic teaching career in Zurich, rather than the rest of his scholarly labor that he is probably most known for today. The German title of this work, *Die Mitte der Zeit* ("The Middle of Time"), was "lost in translation" when the book was translated into English as *The Theology of St Luke* in 1960.[3] I will return to the significance of both titles below. In 1960, Conzelmann accepted an invitation to teach in Göttingen where he remained for approximately thirty years, though with increasing limitations in the latter half of that period due to his decline in health following a heart attack in 1975, increasing reading difficulties with declining eyesight, a stroke in 1985, and a series of severe illnesses until his death

---

1. In this summary, I am indebted to a brief essay in memory of Conzelmann written by one of Conzelmann's colleagues, Dietz Lange, "In Memoriam Hans Conzelmann," in *Gentiles, Jews, Christians: Polemics and Apologetics in the Greco-Roman Era*, trans. M. E. Boring (Minneapolis: Fortress, 1992), xiii–xvii. See also Eduard Lohse, "Theology as Exegesis: In Memory of Hans Conzelmann," in *Gentiles, Jews, Christians*, xix–xxxiii; William Baird, *History of New Testament Research, Volume Three: From C. H. Dodd to Hans Dieter Betz* (Minneapolis: Fortress, 2013), 353–65. I am grateful to Andreas Goldmann, Sigurd Grindheim, Eckhard Schnabel, and Robert Yarbrough for kindly taking the time to read and provide valuable feedback on a previous draft of this essay.

2. John Reumann, "Editor's Introduction," in Hans Conzelmann, *Jesus: The Classic Article from RGG Expanded and Updated*, trans. J. Raymond Lord, ed. with an introduction by John Reumann (Philadelphia: Fortress, 1973), vii–viii.

3. Hans Conzelmann, *Die Mitte der Zeit: Studien zur Theologie des Lukas* (Tübingen: Mohr, 1954). A 7th German edition was published by Mohr Siebeck in 1993. ET Conzelmann, *The Theology of St Luke*, trans. Geoffrey Buswell (New York: Harper & Row, 1960).

on June 20, 1989, at seventy-three years old. A 590-page *Festschrift* focusing on matters related to historical Jesus studies, with contributions from twenty-seven authors, including Peter Stuhlmacher, Jürgen Roloff, Eta Linnemann, Joseph Fitzmyer, E. Earle Ellis, Reginald H. Fuller, Jacques Dupont, and Hans Dieter Betz, was presented to him on his sixtieth birthday.[4] It was during a relatively brief period then, in the 1950s and 1960s, that Conzelmann published his major works in New Testament studies in German (with their English translations usually published in the 1970s and 1980s). These publications cover a broad range of interests in New Testament studies and include the following:

- *Die Mitte der Zeit* (1954; English translation 1960)[5]
- A commentary on the Pastoral Epistles (1955; editing and expanding Dibelius's commentary; English translation in the Hermeneia series in 1972)[6]
- A lengthy article on the historical Jesus (1959) that was translated into English in book form (1973)[7]
- A commentary on Ephesians and Colossians (1962)[8]
- A commentary on the book of Acts (1963; second German edition in 1972; English translation in the Hermeneia series in 1987)[9]
- A comprehensive introduction to the theology of the New Testament (1967; the 1968 second German edition was translated into English in 1969)[10]

---

4.   Georg Strecker, ed., *Jesus Christus in Historie und Theologie: Neutestamentliche Festschrift für Hans Conzelmann zum 60. Geburtstag* (Tübingen: Mohr Siebeck, 1975). See the forward by Georg Strecker for what was said to Conzelmann on that occasion and an explanation for the overarching theme of the book focusing on historical Jesus studies.

5.   See note 3 above.

6.   Martin Dibelius and Hans Conzelmann, *Die Pastoralbriefe*, HNT 13 (Tübingen: Mohr [Siebeck]), 1955; ET Dibelius and Conzelmann, *The Pastoral Epistles*, trans. Philip Buttolph and Adela Yarbro, Hermeneia (Philadelphia: Fortress, 1972).

7.   Hans Conzelmann, "Jesus Christus," in *Die Religion in Geschichte und Gegenwart: Handwörterbuch für Theologie und Religionswissenschaft*, eds. Kurt Galling, et al. (Tübingen: Mohr [Siebeck], 1959), 3:619–53; ET Conzelmann, *Jesus* (see note 2 above).

8.   Hermann Wolfgang Beyer, Paul Althaus, Hans Conzelmann, Gerhard Friedrich, and Albrecht Oepke, *Die kleineren Briefe des Apostels Paulus*, NTD (Göttingen: Vandenhoeck & Ruprecht, 1962).

9.   Hans Conzelmann, *Die Apostelgeschichte*, HNT 7 (Tübingen: J. C. B. Mohr, 1963); ET Conzelmann, *Acts of the Apostles*, trans. James Limburg, A. Thomas Kraabel, and Donald H. Juel, Hermeneia (Philadelphia: Fortress, 1987).

10. Hans Conzelmann, *Grundriss der Theologie des Neuen Testaments* (Munich: Chr. Kaiser Verlag, 1967). A sixth German edition was published by Mohr Siebeck in 1997. ET Conzelmann, *An Outline of the Theology of the New Testament*, trans. John Bowden (New York: Harper & Row, 1969).

- A commentary on First Corinthians (1969; second edition in 1981; English translation in the Hermeneia series in 1975)[11]
- An overview of the history of early Christianity (1969; the English translation, *History of Primitive Christianity*, was published in 1973)[12]
- A comprehensive introduction to the interpretation of the New Testament which he coauthored with Andreas Lindemann (1975; an English translation of the ninth German edition was published in 1988)[13]
- His last book was *Gentiles, Jews, Christians: Polemics and Apologetics in the Greco-Roman Era* (1981; English translation in 1992)[14]

Along with numerous other articles and essays this collection of books and commentaries, largely produced in the 1950s and 1960s, points to an industrious and diligent scholar with a wide-ranging interest and a capacity for broad synthesis as well as an interest in the details of individual texts.[15] His colleague, Dietz Lange, describes Conzelmann as "serious, often brooding, and still, at least in his relatively healthy days, filled with the joy of life, a man of enormous will power and iron discipline, a straight thinker, secure in his independence, direct and explicit almost to the point of rudeness, never merely pleasant, militant but not cantankerous."[16]

---

11. Hans Conzelmann, *Der erste Brief an die Korinther*, KEK 5 (Göttingen: Vandenhoeck & Ruprecht, 1969); ET Conzelmann, *1 Corinthians*, trans. James W. Leitch, Hermeneia (Philadelphia: Fortress, 1975).

12. Hans Conzelmann, *Geschichte des Urchristentums* (Göttingen: Vandenhoeck & Ruprecht, 1969); ET Conzelmann, *History of Primitive Christianity*, trans. John E. Steely (Nashville: Abingdon, 1973). Though in this history Conzelmann focuses primarily on Paul, arguing that the Gospel writers were post-apostolic (20), and that "Jesus' life and teaching are the presupposition of church history" rather than part of it (echoing Bultmann's famous introduction to his theology; see the review by David Dungan in *Int* 28 [1974]: 98–101; see also Peter Balla, *Challenges to New Testament Theology: An Attempt to Justify the Enterprise*, WUNT 2/95 [Tübingen: Mohr Siebeck, 1997], 172–73).

13. Hans Conzelmann and Andreas Lindemann, *Arbeitsbuch zum Neuen Testament* (Tübingen: J. C. B. Mohr, 1975). A fifteenth German edition was published by Mohr Siebeck in 2008. ET Conzelmann and Lindemann, *Interpreting the New Testament: An Introduction to the Principles and Methods of N.T. Exegesis*, trans. from the 8th rev. German ed., 1985, by Siegfried S. Schatzmann (Peabody, MA: Hendrickson, 1988).

14. Hans Conzelmann, *Heiden, Juden, Christen: Auseinandersetzungen in der Literatur der hellenistisch-römischen Zeit* (Tübingen: Mohr [Siebeck], 1981). ET Conzelmann, *Gentiles, Jews, Christians: Polemics and Apologetics in the Greco-Roman Era*, trans. M. Eugene Boring (Minneapolis: Fortress, 1992).

15. See the chronological listing of books and major articles provided by the editor, John Reumann, at the end of Conzelmann, *Jesus*, 97–100. See also the bibliography up to 1975 in the *Festschrift* edited by Strecker, *Jesus Christus in Historie und Theologie*, 549–57.

16. Lange, "In Memoriam Hans Conzelmann," xiii.

Having provided that brief, general background, the rest of this chapter will focus on the work that is the most relevant for our focus on interpreters of Luke and Acts—Conzelmann's earliest and yet most influential study, *The Theology of St Luke* (with elaboration from his other works and his commentary on Acts). Conzelmann's *Theology of St Luke* is widely recognized for its influence in two areas: (1) theologically, the book is viewed as pioneering interest in Luke as a theologian; and (2) methodologically, the book is viewed as establishing the discipline of redaction criticism, particularly with regard to Luke's Gospel. It is true, as Howard Marshall states in his opening summary of previous investigators into Lukan theology in *Witness to the Gospel: The Theology of Acts*, that Conzelmann's book on Lukan theology has "so often been summarized and discussed by writers on Luke–Acts that it is not necessary to do so here."[17] However, since this chapter is a summary of Conzelmann's contribution to Lukan theology, and since *Die Mitte der Zeit* is his most significant contribution to Lukan theology, I will highlight these two areas of theology and methodology that Conzelmann, and *Die Mitte der Zeit* in particular, have brought to the forefront in Lukan studies. I will briefly note both the significance of Conzelmann's contribution in these two areas, and also some general criticisms of each one. At the end of the chapter, I will offer a more general estimate of Conzelmann's overall contribution, noting a fundamental deficiency and also suggesting an area that I think deserves emulation. These two areas in Conzelmann's work (redaction criticism and Luke as a theologian) are overlapping and hard to separate when assessing Conzelmann, but I will summarize Conzelmann's articulation of Lukan theology first before looking at the methodological development in Conzelmann's work that gave rise to this theological framework.

LUKAN THEOLOGY

W. C. van Unnik's 1966 essay on the state of Lukan studies famously called Luke–Acts a new "storm center in contemporary scholarship" in New Testament studies, due largely to the influence of Conzelmann.

---

17.   I. H. Marshall, "How Does One Write on the Theology of Acts?" in *Witness to the Gospel: The Theology of Acts*, eds. I. Howard Marshall and David Peterson (Grand Rapids: Eerdmans, 1998), 8. John Nolland does summarize Conzelmann's book at the beginning of his chapter, "Salvation-History and Eschatology," a little later in *Witness to the Gospel* (64–65).

252 Alan J. Thompson

Van Unnik called Conzelmann's book, along with Haenchen's commentary on Acts, the "high-water mark" and "turning point" in Lukan studies.[18] According to van Unnik, because of Conzelmann's influence, Luke was *now* viewed as a theologian:

> Luke appeared no longer as a somewhat shadowy figure who assembled stray pieces of more or less reliable information, but as a theologian of no mean stature who very consciously and deliberately planned and executed his work. . . . Luke was not primarily a historian who wanted to give a record of the past for its own sake, but a theologian who, by way of historical writing, wanted to serve the church of his own day amid the questions and perils that beset her.[19]

Similar accolades are regularly found in summaries of Lukan studies. In his 1969 book on redaction criticism, Norman Perrin even said that "There can be no discussion of the theology of Luke which does not *begin* with the work of Conzelmann and go on from there."[20] Charles Talbert suggested that the roots of this turning point lay in Bultmann's *Theology of the New Testament*, where Bultmann argued that the very fact that Acts was written shows the shift from an earlier eschatologically oriented community.[21] Nevertheless, according to Talbert, because of the influence of Conzelmann "the door was *now* open to read Luke–Acts as theology rather than as merely history."[22] Similarly, Joel Green opens his account of Lukan studies by stating,

> Contemporary study of the Gospel of Luke takes its starting point from the mid-twentieth-century publication of Hans Conzelmann's redaction-critical study, *The Theology of St Luke*. In Conzelmann's hands, the distinctive voice of Luke the evangelist emerged, leaving in its wake earlier

---

18. W. C. van Unnik, "Luke–Acts, a Storm Center in Contemporary Scholarship," in *Studies in Luke–Acts*, ed. Leander E. Keck and J. Louis Martyn (Nashville: Abingdon, 1966; London: SPCK, 1968), 16, 23.
19. Van Unnik, "Luke–Acts," 23–24. Van Unnik then describes this as a discovery of Luke the theologian.
20. Norman Perrin, *What Is Redaction Criticism?* (Philadelphia: Fortress, 1969), 67 (emphasis added).
21. Charles H. Talbert, "Shifting Sands: The Recent Study of the Gospel of Luke," *Int* 30 (1976): 381–95 (381–82). See Rudolf Bultmann, *Theology of the New Testament*, 2 vols., trans. Kendrick Grobel (London: SCM, 1955 [1953]), 2:117. On this same page, Bultmann cites Philipp Vielhauer's 1950 essay (see below footnote 27). Bultmann is the most cited author in Conzelmann's *Theology of St Luke* with 23 citations listed in the index (see, e.g., Conzelmann, *Theology of St Luke*, 95n1).
22. Talbert, "Shifting Sands," 382 (emphasis added).

judgments of Luke as the voice of Paul (who sometimes misunderstood the Pauline message) or as one so slavishly devoted to his sources that he was incapable of any theological contribution of his own.[23]

Conzelmann's overarching coherent and comprehensive picture in *The Theology of St Luke* of what Luke was doing sparked interest in Luke as an author-theologian, though it also generated ongoing discussions about the validity of Conzelmann's distinct three stage periodization. Conzelmann's *Theology* emphasizes that Luke is not just a collector of miracle stories and parables, or primarily a historian, but is an author and theologian with his own theological development. Therefore, according to Conzelmann, Luke is not primarily concerned with communicating reliably the events in the life of the historical Jesus or those of the early church. Rather, in arranging, adapting, and adding material, Luke is more of a theologian than a historian. This theology of Luke's was developed in response to issues relevant to Luke's own day. In particular, the issue, according to Conzelmann, was a crisis in Luke's life setting (though Conzelmann thinks this cannot be Luke the physician and companion of Paul, so the author and his particular setting are unknown but placed toward the end of the first century).[24] The crisis was the apparent delay of the eschatological end and second coming. The early church thought that this was on the immediate horizon, but then of course it had not happened.

Conzelmann's proposal, then, is that Luke wrote his Gospel and Acts in response to this crisis (Conzelmann thinks that Luke's Gospel was written after AD 70, and Acts was written sometime between AD 80–100).[25] Luke's response was to downplay and remove references

---

23. Joel B. Green, "Reading Luke," in *Methods for Luke*, ed. Joel B. Green (Cambridge: Cambridge University Press, 2010), 1.
24. Conzelmann, *Acts of the Apostles*, xxxiii; Conzelmann, *Interpreting the New Testament*, 233, 236.
25. Conzelmann, *Acts of the Apostles*, xxxiii. Conzelmann provides more discussion of these introductory matters regarding dates in his chapter, "Luke's Place in the Development of Early Christianity," in *Studies in Luke–Acts*, 298–316. There he argues that Luke and Acts were written after AD 70 due to Luke 21:20–24 ("historicizing" as the fate of Jerusalem and the eschaton are separated from each other) and Paul's death is presupposed (from Acts 20:17). According to Conzelmann, the developed stage in eschatology contradicts an early date of composition, and the application of eschatology and a theory of redemptive history to the life of the church in the world is also proof that Luke looks back over an extended development. However, Conzelmann argues that Luke is not so late that he is "early Catholic" (i.e., with "an institutional definition of the ecclesiastical office [priesthood] and the sacraments," "Luke's Place," 304; contra J. C. O'Neill, *The Theology of Acts in its Historical Setting* [London: SPCK, 1961]; cf. also Conzelmann, *Acts of the Apostles*, xxxiii; Conzelmann, *Theology of St Luke*, 149). Similarly, in his commentary (*Acts of the Apostles*, xlviii), he

to the immediate second coming and end of the world. Instead, Luke emphasized salvation history, and a corresponding emphasis on the need for long term perseverance during this extended time of trials throughout salvation history.

More specifically, to facilitate this emphasis on an extended salvation history, Conzelmann argues that Luke has provided a specific periodization of history with three distinct eras:

- first, the time of Israel up to and including John the Baptist (who therefore belongs to the old era);
- second, the time of the ministry of Jesus that is marked off as a Satan free period from after the temptation of Jesus up to the last supper in Jerusalem; and
- third, the life of the church that lasts up until the parousia in the distant future.

In the footnotes, Conzelmann states that he is building on Hans von Baer's (1926) work on the Holy Spirit, and so indicates that he was not the first to develop this threefold scheme.[26] However, he extends and develops the scheme to incorporate all of Luke's theology as a response to this crisis. In this way, Luke shows that the period of the church has its own distinct stage or period and therefore he explains the existence of the church as a distinct period without an immediate end and provides a rationale for the continued perseverance and mission of the church after Jesus's ministry. With the parousia relegated to the distant future, its apparent delay is no longer reason for concern. Jesus, therefore, as the German title states, came not to bring the end of time, but instead lived "in the middle of time." Thus, according to Conzelmann, Luke is decidedly uneschatological and focuses instead on the unfolding of history.[27]

expresses doubt that Luke is expressly opposed to Gnosticism (contra Charles H. Talbert, *Luke and the Gnostics: An Examination of the Lucan Purpose* [Nashville: Abingdon, 1966]).

26. Conzelmann, *Theology of St Luke*, 103, 150, 209, referring to H. von Baer, *Der Heilige Geist in den Lukasschriften* (Stuttgart: Kohlhammer, 1926), 77.

27. In *Theology of St Luke*, 14n1, Conzelmann cites Philipp Vielhauer's 1950 article, "Zum 'Paulinismus' der Apostelgeschichte," *EvTh* 10 (1950–1951): 1–15 (English translation by Wm. C. Robinson Jr. and Victor P. Furnish for *Perkins School of Theology Journal* 17 [1963] reproduced as "On the 'Paulinism' of Acts," in *Studies in Luke–Acts*, 33–50) that Luke's thinking was "uneschatological" ("How uneschatological Luke's thinking is is proved not only by the contents, but by the very fact of the Acts of the Apostles" [the English translation of this quotation in Conzelmann's *Theology of St Luke* differs slightly from the English translation of Vielhauer's in *Studies*, 47]).

Thus, Luke is a theologian of salvation history, but in this Luke departs from early Christian expectation.[28]

Although some adopted Conzelmann's view of Luke's periodization,[29] today many aspects of Conzelmann's threefold division have been rejected. For example:

(1) Regarding the division between the old era of Israel and the subsequent eras including the placement of John the Baptist in the old era and separated from Jesus (even geographically): Conzelmann overemphasizes μέχρι 'Ιωάννου and downplays ἀπὸ τότε in Luke 16:16. He dismisses too quickly the use of εὐαγγελίζω in Luke 3:18 regarding John the Baptist's preaching,[30] other texts such as Acts 1:22 that place John the Baptist in the new era, and the infancy narratives of Luke 1–2, which Conzelmann famously omitted from his analysis.[31] Furthermore, texts such as Luke 16:16 point to two broad eras of promise and fulfilment, rather than three. John is the greatest of the prophets of the old era because he introduces Jesus.[32]

(2) Regarding Conzelmann's so-called Satan-free period of Jesus's ministry: This also downplays the tests and trials of the demonic during Jesus's ministry and misinterprets Luke 22:28. According to Conzelmann, this reference to the disciples standing by Jesus during all his trials only refers to the trials now beginning in Jerusalem.[33] Similarly, with Luke 11:17–23 (regarding Beelzebub and demons) Conzelmann says this is symbolic comfort for the church of Luke's

---

28.   Talbert, "Shifting Sands," 390, cites Conzelmann's *Outline of the Theology*, 149–52 as evidence that Conzelmann later changed his mind about Luke's theology departing from primitive Christianity. Here, however, Conzelmann seems just to reaffirm his earlier argument that Luke is not to be characterized as "early Catholic" (see above note 25).

29.   For example, Joseph Fitzmyer, *Luke the Theologian* (New York: Paulist, 1989), 62–63 (cf. also Fitzmyer, *The Gospel according to Luke*, 2 vols., AB 28, 28A [Garden City, NY: Doubleday, 1981–1985], 181–87, 1115). Fitzmyer modifies some aspects (John the Baptist is more of a transition figure) and questions other aspects (such as the Satan-free period).

30.   Conzelmann, *Theology of St Luke*, 23n1, 221n2, citing Bultmann's *Theology of the New Testament*, 1:86 [87].

31.   Conzelmann, *Theology of St Luke*, 18n1, 22n2, 23n1, 75–76n4, 118. Commenting on Conzelmann's emphasis on Luke 16:16, Paul Minear ("Luke's Use of the Birth Stories," in *Studies in Luke–Acts*, 122) observes that "rarely has a scholar placed so much weight on so dubious an interpretation of so difficult a logion."

32.   See Darrell L. Bock, *Luke 9:51–24:53*, BECNT (Grand Rapids: Baker, 1996), 1351; Alan J. Thompson, *Luke*, EGGNT (Nashville: B&H Academic, 2016), 256–57; Michael Wolter, *The Gospel according to Luke*, 2 vols., trans. Wayne Coppins and Christoph Heilig (Waco, TX: Baylor University Press, 2016–2017), 1:32–33.

33.   Conzelmann, *Theology of St Luke*, 83.

time.[34] Conzelmann's argument that the third era is marked by a significant turning point with ἀλλὰ νῦν in 22:36 misses the fact that ὁ ἔχων
βαλλάντιον . . . πήραν already indicates that a shift from the specific
instructions of 9:3 (and 10:4 for the seventy-two) has taken place.[35]
Furthermore, the connection with 22:37 (γάρ) links the opposition to
Jesus with the opposition that the disciples need to be prepared to face.[36]

(3) Regarding the so-called downplaying of eschatology and the
separation of the period of the church from the period of Jesus's ministry: Although there are certainly distinctions to be made, this separation minimizes the significance of the parallel patterns and promises
that run from Luke to Acts and the references to Jesus's continued
activity in Acts.[37] The eschatology of Luke–Acts is now better understood in terms of inaugurated eschatology, without any radical distinction in Luke between salvation history and eschatological fulfilment,
rather than viewed as supposedly downplaying eschatology.[38] Conzelmann fails to grapple with many texts that emphasize vigilance and
readiness for the eschatological end (e.g., in Luke 12:39, 40 regarding the readiness needed for the coming of the Son of Man like a
thief; and 17:26–27 and the lack of readiness before the flood came in
judgment).[39] Indeed, far from deemphasizing eschatology, Luke often
includes teachings of Jesus that show how the certainty of judgment
and the reality of the age to come, whether at death or when Jesus
returns, should impact ethics and life in the present.[40]

---

34. Conzelmann, *Theology of St Luke*, 188.
35. Conzelmann, *Theology of St Luke*, 13. Minear, "Luke's Use of the Birth Stories," 124, observes that Conzelmann refers to Luke 22:36 as the basis for the shift in epochs no fewer than seventeen times. Wolter, *The Gospel according to Luke*, 2:477 notes the presence of ὁ ἔχων βαλλάντιον . . . πήραν in response to Conzelmann.
36. Cf. Thompson, *Luke*, 347. See Torsten Jantsch, *Jesus, der Retter: Die Soteriologie des lukanischen Doppelwerks*, WUNT 381 (Tübingen: Mohr Siebeck, 2017), 9–14, for an assessment of Conzelmann's threefold division in the context of discussions about Lukan soteriology and its relation to Israel's place in salvation history. I am grateful to Eckhard Schnabel for drawing my attention to Jantsch's work.
37. In *Acts of the Apostles*, Conzelmann does not explain who κύριος refers to in Acts 2:47; 11:21; 16:14; 18:9; 23:11 (and thinks that "begin" in 1:1 is simply a helping verb and that κύριος in 1:24 refers to God, without reference to κύριος in 1:21–22).
38. Building on Conzelmann's contemporaries, Oscar Cullmann and Werner Georg Kümmel. See also the reference to I. Howard Marshall in note 97.
39. Conzelmann, *Theology of St Luke*, 132, states that since "the End is still far away, the adjustment to a short time of waiting is replaced by a 'Christian life' of long duration, which requires ethical regulation and is no longer dependent upon a definite termination."
40. See, e.g., the subheadings for Luke 12:1–13:9; 13:10–15:32; 16:1–18:8 in Thompson, *Luke*, 385–86.

Furthermore, in assessing Conzelmann's contribution more broadly, statements noted above by many such as Perrin and van Unnik that Luke could only now be interpreted as a theologian rather than only a historian, should be tempered with reference to interpreters before Bultmann and Conzelmann. For example, although only brief citations are possible here, three interpreters—John Calvin, Johann Albrecht Bengel, and Adolf Schlatter—comment on Acts in ways that reflect an ongoing interest in this narrative as both a historical and a theological account written for the purposes of providing instruction and assurance.[41] Calvin in his introduction to his (1552) commentary on Acts described Acts as "sacred history" in the pattern of Old Testament history recounting God's saving purposes in history (i.e., seeing theological significance in historical narrative).[42] Bengel's (1734) introduction to his commentary on Acts in his *Gnomon* described Acts as "the continuation of the history of Christ" from Luke's Gospel and what he now does through the Holy Spirit given to his disciples.[43] Adolf Schlatter's comments on Luke and Acts in his second volume on *The Theology of the Apostles* are particularly interesting since the second edition of his *Theology of the Apostles* was published in 1922 when Schlatter was still active as a lecturer at Tübingen, where Conzelmann was soon to study (and Conzelmann occasionally cites Schlatter's commentary on Luke's Gospel[44]). Schlatter also describes Luke and Acts as evidencing Luke's focus on historical processes in order to provide assurance of God's actions.[45] He observes that Luke "directs

---

41. Though not in the sense that a "theological" interest means Luke is creatively correcting, changing, or contradicting his sources so as to provide a theological account with little interest in history and at odds with other New Testament writers.

42. Jean Calvin, *Calvin's New Testament Commentaries: Vol. 6 Acts 1–13*, eds. David W. Torrance and Thomas F. Torrance, trans. J. W. Fraser and W. J. G. McDonald (Grand Rapids: Eerdmans, 1995), 17.

43. Johann Albrecht Bengel, *Gnomon of the New Testament*, 5 vols., ed. A. R. Fausset, trans. A. R. Fausset, et al. (Edinburgh: T&T Clark, 1866), 2:510. On page 513, in commenting on Acts 1:1, Bengel describes Acts as "the Acts of the Holy Spirit." W. Ward Gasque, *A History of the Interpretation of the Acts of the Apostles* (repr., Peabody, MA: Hendrickson, 1989), 17, suggests that Bengel may have been the first to emphasize this as a major theme in Acts.

44. Conzelmann interacts a little with Schlatter's commentary on Luke's Gospel with ten page references to Schlatter listed in Conzelmann's index (often arguing for Luke's free creation of material in contrast to Schlatter's references to Luke's reliability and use of sources, e.g., 32, 63). Although Schlatter officially retired in 1922, he continued to give lectures until 1930, often to hundreds in attendance. See Werner Neuer, *Adolf Schlatter: A Biography of Germany's Premier Biblical Theologian*, trans. Robert W. Yarbrough (Grand Rapids: Baker, 1995 [1988]), 130. I am grateful to Robert Yarbrough for drawing my attention to this timeframe of Schlatter's teaching.

45. Adolf Schlatter, *The Theology of the Apostles: The Development of New Testament Theology*, trans. A. J. Köstenberger (Grand Rapids: Baker, 1999 [1922]), 339.

the community's attention to the chain of events because he sees in them God's sovereign providence."[46] When Schlatter turns to Luke's account of Paul in Acts, he argues that while it is true that Luke as a follower of Paul wrote a historical account, he is writing about Paul as "God's messenger by whose work God reveals himself." Therefore, Luke does not write a biography of Paul and these chapters in Acts are not merely a description of Paul's ministry in "individual selected accounts." Instead, "the issue addressed is what Christ commanded, how he showed himself to be mighty and how he used Paul in his service and gathered the church through him."[47]

Thus, it is unfair to interpreters before Conzelmann to describe him as the one responsible for orienting readers to Luke and Acts as narratives with theological concerns.[48] Nevertheless, it is true that arising out of the specific methodological context in which Conzelmann was operating (as we will see in the next section), Conzelmann's approach was an improvement over the focus on isolated sayings and sources in the immediately preceding years to his work. It is in this context that Conzelmann's focus on Luke as a theologian in his own right was an improvement and certainly gave rise to many discussions about the validity of Conzelmann's schema and provoked critical analysis especially in terms of eschatology.

Furthermore, although his overall view of eschatology and his threefold schema of history are generally no longer followed, aspects of Conzelmann's theology continue to form the basis of some recent discussions. For example, Karl Kuhn's introduction to Luke and Acts highlights Conzelmann's discussions of Lukan style, the role of John the Baptist, Luke's focus on a threefold chronology of salvation-history,

---

46. Schlatter, *The Theology of the Apostles*, 339.
47. Schlatter, *The Theology of the Apostles*, 333–34.
48. A glance at other older English language commentators on Acts also bears this out. For example, J. A. Alexander introduces his (1857) commentary by describing Acts as biblical history and argues that the various omissions are not accidental but deliberate as this sacred history is "a complete and independent history, constructed on a definite, consistent plan, designed to make a definite impression and to answer a specific purpose" (*Acts* [Edinburgh: Banner of Truth, 1963 (1857)], iv). Similarly, Melancthon Jacobus introduces his (1859) commentary by declaring that Acts is "a history of the progress of the Kingdom" and may be called "The Acts of Jesus" in his risen and glorified state (*Notes, Critical and Explanatory, on the Acts of the Apostles* [New York: Robert Carter & Brothers, 1869], 25–26). On Luke's Gospel, see especially N. B. Stonehouse, *The Witness of Luke to Christ* (Grand Rapids: Eerdmans, 1951). Stonehouse's book focuses on Luke's distinctive witness to Christ in the inauguration of God's eschatological kingdom and predates Conzelmann's *Die Mitte der Zeit* by three years (and he indicates in his preface that the initiative for the work goes back to earlier addresses and studies in 1941).

and Luke's view of Rome.[49] Joel Green's book on *Conversion in Luke–Acts* follows Conzelmann's explanation that when Acts speaks of God "granting repentance" the phrase means that God grants "the opportunity to repent."[50] I will return to Conzelmann's theology for a more general assessment toward the end of this chapter. However, to summarize our observations so far: although it would be inaccurate to say that if it was not for Conzelmann no one would consider Luke to be a theologian, and many of the individual theological motifs in Conzelmann's theology had already been developed by others,[51] it is true that within the methodological approaches to the Gospels in Conzelmann's context, he did return the focus to and provoke discussion of Luke's theological interests, particularly in terms of the overarching framework of Luke–Acts. Conzelmann's overarching framework, however, developed out of his methodological approach. This brings us to the second area of Conzelmann's influence.

METHODOLOGY: REDACTION CRITICISM

Conzelmann's *Theology of St Luke* has also been viewed since its German publication in 1954 as a pioneering and classic example of redaction criticism. The main strength of redaction criticism in general is its improvement upon form criticism. Thus, following the focus on individual units in the Gospels and their classification into forms for oral transmission in the life setting of the early church, characteristic of Bultmann (Conzelmann's teacher), Conzelmann's *Theology of St Luke* argued

---

49.   Karl Allen Kuhn, *The Kingdom according to Luke and Acts: A Social, Literary, and Theological Introduction* (Grand Rapids: Baker Academic, 2015).

50.   Joel B. Green, *Conversion in Luke–Acts: Divine Action, Human Cognition, and the People of God* (Grand Rapids: Baker, 2015), 136–39. See, e.g., Conzelmann's commentary on Acts 5:31 in *Acts of the Apostles*, 42. Green's book overlooks passages such as Acts 13:48 (τεταγμένοι), 15:7 (ἐξελέξατο ὁ θεὸς . . . ἀκοῦσαι . . . καὶ πιστεῦσαι), and 18:27 (πεπιστευκόσιν διὰ τῆς χάριτος). See Alan J. Thompson, Review of Joel B. Green, *Conversion in Luke–Acts: Divine Action, Human Cognition, and the People of God*, *BBR* 27.2 (2017): 289–91.

51.   See also note 81. As noted above (note 26), Conzelmann built on von Baer's work on the Holy Spirit for his threefold schematization, and Vielhauer's work for his understanding of Luke as "uneschatological." Furthermore, Conzelmann's view that Luke lacks a theology of the atonement and makes no connection between Jesus's death and the forgiveness of sins specifically builds on C. H. Dodd, *The Apostolic Preaching and its Developments* (New York: Harper & Row, 1964), 25, and H. J. Cadbury, *The Making of Luke–Acts* (New York: Macmillan, 1927), 280. See Conzelmann, *Theology of St Luke*, 201. Conzelmann's subordinationist Christology in which Jesus is merely a subordinate instrument in God's plan specifically builds on Herbert Braun, "Zur Terminologie der Acta von der Auferstehung Jesu," *TLZ* 77 (1952): 533–36. See Conzelmann, *Theology of St Luke*, 175.

that Luke used and shaped his sources for his own purposes related to his own late first-century life setting. Consequently, the interpreter's focus shifted from the oral transmission of individual units to the Gospel as a whole. The focus shifted from a view under form criticism of the Gospel writers as collectors of individual stories to authors with their own interests. Thus, in the introduction Conzelmann describes his work in relation to form criticism as aiming to explain "Luke's work in its present form" and to examine "the structure of Luke's complete work and the essential meaning of this structure."[52] One can see in this approach a step toward later literary approaches and an improvement over earlier more atomistic readings of individual accounts within the Gospels. Having briefly outlined above the main lines of Conzelmann's articulation of Lukan theology, I will provide below some examples and critique of Conzelmann's methodological approach that focused on apparent Lukan changes and additions to his source material.

Conzelmann's 1954 study on Luke, combined with Günther Bornkamm's (Conzelmann's supervisor at Heidelberg) 1948 work on Matthew[53] and Willi Marxsen's 1956 work on *Mark the Evangelist*,[54] consolidated this new method for Gospels criticism. Although Bornkamm pioneered redaction criticism methodologically, and Marxsen clarified the method and coined the term "*Redaktionsgeschichte*," Conzelmann's work on Luke is often viewed as "the most important."[55] In 1966, Perrin described Conzelmann as "the greatest practitioner of this methodology to date"[56] and in 1977 Stephen Smalley stated that Conzelmann's *Die Mitte der Zeit* "marks a watershed in Gospel Studies and an important advance in the method of redaction criticism itself."[57]

---

52. Conzelmann, *Theology of St Luke*, 9, 15.
53. See the English translation, Günther Bornkamm, "The Stilling of the Storm in Matthew," in Günther Bornkamm, Gerhard Barth, and Heinz Joachim Held, *Tradition and Interpretation in Matthew*, trans. Percy Scott (Philadelphia: Westminster, 1963), 52–57; and "End-Expectation and Church in Matthew," in *Tradition and Interpretation in Matthew*, 15–51.
54. Willi Marxsen, *Der Evangelist Markus: Studien zur Redaktionsgeschichte des Evangeliums* (Göttingen: Vandenhoeck & Ruprecht, 1956).
55. David Law, *The Historical Critical Method: A Guide for the Perplexed* (London: T&T Clark, 2012), 190, citing Perrin, *What is Redaction Criticism*, 28. Law (185–88) summarizes the differences between the historical focus in the term *Redaktionsgeschichte* and the more literary focus that arose in the United States under the term "redaction criticism."
56. Norman Perrin, "The Wredestrasse becomes the Hauptstrasse: Reflections on the Reprinting of the Dodd Festschrift," *JR* 46, no. 2 (1996): 297; cited by Law, *The Historical Critical Method*, 190.
57. Stephen S. Smalley, "Redaction Criticism," in *New Testament Interpretation*, ed. I. H. Marshall (Exeter: Paternoster, 1977), 183; cited by Law, *The Historical Critical Method*, 190.

As a classic example of redaction criticism, *Die Mitte der Zeit* also exhibits some of the weaknesses of some applications of that method that have long been pointed out.[58] For Conzelmann, the method for discovering this theology of the Gospel author primarily depended upon the detection of apparent changes that the author has made from his sources. One shortcoming of this method from the outset of course is that it depends on knowing which direction any apparent changes have been made, whether from Mark to Luke, or from Luke to Mark, and the method depends on there being this precise level of literary dependency. Conzelmann assumes the two-source hypothesis, and so operates on the basis that various differences between Mark and Luke evidence changes Luke has made from Mark and that those differences are the key to Luke's theological intentions.[59] I will offer three brief additional and specific criticisms of Conzelmann's application of this method here and observe that in each case Conzelmann himself notes the potential problem.

First, Conzelmann often views such apparent changes as theologically significant, without considering that they might be merely stylistic, virtually synonymous, emphases rather than wholesale changes, or dependent on other historical factors. For example, Conzelmann thought that the removal of the phrase "coming in power" found in Mark 9:1 from the reference to the coming of the kingdom of God in Luke 9:27 was evidence of a change in eschatological perspective. For Conzelmann, this is consistent with the removal from Luke's Gospel of the reference to the "nearness" (ἤγγικεν) of the kingdom found in Mark 1:15 and was viewed as evidence that Luke does not talk of the timing or nearness of the kingdom but merely the nature of it. Conzelmann adds, however, that elsewhere (e.g., Luke 10:9) "Luke is certainly familiar with the statement ἤγγικεν, but it is not part of the

---

58. For example, D. A. Carson, "Redaction Criticism: On the Legitimacy and Illegitimacy of a Literary Tool," in *Scripture and Truth*, eds. D. A. Carson and John D. Woodbridge (Grand Rapids: Zondervan, 1983), 115–42, 376–81; reprinted in Carson, *Collected Writings on Scripture* (Wheaton, IL: Crossway, 2010), 151–78. See also Talbert, "Shifting Sands," 392–94, who identifies three main problems with redaction criticism as practised by Conzelmann: (1) the influence of traditions other than Mark; (2) the problem of only focusing on apparent differences to the tradition rather than also where Luke reproduces tradition; and (3) the rising criticism of the two source theory and Markan priority.

59. Due to the large number of cross references, one needs to read Conzelmann's *Theology of St Luke* alongside a synopsis of the Gospels in order to grasp the observations he makes concerning the apparent changes in Luke's Gospel from Mark.

preaching."[60] The use of ἤγγικεν in Luke 10:11 as "an assertion of the
nearness of the Kingdom" is described as "rare in Luke."[61] Thus, apparent changes may not necessarily be theologically significant.

Second, Conzelmann may have skewed the theology of the Gospel
writer when he focuses only on differences and apparent changes but
overlooks the common material or considers it as only part of the
tradition and therefore contrary to what the author as redactor really
thinks. For example, for Conzelmann, the earlier tradition before
Luke held that John the Baptist stood on the dawn of the new eschatological age, on the dividing line between the old and new epoch,
and was the forerunner. However, in Conzelmann's view, Luke has
downplayed eschatology, and John is removed from being the forerunner of (future) eschatological events;[62] John is instead given a place in a
continuous story of salvation.[63] Nevertheless, Conzelmann states that
(a) he is not taking into account Luke 1:17, 76 and the first two chapters of Luke's Gospel; and (b) Luke's own pronouncements contradict
the "traditions" that Luke has himself preserved such that "he does not
set out his views coherently."[64] Similarly on the topic of the involvement of the Romans in Jesus's death, Conzelmann argues that in Luke
"Jesus is not executed by the Romans" and Luke describes instead the
mockery of the Jews.[65] Nevertheless, two pages later, Conzelmann
states that "in so far as there is any suggestion that the Romans [do]
take part, it is a survival from the sources and is not part of the plan
of Luke's account, but rather, contradicts it."[66] In this instance, rather
than suggest that Luke's combination of redaction and tradition is
inconsistent, it would have been better to question whether this overall construal of Luke's plan overlooks some details in the text and is
perhaps therefore mistaken.

Third, Conzelmann appears not to have correctly understood the
original theological intention of the source (Mark) that he thinks is

---

60. Conzelmann, *Theology of St Luke*, 104, 114n3. He also states that elsewhere Luke can speak of the
coming of the Kingdom, "but this has to be interpreted with the other sayings." Note also page 115
where Conzelmann thinks "it is impossible for Luke to identify Kingdom and Spirit."
61. Conzelmann, *Theology of St Luke*, 107. Luke 11:20 (ἄρα ἔφθασεν ἐφ᾽ ὑμᾶς ἡ βασιλεία τοῦ
θεοῦ) is noted on page 118 but is not discussed. Cf. also Conzelmann, *Theology of St Luke,* 112.
62. E.g., Conzelmann argues that there is evidence of this in the removal of ὀπίσω μου from Mark 1:7
in Luke 3:16 (*Theology of St Luke*, 24).
63. Conzelmann, *Theology of St Luke*, 22.
64. Conzelmann, *Theology of St Luke*, 22.
65. Conzelmann, *Theology of St Luke*, 88. Pilate plays only a passive part.
66. Conzelmann, *Theology of St Luke*, 90.

now a differing theological view on the part of the redactor (Luke). Conzelmann's thesis assumes that Mark and the early church had an imminent eschatology in the sense that they expected the end of the world to take place in the immediate future.[67] Regarding the parable in Luke 19 about the ten servants, Conzelmann states that Luke is contradicting the Christian tradition with this delay. He then admits, however, that even the (supposed) source (Matt. 25:14–30) is aware of the delay, but Luke makes it the main point of the story by adding verse 11.[68] Thus, it appears that even the sources did not advocate only an immediate end but maintained a more complex combination of both the hope and anticipation of the parousia as well as the promise of the spread of the gospel to the nations.

In all of these examples, Conzelmann assumes a very low view of the historical reliability of Luke. In addition to an extreme form of redaction criticism in which he argues that Luke freely changes, adds, and removes material for his own purposes, Conzelmann repeatedly claims that Luke has no knowledge of the historical events. This is particularly evident in his description of Luke's knowledge of geography. Among other claims, Conzelmann says Luke presented Capernaum as though it was in the middle of Galilee rather than by the shore,[69] and didn't know that one would first have to enter Jerusalem before going into the temple.[70] Ward Gasque's overview of the history of interpretation of Acts argues that "[h]istorical scepticism seems to have reached its peak in Conzelmann's treatment of Acts. . . . Haenchen seems rather conservative by comparison."[71]

To summarize this brief reflection on Conzelmann's methodological contribution to the study of Luke's theology in terms of redaction criticism, it is true that as the first full scale redaction-critical study of Luke's Gospel (less so in Acts), Conzelmann's work pioneered a major improvement over form-critical approaches and contributed a link in

---

67. See the above references to Bultmann's *Theology* and Vielhauer's "Paulinisms" in notes 21, 27. Even Matt 23:39 is viewed as treating the entry into Jerusalem as a type of the parousia (Conzelmann, *Theology of St Luke*, 75).

68. Conzelmann, *Theology of St Luke*, 135n2; see also 126, 170 where he notes that Mark 2:19 already signals a delay of the parousia (see also Mark 13:10; 13:32). Note also the discussions in more recent times about the challenges of locating specific Gospel audiences in, e.g., Richard Bauckham, ed., *The Gospels for All Christians: Rethinking the Gospel Audiences* (Grand Rapids: Eerdmans, 1998).

69. Conzelmann, *Theology of St Luke*, 38–39, 60.

70. Conzelmann, *Theology of St Luke*, 75n1.

71. Gasque, *A History of the Interpretation of the Acts of the Apostles*, 248.

the development toward more recent literary approaches. The method as practiced by Conzelmann, however, also exhibits many of the weaknesses that subsequent critics of some forms of redaction criticism have often pointed out. Thus, the more recent approaches that view the Gospels as a whole or complete literary unit generally do not focus on apparent distinctions between tradition and redaction as the primary means of determining Luke's theological emphases.[72] For example, in contrast to Conzelmann's methodology that focuses more on apparent editorial changes, studies on Luke's theology such as those by Joel Green, Mikeal Parsons, and Darrell Bock have a notably decreased emphasis on comparisons with Mark to determine Luke's theology and an increased focus on the narrative as a whole.[73] Compared to the almost three columns of references to Mark in Conzelmann's *Theology of St Luke*, Green and Parsons each have just nine entries referring to Mark in their Scripture indices.[74]

COMMENDATION AND CRITIQUE OF CONZELMANN'S THEOLOGICAL INTEGRATION

In this final section, I will offer an overall assessment of Conzelmann in terms of a fundamental deficiency and also an aspect of his work that provides us with a general example to follow; that is, his overarching integrative framework for understanding Luke–Acts. The overwhelming strength of *Die Mitte der Zeit* is the way in which Conzelmann manages to integrate so many aspects of Luke's work into his overarching scheme.[75] On the one hand, his work is comprehensive in its treatment of topics across Luke–Acts. He manages to cover topics

---

72. Cf. Carson, "Redaction Criticism," in *Collected Writings on Scripture*, 162.
73. Joel B. Green, *The Theology of the Gospel of Luke*, NTC (Cambridge: Cambridge University Press, 1995); Mikeal C. Parsons, *Luke: Storyteller, Interpreter, Evangelist* (Peabody, MA: Hendrickson, 2007); Darrell L. Bock, *A Theology of Luke–Acts: God's Promised Program, Realized for All Nations*, BTNT (Grand Rapids: Zondervan, 2012).
74. Green, *Theology*, 152; Parsons, *Luke*, 220. Cf. Conzelmann, *Theology of St Luke*, 246–48. Bock, *Theology*, 473–74, has twenty-seven references to Mark listed in the index, but many of these do not relate to determining Luke's theology on the basis of changes (though sometimes different emphases are noted).
75. Talbert, "Shifting Sands," 382, notes that although Bultmann and Ernst Käsemann had already identified the issues of eschatology, the delay of the parousia, the Lukan shift to salvation history, and therefore the identification of Luke as a theologian rather than a historian, Conzelmann's influence arose from his integration of these details into an overarching framework. "It remained for Conzelmann to raise the question about the interpretation of the framework as an entity in its own right." See note 51.

such as geographical elements in Luke's Gospel, eschatology, suffering, repentance, the church and empire, the church and Israel, the plan of God, election, the place of Israel's Scriptures, the relationship between God and Jesus, the life, death, resurrection, and ascension of Jesus, the role of the Holy Spirit, the beginnings of the church and the progress of mission, the message and bearers of the message, and conversion and the Christian life.

More than comprehensive, however, *Die Mitte der Zeit* manages to integrate all of these themes into the overarching thesis of Luke's de-emphasis of eschatology and focus on salvation-history due to the crisis of the delayed parousia. No matter what the topic is, whether empire or election, suffering or the Scriptures, Conzelmann views all of these as united through Luke's de-emphasis on (imminent) eschatology and focus on salvation history.[76] Lukan geography serves to separate John the Baptist from Jesus's ministry at the midpoint in time. John the Baptist therefore is not a forerunner in Luke's Gospel and he doesn't preach about eschatology but is merely a preacher of "timeless ethics."[77] Luke's teaching about the kingdom of God does not focus on the timing of it but the need for perseverance because it is entirely future.[78] The destruction of Jerusalem and the temple are not eschatological events but merely a refutation of Judaism in the course of history.[79] Luke's Christology is likewise determined by his focus on the mid-point in time so there is therefore no preexistence of Jesus in Luke's writings and Jesus is viewed as subordinate to God and God's plan in history.[80] Jesus's death is not atoning and has no connection to forgiveness.[81] Instead, Jesus's death is merely a part of the historical

76. "All the central themes in Luke's thought" are to be seen "primarily from the standpoint of the sequence of redemptive history. . . . It is this that gives the various concepts their unity." Conzelmann, *Theology of St Luke*, 184.
77. Conzelmann, *Theology of St Luke*, 25; cf. also 101–2.
78. Conzelmann, *Theology of St Luke*, 56, 104, 122.
79. Conzelmann, *Theology of St Luke*, 78.
80. Conzelmann, *Theology of St Luke*, 173. The relationship of Father and Son "is seen primarily from the standpoint of the sequence of redemptive history" (184). In this discussion, Conzelmann downplays the use of κύριος and dismisses Acts 10:36 as an isolated statement (171).
81. Conzelmann, *Theology of St Luke*, 201. As noted above in note 51, Conzelmann cites Dodd (*Apostolic Preaching*) and Cadbury (*The Making of Luke–Acts*) in support. According to Conzelmann, Acts 20:28 is perhaps used just to give a Pauline impression (201). In his commentary, *Acts of the Apostles* (175), Conzelmann asserts again (and refers to his *Theology of St Luke*, 201, 220n1 for support) that "The blood of Christ plays no independent role in Luke's theology. . . . Here [Acts 20:28] Luke reproduces early Christian tradition."

sequence of events. The Spirit is not associated with the kingdom[82] and is not the eschatological gift but a "substitute in the meantime for the possession of ultimate salvation."[83] The Spirit, therefore, is a solution to the problem of the delay of the parousia[84] and helps disciples to exist in this world, providing power for endurance.[85] Similarly, the discussion of ethics and the Christian life focuses on endurance. Luke's references to the empire also relate to this context of endurance. The state is here to stay and Luke is writing to prepare readers for the long haul and to show that both John and Jesus were nonpolitical and so being a Christian is no crime.[86]

The same overarching framework and integration of themes is found in Conzelmann's commentary on Acts.[87] His subheading to the section entitled "Major Themes" is "View of History," and his introductory sentence asserts that "Fundamental to Acts is a picture of the whole of salvation history divided up into three epochs: the time of Israel, the time of Jesus (as the center), and the time of the church."[88] This framework, says Conzelmann, "determines the ordering of the subject matter in both volumes." He then proceeds to summarize main themes in Acts as seen through this lens. After downplaying the imminence of the end and highlighting the threefold schema, Conzelmann then describes the place of the church, the role of the Spirit, the portrait of Paul, the use of Scripture, subordinationist Christology, Jesus's death and resurrection, the place of Israel, and the place of the empire, all within that schema.

The church, therefore, is "an entity with its own historical dimensions."[89] The Spirit provides the continuity between the time of the apostles and the later church. Luke's "historical schematization" also affects the shape of the picture of Paul who "has to appear subject to the Law."[90] Luke's use of Scripture is also determined by his view

---

82. Conzelmann, *Theology of St Luke*, 115.
83. Conzelmann, *Theology of St Luke*, 95. Cf. also 230.
84. Conzelmann, *Theology of St Luke*, 136.
85. Conzelmann, *Theology of St Luke*, 96.
86. Conzelmann, *Theology of St Luke*, 138–41. In "Luke's Place in the Development of Early Christianity," in *Studies in Luke–Acts*, 298–316, Conzelmann adds that Luke does not have any political interest and that he refers to the Roman Empire only as it impacts the expansion of Christianity (300–1).
87. Conzelmann, *Acts of the Apostles*, xlv–xlviii.
88. Conzelmann, *Acts of the Apostles*, xlv.
89. Conzelmann, *Acts of the Apostles*, xlv.
90. Conzelmann, *Acts of the Apostles*, xlvi.

of history in assuming the continuity of salvation history. This also means that in Luke's Christology there is no doctrine of preexistence as the focus is on Jesus's appearance in the middle of time and therefore Christological subordinationism is dominant throughout.[91] The focus in Acts on Jesus's resurrection is due in part to the assurance that this provides to the believer of God's guidance of the history of the church and future salvation. Jesus's death is also therefore not viewed as atoning; rather, the resurrection is the turning point in the history of the world.[92] The church's relationship to Israel is also understood in terms of the continuity of history with the resurrection being the turning point that marks the end of God's patience.[93] Finally, the relationship between church and empire is likewise understood not in terms of general principles or a view of the state but only in how this relationship impinges on the preaching of the resurrection. For Conzelmann, Luke is not arguing for Roman readers that Christianity is the true Judaism or a *religio licita* (he does not think such a concept existed). Luke's focus instead is on salvation history and the continuity between Israel and the church.[94] The judgment of the empire is supportive, however, of the distinction between Christians and the "Jews."

To arrive at this comprehensive, integrative framework, one might say that, methodologically, Conzelmann's assumptions (1) of an earlier more immediate eschatology and hence the crisis of a delayed end, and (2) that Luke's apparent differences from Mark are the prime location for Luke's theology, were imposed on the text and resulted in a distortion of Luke's material. Furthermore, it is also possible that Conzelmann provides a warning of the potential pitfall of finding one unifying thesis for Luke's writings by illustrating how material that does not fit one's synthesis may be neglected or downplayed. As I have already indicated, with many I am not persuaded by his construal of Lukan theology, his methodology, or his historical skepticism. Talbert concludes his 1976 summary of Lukan studies by stating that "[a]t present, widespread agreement is difficult to find, except on the point that Conzelmann's synthesis is inadequate."[95] Nevertheless, I think

91. Conzelmann, *Acts of the Apostles*, xlvi.
92. Conzelmann, *Acts of the Apostles*, xlvi. Conzelmann again states that an atoning view of Christ's death only occurs in Acts 20:28 as something that is not Lukan but is merely carried through from the tradition (cf. *Theology of St Luke*, 201; see also above in notes 51, 81).
93. Conzelmann, *Acts of the Apostles*, xlvii.
94. Conzelmann, *Acts of the Apostles*, xlvii.
95. Talbert, "Shifting Sands," 395.

Conzelmann's attempt at a comprehensive integration is commendable and still awaits a successor.[96] More recent entries in the genre of books on the theology of Luke–Acts have either focused on one or the other of these books, or have generally tended not to be as integrative as Conzelmann was.[97]

CONCLUSION

In the context of Lukan interpreters, Conzelmann has the dubious distinction of being at the same time both the one who is credited with directing subsequent interpreters to the theological designs of Luke–Acts and the interpreter (as noted above by Talbert) whose framework for the theological intention of Luke–Acts has found almost unanimous rejection. His methodological approach and theological synthesis may serve as a warning of the potential pitfalls that interpreters of Luke and Acts face. The challenges of relating Luke's Gospel to the other Gospels as well as to Acts, of tracing the many themes that run through Luke–Acts and investigating the connections between these themes, and of integrating the literary, historical, and theological interests of Luke–Acts continue to face interpreters today. Conzelmann's methodological and theological framework may have been flawed, but his synthesis generated much interest in Luke's writings in the wake of the inadequacies of form criticism. There is still more

---

96. Furthermore, his association of salvation history with God's plan and the perseverance of the church in the midst of suffering were appropriate and can easily be demonstrated in the texts of Luke and Acts. Contra Conzelmann, however, this can also be found elsewhere in the New Testament.

97. One notable exception to this was I. Howard Marshall who applied his thesis that Luke's central theme was salvation throughout his whole book, *Luke: Historian and Theologian* (Downers Grove, IL: InterVarsity, 1998). This book, of course, is one of the only sustained critiques of Conzelmann's work. Marshall's own method was also an application of redaction criticism, though he recognized Luke's use of common material as well as Luke's own emphases. Furthermore, Marshall did not view the tasks of being a "historian" and a "theologian" as antagonistic to one another but as necessarily interrelated for the goal of providing assurance to readers such as Theophilus. Cf. also R. F. O'Toole, *The Unity of Luke's Theology: An Analysis of Luke–Acts* (Wilmington, DE: Glazier, 1984). O'Toole was criticized for, among other things, focusing on one theme to the neglect of others that did not fit the schema or making the categories too broad in order to include diverse themes. See, e.g., reviews by Walter E. Pilgrim, "The Unity of Luke's Theology: Analysis of Luke–Acts," *Int* 40.3 (1986): 317–22; John F. O'Grady, "The Unity of Luke's Theology: Analysis of Luke–Acts," *TS* 46, no. 3 (1985): 544–45. See also Alan J. Thompson, *The Acts of the Risen Lord Jesus: Luke's Account of God's Unfolding Plan*, NSBT (Downers Grove, IL: InterVarsity, 2011); Mark L. Strauss, "The Purpose of Luke–Acts: Reaching a Consensus," in *New Testament Theology in Light of the Church's Mission: Essays in Honor of I. Howard Marshall*, eds. Jon C. Laansma, Grant Osborne, and Ray Van Neste (Eugene, OR: Cascade, 2011), 146–49. Strauss integrates the major themes of Luke–Acts into the overall purpose of providing legitimization for believers.

work that could be done to explicate Luke's account of the outworking and eschatological fulfilment in history of the triune God's kingdom promises in the saving life, death, resurrection, and reign of the Lord Jesus, through the Holy Spirit, to save and sustain his people until the return of Christ, for his glory. Perhaps approaches that do not assume such contradictions either within the narrative of Luke–Acts itself, or between Luke and other New Testament authors, or between God's action in history and God's interpretation of that action in Scripture offer more promise for a more enduring treatment of Luke's theology.

CHARLES KINGSLEY BARRETT: A HISTORIAN BY NATURE, A THEOLOGIAN BY GRACE

John Byron

C harles Kinglsley Barrett is a name that many if not most students of the New Testament recognize instantly. He has been called one of the greatest biblical commentators of the twentieth century, if not the greatest British commentator. His reputation is such that comparisons with J. B. Lightfoot are not uncommon or undeserved. Both Barrett's and Lightfoot's careers are closely associated with Durham. Both were Cambridge graduates and demonstrated unparalleled familiarity with the New Testament, ancient languages, history, and the classics; all of which they used effectively in their commentaries.

But while many similarities exist, there are also important differences. Lightfoot was an Anglican whose arrival at Durham coincided with being enthroned as Bishop in Durham Cathedral. Barrett, on the other hand, was a local Methodist preacher who came to Durham as a theology lecturer and never attained any particular ecclesiastical office. Lightfoot lived and served in Durham a total of fourteen years, while Barrett taught at the university for thirty-seven years (1945–1982) and lived in Durham another twenty-nine years until his death in 2011. Even in retirement he remained active in New Testament studies and would sometimes participate in the life of the department of theology.

Thus while both men are regularly identified with Durham, it is not a stretch to suggest that it was Barrett who, in many ways, helped to transform Durham into a well-known center for biblical scholarship.

But the name "Barrett" was not only connected with Durham's prestigious university. It was a name well recognized in Methodist circles in the United Kingdom, especially in County Durham. Although a renowned scholar, he was first and foremost a preacher. That was his first calling and it was to that which he remained faithful to the end. While well-known internationally as "Professor Barrett" he was known to most locals simply as "Mr. Barrett," a frequent guest in the pulpits of Methodist chapels. If one wants to fully appreciate C. K. Barrett, his work and identity as a scholar and a preacher must be understood together.

Those who knew Barrett often note how he was a quiet, humble man. As a PhD student at Durham, I had a number of opportunities to interact with him. The first time I met him was during a New Testament seminar. He entered the room, sat next to me, and quietly left at the end of the seminar. It was only the next day that I learned who he was and I am embarrassed to say now that until that day I did not realize he was still alive. On another occasion I was able to escort him to one of his lectures. I not only witnessed his keen mind at work, I also discovered that he had a wonderfully dry sense of humor.[1] If one does not appreciate this part of Barrett's personality, one will miss some of his more witty remarks in what can appear as staid, academic papers.

I present this essay in two halves. In part one I cover Barrett's life from his days as a student and his early influences. I examine the impact he had as a scholar, but also as a Methodist preacher. Part two examines his work on Luke–Acts. I offer a review of his scholarship on the topic with a more concentrated look at his two-volume commentary on Acts, which many have called his magnum opus.

---

1. During the lecture he was provided with a portable lectern positioned on top of a table. As he spoke I noticed that he was leaning on the lectern and it was slowly edging toward the end of the table. After several minutes I sensed near disaster was about to happen. Not wanting to be disrespectful to him but also not wanting to see him become injured, I stood up in the middle of his lecture, walked to the front of the room and said, "Excuse me, Professor Barrett," as I pushed the lectern back onto the table. Barrett paused for a moment, took stock of the situation, and responded with a chuckle: "Ah, I see, I was in danger of depositing myself onto the floor." He then continued the lecture as if nothing had happened.

LIFE AND WORK OF
CHARLES KINGSLEY BARRETT

Son and Cricketer

Charles Kingsley Barrett, son of Fred and Clara Barrett, was born May 4, 1917 in Salford, England. As a child he was frequently ill, causing him to spend much time with his mother, from whom he inherited his quiet personality.[2] His father, Fred, was a well-known Methodist minister and evangelist and an admirer of Charles Kingsley, the nineteenth-century Anglican clergyman, Christian socialist, writer, and early adopter of Charles Darwin's views.[3]

In 1928, three days before his eleventh birthday, Barrett went to Shebbear College in Devon. A small boarding school of about one hundred boys, it was founded by the Bible Christian movement, a nineteenth-century group who focused on poverty and revivalism with a strong reaction against religious hypocrisy.[4] At Shebbear he focused on several subjects including oratory, singing, and history, all of which served him well later in his career. He was also a promising cricket player and rose to be team captain.[5] Barrett never forgot his time at Shebbear College, and they did not forget him as evidenced by the presence of a Shebbear representative at his Durham funeral in 2011. In addition to studying and playing cricket, Barrett began preaching while at Shebbear, a practice that would be part of his weekly routine until his final days. Having observed his father Fred, who was known as a great expository preacher, Barrett commented, "I was soaked in the study of texts, inevitably learning from him ideals of ministry and preaching."[6] Later he would reflect that "I learned from my father that honest biblical criticism was a thing to practice."[7] It seems clear that the influence of his father and the Bible Christian background at Shebbear helped form Barrett's, piety, character, and career trajectory.[8]

---

2. James D. G. Dunn, "Charles Kingsley Barrett 1917–2011," The British Academy, 4, www.thebritishacademy.ac.uk/sites/default/files/01%20Barrett.pdf.
3. John Painter, "Barrett, CK," in *Dictionary of Major Biblical Interpreters*, ed. Donald K. McKim (Downers Grove, IL: IVP Academic, 2007), 155.
4. The movement later merged with the United Methodist Church.
5. "The Reverend CK Barrett, Obituary," *The Telegraph* (September 6, 2011). accessed February 12, 2019, https://www.telegraph.co.uk/news/obituaries/religion-obituaries/8745353/The-Reverend-CK-Barrett.html.
6. Dunn, "Charles Kingsley Barrett," 5.
7. Dunn, "Charles Kingsley Barrett," 8.
8. Dunn, "Charles Kingsley Barrett," 5.

University Student

In 1935 Barrett went to Cambridge University, Pembroke College, where he studied mathematics before changing his focus to theology. Since Pembroke had no theological Fellow, he was assigned to Francis Noel Davey at Corpus Christi College.[9] His first assignment under Davey was to write an essay on the synoptic problem. When preparing to submit the essay Barrett remembers thinking that "it was not a bad essay."[10] But as it turned out, Davey did not like it at all. He had not wanted a summary of the major theories suggested to solve the problem. "He wanted me to dig in to Huck, to examine the text, to describe the phenomena that give rise to the problem."[11] Although he clearly remembers this as a moment of correction and rebuke, it obviously left an indelible mark upon him and this way of approaching the biblical text would forever by part of Barrett's scholarship. The questions driving him would be: "What does the text actually say? What does it mean? What is its place in the Christian tradition?"[12]

It was Noel Davey who steered Barrett to attend what turned out to be Sir Edwyn Hoskyns's last lectures on the theology and ethics of the New Testament.[13] Barrett was amazed to hear from Hoskyns, an Anglo-Catholic, the same character of biblical theology he had imbibed from his father's sermons.[14] In addition, Hoskyns was an early reader of Barth and had translated Barth's commentary on Romans into English, which Davey had Barrett read in his first year.[15] Barrett would later reflect, "If in those days, and since, I remained and continued to be a Christian, I owe the fact in large number to that book and to those in Cambridge who introduced it to me."[16] In spite of their first encounter, Barrett and Davey went on to become lifelong friends.[17]

In 1939 Barrett responded to the call to ministry and moved from Pembroke College to Wesley House, the Methodist theological college at Cambridge. While there he devoted himself to studying the New

---

9. Robert Morgan, "C. K. Barrett and New Testament Theology," *JSNT* 37, no. 4 (2015): 432.

10. C. K. Barrett, "Hoskyns and Davey," in *Jesus and the Word* (Allison Park, PA: Pickwick, 1995), 56.

11. Barrett, "Hoskyns and Davey," 56.

12. Barrett, "Hoskyns and Davey," 56.

13. Robert Morgan, "A Magnificent Seven: C. K. Barrett at 90," *ExpTim* 119 (2008): 227.

14. Robert Morgan, "The Rev CK Barrett Obituary: Biblical Scholar Known for His Acute Analysis of the New Testament," *The Guardian* (October 4, 2011), www.theguardian.com/books/2011/oct/04/ck-barrett-obituary.

15. Barrett, "Hoskyns and Davey," 57.

16. C. K. Barrett, *Romans*, BNTC (London: A&C Black, 1957), vii.

17. Dunn, "Charles Kingsley Barrett," 11.

Testament and added to his knowledge of Hebrew and Greek by teaching himself German, Syriac, and Aramaic.[18] He was able to join C. H. Dodd's senior seminar, study rabbinic literature with Hebert Lowe, and form a lifelong friendship with David Daube, a refugee from Nazi Germany.[19] These friendships with Jewish scholars would be important for Barrett later as he navigated post-World War II New Testament scholarship.[20] He concluded his training at Wesley House in 1942 and was sent to serve as an assistant tutor at Wesley College in Headingly, Leeds. With the Second World War at its height, however, few men were being trained for ministry and the college closed the next year.

In 1943, the same year Wesley College closed, Barrett was ordained and sent to Bondgate Methodist Church in Darlington. The following year he met and married a nurse named Margaret Heap. Together they were married sixty four years and had two children, Penelope and Martin.[21] Anyone who knew the couple well readily commented on how Margaret helped Kingsley to be a productive scholar. Former student and lifelong friend K. H. Kuhn noted in the *Festschrift* presented to Barrett when he retired,

> Margaret presides over the domestic scene while Kingsley enjoys nothing better than talking shop with his friends. And let me add that Margaret's role has been much more than that of a marvelously generous hostess. It is she who had provided . . . the well-ordered and peaceful domestic background so essential to Kingsley's busy life as a minster and scholar.[22]

Margaret confirmed this perception of her role in their marital union many years later in 2007 at a celebration for her husband's ninetieth birthday during which

> She recalled, with a twinkle in her eye, that when they married a friendly Frau Professor took her aside and told her: "Now Margaret, you have married a scholar. You cannot expect him to help in the house and with

---

18. Dunn, "Charles Kingsley Barrett," 6.
19. Morgan, "C. K. Barrett and New Testament Theology," 433.
20. Dunn, "Charles Kingsley Barrett," 6.
21. Margaret passed away in 2008.
22. K. H. Kuhn, "Introduction," in *Paul and Paulinism: Essays in Honour of C. K. Barrett*, eds. M. D. Hooker and S. G. Wilson (London: SPCK, 1982), 1–3, here 3.

the children. He is first and foremost a scholar." Margaret paused, and then added, "And that's more or less how it has been ever since."[23]

Methodist Minister

While Barrett is most often remembered as an eminent scholar, he was first and foremost a Methodist minister. His daughter Penelope recalled that when her father went to Cambridge "His intention was to start with mathematics and then to study theology as preparation for following in his father's footsteps to become a Methodist minister. This is exactly what happened."[24]

Barrett was in fulltime ministry at Bondgate, Darlington for only two years. But his commitment was serious and he never ceased to be a Methodist minister.[25] One revealing anecdote about his commitment to the people of Darlington is found in a sermon he first preached on Luke 15:4–7 in December of 1943. In it he describes how he and other Methodist clergy went down into a coal mine the previous week to speak with miners and learn about their work. Twelve hundred feet below the surface, they worked alongside and interacted with the miners. During a break they were asked by some of the miners, "How do you know God is real?" Miners and minsters talked for a while until it was time to return to work. Sensing the conversation was not yet over, the ministers invited the miners to the Methodist chapel to finish the conversation:

> They laughed. "Could we have a swig of beer while we are at it?" they said. We said goodbye and scrambled up the tunnel. As we got to the end of it, I had an idea. I said to Malcolm, "Where do these fellows go for their swig of beer?" The Victoria Inn, just across from the mine. "Tell them we will be there tonight to finish our talk."[26]

He goes on to recount the warm reception they received at the pub that evening and how one young man came to faith that night. The purpose of the story was to illustrate the lengths God would go to seek

---

23.   Dunn, "Charles Kingsley Barrett," 7.
24.   See the forward by Penelope Barrett Hyslop in Ben Witherington III, ed., *Luminescence: The Sermons of C. K. and Fred Barrett* (Eugene, OR: Cascade, 2017), xv.
25.   Dunn, "Charles Kingsley Barrett," 4.
26.   Witherington, ed., *Luminescence*, 210.

out lost sheep. But it also illustrates that Barrett was willing to go to some lengths to seek out the lost in his Darlington district.

As dedicated as he was to ministry, he also remained committed to his scholarly pursuits. His formidable capacity for hard work allowed him to set aside 10:00 pm to 2:00 am each night to pursue his research.[27] His scholarly commitments not only kept him engaged, they soon led to his departure from Bondgate in 1945 when he moved to Durham to take up an academic career.

Despite his long and very successful career as a New Testament professor and scholar, Barrett never stopped being a Methodist and always followed his first calling and passion, which was preaching. He once reflected, "When you are called to be a minister you are first called to preaching. . . . it was the preaching that has always been first for me."[28] And he never allowed his success in the university setting to overshadow his duty to the chapel. Indeed, it seems that most of those in the pew did not realize a celebrated a scholar was standing before them. This is evident in his daughter Penelope's comments:

> It was a rare occasion that my father wasn't preaching at least twice on Sunday, even well beyond retirement. If necessary, he would preach and play the piano or lead the singing. He worshipped with them as equals and that is how they saw him in return, stripped of his academic titles.[29]

Similarly, James D. G. Dunn, who followed Barrett at Durham, noted, "In my own preaching round Methodist chapels in the region, a typical warmly appreciative remark would refer to Mr. Barrett who taught somewhere in 'the college in Durham.'"[30] And his former student and close friend Morna Hooker remembered,

> Very few—if any—members of the congregations of those Durham village chapels where he faithfully preached over so many years would have realized that they were listening to the foremost New Testament

---

27.   Dunn, "Charles Kingsley Barrett," 7.
28.   Dunn, "Charles Kingsley Barrett," 9–10.
29.   Witherington, ed., *Luminescence*, xvi.
30.   As quoted in Witherington, ed., *Luminescence*, preface.

scholar in the country. Nevertheless, they knew that they were listening to the gospel, and gained great benefit from his exposition.[31]

If there was ever a time Barrett considered no longer being a Methodist, it was during the 1960s. This was a difficult time during the ecumenical movement when a report resulting from conversations between the Methodists and the Anglicans recommended that the two churches should unite. Barrett was one of twelve Methodist representatives to the talks and he along with three others disagreed with the report. These dissenters argued that the proposal did not "recognize adequately the pre-eminent and normative place of Scripture and would lead to the more scriptural church order being swallowed up by the less."[32] The major point of disagreement was Anglican claims that only ordinations performed by bishops were valid and therefore Methodist ministers would need to seek episcopal ordination. Barrett made it clear that if Anglican episcopacy was adopted by Methodism, he would leave the church. "The idea of apostolic succession, he believed, was 'very bad history and worse theology.'"[33] As the final decision for the proposal was approaching in 1969, Barrett was publicly accused of being disloyal to Methodism and attempting to divide it by forming a separate church. In response, Barrett ceased preaching in the Durham Methodist circuit and published a letter in the local newspaper stating that he could not be seen preaching in those pulpits overseen by a superintendent who accused him of disloyalty.[34] The impact of the potential loss of Barrett's preaching was quickly recognized and reconciliation took place. In the end, the proposal was rejected by the Anglicans, not the Methodists. Nonetheless, Barrett ceased to be active in conference affairs and focused on only preaching instead.

Durham Scholar

Barrett became lecturer in theology at the University of Durham in 1945 when Michael Ramsey, then Canon Professor at Durham, convinced him to take up an academic career. The teaching load in those days was considerable and with no formal buildings for departments, Barrett held

31.   Morna Hooker, "Remembering C. K. Barrett," *Methodist Church News*, August 28, 2011, www.methodist.org.uk/about-us/news/latest-news/all-news/remembering-c-k-barrett.
32.   Dunn, "Charles Kingsley Barrett," 10.
33.   Dunn, "Charles Kingsley Barrett," 10.
34.   Dunn, "Charles Kingsley Barrett," 11.

student tutorials in his home and offered lectures on Saturday mornings. Fortunately, one of the other Canon Professors was willing to carry most of the administrative load, which allowed Barrett time for research and writing. He was thus able to settle into a more reasonable fourteen-hour day, a habit he continued into retirement.[35]

Prior to his arrival at Durham in 1945, Barrett had published a handful of articles including notes on a Greek term and the "Q" source.[36] Once in place at Durham, however, he began to flourish as a scholar. His first major publication, *The Holy Spirit and the Gospel Tradition*, was published by SPCK, where his former mentor Noel Davey was editor.[37] This was the beginning of Barrett's long relationship with the SPCK, whom he would consider his chief publisher for much of his career.[38]

Subsequent years witnessed a steady stream of journal articles and book reviews flowing from Barrett's study. But it was his commentary on *The Gospel according to St. John* that established his reputation as an international scholar.[39] Initially it was overshadowed by C. H. Dodd's commentary on John,[40] but in several ways Dodd's work represented the end of an era. While Dodd focused on reading John's Gospel in the context of Hellenistic thought, Barrett's work reflected the impact made by the recently discovered Dead Sea Scrolls.[41] In addition to two major English-language editions (1955, 1978), the commentary was translated into German in 1990 and included in the German New Testament series (*Meyers kritisch-exegetischer Kommentar*), an honor not bestowed upon any other non-German language commentary.[42]

The following year saw the publication of a book for which every student of New Testament is grateful: *The New Testament Background:*

35. Dunn, "Charles Kingsley Barrett," 7.
36. For a complete list of Barrett's publications from 1942 to 1980 see Hooker and Wilson, eds., *Paul and Paulinism*, 373–81. For works published after 1980, see Painter, "Barrett, CK," 160–61 and Dunn, "Charles Kingsley Barrett," 11–19.
37. C. K. Barrett, *The Holy Spirit and the Gospel Tradition* (London: SPCK, 1947). Barrett returned to this topic again in 1967 with two shorter studies: *Jesus and the Gospel Tradition* (London: SPCK, 1967) and *History and Faith: The Study of the Passion* (London: BBC, 1967).
38. Dunn, "Charles Kingsley Barrett," 11–12.
39. C. K. Barrett, *The Gospel according to St. John* (London: SPCK, 1955; 2nd ed., 1978).
40. C. H. Dodd, *The Interpretation of the Fourth Gospel* (Cambridge: Cambridge University Press, 1953).
41. Dunn, "Charles Kingsley Barrett," 12.
42. C. K. Barrett, *Das Evangelium nach Johannes*, KEK (Göttingen: Vandenhoeck & Ruprecht, 1990). See Dunn, "Charles Kingsley Barrett," 13; Painter, "Barrett, CK," 157.

Selected Documents.[43] The volume brought together extracts from many classical texts, inscriptions, and papyri. The value of such a resource for students was underlined by its publication in German in 1959.[44]

Barrett's unyielding energy and focus as a scholar was further confirmed the very next year with his commentary on *The Epistle to the Romans.*[45] This was Barrett's first contribution to the Black's New Testament Commentary series. The series aims for an audience somewhere between scholarly and popular. In that context, Barrett proved himself adept at bringing together his vast knowledge of the Greek language and ancient history when explaining the meaning of Paul's letter. James Dunn has reflected, "Kingsley established the reputation of the Black New Testament Commentary series."[46] Similarly, Robert Morgan noted that "A & C Black owes its reputation in biblical scholarship to Barrett's commentaries on Paul."[47]

In 1958, Barrett was promoted to Professor of Divinity, the first non-Anglican to be given such a chair.[48] The position was especially created for him since the named chairs, Lightfoot and Van Mildert (both former bishops of Durham), were reserved for the Canon Professors. Barrett "objected in principle to the Canon Professorships, not because he was anti-Anglican but simply because it subjected an academic post to a non-academic criterion: the only eligible candidates were ordained (and, at that time, only male) Anglicans."[49]

Barrett's first decade at Durham confirmed that he was a scholar who must be taken seriously. The second and third decades of his career only served to solidify that conviction. In 1961, he was elected a Fellow of the British Academy at the unusually young age of forty and remained a Fellow for more than fifty years.[50] In 1966, he received the Academy's Burkitt medal for biblical scholarship and in 1973 he was elected president of *Studiorum Novi Testamenti Societas*, but only after

43. C. K. Barrett, *The New Testament Background: Selected Documents* (London: SPCK, 1956).
44. C. K. Barrett, *Die Umwelt des Neuen Testaments* (Tübingen: Mohr Siebeck, 1959).
45. C. K. Barrett, *The Epistle to the Romans*, BNTC (London: A&C Black, 1957).
46. Dunn, "Charles Kingsley Barrett," 14.
47. Morgan, "A Magnificent Seven," 226.
48. "The Reverend CK Barrett, Obituary," *Telegraph*, September 6, 2011, www.telegraph.co.uk/news/obituaries/religion-obituaries/8745353/The-Reverend-CK-Barrett.html.
49. Dunn, "Charles Kingsley Barrett," 8.
50. Morgan, "The Rev CK Barrett Obituary."

declining to serve until his more senior colleague, Ernst Käsemann, was honored first.[51]

During this time, Barrett continued to review books, write articles, and comment on the New Testament. In 1963, he published a commentary on the Pastoral Epistles.[52] At the same time, he was publishing essays on the Corinthian correspondences which led to his second commentary in the Black series, 1 Corinthians in 1968 followed by yet a third addition to the series five years later with his commentary on 2 Corinthians in 1973.[53] In addition to his commentaries is a number of books that appeared including *Luke the Historian in Recent Research, From First Adam to Last, Jesus and the Gospel Tradition, Freedom and Obligation*, and *Paul: An Introduction to His Thought*.[54]

Barrett deserves much credit for helping to make the Durham Theology Department known and respected internationally, yet through it all he remained loyal to Durham.[55] "He was a Durham man through and through, turning down attractive invitations to other distinguished universities, and in retirement he moved no further than the edge of Durham."[56] One measure of his success is the number of his graduate students who secured positions in universities and seminaries around the world.[57]

Bridge-Builder

In addition to his work as Methodist minister and New Testament scholar, Barrett is also remembered as a bridge-builder to European scholarship. After World War II, he "did more than most to restore English Academic links with Europe."[58] Some of this may be attributed to Barrett's exposure to Hoskyns who was a student

---

51. Käsemann was president in 1972. Dunn, "Charles Kingsley Barrett," 20.

52. C. K. Barrett, *The Pastoral Epistles in the New English Bible* (Oxford: Clarendon, 1963).

53. C. K. Barrett, *The First Epistle to the Corinthians*, BNTC (London: A&C Black, 1968); Barrett, *The Second Epistle to the Corinthians*, BNTC (London: A&C Black, 1973).

54. C. K. Barrett, *Luke the Historian in Recent Study* (London: Epworth, 1961); Barrett, *From First Adam to Last: A Study in Pauline Theology* (London: A&C Black, 1962); Barrett, *Jesus and the Gospel Tradition* (London: SPCK, 1967); Barrett, *Freedom and Obligation: A Study of the Epistle to the Galatians* (London: SPCK, 1985); and Barrett, *Paul: An Introduction to His Thought* (London: Geoffrey Chapman, 1994).

55. Kuhn, "Introduction," 1.

56. Dunn, "Charles Kingsley Barrett," 3–4.

57. Yet Barrett's students did not come to represent a "school" as sometimes happened in Europe and the United States when particular scholars surrounded themselves with students (Painter, "Barrett, CK," 155).

58. Dunn, "Charles Kingsley Barrett," 8; Painter, "Barrett, CK," 156.

of Harnack, had a close relationship with Albert Schweitzer, and brought his appreciation for German scholarship to Cambridge.[59] Barrett was present when Gerhard Kittel lectured at Cambridge on the *Wörterbuch* and its method (1937?). He remembers Kittel wore a Nazi swastika badge during the lecture, which did not go down well with the faculty. He was also present for a lecture by Karl Fezer of Tübingen, a "German Christian." Hoskyns translated Fezer's lecture and limited students to asking only questions related to theology and not politics.[60] Barrett interpreted Hoksyns's tolerance in these two situations not as sympathetic, but rather as a manifestation of his attitude as an "English gentleman who insists on fair play even for one's enemies."[61] We might surmise that this attitude was adopted by Barrett as well. It is not that Barrett was unwilling or unable to criticize Germany. He was openly critical of the Nazis and the crimes perpetrated by them in a number of his sermons.[62] But it was not a wholesale condemnation of the German people, but a recognition that a darker force stood behind the events leading up to and including the war.

In the early postwar years and throughout his career, Barrett maintained close relationships with German scholars and spent several sabbaticals in Germany. In addition to his early exposure to Barth, Barrett also read Bultmann's *New Testament Theology* in German as it came out in parts. [63] He was able to make both positive and critical use of Bultmann's work and more than any other English scholar, he communicated the measure of Bultmann.[64]

Barrett's impact on English and German scholarship remains to this day. His friendship with his German colleagues at Tübingen University, first with Ernst Käsemann and then Martin Hengel, is evidenced by the existence of the Tübingen–Durham colloquium, a relationship that has benefitted international study of the New Testament among scholars and students alike.

---

59. C. K. Barrett, "Theology at Durham," in *Jesus and the Word* (Allison Park, PA: Pickwick, 1995), 79.
60. Barrett, "Hoskyns and Davey," 59.
61. Barrett, "Hoskyns and Davey," 59.
62. See his sermon on Luke 15:4–7 which he preached six times between April 29 and July 4, 1945 as the horrors of Nazi crimes were beginning to be revealed to the world (Witherington, ed., *Luminescence*, 207–11).
63. Painter, "Barrett, CK," 156.
64. Morgan, "A Magnificent Seven," 228.

Theologian by Grace

Barrett retired from the Department of Theology at Durham in 1982. Yet he never ceased being active in both preaching and scholarship.[65] He was a faithful attendee of the annual meetings of the *Studiorum Novi Testamenti Societas* and was in high demand globally as a lecturer. When not travelling outside of County Durham, Sunday would usually find him in a Methodist chapel somewhere locally where he continued to engage in his first passion, which was preaching. He never lost sight of his connection to the church and his call to Methodist ministry. His last service was sometime in 2009 when he was ninety-two. Even in the last months of his life, his daughter Penelope recalled, he preached and sang hymns to those in the hospital ward. "Preaching was in his blood as his father before him." [66] Charles Kingsley Barrett passed away at age ninety-four on August 26, 2011.

Barrett is often described with such accolades as "the greatest,"[67] "the foremost,"[68] "the outstanding,"[69] or "the finest"[70] British New Testament scholar of the twentieth century. Yet, as is clear from above, his life was lived not just for the academy, but also for the church. He was both a Christian minister and an academic theologian. Together these two sides of him were welded together into one harmonious whole by his strong and positive character.[71] In his own words he saw himself as "a historian by nature, a theologian by grace."[72] Yet, he expressed irritation that others sometimes thought of him only as an exegete rather than a theologian. But for Barrett exegesis was theology. "What did the evangelists, what did Paul wish to say? What was God saying through them? This could only be theology."[73]

We close this section with Barrett's own words, taken from his preface to his commentary on 2 Corinthians:

---

65. The Department of Theology at Durham established the C. K. Barrett Lecture Series in 2007 to commemorate his ninetieth birthday. The series challenges lecturers to bridge the range between academy and chapel as he did so successfully for so long and to the academic and spiritual benefit of so many.
66. Witherington, ed., *Luminescence*, xv.
67. Morgan, "The Rev CK Barrett Obituary."
68. Hooker, "Remembering C. K. Barrett."
69. Painter, "Barrett, CK," 155.
70. Dunn, "Charles Kingsley Barrett," 3.
71. Kuhn, "Introduction," 2.
72. Dunn, "Charles Kingsley Barrett," 18.
73. Barrett, "Hoskyns and Davey,"56.

From the discipline of exegesis I have learnt method; and from Paul
himself, I hope, to understand the Christian faith. Like most people, I
sometimes wonder whether Christianity is true; but I think I never doubt
that, if it is true, it is truest in the form it took with Paul, and, after him,
with such interpreters of his as Augustine, Luther, Calvin, Barth. And, as
I read them, and especially Paul himself, conviction returns, and, though
problems may abound, grace abounds much more.[74]

CHARLES KINGSLEY BARRETT ON LUKE–ACTS

Having laid out an overview of Barrett's life as both a scholar and churchman, I now move to considering his work on Luke–Acts. The climax to
his career is, without doubt, the two-volume commentary on the Book
of Acts, part of the International Critical Commentary series (ICC). [75]
Barrett's longtime Durham colleague, C. E. B. Cranfield, became the
series editor in 1975 and secured him to write the Acts volume. It is a task
Barrett took up in retirement and it consumed sixteen years before both
volumes were completed and published in 1994 and 1998, respectively.

In some ways, Barrett's commentary represents two crowning achievements. First, his work on Acts brings together his impressive knowledge
of ancient languages and Greco/Roman literature combined with his
intimate knowledge of the New Testament documents garnered from
years of study.[76] Second, although the ICC series began publishing in
1895, it never had a commentary on the Acts of the Apostles in its nearly
one hundred years existence. Indeed, some of the older, original volumes
began being replaced starting with Cranfield's Romans commentary in
1975.[77] The choice of Barrett to write on Acts not only filled a long-term
void in the series, it confirmed his status as one of the most distinguished
British New Testament scholars of the twentieth century.[78]

One surprising aspect of Barrett's work is how little he seems to
have focused on the Gospel of Luke.[79] In those articles and essays

---

74. Barrett, *Second Epistle to the Corinthians*, vii.
75. Dunn, "Charles Kingsley Barrett," 18, with reference to C. K. Barrett, *A Critical and Exegetical Commentary on the Acts of the Apostles*, 2 vols., ICC (London: T&T Clark, 1994–1998).
76. J. K. Elliott, review of C. K. Barrett, *The Acts of the Apostles, 2 vols.*, *NovT* 42.2 (2000): 195–96.
77. J. A. Fitzmyer, review of C. K. Barrett, *The Acts of the Apostles*, vol 1, *JTS* 52.2 (2001): 145.
78. Painter, "Barrett, CK," 160.
79. As far as I can determine, Barrett published only one article that focused solely on the Gospel of Luke ("Lk 22.15: To Eat the Passover," *JTS* ns 9 [1957]: 305–7). Most of his other publications were more focused on Acts. One exception is an essay on how Scripture citations are used in Luke–

where the Gospel was examined, it was generally with a view towards learning how the Gospel can aid with interpreting Acts.[80] Much of Barrett's interest and work in Luke–Acts seems to be derived from his interest in ancient history. His publications on Luke–Acts began appearing slowly in the early 1960s and appeared more steadily in the late 1970s and 1980s as he began working on the commentary. Publications from his earlier years reflect the kind of questions that would still be relevant to Barrett more than thirty years later.

The task of reviewing any area of Barrett's scholarship would be challenging. The focus on his work on Luke–Acts is a good example of this challenge, as evidenced by the commentary. It is a densely packed 1272 (+ cxviii) pages in two volumes that include quotations of texts in Greek, Latin, and German.[81] Added to this are his articles and essays published before and after the commentary was completed. With this in mind, my approach below is to review his work chronologically in order to get a sense of his own development in relation to both Luke and him as a scholar. I will then address some of the major thoughts in the commentary, some of which inevitably overlap with his essays and articles.[82]

Luke the Historian in Recent Study (1961)

This was Barrett's first major contribution to the study of Luke–Acts. It was originally written for the sixth A. S. Peake Memorial Lecture which Barrett was invited to give as part of the 1961 Methodist Conference.[83] Although brief, it provides a preview of Barrett's future interpretive trajectory. It seems the seeds that would bloom into his commentary more than thirty years later were already germinating. The lecture/book is broken into three equal parts.

In part one Barrett begins by outlining six ways to understand Luke.[84] Concluding his discussion, Barrett suggests that in the Gospel

---

Acts (C. K. Barrett, "Luke/Acts," in *It Is Written: Scripture Citing Scripture*, eds. D. A. Carson and H. G. M. Williamson [Cambridge: Cambridge University Press, 1988], 231–44).

80. See, e.g., C. K. Barrett, "The Third Gospel as Preface to Acts? Some Reflections," in *The Four Gospels: Festschrift for Frans Neirynck*, ed. F. Van Segbroek (Leuven: Peeters, 1992), 1451–66.

81. For those lacking facility with original languages and in less need of intricate detail, there is a one volume version available: *Acts: A Shorter Commentary* (London: T&T Clark, 2002).

82. One interesting observation is that most of his work published prior to the commentaries is found not in journals, but in *Festschriften*.

83. Barrett, *Luke the Historian*, 5.

84. The six ways Barrett suggests Luke can be viewed are as: (1) a writer, (2) a historian, (3) a religious writer, (4) a Gentile, (5) a Christian, or (6) a Church historian (*Luke the Historian*, 7–26).

Luke is a compiler of traditions, but in Acts he is an author. This conclusion about Acts is a signpost for where Barrett will go not only in this lecture but in later years as well.

In part two Barrett reviews recent interpretations of Luke including well-known scholars such as Dibelius, Conzelmann, and Haenchen.[85] Rather than offer a detailed criticism of each contribution, Barrett simply points out that, while not all in agreement, these scholars represent a revolution in Lukan studies. All of them have abandoned the search for literary sources and instead focus on understanding Luke as an author.[86] In saying this Barrett means Acts rather than the Gospel. This is demonstrated by the selection of material he chose for review. All of the authors but one focus on Acts. This choice not only dictated Barrett's direction in the lecture, but also betrays his own early interest in how Luke writes as a historian of the church. In the rest of the lecture Barrett provides his own assessment of the situation.

He begins by pointing out that Luke is the only New Testament writer to connect the "Jesus of history" to the church, which dictates his motive and format for a two-volume work. "Luke was aware that he was building a bridge between periods of history."[87] Added to this is Luke's double understanding of the ascension, which both declares the end of Jesus's ministry and the beginning of the church. Unlike Mark and Paul who see the ascension as last, Luke sees it as the beginning of a new chapter.[88] It is not the close of history, but the starting point of a new kind of history.[89] At the same time, he believes that Luke as an historian must be understood through his connecting of the Gentile mission to Jesus in Acts. This, for Barrett, is more significant than whether he was influenced by Hellenistic or Jewish models.[90]

One point to which Barrett will return many times over the years is the way in which Luke's portrayal of Paul is not always consistent with the apostle's letters. Barrett suggests that Luke is comparable to the Pastoral Epistles, which were written to combat Gnostic teaching, and treat Paul as a heroic figure.[91] Similarly, he suggests, Acts can be

85. Barrett, *Luke the Historian*, 26–50.
86. Barrett, *Luke the Historian*, 50–51.
87. Barrett, *Luke the Historian*, 55.
88. Barrett, *Luke the Historian*, 57.
89. Barrett, *Luke the Historian*, 58.
90. Barrett, *Luke the Historian*, 61.
91. Barrett, *Luke the Historian*, 63.

understood as a defense of Paul against Jewish (Gnostic) Christians who hated Paul. Contrary to other interpretations, Acts was not addressed to the emperor with the intention of proving Christianity's political harmlessness.[92] Rather, "it was an apology addressed to the Church, demonstrating Paul's anti-gnostic orthodoxy, and his practical and doctrinal solidarity with the church at Jerusalem."[93]

At the same time, Barrett sees Acts tempering early eschatological expectation. He notes how Luke replaces the "abomination of desolation" in Mark's little apocalypse (13:14) with the armies surrounding Jerusalem (Luke 21:20) and argues that by doing so, Luke substituted the more mysterious aspects of the apocalyptic speech for a concrete historical event. "Out of primitive Christian eschatology, which, so far as it insisted upon an early *parousia* of the Son of man, had proved mistaken and misleading, evolved the notion of *Heilsgeschichte*, a continuous historical process which was the vehicle of God's saving purpose."[94] Consequently, Luke held on to the hope of a future coming of the Son of Man, but gave his reader a historical event to focus on that demonstrates God's activity.[95]

Barrett closes by addressing whether or not Luke portrays a form of primitive Catholicism (*Frühkatholizismus*).[96] He argues that with the disappearance of the twelve and the lack of any clear hierarchy in ministry offices, the early church was not "catholic."[97] For Luke, the church is almost always local. While his theme was to see the life and death of ministry as having worldwide significance, it happened through the multiplication of local groups united by a common faith rather than a structure.[98] While this last section may seem to answer a scholarly question, it also betrays Barrett's own thoughts as it related to the church, Methodism in particular. He wrote this in 1961 around the time Methodist and Anglican conversations had suggested a united church under which Methodist bishops needed to submit to Anglican episcopacy. Although there is no clear polemic in this essay, its first audience at a Methodist conference must have understood why such a question about Acts meant so much to Barrett personally.

---

92. Barrett will make this point more forcefully in his commentary on Acts (see below).
93. Barrett, *Luke the Historian*, 63.
94. Barrett, *Luke the Historian*, 64.
95. Barrett, *Luke the Historian*, 65.
96. Barrett, *Luke the Historian*, 71.
97. Barrett will reemphasize this point thirty-six years later in his commentary.
98. Barrett, *Luke the Historian*, 74.

"Stephen and the Son of Man" (1964)

Three years later Barrett returned to Luke's handling of eschatology in Acts. He observes that while the "Son of Man" title appears frequently in the Gospels—twenty-five times in Luke alone—it only occurs once in Acts as part of Stephen's speech (7:56).[99] For Barrett this scene is evocative of the way Luke rewrites primitive eschatology. The Son of Man standing in Stephen's vision to welcome the martyr represents a personal parousia, which is distinct from the coming universal parousia.[100] The long delay after the ascension and the deaths of believers since had raised questions about the return of the Son of Man.[101] Luke, Barrett argues, came to view each individual Christian death as an eschaton. "Thus the death of each Christian would be marked by what we may term a private and personal *parousia* of the Son of Man. That which was to happen in a universal sense at the last day happened in individual terms when a Christian came to the last day of his life."[102] Although brief, the essay provides an early snapshot of Barrett's thinking about Lukan eschatology in light of a delayed parousia.

"Acts and the Pauline Corpus" (1976)

It was a dozen years before Barrett returned to Acts, during which time he was busy completing, among other works, his commentaries on 1 and 2 Corinthians. Yet in this short piece for *The Expository Times*, we see how his work on Paul's letters over two decades raised fresh questions for his work on Acts. In particular, one question Barrett will raise again and again is: Why does Luke not mention Paul's letters?[103] Clearly an admirer of Paul who knew about his travels and career as a missionary, Luke never even hints that Paul wrote letters.[104] Barrett offers some suggestions that are not intended to be conclusive answers, but worthy of consideration.

---

99. C. K. Barrett, "Stephen and the Son of Man," in *Apophoreta: Festschrift für Ernst Haenchen*, ed. Walther Eltester (Berlin: Töpelmann, 1964), 32–38, here 32–34.
100. Barrett, "Stephen and the Son of Man," 36–37.
101. Barrett, "Stephen and the Son of Man," 35.
102. Barrett, "Stephen and the Son of Man," 36.
103. C. K. Barrett, "Acts and the Pauline Corpus," *ExpTim* 88.1 (1976): 2–5.
104. Even some of Luke's contemporaries knew of Paul's letters. Ephesians, which Barrett takes to be pseudonymous, used Paul's letters. The same is true for 1 Clement (47.1) and Ignatius (Eph 12.2) both of whom were aware of Paul's letters. The question is, why is there no comparable reference in Acts? ("Acts and the Pauline Corpus," 2).

First, Paul's letters, although "weighty" (2 Cor. 10:10), were probably not recognized as "canon" at this time. Moreover, some of his letters contain less than complimentary comments about individuals (e.g., Gal. 2:9) that might have motivated some to keep them hidden from public inspection. Furthermore, while the date of Acts is disputed, it shows no evidence of *Frühkatholizismus*. Thus, Acts could be the earliest of the Deutero-Pauline writings in the New Testament, thus explaining Luke's positive portrayal of Paul.

Second, while Luke was an admirer of Paul, he was not a theologian of the same depth as Paul. He worked a generation after Paul and so while he had valuable sources like the so-called We-Source, it should not be confused with a journal. It was most likely an itinerary; a list of places visited and not the kind of document for listing letters.

Finally, Barrett observes that there were several strands of Gentile Christianity at work when Luke wrote. Luke's purpose in Acts is to show how some of these strands became more unified after AD 70; this meant there was no room in the process for mentioning the letters.

"Paul's Address to the Ephesian Elders" (1978)

Two years later, Barrett was addressing the same question about Paul and Acts, this time within a specific passage.[105] Comparing Paul's speech to the Ephesian elders (Acts 20:17–28) with the apostle's letters, he notes once again that although Luke seems to think highly of Paul, he also seems unaware of Paul's letters.[106] Nonetheless, he concludes that, with some historical objections, the Paul of Acts is in harmony with the Paul of his letters.[107]

"Theologia Crucis—in Acts?" (1979)

In this essay, Barrett challenges the claims of some that Acts is missing a theology of the cross.[108] The only place where the doctrine of atonement is mentioned is Acts 20:28 in Paul's address to the Ephesian elders. After an overview of the opinions of those who say that Luke presents no doctrine of the atonement, Barrett argues that while Luke

---

105. C. K. Barrett, "Paul's Address to the Ephesian Elders," in *God's Christ and His People: Studies in Honour of N. A. Dahl*, eds. Jacob Jervell and Wayne A. Meeks (Oslo: Universitetsforlaget, 1978), 107–21.
106. Barrett, "Paul's Address to the Ephesian Elders," 110, 117.
107. Barrett, "Paul's Address to the Ephesian Elders," 116–17.
108. C. K. Barrett, "Theologia Crucis—in Acts?" in *Theologia Crucis—Signum Crucis: Festschrift für Erich Dinkler zum 70. Geburtstag*, eds. C. Anderson and G. Klein (Tübingen: Mohr Siebeck, 1979), 73–84.

is not a "theologian" he certainly understands that being a Christian requires one to take up the cross and suffer (Luke 9:23–27). Luke, he demonstrates, was more interested in showing how people lived rather than articulating theology.[109] He does this by listing many instances in Acts that describe suffering and afflictions experienced by the apostles.[110] Barrett concludes by acknowledging that Luke is not Paul and thus does not articulate theology in the same way as the apostle. But he also says that it would be "dangerous and misleading" to "allege that Luke cannot be a theologian because his Christian cheerfulness keeps breaking in."[111] Barrett acknowledges that it would be incorrect to label Luke a *Theologus crucius*. Nonetheless, Luke "knows that to be a Christian means to take up a cross daily."[112]

"Paul Shipwrecked" (1987)

In this essay, Barrett addresses three topics that arise from his study of Acts 27 in which Paul is shipwrecked while on his way to Rome.[113] In section one he examines the detailed listing of harbors associated with Paul's journey.[114] After evaluating Vernon Robbins's "Sea Journey" essay and comparing several passages from ancient sea journeys with Acts, he decides that Robbins's conclusion cannot be accepted.[115] Barrett then acknowledges how he surprised himself by concluding that the narrative of Acts 27 was written by one who actually made the voyage.[116] In section two he challenges the notion of some commentators that Paul is portrayed as a "Divine Man" in Acts by listing numerous places in Acts where Paul and the other apostles act in direct contrast to that portrayal.[117] In part three he discusses the meal Paul blessed on the ship and concludes it was not a Eucharist. Although Luke certainly describes it in those terms, Barrett thinks it

---

109. Barrett, "Theologia Crucis—in Acts?" 75.
110. Barrett, "Theologia Crucis—in Acts?" 76–83.
111. Barrett, "Theologia Crucis—in Acts?" 84.
112. Barrett, "Theologia Crucis—in Acts?" 84.
113. C. K. Barrett, "Paul Shipwrecked," in *Scripture: Meaning and Method. Essays Presented to Anthony Tyrell Hanson for his Seventieth Birthday*, ed. Barry P. Thompson (Hull: Hull University Press, 1987), 51–64, here 51.
114. Indeed, six times more space is devoted to Paul's sea journey than to his Areopagus speech.
115. Vernon K. Robbins, "By Land and by Sea: The We-passages and Ancient Sea Voyages," in *Perspectives on Luke–Acts*, ed. Charles H. Talbert (Edinburgh: T&T Clark, 1978), 215–42.
116. For Barrett, the list of harbors and geography are too detailed and mundane to not have been provided by an eyewitness document ("Paul Shipwrecked," 55).
117. Barrett, "Paul Shipwrecked," 56–59.

may have been a simple Jewish grace since every meal is a religious meal in Judaism.[118]

"The Third Gospel as Preface to Acts? Some Reflections" (1992)

This article appeared two years before the publication of the first of volume Barrett's commentary on Acts. In it Barrett observes that we often speak about Luke's two volume work as if it was Luke's intention from the beginning to write both. But in reality, we do not know this for sure.[119] Thus Barrett wonders if the Gospel was written in such a way so as to serve as preface to Acts. Over the course of ten pages, he compares many of the parallels between Luke and Acts to see if one can determine the answer to the question.[120] He concludes that one could argue that the Gospel is primary and Acts supports it or that Acts is primary and the Gospel serves Acts by introducing it. Both conclusions are correct since the two books are complementary to one another. But the more important conclusion for Barrett is that Luke–Acts is the first New Testament. That is, it contains all that a Christian needs to know and was probably seen in this light by the author.[121] Adding support to his argument, Barrett suggests that this may be one reason for Marcion's choice of books to include in his "canon." [122] Marcion already had a "New Testament" with Luke–Acts and thus no need for the other three Gospels. Barrett reiterated this point in a later article "The First New Testament," adding more detail to the argument he made in this essay.[123]

"The End of Acts" (1996)

Written between the publication of volume one and two, this essay was part of a *Festschrift* for Martin Hengel.[124] In it, Barrett wrestles with a number of questions that arise from Acts 28 that relate to two main groups Paul interacts with: (1) The Christians of Rome and (2) the Roman Jews. Barrett notes that Paul meets two separate Christian

---

118. Barrett, "Paul Shipwrecked," 62.
119. Barrett, "The Third Gospel as Preface to Acts," 1453.
120. Barrett, "The Third Gospel as Preface to Acts," 1453–62.
121. Barrett, "The Third Gospel as Preface to Acts," 1462
122. Barrett, "The Third Gospel as Preface to Acts," 1466.
123. C. K. Barrett, "The First New Testament," *NovT* 38, no. 2 (1996): 94–104.
124. C. K. Barrett, "The End of Acts," in *Geschichte–Tradition–Reflexion: Festschrift für Martin Hengel zum 70. Geburtstag*, ed. Hubert Cancik (Tübingen: Mohr Siebeck, 1996), 545–55.

groups as he approaches Rome (Acts 28:14–15), leading him to
wonder how unified the church was at that time.[125] He also notes
that while Paul is living in his rented quarters, no other contact with
Christians is mentioned. It is possible, he surmises, that the Christians in Rome did not know where Paul was located. Furthermore,
what happened after the two-year period Paul lived there (28:30)?
Most readers would not think martyrdom, but release. And if Paul
was martyred, why not say so? It is possible he was never released and
simply left there to rot.[126] In the case of the Roman Jews, he finds it
curious that they claimed to have no knowledge of Paul (28:21–22).
Perhaps the expulsion under Claudius in AD 49 might explain it. But
this seems in direct contrast to Acts 21–25 where Paul is presented as
a public enemy to Judaism.[127] In the end, Barrett suggests that Acts
seems to provide historical information from two periods, that of the
past and the one in which Luke was living. Nonetheless, it cannot, he
argues, be treated as a fairytale.

"The Historicity of Acts" (1999)

This is Barrett's final contribution related to Acts. Published one year
after volume two of the commentary was released, in some ways it
serves as a final glance in the rearview mirror as he reflects on Acts
as history.[128] Barrett was invited to write the article for the *Journal of
Theological Studies* on the one-hundredth anniversary of its first issue
in which the historicity of Acts was the topic. Barrett covers the major
contributions to the topic over the twentieth century. He goes on
to demonstrate where Luke is trustworthy as in Roman administration, geography, and when using sources like the We-source. And, as
he has done elsewhere, he outlines the potential problems that exist,
especially between Paul and Acts. In the end, he concludes that Acts
contains good secular history, but that does not mean it is accurate
Christian history.[129] "We cannot prove that it happened in the way
Luke described, but if it did not it must have happened in a similar
way or the result could not have been what it was."[130]

125. Barrett, "The End of Acts," 546.
126. Barrett, "The End of Acts," 549.
127. Barrett, "The End of Acts," 550.
128. C. K. Barrett, "The Historicity of Acts," *JTS* 50 (1999): 515–34.
129. Barrett, "The Historicity of Acts," 530.
130. Barrett, "The Historicity of Acts," 534.

Acts of the Apostles Commentary: Volume One (1994)

Volume one of Barrett's commentary on Acts was published in 1994 and covers the first fourteen chapters of Acts. In addition to lacking an index, it also has no footnotes. Barrett notes in the preface that ever since he read Lightfoot's commentaries it seemed unnecessary to burden a commentary with footnotes. "A commentary ought to be straightforwardly readable, like a monograph, though the reader will of course expect, especially in a work that is not specifically aimed at beginners, to encounter references and quotations, not all of which will be expressed in his native tongue."[131]

Volume one only provides a brief overview of the critical questions related to Acts. It includes what Barrett termed a "Preliminary Introduction." Since he had not yet finished his work on chapters 15–28, which would appear in volume two, Barrett did not think he could offer a complete introduction. Thus, his "preliminary introduction" in volume one was not intended to answer many of the questions raised by the study of Acts. Instead, he was only able to offer some initial material that "introduces" Acts to the reader. More than half of the preliminary introduction focuses on the text of Acts, that is, the manuscript evidence. This is followed by an overview of what tradition has said about Luke, the putative author of Acts. The final section considers Luke's sources.

Although necessarily brief at this point, it is possible to identify a trajectory in Barrett's thinking as it has developed since the early 1960s. In the first twelve chapters Luke was the most challenged in trying to find material about the early church and determining how to arrange it.[132] Barrett seems to think this was a period of history about which Luke knew the least. But when it comes to Paul, the situation is very different. He believes that Luke could have either been a companion of Paul, or represented himself as one, or drawn on the memories of one.[133] Whatever his source, he clearly drew on something for his Pauline information, but certainly not his epistles. Barrett concludes that Luke's focus is on the inclusion of Gentiles into the church that ended up causing such troubles.[134]

---

131. Barrett, *Acts of the Apostles*, 1:ix.
132. Barrett, *Acts of the Apostles*, 1:56.
133. This is also reflected, Barrett believes, in the material related to Philip. Luke's sources must have been traditions about Philip since he claims in Acts 21:8 to have met Philip in Caesarea (1:51).
134. Barrett, *Acts of the Apostles*, 1:51–52.

Acts Volume Two (1998)

Volume two was published four years later. Having completed his study, Barrett was ready to lay out some of his thoughts in a more comprehensive way. An initial observation we can make is that while Barrett used the tools of historical and biblical criticism effectively, he also diverged from what was sometimes viewed as the extreme skepticism of commentators in the past.[135]

Authorship

While tradition has attributed Acts to Luke, a travelling companion of Paul, Barrett finds it difficult to believe that Acts, as a whole, was written by one of Paul's immediate circle. Nonetheless, he does believe that the author was able to draw on one or two sources derived from that circle, including the so-called We-source.[136] He believes that the author of the We-source is responsible for a considerable amount of information in Acts, especially chapters 16–28. Barrett suggests that this person was probably a traveler who was familiar with Corinth, Ephesus, etc., and picked up memories and traditions about Paul along the way.[137] Yet, while there is much about the Paul of Acts that parallels Paul's letters, there are some things that present a challenge. For instance, the author does not seem to fully grasp Paul's theology. Barrett also wonders if he was aware of Paul as letter writer and if he knew about Paul's contentious relationship with Corinth. He also notes the glaring absence of any mention of the Jerusalem decree in Paul's letters.[138] In the end the most Barrett can suggest is that the We-source may be nothing more than a travel itinerary and that Luke was more likely a sailor than a medical doctor.[139]

Historicity

For Barrett, Acts is a history of the Christian mission, rather than a history of the church. As a history, it shows little interest in the structure and development of the church as an institution.[140] He sees Luke as writing at a time when the major issues of contention between the

---

135. David Pao, "Review of Barrett, Acts Commentary vol 2," *JETS* 44, no. 3 (2001): 537–40.
136. Barrett, *Acts of the Apostles*, 2:xxviii–xxix.
137. Barrett, *Acts of the Apostles*, 2:xxx.
138. Barrett, *Acts of the Apostles*, 2:xliv.
139. Barrett, *Acts of the Apostles*, 2:xxix, xlv.
140. Barrett, *Acts of the Apostles*, 2:xxxiii.

Jewish and Gentile segments of the church had been solved and Luke is presenting a history that reveals evidence of past divisions. Luke, however, lives and writes in an age when the atmosphere is different.[141] Consequently, Acts is "the history of the church in a time of conflict written in a time of consensus."[142]

As to his knowledge of history, geography, and Greco-Roman institutions, Barrett says that Luke "was no fool."[143] His knowledge of history can often be corroborated, and where evidence is lacking, he must be taken seriously. Yet, he did have his limitations. "Luke was a man who liked telling stories and was good at telling them. He was less good at the connections between the episodes he narrated; perhaps he was less interested in them."[144]

Theology

In the area of theology, Barrett concludes that while Acts makes a contribution to theology, it is not so much a contribution to specific doctrines, but rather an understanding of the history and course of the Christian mission.[145] Thus, as pointed out in his early work, Christology is not strongly stated or worked out.[146] Instead, Luke focuses on the church as an eschatological community living within the period of fulfillment initiated by the Spirit.[147] The apostles are prominent as evidenced by the great role they play in Acts.[148] Yet, in spite of what at times appears to be an organized movement, one cannot conclude, Barrett argues, that Acts points to the development of a *Frühkatholizismus*. Nor can a case be made for apostolic succession since "the primary function of the twelve apostles was not transmissible."[149] While there may be some hints of a developing catholic structure of the church, they cannot be combined together in such a way as to constitute a structure.[150]

---

141. Barrett, *Acts of the Apostles*, 2:xli.
142. Barrett, *Acts of the Apostles*, 2:lxiii.
143. Barrett, *Acts of the Apostles*, 2:cxiv.
144. Barrett, *Acts of the Apostles*, 2:cxi.
145. Barrett, *Acts of the Apostles*, 2:lxxxii.
146. Barrett, *Acts of the Apostles*, 2:lxxxv.
147. Barrett, *Acts of the Apostles*, 2:lxxxvii.
148. Barrett, *Acts of the Apostles*, 2:lxxxix.
149. Barrett, *Acts of the Apostles*, 2:xcv.
150. Barrett, *Acts of the Apostles*, 2:xcvi.

Purpose

The purpose of Acts is Luke's wish "to hold up before his readers a set of Christian ideals which would show them what their own Christian life should be and at that same time supply them with a strong motivation for following the example."[151] Although there is an apologetic element to the book, it cannot be seen as an apology or even a brief for Paul's defense. As Barrett notes, "no Roman court could be expected to wade through so much Jewish religious nonsense in order to find half-a-dozen fragments of legally significant material."[152] As he stated elsewhere, Barrett views the purpose of Luke–Acts as the author's intention to replace Mark and supplement material about Paul.[153]

Luke's Presentation of History: The Jerusalem Council and Galatians 2

I finish our examination of Barrett's work with a brief look at his conclusions about Luke's presentation of history, particularly as it relates to Paul. The Jerusalem council in Acts 15 provides an opportune case study since Barrett considers it to be the center of Acts.[154]

The topics of Acts 15 are related to problems and patterns found elsewhere in the book: (1) a problem arises; (2) the Christian community addresses it; (3) a solution is found which not only solves the problem but leads to expansion of the community.[155] The story, of course, invites comparisons to Paul's letter to the Galatians. Barrett notes that similarities between the two documents are so striking that it is hard to doubt a single event lies somewhere behind both stories.[156] Some have tried to make these two different meetings, but Barrett is not convinced. He also finds it hard that Luke had ever read Galatians. "Assuming Paul to have been neither stupid nor dishonest, though doubtless like all men fallible in memory, his account, which is first-hand, must be accepted where it differs from Luke's."[157]

---

151. Barrett, *Acts of the Apostles*, 2:ii.
152. Barrett, *Acts of the Apostles*, 2:l.
153. Barrett, *Acts of the Apostles*, 2:li.
154. Barrett, *Acts of the Apostles*, 2:709.
155. Barrett, *Acts of the Apostles*, 2:xxxvi, 709, 710.
156. There are also some incongruities. Acts, for instance, ends with a decree from the church in Jerusalem, whereas no such decree is found in Galatians. Instead a division of labor between Peter and Paul is agreed to—a detail that does not appear in Acts (*Acts of the Apostles*, 2:711).
157. Barrett, *Acts of the Apostles*, 2:711.

Barrett suggests that the events unfolded something like the following. A mission based on Jerusalem's understanding of Gentile inclusion was active among the Pauline churches. This mission demanded circumcision of all and was undermining Paul's work. Paul went to Jerusalem to discuss the problem with the apostles (Gal. 2:2). The meeting was not, Barrett suggests, inharmonious. It ended with the agreement that Paul should go to the Gentiles and the Jerusalem apostles to the Jews. "This sounded well, but was inadequately thought out and the terms remained undefined."[158] It did not take into account what would happen in churches with mixed Jew and Gentile membership. Thus, in Antioch it was assumed that all could experience table fellowship together. However, the messengers from James (Gal. 2:12) insisted the agreement was about circumcision only. James and company agreed that Gentiles did not need to be circumcised, but they did not agree to unrestricted interaction with Jews. James and Paul each dug in their heels. It was the Hellenists, Barrett suggests, who bridged the gap with the Jerusalem decree, which Paul did not accept.[159]

When comparing Paul's and Luke's versions, Barrett concludes that Luke produced the story of the council, but not whole cloth.[160] He knew that envoys from Jerusalem had caused problems in Antioch and perhaps elsewhere. And although he was aware of a number of theological arguments for the inclusion of Gentiles, he did not know Paul's arguments.[161] Luke thought (incorrectly) that the Law was a burden to Gentiles and since he knew that Gentiles received the Spirit the same way as Jews, he concluded that they could not be refused water baptism. According to Luke's presentation, then, all elements of the church agreed with the council's decision. But the informed reader should remember that this is Luke's version. The evidence from Paul's letters strongly suggests that it was not so in his lifetime.[162]

Barrett does not think Luke wrote his version as part of a cover-up. Rather, he wrote in a way that reflected the age in which he lived. A consensus had, in fact, been reached.[163]

---

158. Barrett, *Acts of the Apostles*, 2:712.
159. Barrett, *Acts of the Apostles*, 2:712.
160. Barrett, *Acts of the Apostles*, 2:xxxix.
161. Barrett, *Acts of the Apostles*, 2:xxxix.
162. Barrett, *Acts of the Apostles*, 2:xl.
163. Barrett, *Acts of the Apostles*, 2:xl.

The deaths of Paul, Peter, and James by the end of the 60s allowed for any remaining dissent to be overcome and Luke's version reflects the consensus:

> This is the situation in which Luke lived and wrote. He took it for granted. This makes much better sense than to suppose he invented a fictitious story designed to conceal the horrid truth about the church's past. If Luke was practicing concealment he was an incompetent practitioner: traces of division, of which he himself was perhaps conscious, show through his narrative.[164]

CONCLUSION

There is much more we could say about Barrett's scholarship on Acts. Indeed, additional chapters could and should be written about other areas of his scholarship, his work on Paul's letters in particular. But if there is a final assessment that can be made about Barrett it would be that he embraced honest, rigorous critical methods in his work, but he did not embrace the extreme skepticism that has sometimes manifested itself in New Testament scholarship. Thus, while he was willing to identify and wrestle with difficulties he encountered in Acts, he was not willing to dismiss Luke as a historian. As one reads the totality of his work on Luke–Acts, it becomes clear that the more Barrett studied Luke the more he came to respect him as both an historian and a theologian.

Luke was an historian and so was Barrett. Perhaps there is an element of lifelong self-discovery for Barrett here? As noted above, Barrett said that he was "a historian by nature, a theologian by grace." He was one who clearly understood theology as something that must be rooted in the text. And as his study of Luke–Acts demonstrates, any theology that Luke, or even Barrett himself, developed, needed to be based on what the text said. This is most likely a derivative of Barrett's first calling to preach. Before a preacher can communicate the theology of a particular passage, she or he must first determine what it says, which is what Charles Kingsley Barrett dedicated his life to doing.

---

164. Barrett, *Acts of the Apostles*, 2:xli.

JACOB JERVELL AND THE JEWISHNESS OF LUKE–ACTS

David K. Bryan

In the highly influential collection of essays, *Studies in Luke–Acts* (1966), Willem van Unnik describes Luke–Acts as "a storm center in contemporary scholarship."[1] Towards the end of his essay, he asks a handful of questions that "merit [future] exploration."[2] Among these he asks, "What is the relation of Luke to the Old Testament and to the Jewish picture of the history of that people?" At the time of van Unnik's essay, a critical consensus—often associated with the work of Ernst Haenchen and Hans Conzelmann, supplemented by F. F. Bruce, Philipp Vielhauer, and others—existed among (Luke–)Acts scholars, namely that Luke was a Gentile Christian writing to a Gentile audience.[3] For Haenchen,

---

1. W. C. van Unnik, "Luke–Acts, a Storm Center in Contemporary Scholarship," in *Studies in Luke–Acts*, eds. Leander E. Keck and J. Louis Martyn (Philadelphia: Fortress, 1966), 15–32.
2. Van Unnik, "Luke–Acts, a Storm Center," 28.
3. Tyson claims that the consensus has its ultimate roots in the Tübingen school: "When Jacob Jervell announced what he claimed were revisions in Lukan scholarship, he explicitly did so against the background of a forcefully maintained consensus interpretation. This interpretation was, according to Jervell, primarily associated with the names of Hans Conzelmann and Ernst Haenchen. But Jervell was aware that the roots of this consensus interpretation go back to Ferdinand Christian Baur and the Tübingen school of New Testament scholarship." Joseph B. Tyson, *Luke, Judaism, and the Scholars: Critical Approaches to Luke–Acts* (Columbia: University of South Carolina Press, 1999), 12.

> Luke the historian is wrestling, from the first page to the last, with the
> problem of the *mission to the Gentiles without the law*. His entire presen-
> tation is influenced by this. It is a problem with two aspects: a theologi-
> cal and a political. By forsaking observance of the Jewish law Christian-
> ity parts company with Judaism; does this not break the continuity of
> the history of salvation? That is the theological aspect. But in cutting
> adrift from Judaism Christianity also loses the toleration which the
> Jewish religion enjoys. Denounced by the Jews as hostile to the state, it
> becomes the object of suspicion to Rome. That is the political aspect.[4]

Thus, the book of Acts narrates the proclamation of the gospel to the
Jews first, but their rejection of the Messiah causes the earliest Christians to turn instead to the Gentiles, who are freed from the Jewish
obligations to the law.[5] The purpose of Acts, therefore, is to explain the
Gentile mission and defend the church against any potential political
problems with Rome.

It is at this point in the history of interpretation that Jacob Jervell
(1925–2014) enters the scene. Born in Fauske, Norway[6] in 1925,
Jervell was a student of Nils Dahl[7] at the University of Oslo (in addition to his studies at Heidelberg and Göttingen).[8] His doctoral dissertation in 1959 dealt with the *imago Dei* in Genesis 1:26–27 and its
influence on later Jewish writings, in particular the Pauline epistles.
After completing his doctoral studies, he stayed in Oslo and joined the
faculty at the University, where he taught his entire academic career,
spanning nearly three decades (1960–1988). In the *Festschrift* given
to him on his seventieth birthday, a bibliography of Jervell's publications listed 163 works in Norwegian, German, and English from
1953–1995 (nearly four per year).[9] The topics of his works include

---

4. Ernst Haenchen, *The Acts of the Apostles: A Commentary* (Philadelphia: Westminster, 1971), 100 (emphasis original); cf. Hans Conzelmann, *The Theology of St Luke*, trans. Geoffrey Buswell (New York: Harper & Row, 1961), 211; Tyson, *Luke, Judaism, and the Scholars*, 71. The other common approach to interpretation of Acts was that it was an apology in defense of Christianity to Rome.
5. Jacob Jervell, *Luke and the People of God: A New Look at Luke–Acts* (Minneapolis: Augsburg, 1972), 41.
6. Tyson, *Luke, Judaism, and the Scholars*, 91.
7. Jervell, *Luke and the People of God*, 14 (in the "Preface").
8. Nils A. Dahl, foreword to *Luke and the People of God: A New Look at Luke–Acts*, by Jacob Jervell (Minneapolis: Augsburg, 1972), 9–11, here 10.
9. Svein Helge Birkeflet, "Bibliography of Jacob Jervell's Scholarly Publications," in *Mighty Minorities? Minorities in Early Christianity—Positions and Strategies: Essays in Honour of Jacob Jervell on His 70th Birthday 21 May 1995*, eds. David Hellholm, Halvor Moxnes, and Turid Karlsen Seim (Oslo: Scandinavian University Press, 1995), 213–26.

the historical Jesus,[10] the Gospel of John,[11] an edited volume on the Testament of the Twelve Patriarchs,[12] and, in much of his later works in Norwegian, contemporary bioethics.[13] However, Jervell is known primarily for his work on Luke–Acts, Paul, and early Christianity, in particular *Luke and the People of God* (1972), *The Unknown Paul* (1984), *The Theology of the Acts of the Apostles* in the Cambridge New Testament Theology series (1996), and a German commentary on Acts in the Meyer Commentary Series (1998).[14]

The call in Acts 1:8 for the disciples to be Jesus's "witnesses in Jerusalem, and Judea and Samaria, and to the end of the earth" has long been understood as the pronouncement of the impending proclamation of the gospel to the Gentiles, ending in Rome, the center of the Gentile world (so to speak). To those who have grown accustomed to hearing or reading this summary of the Gentile mission within the book of Acts, Jervell's publications come as quite a shock. For Jervell, the argument that Luke is focused on recounting the successful mission to the Gentiles could not be further from the truth. As he himself later explains with regard to *Luke and the People of God*, Jervell "had two intentions. The first was to show the place of Luke–Acts within Jewish traditions: Luke is not writing from a Gentile point of view. The second was to show that there was a Jewish Christianity even after 70 AD, not only in some small backwater but in the main stream."[15] The focus in much of Jervell's work, therefore, is to bring the Jewish emphases of the Lukan writings, to borrow his expression, out of the

10. Jacob Jervell, *The Continuing Search for the Historical Jesus* (Minneapolis: Augsburg, 1965).
11. Jacob Jervell, *Jesus in the Gospel of John* (Minneapolis: Augsburg, 1994).
12. Jacob Jervell, Christoph Burchard, and Johannes Thomas, eds., *Studien zu den Testamenten der Zwölf Patriarchen*, BZNW 36 (Berlin: Walter de Gruyter, 1969).
13. See Birkeflet, "Bibliography," 222–26.
14. Jervell, *Luke and the People of God*; Jacob Jervell, *The Unknown Paul: Essays on Luke–Acts and Early Christian History* (Minneapolis: Augsburg, 1984); Jacob Jervell, *The Theology of the Acts of the Apostles*, NTT (Cambridge: Cambridge University Press, 1996); Jacob Jervell, *Die Apostelgeschichte*, KEK 3 (Göttingen: Vandenhoeck & Ruprecht, 1998). Jervell's Acts commentary "is the seventeenth edition of the Meyer Acts commentary and the successor in this series to those of Ernst Haenchen." Tyson, *Luke, Judaism, and the Scholars*, 91.
15. Jacob Jervell, "Retrospect and Prospect in Luke–Acts Interpretation," in *Society of Biblical Literature 1991 Seminar Papers*, SBLSPS 30 (Atlanta: Scholars, 1991), 384. He says in the "Preface" to *Luke and the People of God*: "In all these essays the central theme is how Luke deals with ecclesiology, the question of the identity of a church which is heir to the promises given to Israel, a church which claims to be Israel and yet still includes uncircumcised Gentiles within its membership. Alienation of Jewish Christians after the influx of Gentiles into the church and rumors about Paul provide the problems Luke attempts to resolve for his readers." Jervell, *Luke and the People of God*, 17.

shadows into the sun.[16] This "new look" at Luke–Acts dramatically challenged the consensus of the previous half-century, a consensus that, in many ways, still has a foothold today.[17]

In order to clarify his argument, I want to break down his Jewish-centric reading of Luke–Acts into four pieces: (1) a reformulation of the history of early Christianity, (2) Israel as the divided people of God, (3) the restoration of Israel, and (4) the Lukan portrait of Paul. I will then turn briefly in the final section to select critical responses to Jervell's work and the import his work might have for future scholarship.

THE HISTORY OF EARLY (JEWISH) CHRISTIANITY

Hans Conzelmann, in his influential commentary on Acts, says, "For Luke Jewish Christianity no longer has any present significance, but it is of fundamental significance in terms of salvation history."[18] Conzelmann's view of the Jewish people in the early church fits, according to Jervell, with the "consensus . . . that there was a line of development from Palestinian Jewish Christianity through Hellenistic Jewish Christianity, to Paul and Gentile Christianity, ending with the total victory of Gentile Christianity about A.D. 70."[19] In contrast, Jervell argues that this historical account does not cohere with Acts, in particular the Jewish conflict and apologetic speeches in the latter half of Acts.[20] The

---

16. Jervell, *Unknown Paul*, 71.
17. W. Ward Gasque, *A History of the Interpretation of the Acts of the Apostles* (repr., Eugene, OR: Wipf and Stock, 1985), 358; Craig S. Keener, *Acts: An Exegetical Commentary*, 4 vols. (Grand Rapids: Baker Academic, 2012–2015), 1:473.
18. Hans Conzelmann, *Acts of the Apostles: A Commentary*, Hermeneia (Minneapolis: Fortress, 1988), 117 (quoted in Tyson, *Luke, Judaism, and the Scholars*, 87). Jervell says, "When reading current studies of Luke–Acts, I often get the feeling that the author was not a theologian writing in the second half of the first century, dealing with problems of his own time, but that he was a theologian of the Constantinian era. I get this impression principally because the 'established' church that scholars assume to be present in Luke's writings could not possibly have existed in the first century; there we find nothing like an established, united church and nothing which may justifiably be called orthodoxy." Jervell, *Luke and the People of God*, 14.
19. Jervell, *Unknown Paul*, 13, cf. 29; cf. Jervell, "Retrospect and Prospect," 390.
20. Jervell, *Luke and the People of God*, 122–23; cf. Robert C. Tannehill, "Israel in Luke–Acts: A Tragic Story," *JBL* 104 (1985): 69–85, here 81. While acknowledging that he has read it, Tannehill does not interact with Jervell's *Luke and the People of God*, which is odd because both of them reject the notion that Acts is about affirming the Gentile mission. Tannehill's answer is to say that the story is tragic, with little hope remaining for the restoration of the kingdom to Israel. Jervell's response is that the church is a divided people of God and the restoration of Israel is complete at the conclusion of Acts when the mission to the Jews ends. Cf. Tannehill, "Israel in Luke–Acts," 74.

church *in Acts*, says Jervell, consists "primarily of Jews and for the Jews, in Palestine and in the various parts of the Roman empire."[21]

Jervell supports this claim in several ways. (1) The various mass conversions in Acts (2:41; 4:4; 5:14; 6:7; 21:20) are made up of Jews and not Gentiles.[22] Thus, the mission to the Jews should be classified more as a *success* than a rejection.[23] (2) The ecclesiological terms used in Acts to describe the church (λαός, οἶκος, ἀδελφοί, "descendants of Abraham," "the fathers") are consistent with Old Testament usage, connecting the (Jewish Christian) church in Acts to Israel, whereas Luke never uses ἐκκλησία to refer to the church.[24] (3) The conflict experienced by the apostles and missionaries is predominantly, if not exclusively, with Jews.[25] In this vein, Paul's trial narratives in Acts 21–28 do not pertain to Roman conflict but Jewish concerns with Paul's faithfulness to the law and his preaching of the resurrection from the dead.[26] Moreover, the conflict over the law demonstrates that Torah adherence is of the utmost importance for Luke and, therefore, Paul.[27] (4) The use of the Old Testament, and particularly the LXX, in Acts connects the church to Israel, since "the history that Scripture describes is that of Israel, and only that."[28] (5) The Gentiles who do

---

21. Jervell, *Unknown Paul*, 17.
22. Jervell, *Luke and the People of God*, 42, 45; cf. Jervell, *Theology of the Acts of the Apostles*, 13.
23. Jervell, *Luke and the People of God*, 48–49.
24. Jervell, *Luke and the People of God*, 111n78; Jervell, *Unknown Paul*, 133–35; cf. Jacob Jervell, "God's Faithfulness to the Faithless People: Trends in Interpretation of Luke–Acts," *Word & World* 12 (1992): 29–36, here 34; Haenchen, *Acts of the Apostles*, 93.
25. Jervell, *Luke and the People of God*, 42–43. Even the Areopagus speech, for Jervell, is not predominantly about the Gentile mission. "Neither is the Areopagus speech . . . a sermon, but more like a discourse or a lecture on true and false religion. The readers of Acts would have no edification from it. We notice even here Luke's abhorrence. Acts 17:16 tells us about the Jewish wrath against idolatry. The tension between 17:16 and 17:22 clearly is there, but if anything is to be labeled Lukan it is obviously 17:16. . . . Paganism is nothing but sinful, false religiosity only to be condemned. The only possibility—and it is remote—of something else lies in the 'unknown God' (17:23)." Jacob Jervell, "The Church of Jews and Godfearers," in *Luke–Acts and the Jewish People: Eight Critical Perspectives*, ed. Joseph B. Tyson (Minneapolis: Augsburg, 1988), 11–20, here 18.
26. Jervell, *Luke and the People of God*, 163–74.
27. Jervell, *Luke and the People of God*, 138, 141.
28. Jervell, *Unknown Paul*, 133. He goes on to say, "The history of the Gentile nations is not a history of salvation, and for Luke a history of mankind does not exist. For this reason Scripture also does not furnish a history of the individual, but only of Israel, and a history of Gentiles insofar as they have had something to do with Israel." Cf. Jervell, *Theology of the Acts of the Apostles*, 12–13. He later similarly states, albeit with respect to Luke's Greek, "In spite of his ability to write decent Greek, he does so only seldom and sporadically. Most of his work he presents in what may be called biblical Greek, clearly influenced by the Septuagint, a Jewish book, written for Jews and not for Gentiles. Luke's stylistic home was the synagogue." Jervell, *Theology of the Acts of the Apostles*, 5.

accept Jesus in Acts are already familiar with or participants in Judaism, whether as God-fearers or otherwise.[29]

All of this leads Jervell to conclude: "Both Jews and Gentiles accept the gospel [in Acts], but the Jews are the great majority. Our impression [i.e., the consensus position] that it is the other way around does not come from Acts, but from our common conception of the history of early Christianity."[30] In other words, the history of the early church, the history that Acts narrates, is one of early *Jewish*, not Gentile, Christianity. As he says, "Christianity is for Luke the religion of Israel."[31]

With the missional shift to the Gentiles later in the first century, the church gradually becomes more Gentile than Jewish in its ethnic makeup.[32] But this does not mean that Jewish Christianity eventually died out with the Hellenization of the church. Rather, Jervell claims, "The minority, that is, Jewish Christianity in the second part of the first century, remained in the church . . . not *a* but *the* great power, determining the thinking, the theology, and the preaching of the Christian church."[33] In other words, the early church maintains its ties with Israel through the Jewish Christian "mighty minority" at the helm of a Gentile majority. Consequently, when considering the purpose for writing the Acts of the Apostles, it makes sense to understand Luke

---

29.   Jervell, "Church of Jews and Godfearers"; cf. Jervell, *Luke and the People of God*, 45; Jervell, *Theology of the Acts of the Apostles*, 39.

30.   Jervell, *Unknown Paul*, 15. Similarly, "The idea that Luke–Acts, the two-volume work, is a product of Gentile Christianity is in my opinion more based on the common view that it stems from the first great era of Gentile Christianity than on internal reasons. To uphold such an interpretation, one has to neglect the fact that the supposed Gentile-Christian author Luke presents to us more Jewish and Jewish-Christian material than the majority of New Testament authors do. To cling to the general idea about Luke as a Gentile theologian one is forced to regard this material as Jewish-Christian reminiscences, as inactive or nonworking elements within the total Lukan concept." Jervell, *Unknown Paul*, 40.

31.   Jervell, *Unknown Paul*, 16. See also: "There no longer exists any doubt, therefore, what is at stake for Luke. The issue is not legal protection on the basis of *religio licita*. Viewed from the perspective of Luke's ecclesiology, the issue is the justification of the church's existence, and indirectly a concern for the Gentile mission. Hence it is theologically of decisive importance to demonstrate the Jewish orthodoxy as well as the special status of Paul within the church." Jervell, *Luke and the People of God*, 173.

32.   Jervell argues that this "Hellenization of Christianity took place later than we think and that Gentile Christianity became dominant first in the second century." Jervell, *Unknown Paul*, 20; cf. 43. According to Jervell, the majority of scholars hold that "many years lie between events narrated at the end of Acts and the totally different church we have at the time Luke is writing. So 28:28 would mean that Paul looks into the future to a church which has left Judaism and Jewish Christianity behind. Now, in the author's time, the church consists of believing Gentiles who have replaced the Jewish Christians. And Luke knows very well what Jewish Christianity is. . . . Luke would then see the church as the church for the Gentiles without ties to Israel." Jervell, *Unknown Paul*, 19.

33.   Jervell, *Unknown Paul*, 26–27.

as either a Jewish Christian[34] or one who "thinks as a Christian Jew"[35] writing to a church that is predominantly Gentile, yet with a (theologically) strong Jewish "minority."[36] The problem that Luke addresses, therefore, is one in which Jews are harassing and criticizing the Jewish Christians in the church because they no longer adhere to the law and, thus, are no longer counted among the people of God.[37] Luke is not writing to defend the Gentile mission or apologize to Rome, but rather to defend and affirm Paul and his fellow Jewish Christians who are not guilty of apostasy but instead have an assured place in the people of God.[38]

ISRAEL AS THE DIVIDED PEOPLE OF GOD

As van Unnik asked earlier, the question is: How do Israel and the Jews relate to the church and the people of God in Acts? The consensus prior to Jervell, as mentioned earlier, is that "Luke thinks of the Christians . . . taking over the privileges of the Jews as one epoch is

34. He says, "He [Luke] was a Jewish Christian. Maybe he was born a Gentile, but then he came from God-fearers, having his roots in a Hellenistic-Jewish Christianity." Jervell, *Theology of the Acts of the Apostles*, 5.
35. He says, "It is not decisive whether Luke himself was by birth a Jew or Gentile. What is important is that he thinks as a Christian Jew and that he is using the categories typical of Jewish Christianity." Jervell, *Unknown Paul*, 42. David Moessner has recently argued that the παρηκολουθηκότι of Luke 1:3 marks Luke not as one who "has investigated" everything carefully, but rather as one "who was thoroughly steeped in" the events, etc., for a lengthy period of time, thus establishing Luke's qualifications to write his *Doppelwerk* for his audience. David P. Moessner, "Luke as Tradent and Hermeneut: 'As One Who Has a Thoroughly Informed Familiarity with All the Events from the Top' (παρηκολουθηκότι ἄνωθεν πᾶσιν κριβῶς, Luke 1:3)," *NovT* 58 (2016): 259–300. If Moessner is correct, and he makes a fairly compelling case, what might such a new perspective on Luke as qualified "historian" add/change when determining Luke's relationship to Judaism/Israel? Is Luke Jewish or Gentile? Is it possible to tell?
36. He says, "My thesis that Luke–Acts was written chiefly for Jewish-Christian readers—and, I would add, God-fearers, who are closer to Jews than to Gentiles—is dependent upon the theological ideas in his work. I do not find convincing the often-advanced arguments for the opposite view, that Luke wrote for Gentile-Christian readers. That his two volumes were dedicated to Theophilus, someone with a Greek name, is no evidence. Even a Jew, not to mention a God-fearer, could bear such a name." Jervell, "Retrospect and Prospect," 399; cf. Jervell, *Theology of the Acts of the Apostles*, 12–15; Jervell, *Luke and the People of God*, 174–77.
37. Jervell, *Theology of the Acts of the Apostles*, 16.
38. Jervell, *Luke and the People of God*, 146–47; cf. Jervell, "Church of Jews and Godfearers," 20; Jervell, *Theology of the Acts of the Apostles*, 1, 127, 129. On Luke as a historian and theologian, Jervell says, "It is impossible to separate Luke the historian from Luke the theologian, that is the interpreter. History does not confirm the Scriptures, but the Scriptures confirm history." Jacob Jervell, "The Lucan Interpretation of Jesus as Biblical Theology," in *New Directions in Biblical Theology: Papers of the Aarhus Conference, 16-19 September 1992*, ed. Sigfried Pedersen (Leiden: Brill, 1994), 77–92, here 80.

succeeded by the next."[39] The Christian church should thus be understood as the "true" or "new" Israel.[40]

Throughout his works, Jervell challenges this position. For Jervell,
the Old Testament recounts the history of Israel, and the audience to
which Luke writes needs affirmation that its history is the history of
Israel.[41] Luke has no interest in the history of the nations.[42] In terms
of Israel and the church, therefore, Jervell (repeatedly) puts it bluntly:

> In Luke's writings "Israel" always refers to the Jewish people. At no
> time does it serve to characterize the church, i.e., it is never used as a
> technical term for the Christian gathering of Jews and Gentiles. The
> early catholic understanding of the church as a *tertium genus* ["third
> race/nation"] in relation to Jews and Gentiles and ultimately as the *new*
> Israel that is made up of Gentiles and Jews is not present in Acts.[43]

For Jervell, Israel in Luke and Acts[44] does not refer to the "mixed"
notion of the church consisting of Jews and Gentiles as evident in the
second (or third) century and beyond. Israel is Jewish, through and
through, the people of God just as they were in the Old Testament.[45]
There is no "true" or "new" Israel at the time of Luke's writing or at least
in the narrative that he recounts.[46] But how does one explain, then, the
Jewish rejection of Jesus as the Messiah? Why is there so much conflict

---

39. Conzelmann, *The Theology of St Luke*, 163.
40. Jervell, *Luke and the People of God*, 42.
41. Cf. Nils A. Dahl, "The Story of Abraham in Luke–Acts," in *Studies in Luke–Acts*, 139–58, here 151.
42. Jervell states, "The Gentiles have no previous history of any interest to Luke apart from the fact that
     their history shows traces of the Creator, who of course is the God of Israel. When it comes to the
     future the situation is different. The mission to the Gentiles is not an invention of the church or the
     apostles, but solely the responsibility of the Spirit." Jervell, *Unknown Paul*, 106.
43. Jervell, *Luke and the People of God*, 49; cf. 42, 54, 135; cf. Jervell, "God's Faithfulness to the Faithless
     People," 34.
44. Note Jervell's later insistence that he "cannot follow the tendency to speak of 'Luke–Acts' as a single
     book that was later divided and existed in two volumes . . .; Acts is a literary genre other than the
     Gospel, it was written several years later, is dealing with other themes, has other theological ideas
     and corresponds to the largest size of a standard scroll, so that the gospel and Acts as one book
     would be technically far too large." Jervell, *Theology of the Acts of the Apostles*, 117n4; Jervell, "Lucan
     Interpretation of Jesus," 78. However, he does use "Luke–Acts" in earlier works, e.g., Jervell, *Luke
     and the People of God*, 135. Jervell certainly reads Luke and Acts in light of each other (e.g., "The
     Circumcised Messiah"), or, perhaps better said, Acts in light of Luke. He does agree that "there is
     to a great extent a theological unity in the presuppositions behind the books of Luke, especially
     when dealing with christology," but not compositional or, perhaps, narratival unity. Jervell, "Lucan
     Interpretation of Jesus," 78.
45. Cf. Jervell, *Theology of the Acts of the Apostles*, 4, 13, 19, 22.
46. Jervell, "Retrospect and Prospect," 392.

between the Jews and proclaimers of the gospel in Acts? Jervell argues that, in Acts, Israel is a divided people, separated into the repentant and the unrepentant.[47] The former acknowledge Jesus as the Messiah sent by God to redeem and restore them as his people, Israel. The latter "has forfeited its right to belong to the people of God."[48] In other words, "*Israel* has not rejected the gospel, but has become divided over the issue,"[49] with the unrepentant suffering the judgment of God. "Empirical Israel," as he calls them, "are Jews who have accepted the gospel, to whom and for whom the promises have been fulfilled."[50]

A further demonstration of Jervell's view of Israel in Luke and Acts is his unique portrait of the Samaritans.[51] In the Gospel, "the Samaritans . . . rejected Jesus because he was on his way to Jerusalem."[52] They are "Jews who have gone astray."[53] Yet, in Acts, Jervell argues that they "bind themselves to Jerusalem by receiving those who come from Jerusalem. As the listing of missionary territories shows, the restored Israel is found in Galilee, Judea and *Samaria* (1:8; 8:1; 9:31)."[54] The Samaritans are considered a part of the Jewish people rather than as Gentiles, and thus are accorded a possible place in the people of God, depending on how they respond to the Messiah.[55]

One of the reasons the Samaritans and other Jewish groups can still be included in the people of God in Acts is because of circumcision,[56]

---

47. He says, "Luke's view is different: The 'empirical' Israel is composed of two groups, the repentant (i.e., Christian) and the obdurate. It is important for Luke to show that the Jewish Christian church is a part of Israel." Jervell, *Luke and the People of God*, 49.
48. Jervell, *Luke and the People of God*, 54; cf. 43; Jervell, *Theology of the Acts of the Apostles*, 25, 37. He later notes, "Luke is well aware that not all the people will be converted, and furthermore that it is impossible to speak of any salvation for all Israel (cf. 3:23)." Jervell, *Luke and the People of God*, 93. Elsewhere, he says that Luke does not present a picture of the salvation of humankind but, rather, Israel as the people of God. For example, "First, Luke does not view the gospel as addressed to mankind in general, or to mankind without a nationality or history, but to men whose history is Israel's as the chosen people. Luke does not share Matthew's view of making disciples of all nations; he does not view the church as a church of all peoples. His understanding lies closer to the Pauline 'to the Jew first and also to the Greek.' Luke consistently operates within the limits of the conception 'Israel' and 'the nations.'" Jervell, *Luke and the People of God*, 114; cf. 125.
49. Jervell, *Luke and the People of God*, 49 (emphasis added).
50. Jervell, *Luke and the People of God*, 43; Jervell, *Unknown Paul*, 41–42.
51. Jervell, *Luke and the People of God*, 113–32. See also David Ravens, *Luke and the Restoration of Israel*, JSNTSup 119 (Sheffield: Sheffield Academic, 1995), 72–106.
52. Jervell, *Luke and the People of God*, 127.
53. Jervell, *Luke and the People of God*, 124. Other "Jewish" groups, like the Sadducees, also fall under Jervell's rubric of "Jews who have gone astray."
54. Jervell, *Luke and the People of God*, 127 (emphasis added).
55. Jervell, *Luke and the People of God*, 118, 123.
56. Jervell, *Luke and the People of God*, 119.

which points toward another key cog in Jervell's argument about the focus on Israel in Luke and Acts, namely the law. He says, "Most scholars . . . take it for granted that Luke considers the church to be 'the new Israel,' the universal people of God; thus the law is a matter of history, belonging to the old people, now replaced by the church."[57] Jervell disagrees because "the law is to him [Luke] . . . the mark of distinction between Jews and non-Jews. The law is the sign of Israel as the people of God."[58] Luke is consistently positive about the law—"in Luke's Gospel, every criticism is missing. Jesus did not alter anything; the law is permanently valid"[59]—and this is especially true for his portrayal of Paul in the latter half of Acts, a portrayal that has frequently been a source of consternation for scholars. Instead of depicting the church as the new Israel apart from the law, Jervell argues that Luke writes to affirm his Jewish Christian audience of their status as the people of God and demonstrate to them that the earliest (Jewish) Christians as seen in Acts were strict adherents to the law.[60] The law is "Israel's law . . . the sign of the people of God,"[61] and "because the church—consisting of believing Jews—*is* Israel, the church must keep the law."[62] But what does this mean for non-Jews, who are not Israel in Acts? Jervell states unequivocally:

> Luke knows of no Gentile mission that is free from the law. He knows about a Gentile mission without circumcision, not without the law. The [Apostolic] Decree [in Acts 15] enjoins Gentiles to keep that part of the law required for them to live together with Jews; it is not lawful

---

57. Jervell, *Luke and the People of God*, 135; cf. Jervell, "Retrospect and Prospect," 387; Jervell, "God's Faithfulness to the Faithless People," 32. For Jervell, "The term 'the new Israel' cannot be found in the New Testament. I do not question that the idea is present there, at least in germinal form, but not as a general opinion. And this idea can certainly not be found in Luke–Acts." Jervell, *Luke and the People of God*, 135.
58. Jervell, *Luke and the People of God*, 137.
59. Jervell, *Luke and the People of God*, 139.
60. Jervell, *Luke and the People of God*, 141.
61. Jervell, *Luke and the People of God*, 139; cf. Jervell, *Unknown Paul*, 33–34; Jervell, *Theology of the Acts of the Apostles*, 55. In other words, "Luke has not consciously tried to Christianize the law or to interpret it with a view to the Christian church." Jervell, *Luke and the People of God*, 141. "Thus one conclusion can be drawn: Luke's view of the law is bound up with his ecclesiology; it is a sign of the identity of the church. . . . Jewish Christians, being the restored Israel, are the foundation of the church, and so they must be upholders of the law." Jervell, *Luke and the People of God*, 143; cf. Jervell, "Retrospect and Prospect," 396. For his connections between the Spirit and the law, see Jervell, *Unknown Paul*, 99–107, 119–21; Jervell, *Theology of the Acts of the Apostles*, 52–54.
62. Jervell, *Unknown Paul*, 42; cf. Jervell, *Theology of the Acts of the Apostles*, 14.

to impose upon Gentiles more than Moses himself demanded. It is false to speak of the Gentiles as free from the law: the church, on the contrary, delivers the law to the Gentiles as Gentiles. There is no justification by the law; rather it is by the grace of Jesus that Jews and Gentiles are saved (Luke 24:47; Acts 2:38; 3:19f.; 13:39; 15:11 etc.), but this is never contrasted with adherence to the law, otherwise Luke would have jeopardized his ecclesiology. It is impossible that the law should be abrogated, replaced, or conceived as belonging to an epoch now past.[63]

Ultimately, "By insisting on Jewish Christians' universal adherence to the law, he [Luke] succeeds in showing that they are the restored and true Israel entitled to God's promises and to salvation."[64]

THE RESTORATION OF ISRAEL AT THE END OF ACTS

Jervell has argued that Luke presents the Jewish Christian history of the early church in Acts with particular emphasis on Israel as the divided people of God, with the "true" people of God being those who embrace Jesus-Messiah and keep the whole law. The natural response, however, is to ask: When *does* the mission to the Gentiles begin in Jervell's understanding of Acts? The answer—at the restoration of Israel.

Scholars have long recognized the theological importance of the restoration language sprinkled throughout Acts (e.g., 1:6; 3:21).[65] Prior to Jervell, scholars generally understood the restoration of Israel

---

63. Jervell, *Theology of the Acts of the Apostles*, 60; cf. 130–31.
64. Jervell, *Luke and the People of God*, 147.
65. On Acts 1:6, Jervell states, "The restoration of the kingdom is its restoration to Israel (1:6). We have no right to push aside the saying in 1:6 as some sort of nationalistic misunderstanding. This is frequently done without any justification in the text, but from preconceived notions about the history of the early church and Luke's role in it. It is never denied in Acts that the kingdom is the kingdom for Israel. Only so are the repeatedly mentioned promises to Israel in the whole section of Acts 1–15 understandable. . . . The answer to the apostles' question about restoring the kingdom to Israel is that the Spirit will come upon them and they will be witnesses from Jerusalem and to 'the end of the earth' (1:8). This is nothing but a part of the restoration. . . . So far nothing is said about the relation between the kingdom and the Spirit apart from the witness of the apostles as part of the restoration of the kingdom." Jervell, *Unknown Paul*, 98; cf. Jervell, *Theology of the Acts of the Apostles*, 35. One of the more thorough assessments of the restoration of Israel in Acts is in David W. Pao, *Acts and the Isaianic New Exodus*, WUNT 2/130 (Tübingen: Mohr Siebeck, 2000). Pao is also one of the few scholars who appears to engage with much of Jervell's work on this topic. Cf. Ravens, *Luke and the Restoration of Israel*.

as an eschatological hope.[66] In this understanding, the Gentile mission began in Acts *via* Israel's rejection of Jesus as Messiah, so that any notion of the eschatological restoration of Israel corresponds with the conclusion of the Gentile mission at the last day.[67]

Jervell, however, presents a radical counterproposal: the Gentile mission *begins* at the restoration of Israel at the conclusion of Acts.[68] Since Acts does not focus on the Gentile mission, Jervell says, "It is more correct to say that only when Israel has accepted the gospel can the way to Gentiles be opened."[69] The proclamation of the mission to Israel in Acts is a successful one, with Jews either repenting or renouncing membership in the people of God. Therefore, as Jervell states, "the mission to Gentiles is fulfillment of Scripture in the sense that the promises must first be fulfilled to Israel before Gentiles can share in salvation. This fulfillment has occurred in the conversion of repentant Jews. The mission to Jews is a necessary stage through which the history of salvation must pass in order that salvation might proceed from the restored Israel to the Gentiles."[70] In other words, Luke's concern in Acts is to narrate the mission to the Jews, which is a necessary first step—and a fulfillment of God's promises to Israel[71]—before the mission turns to the Gentiles.[72]

---

66. E.g., Haenchen, *Acts of the Apostles*, 143; Conzelmann, *Acts of the Apostles*, 7; cf. Tannehill, "Israel in Luke–Acts," 84–85.

67. For a more recent discussion of the future of Israel, see Michael Wolter, "Israel's Future and the Delay of the parousia, According to Luke," in *Jesus and the Heritage of Israel: Luke's Narrative Claim upon Israel's Legacy*, ed. David P. Moessner, Luke the Interpreter of Israel 1 (Harrisburg, PA: Trinity Press International, 1999), 307–24.

68. Jervell, *Luke and the People of God*, 41–74.

69. Jervell, *Luke and the People of God*, 55; cf. 58. Tannehill, in his essay on "Israel in Luke–Acts," writes, "If the author of Luke–Acts wished only to justify the Gentile mission and a Gentile church, that purpose was already accomplished with the story of Cornelius's conversion (Acts 10:1–11:18) and the decision about the status of Gentile Christians in Acts 15:1–29. There would be no further need to return repeatedly to the problem of the unbelieving Jews." Tannehill, "Israel in Luke–Acts," 81; cf. 74.

70. Jervell, *Luke and the People of God*, 43; cf. 62.

71. Of all his predecessors, Dahl is probably the closest to Jervell's position: "Salvation of Gentiles was from the beginning envisaged by God and included as part of his promises to Israel. Luke does not claim that the church has replaced Israel as the people of God, nor does he call Gentile believers Abraham's children. Gentiles are saved as Gentiles. Luke takes care to adduce prophecies that really spoke of them." Dahl, "Story of Abraham," 151. A subtle difference between Dahl and Jervell, however, is Dahl's belief that "the priority of Israel is regarded as a matter of history; it is no longer a present reality for Luke and for churches like those of Corinth and Rome." Jervell obviously considers Israel as supremely important even up to Luke's day.

72. Jervell, *Luke and the People of God*, 63–64, 122–23.

But what about texts that seem to imply an eschatological restoration of Israel? Jervell responds:

> Strictly speaking, Luke has excluded the possibility of a further mission to Jews for the church of his time because the judgment by and on the Jews has been irrevocably passed. A conversion of the entire Jewish people by the Gentiles in the future, as Paul envisions in Rom. 9–11, is out of the question for Luke.[73]

For Jervell, the church in Acts is Israel, the people of God, and at the conclusion of the mission to the Jews "'a people from the Gentiles' will join Israel (Acts 15:14). The idea is that of a people and an associate people."[74] At the end of Acts, the mission to the Jews is concluded, "Israel is restored, and the time of the Gentiles has come."[75] In summary, "Luke's version of 'the Jew first,' then, is determined by the idea that without 'the Jew first' the Gentiles would have no admission to salvation."[76]

THE LUKAN PAUL AND THE PAUL OF THE EPISTLES

Finally, let me turn to the Lukan Paul. By the time Jervell began to publish on Luke and Acts, the influence of Vielhauer loomed large, as seen in Haenchen's commentary on Acts.[77] Vielhauer examined how Luke employed (or not) the "theological ideas of Paul"[78] as opposed to any semblance of historical verisimilitude.[79] Looking at the Lukan speeches by Paul for his theological positions on natural theology, law, Christology, and eschatology, Vielhauer determined that Luke

---

73. Jervell, *Luke and the People of God*, 64.
74. Jervell, *Luke and the People of God*, 143; Jervell, *Theology of the Acts of the Apostles*, 40. According to Jervell, "The mission to the Gentiles is simply a part of the mission to the Jews. The command to world mission in Acts 1:8 shows the disciples witnessing in Jerusalem, Judaea and Samaria, and to the ends of the earth. 'To the ends of the earth' does not mean the Gentile mission: throughout Acts the mission goes from synagogue to synagogue, ending with a meeting with the Jews in Rome (28:17ff.). There is no specific mission to the Gentiles, separated from the mission to the Jews. It is striking that in their speeches to Jews the apostles emphasize the sharing of the Gentiles in salvation, while in their speeches to Gentiles, they mention their commission to Israel." Jervell, *Theology of the Acts of the Apostles*, 40–41.
75. Jervell, *Unknown Paul*, 42.
76. Jervell, *Theology of the Acts of the Apostles*, 40.
77. Haenchen, *Acts of the Apostles*, 113–16.
78. Philipp Vielhauer, "On the 'Paulinism' in Acts," in *Studies in Luke–Acts*, 33–50, here 33.
79. Vielhauer, "'Paulinism' in Acts," 34.

"presents no specifically Pauline idea" and questioned whether Luke, the companion of Paul, actually wrote Acts.[80]

While several scholars attempted to dispute the growing consensus, Jervell's Jewish-centric reading of Acts contributed new ammunition to the conversation. Rather than attempting to "trace the Lukan portrait of Paul back to the Pauline letters,"[81] Jervell calls attention to the *occasional* nature of the epistles, along with the complexity of Paul, which leads him to conclude that the epistles do not reveal everything about Paul.[82] In other words, one can only find certain "fragments" of Paul in the epistles, and exegetes must be cautious not to extrapolate from these fragments to a complete, unified version of Paul.[83] Thus, "the Lukan portrait of Paul is . . . part of the unknown Paul from the Pauline letters. We have to be aware of the fact that the letters conceal aspects of the genuine Paul. They hide the uncontroversial Paul, what he had in common with all other Christians, especially that which connected Paul and the leaders of the church in Jerusalem."[84] Jervell focuses on the historical, rather than theological, Paul, since the theology of Paul in each letter is dependent upon the letter's specific occasion.[85]

One of the key pieces of Jervell's argument is that it is necessary to examine not only the theology of Paul but also his praxis because one cannot separate the theology from the praxis of Paul, either in Acts or in the epistles.[86] Again, Jervell's stress on Judaism impacts his interpretation. Since Judaism at that time was about "orthopraxy" as opposed to "orthodoxy," it is likely that Paul was more flexible in this theology than his praxis.[87] In order to compare the Lukan Paul with the

---

80. Vielhauer, "'Paulinism' in Acts," 48; cf. Gasque, *History of the Interpretation of the Acts*, 283–91.
81. Jervell, *Unknown Paul*, 58. He argues that there are actually three "editions" of Paul in the New Testament: the Paul of Acts, the Paul of the Pauline epistles, and the Paul of the Pastoral epistles. Jervell, *Unknown Paul*, 55.
82. Jervell, *Unknown Paul*, 55. Elsewhere, he states: "We overlook that Paul actually was a manifold and complex figure, with obvious tensions, and one whose theology developed and underwent changes in the course of the years, not least in relation to important theological ideas such as law, justification, and the fate of Israel and the Gentiles. . . . You can find all Pauline theological conceptions in Acts, even if sometimes in a rudimentary form. And all the concepts of Paul in Acts can be traced to the Pauline letters, but there more in the background and in the shade, without significant theological importance. What we find in Acts is the average, unpolemical theology, which characterizes Paul apart from his most polemical letters in the times of his hardest controversies." Jervell, *Theology of the Acts of the Apostles*, 3.
83. Jervell, *Unknown Paul*, 52.
84. Jervell, *Unknown Paul*, 57.
85. Jervell, *Unknown Paul*, 56–58; cf. 76.
86. Jervell, *Unknown Paul*, 58–59.
87. Jervell, *Unknown Paul*, 58, 69–70.

Paul of the epistles, one needs to look more closely at the orthopraxy of Paul in his epistles rather than his theological orthodoxy, which changes depending upon his intended audience. According to Jervell, the orthopraxy seen in the Paul of the epistles reveals that Paul

> lived as a Jew. He . . . observed the law meticulously (Phil. 3:5), although his compatriots transgressed it (Rom. 2:17ff.; 7:14ff.). He can even say that the Jews do not possess the law (Rom. 8:4ff.; 9:31). But Paul adheres to the law as a Jew and as a Christian. The unknown Paul, whose Judaism has consequences for his theology, maintains that he remains a Jew and a Pharisee, and that the traditions of the fathers are important to him (Rom. 9:7; 11:2; Gal. 2:15; 2 Cor. 11:22).[88]

It is this portrait of the Torah praxis of the "unknown Paul" of the epistles that Jervell claims is also readily observable in Acts.[89] In particular, Luke presents Paul as a law-abiding Pharisee.[90] Luke is concerned with defending Paul against rumors of false teaching against Judaism as seen in Acts 21:21 and the other speeches of Acts 21–28, countering that Paul is the quintessential "teacher of Israel."[91] Previous scholars saw this emphasis on Torah observance in Acts as a Lukan "re-Judaizing" of Paul; Jervell finds this untenable because these same scholars argue that Paul and early Christianity had already long turned to an exclusive focus on the Gentiles.[92] Thus, rather than being contradictory, Jervell says,

> The Lukan Paul, the picture of Paul in Acts, is a completion, a filling up of the Pauline one, so that in order to get at the historical Paul, we cannot do without Acts and Luke. . . . Luke's picture completes partly what lies in seclusion or restrained in Paul's own letters, thanks to their specific purpose, and partly what can be found in the "outskirts" or in

---

88. Jervell, *Unknown Paul*, 59; cf. 73.

89. Cf. Jervell, *Unknown Paul*, 75–76. He says, "In Paul's letters we have only fragments of the unknown Paul—the law-observant, Pharisaic, Jewish-Christian Paul. . . . If you interpret Paul solely by means of his letters you easily lose Paul the Jew. It has, however, been preserved in the oral tradition that lies behind the Acts of the Apostles." Jervell, *Unknown Paul*, 59.

90. Jervell, *Unknown Paul*, 71; cf. Jervell, *Theology of the Acts of the Apostles*, 14, 92. Another Lukan emphasis is of Paul as miracle worker. On this, see esp. Jervell, *Unknown Paul*, 77–95. On the historicity of Luke's presentation of Paul, see Jervell, *Unknown Paul*, 68–76.

91. Jervell, *Theology of the Acts of the Apostles*, 86–88. On the Jewish emphases for Paul and the speeches in Acts, see esp. Jervell, *Luke and the People of God*, 153–83. Many prior to Jervell saw the speeches as affirming the Gentile mission. See Tyson, *Luke, Judaism, and the Scholars*, 74.

92. Jervell, *Unknown Paul*, 57.

the margin of his former and first letters, and partly what we detect, when we realize what became of Paul in the end theologically; I am thinking of Romans 9–11. We could say regarding the Lukan Paul that that which lies in the shadow in Paul's letters Luke has placed in the sun in Acts.[93]

Ultimately, for Jervell, "The apostle to the Gentiles of Paul's letters is, in Acts, the missionary to the Jews. This and other differences have to do with different answers to the question about Israel and the people of God."[94]

CRITIQUE OF JERVELL AND POSSIBLE IMPACT ON FUTURE SCHOLARSHIP

In the history of interpretation, one of the areas in which Jervell has dramatically advanced the conversation has been with regard to the Jewish emphases of the Lukan writings. In his recent commentary on Acts, Craig Keener states, "However we reconstruct Luke's audience, the polemic within the narrative itself . . . is mainly intra-Jewish."[95] Such a position *prior to Jervell* would have been extremely uncommon.[96] However, in many scholarly (and ecclesial) circles, the Haenchen–Conzelmann consensus regarding the history of early Christianity endures unabated.[97] The (growing?) position holding that the genre of Luke is akin to Greco-Roman biography and Acts to Greco-Roman historiography has further turned attention away from the Jewishness of Luke's *Doppelwerk*.[98]

---

93. Jervell, *Unknown Paul*, 70–71; cf. 73–74. On Romans 9–11, see Jervell, *Unknown Paul*, 65–67, 74–75. For a comparison of Paul's proclamation to "the Jew first, then the Greek" in both Acts and the Pauline writings, see Simon Butticaz, "'Has God Rejected His People?' (Romans 11.1). The Salvation of Israel in Acts: Narrative Claim of a Pauline Legacy," in *Paul and the Heritage of Israel: Paul's Claim Upon Israel's Legacy in Luke and Acts in the Light of the Pauline Letters*, eds. David P. Moessner, et al., trans. Nicholas J. Zola, LNTS 452 (London: T&T Clark, 2012), 148–64, here 159–60.
94. Jervell, *Theology of the Acts of the Apostles*, 117. For some of the differences between Paul in Acts and Paul in the epistles, see Jervell, *Theology of the Acts of the Apostles*, 118. See also Ravens, *Luke and the Restoration of Israel*, 173–211.
95. Keener, *Acts*, 1:469.
96. See, e.g., Tyson, *Luke, Judaism, and the Scholars*.
97. See Keener's own remarks on their eschatological view of Acts 1:6. Keener, *Acts*, 1:686.
98. See, e.g., Richard A. Burridge, *What Are the Gospels? A Comparison with Graeco-Roman Biography*, 2nd ed., BRS (Grand Rapids: Eerdmans, 2004); Craig A. Keener, *Christobiography: Memory, History, and the Reliability of the Gospels* (Grand Rapids: Eerdmans, 2019).

Which Judaism?

Some remain, therefore, unconvinced, or only partially convinced, by Jervell's Jewish assessment of Luke and Acts. John Carroll says that Jervell has little to no engagement with Judaism *outside* of Luke's narrative, so that Jervell does not "take seriously the fundamental distinction between the setting within the narrative and Luke's own (later) social setting."[99] There is no doubt that the historical analysis of the first-century world is underdeveloped in Jervell, although, to be fair, his method is, to put it in contemporary terms, far more narratological than historical.[100] But Jervell does talk about Israel in an almost "idealized" way to the point that, in many ways, Jervell makes Israel a monolith, ignoring or unaware of the diverse strands of Judaism in the Second Temple period.[101] Recent studies delineating the complexity of ethnicity in the ancient world also push against Jervell's assessment of Judaism in Luke and Acts.[102] To say that Luke writes to affirm *Jewish* Christians of their heritage as the people of God ignores or, at least, undervalues the Hellenized identity of these Jews-turned-Christians. Many scholars, especially in light of the increase in textual materials from the Second Temple period, would push back against Jervell, affirming that both Jewish *and* Greco-Roman contexts both within *and* outside the narrative are vital to the interpretation of the Lukan writings.[103]

---

99. John T. Carroll, review of *The Theology of the Acts of the Apostles* by Jacob Jervell, *ATR* 79 (1997): 437–38, here 437.

100. In comparison to Haenchen and Conzelmann, Dahl says, "In his methodological approach, he [Jervell] sides with them. But like all scholars, Jervell has not let his questions be determined by current opinions and controversies." "Jervell has returned to the point at which Dibelius and Cadbury started more than half a century ago: fresh analysis of the text. . . . He tries to trace the questions that were of primary interest to the author of Luke–Acts himself." Dahl, foreword to *Luke and the People of* God, 10.

101. See, e.g., John M. G. Barclay, *Jews in the Mediterranean Diaspora: From Alexander to Trajan (323 BCE–117 CE)* (Berkeley: University of California Press, 1996); Steve Mason, "Jews, Judaeans, Judaizing, Judaism: Problems of Categorization in Ancient History," *JSJ* 38 (2007): 457–512; John J. Collins, *The Invention of Judaism: Torah and Jewish Identity from Deuteronomy to Paul*, Taubman Lectures in Jewish Studies 7 (Oakland: University of California Press, 2017).

102. E.g., Eric D. Barreto, *Ethnic Negotiations: The Function of Race and Ethnicity in Acts 16*, WUNT 2/294 (Tübingen: Mohr Siebeck, 2010).

103. Even within his commentary on Acts there is often far less discussion of the first-century context of Acts than most scholars would prefer, especially considering its publication date in the late 1990s. For example, his explanation of the ascension accounts hardly mentions the myriad ascension accounts in Second Temple Jewish and Greco-Roman literature, much less those of the Old Testament. Jervell, *Die Apostelgeschichte*, 116–21.

The Restoration of Israel at the Conclusion of Acts

Turning to the narrative of Acts, Robert Tannehill questions Jervell's conclusion that the unbelieving Jews are permanently rejected at the end of Acts,[104] while Max Turner calls it "artificial."[105] Turner says that "Jervell distorts the Jewish Christianity depicted by Luke by making it too Torah-centric," and thus "does not allow sufficiently for the decisive effects of Jesus' ministry in transforming Israel."[106] Moreover, the conditions in the Apostolic Decree "were not the full demands made on an associate people of God, but the minimal requirements that would allow continued fellowship between Gentiles and scrupulous Jews."[107] Turner concludes that Jervell "misrepresents" the theological emphases of Luke, obscuring "the lordship of Christ by the Spirit and its corollary, a new covenant people."[108]

Turner is correct to note that Jervell leaves the reader of Acts with a large amount of uncertainty as to how the Gentiles participate as an associate people in the people of God.[109] This can be seen in Jervell's discussion of the implications of Acts for today at the conclusion of his *Theology of the Acts of the Apostles*: "we can even cross out the idea that the church is Israel, a meaningful notion only when the members of the church are themselves Jews coming from the synagogue. This was replaced in the second century by the idea of the church as the new Israel, where the church members were neither Jews nor Gentiles, but looked upon themselves as '*tertium genus*', 'the third nation.'" So, the church in the second century is no longer Israel, but a "third nation"— how does this work? And is it so bold as to question whether such a notion of a *tertium genus* was present for Luke in Acts as so many

104. Robert C. Tannehill, review of *The Theology of the Acts of the Apostles* by Jacob Jervell, *JBL* 117 (1998): 147–49, here 149. He says, "The restoration of Israel is not complete with Paul's preaching in Rome. It will only be complete when the twelve tribes—Israel in its fullness—are assembled under their Messiah and living in political freedom from their 'enemies' (Luke 1:69–75), as God spoke through the prophets (Luke 1:70)."
105. Max Turner, "The Sabbath, Sunday, and the Law in Luke/Acts," in *From Sabbath to Lord's Day: A Biblical, Historical and Theological Investigation*, ed. D. A. Carson (Grand Rapids: Zondervan, 1982), 100–157, here 116.
106. Turner, "Sabbath, Sunday, and the Law," 117.
107. Turner, "Sabbath, Sunday, and the Law," 117–18.
108. Turner, "Sabbath, Sunday, and the Law," 119; cf. Robert J. Cara, review of *The Theology of the Acts of the Apostles* by Jacob Jervell, *WTJ* 58 (1996): 333–35, here 334–35. To defend Jervell, it is not clear to me that Turner has considered one of the chief supports for Jervell's position, namely the history of early *Jewish* Christianity in Acts.
109. Max Turner, review of *The Unknown Paul: Essays on Luke–Acts and Early Christian History* by Jacob Jervell, *JETS* 29 (1986): 215–16, here 216.

exegetes have observed? Jervell's emphasis on the Jewishness of Acts is certainly welcome and significant, but one wonders if he goes too far to the other extreme.

The Lukan Paul Within Judaism

Apart from this criticism, there remains a (larger?) fraction of scholarship whose response to Jervell could be characterized almost as one of inattentiveness, especially with regard to Jervell's *The Unknown Paul*. Whether this is mere oversight, implicit criticism, or simply rejection is difficult to say. In a 1991 paper given at the annual SBL meeting in Kansas City, Jervell was asked, as he put it, "to deal particularly with my own work and its impact on the American and European scene."[110] He says, honestly, "The books have made almost no impact whatever on the German-European scene," but "the situation in American exegesis has been quite different. There has been a new and very lively discussion and a stream of books and essays dealing especially with the Jewishness of Luke–Acts, Luke's milieu, his readers, and the law."[111]

One opportunity for the inattentiveness to Jervell to be corrected could be through the renewed attention in recent years to the relationship between Paul and Judaism. Gabriele Boccaccini says in *Paul the Jew* (2016): "A new paradigm is emerging today with the Radical New Perspective—a paradigm that aims to fully rediscover the Jewishness of Paul. Paradoxically, 'Paul was not a Christian,' since Christianity, at the time of Paul, was nothing else than a Jewish messianic movement, and therefore, Paul should be regarded as nothing other than a Second Temple Jew."[112] Mark Nanos says "that the writing and community building of the apostle Paul took place *within* late Second Temple Judaism, *within* which he remained a representative after his change of conviction about Jesus being the Messiah (Christ). This also means that the assemblies that he founded . . . were also developing their (sub)culture based upon their convictions about the meaning of Jesus for non-Jews as well as for Jews *within*

110. Jervell, "Retrospect and Prospect," 383n1.
111. Jervell, "Retrospect and Prospect," 384. William Baird, in the final volume of his history of New Testament research, makes no mention of Jervell at all. William Baird, *History of New Testament Research, Volume 3: From C. H. Dodd to Hans Dieter Betz* (Minneapolis: Fortress, 2013).
112. Gabriele Boccaccini, "Introduction: The Three Paths to Salvation of Paul the Jew," in *Paul the Jew: Rereading the Apostle as a Figure of Second Temple Judaism*, eds. Gabriele Boccaccini and Carlos A. Segovia (Minneapolis: Fortress, 2016), 2.

Judaism."[113] This approach to Paul recognizes the diversity of Judaism in the first century, which helps explain the "controversial nature" of Paul in his letters.[114] More importantly, Paul was not *opposed* to Judaism in competition with Christianity; rather, Paul was highly concerned with Torah obedience as a faithful Jew who believed in Jesus the Messiah.[115]

Reading the recent scholarly examination of the Paul of the epistles within Judaism, it sounds remarkably similar to Jervell's claims for Paul in *Acts*.[116] Jervell has argued that Luke and Paul (and much of the early history of Christianity) are *Israel*-focused. Luke presents the church as "Israel, the one people of God." Torah (i.e., orthopraxy) is supremely important in Acts, especially for Paul the Pharisaic Jew.[117] Luke's audience, like the Pauline "assemblies" in the "Paul within Judaism" perspective, remains determined to understand properly their relationship to the God of Israel and his people. Note what Jervell states in his discussion of the four speeches of Paul in Acts 21–28: "Thus whatever Paul was as a Pharisee, he still is as a Christian, except that now he is no longer a persecutor. Thus Luke can say that it is impossible for Paul to teach what he is charged with. To put it positively, if anyone is suited to be the teacher of Israel, it is Paul."[118] Jervell would also likely embrace the diversity of Paul and the Judaism of the first century that is also appreciated by the "Paul within Judaism" perspective. No matter one's stance on Paul and Judaism in the epistles, the comparison here with recent Pauline scholarship thus invites renewed attention to (1) the portrayal of

---

113. Mark D. Nanos, "Introduction," in *Paul within Judaism: Restoring the First-Century Context to the Apostle*, eds. Mark D. Nanos and Magnus Zetterholm (Minneapolis: Fortress, 2015), 1–30, here 9.
114. Boccaccini, "Introduction," 4.
115. Boccaccini, "Introduction," 18.
116. Perhaps the first to call for a new examination of the Paul in Acts in light of the "Paul within Judaism" perspective is Joshua W. Jipp, "What Are the Implications of the Ethnic Identity of Paul's Interlocutor? Continuing the Conversation," in *The So-Called Jew in Paul's Letter to the Romans*, eds. Rafael Rodriguez and Matthew Thiessen (Minneapolis: Fortress, 2016), 183–203, esp. 191–96. Jipp mentions Jervell briefly in light of the Lukan Paul's Torah observance, but there are even more parallels between Jervell's work and the recent ("radical") Pauline perspective.
117. Jipp, "What Are the Implications," 193; cf. Daniel Marguerat, *Paul in Acts and Paul in His Letters*, WUNT 310 (Tübingen: Mohr Siebeck, 2013), 48–65.
118. Jervell, *Luke and the People of God*, 169–70.

Judaism and Paul in Acts,[119] and (2) the relationship between the Lukan Paul and the Paul of the epistles.[120]

CONCLUSION

For Jacob Jervell, "The Jewishness of Acts, compared to all other New Testament writings, is conspicuous: in the pre-Pauline Christology; in the ecclesiology; where the church is Israel; in the soteriology, with the promises of salvation given only to Israel; in the law, the Torah, with its full validity for all Jews in the church; in Paul being the missionary to Israel and the Dispersion."[121] Contrary to the consensus of Lukan scholarship on several issues, Jervell unabashedly reinterpreted the ways in which exegetes should understand the church in its earliest form. Acts was not written to defend the Gentile mission, but rather to defend the Jewish Christian minority remaining in a rapidly expanding Gentile Christianity at the close of the first century. To summarize it differently, as Jervell states, "The concept of Israel as the church is not merely one element in the theological thought of Luke–Acts. It is the very center of Luke's preaching and theology."[122]

119. Todd Penner wonders how we would understand Paul if we only had the book of Acts. Todd Penner, "Madness in the Method? The Acts of the Apostles in Current Study," *CBR* 2 (2004): 223–93, here 247. He says, "An interesting thought experiment would be to query what our image of Paul would look like if we only had Acts with which to work. Would we find/recognize the Paul of the letters? There would definitely be some broad patterns of agreement (Paul was a missionary to the Gentiles; Paul had a connection to Antioch), but it is not evident that we would have the same fundamental (especially theological) conception of Paul that we now do."

120. This latter point has been pursued more extensively in the last few years. See esp. Moessner, et al., eds., *Paul and the Heritage of Israel*.

121. Jervell, *Theology of the Acts of the Apostles*, 5.

122. Jervell, "God's Faithfulness to the Faithless People," 35; cf. Jervell, *Luke and the People of God*, 141; Jervell, *Theology of the Acts of the Apostles*, 22.

RICHARD I. PERVO: LUKE AS NOVELIST AND ACTS AS ENTERTAINMENT

Ron C. Fay

INTRODUCTION

R ichard Ivan Pervo (May 11, 1942–May 20, 2017) spent his life enjoying the book of Acts. He was born in Lakewood, Ohio, and lived in Fairview Park, Ohio, until his junior year of high school.[1] His parents Ivan and Elizabeth then moved the family to Wisconsin, where he finished high school and began college. He received his bachelor's degree from Concordia Senior College in Fort Wayne, Indiana. He married his wife Karen on April 2, 1967. After five years of social work and community organizing in Saint Louis, they moved to Massachusetts where he began his graduate work. He finished his Master of Divinity at the Episcopal Divinity School (EDS), in Cambridge.[2] He graduated from Harvard University with a ThD in 1979, where he did his dissertation under Dieter Georgi.

---

1. The information on Richard Pervo's life comes mostly from Mary Mergenthal, "Lives Lived: Richard Pervo," *The Park Bugle*, St. Paul, MN (July 2017): 17.
2. Academic information comes from Clare K. Rothschild, "Richard I. Pervo," n.p. [cited May 28, 2018], https://www.sbl-site.org/assets/pdfs/Pervo-Obituary-SBL.pdf.

Pervo wrote extensively on Luke–Acts, focusing mostly on Acts, throughout his career.[3] This likely was the natural result of work done for his dissertation, "The Literary Genre of the Acts of the Apostles,"[4] which jumpstarted his lifelong fascination with the book. During his doctoral work, he taught Greek at EDS (1971–1975). He then became an assistant professor at Seabury-Western Theological Seminary in Evanston, Illinois, in 1979. He taught there until 1999, while also being elevated first to associate professor then to full professor. In 1999, he became Professor of Classical and Near Eastern Studies at the University of Minnesota where he worked until he resigned in 2001.[5] He continued to serve as an Episcopal priest until 2003. He published as a member of the Westar Institute until the time of his death from leukemia on May 20, 2017.

Pervo took to heart the advice "to be skeptical about 'assured results.'"[6] He never met an opinion about Acts he did not question. If Acts was considered a history, he would challenge the genre.[7] If Acts was considered written in the late first century, he would challenge the dating.[8] If Luke–Acts was considered a unified work, he would challenge that unity.[9] If Acts was historically considered a Lukan work, he would challenge that historical attribution.[10] He did not undertake such activities to be difficult but merely wanted his work to be data-driven, historically nestled, literarily situated, and intellectually satisfying. His work in the Lukan corpus should make Luke and Acts more accessible and less tangled to the

3. See the bibliography of his works in the *Festschrift* dedicated to him by Harold W. Attridge, Dennis R. MacDonald, and Clare K. Rothschild, eds., *Delightful Acts: New Essays in Canonical and Noncanonical Acts*, WUNT 391 (Tübingen: Mohr Siebeck, 2017), 247–72.
4. Later published as Richard I. Pervo, *Profit with Delight: The Literary Genre of the Acts of the Apostles* (Philadelphia: Fortress, 1987).
5. Pervo pled guilty to one count of distribution and five counts of possessing child pornography. See Margaret Zack, "Professor Pleads Guilty to Child Porn Charges," *Star Tribune*, Minneapolis, MN (May 31, 2001). In no way do the editors of this volume condone, dismiss, or even wish to disregard the behavior of Pervo. This volume collects the work of those who contributed to the growing body of knowledge about Luke–Acts, and Pervo has brought up issues with which all further scholars must interact, even if the person behind those ideas committed reprehensible acts.
6. Pervo, *Profit with Delight*, xi. He notes this advice came in cumulative fashion from various professors.
7. The main thesis of *Profit with Delight* posits a different genre for Acts than history, though this stance seemed to have softened later according to Richard I. Pervo, *Acts*, Hermeneia (Minneapolis: Fortress, 2009). 15.
8. Richard I. Pervo, *Dating Acts: Between the Evangelists and the Apologists* (Santa Rosa, CA: Polebridge, 2006).
9. Mikeal C. Parsons and Richard I. Pervo, *Rethinking the Unity of Luke and Acts* (Minneapolis: Fortress, 1993).
10. Richard I. Pervo, "When in Rome: The Authorship of Acts in the Late Second Century," *Biblical Research* (2015): 15–32.

common layperson.[11] He wrote about who Paul was both as a historical person and as he was framed by others.[12] Pervo wanted to answer the basic questions of who, what, when, where, and why for the book of Acts; the "how" questions he essentially left to others, as will be discussed below.

THE GENRE OF ACTS

Pervo began by accepting the idea that Acts was the second volume of Luke–Acts. What this specifically means he dealt with later in his career. He thought the question of genre, or "what is Acts?" would help connect the New Testament work to the surrounding culture of first-century readers by comparing it to synchronic works.[13] In order to find parallels, Pervo dissected the style with which Luke composed Acts. He did this by noting instances of Lukan repetitions with variation. Luke repeats stories of persecution, arrests, and trials. Each of these various types of tropes has enough variance in form, ordering, and details that instead of losing the reader, they tend to heighten the tension and build toward a climax.[14] For Pervo, this serves to draft the outline of a pattern that points to Acts being a written form of entertainment.

Entertainment as an end in itself within the Bible strikes a discordant note in many readers. The Bible should contain serious theological works or important moments of history. Yet John contains moments of humor,[15] Mark depicts moments of absurdity,[16] Paul insults his readers and opponents,[17] so why be surprised that Acts is popular literature?

---

11. See the preface to Richard I. Pervo, *The Mystery of Acts: Unraveling its Story* (Santa Rosa, CA: Polebridge, 2008), vii–ix. He wrote this book specifically to take all the jargon and technical issues out of dealing with Acts so that, according to him, the logical inconsistencies of story, place, and history would be smoothed for the typical reader.

12. Richard I. Pervo, *Luke's Story of Paul* (Minneapolis: Fortress, 1990) and Pervo, *The Making of Paul: Constructions of the Apostle in Early Christianity* (Minneapolis: Fortress, 2010).

13. Per his explanation in Pervo, *Profit with Delight*, xii.

14. E.g., "Luke has transformed a potentially depressing account of Paul's incarceration into a narrative of high suspense and broad appeal." Pervo, *Profit with Delight*, 48.

15. E.g. the definition of irony in John given by R. Alan Culpepper, *Anatomy of the Fourth Gospel: A Study in Literary Design* (Philadelphia: Fortress, 1983; rev. ed., 1987), 166–67. Cf. R. Alan Culpepper, "Reading Johannine Irony," in *Exploring the Gospel of John: In Honor of D. Moody Smith*, eds. R. Alan Culpepper and Clifton Black (Louisville: Westminster/John Knox, 1996), 193–207.

16. Specifically, one can look at Mark 14:15–52. The options laid out in the commentaries show how strange this episode appears to modern eyes. E.g. Craig A. Evans, *Mark 8:27–16:20*, WBC 34B (Nashville: Thomas Nelson, 2001), 427–29 and R. T. France, *The Gospel of Mark*, NIGTC (Grand Rapids: Eerdmans, 2002), 595–97.

17. Paul labels the Galatians as foolish (Gal. 3:1) and wishes his enemies would castrate themselves (Gal. 5:12).

After all, the book contains "arrests and escapes, stonings and beat-
ings, trials and riots, travel to various places, and as a grand finale, a
shipwreck."[18] This only begins the quest for the genre of Acts, as these
episodes clearly delineate a different content and structure from the
Gospel of Luke. Even if one were to argue for a close unity of Luke's
two putative works—based on grammar, syntax, writing style, and the
like—one can hardly call the genres comparable. While Luke's Gospel
follows the life of Jesus from birth to death, focusing mostly on his
journey toward his death and the week of his death, Acts does not have
a central character around which the entire narrative revolves.[19]

The differences between the Third Gospel and Acts force the reader
to consider what Acts could be. Though some scholars claim Acts
continues the biographic genre from Luke, this hardly seems plausible since Acts does not focus on a single character throughout.[20] The
Gospel is a biography of a "popular type" that can be called "a story
of Jesus comparable to other ancient lives."[21] At the same time, one
can argue that both Luke and Acts seem to follow a biblical pattern of
historical reference, such that the lives of Jesus, Peter, and Paul model
those of Elijah, Elisha, and other Old Testament figures.[22] If this
adheres, then Acts moves beyond historiography and into apologetics.
This understanding of Acts, championed by such authors as Gregory
Sterling,[23] begins to point toward Acts having comparable features
of popular level literature. Combine this with the work of Eckhard
Plümacher,[24] arguing that Acts exhibits the traits of a monograph, and
a clearer picture begins to form.

---

18. Pervo, *Profit with Delight*, 12.
19. Though Pervo does seem to see Acts as about Paul and Peter thus functions as only a "prop" used
    by Luke to transition from Jesus to Paul. See his description of the relationship between Luke's
    characterization of Peter and Paul in *Dating Acts*, 59–61, 91–95.
20. However, see the idea of "double biography" in, among others, Sean A. Adams, *The Genre of Acts
    and Collected Biography*, SNTSMS 156 (Cambridge: Cambridge University Press, 2013), and
    Walter Berschin, "Biography: Late Antiquity," *BrillPauly* 2:653–55.
21. Richard I. Pervo, *The Gospel of Luke*, The Scholars Bible (Salem, OR: Polebridge, 2014), 1. That
    the Gospels are indeed biographies written as those of their time is no longer controversial since
    Richard A. Burridge, *What Are the Gospels? A Comparison with Graeco-Roman Biography*, SNTSMS
    70 (Cambridge: Cambridge University Press, 1992), even if not all scholars are convinced.
22. Pervo claims Luke has a "'Deuteronomic' viewpoint" (*Acts*, 15).
23. Gregory Sterling, *Historiography and Self-Definition: Josephos, Luke–Acts and Apologetic
    Historiography*, NovTSup 64 (Leiden: Brill, 1992).
24. Eckhard Plümacher, "Cicero und Lukas: Bemerkungen zu Stil und Zweck der historische
    Monographie," in *The Unity of Luke–Acts*, ed. Joseph Verheyden, BETL 92 (Leuven: Leuven
    University Press, 1999), 759–75.

What, however, is meant by the term "entertainment"? One can just as easily be entertained by a scholarly essay as a Monty Python skit. In this case, however, entertainment refers to "the kind of humor most likely to appear in popular literature,"[25] and includes various forms. Pervo lists and describes irony, burlesque and "rowdy" episodes, cleverness and wit, pathos, colorful scenes, exotica, forms of revelation, oratory, and life in high society. Each of these criteria comes with a specific idea, though with a large enough understanding that some episodes can fit into more than one category. Pervo gives some examples from Greco-Roman literature and then shows how these have parallel accounts in different parts of Acts. For example, citing Helidorus 8.7 as an example of irony (a poisoner being poisoned),[26] he then goes on to note that Elymas being struck blind in Acts 13:11 represents irony since he was supposed to keep the proconsul from being fooled. Hence the one to protect from blindness (being fooled) is himself struck blind (for being a fool).[27] In the same way, Acts 19:21–41 demonstrates a rowdy episode, Eutychus in 20:7–12 shows humor, and pathos occurs throughout Paul's "farewell journey."[28] The summaries of 2:44–45 and 4:32–35 are paired with descriptions of the Essenes by Josephus to demonstrate utopian ideas, the mention of Ethiopia is coupled with the *Alexander Romance* 3.18–24 to demonstrate the appeal of exotica, while the significance of speeches is obvious throughout the book. The glimpses into high society occur in certain characters throughout, notably in Felix, Festus, centurions, those connected to Herod, and other rich and powerful people.

In seeing these various characteristics of popular novels appear in Acts, Pervo argues that Acts itself must then be a type of entertainment. A quick word of caution here, however, as entertainment is neither a genre itself nor a mark of discrediting other genres. One can read a history textbook and be bored or delighted, depending on how it is written and the emphases the author chooses. The most likely ancient parallel, it follows, should be that of novels.

---

25. Pervo, *Profit with Delight*, 59. He is not describing entertainment per se, rather directly describing the two types of humor listed by Cicero (essentially coarse and refined) and mentioning that the former fits within the popular sphere consumed by most people (*mobile vulgus*), and thus fits the idea of common entertainment.
26. Pervo, *Profit with Delight*, 160n16.
27. Pervo, *Profit with Delight*, 59–60.
28. This is the title that Pervo gives to it, *Profit with Delight*, 67.

The final chapter of *Profit with Delight* gives away the game: "Historical Novels." Pervo spends time looking at pagan, Jewish, and Christian novels to see how they line up with Acts. Using the taxonomy of entertainment previously introduced, Pervo digs into various romantic novels from the Greco-Roman world. Taking Xenophon's *Cyropaideia* as a starting point, he notes how instructive and useful this novel was found by various authors and statesmen.[29] He then examines Jewish and Christian novels to see how those fit his argument. It is in the latter that the most useful comparisons arrive, using apocryphal acts such as the *Acts of John*, *Acts of Andrew*, and of course the *Acts of Paul*. It then leads to the conclusion by Pervo that Acts is a historical novel.

This conclusion, however, comes with various accompanying addendums. Though the term "novel" brings to mind concocted plotlines and fictional events, the "historical" tag admits the author intentionally links his work to historical occurrences. The truth or validity of the work does not rest on the generic label since the author need only report events in a specific (in this case entertaining) way to encompass both aspects of the "historical novel" type. Pervo's take from this, however, is to question Luke's theological motives, wondering if his theology fits the current day, and to chastise the author for "activity at least partly frivolous" and "not always tell[ing] the truth."[30] Pervo's closing lines best explain how he understands Luke as an author after coming to this conclusion. "Had Luke pursued different ideals we might have a far clearer grasp of primitive Christian history. . . . As a historian he leaves much to be desired. What he did have were vision and the means to express it."[31]

THE DATE OF THE WRITING OF ACTS

Upon concluding that Acts follows the genre of historical novel from around the first century, Pervo decided to engage the question of when Acts was written. Though originally uncertain about how to trace the use

---

29. E.g. Cicero, *Letter to Quintus* 1.1.23, Diogenes Laertius 6.16 about Heracles, and some "histories" about Alexander. Cf. Pervo, *Profit with Delight*, 115–16, and 177nn1, 4.
30. *Profit with Delight*, 137–38, quotations coming from 138. Pervo does seem to slightly contradict himself here as he speaks both of Luke writing history and of Luke lying. This would seem to fit the idea of propaganda. This discrepancy will be explored more fully below.
31. Pervo, *Profit with Delight*, 138.

of sources,[32] he began to look at what sources could possibly have been used in authoring Acts.[33] From the start, he acknowledges the burden of proof rests fully on his proposal of a later date, since the scholarly consensus of a date for Acts settled down to around AD 80–90.[34] In addition, his purpose is not to propose a new date for the sake of being novel, rather he wants to show why the dating has significance.[35]

Methodologically, Pervo moves slowly and carefully in examining evidence to rule out ranges of dates. He uses quotations, allusions, and echoes of Acts in other literature to consider an end date and looks for quotations, allusions, and echoes in Acts to set an opening date. Realizing an end date is easier and less controversial, Pervo starts by setting a hard end date, a *terminus ad quem*, of AD 175–180 based upon Irenaeus, Tertullian, and Clement quoting from and using Acts.[36] Due to the way the apocryphal Acts used the canonical version, the appearance of Luke in Marcion's canon, and Justin Martyr's apparent echoes of Acts 1:8 in *1 Apology* 50.12,[37] the latest date becomes pushed down to AD 150 and, ultimately, most likely around 130.[38] Now that this becomes a firm *terminus*, the question as to the earliest date, *terminus a quo*, becomes the focus of much of the rest of *Dating Acts*.[39]

This begins the hunt for sources for and in Acts. Pervo tackles the most obvious sources first: the Septuagint and the Gospels. That Luke used the Septuagint in authoring Acts comes as no surprise, so the question is not the activity of the use but the style of that use, since the specific methodological approaches and stylistic choices

---

32. See his comments in Pervo, *Profit with Delight*, 136. There was never a question as to whether Acts was composed with sources, but only what sources those might be and how they were used. For example, Pervo translates παρηκολουθηκότι as "researching" in Luke 1:3 (*Gospel of Luke*, 14–15).
33. Pervo, *Dating Acts*, viii.
34. Pervo, *Dating Acts*, vii. Craig S. Keener, *Acts: An Exegetical Commentary*, 4 vols. (Grand Rapids: Baker, 2012–2015), 1:383, widens the window to between 64 and 90. The original assessment by Pervo is also contradicted by Pervo's own count later in *Dating Acts*, 359–63, as he lists the most scholars adhering to a 70–80 range as opposed to other ranges.
35. Pervo, *Dating Acts*, vii. He states, "Formally, this monograph is about the date of the book of Acts. . . . The subject of this book is the *significance* of the date of Acts" (emphasis original). This chapter, however, will focus only on the dating itself and not the significance, as the conclusion reached by Pervo holds enough significance in itself.
36. As Pervo notes (*Dating Acts*, 15), there exists no debate about this dating.
37. Following Ernst Haenchen, *The Acts of the Apostles*, eds. and trans. R. McL. Wilson, et al. (Philadelphia: Westminster, 1971), 8.
38. Pervo, *Dating Acts*, 26.
39. Pervo, *Dating Acts*, 26. Pervo states it as the purpose of "the rest of the book," but he deviates from this stated purpose from time to time looking at some other issues and later argues about the significance of the dating.

could shed light on what type of influences were active when Luke wrote.[40] Pervo notes that Luke appropriates language, style, and even episodic content from the LXX. The patterning in Luke and Acts of Jesus and/or Paul recreating specific Old Testament events, or even superseding them, fits the "possibility of invention" of some of these stories to help the theological aims of Luke.[41] Aside from the Old Testament typology that stems from the LXX, some stories are retellings of accounts from the Gospel of Mark. For example, the shadow of Peter and the clothing of Paul healing those nearby in Acts parallel Mark 6:55–56, especially how it was the power of the prophet and not the faith of the person that brought healing.[42] Numerous other tropes from Mark appear in some form in Luke and then become reimagined in Acts. Pervo points to certain exorcisms in Mark having didactic and temporal parallels in Acts, while other themes have thematic parallels.[43] That Mark functioned as a source for Acts comes as no surprise since the challenged consensus of scholarship is that the Second Gospel was a source for Luke, which most likely came before Acts anyway.

The early church posited Luke as the author of Acts, and as he was a companion of Paul, it would only be logical for Acts to depend in some part upon Paul as an oral source and his letters as a written source. Critical scholarship, however, has considered the timeline of Acts and the historical episodes within the Pauline epistles to be generally at odds. For example, correlating the visits of Paul to Jerusalem in Acts with the visits mentioned in Galatians causes numerous chronological

---

40. A keen observation that not many scholars have followed since. Pervo points to the work of W. K. L. Clarke, "The Use of the LXX in Acts," in *The Beginnings of Christianity, Part 1: The Acts of the Apostles*, eds. F. J. Foakes Jackson and Kirsopp Lake, 5 vols. (London: Macmillan, 1920–1933), 2:66–105 and T. L. Brodie, "Greco-Roman Imitation of Texts as a Partial Guide to Luke's Use of Sources," in *Luke Acts: A New Perspective from the Society of Biblical Literature Seminar*, ed. Charles H. Talbert (New York: Crossroad, 1984), 17–46.

41. Pervo, *Dating Acts*, 31–32.

42. See especially Robert H. Stein, *Mark*, BECNT (Grand Rapids: Baker, 2008), 332. Pervo notes the parallel in form but not the parallel in terms of power versus faith. See *Dating Acts*, 38. A Lukan parallel that would strengthen his case might be Luke 8:44, though that does come from a faith vantage point. Cf. Darrell L. Bock, *Acts*, BECNT (Grand Rapids: Baker, 2007), 232 and Eckhard J. Schnabel, *Acts*, ZECNT (Grand Rapids: Zondervan, 2012), 293. Joseph A. Fitzmyer (*The Acts of the Apostles*, AB 31 [New York: Doubleday, 1997], 329) calls the episode with Peter's shadow "strange" but "similar" to Paul's clothing bringing about healing without looking beyond those.

43. Pervo, *Dating Acts*, 38–45, esp. 42–44. This section of the chapter has multiple tables showing various connections, allusions, and parallels.

and logical problems.[44] The major commentaries on Acts assume with little to no argument that Luke either did not know or did not use Paul's letters when writing.[45] Pervo not only disagrees with the scholarly consensus, he actively pokes fun at it arguing that true scrutiny of this hypothesis "reveals the utter risibility of any contention that the author of Acts was unaware of Paul's epistolary creations; indeed, it renders that claim unworthy of serious scholarly consideration."[46]

Part of Pervo's contention rises from a mistake he believes many scholars make in not noting genre differences. Paul wrote occasional letters to specific audiences to address momentary issues. Luke wrote a "history of Paul" (when dealing with the historical figure of Paul unlike his treatment of Paul in other parts of Acts) that has to do with his actions and speaking. Adding to this, Luke's purpose in telling Paul's story was about Luke's own goals. As Pervo tells it, Luke did not use sources "to discover 'what actually happened,' but as aids in imposing his own construction of the past."[47] The Paul of Acts "does not write; he visits."[48] It is in recognizing the purpose of Acts that one can see Luke may have used the letters not as historical research, but as jumping off points for his own agenda. Just as Luke rewrote Mark, so could Luke rewrite Paul.[49]

The initial case for Acts relying upon the letters comes from the theology exhibited in various episodes. Acts 13 climaxes with Paul acknowledging the defectiveness of the law toward freeing humanity

---

44. E.g. see the brief description in Richard N. Longenecker, *Galatians*, WBC 41 (Nashville: Thomas Nelson, 1990), lxxiii–lxxxiii.

45. Taking C. K. Barrett (*A Critical and Exegetical Commentary on the Acts of the Apostles*, 2 vols., ICC [New York: T&T Clark, 1994–1998], 1:51–52) as representative, he simply asserts that Luke "seems not to have used the epistles." Fitzmyer (*Acts*, 133) contends that Luke could not have known the letters, since "we would scarcely encounter the discrepancies commentators often point out today." While a majority view, this certainly is not unanimous. See the brief rejoinder and apologetic in Keener, *Acts*, 1:227.

46. Pervo, *Dating Acts*, 52.

47. Pervo, *Dating Acts*, 52. Pervo notes that this does not change the consensus about Luke's purpose, only his methods.

48. Pervo, *Dating Acts*, 53. Pervo takes this nonepistolary Paul too far when he states that Paul accompanies those who take the letters after Acts 15, and so Luke's Paul is "scarcely allowed to touch" a letter (54).

49. The analogy Pervo gives considers the later letters attributed to Paul as "revised" Paul, and so Luke is doing the same thing in terms of reshaping and refocusing the historical Paul. See especially *Dating Acts*, 55–56. For a complementary though more complex recounting, see Daniel Marguerat, "L'image de Paul dans les Actes des Apôtres," in *Les Actes des Apôtres: Histoire, récit, theologie; XXᵉ congrès de l'Association catholique française pour l'étude de le Bible (Angers 2003)*, ed. M. Berder, LD 199 (Paris: Cerf, 2005), 121–54.

from all sins whereas God's grace through Jesus covers all sins and all
who believe.[50] If the law then is unable to save and impossible to fulfill,
it lends itself to a Gentile view of the law. Justification in Lukan terms
comes from humility and belief (putting Acts 13:38–39 together
with Luke 18:13–14), a less robust understanding than Paul's typical
justification by faith tenet, but not opposed to it. Luke's Paul, Luke's
Jesus, and Luke's Peter (Acts 15:7–11) all proclaim the same gospel:
that conversion comes about due to God's work in faith. Though this
conveys less stringently the doctrine Paul strongly emphasizes, it does
in fact convey it.[51] The theology of Acts builds on the theology of Paul
and assumes it as settled; it does not need to be further substantiated,
only amended.

Pervo strengthens his argument by compiling a list of numerous
passages from Paul that Acts either parallels closely or echoes. The
strongest of these, 2 Corinthians 11:32–33 with Acts 9:23–25, has
both allusion and direct lexical connection.[52] Pervo demonstrates
other parallels between Acts and other Pauline works, specifically 1
and 2 Corinthians and Romans. Galatians then becomes the biggest
question mark for scholars, and the largest mine for Pervo's cumulative case approach. He argues that for no fewer than twenty-five
possible times Acts relies upon or echoes Galatians, with numerous
lexical and thematic connections. Of course, he argues that Luke does
not preserve Paul's meaning in Galatians, often using the epistle to
further his own writing aims and possibly subverting Paul's.[53] The largest conundrum facing those who desire to understand the connection
between Acts and Galatians revolves around the relationship between
Acts 15 and Galatians 2. While both have the same major players,
location, main controversy, and resolution, the details differ drasti-
cally. Galatians recounts a heated confrontation that cut to the heart of
Christianity's character. Acts describes a group of disparate viewpoints

---

50. A disputed view of the law, to be sure. Schnabel (*Acts*, 584) notes that the issue likely focused on
the completion of forgiveness (once for all) rather than the extent of the forgiveness (which sins are
covered). Cf. the discussions in Sigurd Grindheim, "Luke, Paul, and the Law," *NovT* 56 (2014):
335–58; and Craig L. Blomberg, *A New Testament Theology* (Waco, TX: Baylor University Press,
2018), 434–41.

51. Pervo considers this more Deutero-Pauline than Pauline (*Dating Acts*, 59–60). Cf. Marguerat,
"L'image de Paul," who sees Paul split among three different axes: Lukan Paul, Paul of the authentic
letters, and Deutero-Paul.

52. Pervo, *Dating Acts*, 60. Note table 4.1a to see the connections clearly laid out.

53. Pervo, *Dating Acts*, 74. Pervo believes Luke reinvents Pauline history so that Acts shows more unity
than Galatians does, which fits within the major purposes of writing Acts.

amicably working toward a mutually agreeable conclusion. Pervo eloquently describes this: "Luke transformed the dross of Galatians 2 into the gold of Acts 15."[54] Once one strains out the Lukan material, Galatians 2 fits the skeleton of the remaining story without needing to posit an Antiochene source or another tradition upon which Luke drew.[55] Further, the episodes in Acts that describe Paul's work that are vaguest occur in time periods about which Galatians is silent. Much like Bauckham's argument that John knew Mark as evidenced by intentional shifts in John's text that complement material in the First Gospel,[56] so Pervo argues that Luke knew Galatians inasmuch as Acts provides less detail than corresponding portions of Galatians where the text jumps years.[57] Acts 20:17–35 provides numerous parallels to Pauline texts, with connections to, in the order of Paul's speech, 1 Thessalonians, Philippians, Ephesians, Romans, 2 Corinthians, 1 Corinthians, Galatians, and Colossians, with numerous occurrences of most of these.[58]

Finally, Pervo refutes arguments from silence.[59] Many critics claim Luke did not know Paul's letters since he fails to record any strife within early Christianity,[60] yet Paul typically writes to handle controversies within his churches. Contrary to this point of view, Acts 15 relays a major controversy yet minimizes the conflict and exaggerates the unity of the early movement. In this, Luke recounted the largest problem such that, fitting with his purpose of presenting the Way in the best possible light, all other internal disputes would be ignored. Critics assert Luke bypasses the issue of the collection for Jerusalem yet Acts 24:17 specifically mentions it! Luke must have had knowledge of

54. Pervo, *Dating Acts*, 87. Pervo combines his argument on the Jerusalem council with that of the collection, but the contrasting tables and lines of argument he utilizes work better separately, and his discussion and writing about the Jerusalem council is the stronger of the two, which determined the focu~ 'iere.
55. Pervo (*Dating Acts*, 89) points to Martin Dibelius, *Studies in the Acts of the Ap ..es*, ed. Heinrich Greeven, trans. Margaret Ling and Paul Schubert (London: SCM, 1956), 93–101, esp. 99.
56. Richard Bauckham, "John for Readers of Mark," in *The Gospels for All Christians: Rethinking the Gospel Audiences*, ed. Richard Bauckham (Grand Rapids: Eerdmans, 1998), 147–71.
57. Pervo, *Dating Acts*, 96–100. He relies heavily on the work of Anthony J. Blasi (whom he calls Blassi), *Making Charisma: The Social Construct of Paul's Public Image* (New Brunswick, NJ: Transaction Publishers, 1991).
58. Pervo, *Dating Acts*, 111–31. Pervo even notes parallels to the Pastoral Epistles in some content. This section of *Dating Acts* displays some of the best data gathering, analysis, and argumentation in the book.
59. Though this summarizes a lot of his previous comments in the chapter, for this paragraph see the brief thoughts in Pervo, *Dating Acts*, 134.
60. Pervo only argues against this from a Pauline perspective. Otherwise one would expect Acts 5, including Ananias and Sapphira, to be mentioned, along with picking the seven in Acts 6.

it and yet chose to not include it throughout his narrative. Luke also never describes how controversial Paul is among the believers. This fits within the framework of the first objection, as Acts does not put internal church matters on display except for the Jerusalem council. These different pieces of evidence pooled together point toward the author of Acts knowing of and, in some part, using a collection of Paul's letters for constructing his book.

Josephus appears as the next possible source for moving the *terminus a quo* of Acts. This would push the date back to AD 95 at minimum. Though not necessarily a popular theory, the possibility that Luke used Josephus had proponents in the nineteenth and twentieth centuries, such as Francis Crawford Burkitt, Max Krenkel, Morton Scott Enslin, and Joseph Klausner, to name a few.[61] Based on the work of Krenkel and Burkitt, Pervo notes the major argument against Luke using Josephus focuses on how Luke contradicts or gets wrong much of what Josephus wrote. Pervo pushes back on this idea noting that Luke did not use Paul's letters as a scholar or typical historian would, so why the same assumption that Luke would faithfully and meticulously use everything Josephus produced? If Luke functions as an entertainer and purveyor of story rather than a historian, the assumption that Luke would not deviate from a source comes up as invalid and no longer a useful criterion for consideration if Luke used a specific writing. Pervo notes that the Tübingen school pushed such a specific understanding of how biblical authors were supposed to write, so that any deviation from this pattern caused skepticism about the appearance of the source at all.[62] Rather than the use of Judas of Galilee and Theudas in Acts 5:36–37 showing no connection to Josephus, Pervo argues that it shows rather a misuse of *Ant.* 20:97–102 instead.[63] This sets the pattern for Luke's reading and reliance on Josephus: instead of quoting him and using his works as a blueprint or timeline, Luke takes the words of Josephus and places them whenever and however he

---

61. See Pervo, *Dating Acts*, 149–50, 409nn4–5.
62. Pervo, *Dating Acts*, 150–51. Tongue firmly in cheek, Pervo adds that biblical authors "were to follow this practice for the convenience of modern scholars, who were thereby able to identify and isolate those sources with relative confidence and ease." Pervo's writing consistently pokes fun at what he considers obviously unrealistic expectations from certain scholars.
63. The argument that more than one Theudas could have led a revolt comes essentially to a standstill as both Pervo (*Dating Acts*, 411n35) and his detractors (e.g. Schnabel, *Acts*, 316) use the same set of data to argue opposing conclusions. Namely, there are multiple people named Theudas, yet it is not a common name. Pervo leans on the "not common" and his detractors lean on "multiple people."

wants within his narrative world.[64] This allows Luke creative freedom to shape his story according to his needs while retaining historical points of contact with the surrounding world.

The last major push in setting a date for Acts comes from how the book appears in and is used by the Apostolic Fathers.[65] Just under a third of *Dating Acts* wrestles with the data found in the various extant manuscripts, records, and writings from the Fathers or about the Fathers.[66] The first step in this process comes from recognizing that the more primitive or more developed an idea becomes does not imply the chronology of that idea follows. Acts was written before the *Acts of Paul* even though the latter carries a more primitive theology.[67] However, succession and anachronism do show chronological development. For example, Paul handing off leadership to the presbyters of Ephesus shows a notion of church government that did not exist at that time, pushing the writing of Acts into a later period.[68] This directly ties in with the Pastoral Epistles' view of the developing church structure, also pushing back the date. In other passages, Luke changes the language of Jesus's words from "general exhortations . . . into paradigms of leadership," which seem to be from the culture of "the late Deutero-Pauline world, from the Pastoral Epistles and Polycarp."[69] This type of development and connection forms the heart of Pervo's argument for the rest of the book.

Certain themes in the Lukan writings rely on the development of ideas or formulas in the Apostolic Fathers. The concept of giving comes across in both of Luke's books as essential to following Christ.

64. See Pervo, *Dating Acts*, 198. He concludes by speaking of Luke using "Josephus as inspiration very much as he used the LXX."
65. Pervo seems to define this group as Ignatius of Antioch, *Barnabas*, Polycarp, *Didache*, *Hermas*, and *1–2 Clement* per his explanation in *Dating Acts*, 202. However, this also seems to include the Deutero-Pauline works, the Pastoral Epistles, and some postbiblical authors not previously listed. This designation in the long run does not have a firm group in mind, and the actual dates involved are not specified. On the one hand, Pervo wants to focus on non-biblical writings, while on the other hand continually dropping references about the Deutero-Pauline (including the Pastoral Epistles) ethos or theological slant (such as being against women in ministerial leadership).
66. Of the 346 pages of main text in Pervo, *Dating Acts*, 108 pages deal with these Fathers, an astonishing 31%.
67. Pervo, *Dating Acts*, 201–202. He compares the "primitive" vs. advanced schema to his own filing system, which he then amends to "primeval" with his typical humor (201).
68. This claim seems problematic, as Luke slides between presbyter and episkopos for his designations of the group, which contradicts this hierarchy upon which Pervo bases his argument. See Fitzmyer, *Acts*, 675–76 and 679.
69. Pervo, *Dating Acts*, 225.

It forms a core part of the teaching of Jesus in Luke (e.g. 6:34–38) and it carries significance in multiple and varied instances in Acts (e.g. 5:1–11 and 20:35). Pervo argues that the introductory formula used by Paul in Acts 20:35 directly parallels *1 Clement* 13:1–2 and 46:7.[70] While Pervo admits that traditionally the dependence has been considered in the other direction, he notes the "rarity of the Christian use of the proverb . . . and the close similarity of the quotation formula"[71] point toward Acts using *1 Clement*. In a similar fashion, Luke changes the immediate and visceral urgency of Mark's Gospel and the spiritual teaching of Matthew's Gospel into a focus on sustained Christian living. In other words, Luke softens the eschatological view of the first two Gospels into an understanding of how to live according to the principles laid out by Jesus and the apostles. The theological world of *1 Clement*, the Pastorals, and the Deutero-Pauline works also coheres with Luke–Acts in nuances of language. Righteousness loses the pure Pauline understanding and progresses to include behavior, salvation comes from faith and hospitality, and holiness becomes a dominant virtue.[72] Pervo continues to find other parallels in theological thought between Acts and the Apostolic Fathers beyond the examples cited.

Pervo turns from more concrete examples of the development from Pauline thought to post-Pauline thought to other, less substantial data. Nonetheless, Pervo believes that a cumulative case approach to vocabulary, phrases, and intellectual connections will help lend weight to his thesis, where each piece of data stands alone such that one clue falsified does not negate the entire picture. His intention with this investigation is to show a trajectory in the evidence, even if some of it does not convince. Approximately thirty pages of the text move through various words or roots to discuss the general usage of each as they appear in Luke–Acts as opposed to biblical and nonbiblical writings.[73] *Metanoia* stands as a typical, if longer, entry in this list.[74]

---

70. See the Greek laid out in parallel columns in the helpful Table 6.7 in Pervo, *Dating Acts*, 229.
71. Pervo, *Dating Acts*, 229.
72. See the full discussion, including applicable tables showing parallel Greek constructions, in Pervo, *Dating Acts*, 231–39. That *1 Clement* pushes Paul's theology in a different direction is not surprising or controversial, yet Joshua Jipp (*Saved by Faith and Hospitality* [Grand Rapids: Eerdmans, 2017]) argues for these meanings to be normative in the New Testament, just misunderstood by modern Christianity.
73. Pervo, *Dating Acts*, 260–91.
74. Pervo includes the word as both μετάνοια and *metanoia* in the text due to it having a "popular philosophical tradition." See Pervo, *Dating Acts*, 275.

Pointing to a previous section of his work, Pervo continues with the idea that Acts and *1 Clement* both turn the study into an ethical issue. While sins in the earlier writings can be forgiven by turning to Jesus, those after the beginning of the church enter into a more complex matrix, since postbaptismal sin becomes theologically problematic. This allows Luke and Acts "to represent a compromise approach"[75] between the position of early Christianity and more developed theological considerations. This type of comparison persists in Pervo's work, with terms from Luke and Acts placed next to the same terms in such books as the Deutero-Pauline works, Hebrews, 1 and 2 Peter, and then Ignatius, the *Didache, Hermas*, the Pastorals, and *1 Clement*. The cumulative case approach ends with Pervo pointing out possible allusions and parallels in various literature dated AD 125 or later. He looks at the longer ending of Mark, Ephesians, *1 Clement*, and the *Didache* among others before ending with Polycarp, calling the last "a *terminus ante quem* for Acts."[76]

The last piece of the puzzle in determining the date of the writing of Acts comes from looking at smaller data points such as anachronisms in the text, problematic accounts of certain individuals, and theological, social, and legal issues. Anachronisms occur in most writing when there is a distance of time between the events and the recounting. One such anachronism comes from the use of οἱ ἐκ περιτομή in a setting where such a distinction is moot (Acts 10:45 and 11:2).[77] Coupled with the distinctive language in the speeches of Peter, Stephen, and Paul where the speaker clearly separates himself from the ethnicity and connectivity of the Jews by using second person instead of first person in direct address,[78] these two pieces of evidence point toward a later date for Acts. Luke injects the language and disjunction between Judaism and Christianity back into the early church period. In terms of characterization, the apostles become idealized heroes as much in Acts as in second-century Christian literature. Numerous scholars have made the comparison between the descriptions in Acts and those of *1 Clement* with respect to Peter and Paul, which romanticizes and idealizes them.[79]

---

75. Pervo, *Dating Acts*, 274.
76. Pervo, *Dating Acts*, 305.
77. Pervo, *Dating Acts*, 310.
78. Pervo says the three men "speak of 'your forebears' as if they were not themselves Jews (e.g. Acts 3:25; 7:52; 28:25)" in *Dating Acts*, 310.
79. Frustratingly, Pervo does little to back this assertion, only pointing to a previous part of his work which also cites few other scholars. See Pervo, *Dating Acts*, 62, 319, and 451n73.

Finally, Pervo ends this section of evidence with theological reflections. He notes that the earlier texts of the New Testament focus on realized eschatology rather than on what he calls "individualized eschatology," such that Paul answers questions about the significance of salvation for now without addressing the question of what happens to the individual upon death.[80] *Hermas* and *1 Clement* lean away from daily living and point toward a glorious future in heaven with those who went before. Pervo sees direct parallels in language and tone in Acts 1:25 and Luke 12:16–20; 16:19–31.[81] Legal and social problems also show the same bent, as Acts evinces a later reflection of how the Roman world interacted with Jews and Christians and the conflicts between them. All of these smaller arguments of theology, social issues, anachronisms, and character portraits point toward a late date for Acts.

In bringing his various arguments together, Pervo ends with a *terminus a quo* for Acts of AD 110–120 and a *terminus ad quem* of AD 130.[82] Each step along the path was taken carefully, from forming an initial end point by looking at the use of Acts in Irenaeus and Tertullian to concluding on a final range of dates. Though most scholars disagree with where Pervo's work has taken him in terms of dating, his work still commands respect due to his careful argumentation, his building from multiple streams of data, and how he set aside his own preconceptions in reassessing the dating of Acts.

THE UNITY OF LUKE AND ACTS

While Pervo's scholarly tomes pushed the boundaries in different areas, none so shook the pillars of biblical academia as his combined work with Mikeal Parsons on arguing against the two-volume unity of Luke–Acts.[83] What makes this case different from the previous two, aside from authoring with Parsons, comes from its brevity and focus.

---

80. Pervo, *Dating Acts*, 321–22. This seems to be a common issue in religion of that time. See Ron C. Fay, "Greco-Roman Concepts of Deity," in *Paul's World*, ed. Stanley E. Porter, PAST 3 (Leiden: Brill, 2008), 51–80, here 77.
81. The verbal parallels are minute, but the tonal connections compensate for his argument. See Pervo, *Dating Acts*, 322–23.
82. Pervo, *Dating Acts*, 343.
83. After noting that the scholarly consensus from Cadbury onward linked Luke and Acts together into Luke–Acts, Parsons and Pervo (*Rethinking the Unity of Luke and Acts*, 7) state, "perhaps the time has come to re-open the debate."

The two authors limit the discussion to three basic areas: genre, narrative, and theology.

Setting aside authorial and canonical issues, the authors first tackle the question of genre.[84] The problem the authors see stems from what Pervo had already argued in his dissertation, namely that Acts does not tell the story of a singular person and Luke does not fulfill the conventions of popular literature. The stories follow different trajectories from each other. Luke and Acts have completely different textual histories, with Luke joining the Gospel collection and Acts standing on its own.[85] Various theories regarding a unified genre are named, introduced, then argued against in quick succession, such as monograph, general history, antiquities, and apologetic history among others.[86] In terms of arguing for different genres, the first step in the process comes from noting the different sources of each. Luke combines sayings, parables, miracles, and other typical episodes of a Gospel, whereas Acts shows speeches for different speakers crafted by the same author. Both have a prominent journey motif; for Luke the focus remains on the destination (Jerusalem), while for Acts the focus is on the person journeying. Luke has the destination as the goal, so few details about the trip itself emerge, whereas Acts includes all sorts of different anecdotes.[87] The objection that an author must write within a single genre, even for a two-volume work, does not hold historical merit: numerous authors both ancient and recent have created within varied genres.[88] The final nail in the coffin for generic unity comes from Acts itself,

---

84. Parsons and Pervo, *Rethinking the Unity of Luke and Acts*, 7–9. There is no claim made about authorship, other than to say the same author likely wrote both, and canonical unity is pointless since Luke and Acts have John sitting between them.

85. See Brevard Childs, *The New Testament as Canon: An Introduction* (Philadelphia: Fortress, 1984), 236. A surprising oversight in this argument would be the history of the actual texts: Luke shows the normal variation found within the Gospel genre whereas Acts has a completely different history depending on the text type. Though some still want to push for connection (see David E. Aune, "The Text-Tradition of Luke–Acts," *Bulletin of the Evangelical Theological Society* 7/3 [1964]: 69–72), the evidence does not point toward a unified textual transmission and thus instead early differentiation. See the comments in Andrew F. Gregory and C. Kavin Rowe, eds., *Rethinking the Unity and Reception of Luke and Acts* (Columbia: University of South Carolina Press, 2010), xi. They point out that this missing line of argumentation undercuts the thesis and limited the impact of the book.

86. Parsons and Pervo were not dismissive in their work, rather the flaws for each designation become quickly apparent in the original authors' own work. See *Rethinking the Unity of Luke and Acts*, 29–31 for a solid example.

87. Parsons and Pervo, *Rethinking the Unity of Luke and Acts*, 38.

88. One need only think of the works of Isaac Asimov (science fiction, mystery, physics, biblical criticism, etc.), Shakespeare, John (as putative author of the Fourth Gospel, Revelation, and 1–3 John), or Josephus.

as the opening verses declare the previous volume to be about Jesus (singular, thus biographical) and this volume to be about the apostles (plural, and thus not a biography).[89] So if Luke functions as part 1 and Acts as part 2, Luke could not be a biography (or part of the *bioi* genre) as commonly argued since it would no longer have a single focus as Acts covers a larger group of people.[90]

The closest connection between Luke and Acts comes from the nature of the ongoing story. Luke tells the story of Jesus founding the church and Acts tells the story of the development of the church. This would require unity to be found in the narrative.[91] However, numerous disjunctions appear between the two. The main Lukan speaker within the story, Jesus, has a distinctive voice and method of discourse. He often utilizes stories and parables to make his points. In Acts, the apostles, who spent time with this same Jesus, do not use those same rhetorical tools (though mirroring the miraculous activities).[92] Luke and Acts use parallels differently, such that Jesus traveling toward Jerusalem serves as a setting for his teaching while the journeys of the apostles, especially Paul, heighten excitement of reading the narrative.[93] While Luke and Acts connect with their prologues, other places where overlap should occur (or occur more tightly) have discrepancies, such as the two different ascensions (Luke 24:50–53 and Acts 1:6–11). Though the prologues tie the books together, Luke does not offer any clues to the reader to expect a second volume. The function of narrators within the text also points toward a disunity, as the "we" passages occur only in Acts, and Jesus never places himself within a parable, but Paul tells autobiographical stories. These differences display a varied approach to writing.[94] Discontinuity should not be

---

89. Parsons and Pervo, *Rethinking the Unity of Luke and Acts*, 43. Bock argues that Acts continues the work of Jesus from the Gospel of Luke but does so through the Holy Spirit acting through the apostles. See Bock, *Acts*, 2–3.
90. Parsons and Pervo conclude with, "If the unity of Luke and Acts is not a modern construct, the demand for generic unity very probably is" (*Rethinking the Unity of Luke and Acts*, 44).
91. Seemingly one of the arguments in Robert Tannehill, *The Narrative Unity of Luke–Acts: A Literary Interpretation*, 2 vols. (Philadelphia: Fortress, 1986–1990), 1:xiii.
92. Parsons and Pervo, *Rethinking the Unity of Luke and Acts*, 51. They directly mention Peter when making this point, but Peter's speeches function very differently than the words of Jesus according to Hans F. Bayer, "The Preaching of Peter in Acts," in *Witness to the Gospel: The Theology of Acts*, eds. I. Howard Marshall and David Peterson (Grand Rapids: Eerdmans, 1998), 257–74.
93. This idea comes naturally from Pervo's labeling of Acts as entertainment.
94. This simplifies a more complex argument based on types of narrators both above and within the text. See Parsons and Pervo, *Rethinking the Unity of Luke and Acts*, 49–51 and 65–67 for the more robust argument.

a problem in narrative, as the narrator must always make choices and leave out details to make a story. Luke 1–2 differs greatly from 3–24 and Acts 1–12 differs greatly from 13–28, yet these differences do not mean there is disjunction or new authors for each section. Further, the two books have dissimilar methodology in how discourse functions, pointing to a narrative dissonance.[95]

Theology comes as the final area Parsons and Pervo tackle to make their case against unity. The theology of the Third Gospel has had numerous works devoted to it, with Conzelmann placing it front and center for all of Luke's theology.[96] Finding the theology of the Gospel, however, takes a redaction-critical approach, whereas the theology of Acts comes from assessing the speeches of the characters within the narrative framework used by the author.[97] Few authors have clearly explored the problem of finding the theology of a single author in two opposite ways due to the genres or tools which one can bring to bear.[98] The first volume covers Jesus the person and the second covers Jesus as the message. If Luke–Acts can have a unified theology, it must be found in bridging this divide.[99] Since Luke followed the formula of the other Gospels, Acts would be more fertile ground for divining the true theology of the author. The resurrection as event separates Luke from Acts, and so how Acts defines salvation based upon the resurrection should give rise to the author's theology. The crucifixion and death of Christ seem to hold no special place.[100] Anthropology comes across as one unifying theme across the two volumes such that humankind has redeemable qualities and Jesus functions as the epitome of these qualities.[101] Rather, Christology and anthropology then merge,

---

95. Parsons and Pervo, *Rethinking the Unity of Luke and Acts*, 81. They summarize this argument by saying, "The literary techniques distinguished in Luke and Acts, like the textual connectors, the framing devices, first-person narration, are significant in establishing disunity at the discourse level."
96. Hans Conzelmann, *The Theology of St Luke*, trans. Geoffrey Buswell (repr., Philadelphia: Fortress, 1960). This, however, has changed since Parsons and Pervo wrote. See, e.g., Marshall and Peterson, eds., *Witness to the Gospel*, as an example of Acts taken by itself and an example of Luke and Acts combined in the work of Darrell Bock, *A Theology of Luke and Acts: God's Promised Program, Realized for All Nations*, Biblical Theology of the New Testament (Grand Rapids: Zondervan, 2012).
97. Parsons and Pervo, *Rethinking the Unity of Luke and Acts*, 85.
98. Tannehill, *Narrative Unity*, seems close to seeing this problem in his second volume, but then never follows through.
99. Parsons and Pervo, *Rethinking the Unity of Luke and Acts*, 86–87.
100. Parsons and Pervo, *Rethinking the Unity of Luke and Acts*, 87–88.
101. This argument comes from Luke focusing on the marginalized as people of value, Jesus as a continuance of Adam instead of replacing him, and the utopian idealized version of true community present in both Luke and Acts and how all of this rests upon a Greco-Roman understanding of

making the Gospel superfluous and Acts more significant. "Probes of such themes as eschatology, soteriology, and ethics have not yielded a unified picture."[102]

In taking these three major concepts together (genre, narrative, theology), the disunity of Luke–Acts has been strengthened. Rather than Luke–Acts being an assumption of scholarship, once again this concept needs to be proven. It is in seeing how Luke and Acts stand apart from each other, and how Luke stands with the other Synoptics, that the question becomes reopened to scholarship.

AUTHORSHIP: WHO DECIDED LUKE WROTE ACTS?

The last major area where Pervo sought to question the status quo came in looking at the authorship of Acts. To be specific, Pervo posits the view that Luke the physician was the author of Acts came directly from Irenaeus, and other lines of traditional ascription to Luke trace their origins from this attribution.[103] He follows multiple lines of evidence to come to this conclusion.

The earliest stratum of data concerning Acts does not include authorship, even though it and the Third Gospel were widely accepted works.[104] Acts has less historical connection to Luke than the Third Gospel does. According to Pervo, Luke as author of the Third Gospel occurs early in the manuscript tradition, based upon Gospel prologues appearing in both Latin and Greek.[105] The Muratorian list includes Luke as the author of the Third Gospel and Acts, and does so based on Luke being present at these events. The problem comes in realizing that the "we" passages function as the crux of the argument, which assumes a more complete presence for that narrator than actually happens.[106]

---

culture. See Parsons and Pervo, *Rethinking the Unity of Luke and Acts*, 105–106 for the summary of these issues.
102. Parsons and Pervo, *Rethinking the Unity of Luke and Acts*, 113.
103. Pervo, "When in Rome," 15.
104. Andrew Gregory, *The Reception of Luke and Acts in the Period Before Irenaeus: Looking for Luke in the Second Century*, WUNT 2/169 (Tübingen: Mohr Siebeck, 2003).
105. Pervo, "When in Rome," 19.
106. Pervo, "When in Rome," 22. He continues, "The Muratorian list does not, whatever its date, strengthen the tradition" in terms of being independent.

Irenaeus comes to the forefront and clears the air about Acts. He places Mark and Luke as parallel figures, both functioning as amanuenses for their respective apostles, Peter and Paul. Luke did not write the Gospel of Paul, in that his theological inclinations and Paul's do not harmonize to a great degree.[107] Once Luke has the apostolic authority to write a Gospel, allowing more makes sense.[108] Luke as author of Acts then becomes a logical deduction based upon the available data within the New Testament canon, specifically linking together the "we" passages in Acts with Colossians 4:14 and 2 Timothy 4:10–11. This deduction, however, comes from disputed letters that build off of genuine Pauline letters, so the data is tainted. This can be gleaned from comparing Colossians 4:10–14 with Philemon 23–24. The former expands and clarifies the latter.[109] If Irenaeus includes these details for the purpose of arguing against Marcion, then the idea of Luke writing his two volumes stems from this defense of orthodoxy. While possible that he takes this argument from someone else, the more probable and only extant versions come from Irenaeus.[110]

The last portion of the dispute involves looking at a parallel case, a contemporary account, and problems of narration. First, the Gospel of John functions as a warning sign in that John the apostle as the author can very well be an invention of Irenaeus.[111] This creates an obvious parallel. Second, the *Acts of Paul*, typically dated around AD 175, uses Paul and Acts.[112] In taking the narrative together with the "we" passages in Acts, there is no viable way to understand how the *Acts of Paul*, which mentions Luke multiple times, would fail to

---

107. Pervo ("When in Rome," 24) argues, "Luke favors an exemplarist Christology, rates miracles higher and the death of Jesus lower than does Paul, is familiar with but does not emphasize Paul's theology of justification, and, in general, does not place apocalyptic method at the center of his theology."

108. See Irenaeus, *Haer.* 2.75.

109. Pervo ("When in Rome," 25) uses a table to show the comparison, with the list in Philemon including names with very little description and the list in Colossians containing more specific attributes for each person except Demas and adding a name (Jesus Justus).

110. The other external evidence cited by contrary scholars, Pervo ("When in Rome," 26) contends, does not have proven independent attestation.

111. This is the proposal of Helmut Koester, "Ephesos in Early Christian Literature," in *Ephesos: Metropolis of Asia*, ed. Helmut Koester, HTS 41 (Valley Forge, PA: Trinity, 1995), 119–40.

112. Though disputed, see the positive case made in Richard Bauckham, "The *Acts of Paul* as Sequel to Acts," in *The Book of Acts in its Ancient Literary Setting*, ed. Bruce W. Winter and Andrew D. Clarke, BAFCS 1 (Grand Rapids: Eerdmans, 1993), 105–52. He traces how the extant portions assume a familiarity with parts of Acts and when combined with other data build the possibility that the *Acts of Paul* was written to be the second volume of Acts.

mention his authorship of Acts if known.[113] Either Luke was known to be the author and the *Acts of Paul* ignored or rejected it or else the author did not know of this. The simplest explanation favors the latter. Third, the problem of the levels of narration raises its head. The early church unanimously understood Acts as history written by someone who experienced at least some of the story. At the same time, Acts displays itself at multiple levels: the preface builds the picture of a researcher, but the book then assumes an omniscient narrator.[114] Even if one researched all of these events, the author revised Acts to the point where it no longer has the "voice of an eyewitness"[115] so the "we" misleads rather than leads.

These various strands of evidence, taken together, point to the conclusion that Irenaeus did not get the idea of Luke as author of Acts from any written source before him. Instead, this tradition starts with him. Irenaeus brought together Colossians, 2 Timothy, and his reading of Acts to conclude that Luke wrote Acts even though Luke and Acts circulated separately.

PAUL AS CHARACTER

The various quests for the historical Jesus have led down numerous false paths, reflective surfaces, and biased accounts until scholars attempted to systematize rules which have come under fire themselves. At the same time, the historical Paul, while of a less contested nature, certainly has been the subject of its own scholarship. Instead of tackling the historical Paul, however, Pervo wrote about how Paul appeared as a character in various literary works. Though most scholarship places the Paul of Acts against the Paul of the epistles, Pervo bypasses that issue to see how Paul functions as a character in the canonical Acts, Deutero-Pauline epistles, noncanonical Acts, and noncanonical epistles.[116]

---

113. Pervo, "When in Rome," 28. He summarizes: "Acts of Paul 14 does not allow for Lucan authorship of Acts." He is arguing that the author of the *Acts of Paul* did not know of Luke as author rather than that Luke was not the author, a fine but important distinction.
114. Pervo, "When in Rome," 29–30. He notes that Luke and Acts "present an omniscient narrator who can enter closed rooms, overhear private conversations, read minds, and so forth."
115. Pervo, "When in Rome," 30.
116. For Paul in Acts, see Pervo, *Luke's Story of Paul*, though it is more of a stylized account of Acts than a true character story about Paul. For Paul in the Deutero-Pauline and noncanonical works, see Pervo, *The Making of Paul*.

The Paul of Acts is also the Saul of Acts, and Pervo labors to make them a contiguous character. He tells the story of Saul the persecutor turned Saul the evangelist, who begins by plotting against the church and ends up plotted against because of his expanding the church.[117] Saul leaves on his first missionary journey with Barnabas and the two are assisted by Mark. Paul, his name changing due to the geography, knocks Bar-Jesus blind and announces himself on the stage of Acts through miraculous powers and the conversion of a significant person. The imprint of the Holy Spirit on Paul, so soon after the Spirit poured out on the Gentiles through the preaching of Peter, signifies both Paul's newfound station and his position as the focal point for the unfolding drama of Acts.[118] Paul continues to preach as he travels, including the intentional pattern of visiting synagogues first. His sermons have parallel, though not exactly the same, content as those of Peter. This displays Paul's continuity with the Jerusalem church except that Paul's converts tend to generally be Gentile instead of Jewish.[119] Paul comes across as a heroic figure who withstands numerous attacks, privations, disasters, and plots.[120] He becomes increasingly independent, such that those no longer part of his circle disappear from the story and from importance to the story.[121] Paul continues to perform miracles and preach, but the results vary from jail time (due to the owners of the slave girl freed from demonic possession), to household conversions (the jailer's family), to Jews chasing them from the city, to a debate in Athens. Only in Corinth and Ephesus does preaching bring about large positive results. The return to Jerusalem and the long road to Rome are characterized by specific occurrences: Paul heals someone (including himself, as in Acts 28:3–6), Paul is falsely accused, Paul tells his story, and Paul's judgment is delayed.[122] In the midst of his return to Jerusalem and original arrest, the Paul of Acts maintains and strengthens his Jewish identity without sacrificing his Christian faith.[123] Acts holds up Paul as a model prisoner who does not escape

---

117. Pervo, *Luke's Story of Paul*, 35.
118. Pervo, *Luke's Story of Paul*, 46.
119. Pervo, *Luke's Story of Paul*, 47–48.
120. Pervo (*Luke's Story of Paul*, 51) begins noting this type of description of Paul.
121. Pervo (*Luke's Story of* Paul, 55) stresses the point that at the start of his second trip, Antioch no longer gives him direction as it did at the beginning of his first journey.
122. Pervo, *Luke's Story of Paul*, 80. This is not precisely what Pervo says, but it incorporates the main ideas.
123. Pervo, *Luke's Story of Paul*, 77.

when given the chance (both in Philippi and at his shipwreck), helps everyone that he can when they come into contact, speaks boldly, balances his Jewish life with his Christian faith, performs miracles, and preaches the gospel to both high and low.

The Paul of the Deutero-Pauline and noncanonical works has different emphases. Rather than focusing on salvation through belief or justification, this Paul teaches ethical living and eschews eschatological leanings for practical considerations.[124] The Christian life includes fitting in with society when possible and not making waves.[125] The epistles cast Paul as more a "model Gentile convert" than a Jewish believer.[126] The noncanonical works, no matter the genre, picture Paul as either an equal apostle or coequal with Peter and above the rest. This can be seen in the changing narrative of Paul and Peter as replacements and then partners in Rome.[127] The noncanonical Paul was more miraculous, less Jewish, more focused on ethics, and less focused on Jesus. The noncanonical Paul became the story, and the religion became Paulinism instead of Christianity, such that authors arose producing works to counteract and negate the works of Paul.

CRITIQUE AND CONCLUSION

The various scholarly conclusions of Pervo landed with bumps. None of his major proposals have become the new consensus. His most powerful work, seeing Acts as popular-level literature written to entertain, seemingly did not even fully convince his older self as he allows for a more historical understanding of Luke's book.[128] Scholars still argue over the genre of Acts, as Pervo's case does not convince for many reasons.[129] One major reason comes from how he never defines or gives genre markers for the popular level novel. Instead of beginning with a list of genre identifiers or commonalities among the type, he moves

---

124. This comparison does blend the Paul of Acts and the undisputed epistles, but it fits within the sphere of what Pervo seeks to accomplish. See Pervo, *Making of Paul*, 18 and 75.

125. Pervo, *Making of Paul*, 93.

126. Pervo, *Making of Paul*, 118.

127. Pervo, *Making of Paul*, 185. Pervo carefully notes how the story of Paul and Peter changes over time, with Paul annoyed with Peter in Galatians, to Peter substituting for an absent Paul in the *Acts of Peter*, to the two ministering in tandem in the sixth-century work the *Decretum Gelasianum* 3.2.

128. Though sticking with the idea of Acts as a popular level work, he nonetheless recognizes that it fits in the context of a historical novel. He still contends that Luke is a better novelist than historian, yet he seems to walk back some of his previous harsh words about Luke as a liar. See Pervo, *Acts*, 18.

129. For example, see the discussion in Keener, *Acts*, 1:51–220, especially 63–83.

into comparing individual snippets of various novels to Acts.[130] This method opens Pervo up to the charge of selection bias or parallelomania. In pushing for this classification for Acts, Pervo commits some historical mistakes, privileging noncanonical works and dating them potentially earlier to show how Acts draws on them instead of vice versa.[131] He also does not situate the noncanonical Acts into their own genre discussion and instead assumes a specific type without arguing for it.[132] Some of these same problems appear when he dates Acts using parallels most scholars would contend have Acts as a source. Pervo sees Luke as the one incorporating them into Acts. Since Luke as author composes creatively, Pervo justifies his stance by describing Luke as imaginatively changing his sources to fit with his message. This allows Luke's words to be far removed from any source, and therefore it is all the more difficult to detect how and what sources are being used. If the genre of Acts is wrong, however, then this case for the dating falls with it since the evidence for the latter is based foundationally on the former. With respect to his take on the unity of Luke–Acts, he and Parsons made a strong case about the disunity of genre and narration, and the reception history bears out this disconnect.[133] In seeing a common author and common style, scholarship jumped to a more unified take than necessarily should have been the case, and Pervo's work rightly challenged the assumptions made about reading Luke's two volumes.[134] One disappointment in Pervo's scholarship comes in his handling of Paul. In looking through the various genres and early Christian works that include or feature Paul, Pervo would have been in the perfect spot to analyze how Paul was understood theologically, used authoritatively, and characterized in narrative. Rather than

---

130. The selective nature of these comparisons also tells against his case, as he rarely justifies his decisions other than by noting a similarity to Acts. To strengthen his argument, he should have defended his choice of works to be used.

131. See Ben Witherington III, *The Acts of the Apostles: A Socio-Rhetorical Commentary* (Grand Rapids: Eerdmans, 1998), 376–81.

132. With the problems in classifying genres in the noncanonical Acts, see Jean Daniel Kaestli, "Les principals orientations de la recherche sur la Actes apocryphes," in *Les Actes Apocryphes des Apôtres: Christianisme et monde païen*, eds. François Bovon, et al. (Geneva: Labor et Fides, 1981), 49–70, here 57–67. For particulars in tying Acts to the genre of the noncanonical Acts following the work of Kaestli, see Bauckham, "The *Acts of Paul*," 139–41.

133. Cf. Gregory, *Reception of Luke and Acts*; C. Kavin Rowe, "Literary Unity and Reception History: Reading Luke-Acts as Luke and Acts," *JSNT* 29.4 (2007): 450–57, and the essays in Gregory and Rowe, eds., *Rethinking the Unity and Reception of Luke and Acts*.

134. Cf. Richard I. Pervo, "Fourteen Years After," in *Rethinking the Unity and Reception of Luke and Acts*, 23–40.

pulling together a comprehensive if disparate portrait, Pervo opted to leave each use of Paul separated.

Richard I. Pervo wrote to challenge the status quo. He sought to push the conversation on Acts with respect to genre, dating, and the presupposition of the unity of Luke–Acts. He wrote with verve, daring, an eye on primary and secondary literature, and a dry humor that made his own volumes entertaining to read, something atypical in scholarly fields. In terms of opening or reopening discussions, he succeeded. In terms of his conclusions carrying the day, he failed. Yet what he wanted most of all was to spur further research into Acts and create more excitement and interest in the book among laypeople, and in that goal he exceeded his own expectations.

LOVEDAY C. A. ALEXANDER: LUKE-ACTS IN ITS ANCIENT LITERARY CONTEXT

Laura J. Hunt

INTRODUCTION

The focus of Reverend Canon Professor Loveday C. A. Alexander's work has been, as we will see, on "the literary talents of Luke" as she examined his prefaces, his historicity, and discussions of genre surrounding his works. But she has also examined questions regarding the development of Christianity, the passing on of traditions about Jesus using practices comparable to Hellenistic schools, and stories of Paul that look similar in some ways to Greek novels. Insights into Luke's ecclesiology become relevant for both scholarly reconstructions and church life today. This chapter will address these studies in topical fashion after a brief look at Professor Alexander's life and nonacademic contributions.

BIOGRAPHY

Professor Alexander's life has crossed many of the boundaries often erected between scholarship and the rest of life. She was born in Belfast, Northern Ireland, on August 15, 1947, but she grew up in the north of England and still enjoys walking in the hills and by the sea. She has two children and two grandchildren and is married to Philip Alexander, Emeritus Professor of Jewish Studies at the University of Manchester. Her career has successfully crossed between the disciplines of classics and biblical studies and the responsibilities of academia and the church, which have offered both their gifts and their demands.

Alexander completed her first degree in classics at Somerville College, in the University of Oxford; she then went on to complete her DPhil in the Faculty of Theology. Her classical background provided her with expertise in ancient languages and a wide familiarity with nonbiblical Greek texts. Hellenistic schools and Greek technical writing have become part of her approach to the Gospel of Luke and the Acts of the Apostles.

Loveday Alexander was appointed Canon Theologian at Chester (2003–2014) and Chichester Cathedrals (2011–2016), and her many publications for lay and clergy readership demonstrate her commitment to sharing the fruits of her academic research with the church. She continues this work today as a member of the Church of England's Faith and Order Commission (2008–2022).

Alexander has published a *Guide for Reflection and Prayer* on the Book of Acts.[1] She engaged discussions about church offices with "Are There Any Bishops in the Bible?" which was the Canon-Theologian's Chester Cathedral Lecture, 2012,[2] and she reminded readers about the "reticence of the Creeds" to define more than is necessary in "Homosexuality and the Bible: Reflections of a Biblical Scholar."[3] Furthermore, she continues to engage with both academic and confessing communities with lectures such as the 2016 Clark Lecture at Duke Divinity School, "Is Luke a Historian? Writing the History of the Early Church," and a Bible Talk at Chester Cathedral, in March 2021, "'Love bade me welcome': George Herbert and Nicholas Ferrar."

These examples, and those discussed below, demonstrate the breadth of her writing abilities, from her thorough engagement

---

1. Published in the UK in The People's Bible Commentary series by Oxford: Bible Reading Fellowship, 2006 and in the Daily Bible Commentary series by Peabody, MA: Hendrickson, 2006 in North America.
2. See also Loveday Alexander and Mike Higton, eds., *Faithful Improvisation? Theological Reflections on Church Leadership* (London: Church House Publishing, 2016).
3. Loveday Alexander, "Homosexuality and the Bible: Reflections of a Biblical Scholar," in *Grace and Disagreement: Shared Conversations on Scripture, Mission and Human Sexuality*, ed. by The Archbishops' Council (London: The Archbishops' Council, 2014), 24–51.

with Greek in *The Preface to Luke's Gospel*, to her French article on intertextuality,[4] her student-level chapter on the importance of (and cautions about) using Greco-Roman literature and culture for New Testament studies,[5] and two very similar articles on the topic of biblical interpretation and application, one more accessible ("This Is That"), and one more academic ("God's Frozen Word").[6] Although the discussions below focus primarily on Alexander's academic work as opposed to her ministerial, it occasionally becomes difficult to separate the two.

PREFACES AND HISTORICITY

This section covers the beginning of Alexander's academic inquiries, her thesis comparing the prefaces of Luke's Gospel and the Book of Acts with those of various other ancient Greek works. While she distances Luke's style of preface-writing from ancient Greek historiographies, she points out that such a determination does not affect conclusions about the historicity of Luke–Acts. As we will see, Alexander looks at the name of the recipient of the dedication, Theophilus, and concludes that he was likely a real person and perhaps a patron who provided space for Christian teachers to perform their works. The trials of Luke–Acts offer evidence for the dating of the works to the reign of Claudius. The preface to Acts is judged to be like that of the Gospel, differing only in its reference to the other work. However, Alexander concludes that the two books should be read as one two-volume work since several scenes and references at the end of Acts mirror the beginning of Luke's Gospel.

While some previous scholars had classified the Gospels within the genre of historiography, Alexander concluded that the preface to Luke's Gospel is shorter, barely mentions sources, methodology, subject-matter, or usefulness, nor does Luke introduce himself or write in a sufficiently high literary register to qualify as an attempt

4. Loveday Alexander, "L'intertextualité et la question des lecteurs : Réflexions sur l'usage de la Bible dans les Actes des Apôtres," in *Intertextualités: La Bible en échos*, eds. D. Marguerat and A. Curtis (Geneva: Labor et Fides, 2000), 201–14.
5. Loveday Alexander, "The Relevance of Greco-Roman Literature and Culture to New Testament Studies," in *Hearing the New Testament: Strategies for Interpretation*, ed. Joel B. Green (Grand Rapids: Eerdmans, 2010), 109–26.
6. Loveday Alexander, "'This is That': The Authority of Scripture in the Acts of the Apostles," *PSB* NS 25 (2004): 189–204; Alexander, "God's Frozen Word: Canonicity and the Dilemmas of Biblical Studies Today," *ExpTim* 117.6 (2006): 237–42.

to mimic historians' prefaces.[7] Rather, it more likely participates in a register she sometimes refers to as "scientific tradition" but prefers to call *Fachprosa,* "a range of technical handbooks in subjects as diverse as engineering, rhetoric, and medicine."[8] In comparing the preface of the Third Gospel to other prefaces in the ancient world, including Jewish writing, Greek rhetoric, Greek histories, and Greek technical writing, Alexander notes the following frequent characteristics of technical writing: a mention of the author's decision to write, with qualifications and methodology; the subject matter and its nature; a recipient of a dedication addressed in the second person; and a mention of other authors who have written on the same topic.[9] The Greek employed usually consists of periodic sentences, rhetorical devices such as litotes and alliteration on the p-sound, distinctive vocabulary (particularly on the topics of presentation, evaluation of the contents and author qualifications), and verbal periphrasis and compound verbs.[10]

In an appendix to *Preface,* Alexander analyzes the structures of four of these prefaces along with Luke 1:1–4. While Alexander engages with them in Greek, I list them here in English translation:

> Diocles to King Antigonus. Since you happen to have become the most cultured of all kings and to have lived longest and to be experienced in all intellectual activity and to be a frontrunner in the sciences, I thought that the learning and theoretical study of matters related to health would be a royal and appropriate intellectual activity. I am therefore writing to you [about the question] whence diseases in human beings originate and what signs precede [them], and how one might be successful in treating them. For just as a storm does not at any time come about in the atmosphere without certain signs preceding it, which sailors and people with much experience attend to, likewise an affection does not originate in the bodily nature of a human being at any time without some sign occurring prior to it. If you are persuaded by our words, you

---

7. Alexander notes in particular the work of Meyer, Toynbee, van Unnik, and Barrett; Loveday Alexander, *The Preface to Luke's Gospel: Literary Convention and Social Context in Luke 1.1–4 and Acts 1.1,* SNTSMS 78 (Cambridge: Cambridge University Press, 1993), 2.
8. Alexander, *Preface,* 102–103; Loveday Alexander, "On a Roman Bookstall: Reading Acts in Its Ancient Literary Context," in *Acts in Its Ancient Literary Context: A Classicist Looks at the Acts of the Apostles* (London: T&T Clark, 2006), 1–20, here 3.
9. For a definition of technical writing, see below.
10. Alexander, *Preface,* 67–101.

will attend to the accurate [indications] about them. (Diocles of Carystus, *Letter to Antigonus* 1–10, fourth/third century BCE)[11]

According to the theory that governs epistolary types, Heraclides, (letters) can be composed in a great number of styles, but are written in those which always fit the particular circumstance (to which they are addressed). While (letters) ought to be written as skillfully as possible, they are in fact composed indifferently by those who undertake such services for men in public office. Since I see that you are eager in your love to learn, I have taken it upon myself, by means of certain styles, to organize and set forth (for you) both the number of distinctions between them and what they are, and have sketched a sample, as it were, of the arrangement of each kind, and have, in addition, individually set forth the rationale for each of them. (I do so), partly assuming that this pleases you too, since you will know that you are making your splendid life surpass others, not in banquets, but in professional skills, and partly believing that I shall share in the praise that will properly (redound to you). (Demetrius, *Formae Epistolicae* 1–8, 1 BCE)[12]

The investigation of the properties of Atmospheric Air having been deemed worthy of close attention by the ancient philosophers and mechanists, the former deducing them theoretically, the latter from the action of sensible [i.e., able to be apprehended by our senses] bodies, we also have thought proper to arrange in order what has been handed down by former writers, and to add thereto our own discoveries: a task from which much advantage will result to those who shall hereafter devote themselves to the study of mathematics. We are further led to write this work from the consideration that it is fitting that the treatment of this subject should correspond with the method given by us in our treatise, in four books, on water-clocks. For, by the union of air, earth, fire and water, and the concurrence of three, or four, elementary principles, various combinations are effected, some of which supply the

---

11. Translation by Philip J. van der Eijk, *Diocles of Carystus: A Collection of the Fragments with Translation and Commentary*, vol 1: *Text and Translation* (Leiden: Brill, 2000), 310–13.
12. Translation from Abraham J. Malherbe, *Ancient Epistolary Theorists*, SBLSBS 19 (Atlanta: Scholars Press, 1988), 31. Note that in this case the preface continues as the author explains that he designed his words for older people just as much as for youths; Alexander, *Preface*, 215.

most pressing wants of human life, while others produce amazement and alarm. (Hero of Alexandria, *Pneumatica* 1. 1–5, first century CE)[13]

Many having more extensively considered the theory of wounds, I myself considered it necessary to be more descriptive and to work these topics out according an outline, thus intending this matter to be well enumerated and easily understood for those approaching the discipline for the first time. It is simple, and comparatively easily dealt with after relatively simple apprehension as indeed it has readily been found to be by many. Now one must begin. (Galen of Pergamon, *De Typis* 1–6, second century CE)[14]

Alexander offers the following translation of Luke's Prefaces:

Inasmuch as many have undertaken the task of compiling an account of the matters which have come to fruition in our midst, just as the tradition was handed down to us by the original eyewitnesses and ministers of the word, it seemed good to me also, having followed everything carefully and thoroughly, to write it all up for you in an orderly fashion, most excellent Theophilus so that you may have assured knowledge about the things in which you have been instructed. (Luke 1:1–4)[15]

The previous treatise which I wrote, Theophilus, about all that Jesus began to do and to teach. (Acts 1:1)[16]

In these prefaces, Alexander notes the regular occurrences of causal clauses; mentions of other writers; description, nature, and methodological treatment of subject-matter, the author's decision to write as the main verb; a rhetorical address, and the results for the dedicatee or the readers.[17] Furthermore, since the style of Luke's writing shifts immediately after the preface to a register more in line with biblical

---

13. Translation from Bennet Woodcroft, *The Pneumatics of Hero of Alexandria: From the Original Greek* (London: Taylor, Walton and Maberly, 1851), 1. This preface, too, contains an additional sentence not included in Alexander, *Preface*, 215.

14. Translation from Zachary K. Dawson, "Does Luke's Preface Resemble a Greek Decree? Comparing the Epigraphical and Papyrological Evidence of Greek Decrees with Ancient Preface Formulae," *NTS* 65.4 (2019): 552–71, here 559.

15. This is a compilation of her translations in *Preface*, 107, 116, 125, 136.

16. Alexander, *Preface*, 142.

17. Alexander, *Preface*, 213–16.

Greek, Alexander proposes that Luke wrote the preface he did because such a style seemed normal to him, "what one does when one writes a preface."[18] Luke's Greek fits within the middle level of craftsmen, artisans, and practitioners.[19]

Alexander was careful, in this comparison, to anticipate arguments motivated by concerns about historical reliability, pointing out that historiography itself had rules that differed from those of our own historians. One way to check for the truth of a text is to compare it to outside historical events. But there are two other ways. The first has to do with a subjective evaluation of how likely the events described are to have happened. The second has to do with genre.[20]

It has often been assumed that if Acts is an ancient history, then it was presenting itself as a reliable account of events. But that correlation does not always hold in the ancient world. Furthermore, classifying Acts as another genre does not necessarily destroy its truth claims. Greek and Roman historiographers and biographers, to be sure, speak in the third person and carefully distinguish between what they themselves have seen and therefore know to be true, and things told to them by others which can be questioned. Thus, they present an aura of objectivity. However, the reporting of the tales or experiences of others often brackets reports of fantastic fictions that were told to hold the attention of readers. This practice contributed to the reputation of historiographers, geographers, and biographers as liars.

Thus, one cannot prove the facticity of Acts simply by categorizing it as a historiography. With its variations of ethnicities and far-flung geographies, Acts opens the door to the possibility that its tales are inventions. On the other hand, the thoroughly Roman settings, the lack of a happy ending, and the businesslike preface all suggest facticity.[21] "Acts is a narrative which both implies and creates the presumption of a shared religious experience: and that is something difficult

---

18. Loveday Alexander, "Luke's Preface in the Pattern of Greek Preface-Writing," *NovT* 28 (1986): 48–74, here 64–66. Alexander also goes through 2 Macc. 2:19–32; Eccles. 1–36; *Letter of Aristeas*; Philo of Alexandria; and Josephus. She finds "a diverse group of Jewish writers whose prefaces plug into Greek literary convention in different ways"; *Preface*, 166.

19. See Alexander, *Preface*, 184–86, for Luke's attitude toward epics, manual labor, and orality that also support this conclusion.

20. Loveday Alexander, "Fact, Fiction, and the Genre of Acts," *NTS* 44 (1998): 380–99, here 380.

21. Luke's characterization of Felix and the arrival of Bernice and Agrippa (Acts 23–26) coheres with other reports of the time; Loveday Alexander, "Acts," in *The Oxford Bible Commentary*, eds. John Barton and John Muddiman (Oxford: Oxford University Press, 2001), 1028–61, here 1057–58.

to accommodate within the standard fact/fiction grid of Greek literature."[22] While those who know other Jewish writings might recognize the genre from the LXX, those familiar only with Greek writings might legitimately be confused.[23]

Issues of facticity come up again with regard to Luke's dedicatee, Theophilus. It is possible that Theophilus was a colleague of Luke's, the patron of a house church who provided a space in which Luke could perform his oeuvre. Alternatively, Alexander points out that his name was common among the Jewish diaspora.[24] This suggests that, rather than a powerful Roman, he might be part of the Jewish community in Rome, perhaps, "(let us hypothesize) . . . a prominent and amenable representative of the same Jewish community in Rome to which Luke has Paul make his last impassioned plea for hearing in Acts 28."[25] If Luke were writing to a Jewish diaspora community, his frequent references to the LXX would need no apology or explanation. Whether this seems plausible or not, Alexander notes that the book of Acts provides a history of Paul's life which gives a backdrop to his letters. Christianity or at least our conception of its origins would look quite different if John, or James, or Peter had had an associate similarly interested in taking notes about their activities.

Alexander also analyzes the speeches in Acts and compares them to later Roman discussions about prosecuting Christians (Pliny, *Ep.* 10.96–97).[26] The Roman judicial system required a judge (but for capital cases, one needed a governor who was often rarely available), a prosecutor, the accused (who could give a defense in some cases; Acts 25:16), and a verdict (which governors sometimes decided idiosyncratically). In general, the motives for accusing Christians (*odium humani generis*, "latent political disobedience," or a loss in temple sacrifices) were different from the charges: "disorder . . . disloyalty . . . illegal assembly . . . atheism."[27] Alexander looks at these elements in the various trials in Acts and draws the following conclusions:

22. Alexander, "Fact," 399.
23. Alexander, "Fact," 397.
24. Loveday Alexander, "What if Luke Had Never Met Theophilus," *BibInt* 8 (1999): 161–70, here 165.
25. Alexander, "What if Luke," 165.
26. Loveday Alexander, "Silent Witness: Paul's Troubles with Roman Authorities in the Book of Acts," in *The Last Years of Paul: Essays from the Tarragona Conference, June 2013*, eds. Armand Puig i Tàrrech, John M. G. Barclay, Jörg Frey, and Orrey McFarland, WUNT 352 (Tübingen, Mohr Siebeck, 2015), 153–73.
27. Alexander, "Silent Witness," 158.

1. Paul's troubles occurred not because the authorities appre-
    hended him contravening the law but because locals prose-
    cuted him. This presentation of Paul's history could be attrib-
    uted to Luke's desire to exonerate Paul, but it also fits with
    Roman behavior.

2. The locals are identified as immigrants or tradespeople, but not
    slaves.[28] They are often motivated by financial concerns; they see
    Paul as a competitor who would further impoverish them.

3. Those adjudicating his case are often motivated by a fear of
    being unable to keep the peace.

4. There is also, and this became a stronger motivating force in
    later Christian persecutions, the Roman fear of diminishing
    respect for the gods.[29]

Comparing these conclusions to the situation at the time of Pliny,
Alexander points out that by then Christians are seen as clearly separate
from Jews. Christianity has gone from an annoyance to a threat, and
to simply call oneself a Christian has become a crime.[30] If G. E. M. de
Ste. Croix is correct that these changes occurred after 64 CE (after the
persecution of Christians as responsible for the great fire in Rome),
Alexander's analysis of the conflicts in Acts places them under the reign
of Claudius, i.e., 41–54 CE.[31]

What about the preface to the book of Acts? Multivolume works
in the ancient world often started with a sentence of recapitulation, as
does Acts. Luke's care to alert his readers to the existence of his Gospel
might suggest that he saw the two works as integral. Consonances
with the preface to Luke's Gospel also suggest that Acts is not a second
work or a different genre.[32] However, recapitulations do not always
refer to the first half of the work in progress but sometimes to another
of the author's works. Luke's recapitulation (Acts 1:1), then, tells us
little about the way he conceived of the two volumes.

---

28. Alexander, "Silent Witness," 169.
29. Alexander, "Silent Witness," 171.
30. Alexander, "Silent Witness," 172.
31. Alexander, "Silent Witness," 172; G. E. M. de Ste. Croix, "Why Were the Early Christians
     Persecuted?" *Past and Present* 26 (1963): 6–38, here 8.
32. Loveday Alexander, "The Preface to Acts and the Historians," in *History, Literature and Society in the
     Book of Acts*, ed. Ben Witherington III (Cambridge: Cambridge University Press, 1996), 73–103,
     here 82–100.

Alexander initially thought the idea of Luke intentionally composing a two-volume work unlikely given the lack of references in the
Gospel to Acts as a continuation of the story.[33] However, in her chapter,
"Reading Luke–Acts from Back to Front," she uses Genette's concept
of paratext to note some of the ways that the end of Acts resumes
themes and references from the beginning of the Third Gospel.[34]
The Gospel and Acts generally focus on Jerusalem and specifically in
the transition from one to the next leave out any of the references
to Galilee found in Matthew, Mark, and John. This helps the reader
move smoothly from the ascension in Luke to the ascension in Acts.
However, Acts does not end in Jerusalem but in Rome, and in the
Gospel, the birth of Jesus is framed in a Roman construction of time
(Luke 2:1). Moreover, the discussion with the Jews at the end of Acts
mirrors the discussion with Simeon at the beginning of the Gospel,
and "the rare septuagintal word σωτήριον" occurs in both of these
passages (Luke 2:30; Acts 28:28) and also in Luke's Isaiah quotation
describing John the Baptist (Luke 3:6). These are three out of only five
occurrences of this word in the New Testament.[35] Isaiah 6:9–10 seems
to have been quite constitutive for early Christianity.[36] Luke includes
only a shortened quotation when he takes over the Parable of the Sower
from Mark (Mark 4:12; Luke 8:10). He waits until Acts 28:26–27 to
offer a longer version in his final explanation of the general (although
never complete) rejection of the gospel by the Jewish leaders, thus
tying the two works together.

The ending of Acts focuses on Paul and his act of proclamation,
described as "testifying to the kingdom of God" and "persuading
them about Jesus from the Law of Moses and also from the Prophets" (28:23; cf. 28:31). The beginning of Luke's Gospel, too, focuses
on prophets and prophecy (Mary, Zechariah, Anna, and Simeon).[37]
John the Baptist's story is told all at once in Luke, unlike in the other

33. On Alexander's reluctance to come to this conclusion, see Loveday Alexander, "Reading Luke–Acts
    from Back to Front," in *Acts in Its Ancient Literary Context*, 207–29, here 224; reprinted from *The
    Unity of Luke–Acts*, ed. Joseph Verheyden, BETL 142 (Leuven: Peeters, 1999), 419–46.
34. Alexander, "Reading Luke-Acts," 209–10.
35. Alexander, "Reading Luke–Acts," 220. Alexander says σωτήριος occurs "only four times," but the
    word can also be found in Ephesians 6:17 and Titus 2:11 (that last is possibly disputed).
36. It is cited in Mark 4:12 (and parallels); 8:17–18; John 12:39–40; Alexander, "Reading Luke–Acts,"
    216.
37. Note that kingdom (Luke 1:33) and the Law of Moses (2:22) feature at the beginning of Luke's
    Gospel as well, and John the Baptist also seeks to persuade people about Jesus (3:15–18).

Gospels, foregrounding him as a prophet (1:76). In this way, both the beginning of the Gospel and the end of Acts highlight those who proclaim Jesus.

Then, too, the opening of Luke's Gospel slowly ushers its listeners from everyday life into the world of the narrative, one with angelic appearances and a miraculous conception. Similarly, the ending of the book of Acts brings us from the miraculous (28:1–10) "back to the everyday world where the rest of us live, a world where prophets and angels have receded back into a mythical past, but where the more mundane and open-ended tasks of teaching and persuasion continue 'unhindered.'"[38]

These similarities between the beginning of the Third Gospel and the end of Acts would not allow a reader or hearer to foresee the end of Acts from the Gospel's beginning. Still, ancient readers like Theophilus (Luke 1:4) would have already been taught what happened to Paul, and these texts would have been read not just once but many times. In this way, the resonances between the beginning of the Gospel and the end of Acts would emerge. The mirroring of themes from the beginning of Luke's Gospel at the end of Acts suggests to Alexander that Luke intends from the beginning of his Gospel to communicate the tragedy of the closed ears of Israel (Luke 1:16–20, 54–55, 67–79; 2:28–38; Acts 28:23–30). The two volumes are one book.[39]

LUKE–ACTS AND GENRE

While Alexander's studies regarding historiography have already been discussed, this section will describe her further work on the topic. She dismisses the genre of epic for both volumes, and the genre of *apologia* for Acts, and she argues instead that once Luke gets into the narratives proper his style is most like that of the LXX. Furthermore, although Alexander notes similarities with ancient biographies, she suggests that Luke's work fits that genre only as a broad umbrella term. Functionally, Luke–Acts provides grounds for the emerging Christian teaching

---

38. Alexander, "Reading Luke–Acts," 229.
39. For a summary of *Preface* with echoes of "Reading Luke–Acts," see Alexander, "Formal Elements and Genre: Which Greco-Roman Prologues Most Closely Parallel the Lukan Prologue?" in *Jesus and the Heritage of Israel*, vol. 1: *Luke's Narrative Claim upon Israel's Legacy*, ed. David P. Moessner, Luke the Interpreter (Harrisburg, PA: Trinity, 1999), 9–26.

and for the self-understanding of Christianity as a development of
God's revelation in the Jewish Scriptures.

In a 1998 book chapter, Alexander recounts a classroom exercise
in which she asked students to compare battle scenes in the writing of Thucydides and the Septuagint.[40] Her students noticed that
Greek writers went into more detail, included more characters, and
constructed more complex narratives. They used direct speech less, but
the speeches themselves were longer. The ethical behavior of combat-
ants was important to both kinds of authors, but most evident in the
biblical accounts. Biblical narratives included women, while Greek
war stories did not. Also, Greek histories were expected to deal with
events of importance to the largest number of people and nations,
which often meant war. The topic of Luke–Acts was not likely to be
considered noble or important to Greek readers.

Greek authors inserted authorial comments into their writing,
guiding their readers through what they themselves saw or experienced
and what they only heard. The biblical author however is mostly invis-
ible. In biblical narratives, God is one of the characters, and miracles
occur often.[41] In Greek histories, the supernatural is not frequently
mentioned and when it is, it is often subject to skepticism. Thus,
Greek historians deployed the authorial voice to bolster the truth of
their words and yet were generally perceived to be liars. Students, as
opposed to ancient readers, found the Greek histories more reliable
than the biblical stories, perhaps because of their bias towards objectivity, a bias which is satisfied by the seemingly objective authorial voice.
Furthermore, students were more entertained by the Greek histories
because they include details and amusing side bars that kept them
interested, as opposed to the "war bulletin" style of the biblical story.[42]

Which of these two approaches does Luke follow? "What seems
to emerge clearly from this survey is that where there is a significant difference between the two traditions, Luke follows the biblical
approach to historiography almost every time."[43] Acts is shorter; it uses
less characters, although it includes women; and Luke's narrative style

---

40.   Loveday Alexander, "Marathon or Jericho? Reading Acts in Dialogue with Biblical and Greek
        Historiography," in *Auguries: The Jubilee Volume of the Sheffield Department of Biblical Studies*, eds.
        David J. A. Clines and Stephen D. Moore, JSOTSup 269 (Sheffield: Sheffield Academic, 1998),
        92–125.
41.   Alexander, "Acts," 1034, 1042.
42.   Alexander, "Marathon," 115.
43.   Alexander, "Marathon," 119; cf. Alexander, "Acts," 1043.

is "straightforward and concise."[44] Except for the prefaces, Luke does not take an authorial voice; he frequently comments on the narrative, but through the prayers of the characters.[45] His speeches are unequal in length and his storytelling often occurs as anecdotes.[46] Thus, while Alexander characterizes Luke's prefaces as written in a technical register appropriate for *Fachprosa*, the bulk of Luke's narrative follows the model of the Septuagint.

In 2003, Alexander continued her discussion of genre responding to some scholars, such as Marianne Palmer Bonz and Dennis MacDonald, who argued that Luke–Acts and Mark were modeled on ancient epics.[47] She begins by defining an epic, noting that the word can be used casually to mean a long, important foundational narrative, but when used specifically as an ancient genre it includes: "verse narrative" of some "length [and] complexity," having "a certain grandeur" and heroism.[48] It is true that within the Hebrew Bible we might find some narratives comparable to epic works; however, that is not the case in the New Testament. And while Acts might be a foundational narrative, construing it as epic in that casual sense does not imply that it is epic as to genre as well. Even if the New Testament shows awareness of Homer and Virgil, those stories were retold outside of the poetic form in the ancient world, so texts could echo the stories without imitating the genre. Indeed, when *lexis* ("diction . . . accidence and syntax . . . rhythm and metre") is taken into account, Alexander shows that the book of Acts is imitating biblical Greek, rather than Homer or Virgil.[49] The importance of *lexis* also brings into question the validity of the concept of a "prose epic."[50]

Some passages in Acts reward comparison, however. Just as Aeneas's arrival at the site where Rome would be founded is described

---

44. Alexander, "Marathon," 120.
45. Alexander, "Acts," 1034.
46. Alexander, "Marathon," 121.
47. Marianne Palmer Bonz, *The Past as Legacy: Luke–Acts and Ancient Epic* (Minneapolis: Fortress, 2000); Dennis R. MacDonald, *The Homeric Epics and the Gospel of Mark* (New Haven, CT: Yale University Press, 2000); MacDonald, *Does the New Testament Imitate Homer? Four Cases from the Acts of the Apostles* (New Haven, CT: Yale University Press, 2003).
48. Loveday Alexander, "New Testament Narrative and Ancient Epic," in *Acts in Its Ancient Literary Context*, 165–82, here 167; reprinted from "New Testament Narrative and Ancient Epic," in *Raconter, interpreter, annoncer: Parcours de Nouveau Testament. Mélanges offerts à Daniel Marguerat pour son 60ᵉ anniversaire*, eds. Emmanuelle Steffek and Yvan Bourquin, Le Monde de la Bible 47 (Geneva: Labor et Fides, 2003), 239–49.
49. Alexander, "New Testament Narrative," 172. Note, however, Acts 27:41 where Luke uses Homeric language to describe the grounding of the ship; Alexander, "Acts," 1060.
50. Alexander, "New Testament Narrative," 173.

as a homecoming even though he has never been there, the welcoming party for Paul (Acts 28:15) gives his arrival in Rome the feeling of coming home even though it is his first visit.[51] Occasionally, such as with the Socratic allusion (καινὰ δαιμόνια; Plato, *Apol.* 24b, DL 2.40) in Paul's trip to Athens (ξενὰ δαιμόνια; Acts 17:18) and the nautical language in Acts 27:2–5, Luke changes his register to aid his literary allusions.[52] The epic symbolism of the storm at sea as an unruly mob is used by Luke, as well: Paul is not only more composed than even the sailors because of his *pietas*, but the unruly sea alludes to Paul's troubles in various ports of call (e.g., Acts 19:28–41), as well as the Psalms that mention the nations who do not obey God (e.g., Ps. 46). However, Luke's realistic portrayal of events is a far cry from Virgil's eloquence.[53] Luke's orderly account is also nothing like Virgil's flashbacks and his prophecies about the future which refer to Virgil's present day. There might be value in comparisons with ancient epics, but the genres are not the same.

Another genre which has been proposed for the book of Acts is that of *apologia*.[54] However, Alexander points out that ancient *apologiae* constructed dramatic situations in which the defendant must present an oral defense before judges and spectators.[55] Setting up the drama in this way puts the narrator in the persona of the defendant and provides the opportunity for those listening to place themselves in the drama as part of the gallery. However, this clear setting of a dramatic trial is missing for the book of Acts, which immediately puts its categorization as an *apologia* into question. Acts, in fact, is not the narrative of a trial, but rather a narrative that contains accounts of several trials. "[I]t is the characters, not the narrator, who make these apologetic speeches, and . . . the narrator never intervenes in his own person to drive home the

---

51. Alexander, "New Testament Narrative," 174.
52. Loveday Alexander, "Acts and Ancient Intellectual Biography," in *The Book of Acts in Its Ancient Literary Setting*, eds. Bruce W. Winter and Andrew D. Clarke, BAFCS 1 (Grand Rapids: Eerdmans, 1993), 31–63, here 59; Alexander, "New Testament Narrative," 175. For more on Socratic allusions, see below.
53. Alexander, "New Testament Narrative," 178.
54. Loveday Alexander, "The Acts of the Apostles as an Apologetic Text," in *Acts in Its Ancient Literary Context*, 183–206; reprinted from "The Acts of the Apostles as an Apologetic Text," in *Apologetics in the Roman Empire: Pagans, Jews, and Christians*, eds. Mark Edwards, Martin Goodman, Simon Price, and Christopher Rowland (Oxford: Oxford University Press, 1999), 15–44.
55. Alexander, "The Acts of the Apostles," 187–88. For Romans, the defense would be given by an advocate discussing the defendant in the third person.

point to the text's inscribed audience."[56] What these speeches in Acts do offer, however, are multiple opportunities to demonstrate how to turn trials into opportunities for gospel witnessing, and to show how "the gospel story . . . changes and adapts to different cultural contexts."[57] For example, in Acts 25–26, Paul's *apologia* before Festus allows Luke to show "that Christian practice is not contrary to Roman law," nor to Jewish traditions, and that, in fact, following Christ is obedience to God.[58] Furthermore, in Acts the speeches and the narratives mutually reinforce one another as the addresses both repeat the narrated events and explain them with references to the Jewish Scriptures.[59]

Delving more deeply into distinguishing Acts from the language both of ancient epics and of ancient historiography, Alexander sets forth and defends a series of propositions regarding Luke's language and some sociological conclusions to which they point.[60] These propositions build on works by Albert Wifstrand and Eduard Norden. According to Norden, "Luke consistently adapts Mark in the direction of a more refined and elegant Greek."[61] Wifstrand, similarly, shows that "Luke's Greek is consistently more refined and elegant than Mark's," whether in original compositions or in his editing.[62] Norden had thus concluded that "Luke was an Atticist in his Greek."[63]

At this point in the argument, Alexander distinguishes between several Greek varieties: Attic Greek which spread from Athens from the fifth century BCE; *koine* Greek which was the vernacular written and spoken from the fourth century BCE; classicism, the higher registers of literary Greek in the first century CE; and Atticism which was

---

56. Alexander, "The Acts of the Apostles," 194.
57. Alexander, "What if Luke," 161; Alexander, "Acts," 1034.
58. Loveday Alexander, "Luke's Political Vision," *Int* 66.3 (2012): 283–93, here 287, 289, 290–91.
59. Alexander, "The Acts of the Apostles," 203. This practice of interpreting experiences using the resources of Jewish Scriptures will be seen again in Alexander's article, "This is That" (below).
60. Loveday Alexander, "*Septuaginta, Fachprosa, Imitatio*: Albert Wifstrand and the Language of Luke–Acts," in *Acts in Its Ancient Literary Context*, 231–52; reprinted from "*Septuaginta, Fachprosa, Imitatio*: Albert Wifstrand and the Language of Luke–Acts," in *Die Apostelgeschichte und die hellenistische Geschichtsschreibung: Festschrift für Eckhard Plümacher zu seinem 65. Geburtstag*, eds. Cilliers Breytenbach and Jens Schröter (Leiden: Brill, 2004), 1–26.
61. Eduard Norden, *Antike Kunstprosa vom VI. Jahrhundert v. Chr. bis in die Zeit der Renaissance*, cited in Wifstrand (below) and in Alexander, "*Septuaginta*," 232n6.
62. Alexander, "*Septuaginta*," 233; Albert Wifstrand, "Luke and Greek Classicism," in *Epochs and Styles: Selected Writings on the New Testament, Greek Language and Greek Culture in the Post-Classical Era*, eds. Lars Rydbeck and Stanley E. Porter, trans. Denis Searby, WUNT 179 (Tübingen: Mohr Siebeck, 2005), 17–27; Wifstrand, "Luke and the Septuagint," in *Epochs and Styles*, 28–45.
63. Alexander, "*Septuaginta*," 234.

a literary Greek different from Attic but aspiring to imitate it, popular among the *literati* in the second century CE.[64]

Based on these distinctions, Alexander restates Norden's conclusion: "Luke operates towards the high (H) end of the linguistic spectrum."[65] She points out that "'Classicism' [was] a broader and earlier phenomenon than the high Atticism of the second century."[66] And, with Wifstrand, notes that "Luke's language is a direct continuation of standard Hellenistic prose (SHP), which was untouched by classicism but was itself significantly more 'Attic' in character than everyday spoken Hellenistic Greek."[67] This dialect, "SHP, though it may have belonged originally to the H code, had moved down the scale by the 1st century CE under the emergent influence of classicism."[68]

This discussion leads Alexander to the following conclusions:

1. "Luke, in contrast to the other synoptics, gives his language a more elevated and dignified style associated with the peculiar style of Greek prevalent in the Greek Bible."[69]
2. "Luke's use of biblical Greek represents a form of *imitatio* analogous with the use made of the literary classics by Greek and Roman authors."[70]
3. "Within the Jewish communities of the Greek-speaking Diaspora, 'biblical Greek' functioned as a prestige H-code."[71]

---

64. Besides Alexander, "*Septuaginta*," this discussion can also be found in Sean A. Adams, "Atticism, Classicism, and Luke-Acts: Discussions with Albert Wifstrand and Loveday Alexander," in *The Language of the New Testament: Context, History, and Development*, ed. Stanley E. Porter and Andrew W. Pitts, Linguistic Biblical Studies 6 (Leiden: Brill, 2013), 91–111, here 92–93 and 101–102. Following Alexander, I have called the "initial phase of Atticism," classicism.

65. Alexander, "*Septuaginta*," 239. Alexander proposes a culture of diglossia, a language situation where the higher-status élite speak one language or dialect (H) and the lower-status population speaks another (L). This proposition depends on Ferguson, "Diglossia," *Word* 15 (1959): 325–40.

66. Alexander, "*Septuaginta*," 239.

67. Alexander, "*Septuaginta*," 240.

68. Alexander, "*Septuaginta*," 242.

69. "The paper thus presents a succinct and forceful statement of a position now widely accepted in Lukan studies, namely that 'Luke, in contrast to the other synoptics, sought to give his narrative a more elevated and dignified style by consciously and deliberately associating it with the peculiar style of Greek prevalent in the LXX which, so often reflecting the phraseology of a different language, had acquired a sacred status in the eyes of Hellenized Jews and proselytes as well as of the first Christians'"; Alexander, "*Septuaginta*," 242; Wifstrand, "Septuagint," 41.

70. Alexander, "*Septuaginta*," 244. The language of the Greek Bible is, in fact, quite close to the SHP, except for the Hebraisms.

71. Alexander, "*Septuaginta*," 245. In "L'intertextualité," 208–209, Alexander had argued for Luke's register as an *imitatio* of the Greek Bible, but in "*Septuaginta*," 246–49, she broadens this model to "biblical Greek." See also Adams, "Atticism," 104.

4. "But in the wider world of Greek culture, 'biblical Greek' would rank with SHP, lower down the code spectrum than Atticizing Greek."[72]

Alexander notes that we cannot tell from Luke's use of SHP whether classical Greek was part of his repertoire. But it is possible that SHP was the only dialect available to him as a member of "the bureaucratic circles educated to use Greek for administrative, business and professional purposes."[73] Luke's deployment of biblical Greek, somewhat similarly, shows that he had access not just to the Greek OT but to a broader range of Jewish Greek works.[74] Alexander concludes, then, that "it seems . . . reasonable to suggest that we are dealing with a prestige code of heightened, formal, religiously-charged language deployed at the very least in the preaching and the liturgy of Greek-speaking Diaspora communities."[75] This study dovetails with Alexander's previous works, demonstrating that Luke chose a technical dialect with which to begin his volumes but then wrote the rest of his work in language congruent with literate Greek-speaking Jews.

With this nuanced distinction in place, we come back to the topic of genre. In 1992, Richard A. Burridge published *What Are the Gospels?* where he argued that the Gospels are Greco-Roman biographies, or *bioi*.[76] Alexander is appreciative in her review, although she notes that by placing the Gospels in this genre, Burridge has not said very much because the genre is so broad.[77] In her 1993 article, "Acts and Ancient Intellectual Biography," Alexander interacts with Charles Talbert's proposal that Luke–Acts is likely modeled on the same kinds of source documents as those used by Diogenes Laertius in his *Lives of the Philosophers*.[78] Talbert focuses attention on the "intellectual biographies" of

72.   Alexander, "*Septuaginta*," 245.
73.   Alexander, "*Septuaginta*," 251.
74.   Alexander, "*Septuaginta*," 245.
75.   Alexander, "*Septuaginta*," 251–52.
76.   Richard A. Burridge, *What Are the Gospels? A Comparison with Graeco-Roman Biography* (Cambridge: Cambridge University Press, 1992).
77.   Loveday Alexander, "What Are the Gospels: A Comparison with Graeco-Roman Biography," *EvQ* 66 (1994): 73–76.
78.   Loveday Alexander, "Acts and Ancient Intellectual Biography"; Charles H. Talbert, *Literary Patterns, Theological Themes and the Genre of Luke–Acts* (Missoula, MT: Scholars Press, 1974); Talbert, *What Is a Gospel?* (Philadelphia: Fortress, 1977); Talbert, "Biographies of Philosophers and Rulers as Instruments of Religious Propaganda in Mediterranean Antiquity," *ANRW* II.16.2 (1978): 1619–51; Talbert, "Biography, Ancient," *ABD* (New York: Doubleday, 1992), 1:745–49.

thought leaders rather than political leaders.[79] He develops five functions for these biographies, but Alexander notes the importance of two
of them: "To validate and/or provide a hermeneutical key to a teacher's
doctrine" and "[t]o provide the readers with a pattern to copy."[80] The
first of these fits especially well with Acts' description of Paul's life. The
second supports the conception of early Christianity along the model
of a Hellenistic school.[81]

When Alexander compares the stories of Paul in Acts to Diogenes
Laertius's fifth book (on Aristotle), however, the topics are similar but
important differences emerge. Luke's voice only appears in the preface
whereas Diogenes steps in often to draw attention to the identity or
existence of his sources and to differences between them when they
occur. Luke offers complete narratives and characterizations through
speeches. Diogenes keeps his narrator at a distance from events and
describes philosophers without committing himself to any one school.
Although we perhaps see Luke's voice emerge in the "we-passages,"
Alexander argues that this is not an authorial voice but rather "the
narrator there simply (and oddly) becomes a temporary character in
his own narrative."[82]

These differences lead Alexander to conclude that "intellectual biography . . . fails to provide a clear literary model for Acts."[83]
However, the elements and ordering they provide, if taken as evidence
of expected features of a biography, do cohere in some ways with
Luke's telling of Paul's life, particularly as we see them expressed in
various retellings of the life of Socrates.[84] This framework allows the
story of Paul to reach ancient readers as a familiar tune in a new key,
and it gives scholars today the tools to classify a structure that looks
unfamiliar within a known framework.[85]

---

79. Alexander, "Acts and Ancient Intellectual Biography," 34.
80. Alexander, "Acts and Ancient Intellectual Biography," 35.
81. Both of these topics will be explored further in the next section.
82. Alexander, "Acts and Ancient Intellectual Biography," 48.
83. Alexander, "Acts and Ancient Intellectual Biography," 56.
84. Alexander, "Acts and Ancient Intellectual Biography," 58–62. These common features include: "The
    divine call"; "The mission"; "The daimonion" (Acts 16:6–10 and especially 17:18); "Tribulations";
    "Persecution"; "Trial"; "Prison"; "Death." Although Paul's death is not explicitly narrated, his stated
    willingness to face death (Acts 20:22–24) and the presence of women and children at the tearful
    farewell (21:5, 12) provide Socratic parallels. See also Paul's determination to go to Jerusalem;
    Alexander, "Acts," 1054.
85. Alexander, "Acts and Ancient Intellectual Biography," 63. Note that in her 2001, "*Ipse dixit*" (see
    below), Alexander draws no conclusions about genre; Alexander, "Acts," 1029.

HELLENISTIC SCHOOLS AND MEMORY

The topics discussed so far led into (and emerged from) Alexander's interest in Hellenistic schools. Alexander's thorough knowledge of Hellenism gives her plenty of resources for discussing the practices of ancient manuscript copying and circulation. She dedicates several articles to those topics, frequently connecting their focus on orality and their emphasis on creative repetition with the episodic nature of Luke–Acts. Thus, although the repeated retellings of events in Acts include variations uncomfortable to modern ears, they would have fit comfortably within ancient practices.

The dissemination of the Gospels has sometimes been thought to depend on patrons, such as Theophilus. However, we cannot assume that patronage included an obligation to create copies of an author's work in an ancient version of publication. Rather, patronage in the ancient world usually meant providing a social setting where the works could be performed.[86] Besides this oral dissemination "the two books which Luke dedicated to Theophilus could have become part of his library, available to the church which met in his house, and ultimately becoming the nucleus of that church's library."[87] The Gospels have sometimes been compared to the lives of philosophers. The lives were concerned with passing on the teachings of the philosophers. Biographical anecdotes were primarily compiled to back their teachings with stories of their conduct. In fact, the book of Acts would function this way for the letters of Paul, reporting not only his life but also passing on some of his speeches.[88]

The dissemination of these works occurred as private owners copied texts and traded for texts they did not yet own. Lecture notes were sometimes circulated without the author's name and then used for oral performances by new orators, only slightly revised, if at all. Social networks among early Christians would have provided a natural avenue for such exchanges. Also, Christian works were written on codices, long before they became an accepted format for literary compositions. This reticence among the *literati* may be related to a

---

86. Alexander, *Preface*, 195–96.
87. Alexander, *Preface*, 198.
88. Alexander, "What if Luke," 168; Alexander, "Acts and Ancient Intellectual Biography," 35–36; Alexander, "Luke's Preface," 68–69.

prejudice that connected the codex with draft copies, schoolwork, household expenses, and tax records.[89]

The setting where early Christian texts and ideas were exchanged would have looked to an outsider much like Jewish synagogues and philosophical schools.[90] Galen, in fact, critiques some schools for relying too much on faith, calling them just like "the school of Moses and Christ," thus demonstrating his perception of the similarities among these gatherings.[91] Alexander elucidates:

- Plato founded what we might call a school whose traditions were based on his written dialogues and their exegesis in oral teachings in an academy. These were taught by a local Platonist teacher to philosophy students in a class in the *polis*.[92]
- Similarly, Hippocrates founded what we might call a school whose traditions were based on his *Corp. Hipp.* and their exegesis in oral teachings at the Cos school. These were taught by a local medical teacher to medical apprentices or *philiatroi* (lay advisors or practitioners) in a master's house, or at a lecture or in a professional guild in the *polis*.
- Moses, too, founded what we might call a school whose traditions were based on Torah and their exegesis in oral Torah at the Great Synagogue. This was taught by a local rabbi or synagogue leader to *talmids* or any Jews in the rabbinic "academy" or synagogue in the Jewish community.[93]
- And finally, Christ founded what we might call a school whose traditions were based on Scripture and their exegesis in the oral word of the Lord among the disciples who were rhetorically constituted as a family. These were taught by an apostle, prophet, or teacher to apprentices or any Christian in the

---

89. Loveday Alexander, "Ancient Book Production and the Circulation of the Gospels," in *The Gospels for All Christians: Rethinking the Gospel Audiences*, ed. Richard J. Bauckham (Grand Rapids: Eerdmans, 1997), 71–111.

90. Alexander, "Acts and Ancient Intellectual Biography," 39.

91. Loveday Alexander, "Paul and the Hellenistic Schools: The Evidence of Galen," in *Paul in His Hellenistic Context*, ed. Troels Engberg-Pedersen (Minneapolis: Fortress, 2003), 60–83, here 65. She notes in this article Galen's use of the phrases "the school of Moses and Christ" (Μωσοῦ καὶ Χριστοῦ διατριβή) and "the followers of Moses and Christ" (οἱ ἀπὸ Μωσοῦ καὶ Χριστοῦ).

92. These sentences describe Alexander's chart in Loveday Alexander, "*Ipse dixit*: Citation of Authority in Paul and in the Jewish and Hellenistic Schools," in *Paul Beyond the Judaism-Hellenism Divide*, ed. Troels Engberg-Pedersen (Louisville, KY: Westminster John Knox, 2001), 103–27, here 106.

93. Alexander, "*Ipse dixit*," 106.

"school of Paul" or at an *ekklēsia* in the Christian communi-ty.[94] And just as the lives of the philosophers legitimated these traditions, so the Gospel of Luke could have functioned to legitimate Christian teachings, and the stories of Paul's life in Acts might have legitimated the "school of Paul."[95]

Despite these similarities, Christian gatherings differed in their preach-ing locations.[96] Some philosophical schools would have had access to public spaces in towns and cities while others were precluded from spaces belonging to the public (i.e., the *polis*). Christianity would likely not have had access to public spaces either and thus would have needed to (1) attempt to share Jewish spaces (synagogues) and when that did not work (2) meet in spaces provided by patrons—likely houses that were, in Roman fashion, open to the public.[97]

Luke describes the preaching there, what he calls the teaching of the apostles (Acts 2:42) or the service of the word (6:2), in terms of witnessing to Jesus, an activity that brings us to a discussion of memory and tradition.[98] Using Birger Gerhardsson's work on memory within rabbinic schools as a backdrop, Alexander shifts her focus to Helle-nistic practices.[99] She starts with Justin's name for the Gospels: the ἀπομνημονεύματα (memoirs) of the apostles. But this Greek word includes three aspects of the passing on of tradition, two of which are often not included in English translations. First, it refers to the

---

94.   Alexander, "*Ipse dixit*," 106.

95.   Alexander, "What if Luke," 168; Alexander, "Acts and Ancient Intellectual Biography," 35–36; Alexander, "Luke's Preface," 68–69. For more on the legitimation of texts, see Loveday Alexander, "Canon and Exegesis in the Medical Schools of Antiquity," in *The Canon of Scripture in Jewish and Christian Tradition: Le canon des Écritures dans les traditions juive et chrétienne*, eds. Jean-Daniel Kaestli and Philip S. Alexander, Publications de l'Institut Romand des Sciences Bibliques 4 (Lausanne: Zèbre, 2007), 115–53. For the importance of memory in Hellenistic schools and the way that affects our understanding of the transmission of the Gospel stories, see Loveday Alexander, "Memory and Tradition in the Hellenistic Schools," in *Jesus in Memory: Tradition in Oral and Scribal Perspective*, eds. Werner H. Kelber and Samuel Byrskog (Waco, TX: Baylor University Press, 2009), 113–54.

96.   Alexander, "Paul and the Hellenistic Schools," 73–76.

97.   For more on the negotiation of these spaces, see Loveday Alexander, "'Foolishness to the Greeks': Jews and Christians in the Public Life of the Empire," in *Philosophy and Power in the Graeco-Roman World: Essays in Honour of Miriam T. Griffin*, eds. G. Clark and T. Rajak (Oxford: Oxford University Press, 2002), 229–49.

98.   Loveday Alexander, "Memory and Tradition," 113–54.

99.   Gerhardsson's work was originally published in 1961. See today Birger Gerhardsson, *Memory and Manuscript: Oral Tradition and Written Transmission in Rabbinic Judaism and Early Christianity with Tradition and Transmission in Early Christianity* (Grand Rapids: Eerdmans, 1998).

"memories of the apostles"; it can refer to the "anecdotes of the apostles," and finally, as mentioned, the "memoirs of the apostles," i.e., the
texts themselves.[100] These different glosses for ἀπομνημονεύματα
each have counterparts in the enactment of memory in the Hellenistic
world.

Starting with the last, Alexander notes that memory can be
embodied in a text. Xenophon writes his *Apomnemoneumata Xeno-
phontis* in which his memories of Socrates are written down, "already
molded by the literary forms and expectations of the larger society."[101]
Memories circulated in stories, but then were written down and gathered together. These compilations could become collections of sayings,
collections of anecdotes, sometimes organized by topic. Their roots in
orality are evidenced by the way the same report will show up in more
than one collection or attributed to a different teacher. Thus, it is not
self-evident that these collections would ever be compiled into a fully
narrated biography.

Memory could be performed, as well, in short anecdotes, attributed *chreia*, or anonymous aphorisms.[102] These memories and their
settings became important as exemplars of virtue, which were thought
to be more easily imitated than mere definitions.[103] They were also used
to attack or defend one school or another according to the congruity
between the teacher's life and teaching. Thus, life settings and stories
about a founder were important as moral examples, rather than as
biographical material.

Memory was practiced within a variety of genres. Histories were
read, as other genres were, for both their content and their style.
Students memorized the content, in fact, before approaching the
texts. Later in the students' progression, passages became models for
imitation and themes for compositions.[104] It was understood that texts
could demand that readers acquire the necessary background information to fill in gaps in expected knowledge.[105] Luke, similarly, presupposes knowledge of the Gospel story and elements of the history of the

---

100. Alexander, "Memory and Tradition," 119.
101. Alexander, "Memory and Tradition," 121.
102. Alexander, "Memory and Tradition," 126–32.
103. Alexander, "Memory and Tradition," 145.
104. Alexander, "L'intertextualité," 205–206.
105. Alexander, "L'intertextualité," 212–13, 210–11.

Hebrew people by simply referring to characters or concepts without explanation, thus grounding his story in tradition (Acts 1).[106]

Memory performed in texts and in oral performance both grounds and is grounded in memory as tradition.[107] Bits of wisdom were crafted expressly for the purpose of easy memorization, and memorization itself was highly valued and trained, and its use throughout life displayed one's *paideia*. Students first learned passages by heart and later "worked and reworked" them in their own words, thus building both "stability and fluidity . . . into this model."[108] Empiricists and Epicurians were especially dedicated to this process, and Alexander notes a repetition of narrative patterns with variations throughout Acts.[109] Personal connections with the founder were not emphasized, only embeddedness in the tradition.[110]

All of this means that there was a general culture of memory in the ancient world, in Hellenistic schools as well as in rabbinic ones, which legitimated one's tradition by grounding it in the past.[111] Knowing the way traditional learning worked helps us understand Luke when he "states that his gospel provides written confirmation (ἀσφάλεια) of the oral instruction Theophilus has already received (κατηχήθης)—a term from the medical schools that was already gaining currency for Christian instruction."[112] Irenaeus describes the transmission of the gospel with the same balance of memorable content and exemplary way of life.[113]

Thus, it is not so much the written tradition but the practice of tradition in all its modes that schools transmit: "Someone once told Diocles the doctor that he would not need any more teaching because he had bought a medical book. Diocles responded: 'For those who have studied, books are reminders, but for the unlearned, they are tombs.'"[114] Written texts thus simply "captur[e] a fleeting moment

---

106. Alexander, "L'intertextualité," 211–12.
107. Alexander, "Memory and Tradition," 132–41.
108. Alexander, "Memory and Tradition," 135, 146.
109. Alexander, "Acts," 1033, 1043, 1054–55.
110. Alexander, "Memory and Tradition," 141.
111. Alexander, "L'intertextualité," 213; Alexander, "Memory and Tradition," 142.
112. Alexander, "Memory and Tradition," 146. See an overview of Gospels and transmission practices in Loveday Alexander, "What is a Gospel?" in *The Cambridge Companion to the Gospels*, ed. Stephen C. Barton (Cambridge: Cambridge University Press, 2006), 13–33.
113. Alexander, "Memory and Tradition," 147.
114. Alexander, "Memory and Tradition," 148.

between performance and re-oralization."[115] The four Gospels, too, are not the end or the goal of a previously oral process. They are a moment in time, and Jesus stories continued to be told and condensed and reused in new configurations even after they were written down. Stories told in the third person that foreground disciples (of Diogenes as well as of Jesus) invite those who listen to join the circle.[116] Alexander thus grounds her study of Luke–Acts within her broader understanding of instruction and oral transmission in the first century CE.

GREEK NOVELS AND THE BOOK OF ACTS

Alexander's wide knowledge of texts outside of those commonly used in comparisons with the New Testament allows her to engage in several unusual studies. This section will summarize her comparison of the book of Acts to the Archive of Theophanes and her suggestion that one possibility for the "we-passages" and the redundant details of the travel narratives in Acts could be that it was constructed based on the travel notes of one of Paul's companions. Still within the context of Paul's travels, Alexander notes the way, on the one hand, Acts turns Greek approaches to the world upside-down, constructing the east as familiar and the west as barbarian. On the other hand, however, as we have discussed already, the final scene in Acts when Paul is welcomed on his way into Rome by a group of brothers and sisters (28:15) "has almost an air of homecoming."[117] One of the most intriguing comparisons Alexander makes is between the scattered nodes of the ancient ἐκκλησίαι and today's internet.

In "The Pauline Itinerary and the Archive of Theophanes," Alexander explores the archive of Theophanes, the records of a journey from the fourth century CE.[118] Her conclusions are, first, that these archives show that records of Paul's journey could also have existed and then

---

115. Alexander, "Memory and Tradition," 149. For more on the importance of orality, see Loveday Alexander, "The Living Voice: Scepticism Towards the Written Word in Early Christian and in Greco-Roman Texts," in *The Bible in Three Dimensions: Essays in Celebration of Forty Years of Biblical Studies in the University of Sheffield*, eds. David J. A. Clines, Stephen E. Fowl and Stanley E. Porter, JSOTSup 87 (Sheffield: Sheffield Academic, 1990), 221–47.
116. Alexander, "Memory and Tradition," 153.
117. Alexander, "Reading Luke-Acts," 214.
118. Loveday Alexander, "The Pauline Itinerary and the Archive of Theophanes," in *The New Testament and Early Christian Literature in the Greco-Roman Context: Studies in Honor of David E. Aune*, ed. John Fotopoulos, NovTSup 122 (Leiden: Brill, 2006), 151–65.

been used as sources for the book of Acts. Second, one could acquire information about an upcoming journey from circulating recommendations, and this was likely true in the first century CE as well. Also, some of Theophanes's records of expenses use various pronouns including first person plural, such as when wine is bought "for us."[119] This might provide an explanation for the we-passages in Acts. However, Theophanes's records contain no redundant place names and no verbs, particularly vivid seafaring verbs such as we find in Acts.[120] Thus, these records do not answer all the questions Alexander raises. Still, they remind us that narratives were not the only written texts documenting ancient travel.[121]

The possibility that someone kept Paul's records and receipts becomes more likely when one attends to one of Alexander's important insights:

> Paul himself . . . describes his experiences of sea-travel in lurid terms scarcely bettered by the novelists (2 Cor. 11), and carefully avoids drawing attention to the practicalities of his journeys. Like a presidential candidate on the campaign trail, the apostle travels from venue to venue without having to think about the means of travel at all, relying on his team to study the timetables and make the reservations. For the narrator of Acts, by contrast, sea travel is a matter of consuming interest.[122]

Alexander examines two Greek novels in which journeys feature prominently, *Chaereas and Callirhoe* by Chariton and *Ephesiaca* by Xenophon of Ephesus.[123] In Acts, Paul's voyages are not clearly demarcated one from the other. Furthermore, they feature Jerusalem as Paul's departure point and end goal. However, as Acts progresses, the center shifts so that by the end of the narrative, Jerusalem is on "the eastern edge of a westerly voyage which follows the sea-routes more familiar to

---

119. Alexander, "The Pauline Itinerary," 160, 164.
120. See also Alexander, "Acts," 1046.
121. Alexander, "The Pauline Itinerary," 165.
122. Loveday Alexander, "'In Journeying Often': Voyaging in the Acts of the Apostles and in Greek Romance," in *Luke's Literary Achievement: Collected Essays*, ed. C. M. Tuckett, JSNTSup 116 (Sheffield: Sheffield Academic, 1995), 17–49, here 36. Note that Alexander also compares 1 Corinthians 11 to Greek novels; see Loveday Alexander, "'Better to Marry Than to Burn?': St. Paul and the Greek Novel," in *Ancient Fiction and Early Christian Narrative*, eds. Ronald F. Hock, J. Bradley Chance, and Judith Perkins (Atlanta: Scholars Press, 1998), 235–56.
123. Alexander, "In Journeying Often." In this essay in particular, Alexander retells the novels' plots quite humorously. For more on Acts and Greek novels, see the chapter in this volume on Richard Pervo.

the Greek reader than to the Bible."[124] In the passages that emphasize seafaring, notable for their first-person plural pronouns, Paul displays confidence and competence beyond that of captain or crew.[125] While in the novels, Rome is the center of the world, Greece rules the sea, and everything else is barbarian, in Acts, Paul comes from the east, which is the center of the narrative, and ultimately conquerors Greece and the sea with his wisdom and knowledge.

In "Narrative Maps," Alexander delves into this topic even more extensively and lays out the primary toponyms which describe where the characters go, secondary toponyms which come from other characters' reported journeys, and tertiary toponyms which come from other narrative references.[126] She also pays attention to the repetition of some place names. This allows her to create maps that reflect not the actual geographical space but rather the mental maps created by the story. Acts, as opposed to the Greek novels, has more interior place names and constructs the east as home and Athens as foreign. Yet Paul, while refusing even more emphatically than Callirhoe to worship other gods, strides across the Mediterranean with "the inexorable progress" of Jesus just as Callirhoe did for Aphrodite.[127]

Picking up again on the feeling of coming home as Paul arrives in a city where brothers come out to welcome him (after a voyage through barbarian lands), Alexander looks at Eusebius's descriptions of Paul.[128] Eusebius is concerned to show a tight succession (as with the philosophers) from Jesus, radiating out from Jerusalem, that eventually reaches the real center of power, Rome. As he continues his history, one notices another mental map, one that conforms to Roman

---

124. Alexander, "In Journeying Often," 32.
125. Alexander, "In Journeying Often," 38. Alexander notes that in this passage "Jonah's situation is reversed."
126. Loveday Alexander, "Narrative Maps: Reflections on the Toponymy of Acts," in *The Bible in Human Society: Essays in Honour of John Rogerson*, eds. M. Daniel Carroll R., David J. A. Clines and Philip R. Davies, JSOTSup 200 (Sheffield: Sheffield Academic, 1995), 17–57.
127. Loveday Alexander, "The Virgin and the Goddess: Women and Religion in Greek Romance," in *Women and Gender in Ancient Religions: Interdisciplinary Approaches*, eds. Stephen P. Ahearne-Kroll, Paul A. Holloway, and James A. Kelhoffer, WUNT 263 (Tübingen: Mohr Siebeck, 2010), 11–37, here 34. Alexander notes in this essay, too, that women's prayers and women's agency find their counterparts in Luke–Acts as in Greek romances, although the independence of the women is quickly hidden in reception history if not in Paul.
128. Loveday Alexander, "Mapping Early Christianity: Acts and the Shape of Early Christianity," *Int* 57 (2003): 163–73. For the term "barbarian," see the use of βάρβαροι in Acts 28:2, usually translated 'islanders'; Alexander, "Mapping Early Christianity," 164.

provinces: local churches with authority over all the other churches in their region.

This localization of power mirrors the connection between Jerusalem and the diaspora Jews, with their שליחים (šĕlîḥîm, sg. שליח šālîaḥ), who were commissioned with letters from authorities in Jerusalem, at least until the destruction of the temple.[129] In contrast, Luke does not depict the apostles as authoritative. Instead, Acts presents a rather loose network of churches, each with autonomy, but connected through Paul and the other apostles. There may, in fact, have been several networks, such as Pauline, Johannine, and Petrine, in larger cities where greetings and information were exchanged. Alexander suggests that "the communication superhighways of the Internet—a polycentric and infinitely expandable network with no clear authority structure" might provide a relatable model for churches in our postmodern world.[130]

ECCLESIOLOGY AND THE BOOK OF ACTS

Ecclesiology is another topic of interest to Alexander, one that bridges her academic and practical responsibilities.[131] She notes both continuity and diversity between Luke's Gospel and Acts. She describes the way Luke repeatedly constructs the early believers' reliance on the Jewish Scriptures (usually in Greek translation) to explain the Holy Spirit's activity. On issues of authority and leadership, she concludes that Acts relies on a balance of charismatic leading and traditional explanations, of local leadership with trans-local communication. Many Christian denominations, of course, rely on Acts to justify their polity even though, for Luke, "ecclesiology as such plays a relatively minor part."[132] Still, Alexander also notes that the New Testament and

---

129. Alexander, "Mapping Early Christianity," 167–68.
130. Alexander, "Mapping Early Christianity," 171.
131. Further reflections include Loveday Alexander, "Women as Leaders in the New Testament," *Modern Believing* 54 (2013): 14–22. See, too, her review of Twelftree's *People of the Spirit* where she notes that he suggests that while contemporary churches preach the gospel to themselves and work for social justice in the world, the early church preached the gospel to the world and worked for social justice within the church; Loveday Alexander, "People of the Spirit: Exploring Luke's View of the Church," *Theology* 114.1 (January 2011): 56–57.
132. Loveday Alexander, "Community and Canon: Reflections on the Ecclesiology of Acts," in *Einheit der Kirche im Neuen Testament: Dritte europäische orthodox-westliche Exegetenkonferenz in Sankt Petersburg, 24.–31. August 2005*, eds. Anatoly Alexeev, Christos Karakolis, and Ulrich Luz, WUNT 218 (Tübingen: Mohr Siebeck, 2008), 45–78, here 46.

even the Gospels teach ecclesiology even when they do not mention it as such.[133]

Luke's Gospel focuses on hospitality, so that discipleship is about encounter, repentance, the renunciation of wealth and privilege, and suffering.[134] The call begins with Israel and the twelve, but extends to women, the seventy, and the world. But Luke also picks up Mark's emphasis on the renewal of God's kingdom. Through the Holy Spirit, disciples are brought in, listen to the Word, learn the tasks of healing and restoration, and then are sent out as apostles. Disciples and apostles encounter suffering and endure with hope, centering their faithfulness on the remembrances of Jesus. While Matthew adds a tension between present hospitality and future judgment, and disciples (as prototypical church leaders) humbly exercise both care and oversight, Luke focuses less on the prototypicality of the disciples in his Gospel and instead saves most of his ecclesiology for Acts.

Alexander recognizes the difficult gap between the story of the early church as it happened and the story as Luke tells it. However, it is the latter that became constitutive for the church so, without ignoring the former, she focuses on Luke's text.[135] She points out that the book of Acts exhibits both continuity with and distinctiveness from the synoptic Gospels, as one might expect. On the one hand, the disciples stop focusing on the end times, but also Jesus is now in heaven and the disciples take over the proclamation of the kingdom by the power of the Spirit Jesus sends.[136]

Luke's usage of the term usually translated church, ἐκκλησία, refers to "the body of God's people in a given place," rather than any conception of a universal church.[137] It is not a fragment of some larger entity, but rather "a locally-grounded instantiation of something bigger which is the church of God."[138] Only when Luke has described the believers in Syria and Cilicia (15:41) does he begin to use the plural form. Luke's lack of further specificity allows for unity and diversity among churches from their beginnings.

---

133. Loveday Alexander, "The Church in the Synoptic Gospels and the Acts of the Apostles," in *The Oxford Handbook of Ecclesiology*, ed. Paul Avis (Oxford: Oxford University Press, 2018), 55–98.
134. For this whole paragraph, see Alexander, "The Church."
135. Alexander, "Community," 50–51; Alexander, "The Church," 57.
136. Alexander, "The Church," 80.
137. Alexander, "Community," 52–53. Luke uses terms that echo the people of God language from the Jewish Scriptures ("The Church," 87).
138. Alexander, "Community," 53.

For Luke, the unity of the church starts with the believers in Jerusalem, constituted by Jesus and the Holy Spirit now sent by him from heaven.[139] Initially, this Jerusalem-centered community was able to grow into the immediate environs while remaining unified through the travels of the apostles, a unity of heart and soul, the sharing of food, prayer (sometimes but not always formal prayers), teaching, and a fellowship that prioritized the sharing of goods.[140]

Luke describes diversity in the church, as well. The shift from twelve disciples of one Lord to twelve apostles following the Holy Spirit built diversity into the leadership of the church from the beginning. And although Luke shows the primacy of the Holy Spirit, it is that very Spirit who multiplies their ministries and practices, as the apostles (in imitation of Jesus) travel and preach. Acts describes some of the leaders giving up their oversight in the distribution of food, too, and those who continue that ministry are not confined to their new tasks.[141] As ministry moves out from Jerusalem, the apostles' authority (including Paul's) remains grounded in the Spirit whose presence signals the restoration promised by God.[142] Furthermore, Luke tells us little about the elders in Jerusalem which has the effect of creating an "empty centre."[143]

Yet the church does have what Alexander calls "a catholicity of κοινωνία-in-diversity."[144] She points out that the church in Antioch shows no appearance of submission to Jerusalem as it got started, nor even of intentional planning. Rather it came about simply by refugees from persecution "gossiping the gospel" (Acts 11:19–20).[145] The book of Acts describes various patterns for conversions, moreover. They always include repentance, baptism, forgiveness, and the gift of the Spirit, but there is no prescribed order.[146] As the center disappears, Luke is not eager to replace it. Even when Antioch sends out Paul and Barnabas, the ministry crosses back and forth between Jews and

---

139. Alexander, "Community," 54; Alexander, "The Church," 58, 84–85; Alexander, "Acts," 1042. The way the early community explains their experiences with Jewish Scriptures will be discussed below.

140. Alexander, "Community," 56–59.

141. Alexander, "Community," 60.

142. Alexander, "The Church," 85–86.

143. Alexander, "Community," 65.

144. Alexander, "Community," 67; Alexander, "The Church," 87.

145. Alexander, "Community," 68.

146. Alexander, "The Church," 86; Alexander, "Acts," 1032.

Gentiles across the northeastern Mediterranean, and Antioch does not become authoritative.

At the council, charismatic Antioch, led by "prophets and teachers" (13:1), and tradition-centered Jerusalem, led by "apostles and elders" (15:4, 22), come together.[147] Elders in Jerusalem and in Paul's churches exercise organizational leadership, but apostles' commissions come from Jesus. James has some sort of authority but only "as *primus inter pares*," and he gives "due weight to the testimony of Peter and Paul" and adds the "authority of the Jewish scriptures."[148] Only after listening carefully to one another do they come to a decision.[149] As a result, the only ones who are shut down are those who wanted "to impose uniformity of practice on a far-flung constituency."[150]

In an ecclesial setting where itinerancy is common, practices of hospitality carried great importance. Alexander writes about Luke 10:38–42 and points out that categorizing Mary as good and Martha as bad seems to liberate women by allowing them to become disciples.[151] However, that interpretation delegitimizes a life of acts of service. Alexander suggests that instead we categorize the story as one about good and better. The story is principally about Martha. Mary is a background character. Martha is doing all the things considered good in the Gospel except that she worries. For women as for men, the lesson is not that hospitality or active service is bad, but rather that hospitality should not mean that chores get more attention than the guest, especially when the guest is Jesus.

Israel's Scriptures also continue to function within these new communities (e.g., Acts 1:20).[152] Alexander locates the authority of Scripture in an interpretational practice that searches for the explanation of God's present revelation in God's past revelatory acts, depending on the Holy Spirit and navigating a multiplicity of meanings.[153] The results,

147. Alexander, "Community," 72.
148. Alexander, "Community," 74.
149. Alexander, "Community," 75. Note that this conclusion in 2008 corrects her earlier statement about the authority of the Jerusalem council; Alexander, "Acts," 1047.
150. Alexander, "Community," 76.
151. Loveday Alexander, "Sisters in Adversity: Retelling Martha's Story," in *Women in the Biblical Tradition*, ed. George J. Brooke, Studies in Women and Religion 31 (Lewiston, NY: Edwin Mellen, 1992), 167–86.
152. Alexander, "This Is That," 189–204; Alexander, "God's Frozen Word," 37–42; Alexander, "Acts," 1031.
153. Alexander, "This Is That," 191–93.

for Luke, are then judged against "the fundamental canon . . . the person of Christ himself."[154]

RECEPTION

One of the challenges of Alexander's work is the nuanced nature of her study and its conclusions.[155] Darryl Palmer, for example, suggests that "one of the main problems" regarding the nature of Acts is "the discrepancy between the technical features of the Lucan preface and the biographical and historical content of Luke and Acts."[156] Daryl D. Schmidt also notes some confusion between these two elements which Alexander "seeks to clarify" in "Formal Elements and Genre" and later further discusses in "Septuaginta."[157] Gerald Downing builds on Alexander's insights, noting that in the first reading of Luke–Acts, the preface would let the auditors know what genre they were *not* going to hear but not what they *would* hear.[158] Alexander, in fact, draws no firm conclusion about genre in her 2009 entry on "Acts" in the *Oxford Bible Commentary* but looks instead at its affinities with histories (both Greek and biblical), biographies (particularly philosophical biographies), novels, and apologetic texts.[159] The importance of Alexander's initial work was in spurring discussions about the relationship of *Fachprosa* to Attic and Koine Greek.[160]

---

154. Alexander, "This Is That," 194–95.
155. For a summary of initial reviews, see David E. Aune, "Luke 1.1–4: Historical or Scientific Prooimion?" in *Paul, Luke and the Graeco-Roman World*, ed. Alf Christophersen, Carsten Claussen, Jörg Frey, and Bruce Longenecker, JSNTSup 217 (Sheffield: Sheffield Academic, 2002), 138–48, here 138–39. Note that Alexander's initial hesitancy to connect Luke and Acts together, which Marshall called "carrying a proper scholarly caution to excess," was criticized. As we have seen, her later studies led her to different conclusions. See I. H. Marshall, "Acts and the 'Former Treatise,'" in *The Book of Acts in Its Ancient Literary Setting*, 163–82; Alexander, "Reading Luke–Acts from Back to Front."
156. Darryl W. Palmer, "Acts and the Ancient Historical Monograph," in *The Book of Acts in Its Ancient Literary Setting*, 1–29. Cf. Adams's concern that Alexander only compares the length of Luke's preface to that of Thucydides (183) with Alexander's discussion in *Preface*, 30, 103; Sean A. Adams, "Luke's Preface and Its Relationship to Greek Historiography: A Response to Loveday Alexander," *JGRChJ* 3 (2006): 177–91, here 183. See similar concerns in Dawson, "Luke's Preface," 554, who reproduces Adams's critique without addressing Alexander's other examples.
157. Daryl D. Schmidt, "Rhetorical Influences and Genre: Luke's Preface and the Rhetoric of Hellenistic Historiography," in *Jesus and the Heritage of Israel*, 27–60; Alexander, "Formal Elements."
158. F. Gerald Downing, "Theophilus's First Reading of Luke–Acts," in *Luke's Literary Achievement*, 91–109, here 97–98.
159. Alexander, "Acts," 1029–30.
160. Aune, "Luke 1.1–4," 141. See also Stanley E. Porter, "Thucydides 1.22.1 and Speeches in Acts: Is There a Thucydidean View?" *NovT* 32.2 (1990): 121–142, here 124–27.

David Aune, however, points out the speculative nature of Alexander's conclusions given the paucity of evidence of prefaces (many more works are known to have existed than have survived) and her failure to address "the function of prefaces in scientific literature" and the disconnect apparent between Luke's use of a scientific preface for a work that is clearly not scientific in its genre.[161] Aune's strongest critique comes when he compares Luke 1:1–4 to Plutarch's *Septem sapientium convivium* which parodies a report of a symposium. The twelve similarities he finds between the two, some of which Alexander noted in scientific prefaces, do not disprove her argument that Luke had the latter model in mind but do problematize categorizing *Fachprosa* as an isolated register.[162]

John Moles responds to Alexander's work and concludes that Luke's preface resembles a Greek decree.[163] Zachary K. Dawson refutes Moles but also characterizes Alexander's work as "claim[ing] that the whole work of Luke–Acts should be read as a technical or scientific work."[164] This seems to go beyond Alexander's proposal that "the biographical content of the Gospel and Acts is by no means an insuperable obstacle to viewing Luke as a writer set firmly within the context of the scientific tradition," and that Luke's "situation in presenting his Gospel in written form must have been in some important sense like the situation of other writers who used the same sort of preface."[165] Vernon K. Robbins extends Alexander's insights to argue that the prefaces rhetorically line up auditors' expectations with a narrative grounded in the stories and practices of nascent Christianity.[166] Stanley E. Porter approaches the issue of genre from the perspective of ancient discourses on ethics and brings attention back to biographies.[167] Sean A. Adams extends the discussion and argues that the broad biographical genre can be narrowed by focusing on collected biographies.[168] Adams also

161. Aune, "Luke 1.1–4," 143–44.
162. Aune, "Luke 1.1–4," 144–47. See also Porter, "Thucydides." 125.
163. John Moles, "Luke's Preface: The Greek Decree, Classical Historiography and Christian Redefinitions," *NTS* 57.4 (2011): 461–82.
164. Dawson, "Luke's Preface," 554.
165. Alexander, "Luke's Preface," 70; Alexander, *Preface*, 174.
166. Vernon K. Robbins, "The Claims of the Prologues and Greco-Roman Rhetoric: The Prefaces to Luke and Acts in Light of Greco-Roman Rhetorical Strategies," in *Jesus and the Heritage of Israel*, 63–83.
167. Stanley E. Porter, "The Genre of Acts and the Ethics of Discourse," in *Acts and Ethics*, ed. Thomas E. Phillips (Sheffield: Sheffield Phoenix, 2005), 1–15.
168. Sean A. Adams, *The Genre of Acts and Collected Biography*, SNTSMS 156 (Cambridge: Cambridge University Press, 2013).

points out that to simply compare the life of Paul to ancient biographies is to leave out the first half of the book of Acts.[169]

Another critique of Alexander's work centers on her discussion of αὐτόπτης (eyewitness or "first-hand experience").[170] She argues that while the *concept* of firsthand experience was important for historians, it is not always represented by the word αὐτόπτης. Thucydides uses the concept but not the word, and Herodotus uses the word but in the context of geographical knowledge.[171] It is a common word among Empiricists, however, and Alexander posits that they influenced Polybius (and from him, Josephus).[172] Grounding Luke's use of the word in *Fachprosa* instead of in histories, then, suggests that Luke was gathering information from those with personal experience with Jesus and the developing tradition just as, within school traditions, practice and oral tradition superseded written knowledge.[173] Similarly, "for Justin, the key 'proofs' of the gospel message are supplied by the prophets, not the 'eyewitnesses.'"[174] Clare K. Rothschild, however, by looking at the importance of eyewitnesses throughout Luke–Acts, problematizes the conclusion that Luke in his preface was differentiating between the two.[175]

Sean A. Adams agrees that trustworthy sources are important to historians. He, too, cites Thucydides's concerns and Herodotus's geographical use of the word αὐτόπτης. He discusses its uses in Polybius and Josephus, but not their possible connection to Empiricists nor dependencies between them. Therefore, noting that Luke's use is unique in the New Testament, he concludes that "Luke borrowed this word from Greek historians in order to associate his work with that genre."[176] Dawson, citing Adams, further suggests that Alexander's argument is "a case of special pleading."[177] He argues, too, that

---

169. Adams, *The Genre*, 21.
170. Alexander, *Preface*, 123. See further discussion in John J. Peters, "Luke's Source Claims in the Context of Ancient Historiography," *Journal for the Study of the Historical Jesus* 18 (2020): 35–60, here 36–42.
171. Alexander, *Preface*, 34–41.
172. Alexander, *Preface*, 80–82, 87, 40.
173. Alexander, *Preface*, 120, 123–24.
174. Alexander, "Memory and Tradition," 141. Schmidt echoes Alexander; "Rhetorical Influences," 29.
175. Clare K. Rothschild, *Luke–Acts and the Rhetoric of History*, WUNT 2/175 (Tübingen: Mohr Siebeck, 2004), 225; cf. 213–90. For her other substantial critique of Alexander, see 68n31.
176. Adams, "Luke's Preface," 188; cf. 187–90. See also Adams's extension of Alexander's work already cited, "Atticism."
177. Dawson, "Luke's Preface," 556.

a way forward might be to categorize all prefaces as one genre, in which case the similarities Alexander discovered would be reasonable when compared both with "shorter historiographical *and* scientific prefaces."[178] Schmidt looks more broadly at historiography and concludes that Luke was "a writer of 'historical' narrative, but not necessarily a 'historian.'"[179] He, like Alexander, notes the imitation of Jewish as well as Hellenistic Greek models.

Such distinctions, those between the genre of a work and the register of its preface and the possibility of *imitatio* in each, should be maintained. Moreover, this discussion as well as the debates about the style of prefaces, it seems to me, might benefit from considering Umberto Eco's category of "cultural units."[180] Eco's semiotics recognizes the way words reference meanings in a variety of cultural frames. He thus provides tools for bridging textual and cultural contexts. The use of a word such as αὐτόπτης would raise (for listeners aware of them) only the broader conversations in which the specific word was used, even if other authors referred to that concept. Yet it is the immediate textual context that guides the listener through the cultural possibilities.

Alexander's descriptions of Hellenistic schools provide an important backdrop, particularly for the repetition of events in Acts' speeches and Luke's concern for passing on not only the activities of the early church but also the contents of Peter and Paul's speeches. Alexander's work often suffers from a lack of attention to recent approaches, for example in the rare mention of the Roman presence either in the world or in the texts. However, because she grounds her work in dialogue with scholars with deep roots in the classics and ancient Greek, her work provides an important bridge between the approaches to Luke–Acts from the past and in contemporary studies. Her scholarship continues to provide fruitful material with which to engage and will continue to do so with her upcoming work on discipleship in the Gospels and Acts, and leadership and authority in the Pauline Letters.[181]

---

178. Dawson, "Luke's Preface," 556, emphasis mine.
179. Schmidt, "Rhetorical Influences," 59.
180. Laura J. Hunt, *Jesus Caesar: A Roman Reading of the Johannine Trial Narrative*, WUNT 2/506 (Tübingen: Mohr Siebeck, 2019), 53–55.
181. Loveday Alexander, "Discipleship and the Kingdom in the Gospels and Acts," in *Discipleship: Then and Now*, eds. Stephen Cherry and Andrew Hayes (Norwich: SCM Press, 2022); Alexander, "Paul the Apostle: Leadership and Authority in the Pauline Letters," in *Oxford Handbook of Pauline Studies*, eds. Barry Matlock and Matthew Novenson (Oxford: Oxford University Press, forthcoming).

CONCLUSION TO *LUKE–ACTS IN MODERN INTERPRETATION*

Stanley E. Porter and Ron C. Fay

This volume covers approximately two hundred years of Lukan scholarship. For some of that time, Luke–Acts had relatively little written about it. Paul and John were major sources of controversy and Luke's writings were a concern only in how the historical Jesus appeared or in how the Synoptic Gospels were used as a trio. Nevertheless, there have been various controversies and contours followed in the debates over Luke–Acts, and this volume includes many of them, associated with their major proponents. As becomes evident, virtually everything has been questioned in the history of Luke and Acts, including authorship, date, audience, purpose, destination, theological emphases, genre, and the unity of these two works. This highlighting of historical tendencies does not seek to answer these questions; rather, we look to frame the discussions within their times and to watch how the interpretation of this corpus has unfolded.

Our introduction to this volume began with F. C. Baur, because in some ways he set the agenda for subsequent discussion of Luke–Acts. However, in terms of detailed discussions of major figures in the debate, this volume begins with Adolf Harnack and ends with Loveday C. A. Alexander, meaning that the lens through which we view Luke–Acts is limited in time from about 1870 to the present. Though certainly many twists and turns in the history of Lukan interpretation occurred before Harnack or even Baur, it was these giants (and a few we were unable to cover) who encouraged the study of Lukan works by setting the groundwork and asking questions that resonate with scholars today and will continue to do so in the years to come.

Adolf Harnack certainly wrote on more than just Luke–Acts. His scholarship spanned more than forty years and moved beyond the bounds simply of New Testament studies, let alone Lukan scholarship. He worked on redefining what it meant to be Christian, following the path set down by his German liberal predecessors. While other major scholars disagreed with his work (e.g., Rudolf Bultmann), they all responded to it, which in itself shows the depth and breadth of his work. Harnack wanted to communicate what the true gospel was, the true message of Jesus, and he looked to do this by using sound historical methodology instead of seeing his own reflection in the historical Jesus. In this, he took a step away from the nineteenth-century liberal tradition. In following them, however, he also displaced Jesus from his own time period. Harnack, however, held remarkably conservative views on authorship and dating for Luke and Acts. He argued for both to be written by Luke the physician, who was from Antioch, and both were completed before the death of Paul. Much of Harnack's argument comes from his brilliant use of source criticism and his ability to see similarities and differences between different passages. It is from this study, and comparing how Matthew and Mark use sources, that Harnack concludes that Luke transforms his sources to fit his own style of writing, thus blending it into a coherent and smooth finished document. Thus, Adolf Harnack has a solidly conservative take on the historical and textual issues, but a strong liberal understanding of the theological implications.

Though the "form criticism" school started before him, Martin Dibelius pushed it into the consciousness of scholarship. He developed his methods after learning in the history of religion school, primarily from Hermann Gunkel. This focused Dibelius's thinking that oral history had less accuracy and truth whereas written history conveyed more faithfully what actually happened. In order to build on these ideas, he constructed *Sitze im Leben* for Luke and Acts. Luke distinguishes itself as literature and not popular level writing. This means that Luke was written for those outside the church but not for low level amusement. Instead, it contained the essence of Christian preaching: the life and teachings of Jesus were recounted by those who were there and then passed on to those who were not. Dibelius wanted to isolate the teaching of Jesus within the Gospels in order to pull out the original meaning to those first-century audiences. He sees many of the parables and stories Jesus tells as built around *chriae* (original sayings, whether from him or someone else) in order to illustrate a specific point. Luke does this more than Mark or Matthew, as Luke's stories tend to be more elaborate and developed. Dibelius believes Luke used legends (stories about holy people) to fill in details around Jesus, such as those concerning Mary, the shepherds, and Simeon. Legends are not necessarily false; rather, they are a specific subgenre used to build a larger story. Luke uses these various *chriae* and legends to build a biography. In the same way, Luke builds out Acts by using the same methodology: putting together legends and teaching, and then adding his own words as the speeches to demonstrate how the early church arose. Acts ends up being of higher literary quality than the Gospel since Luke is able to mold his story without needing to bend to the tradition or include stories that do not fit his purpose. In all of this, Dibelius comes across as someone who wants to dissect the text to find the original meaning while still seeing the sum as greater than the parts due to Luke's literary talent.

Henry J. Cadbury, though born the same year as Dibelius, lived longer and wrote more specifically on the Lukan corpus, likely coining the term "Luke–Acts." His initial work examined the Greek of Luke–Acts. Rather than postulating a special dialect of Greek for the New Testament, Cadbury's research showed the close proximity to LXX Greek as well as there being commonalities with contemporaneous compositions. Further, he examined the thesis that the language of Luke–Acts pointed specifically to a physician and rejected it, as the vocabulary and syntax echoed such writers as Josephus and Plutarch. Cadbury also conducted a detailed investigation of the prefaces to Luke and Acts. He concluded that his understanding of the language of the New Testament was coherent with the evidence gathered from these two works, that Luke intended to write history based on his style and choice of wording, and that Luke intentionally used writing conventions to make the connection to that genre. However, Luke's speeches were purely his own creations, though this does fit within the historian's purview according to Cadbury. This leads to a major theme in Cadbury's scholarship: he claimed and tried to achieve objectivity in his work yet seemed to equate objectivity with a lack of theological bias or even theological apologetic. Cadbury's influence moving forward can be seen in how other scholars have tried to be objective, how he nurtured students from disparate theological backgrounds, and how future academics needed to respond to his ideas on Luke–Acts.

Ernst Haenchen concentrated more on Acts and fueled the revival in the Acts area of research. While not incorporating research into sources of Acts, he assumed there were sources in his own writing on Acts. He seemingly equivocates in this area by seeing Luke, a skilled writer and researcher, using sources but blending them in such a way that they essentially become his own writing. This comes from Haenchen's intentional correction to scholarship in focusing on Luke as a writer when previous works had highlighted his work as an historian and then later as a theologian. Haenchen contended that Luke's writing supersedes and, in some sense, precedes those other two roles, at least in how readers can apprehend him. He looked to build upon and moderate the work of Dibelius and Conzelmann (the latter was a contemporary). He saw Luke as a Gentile first, who softened the Jewishness of the gospel and was a precursor to early Catholicism. Haenchen argued for a less systematic and more practical theology in Luke, such that he realized immanent understandings of the final resurrection were untrue since he lived to see the deaths of the apostles, including Paul. Instead, Luke shifted to the resurrection being a practical outworking in the life of all believers. The return of Christ, therefore, will happen at an unknowable future date, which turns the believer toward a life lived in the Holy Spirit now. This theological struggle then informs the historical one: how would the Jewish-centered Christian faith create a mission that could reach out to Gentiles? The gospel without the law then becomes the focal point of both the theological and historical movement from Jew to Gentile in terms of the population of the Christian faith. Luke's skill as a writer appears in how he turned these problems into themes and answered them with condensed scenes. Luke's amazing gift of writing enabled him to take protracted struggles of the church and fit them into short narratives that convey truth without necessarily being historically precise. This allowed Luke to paint a portrait of Paul that includes his skilled verbal defense of himself and his mission while setting aside other questions not central to the Gentile mission. Haenchen described a Luke fascinated by the question of the Gentile mission and how the gospel functioned apart from the law in a Christian theological era dominated by Jewish concerns.

The last great New Testament scholar who in fact never formally studied the New Testament was F. F. Bruce. He approached the Lukan corpus through his background in classics. He began by looking at the composition of the speeches in Acts. Using his previous education, he took a Thucydidean view in claiming the speeches would be considered accurate representations of what was actually said, even if not verbatim. He used the language and patterns in Luke to back his claim about Acts. He repeated this claim multiple times and added different layers to his defense of it as time progressed. The problem becomes that Bruce does not progress, using the same arguments and the same views without seeing the underlying assumptions and evidences are themselves elements that need to be discussed if not defended. His work in situating the events of the New Testament in history sensibly and uncritically follows the outline of the Gospels and Acts. Bruce creates a Pauline timeline based on Acts, yet he does not include the Pastorals in his chronology as he does not consider them Pauline (nor Ephesians, though he does give that a date). Bruce's commentary on the Greek text of Acts would perhaps be his greatest contribution to Lukan studies. This volume has gone through three editions, and they all characteristically take the text as reliable and respond to those who do not consider it so. His English text commentaries take a step beyond the grammatical interaction in his Greek text editions and move more toward theology and application. Bruce's greatest contribution comes from his steady and rational support of Acts (and subsequently Luke) as historically valuable and accurate. He positioned his defense to counter the prevailing German criticism based on his education as a classicist and his understanding of how Greek historians viewed their own work. His greatest weakness, however, is found within his strength: he never changed or updated his work according to the latest scholarship or critical arguments against his views.

Luke–Acts often sat behind Paul in terms of where scholarship focused, but Hans Conzelmann put the spotlight back onto the Lukan corpus in the 1950s and 1960s with his works. Along with Haenchen, Conzelmann shifted how scholars viewed Luke the author. Rather than seeing him as an editor or historian, Conzelmann proposed and defended Luke as a theologian. This shifted the work away from how Luke composed to why he composed. Rather than seeking sources or seams, scholarship looked at how Luke's wording and choices display a specific and developed theological understanding of Jesus and the early church. Conzelmann supported and developed three stages of salvation history within Lukan studies, seeing Luke as dividing time into the time of Israel (including John the Baptist), the ministry of Jesus (during which Satan was bound), and the time of the church (which lasts until the second coming). This shift in thinking comes from Conzelmann's refusal to see any realized eschatological teaching in Luke or Acts and the fact that he ignores or downplays the initial chapters of Luke and the descriptions of John the Baptist's ministry and teaching. This seeming inconsistency finds some foundation in Conzelmann's methodology in that his choices stem from his use of redaction criticism in formulating his understanding of Luke as author and theologian. In making discrete choices, Luke's own thoughts and ideas shine through and allow the reader to understand his theology. Upon examining what Luke chooses to highlight and downplay, the theology of both Luke and Acts becomes clear and, according to Conzelmann, consistent. For Conzelmann, then, Luke was not attempting to write history or in an historical way; rather he was intentionally creating a theological grid to understand how Jesus and the early church point toward a delayed parousia and how the church should function now in light of these theological rather than historical truths.

Though often noted for his Pauline scholarship, C. K. Barrett wrote a magnificent two-volume commentary on Acts for the ICC series that stands as the high point of his academic work in the Lukan corpus. Barrett labored in both the academy and the church, with his love for the latter often shining through in his work for the former. His unique outlook on life allowed him to build bridges within scholarship that had begun to collapse, such as the connection between British universities and European higher education. Strangely typical for many scholars in this volume, his work on the Gospel of Luke only served as a precursor or foundation for his research in Acts. Just as Barrett built bridges in his life, so did he see Luke building bridges between the Jesus of history and the church. It is this tendency in Luke that propelled Barrett into his focus on Acts. He saw evidence of this in the Paul of the letters differing from the Paul of Acts, as this helps show Paul's unity with the Jewish church as the leader of the Gentile mission. The unity that Acts observes would in some respects be undercut by the nature of Paul's epistles, in that Paul undertakes the task of critiquing and correcting the behavior of various Gentile churches, which Barrett sees as various strands of Gentile Christianity. Since Luke wanted Acts to defend and demonstrate unity within the church, the letters of Paul and the Paul of the letters would not fit his aims. Luke, the purported author of Acts, clearly did not understand the theology of Paul and, while acquainted with his work, was likely not an actual companion of Paul. Acts then contains the history of the development of Christian mission but not the historical development of the church. Luke's version of the inclusion of the Gentiles does not come from historical events but from historical conclusions, such that his outcome of the Jerusalem council is what the church used but does not show how the church actually got to that position. Paul argued and struggled for Gentile inclusion throughout his ministry, and it was only with the death of the first generation of Jewish Christian leaders that this rapprochement came about. Barrett's Luke writes as a reconciler of mission rather than as an astute historian or theologian.

Jacob Jervell was a major voice in Lukan studies due to his unique take on Luke as a Jewish-centered writer. Jervell's work came on the heels of Haenchen, Bruce, Conzelmann, Barrett, and others that Luke was a Gentile focused on the Gentile mission. Jervell argued the opposite, and he did so by starting with the Gospel of Luke, thus giving himself a broader and more sweeping narrative upon which to call. In discussing the church and its relationship to Israel, Jervell disagreed with the notion that Acts followed the church as opposed to Israel. Jervell argued that Luke saw the church as a continuation of Israel and thus primarily a Jewish institution. Only the historical development of the church being predominantly Gentile today, he observed, caused scholarship to read back into Luke's writing a primarily non-Jewish conception of the narrative. Instead, Jervell saw the mass conversions throughout Acts as consisting mostly of Jews. Luke did not write to defend the Gentile mission, he wrote to show that Israel consists of those who follow God. The Samaritans should be understood as part of Israel when they follow God, as Israel itself divides over what it means to be part of Israel. The law in Luke (and also therefore in Acts) still functions and Israel still must hold to it. Jesus did not set it aside, rather Jesus scrupulously adhered to it. The Gentile mission fills the properly constituted Israel, as the people of God means Israel, and the point of the gospel message is to force a decision either to be a part of God's people or not to be.

Those who reject the gospel, therefore, forfeit the right to be called Israel and those who accept the gospel become adopted into Israel, no matter the previous ethnic origin. The mission to the Gentiles follows both chronologically and logically after the mission to the Jews. With respect to the Paul of Acts and the Paul of the epistles, Jervell switched the emphasis by focusing on the occasional nature of the epistles versus the intentional characterization of Acts. For Jervell, Acts describes Paul as a whole, and the epistles only touch on snippets of him due to the occasional and limited nature of those letters. Jervell caused Lukan scholarship to reassess the Jewish nature of Luke–Acts and how one reads the emphases through Luke's works.

As we reached the twenty-first century in our conspectus, we next included Richard I. Pervo. His scholarship helpfully summarizes the state of Lukan studies based on his desire to challenge each part of the status quo, specifically in his focus on Acts. Pervo first targeted the genre of Acts. Instead of seeing it as history, Pervo built the case that Acts is written as an historical novel designed to entertain those at the common level. In terms of dating Acts, Pervo used the various sources and parallels of Acts to push for a date between AD 110 and 130. With respect to Acts being written by the author of Luke and functioning as part of a unified Luke–Acts, he catalogued the differences and breaks between the two volumes to argue that this unity of purpose, authorship, and genre should be reassessed, especially in light of how tightly Luke coheres to the other Synoptic Gospels while none of them has a second volume. Luke and Acts circulated separately, have different genres, and have clearly different aims, and thus Pervo argued they most likely had different authors as well. In terms of provoking scholarship, Pervo did not stop with "introductory" matters but also looked at content. The picture of Paul, he argued, changes over time within the Bible. Paul of Acts and the early epistles shows an apostle who argued for the faith and reasoned within his Jewish understanding of the law and Israel's God. The Paul of the later epistles produces the prototypical and perhaps even perfect Gentile convert who inhaled the Jewish Bible and exhaled a developed theological position as the underpinning to early Catholicism. Each step along the way, Pervo challenged the consensus and has forced others to react to his ideas.

The last scholar, and only one still living, that we included within this volume was Loveday C. A. Alexander. While not groundbreaking in terms of content, her approach and specific areas of study moved scholarship forward. With a background in classics and a deep appreciation of that style of writing, Alexander challenged the notion that Luke wrote his introductions in an elevated style. Instead, she placed him at a more popular level and then compared his introductions to those of other writers. In doing so, she concluded that he did not intend to write in a technical fashion; rather, Luke wrote like a typical craftsman in a style that fit who he was. She waded into the morass that is the discussion of the genre of Acts, and after ruling out some options, never gave a definitive answer. In looking at how Luke and Acts were composed, she made comparisons to the various Hellenistic schools and showed both similarities and differences. Being the ecclesial leader that she is, Alexander made sure to relate her scholarly pursuits to her function within the church, as she applied the structures of Luke and Acts to her practical ministry. Alexander used her work to inform her ministry, and her background in classics to inform her work in Lukan studies.

These scholars and their works have challenged how we read and understand the Gospel of Luke and the Acts of the Apostles. Are these two volumes written by one person? Are they heavily influenced by Jewish views? Did Luke write to placate the Romans or to defend the Gentile mission? Was Luke just a man who pasted some stories together based on Mark, Matthew, and what he learned as a third-generation believer? Or was Luke a master theologian and historian who carefully researched, selected, and combined the various pericopes into thematic units that capture theological truths while also faithfully recording history? These various authors come to vastly different conclusions based on the same evidence. While this volume will not give definitive answers, it does show how these views grew from the different scholars and how they influenced Lukan studies in their time and will continue to influence the field for decades to come.

SCRIPTURE INDEX

AUTHOR INDEX